EUROPE
1815–1960
Second Edition

ANTHONY WOOD

LONG

D0227919

LONGMAN GROUP UK LIMITED
Longman House, Burnt Mill, Harlow, Essex CM20 2JE, England
and Associated Companies throughout the World

First published 1964
Second edition 1984
Third impression 1986

ISBN 0-582-35349-1

Set in 10/11 pt. Baskerville, Linotron 202

Produced by Longman Group (FE) Ltd
Printed in Hong Kong

Cover: Detail from the painting
by French artist Eugène
Delacroix, entitled *Liberty*
Leading the People (1830). Louvre,
Paris.

Preface

The purpose of this book is to trace the general course of European history from the time of Napoleon onwards. To cover a period of such intense development at once poses the problem of method. The aims and difficulties of individual countries are a vital element in the story of these years: and yet it is also a fact that the forces of nationalism, industrialization and social changes, and the complexity of language, peoples, and classes in central and eastern Europe raise questions that cut clean across all political frontiers. Indeed, I believe that these general factors are so essential to the understanding of the period that I have purposely treated the history of the Continent as a whole; I have, however, tried to strike a balance by elaborating the detail of national development within the wider framework, although I have not included the purely domestic history of Great Britain, except where this directly impinges on events abroad.

Over Christian names I have aimed chiefly at the convenience of the reader rather than at any consistent principle, and I have anglicized most titles, although it is not always possible to observe precise distinctions —as, for example, between the German *Fürst* and *Prinz*. Place-names are more controversial, since their different German and Slavonic forms reflect in themselves the rivalries of central and eastern Europe. I have added a glossary of these at the back of the book, and in the text, when no neutral anglicized form existed, I have simply used the one most commonly adopted in this country.

There are many acknowledgements to be made—to my teachers at Oxford, to the London Library and the Deutsches Kulturinstitut who supplied me with many of the necessary books, and to my colleague Count Sollohub who allowed me to make use of his thesis on German nationalism. In compiling the statistics at the end of the book, the publishers have kindly given me permission to quote from the following: *Eastern Europe between the Wars 1918–41* by H. Seton-Watson, published by the Cambridge University Press; *The Struggle for Mastery in Europe 1848–1918*, by A. J. P. Taylor, published by the Clarendon Press, Oxford; *French Electoral Systems and Elections since 1789* by P. Campbell, published by Faber and Faber Ltd; *The Growth of the American Republic*, by S. E. Morison and H. S. Commager, published by the Oxford University Press Inc.; *Modern Germany: Its History and Civilization*, by K. S. Pinson, published by the Macmillan Company, New York, © 1954, by the Macmillan Company; and the 1959 edition of the *Encyclopaedia Britannica*.

In addition to this practical assistance I must also mention debts of a more intangible kind. There is an atmosphere, a background of assumptions, which it is not easy for an English person to grasp in attempting to explain Continental history, and a number of circumstances have helped me to realize, if not to resolve this difficulty. The experience of the Second World War seemed at the time to be of little academic value; yet the sight of the shattered orchards of Normandy and the ruin of the German cities did at least give a glimpse of the stakes for which twentieth-century politics are played. It was as a student at the University of Basle that I first became aware of the social and linguistic complexity of central Europe and I take this opportunity of expressing my thanks to Professor H. Lüdeke for all his kindness to me while I was there; also to the authorities of Winchester College for later allowing me leave of absence for an invaluable year as Lecteur at the Sorbonne. Lastly, my greatest debt is to my wife not only for enduring another bout of authorship, but also for adding a Scandinavian flavour to my appreciation of European history.

A. C. W., *Winchester*, 1963

Note to the Second Edition

The immense amount of fresh material that has been published since this book first appeared has added particularly to our knowledge of the twentieth century, and I am grateful for the opportunity to revise and expand some of the later sections in this new edition. When I originally stopped at 1945, the ruin of Europe seemed to be an appropriate conclusion to the tensions and animosities of the previous hundred and fifty years. I have now moved the story on to 1960. This is bound to be a rather more open-ended closing date, but I felt that it was important to describe the shaping of a post-war Europe that has formed the immediate background of our lives, and the needs of the student had to outweigh the niceties of dramatic unity. Apart from that, I have rearranged some of the topics in the nineteenth-century sections. This is simply in order to make it easier to refer to individual countries for which I have also compiled a separate index at the back. It does not affect the principal aim of the book which remains the presenting of the major forces of change on the Continent as a whole.

A. C. W., *Winchester*, 1983

Contents

Contents   ix

MAPS

Introduction

The Significance of the French Revolution

It used to be said that when France sneezes, Europe catches cold. In recent years historians have sometimes questioned the precise extent of social change brought about by the French Revolution, but on the whole it would be hard to deny that between 1789 and 1815 France was the centre of events after which Europe was never quite the same again.

The most striking feature of the *ancien régime* in Europe in the eighteenth century had been the existence of a highly privileged class of nobility, upper clergy, and *bourgeois vivant noblement*. To belong to this exclusive caste had meant to avoid the main burden of taxation and to enjoy the right of entry to the highest posts in the country. This was a system of society so interwoven with the legal and administrative complexities of the *ancien régime* that it is tempting to regard the French Revolution as a concerted effort on the part of the unprivileged to wipe the slate clean and to draw the whole of government and society afresh. Yet throughout the revolutionary turmoil in France there was little unity among the unprivileged. Each small section of society was thinking in terms of a readjustment that would simply enable it to enjoy more fully the benefits of the existing system. The significance of the year 1789 is that each group imagined that its hour had come, and the consequence was a struggle between conflicting ambitions in which the *ancien régime* was torn asunder.

At Versailles, where the Estates General assembled in May 1789, it was the Third Estate, aided by King Louis XVI's fears of an outbreak from Paris, who threw off the control of the nobility and upper clergy and established the three Estates as an indivisible National Assembly pledged to redefine the governmental structure of France. Yet the Third Estate themselves, representing the ambitions of a mainly professional class, were barely in control of other discordant forces on whom they depended for their own survival— artisans and unemployed in the towns, who, in Paris, were instrumental in the taking of the Bastille on 14 July, and peasantry in the countryside, who forced the deputies in August to decree the ultimate abolition of all forms of aristocratic privilege.

Nevertheless, by the autumn of 1791 the National Assembly had devised a constitutional monarchy for France in which wealth was largely to replace birth as the source of political influence. A representative Chamber with the sole right of initiating legislation was to be elected on an extremely limited franchise which favoured the richest section of society. Royal officials were no longer to manage local government; its structure was simplified and almost totally decentralised in a pattern of some eighty regional *départements*, which were then broken down again into smaller units. This formed the basis for administering taxation and the law and for the reorganization of the Church, and the same preponderance of the richer classes was reflected in the membership of the various councils that operated at these levels.

For those who were comfortably established it seemed that the Revolution had gone far enough. Yet it was soon clear that they had failed to create a lasting settlement. Their principal difficulty was that they had to rely upon a constitutional monarchy in which the monarch himself apparently had no faith. The tragedy for Louis XVI was that although, like Charles I of England, he had many commendable personal qualities—deeply religious, a devoted father, a Bourbon without a mistress—none of them were relevant to the problems that faced him. He did not have the ability to outwit the new type of middle class politician with whom he had to deal; and he certainly did not have the inclination to give them a firm lead, as he had already made clear in an ignominiously unsuccessful attempt to escape from France in the summer of 1791. As a consequence, the politicians were hardly in a strong position to counter a growing criticism from different quarters. On the right the reorganization of the Church caused a great rent that cut through every class division in France, creating new support for the *émigrés* who were forming their army at Coblenz. At the same time, *assignats*, bills of credit issued against the confiscated lands of the Church, began to circulate as paper currency, and in the consequent inflation the urban poor faced not merely political disillusionment, but also the much sharper prick of hunger, of which the radical politicians were quick to take advantage.

It was the outbreak of hostilities with Austria and Prussia in April 1792 that brought these problems to a head. For the Powers of Europe war meant nothing less than a crusade in defence of the existing order of society. For France it was to mean a struggle for survival which eventually opened the way to democratic republicanism. There were to be three periods when national disaster seemed imminent and each was to have striking consequences on the French domestic scene.

The first came in the summer of 1792, when the news of military retreats and surrenders led to a *coup d'état* in Paris that ended the monarchy, established a National Convention elected by universal suffrage, and in January 1793 sent Louis XVI to the guillotine.

The second came in the spring and summer of 1793, when fresh disasters and the fear of counter-revolution at home brought the two principal political groups into direct conflict. The Girondins had strongly supported the revolutionary war, but wished to preserve a system of political federalism and economic *laissez faire*, and it was the Jacobins who won the support of the masses in Paris with an emergency wartime policy of centralization, economic controls, and Terror exercised through the Committee of Public Safety and the Revolutionary Tribunal.

By the summer of 1794 the situation at the front had vastly improved. Robespierre and his supporters, who had destroyed two rival factions under Danton and Hébert, were themselves dispatched to the guillotine, and, in the right-wing reaction that followed, the controls were relaxed and the Jacobins became the victims of a new White Terror. For four years a Directory of five attempted to ward off the political extremes of right and left in a series of *coups*, through which they became increasingly dependent upon the army, but when in the summer of 1799 France suffered a number of defeats at the hand of the Second Coalition of Great Britain, Russia and Austria, a new Jacobin revival appeared imminent and the third moment of crisis had come.

In fact, the advance of France's enemies was checked and the hopes of the Jacobins with it, but there was little confidence in the power of the Directory to continue to survive such shocks. For the bourgeois the memories of economic controls, reinforced by a policy of Terror, were still too recent, and a small group of conspirators looked hastily for a military figure who might stand nominally at the head of a revised constitution which would offer the newly established classes greater security. In the event they underestimated the man whom they chose, for the *coup d'état* of Brumaire* brought Napoleon Bonaparte to a position of supreme power which he was to hold for the next fourteen years.

The significance of Napoleon's work within France was not that he created a totally new system of government; rather that he consolidated certain aspects of the Revolution at the expense of others. Constitutional rule based on a separation of powers, decentralization of local government and the great tangle of electoral processes were all swept aside in the creation of a simplified autocracy in which the executive power in the person of Napoleon dominated the so-called legislature and the courts of law, and through the appointment of Prefects in the provinces brought the government of the entire country directly under the central authority. On the other

---

* The name of a month in the calendar introduced by the revolutionaries in 1792. The date was actually 9–10 November.

hand, strong rule was able to solve the two great problems which
the revolutionaries had created for themselves—the currency and
the Church. The *assignats* were abolished, the national finances were
re-established through a newly organized Bank of France, and a
Concordat with the Pope restored relations between France and
Rome. One thing, however, Napoleon knew he could not touch. The
Church lands, in which the peasantry and middle classes had been
investing during the past ten years, were not given back. Similarly,
any reappearance of the old social privileges of the aristocracy was
out of the question. Equality before the law, a reasonably equitable
system of taxation, *la carrière ouverte aux talents* in the army, government service and the professions, all these aims of the early years
of the Revolution were now guaranteed by the emergence of what
appeared at last to be a stable government. By and large, it·was a
bargain that suited the French, since it seemed to secure peasantry
and middle classes both from a restoration of the *ancien régime* and
from the alarming tendencies of revolutionary Jacobinism.

But for Europe there was another aspect of Napoleon's rule that
was to be of startling significance. By 1808 the wars in which he had
defeated the Continental Powers had placed his country in an
absolutely unprecedented position of authority. His relations and
marshals occupied the thrones of kingdoms in the Netherlands, Germany, Italy, and Spain; the government of the Swiss cantons had
been remodelled and a Grand Duchy of Warsaw created on the borders of Russia. Almost everywhere throughout these territories ran
the writ of the Civil Code, embodying the Napoleonic version of the
social and political message of the French Revolution.

Napoleon himself was not to last. The fatal attack on Russia in
1812, the retreat from Moscow, and the campaigns against the Powers of the Fourth Coalition in Germany in 1813 led on to the surrender of Paris and the proclamation of the deposition of Napoleon
by the French Senate in April 1814. Yet the defeat of France was
not to mean the end of the Revolution. It was only twenty-five years
since the meeting of the Estates General at Versailles, but in that
short time the classes and peoples of Europe had caught a glimpse
of a different order of society and government that they could never
forget. They had, too, begun to grow aware of a sense of national
individuality, partly because of the way in which the Napoleonic
conquests had been followed by an immense simplification of the
political frontiers of the eighteenth century, but principally because
of the antagonism which the imposition of French authority had
aroused. Thus Napoleon had bequeathed to Europe more than he
could ever have imagined; the history of the nineteenth century is
the story of that inheritance and of all the contradictory ambitions
to which it gave rise, as a growing economic revolution added
strength to the attack on the assumptions on which the old order
had been based.

Part 1

Europe in 1815

Chapter 1

The Congress of Vienna

Three times since 1814 a new map of Europe has emerged from the ruin of the old. Earlier conflicts had often been widespread—in the eighteenth century reaching as far as America and India—but the objectives of the combatants had remained limited and the terms of the subsequent treaties restricted to local territorial readjustments. It was the threat of political and social revolution implicit in the Napoleonic wars that gave a different character to the terms of the peace that followed, and in this sense it is easy to imagine a link between the Congress of Vienna and the peace-making of 1919 and 1945 in a new era of European settlements.

Two major features, however, distinguish the treaties of Vienna from those of Versailles and Potsdam. The first point of difference lies in the general aim of the diplomats. After the two World Wars of the twentieth century there was no question of recreating the situation that had existed before the outbreak of hostilities; the statesmen of 1814, on the other hand, were definitely seeking some sort of return to the eighteenth-century system. It was not merely that their pride had been bruised by the impact of Napoleon's armies; the whole basis of the *ancien régime* had been challenged by the extension of revolutionary principles in the lands adjoining France, and for the Allies the purpose of victory was to restore the political and social framework that had been so roughly shaken since 1789.

This determination to re-establish the old legitimate governments helps to explain the second point of difference. All three settlements were primarily the work of the great Powers, but in one respect Vienna was a more genuine congress than the others, since it had been preceded by a logical sequence of agreements with France, restoring the Bourbon monarchy and ending the state of war, so that, when the Congress met, France could take her place alongside the victorious Powers. In contrast to this, at Versailles in 1919, the problems of the peace terms and the redrawing of the frontiers were dealt with in a combined process in which Germany was treated purely as a defeated country. After the second World War, there was no congress at all; the leaders of Germany were all dead, missing, or captive, and the victors already at loggerheads had to content themselves with organizing their areas of occupation in their own ways.

On 6 April 1814 at Fontainebleau, Napoleon, having failed to establish a Regency for his son, the King of Rome, had agreed to unconditional abdication. The terms which the allied Powers imposed on the former ruler of France were by no means severe; he was granted the island of Elba in full sovereignty, as well as an annual revenue of two million francs from France, while the Empress Marie Louise was to hold the Duchies of Parma, Piacenza, and Guastalla in perpetuity, and the numerous members of his family were to retain their titles and to receive annuities, including a pension of a million francs a year for Josephine.

Once Napoleon had been removed, the second problem was to persuade the French that they really wanted a restored monarchy after all. Here they were fortunate in that Talleyrand, the ex-bishop of the *ancien régime*, who had played a leading part in almost every French government since 1789, was able to talk the French Senate into proclaiming the return of the Bourbons and was thus able to contrive the fiction that Louis Stanislav Xavier, Count of Provence, brother of the guillotined Louis XVI, had been recalled by his own country to the throne of France to rule as Louis XVIII. On 23 April an armistice was signed between France and the Allies, and on 3 May Louis made his official entry into Paris. Restored sovereigns should not appear to depend upon foreign bayonets, and this was not an easy moment for Louis with the city full of troops of the Allies. From the Pont Neuf to Notre Dame the route was lined with Napoleon's Old Guard. 'Ces mêmes hommes,' wrote Chateaubriand in his *Mémoires d'outre-tombe*, 'privés de leur capitaine, étaient forcés de saluer un vieux roi, invalide du temps, non de la guerre, surveillés qu'ils étaient par une armée de Russes, d'Autrichiens et de Prussiens dans la capitale envahie de Napoléon.'

The moment passed. Provided that the general principles of 1789 were guaranteed, restoration was acceptable to most of the French, weary of war and of the economic consequences of Napoleon's Continental schemes, and the Allies could move quickly on to the next step—the signing of the Treaty of Paris with France on 30 May. The terms reduced her eastern frontier to what it had been in 1792, with the addition of a part of Savoy, including Chambéry and Annecy, but overseas she had to surrender Tobago, St Lucia and Mauritius to Great Britain and the Spanish half of San Domingo to Spain. In the main, however, this first Treaty of Paris was remarkable for its moderation. Under Napoleon France had imposed her will upon almost every country in Europe, achieving a dominion beyond the wildest dreams of the monarchy of the *ancien régime*, and now at the end, when her power was broken, her original frontiers were respected, no indemnity or reparations were demanded at all, and even the art treasures looted from all over Europe were left in her possession. There was wisdom in such forbearance, for by this means it was hoped that Louis XVIII might be eased on to his throne and Bonapartism die a natural death.

These were the diplomatic preliminaries that preceded the meeting of the Congress of Vienna which in accordance with the Treaty of Paris was attended in the autumn of 1814 by the sovereigns and plenipotentiaries from 'all the Powers engaged on either side in the present war'. Certain questions such as the independence of Switzerland, the creation of a large Kingdom of the Netherlands and the realigning of local frontiers in Germany and Italy had already been discussed among the great Powers, and it was never intended that the Congress should do much more than ratify the final decisions. Vienna, during these months, became a dazzling scene of royalty *en fête*. At a cost of some thirty million florins the Emperor Francis offered a lavish hospitality to most of the reigning sovereigns of Europe, as well as more than two hundred princely families; public balls, banquets, amateur theatricals, sleighing trips through the Wienerwald, all formed a glittering background to the intrigues of the ladies and to Sir Sidney Smith's interminable narration of the siege of Acre, while the great Powers deliberated and the Austrian secret police rummaged through the waste-paper baskets of the diplomats.

To one side of the Hofburg stood Metternich's house on the Ballhausplatz and it was here that the real work of the Congress was carried on. The British delegation consisted of four plenipotentiaries headed by the Foreign Secretary, Lord Castlereagh, an aloof, cold, handsome figure, whose principal aim at the Congress was to bring about a balance of forces in Europe that would remove any danger of expansion by France or Russia. Apprehensiveness over a possible revival of French power was natural, and his wariness of Russia's possible designs westward was a direct legacy from William Pitt's policy during the Otchakov crisis of 1791. Thus for Castlereagh it was essential, first, to guard the eastern frontier of France with a strong Netherlands, Piedmont and an independent Switzerland, and second, to create a central European *bloc* out of Prussia and Austria who might stand firm against France or Russia.

The Russian delegation was large and highly international. The Foreign Minister, Count Nesselrode, and two other plenipotentiaries, Count Razumovski and Count Stackelberg, were accompanied by the German Freiherr vom und zum Stein, the Polish Prince Adam Czartoryski, and the Swiss Laharpe, each to give advice on his own region, while Count Capo d'Istria of Corfu and the Corsican Pozzo di Borgo, Russian ambassador at Paris, exercised a rather more general influence. In fact, Tsar Alexander never relied entirely on any single one of his advisers and the other Powers could never be sure that he would not revoke what his subordinates had just negotiated. Alexander, his round cherubic face shining with benevolence, his tight-fitting uniform almost bursting at every seam, was a strange unpredictable character, oscillating wildly between authoritarianism and liberal gestures, a complicated psychology in which pious aspiration often blended with deep cunning. This duality of outlook was reflected in his schemes for Poland, where he wished to recreate the old Kingdom, granting it a liberal constitution, but at the same time making it part of his own dominions. This would have deprived Prussia and Austria of some of the Polish provinces that they had gained in the partitions of the eighteenth century, and the re-emergence of an undivided Poland completely in the pocket of Russia would have seen the fulfilment of Catherine the Great's original plans before she had had to abandon them in favour of sharing the spoil with Prussia and Austria.

Frederick William III of Prussia, much enamoured of the Russian Tsar, was prepared to accept the idea, tempted by Alexander's suggestion that he should take the Kingdom of Saxony by way of compensation; his delegation, headed by Prince Hardenberg, and mainly bound by the considerations of the Prussian General Staff, was content so long as Prussia's position in Germany was assured. Much stronger objection came from Austria, since Metternich was determined that Russia should not gain Poland, while Count Stadion and Prince Schwarzenberg, although they cared little about Poland, had no liking for the suggested Prussian acquisition of Saxony.

For Talleyrand, now Foreign Minister to Louis XVIII, this quarrel among the Allies offered an ideal opportunity. There was no question of territorial acquisition for France; his sole aim was to restore her prestige and to end her isolation. Before his arrival at Vienna the Powers had drawn up a *protocole séparé* prescribing a procedure which would have left all major decisions in the hands of the four Powers of the Quadruple Alliance, but it did not take long for Talleyrand to use the Allies' own principle of legitimacy to demolish this scheme. 'The intervention of Talleyrand', wrote Gentz, Metternich's secretary, 'hopelessly upset our plans. It was a scene I shall never forget.' By November Talleyrand had secured the inclusion of France, Spain, Portugal, and Sweden, thus creating a directing committee of the eight signatories of the Treaty of Paris who had convened the Congress.

It was the Polish–Saxon question that enabled him to take the next step. In December he openly supported the Austrians in their resistance to Prussian acquisition of Saxony, and when Hardenberg announced in anger that any further interference with the Prussian claims would be tantamount to a declaration of war, Talleyrand

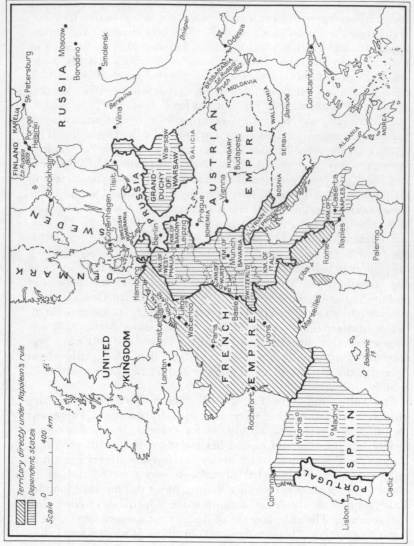

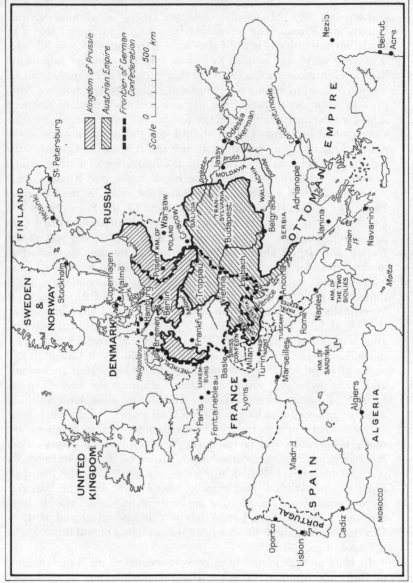

EUROPE AFTER THE CONGRESS OF VIENNA 1815

seized his chance during the momentary panic to propose to Castlereagh and Metternich a secret treaty of alliance against Prussia and Russia. The treaty was signed on 3 January 1815. 'The Coalition is dissolved,' wrote Talleyrand in triumph to Louis XVIII; 'France is no longer isolated in Europe.' In fact, neither side would have been prepared to go to war at this moment and the mere shock of such a division among the Allies was sufficient to produce a compromise solution to their difficulties. For Talleyrand, however, it remained a considerable diplomatic victory, since the price of his support had been that France should join the major Powers in the detailed negotiation, and thus during the rest of the Congress the significant decisions were taken by a Committee of Five in which France sat with Great Britain, Austria, Prussia, and Russia.

The treaty was eventually signed in June 1815 by the five great Powers as well as by Sweden and Portugal. Of the Polish territories Prussia was to regain the province of Posen, Austria retained Galicia, while Cracow was to become a Free City. The rest of the Napoleonic Grand Duchy of Warsaw was to become the Kingdom of Poland under the Tsar. Prussia's compensation for this Russian gain was only two-fifths of Saxony, including about 850,000 inhabitants, but she received in addition a large area of the Rhineland, Westphalia, and Swedish Pomerania. Sweden had lost Finland and the Åland Isles after the Russian invasion of 1808, but, in accordance with an agreement of 1812, now received Norway from Denmark, who in return gained only the small duchy of Lauenburg.

No attempt was made to recreate the old Holy Roman Empire, and the thirty-eight sovereign states including the Free Cities of Lübeck, Bremen, Frankfurt, and Hamburg, were loosely linked together in a German Confederation with a Diet at Frankfurt under the presidency of Austria. Within this confederation Hanover was made a kingdom and received small additions of territory, while Bavaria gained Bayreuth and Anspach in return for the territory she restored to Austria. British interests were served by the incorporating of the United Provinces of the Dutch and the Austrian Netherlands into a Kingdom of the Netherlands under the House of Orange, King William I holding the title also of Grand Duke of Luxemburg, although the city itself was to be a Federal fortress with a Prussian garrison.

In Italy no appearance of unity was created at all. The Kingdom of Sardinia rounded off its mainland possessions of Piedmont, Savoy, and Nice with the former territories of the republic of Genoa as a bulwark against French expansion; Austria regained Lombardy and retained Venetia which, until Napoleon's invasion in 1796, had been an independent republic. In central Italy the Papal States including the legations of Ferrara, Bologna, Ravenna, and Forli straddled the peninsula, while to the north of them the duchies of

Parma, Modena, and Tuscany were given back to members of the Habsburg family. To the south it was the ruler, rather than the frontiers, of the kingdom of Naples that presented the problem. Murat had fought alongside Napoleon at Leipzig in 1813, but this had not inhibited him from opening negotiations with the Allies, and in January 1814 he had signed a treaty with them, offering his army of 30,000 in return for a guarantee of his throne. By 1815, however, the need that Castlereagh and Metternich felt to conciliate Louis XVIII, who naturally hated any survivor of Napoleon's Europe, had caused them to agree secretly that Murat should be expelled to allow the restoration of the Spanish Bourbon, King Ferdinand, and, in the event, Murat's support of Napoleon on his return from Elba was to give them all the justification that they needed.

In addition to this redrawing of the map of Europe the Powers also reached a number of other more general agreements. In the same year they were to sign a guarantee of perpetual neutrality for the Swiss Confederation, whose cantons the Congress had made up to twenty-two in number with the addition of Geneva, Valais, and Neuchâtel, the last of these being a Prussian enclave. The question of the navigation of rivers which ran through several countries was dealt with by a special committee, and it was established that such rivers should be open to all commerce with no further increase of duties then in force. Another matter that particularly exercised Castlereagh was the abolition of the slave trade. Great Britain, the United States, and Denmark had already abolished it; Sweden and the Netherlands were prepared to do so and Louis XVIII had promised Castlereagh that France would also suppress it within five years. Negotiation with Spain and Portugal took rather longer, but eventually each responded to the offer of a cash payment from the British government by way of compensation.

Castlereagh had been anxious to keep the question of overseas possessions outside the scope of the Congress, mainly because British naval power during the war had enabled her to make great gains at the expense of France and the Napoleonic kingdom of Holland. Here agreement was reached simply through a series of private treaties. Great Britain gave back the East Indies to the Dutch, but retained Ceylon, as well as Cape Colony in South Africa and a part of Dutch Guiana. France had lost Tobago, St Lucia and Mauritius to Great Britain by the Treaty of Paris, but received back French Guiana from Portugal and also Guadaloupe, after Sweden had been persuaded to give up her claim in return for an indemnity of one million pounds from the British.

The diplomatic shifts and quarrels which had inevitably attended this vast readjustment of territories inside and outside Europe were overshadowed towards the end of the Congress by a new and unexpected development. On 1 March 1815, after slipping out of Elba,

Napoleon landed in the south of France near Antibes. At Vienna
the great pageant of entertainment came suddenly to a halt. 'It
seemed', wrote an eye-witness, 'as if a thousand candles immediately went out.' In France the Bourbon restoration, so carefully
stage-managed by Talleyrand, fell in ruins, as Napoleon, on his
progress northwards, was welcomed by the troops sent to resist his
advance. 'I will receive you,' he wrote to Marshal Ney, who had
promised Louis that he would bring Napoleon back in an iron cage,
'as I did on the morrow of the battle of the Moskowa,' and Ney
found it impossible to resist the old magic. Louis fled hastily to Lille
and on 20 March the Emperor once more entered his capital in
triumph, while in Naples Murat, hearing the news, declared war on
Austria and advanced north towards Milan.

On both sides frantic preparation followed. In France, in order
to compete with the Charter (see p. 34) already granted by Louis
XVIII, Napoleon gave a promise of constitutional government,
later embodied in the *Acte additionnel*, and tried to play on the divisions among the Allies by a peace offer to Great Britain and Austria.
When this failed, he set off on 12 June with 120,000 troops, intend-
ing to strike at Brussels. At Vienna the Allies immediately renewed
the Treaty of Chaumont, determined on the expulsion of Napoleon,
although doubtful whether they could impose the Bourbons a second time on France. By now, however, the Russians had withdrawn
to Poland and the Austrians were engaged with Murat in Italy.
Thus the only forces available to face Napoleon were a combined
army of British, Hanoverians and Netherlanders under the Duke of
Wellington and the Prussians under Blücher, and it was consequently those two who fought the series of fluid defensive actions
that culminated in the battle of Waterloo on 18 June. Here Wellington's squares stood firm against the French attack throughout
the whole day, until the Prussians, whom Napoleon believed he had
driven from the field two days before at Ligny, came up on the flank
in the evening and the Allied cavalry swept in to victory.

'I hasten to congratulate you', wrote Metternich to Wellington,
'on the brilliant opening of the campaign.' But, as it turned out,
Napoleon's fate had depended not on a campaign, but on a single
battle. This time it was Fouché, Napoleon's Minister of Police, who
played Talleyrand's role in organizing the capitulation of France;
the Chamber set up a provisional government and Napoleon fled
westwards to Rochefort to avoid being shot by Blücher who was
advancing on Paris with his Prussian army. It was four months
before any agreement could be reached among the Allies over the
terms of the second Treaty of Paris. Prussia, the Netherlands, and
many of the smaller German states were in full cry, demanding
heavy indemnities as well as the loss of Alsace, Lorraine, French
Flanders, and Savoy, but eventually Castlereagh, angered by the

brutalities of the Prussian army in France and anxious not to create a lasting sense of grievance among the French, was able, with the support of the Tsar, to bring Austria round, after which the Prussians had to give way. The second Treaty of Paris was finally signed on 20 November; in the north-east, thin strips of territory were surrendered to the Netherlands and the Prussian Rhineland, including the frontier fortresses of Philippeville, Marienbourg, Saarlouis, and Landau; in Savoy, the *département* of Mont Blanc was given to the Kingdom of Sardinia. An army of occupation numbering 150,000 was established in the northern *départements*, the fortress of Hüningen near the Swiss border dismantled, and an indemnity of 700 million francs imposed, as well as liability for claims for losses suffered by private individuals.

Thus the Hundred Days cost France dear—and not only France. After his surrender to the captain of *HMS Bellerophon* outside Rochefort, Napoleon was to spend the remainder of his life, closely watched, on the island of St Helena in the south Atlantic—a poor exchange for Elba. In Italy, a month before Waterloo, Murat had been defeated at Tolentino by the Austrians and had fled to the south of France; in September he returned by sea, landed in Calabria, and attempted to gain support, as Napoleon had done on his return from Elba, but the *coup* failed utterly. He was arrested and later executed by a firing squad on the beach at Pizzo. And even for Louis XVIII, as he wearily retraced his steps back into France, there was the bitter knowledge that the King of France was returning, in Chateaubriand's words, 'derrière ces uniformes rouges qui venaient de reteindre leur pourpre au sang des Français'.

Chapter 2
Classes and Peoples

A violent oscillation of frontiers amid more than twenty years of revolutionary war had wrought little fundamental change in the European way of life. All but a small fraction of the 200 million inhabitants were peasantry, and across the great northern plains that stretched from the north-east of France to the steppes of Russia, tiny villages still practised a communal system of farming on the surrounding open fields, where the peasant held his scattered strips. Naturally, there were many local exceptions to this pattern in regions where geography demanded a more individual type of agriculture—among the vineyards of the south of France, in the Alpine districts and the Balkans, and along the shores of the Norwegian fiords. In Finland and the north of Sweden there could be no open fields where the peasant had to struggle against the encroaching forest and the long seasons of heavy snow, while on the polders of the North Sea coast and among the Masurian marshes of East Prussia the farmhouses stood perched along the dykes, each at the head of its own holding.

By any twentieth-century standard the cities throughout the entire Continent would seem minute. The population of Paris, the largest of them by far, was 600,000; few others numbered more than 200,000—St Petersburg and Vienna—while the rapid growth of Berlin in the eighteenth century had only brought her to 180,000 by 1815. Commercial towns such as Lyons, Marseilles, and Hamburg could boast 100,000 inhabitants, Genoa rather less, while the Baltic ports were even smaller.

The general aspect of most towns was still of an earlier epoch; houses of timber and plaster formed an untidy pattern of rambling streets around the church and market place; sanitation was primitive and the plash of fountains indicated the main source of water supply. In the larger cities, however, the eighteenth century had brought many changes. The old surrounding walls were coming down and in their place planned vistas of gardens and public walks lent a new air of spacious dignity—in Paris the Champs-Élysées, in Frankfurt the Palmengarten, in Berlin Unter den Linden. In an age of absolutism the palace had become a symbol of vital importance in the effort to keep up with the Bourbons. Every German prince had toiled at his miniature Versailles. The rococo charm of Frederick the Great's Sans Souci, the simple French style of Drottningholm to the west of Stockholm, the richly embroidered classicism of the Spanish Bourbon Charles III's palace at Caserta, and the still more elaborate splendour of the Winter Palace at St Petersburg were all evidence of this same determination; indeed, the original plans submitted to the Habsburg Emperor Joseph I for the Schönbrunn would have outshone Louis XIV's Versailles, had the finances been equal to it, and even the more modest palace completed in the reign of Maria Theresa was a fair rival.

No single style of building was dominant throughout the eighteenth century. Italian baroque had a marked influence in Austria, Bohemia and the south of Germany, and Vienna itself had been transformed into a city of elaborate façades, in which classical form was almost submerged amid a wealth of fantastic embellishment. The gardens, which were part of the architectural plan of the palaces, tended to imitate the careful geometrical patterns of Versailles, although by the second half of the eighteenth century the artless naturalism of the English park was becoming popular. In the north, on the other hand, baroque never really took root, and the neo-classical style predominated in the Christiansborg at Copenhagen, rebuilt after the fire of 1794, in the rectangular simplicity of the King's palace on the central island of Stockholm, and in the Great Square at Helsinki, which became the administrative capital of Finland under Russian rule.

The system of roads linking the towns varied enormously in quality. The French had long been known to have the best in Europe, and it had been part of Napoleon's Imperial design to extend these beyond the borders of France, so that Paris had become the centre of a great network of paved highways reaching out to Hamburg, Madrid and Amsterdam and over the Mont Cenis and Simplon passes. There was, too, quite a good system of metalled roads linking Vienna with Prague and most of the large towns of south Germany, but to the north and throughout eastern Europe they were little more than stony tracks and a journey by coach was a hazardous and expensive undertaking.

Two particular features emerge from this general picture of the Continent in 1815. The first was a strongly established sense of local feeling, due principally in eastern Europe to the poor communications, and reinforced in Germany, Italy, and Switzerland by the historic rivalries among the old duchies and cantons; throughout most parts of Europe, each large town with its cathedral, university, or trading connections formed an entity in itself with its own leading

families and traditions, providing amid the general vagueness of
national sentiment a focal point for regional loyalties, strongly
emphasized by marked differences in dialect.

This parochialism was to some extent counter-balanced by the
second feature, a landed aristocracy for whom the distinction of class
cut horizontally across the local and national divisions of Europe;
the great mansions on the country estates, the town houses, the lavish entertainments, all pointed to a common way of life based on
the assumption of a social pre-eminence, and greatly strengthened,
in central and eastern Europe and Scandinavia, by a long process
of intermarriage. From Paris to St Petersburg French had become
the language of diplomacy and of high society. Count Cavour was
happier speaking French than the language of the country that he
was later to help create, and it was in French that Metternich, a
Rhinelander, exchanged his letters with Madame de Lieven, the
daughter of a Prussian family living in Estonia. Allegiance to their
class was the dominant loyalty and a foreign origin was of little
account; the Duke de Richelieu as Governor of Odessa, Stein in the
service of the Russian Tsar and Sir John Acton as Prime Minister
to the King of the Two Sicilies were only more recent instances of
a social system that had earlier accepted Bouquoys and MacNevens
in Bohemia, Hamiltons in Sweden, and Greigs and Barclays in
Russia.

Thus far, the natural diversity of regional peculiarities would
seem a small detail in comparison with the general factors common
to most parts of Europe in 1815. There were, however, within this
scene certain profound differences between eastern and western
Europe that would suggest a line of demarcation running very
roughly down through the centre of Germany.

The first of these differences lay in the general form of society. To
the west of the Elbe and in Denmark there had developed between
aristocracy and peasantry a complexity of professional, commercial,
and industrialist classes, while the middle class to the east of the
Elbe was so slight as to be politically and socially insignificant.
There was a corresponding difference in the peasantry. To the west
the bulk of the land was farmed by a variety of tenants and small
owners, whereas the pattern of landholding in the east consisted
mostly of vast estates which the landlords farmed with serf labour.

In France royalty and aristocracy had been restored, but without
the trimmings of the *ancien régime*. *Émigré* land that had been confiscated by the government since 1789 could be given back only if it
had not been sold or granted away, but it has been reckoned that,
by 1820, the old nobility had regained about half of what they had
lost. Their ancient privileges, however, were gone for ever; they paid
taxes, their relationship with their tenants was on a purely business

footing, and their estates lay side by side with those of a new aristocracy—merchants, lawyers, and government officials who had
seized the chance offered by *la carrière ouverte aux talents*. Restoration
France presented a scene of a vigorous *arriviste* society imbued with
a belief in 'room at the top'—the France of Balzac's novels. Three-
quarters of a population of 29 million were still peasantry, but many
now owned their plots of land and consequently had no further
interest in revolution, although there was a high proportion of landless wage-labourers and a considerable class of tenant farmers;
métayage, the system whereby owner and farmer shared the profits,
still continued, mainly because it had been practised by the gentry
who on the whole, had tended to survive the Revolution.

In Spain and Italy restoration was distinctly less of a compromise.
In both countries the clergy and nobility regained their privileged
positions. The Spanish peasantry in the Peninsular War had fought,
not for freedom, but in order to expel the foreign invader; in Italy
the peasant, sometimes owning a little land, more often a tenant or
farming under the *mezzadria* (*métayage*) system, lived in a state of
poverty which reached the lowest form of life in the south, and in
neither country was the middle class numerous enough to make any
effective claim to the fruits of the Revolution.

The Swiss and Dutch peasantry had long enjoyed personal freedom, but their upper classes were of a kind slightly different to the
general European pattern. In the large merchant houses along the
canals of Amsterdam and in the splendid eighteenth-century
baroque mansions of Basle and Berne there dwelt the patrician families whose power lay not primarily in land, but in capital accu-
mulated during a long trading past and in the prestige of their name
within the confines of their city. A similar hierarchy of old families
was also to be found in the German Free Cities of Bremen, Lübeck,
Hamburg, and Frankfurt, still holding fast to the greatness that the
days of the Hanse had once given them, although by now conscious
of the challenge from a new middle class growing slowly in their
midst.

Immediately to the east of the Rhine the relationship of the peasant to his lord varied considerably from serfdom to the payment of
a nominal quit-rent. This process of change had already begun in
the eighteenth century and the most striking form of emancipation
was to be seen in Denmark in the 1780s, where enlightened despotism had abolished personal service and various forms of feudal
obligation and had carried through a process of enclosure in the
interests of the small farmer rather than of the great landlord. Elsewhere among the states of western Germany the changes had been
stimulated by the Napoleonic reforms and were hardly checked by
the restoration. But although, throughout the first forty years of the
nineteenth century, legal ties continued to be removed or curtailed

and feudal payments commuted into rents, the development of an independent landholding peasantry remained very slow, owing partly to the cost of commutation, partly to a land hunger among a growing population.

These social developments among bourgeois and peasantry west of the Elbe contrasted sharply with the scene in eastern Europe. It is true that, since 1807, a series of edicts in Prussia had broken down something of the barrier of caste, enabling nobility to enter commerce and the professions, the middle class to buy manorial estates, and the higher grade of peasant to become the owner of two-thirds of his original holding. But the main effect of this was to provide an economic outlet for the younger sons of impoverished nobility, for whom there had been insufficient opportunities in state service. It did not transform the situation, and although the numbers of bourgeois families increased among the holders of estates, the nobility continued to enjoy pride of place. In the countryside as a whole, the scene was dominated by the Prussian Junkers, a hard-working, intensely conservative class of gentry, who farmed their entire estates themselves with serf labour, and, far from breaking up, the tendency was for these great *latifundia* to increase, as they constantly absorbed new land that had originally been held by the peasantry.

In the Habsburg dominions and Russia the middle class did not amount to more than a tiny section of the population—merchants and civil servants scattered among the towns. Under Habsburg rule ownership of land, which was almost entirely a monopoly of the Crown and the nobility, carried with it considerable control over the resident peasantry, serfs who farmed smallholdings in return for a variety of dues, goods and days of labour-service—the *Robot*. In the German-Slav provinces the peasant did enjoy a certain freedom of movement and some could even dispose of their holdings as they wished, but this did not apply in Hungary, where the power of the Crown was more limited and the peasant was almost entirely at the mercy of the magnate.

In Russia the chief positions of state were the preserve of the nobility and although service in the army, navy, or bureaucracy, which Peter the Great had imposed upon them, was no longer obligatory, there were many families for whom such service had become a traditional function. The centre of peasant life was the village commune, the *mir*. 'Crown peasants', who belonged to the State, paid an *obruk* in kind or in cash for the right to cultivate the land; a few of the privately-owned serfs also paid an *obruk*, but the majority had to render *barshchina*, compulsory labour of about three days a week on their lord's land, for which they had to provide the implements. These *barshchina* serfs depended completely upon their masters, who could flog them, send them into the army or to Siberia with hard labour, use them as gambling stakes or sell them outright. 'Land-owners do whatever seems good to them on their estates, except inflict capital punishment; that is forbidden,' wrote Catherine the Great to Diderot. The consequence of such a system was that masters sometimes went in fear of their lives; Dostoevsky's father was killed by one of his own peasants, and later, if ever a landowner—as Tolstoy described in his novel *Resurrection*—attempted to intro-duce reforms, he was often frustrated by the mistrust of the very people that he was trying to help. 'God, how sad our Russia is,' sighed Pushkin, as Gogol read to him the manuscript of his novel *Dead Souls*. One has only to consider the penal code in Great Britain at this time to realize that harshness was a general feature of Euro-pean life, yet the social inequalities, which in the west might move reformers to anger, were so enormous in Russia that they could inspire nothing but a sense of despair.

Only on the periphery of the Russian dominions were there any regions free from serfdom. Throughout the period of Swedish col-onization the Finnish peasant had farmed his land as a free man and now continued to do so. In the Baltic provinces Tsar Alexander I, shortly after his accession, had proposed the emancipation of the serfs, but the scheme had been acceptable to the landlords mainly because serfdom had been found to be a hindrance to effective capitalist farming, and freedom without land was simply to turn the majority of the peasantry into an agricultural proletariat as depen-dent as before on their masters. In the Kingdom of Poland serfdom, which had been abolished in Napolean's Grand Duchy of Warsaw, was not restored, while on the Caucasian frontier the various Cos-sack communities, whom Tolstoy depicted in an early novel, were also free and in their capacity as military outposts even enjoyed immunity from taxation.

A second point of difference between east and west is to be seen in the varying levels of economic development. It would not be true to suggest that there was no industry at all in the east, since local centres of silk weaving in Saxony and coal and iron production in Silesia had flourished for a long time. Yet the principal activity in the east was agricultural, and the main commercial and industrial advantages lay with the west. In the eighteenth century the British, French, and Dutch with their sea power and overseas possessions had developed a considerable world trade, although their relative positions had changed somewhat during the recent war. By 1815 Great Britain's command of the sea routes was unchallenged and her early industrial revolution had enabled her to treble her exports since 1789; French trade now concentrated more on Europe and the

Near East, while in the Netherlands it was the Belgians rather than the Dutch who first seized on the opportunities offered by industrialization (see p. 86).

In Germany the desire for greater economic freedom, which had been one of the motive forces of the French Revolution, had led to a considerable weakening of the guilds within which the labour of the handcraftsman had been organized and protected. In the years immediately following 1815, however, industry in Germany was still too undeveloped to keep up the attack on the regulation of labour, and although guilds were abolished in Nassau in 1819, they had by 1830 been re-established in Hesse-Cassel, Hanover, and Oldenburg and retained some power in Bavaria.

National unity, which still eluded central Europe, greatly aided the commercial development of the states of the west in two other ways. The British and French merchant was free from the hindrance of internal customs boundaries. He had, too, a reasonably uniform monetary system. In 1815 the Bank of France, founded by Napoleon, had at first retained an exclusive right of note issue, although a little later under the restored monarchy this was extended to provincial banks; in 1814 the Netherlands Bank was given a similar monopoly; in Scandinavia inconvertible government notes circulated, while in Great Britain the single gold standard had been established in 1816.

In contrast to this the customs barriers between the thirty-eight states of the German Confederation, the twenty-two Swiss cantons and the various kingdoms and duchies in Italy seriously hampered the activity of the merchant in his own country, while making a concerted policy of protection against foreign competition highly problematical. This particularism in central Europe was also reflected in a diversity of monetary systems. Twelve different currencies were in circulation in Switzerland, some restricted to their own canton. Among the states and Free Cities of Germany the silver thaler varied greatly in worth and there were differing relations between gold and silver. In Italy every state had its own currency. Such a confusion provided a roaring trade for the money-changers, but in almost every other respect was disastrous for any profound economic development. Thus the idea of unification that came increasingly to occupy men's thoughts in this part of Europe was to be prompted not simply by nationalist aspiration, but by a growing desire to overcome these economic consequences of particularism.

Finally, the third major difference lay in the confusion of peoples and classes that was to be found in eastern Europe. This is not to suggest that the west had yet attained a homogeneity of nation and state. Regional differences in sentiment and dialect have already been noted in Germany and Italy. Three main languages were in use in Switzerland, while German dialect was common in Alsace, and French in parts of Savoy. Yet, with the exception of the Belgians, whose upper and middle classes spoke French rather than the Flemish and Walloon of the peasantry, class divisions in the lands west of the Elbe and in Denmark did not rest primarily on differences of race or language.*

The reason for the contrast east of the Elbe lay in the constant shifting of peoples across the great plain-lands of Europe ever since the decline of the Roman Empire. The movement of the German and Slav tribes westwards, the violent incursions of the Huns in the fifth century, the Magyars in the ninth and the Tartars in the thirteenth, and the great surge of the Ottoman Turks through the Balkans, which by the sixteenth century had brought the frontier of Islam to within seventy miles of Vienna, had all to some extent been balanced by a series of movements eastwards—the Swedish colonization of the south coast of Finland, the conquest of the Baltic provinces by the Teutonic Knights, and the peaceful settlement of German farmers and traders across the mountains of Bohemia and over the plains of Poland. Except in the lands immediately to the east of the Elbe this interweaving did not result in any general assimilation, and the consequent stratification of conquerors, immigrant settlers and subject peoples, divided by race and language, created social divisions of a type totally different from those found in western Europe.

The situation within the Habsburg dominions provides the most striking instance of this strange medley. The three dominant classes were of totally different origin—German, Magyar, and Polish. The German element were well established in the Alpine regions, the Tyrol, Austria, and the Sudetenland, where the old Bohemian nobility had become germanized since the battle of White Mountain in 1620. From this German group most of the government bureaucracy were recruited and their hold on the towns was everywhere considerable—even in Budapest the local council carried on its business in German until the 1880s. In Hungary, the great nobility were essentially Magyar, but, speaking French, German, or Italian, remained a caste apart, entrenched in their enormous estates with their town and country palaces, and it was only the gentry who maintained a real contact with the peasants, many of whom were by now magyarized, although less than half the total population of Hungary were actually Magyar-speaking. On the other hand, if one excludes the Slovak, Croat, and Rouman peasantry, the thought of

---

* This refers simply to the Continent. The social divisions in Ireland with an upper class of Protestant Anglo-Irish stock were not unlike those to be found in eastern Europe.

a historic past did give Hungary a greater sense of national unity
than existed elsewhere in the Habsburg lands. In Galicia, the Polish
ruling class had been left unaffected by their transference to the
Habsburgs, their peasantry consisting of Poles, Little Russians, and
Roumans.

Below these three dominant groups of German, Magyar, and Pole
there remained a mass of subject peasant peoples—Bohemians and
Slovaks to the north, Slovenes in Carniola, Croats to the south, and
Roumans to the east in Transylvania—and among all these the only
hope of personal advancement lay in settling in a nearby town and
in acquiring a knowledge of the German language.

Along the south coast of the Baltic the same dovetailing of peoples
by classes was equally common. In East Prussia and the Polish
provinces of West Prussia the German Junker was overlord of a
German and Slavonic peasantry. In the adjoining borderland of the
Russian dominions this German upper class did not extend into
Lithuania, where in the great days of its independence as a Principality there had been a local aristocracy. Their descendants, however, were by now Polish-speaking and lived in a style very similar
to the Polish nobility, working their estates with Lithuanian, Polish,
and White Russian peasantry. Farther up the coast still, the upper
class became German again, the Baltic barons, descendants of the
Teutonic Knights, using the labour of Estonian and Lettish serfs,
while to the north of the Gulf, in Finland, centuries of Swedish rule
had established a Swedish-speaking nobility divided by language
and origin from the peasantry who were almost entirely Finnish.

East of this borderland social differences were equally marked in
the major areas of European Russia. The Russian nobility and many
of the gentry had become westernized, spoke French, and divided
their time between their town houses in Moscow or St Petersburg
and their country residences. Yet although they led a life remote
from the serfs on their estates, the differences of language and west-
ernization were in a sense more artificial than in the Russian bor-
derlands and the Habsburg territories, and despite the enormous
gap between upper and lower classes, a patriotic fervour could still
unite them, as Napoleon had learnt to his cost in 1812.

To the south of Croatia, Hungary, and Russia lay all that part
of Europe still under the rule of the Turkish Sultan. The Balkans
were a maze of different peoples, Macedonians, Bulgars, Greeks,
Serbs, Vlachs, and Albanians intensely jealous of each other, and
speaking a variety of dialects. There had been no great colonization
by the conquerors, although about 150,000 Turks had settled in
Greece. Religion was the fundamental point of distinction; the mos-
ques of Islam were to be found in most of the towns of the Balkans,
particularly among the Albanians who were very largely Moslem,

but the Turkish pashas made no attempt to convert the Christian Slavs and Greeks, mostly of the eastern Orthodox Church, whose religion simply marked them as a subject class, liable to heavy taxation. The main feature of Balkan society was the family or small village headed by its local patriarch, and the only people who had been able to establish a general influence outside their own region were the Greeks; they enjoyed a commercial superiority over all the races of the Ottoman empire and their skill in finance and their knowledge of languages, which was forbidden to Moslems, made them invaluable as tax collectors and local officials in the day-to-day government of Turkish territories in Europe. In Greece itself Greek and Moslem poor alike were harried by a Turco-Greek officialdom; since the beginning of the eighteenth century Greeks had been nominated by the authorities in Constantinople as rulers of the Danubian provinces of Moldavia and Wallachia; the Bulgarian Church was by now under their control, and the Bulgars, who were entirely peasant, had almost as great a hatred for the Greek as they had for the Turk.

Thus, in conclusion, while it is undeniable that the statesmen who devised the new frontiers at the Congress of Vienna paid little attention to national sentiment, it is also clear that any political organization of central and eastern Europe could only be on a non-national basis. The problem for the governments was how long such an assumption would remain valid after the excitement of the Napoleonic interlude.

Chapter 3

Governments and Churches

1. The governments of Europe

It is perfectly understandable that the very thought of the Revolution as it developed after 1789 should be anathema to the sovereigns of Europe; yet some of its ideas, at least, had already found expression in their notions of government long before the National Assembly in France had begun its work. The last half of the eighteenth century had been a period of enlightened despotism in which the monarchs had seriously attempted to introduce striking changes aimed at a greater economic and administrative efficiency and at an improvement in the position of the peasantry. These reforms, imposed from the throne, had come up against a dogged resistance from the upper class, and the strength of this opposition revealed the fundamental paradox of the *ancien régime* that there were considerable limits to the power of the sovereigns. Frederick the Great of Prussia and Catherine II of Russia avoided disaster only because they did not try their nobility too far; in the Empire the more radical policy of Joseph II led to open revolt in Hungary and the Austrian Netherlands, while in France it was the attempt of Louis XVI's government to lay a general land tax on the nobility that ultimately brought about the *révolte nobiliaire* in 1788 and the demand for a summoning of an Estates General, which the privileged Orders believed they could control. By 1815 the sovereigns knew well that they had more to fear than a turbulent aristocracy, who by now clung to them for support, and the effect of the Revolution was naturally to make them far more conservative in their outlook. Yet, at the same time, the practical achievement of the French had confirmed the need for a greater efficiency in mobilizing the general potentiality of their states, and the more intelligent of the rulers had realized the importance of anticipating any outbreak by introducing reform themselves, before it was forced upon them through pressure from below.

This need for change was reflected particularly in all those countries whose governments Napoleon himself had not personally altered. It was in Prussia, after the shock of her military defeats in 1806, that the most radical reforms had taken place. Stein and

Hardenberg had carried through a partial emancipation of the peasantry from personal servitude to their landlords (see p. 20); the system of education was remodelled, so that the pupil passed through the primary school and the Gymnasium on to the newly founded University of Berlin, and governmental administration was reorganized with a council of state which included the heads of departments under the presidency of the King. At the same time, Scharnhorst and Gneisenau endeavoured to make the best of Napoleon's decree of 1808 that the Prussian army should be no stronger than 42,000 by introducing a short-service system of conscription, from which the citizen passed into the reserve. In the regular army promotion was to be based rather more on merit, although, within itself, the Officer Corps was to retain that character peculiar to Prussian history, whereby it stood apart from the ordinary institutions of, government, and thus enjoyed its own personal relationship to the sovereign. The only concessions to liberal hopes consisted of Stein's municipal law of 1808, which allowed the towns their own elected councils, and, in 1823, the recognition of the provincial assemblies, the *Landtage*, based usually on the old division of Estates. Important though these two types of institution were to be later, however, they still did not constitute an effective check, in 1815, on the central executive of King and bureaucracy.

In Russia, government remained entirely in the hands of the Tsar, and although Alexander, who prided himself on his liberal outlook, had carried through various reforms, they were less sweeping than in Prussia. The administrative colleges established by Peter the Great were turned into eight ministries, each with its departmental head. Torture was abolished, as well as serfdom in the Baltic provinces, and there was an extensive promotion of schools and universities. The principal field for Alexander's liberalism, however, was not in Russia itself, but in the newly acquired territories of Finland and Poland.

In 1809, before the four Estates of the Finnish Diet at Porvoo, Alexander promised to maintain 'the religion and fundamental laws of the land as well as the privileges and rights which each class in the said Grand Duchy in particular and all the inhabitants in general, be their position high or low, have hitherto enjoyed according to the Constitution'. This confirmation of the position that Finland had enjoyed under Swedish rule granted rather less than might be imagined, since, although Sweden had been a constitutional monarchy throughout the major part of the eighteenth century, the two *coups d'état* of Gustavus III in 1772 and 1789 had considerably strengthened the powers of the sovereign, and Alexander never actually summoned another Finnish Diet, although he constantly talked about it. Nevertheless, Alexander was determined to reconcile the Finns to his rule. He styled himself Grand Duke of Finland, gave back for inclusion within the Duchy the Karelian districts taken by Peter the Great in 1721, appointed a Swedo-Finn Baron Sprengt-porten as his first governor, and established a Finnish Committee at St Petersburg to advise him on questions of administration.

In Poland his liberalism went still further. 'Gentlemen,' he said to the Poles at Vilna on his way back from Paris in 1814, 'yet a little patience, and you will be more than satisfied with me.' The consti-tution, which Alexander granted as King of Poland in 1816, owed much to the Napoleonic system in the Grand Duchy of Warsaw. Poland was to have complete autonomy with her own budget and an army of 40,000, while Polish was recognized as the sole official language, and the Napoleonic Code, freedom of the press and re-ligious toleration were all guaranteed. The Diet was to consist of an upper House, whose members were chosen for life by the King, and an elective Chamber of Deputies with seventy-seven seats for the lesser nobility and fifty-one for the Third Estate. An electorate of 100,000 out of a population of slightly more than three million was a considerably higher proportion than that which existed in Res-toration France and was roughly on a par with the British. In fact, the power of the Diet meant little more than the right of petition, and the government of the country was mainly vested in an exec-utive council under the direction of a viceroy appointed by the King. Nevertheless, the Polish constitution was in many ways a remark-able concession, and although Alexander later fell out with the Diet, the only major grievance still outstanding among the Poles in 1815 was Russia's retention of the lands that she had taken in the par-tition of 1772.

In Denmark the King's power had been absolute ever since 1661, and in 1815 Frederick VI could still rule without the hindrance of any parliamentary institution. In contrast to this, the deposition of Gustavus IV of Sweden in 1809 had been followed by the sum-moning of the Estates of the *Riksdag*, who offered the crown to Gus-tavus's uncle as Charles XIII, on condition that they should be able to exercise the constitutional check on the King's actions, of which they had been deprived by Gustavus III's Act of Union and Security in 1789. The Estates retained their influence on the suc-cession, for, on the death of Charles XIII's heir in 1810, they eventually elected as Crown Prince Marshal Bernadotte, who had impressed Swedish envoys favourably while he had been acting on Napoleon's behalf in Denmark. Bernadotte soon adopted the inter-ests of his new country, joined with the Russians in 1812 against his former master, and was chiefly responsible for the taking of Norway in 1814. This was not merely a blow for Denmark; the Norwegians themselves, who had just established their own Parliament, the *Stort-ing*, and elected a Danish prince as their king, had no wish to be absorbed by Sweden and insisted that their constitution should be safeguarded before they would accept a personal union under the Swedish crown.

Of all the governments of Europe there was one essential characteristic that marked the Austrian empire off from the others. Prussia and Russia both included alien peoples within their frontiers, but these were mostly on the periphery of their domains, whose core remained essentially Prussian or Russian. The remarkable feature of the Austrian empire was that it lacked a basic national characteristic. The origin of the Habsburg fortunes had lain in the Alpine lands, but the acquisition of the crowns of Bohemia and Hungary, Galicia, and the Italian provinces of Lombardy and Venetia had given their possessions the character of a vast family estate, in which the separate regions simply owed a personal allegiance to the Emperor. The principal problem in the management of so unwieldy an estate was the precise sharing of government between Vienna and the provinces. Decentralization, which such a diversity of territories seemed to demand, might mean weakness in the face of powerful neighbours, and, in an age of rising nationalism, even disintegration. Instead, centralization, which Maria Theresa and her son Joseph II had attempted to impose in the last half of the eighteenth century, had resulted in overburdening the bureaucracy at Vienna to such an extent that administration moved at a snail's pace. Beneath the Council of State, the *Staatsrat*, there existed a confusion of departments and committees whose responsibilities constantly overlapped and whose work was seldom governed by a clear line of policy. The ministers were the personal servants of the Emperor, appointed and dismissed as he wished. 'He overwhelms me with kindness,' said Metternich of his master in 1829, 'and gives me his confidence, but he does this because I follow the direction which he lays down for me. If I had the misfortune to leave this prescribed path, Prince Metternich would not be Minister of Foreign Affairs for twenty-four hours longer.' At least Metternich, who gained the official title of Chancellor in 1821, knew that he was responsible for foreign policy; the duties of the other ministers varied from month to month and they could never know that the Emperor had not gone behind their backs to deal directly with a civil servant. 'Administration', commented Metternich's colleague Hartig, 'has taken the place of government.' Thus the cumbersome system of centralization not merely had the effect of reducing provincial assemblies to a state of powerless make-believe; it was utterly frustrating for the local officials. 'The want of some all-controlling hand', wrote the British Consul-General in Lombardy in a dispatch to Palmerston in January 1848, 'is most severely felt and is admitted by the local authorities who bitterly complain of the delays of the Government at Vienna from whence they can get no answer to their repeated Representations.'

Only in Hungary was there some check to centralization. The Magyars had always insisted that they recognized the Habsburg as their King, never as the Emperor. This was not a nationalist movement in the nineteenth-century sense. The Hungarian Diet, at which Latin was used as the only acceptable *lingua franca* among so many different languages, was dominated by the nobility and used as a bulwark against Habsburg interference which threatened to undermine their privileges, and even when Francis refused to summon a Diet between 1811 and 1825, provincial government remained in the hands of *comitats* of local nobility which controlled the raising of taxes and recruits for the army.

Other countries could later come to terms with nationalism or liberalism; for Austria no such compromise was possible without jeopardizing her very existence. 'My realm resembles a worm-eaten house,' said the Emperor Francis I to a Russian diplomat. 'If one part is removed, one can never tell how much will fall.' Yet, although the coincidence of differences of class with those of language and origin was to lend impetus to nationalist aspirations, it did also supply the key to Habsburg survival. If any of the dominant groups—Germans, Magyars or Poles—were to present the government with a demand for political autonomy or independence, they seldom had the support of the peasantry, who felt that Habsburg rule, however remote, might to some extent hold their masters in check. On the other hand, any national movement among the subject peoples naturally implied a challenge to the order of society as unpalatable to the German, Magyar, and Polish landowners as it was to the Habsburgs themselves. 'My peoples are strangers,' commented Francis I. 'Out of their dislike order is born, and of their hatred universal peace.' This realization did at least give the monarchy a policy for self-defence; a final solution to the problem of its inheritance it was never to find. The struggle to do so lies behind much of its history in the later years of the nineteenth century, and its ultimate failure was to bring down a whole European society in the collapse of the Central Powers at the end of the first World War in 1918.

In the lands surrounding France, which had come more directly under Napoleonic forms of rule, the forces of restoration were determined to root out the revolutionary principle. It is true that, in 1815, the Fundamental Law of the Kingdom of the United Netherlands included a States General of two Chambers, one of which was a representative assembly, but this was actually little more than a façade of constitutional government. The Belgians had never accepted it when it had been presented to them for ratification, and despite the fact that the seat of government alternated every year between Brussels and The Hague, they never forgot their resentment at being incorporated with the Dutch (see p. 71). In any case, the new system did not include ministerial responsibility, and the deputies had only a limited control over finance. 'I can reign without ministers,' stated King William I; 'it is I alone who govern and I alone am responsible.'

In Germany, although the general effect of Napoleon's simplification of the map was preserved, the ghost of the Holy Roman Empire still seemed to haunt Europe in the form of the German Confederation devised at the Congress of Vienna. The frontiers of the Confederation, with its thirty-eight states, excluded a part of the Habsburg and Prussian territories and included a non-German element among rulers and populations; Bohemia and Moravia lay within its borders; the King of the Netherlands was Grand Duke of Luxemburg; the personal union of the British and Hanoverian crowns was to last until 1837; and Holstein was governed by the King of Denmark in his capacity as Duke of Slesvig-Holstein.

The most that could be said for the German Confederation was that it had defined a frontier within which the individual states, in time of war, would be unable to sign separate treaties of peace. Beyond this, as with most confederations, the *Bundestag*, the Federal Diet sitting at Frankfurt under an Austrian president, was no more than a collection of ambassadors, each concerned to safeguard the sovereignty of his own state. The system of voting in a plenary session was such that a combination of Prussia, Austria and the four major kingdoms of Bavaria, Württemberg, Saxony, and Hanover could destroy any chance of the two-thirds majority needed to carry a measure, while for a change in the constitution itself a unanimous vote was required. The Federal Act, drawn up at the Congress, had authorized the *Bundestag* to organize a military force, as well as some common economic system, but the local jealousies to which the whole system gave full play made it impossible for any executive machinery to emerge at all. The German Confederation represented no more than an arrangement whereby those areas of Germany which lay beyond the frontiers of Prussia and Austria might be sufficiently organized to be drawn within Austria's sphere of influence without becoming a positive political force of their own. Two possible dangers threatened to undermine this scheme—discord between Austria and Prussia over supremacy in Germany, and German nationalism demanding the creation of a stronger central government, which might curtail the sovereignty of the individual states. In fact, particularism in 1815 was strong enough to check either of these dangers. The conservative element in the Prussian government had no wish to become further involved in Germany, for fear of Prussia losing her identity, and consequently had no objection to Austria holding the presidency of the *Bundestag*, while against German nationalism Metternich could rely on the princes, who were determined to preserve their own sovereign power.

Within each of the German states themselves the Federal Act had declared that *eine landständische Verfassung* should be set up. The problem here was that *Verfassung* had a wider connotation than the word 'constitution' in English; it could simply mean a series of governmental edicts of purely executive significance, while *landständische* referred to a gathering of various Estates drawn from different strata of society and often antagonistic to each other—the same difficulties as hampered the full development of the Swedish *Riksdag* and the Hungarian Diet. Thus, many of the thirty-eight governments were virtually absolutist. It would, however, be wrong to apply this judgement to the whole of Germany. A parliamentary tradition of a sort had survived in Württemberg, Saxony, and the Rhine Duchies where the Estates had continued to exercise some control over taxation and the local military establishment; and it was partly owing to this tradition that, in the years following 1815, the princes of the larger states in the south-west, Bavaria, Baden, and Württemberg, governed within the framework of two-chamber assemblies. Yet, while it would be wrong to picture a scene of absolute authoritarianism in every state in Germany, there could be no denying the general weakness of parliamentary life, even where it existed. An upper House of local aristocracy had little contact with a lower House, from whom they regarded themselves as socially apart, while the lower House, elected through an extremely narrow franchise, often consisted of many of the same individuals who composed the local bureaucracy. The existence of such bodies might help to keep alive the idea of constitutional government; they were hardly likely in themselves to constitute a real bulwark of resistance to the prince.

In Switzerland a similar settlement was to emerge. For centuries the Swiss cantons had each pursued their independent policies, only loosely bound by a variety of local agreements, the French-speaking area round the Lake of Geneva and the Italian-speaking communities of the Ticino Valley being generally in a state of subjection to the German-speaking cantons to the north. In 1798 French intervention had cut through all forms of cantonal autonomy and imposed a centralized system which, although it made all individuals equal before the law and was nominally based on an elective principle, really placed all power in the hands of an executive directory. Napoleon's Act of Mediation in 1803 abolished this rigid centralization, which was historically alien to the spirit of Swiss institutions, and established in its place a federal system which restored many of the old sovereign rights of the cantons, while preserving a general Swiss citizenship with freedom of settlement and equality among the cantons.

The fall of Napoleon brought two different groups to the fore. The conservatives wished for a complete restoration of the situation before 1798. Berne was particularly anxious to re-establish her rule over Vaud and Argau, the Alpine cantons wished to return to their old democratic autonomy, and the patrician families of the large towns wanted to regain their privileged position of local authority. The second group, liberals who had enjoyed social freedom under the Napoleonic system and feared the loss of the cantons' new equality of status, pinned their hopes to the maintenance of a strong federal authority, and the conflict between the two became so fierce that it was only the threat of Allied intervention, together with a good deal of negotiation in the Swiss committee at Vienna, that prevented the outbreak of civil war.

The Federal Pact was eventually drawn up in September 1815. The most that the liberals were able to achieve was the preservation of the existing cantons on a basis of equality, including the three additions of Geneva, Valais, and Neuchâtel. Thus, since the French- and Italian-speaking regions were not to be reduced once more to the level of subject cantons, French and Italian remained on a par with German as official languages. Apart from this, the conservatives gained all that they had wanted. In matters of coinage, posts, local customs duties, and education the cantons were to enjoy complete autonomy. They could pursue their own political arrangements, including private military and economic agreements with other countries, provided that these did not affect the Confederation. The recognition of a general Swiss citizenship and of freedom of worship was withdrawn, although Roman Catholic religious houses were to be guaranteed. The central government, the Diet, was correspondingly weak, merely a collection of representatives, each voting on instructions from his canton. There was not even a federal capital, Zürich, Berne, and Lucerne acting in turn as the *Vorort*, the canton representing the Confederation. Unlike the German Confederation, however, the Swiss did have a Federal army, over 32,000 strong, in order to be able to defend their neutrality. In this way, virtually free from any over-riding authority, the patrician families of Berne, Basle, Lucerne, Solothurn, and Fribourg regained their old authority, while even in the cantons which drew up new constitutions the franchise was so restricted by qualifications of property and education that government was mostly in the hands of a local oligarchy. The liberal elements, although defeated, kept up the struggle in the towns, but, as in Germany, they knew that the crux of the problem lay in the creation of a stronger central government which would be in a position to impose their solution on the whole of Switzerland.

Thus, in Germany and Switzerland, only a battered fragment of the Napoleonic régime survived the general restoration. Still less remained in Italy and Spain. Nowhere in Italy was there even the pretence of a constitutional government under the restored sovereigns, who, ironically, had been welcomed back by their subjects. Victor Emmanuel, ruling his enlarged dominions from Turin, the Habsburg princes in the central duchies, Pius VII, the gentle Pope whom Napoleon had carried off into captivity, Ferdinand of Naples who promised a constitution in order to outdo Murat and then suppressed it, all ruled through a handful of ministers who were responsible only to them, while in the north Lombardy and Venetia lay under the control of Austrian governors. In fact, with the exception of Naples, this despotism was reasonably mild, particularly in Tuscany, where the Grand Duke restored the code of his Habsburg predecessor, Leopold, but in the last analysis the strength of most of these governments rested not on the support of their subjects, but on the Austrian emperor, firmly established in Lombardy and Venetia, and with a private agreement whereby he could call for troops from Naples and Tuscany.

In Spain the transformation was as complete. Joseph Bonaparte had at least approved a draft constitution, although it was never put into effect, and the Spanish *Cortes*, summoned by the leaders of the resistance to Napoleon's armies, had produced a constitution in 1812 at Cadiz, which would have established a parliamentary monarchy. Yet, when Wellington's forces had reached the Pyrenees and King Ferdinand VII had returned from a fairly comfortable retirement in France, his first action was to annul the entire constitution by royal decree, after which he proceeded to rule as he wished with all the apparatus of censorship and secret police.

In contrast to this whole-hearted restoration of an earlier system in the territories whose governments Napoleon had completely remodelled, Louis XVIII issued to his people, on 4 June 1814, a Charter whose purpose was to convince all classes that the work of the Revolution would not be undone. The inviolability of property reassured those who had bought their lands since the Revolution, and the guaranteeing of the public debt naturally suited the investing class; there was to be liberty of the press, provided that there was no infringement of the 'lois qui doivent réprimer les abus de cette liberté', and all Frenchmen were to enjoy equality before the law and freedom from arbitrary arrest. The pattern of government came closer to the English system than any of the French constitutions drawn up since 1789. Although the King alone had the right to propose new laws, they had to be passed by a Chamber of hereditary peers and a Chamber of Deputies, one-fifth of whose seats were to come up for election every year. The strength of this lower House, whose size was first put at 258 seats and, after Waterloo, increased to 402, lay in its right to sanction all taxation for one year at a time. The deputies, to be resident in the *département* that they represented,

were drawn from a relatively small class who paid 1,000 francs in
direct annual taxation, and the franchise itself was restricted to men
of not less than thirty years of age who paid 300 francs a year—an
electorate of approximately 100,000 out of a total population of
about 29 million.

Within this framework the King had reasonable freedom to
govern. As supreme head of the executive he had the right to choose
his ministers from within or outside the Chambers and they
remained individually his personal servants without any form of
Cabinet solidarity. The centralized Napoleonic system of Prefects
in the provinces survived the Restoration, and here the King's right
to appoint all public officials gave him considerable control over
local administration. Certain clauses, too, in the Charter were open
to wide interpretation, as, for example, over the Press laws or over
the King's power to issue ordinances 'nécessaires pour l'exécution
des lois et la sûreté de l'État'. Naturally home or foreign policy
might always be criticized in the Chambers, but the royal government had a little room in which to manoeuvre, since there was no
limit to the number of peers that the King could create, and his
right to dissolve the Chamber of Deputies (provided that a new one
was elected within three months) did give him a chance to appeal
to the electorate.

On the whole, the Charter represented a serious attempt to heal
the wounds of France and to establish a reasonable balance of government, but inevitably it left much to the good sense of the reigning
sovereign and to the temper of the upper classes. It was always open
to amendment by constitutional means; thus conscription, which it
declared abolished, was restored in 1818, and the continual alterations in electoral procedure reflected the various changes in the
political outlook of the Chamber of Deputies during the next ten
years (see pp. 52–4). The French by now had had ample experience that a written constitution could never be foolproof, but the
Charter was at least the best compromise that could satisfy the conditions of 1814, and the average Frenchman could feel that, in
France at least, the turmoil of the preceding twenty-five years had
not been entirely in vain.

2. Religion

For the Papacy the fall of Napoleon restored rather less than it did
for the secular governments. In Spain, Italy, and Bavaria its powers
were almost entirely re-established, but the old prince bishoprics in
Germany were not recreated, and in Austria Francis I retained a
good many of the restrictions imposed on the Church by Joseph II
in the 1780s. Louis XVIII's Charter of 1814, had declared that
'la religion catholique, apostolique et romaine, est la religion

d'État', but the French clergy were far from regaining the position
of a privileged Estate. They continued to be largely dependent upon
a salary from the State, and although they were allowed to develop
institutions of secondary education parallel to the state system,
education still remained technically the monopoly of Napoleon's
University of France.

The question of the precise relation of a Catholic sovereign to his
own clergy was of long standing in Europe, and the recent trials of
the Church at the hands of secular power in France, Italy, and Germany were to give renewed force to the Ultramontane movement,
causing the clergy and laity to turn to Rome for practical as well as
spiritual leadership. 'Point de christianisme sans le catholicisme,'
wrote Joseph de Maistre, 'point de catholicisme sans le pape, point
de pape sans la suprématie qui lui appartient.' In France Ultramontanism appealed mostly to the lower clergy as a means of escape
from the authority of the bishops; in Germany the movement spread
rapidly, particularly in Bavaria where King Ludwig I (see genealogical table, p. 484) was determined that Munich should become
the cultural and political centre of German Catholicism. But, however much they might differ over the precise relation of the secular
and spiritual power, most Catholics believed profoundly that they
should work together in a closely knit harmony; the notion of
Throne and Altar in some form governed their political thinking.
In regions where Catholics were under Protestant rule, no such ideal
was immediately within reach, and it was in Belgium and Ireland
that the struggle for Catholic independence was later to encourage
the rise of a movement of Liberal Catholicism aiming at a divorce
between the secular and the spiritual authority.

In Protestant countries the counterpart to Throne and Altar was
the doctrine of Church and State. In Great Britain, where there were
large numbers of Nonconformists, Anglicans technically held a
monopoly of all national and local positions of authority. 'Westminster Abbey', as a contemporary wrote, 'is part of the constitution.' In the State Churches of Scandinavia the monopoly was less
irksome, since all but a tiny fraction of the population of Denmark,
Sweden, and Norway were Lutheran. In Prussia many of the more
conservative saw the union of Church and State as a bulwark
against unbelief and supported Frederick William III's advocacy
of a common liturgy among all Protestant Churches under the aegis
of the State, although one group under Schleiermacher strongly
resisted the tendency of the Prussian bureaucracy to control the
bishops and pastors.

In Russia there was no debate at all over the problem, since the
Orthodox Church had long existed within the framework of the
State, although there were by now, as a result of recent acquisitions,
a variety of religious minorities on the fringe of her territories—

Lutheran Finns and Balts, Catholic Poles, Uniate Ruthenians, who observed Orthodox rites, but were obedient to the Pope, and, in the regions of the Black Sea and the Caspian, pockets of Moslem and Buddhist Tartars. It was outside the frontiers of Russia that the political significance of the Eastern Church was most marked. The Orthodox Christian Slavs under the rule of the Turk in the Balkans naturally looked towards the Tsar as their protector, and throughout the nineteenth century Russia was able to use this situation as a means of weakening the Turkish hold. Among the Balkan Slavs as a whole, however, the religious background created considerable division, since the Albanians had largely accepted Islam, the Bulgars resented the hold of the Greeks over their Church, and the gulf between Catholic Croats under Habsburg rule and the Orthodox Serbs was later to make the creation of any large South Slav state extremely difficult.

In contrast to the laxity and secularism of the eighteenth century the early half of the nineteenth does mark an important period of religious revival. This naturally reawakened the old mistrust between the Christian sects, which was to become bitter over the question of national systems of education, and the re-establishing of the Jesuit Order by Pope Pius VII in 1814, followed by their rapid infiltration into most Catholic areas, tended to exacerbate the latent antagonism. In the main, however, this revival did not upset the general tendency towards a toleration of dissenting minorities. The 680,000 Huguenots in France had full rights of citizenship and their clergy even received a salary from the State. Prussia treated her newly acquired Roman Catholic subjects in the Rhineland with reasonable tact, as did Bavaria her Protestant subjects in Franconia. In the southern Netherlands, now under a predominantly Dutch government, the Roman Catholic clergy had complete religious freedom, and in Russia Alexander I went so far as to include a Roman Catholic archbishop and a leader of the Lutheran congregations in the Holy Synod of the Orthodox Church, and even toyed with the idea of a union of the Eastern and Roman Churches.

This ideal of mutual toleration did not extend, however, to the Jews, who at this time numbered about 10 million in Europe. The reasons for the antagonism from which they had always suffered were partly economic, partly racial —economic, because the laws which forbade them to hold land had caused them to concentrate on commercial enterprise in the towns, at which they were remarkably skilful—racial, because their own religious exclusiveness had prevented their assimilation in the countries where they settled. In the west their numbers were small, and after 1815 they were allowed, in France and the Netherlands, to retain the full rights of citizenship that Napoleon had granted them. In central Europe anti-Semitism was much fiercer. The Catholic states, and particularly the Free Cities of the German Confederation, had strongly opposed the plea which Metternich and Hardenberg had made at the Congress of Vienna for a continuation of the toleration which they had enjoyed under Napoleon. In the end, the matter had had to be left to the Diet at Frankfurt, where no ruling was ever given, and thus, in many towns in Germany, the Jews were once more banished to the ghetto. In the Swiss cantons and the Italian states they lost their civic rights, and although they gained a few concessions in Hungary, none were made in Bohemia and Galicia, while Vienna remained a closed city to them, except for two hundred 'tolerated' families. The Jews were most numerous in Poland; here the hatred was particularly strong, and indeed, throughout the whole of central and eastern Europe, the temporary disorders during successive periods of revolutionary upheaval usually provided an opportunity for a *pogrom* of the local Jewish population.

For the Jews themselves the question of assimilation was as difficult as it was for the Christians who resented their presence. Lacking a country of their own, harried by constant antagonism and frequent persecution, they clung to their religion, their customs, and their use of Yiddish in everyday life as the only means of maintaining their identity. At the end of the eighteenth century the massacres in the Ukraine had given rise to a new conservative sect, the Hassidim, demanding complete isolation from the Christians around them, and the majority of Jews at this time shared this outlook. There were, however, some signs of a desire for assimilation. In Germany Mendelssohn, the friend of Lessing, and, in Russia, Levinsohn each worked towards this end; in Alsace the Jewish population became mainly French-speaking. Some of the more ambitious, such as the poet Heine or the Socialist Lassalle, renounced their Jewish faith—Disraeli and Karl Marx were both the sons of converts but, on the whole, conversions to Christianity among the Jews were rare—less than 200,000 in the whole of the century. In any case, conversion was a factor of minor importance. The roots of European anti-Semitism lay far deeper than any mere religious antagonism, and the restrictions imposed on Jews were not simply the result of a governmental tyranny; they reflected the general sense of aversion among the non-Jewish peoples themselves and in a century which was to bring greater power to the masses, anti-Semitism was to become a factor of increasing importance throughout the Continent.

Chapter 4

The Outlook for the Future

1. Diplomatic considerations

It was not unnatural that for many decades after the Napoleonic war France should be regarded as the greatest potential threat to the peace of Europe. Her military prowess was obvious, and, with the exception of Russia, her population (see Appendix 7, p. 492) was still the largest of any state on the Continent. These fears over a possible revival of French acquisitiveness were to have a marked effect on the course of later events. They played their part in the emergence of Belgium as an independent state; they were an essential feature in the story of Italian unification; Bismarck was to make skilful use of them in the three wars with which he created the German Empire, and even after 1870, Great Britain, whose naval bases were planned mainly on the assumption of French hostility, continued to regard France as her major opponent in the colonial field until the end of the century.

The other source of tension lay in Russia. The great circumference of her land frontier through central Asia naturally created a sense of uneasiness among the British with their vast interests in India, and after the building of the Trans-Siberian railway in the 1890s the Far East was to become a new area of rivalry among the great Powers. In 1815, however, it was Russia's expansion westwards that awoke the gravest concern. In Scandinavia her long duel with Sweden throughout the eighteenth century had culminated in her annexation of Finland in 1808. As it transpired, this was to be the end of the struggle, for although the Swedes had accepted Bernadotte as their Crown Prince in the hope that the presence of a Napoleonic marshal might enable them to recover their former position, Bernadotte himself, seeing the futility of any further attempt, had persuaded them to accept Norway as adequate compensation for the loss of Finland; from this time on, so long as some form of balance existed among the Continental Powers, Sweden could reckon to avoid being dragged into the major crises of the nineteenth and twentieth centuries.

But if the dispute in the extreme north appeared now to be closed,

a new issue had already arisen in the south-east of Europe, where
the gradual decline of Turkish rule in the Balkans was to offer a
vast field for Russian expansion. The ultimate fate of these Turkish
territories in Europe constituted the Eastern Question and particularly concerned two of the Powers—Great Britain and Austria.

For the British the principal aim was to ensure that the Russian
Black Sea fleet might not enter the eastern Mediterranean. It had
been established by the Anglo-Turkish agreement of 1809 that the
Dardanelles should be open to merchant vessels and closed to warships in time of peace, and open to Turkey's friends and closed to
her enemies in time of war, and since the absorption of Balkan territories by Russia might eventually rob Turkey of her freedom of
action in maintaining this agreement, the policy most likely to be
followed by the British government was one of supporting Turkey
against Russian encroachment. In this, however, the British were
hampered by two other factors—first, the weakness of Turkish
domestic government which British ambassadors at Constantinople
in the early nineteenth century were constantly endeavouring to
reform, and, second, the growing nationalism among the Balkan
peoples who, as Slavs and Orthodox Christians, naturally looked to
Russia for assistance in throwing off the Turkish yoke. Whenever
these factors combined to make the loss of some part of the Turkish
dominions inevitable, the only alternative for the British, in order
to avoid Russian gains, was the recognition of independent national
states in the Balkans under a European guarantee. Over the creation
of the kingdom of Greece in 1830, this second course was adopted
in agreement with Russia; over the creation of Rumania out of the
Danubian provinces of Moldavia and Wallachia it followed her
defeat in the Crimean War. Thus Great Britain's support of Turkey
was only incidental to her suspicion of Russia; she would not necessarily preserve Turkey's possessions in the Balkans, and when the
emergence of the German Empire in 1871 was followed by the gradual succumbing of Constantinople to German and Austrian influence, Great Britain was to swing round to friendship and eventually
wartime alliance with Russia, to whom, by 1915, she was even prepared to offer the control of the Straits.

For the Habsburgs any kind of change in the Balkans was bound
to be for the worse. They naturally objected to further Russian
expansion in their direction; a partition of the Balkans with Russia
had little appeal, since it would only add to the complications of
Habsburg domestic government which were already considerable;
nor did the carving of independent states out of Turkey-in-Europe
offer any solution to the problem, since these would become a
focal point for the Slav nationalist groups within the Habsburg
dominions. The only hope for Austria was the maintenance of the
status quo, as Metternich's secretary Gentz realized, when he wrote in

1815: 'the end of the Turkish monarchy could be survived by the Austrian for but a short time.'

In fact, Russian policy did not aim at immediate acquisition. The sensitiveness of Great Britain and Austria would make any absorption of Turkish territory an international question which might result in the establishment of greater western interests in the Balkans; there was also the possibility that a smaller Turkey, once shorn of her unwieldy European possessions, might be capable of internal reform and hence become a stronger state on Russia's borders. Thus, although the eventual partition of Turkey-in-Europe remained a talking point in diplomatic circles throughout the nineteenth century, none of the Powers seriously desired it and Russian plans were based rather on a gradual extension of influence throughout the whole of the existing territories of Turkey under the guise of a protectorate over all Orthodox Christians in the Balkans. Besides, other interests which they had in common tied Austria, Prussia, and Russia to a policy of preserving the *status quo*; they were all three autocratic monarchies, mistrustful of western liberalism, and the territories of Poland, which they had earlier shared out among themselves, gave them a considerable stake in the maintenance of existing frontiers.

These various hopes and fears were reflected in two agreements signed in the autumn of 1815. The Holy Alliance drawn up by Tsar Alexander was a personal document to be signed by the sovereigns of Russia, Prussia, and Austria, promising mutual support in the spirit of Christian brotherhood. Despite the scornful amusement with which Metternich and Gentz treated the whole idea, Frederick William and Francis saw no objection to signing an agreement which was too general and high-minded to involve them in any precise commitment. Alexander may simply have seen the scheme as a further guarantee of the existing order, although it is possible that when he suggested that it should be offered to all the other Christian sovereigns in Europe, he may have had some plan at the back of his mind for isolating Turkey, with whom Russia had been at war at the time of Napoleon's invasion in 1812. Whatever Alexander's motives, Castlereagh fought shy of it and was able to plead the madness of George III as an excuse for standing aside. Nothing very much ever came of the Holy Alliance, but its name was to stand as a general term for the autocratic governments of Prussia, Russia, and Austria until the middle of the century.

The second agreement was a more orthodox diplomatic document. By the Treaty of 20 November 1815 Great Britain, Austria, Prussia, and Russia renewed the Quadruple Alliance of 1814 for twenty years as a means of safeguarding themselves against any revival of French aggression. Castlereagh was careful to insist that the terms should be limited to an agreement on collective action

against any Bonapartist restoration or any attempted revision of the
frontiers of France as established by the second Treaty of Paris.
Once again, Alexander would have liked to include a general guarantee of all frontiers and governmental régimes throughout Europe,
but Castlereagh had no intention of binding British foreign policy
to the requirements of the autocratic Powers. Article VI of the treaty
did contain the famous proposal for periodic congresses of the signatory Powers 'for the purposes of consulting upon their common
interests', but although this was an interesting innovation, the system of congresses, in Castlereagh's view, was really no more than
a convenient method whereby the great Powers might carry on the
normal processes of diplomacy. The autocratic Powers, however,
certainly saw them as a possible way of exercising a *general* supervision and of coordinating the suppression of revolutionary activity
anywhere on the Continent, and this divergence of aim was soon to
weaken the united front that the Powers had hoped to preserve, and,
by 1822, had led to Great Britain's withdrawal.

2. Liberal and authoritarian notions of government

Political theories are as diverse as the personalities of the men who
produce them and it would be rash to trace the steady development
of a line of doctrine through a whole series of thinkers. It is, however,
possible to outline very generally two attitudes towards the reform
of government which derive from writers before the French Revolution and whose effects have continued until the present day. Both
were strongly influenced by the new empirical methods of the eighteenth-century scientists, yet the lines of thought that they suggest
were to run in two entirely different directions.

The first lies at the root of the movements that were to adopt the
course of constitutional government, liberalism, and humanitarian
legislation. The emergence of a limited monarchy in England helped
to inspire the theories of John Locke, in which government existed
for the sake of a society of property-owning individuals, who were
therefore entitled to resist any infringement of their natural rights.
The interest that the English pattern of life had held for Voltaire
and Montesquieu had been translated in eighteenth-century France
into terms of growing criticism of governmental despotism, economic monopolies, and social privilege. Montesquieu's *L'Esprit des
Lois*, for example, was strongly influenced by English ideas and his
notion whereby despotism might be avoided by a balance of powers
between legislature, executive, and judiciary may be clearly recognized in the American and the French Revolutionary constitutions.
Naturally, after they had crossed the Channel, these ideas under-
went a certain transformation. The rights of the English, rooted in
Common Law, were based on a long historical tradition and the

events of 1688 never implied any great social revolution. On the Continent, these traditional links had mostly perished and French political thought before the Revolution was a highly literary philosophy, devised by an intelligentsia who lacked all experience in government, and, since it concentrated on the definition of abstract principles, tended to be far more dogmatic, challenging the social as well as the political order.

This first theme is particularly noticeable in the revolutionary mutterings of the early half of the nineteenth century. Within the wide bracket of that general term 'the middle classes', industrialists, merchants, and professional men represented the most active form of discontent, desirous of political power and economic advantage. The degree of subjection against which they protested, the width of the gap between upper and lower bourgeois and the extent to which they concerned themselves with nationalism, all varied from one region of Europe to another; yet, in the outbreaks of 1830 and 1848 there is a striking similarity of demand among these groups—the preservation of monarchy within a constitutional framework, a legislative Assembly elected on a franchise based on a property qualification, freedom of the press, the abolition of social privilege by birth and the removal of internal restrictions on trade and industry—in short, the replacement of absolutism and a privileged aristocracy by a constitutional monarchy ruling in the interests of a business and professional class—the situation established momentarily in France in 1791, and, to some extent, restored in 1814.

The aspirations of this middle-class liberalism naturally represented a growing threat to the established government and society of Europe and in their initial attacks on the old order in the first half of the century liberal and democrat shared a common objective. Like their sovereigns, however, the business and professional classes looked with loathing on the prospect of revolutionary Jacobinism, a republicanism of the masses in which political democracy implied a social equality with all its economic consequences. 'Sir, your levellers wish to level down as far as themselves,' Dr Johnson once remarked, 'but they cannot bear levelling up to themselves.' The same thought is implicit in a statement made by a German liberal, David Hansemann, in 1830. 'By majority . . . we are never to understand one determined by counting heads, but rather the true strength of the nation, which, while it is also to have no interest other than that of the numerical majority, yet differs essentially from it, since by its better education, greater insight and its property, it has a larger stake in the maintenance of a stable, vigorous and good government.' Thus, whenever revolutionary action seemed to be on the point of success, the latent antagonism between the two groups flared up, causing the liberals to retreat towards the old order as a bulwark against extreme social revolution.

The second theme that may be discerned in the eighteenth-century theorists points to a new form of authoritarianism, although the character of the arguments that led up to it varied enormously. For Helvetius the evidence of the senses suggested that pleasure was good and pain was bad, but since men were not sufficiently wise to see how to attain the one and to avoid the other, the aim of government must be to establish through the work of a few enlightened legislators a series of incentives and deterrents by which men would be guided towards the happiest possible life. In contrast to this, Rousseau's ideas were based on a mystical conception of the community. For him the fundamental dilemma lay in the fact that although a man ideally should be completely free, he had to live in a society, which must automatically mean the curtailing of that complete freedom. The solution that Rousseau conceived was a society of naturally good men for whom the expression of their own personal liberty lay in spontaneous surrender to the whole community. Only through this fusing of individual wills in a general will could a society of genuinely free men be established; yet although men should want to attain this state, only a handful actually realized that they did want it. This was the link with Helvetius, for in Rousseau's view it was the duty of those few to lead the rest. Thus Helvetius believed that men must be forced to be happy, Rousseau that they must be forced to be free. Both postulated rule by a small group who knew what was best for all.

Jacobinism and the rule of Napoleon were both instances of this second theme of authoritarianism in the general interest, but it was not really until the second half of the nineteenth century, when the struggle between the classes had become intensified, that it took on a practical form. Nationalists struggling to achieve unification or independence, bourgeois fearful of Socialism, Socialists seeking to transform the whole economic basis of society, all tended to move towards the surrender of freedom to a small group who claimed the right to impose their own solutions on the whole community. This process was to be aided by two further developments of the nineteenth century. First, the startling increase in technical means opened up possibilities of control by the State which was to give the dictatorships of the twentieth century a unique character in the history of the world, and which in all forms of government hastened the general assumptions of collectivism. Second, the need to capture the support of the masses in a new industrial age caused both left and right wings to make increasing use of the doctrine of popular sovereignty. Yet the paradox of this creed was that it accelerated the growth of a simplified form of government under one man, the cult of personality. Mistrust of social extremists caused liberals to fall back on the Second Empire of Napoleon III and the German Reich of Bismarck's creation, just as the fear of Communism in the twentieth century opened the door to the Nazi and Fascist dictatorships; among the Socialists themselves a new highly disciplined organization was to take the place of romantic aspiration, and the Russian revolution of November 1917, which established the dictatorship of the Bolshevik party, was simply another facet of the same argument propounded by Helvetius and Rousseau a hundred and fifty years before.

3. The Romantic movement and its influence on nationalism

Although the calculations of diplomacy and the ambitions of social groups naturally vary according to the circumstances of each epoch, they remain common as general factors to most periods of history. Their distinguishing feature in the early nineteenth century, however, lies in the fact that they became charged with a new intensity through the great emotional storm of the Romantic movement whose repercussions were felt in every side of life and in every region of Europe.

It is in the arts that the significance of this extraordinary transformation may be most simply illustrated. The classicism of the seventeenth and eighteenth centuries had established an absolute ideal of beauty only to be realized through obedience to certain rules of balance and harmony, by which the individual promptings of the artist were to be restrained and disciplined. The central theme of the Romantic movement was that it broke violently with these rules and in their place concentrated purely on imaginative insight and emotional impact; thus, in his Preface to the *Lyrical Ballads*, Wordsworth claimed that the purpose of the poems was 'to illustrate the manner in which our feelings and ideas are associated in a state of excitement'. The movement was already clearly established before the end of the eighteenth century—particularly in Germany during the 1770s and 1780s, the period known later as *Sturm und Drang*—and was to gather overwhelming force throughout the first half of the nineteenth. The delight in nature, so marked in the poems of Wordsworth and Goethe, was to be the inspiration of Lamartine, Mörike, Lenau, and Eichendorff; the great outpouring of love poetry of Keats, Shelley. Byron, and Heine; the flamboyance of gesture in the paintings of Géricault and Delacroix; the vast orchestration of Beethoven and Schubert; and the lyrical compositions of Schumann, Liszt, and Chopin, were all later manifestations of this new mood of emotionalism that took possession of every art.

Romanticism, however, went far deeper than any experimenting with new technical forms. The concentration on personal feelings led to a yearning for the unattainable that caused men to look not only within themselves, but also backward in time. Goethe's *Götz von Berlichingen* and Schiller's *Wallenstein* and *Wilhelm Tell* were not simply new types of play, free from the classical rules of the three unities; they heralded that nostalgia for Europe's past from which the historical novels of Walter Scott and Alexandre Dumas were soon to find such a response. In the academic world there awoke an interest in the study of local *patois*—old Provençal and Breton—and Herder's *Volkslieder*, the poems of Robert Burns, the Grimm Brothers' fairy tales, and the great Nordic sagas of the immemorial past appeared as glimpses of some great treasury of regional cultures and folklore. For centuries the deserted monuments of earlier ages had been left untended and often, like the Colosseum at Rome, the shattered Parthenon at Athens or the dissolved monasteries in England, had been plundered by local inhabitants who saw them merely as a quarry of easily available building material. To the tourist of the twentieth century their preservation may seem natural enough; yet it was the Romantic movement, with its passion for ruin, that first caused men to see them with new eyes, stimulating the beginning of serious archaeological exploration in Italy and Greece and turning the English to express a growing love of the medieval in the architecture of the Gothic revival.

In the wider sphere of everyday life whole generations of young people became imbued with the romantic despair of Goethe's *Werther*, a Byronic melancholy in revolt against the orderly assumptions of the eighteenth century. Naturally, in so personal a movement this revolt took a variety of forms. The Romantic might praise Rousseau's 'noble savage', the primitive man uncorrupted by the artificiality of civilization; he might applaud the advent of the French Revolution—'Bliss was it in that dawn to be alive'—or the rise of Napoleon as one of history's great men; or he might succumb to the mystique of royalty, anointed with holy oil and tracing its lineage back through the dim ages. He might proclaim a fierce atheism, or he might retreat from the rationalism of the eighteenth century to a deep reverence for the ritual splendour and historic power of Rome. But whatever the attitude, its expression had always a rich exaggeration, at its best creating a new cultural epoch in Europe, at its worst, morbid, introspective, dallying with drugs and thoughts of suicide.

The most notable consequence of Romanticism was the great stimulus that it gave to the new emotions of nationalism. In France this meant simply an ardent patriotism inspired by the revolutionary ideal and the extraordinary achievement of Napoleon's armies. Although by 1814 the French were glad of peace, the sense of anticlimax among the younger generation in the years that followed is a constant theme in de Vigny's *Servitude et grandeur militaire*, de Musset's *Confession d'un enfant du siècle*, and the early poems of Victor Hugo, and the strength of latent Bonapartism rested not so much on the desire for a new political programme, as on the vague mystical attraction of the Napoleonic legend, a hunger for *la gloire*.

But it was in the regions where national unification had not yet been attained that Romanticism, with its interest in folklore and its sense of a historic past, suggested a new basis for establishing the collective identity of peoples. 'Der naturlichste Staat ist also *ein* Volk mit *einem* Nationalcharakter,'* wrote Herder in his *Ideen zur Philosophie der Geschichte*. The true nation, in fact, was derived from the tribal group knit together by a blood relationship, and this tie, in the opinion of Schlegel and Fichte, was to be recognized in the possession of a common language. 'Whenever a separate language is found,' declared Fichte in his *Reden an die deutsche Nation*, 'there is also a separate nation which has the right to manage its affairs independently and to rule itself.' The doctrine of German cultural and historical unity preached by Schelling at Munich, Dahlmann at Göttingen, Strauss at Tübingen, and Ranke, Fichte, and Savigny at Berlin gave the Universities the leadership of the movement, but the enthusiasm ran far beyond the bounds of the lecture room. In Germany it found practical expression in the war of liberation of 1813; in Italy the new academic interest in the classical past was to blend with the aspirations of extreme Italian nationalists who were later to see Rome as the only possible capital for a united Italy; farther east, although Slovenes, Ruthenians, Letts, and Estonians had been subject too long for the movement to make any immediate appeal, it was soon to have its effect on Bohemians, Poles, Magyars, and Greeks, for whom an awareness of their past was bound to excite thoughts of independence.

The full implications of this nationalist emotion were not to be apparent until the 1840s. Most of the early academic enthusiasts genuinely believed that only good could come of the emergence of a collective identity of national groups. *Frisch, fromm, fröhlich und frei* ('brisk, pious, joyous, free') ran the watchword of the *Burschenschaften*, the student groups organized by Jahn—quasi-religious rather than militant—and it was ironical that much of the revival of the old Slavonic languages was the work of German scholars. Similarly, in Italy the *Carbonari*, a network of secret societies motivated by a hatred of Bonapartist rule, stood for the highest moral ideals, and the complicated ritual of their Lodges, reminiscent of the Free Masonry from which they had sprung, was bound up with the expression of vaguely Christian and democratic hopes for the complete purification of society. Yet it is possible to see in these origins the contradictions that were later to play so great a part in the history of nineteenth- and twentieth-century Europe. The idealists

---

* 'The most natural kind of State is therefore a single people with a single national character.'

overlooked the competing claims that would be made, when the mystique of *das Volk* came to be translated into terms of nation states with clearly defined frontiers, and when existing differences of language were found no longer to coincide with old historic boundaries; more particularly, the overlapping of peoples divided by class and language was to add a sterner note of social revolution to the rhapsody of national self-determination. But, whatever its dangers, the spirit of nationalism, once it was awakened, was too strong ever to be finally denied. 'Art and science are universal,' said Goethe after the battle of Leipzig in 1813, 'and in view of these the bonds of nationality disappear. But the consolation they afford is but hollow comfort and cannot replace the proud consciousness of belonging to a great, strong, feared and respected nation.'

Part 2

The Defence of the
Vienna Settlement
1815–48

Chapter 5

The Early Days of the Settlement 1815–30

'Depuis longtemps l'Europe a pris pour moi la valeur d'une patrie.' This remark of Metternich's to the Duke of Wellington in 1815 throws a profound light on the character of the man who was to attempt to order the destiny of Europe for the next thirty-three years. By upbringing Metternich was a Rhinelander, educated at the Universities of Strasbourg and Mainz; by profession a diplomat, serving the Emperor at Dresden, Berlin, and Paris before becoming Minister of Foreign Affairs in 1809; by birth an aristocrat for whom the *ancien régime* of the eighteenth century meant the very essence of civilization. In many ways there could have been no more suitable representative of the Habsburg Empire, resting, as it did, on an utterly non-national structure of classes and peoples. It is understandable that the picture which has been preserved of him is of a great despot; a conservative in a time of irresistible change is hardly likely to be popular. Yet the picture is untrue, for Metternich was neither great, nor a despot. He was a charming cultivated *seigneur*, fond of the lighter side of society, confessing to Madame de Lieven, with whom he carried on a correspondence over the years, that 'la vie d'un ministre est une vie affreuse'. He was conceited, but seldom malevolent. Although suspicious of change, he was fully aware of the need for reform within the system of Habsburg government at Vienna. 'Je passe ma vie à étayer un édifice vermoulu,' he said, but, lacking the brilliance of a Talleyrand, he had to rely on hard work and a constant attention to detail. 'Il prend l'intrigue pour la politique,' Napoleon had scoffed at him; yet the charge was a little unfair, since Vienna imposed not only the objects, but also the methods of government.

In his Political Testament of 1820 the positive aims which he defined suggest an essentially eighteenth-century ideal of balance and harmony. He believed that the only consequence of liberalism would be to shatter an ordered society, after which liberalism itself would succumb to the forces of demagogy—an odd source for an anticipation of Marxist doctrine! He hated, above all, 'the presumptuous man', the term with which he summed up the ambitious bourgeois and the discontented nationalist, and since these two forces directly challenged the old European pattern of society and government, the defence that he planned had also to be on a European scale; 'union between monarchs is the basis of the policy which must be followed to save society from total ruin'. Hence his determination that Austria stand guard over the Vienna settlement in Germany at Frankfurt, and in Italy at Milan; hence his suspicion of the vague liberal whims of Alexander I and Frederick William III.

Certainly, by the end of 1815, Metternich might rest content with the situation in Europe. Napoleon was far away in St Helena; it was already clear that the Diet of the German Confederation at Frankfurt was sufficiently weak to be a mockery of any scheme for more positive unification, and military alliances with Tuscany and Naples had consolidated the control of Vienna over Italy. All this, however, was only a beginning and for the next thirty-three years he was to conduct a vigilant defence of the settlement that had been established after the Napoleonic wars.

1. France under the Bourbons

Even under a Bourbon monarchy France was bound to remain suspect, particularly when Louis XVIII, on his second restoration, placed Talleyrand at the head of a government which included Fouché as Minister of Police. 'Le vice appuyé sur le bras du crime', ran Chateaubriand's biting comment in his *Mémoires*, and although Louis may have owed much to Talleyrand's efforts at Vienna and to Fouché's at Paris after Waterloo, royalist opinion was utterly shocked and the appointments did not last long. The narrowness of the franchise and the fury of the royalists after the perils of the Hundred Days resulted in an electoral victory for the Ultras, the extreme conservatives, so overwhelming that it took even Louis XVIII by surprise. *La Chambre introuvable*—out of this world—he called it, and the banishment of Fouché and the retirement of Talleyrand followed almost at once.

The irony of the situation was that Louis was far more shrewd than many of his supporters and during the next year was greatly embarrassed by their ardour, which might well have provoked a Bonapartist or Jacobin reaction. Accordingly, he selected his new ministers from more moderate elements who, together with the Chamber of Peers, which still included many officials of the Empire, might be able to tone down the zeal of the Ultras in the Chamber of Deputies. His principal minister was the Duke de Richelieu, an *émigré* who had already proved his ability in the service of the Tsar as governor of Odessa. 'He is certainly the Frenchman who is best acquainted with the Crimea,' sneered Talleyrand at his successor, but, with the inevitably sterner second Treaty of Paris still to be ratified, Talleyrand may not have been entirely sorry to go. In any case, Richelieu proved to be a most happy choice; a bizarre figure with his untidy dress and Russian boots, he was the very man that Louis needed at this time—an aristocrat of whom it could not be said that, unlike many of his contemporaries, he had forgotten nothing and learnt nothing.

For the following twelve months the King and his ministers tried to ride out the storm and the Ultra reaction. Eighteen Bonapartist generals were court-martialled and shot—including Marshal Ney, who was tried before the Chamber of Peers—and if La Bourdon-naye, an Ultra in the Chamber of Deputies, had had his way, there would have been many more. In the provinces an unofficial White Terror claiming some 250 victims raged unchecked; new press laws, passed in November 1815, made liberal newspapers increasingly liable to prosecution, and in December *cours prévôtales* were re-established in the *départements*, summary courts whose death sentences were to be carried out within twenty-four hours. The government did what it could to restrain this Ultra fury, but in May 1816 an unsuccessful Bonapartist outbreak at Grenoble was sufficient warning that the passion for revenge was endangering the whole of the Restoration settlement, and when the British and Russian governments had expressed their concern at the Allied conference of ambassadors, Louis decided, in September 1816, to exercise his right to dissolve the Chamber and to hold a general election.

Apart from the Ultras, there were two principal groups from whom Richelieu might hope for a more moderate Chamber—the Independents, liberal bourgeois suspicious of the old nobility and hankering after the tricolour and the glory of the Empire; and a centre party, the Constitutionalists under Royer Collard and Guizot, Louis' main hope for a balance between extremes. The general election of the autumn of 1816 gave the King and his ministers precisely the moderately royalist assembly that they wanted; the pendulum, however, continued to swing and with each subsequent annual election of one-fifth of the seats the liberal element grew larger, until by 1819 they held 90 out of the 258 seats to which Louis had reduced the Chamber in 1816.

This increase, reflecting to some extent the reaction against the Ultras, was also partly explained by changes brought about with the electoral laws of 1817 and 1818. At first, after 1815, elections had been in two stages, whereby the electors had only exercised an indirect vote at the level of the *arrondissement*, a method which was naturally popular with the wealthier landowning class, since it allowed them to exercise considerable influence. The new procedure lowered the age for the electors from thirty to twenty-five and centred the polling on the chief town of the *département* where they voted directly for all the deputies of that *département*. Thus the working of the electoral system was itself a weapon in the struggle between the political groups, perhaps the greatest weakness of constitutional government under the Charter.

At the time, however, the fortunes of the restored French monarchy were aided by a remarkable national recovery after the collapse of 1814. The finances were placed on a more stable footing than ever before, enabling France to pay off the indemnity imposed by the second Treaty of Paris and thus to rid herself of the army of occupation. Gouvion-Saint-Cyr's conscription law of 1818 added greatly to the forces at the King's disposal to resist any threat of a Bonapartist *coup*, and the Allies, anxious to strengthen the position of the restored monarchy, were well aware that it would gain greatly in prestige from the withdrawal of the Allied army. The final agreement over financial settlement and military evacuation was reached at the Congress of Aix-la-Chapelle in 1818, the first of those meetings envisaged in the Treaty of November 1815. Richelieu was hoping for something more—the inclusion of France in the counsels of the great Powers—and through his Russian connections looked for support from Tsar Alexander who still dreamed of some general political guarantee of all existing régimes throughout Europe. This possibility of Franco-Russian collaboration either within or outside a European concert confronted Great Britain and Austria with a dilemma which resulted in a compromise—the inclusion of France in all future Congresses, balanced by a renewal of the Quadruple Alliance as a safeguard against a reawakening of French ambitions. 'It is owing to the Emperor of Russia,' wrote Richelieu to Louis XVIII, 'and to his all-powerful intervention that we have attained the end which for the last four weeks seemed always to elude us,' and, on the whole, he could return to Paris well pleased.

Ironically, however, his own position at home had by now deteriorated. He feared that the balance in the Chamber of Deputies was swinging too far in the direction of the liberals. 'Let us think no more of liberal concessions,' he said to Decazes, the Minister of Police. 'We have made enough, and much good they have done us.' But Decazes, together with several others of the ministers, did not agree, and since he was a firm favourite of Louis XVIII, Richelieu, tiring of the situation, decided at the end of 1818 to resign.

The greater liberalism of Decazes, who took his place as Minister of the Interior, was marked principally by the introduction of a new press law. Under Richelieu control of the press had continued to be exercised by the government, even after the dissolution of *la Chambre introuvable*—an untidy system whereby editors had to satisfy both the police and the censorship committee—mainly because Richelieu had feared that an unbridled press might suggest to the Allies that France was not yet to be trusted. The new law of 1819 abolished the police control so that, in future, editors could only be charged with a breach of the penal code, in which case they were assured of a trial by jury. This new freedom of the press, was largely a matter of interest for the middle classes, since a stamp tax, combined with a system of annual subscription, made newspapers too expensive a luxury for the masses.

Within a year the liberal trend in France had been brought to a halt, when in February 1820 Louis XVIII's nephew, the Duke de Berri, the main hope for the Bourbon succession, was stabbed to death by a lunatic outside the Opera in Paris. The immediate alarm subsided a little when it appeared that the assassination was not part of any larger conspiracy, and since the Duchess was now known to be expecting a child, *l'enfant du miracle*, the Bourbon succession might still be secure. The episode, however, had happened to coincide with a flurry of revolutionary outbreaks elsewhere in Europe and as the conservatives tightened their defences, public opinion forced Louis to dismiss the Decazes ministry.

He was able to recall Richelieu, but the new government was inevitably strongly Ultra in character. In the spring of 1820 censorship of the press was restored, and a new electoral law was passed in favour of the upper class. Groups of *arrondissements* were turned into single-member constituencies, where local landed interests might once again make themselves felt more effectively, and, in addition, that quarter of the electorate which paid the highest taxes in each *département* was to enjoy a second vote for the purpose of returning a further 172 deputies to the Chamber. The growing bitterness of feeling between Ultras and liberals soon made it impossible for Richelieu to pursue a central course of action, and on his resignation at the end of 1821 the appointment of the Duke de Villèle increased the strength of the Ultras still more. A few outbreaks in 1822 were easily put down and at the beginning of 1824 the government decided to reinforce its position by holding a general election. The outcome of this appeared decisive. The new electoral procedure, combined with every form of pressure exercised by the Prefects on electors in the provinces, resulted in the return of a Chamber in which the liberals were reduced to fifteen seats—*la Chambre retrouvée*, as the Ultras called it in delight—and Villèle had no difficulty in consolidating this success with a further amendment to the Charter, abolishing the annual elections of one-fifth and prolonging the life of the existing Chamber for seven years.

Meanwhile, the Powers of the Holy Alliance had been more concerned with risings in Italy, Spain and Portugal, where military groups had momentarily forced the sovereigns to yield to their demands for constitutional reform. It had been Alexander who suggested a new Congress, which met at Troppau in October 1820, in order to discuss the means of intervention. Austria and Prussia were only too willing to attend, but, in France, Richelieu, wishing to restrain the ardour of the Ultras, would only agree to send two representatives to act as observers. In Great Britain Castlereagh, who was as suspicious as ever of the intentions that might lie behind general schemes of intervention, had already in May circulated a State paper declaring that his government could never be party to a guarantee of existing régimes in every state in Europe, and emphasizing that the Treaty of November 1815 was concerned only to prevent a Bonapartist restoration in France. Thus the British, too, only sent an observer, and when the three Powers of the Holy Alliance at Troppau published a manifesto claiming the right to intervene when revolutions outside their frontiers appeared to threaten their own internal order, the breach between British policy and the Continent was finally apparent.

In Italy Metternich eventually decided to act on his own initiative (see p. 59). Spain, however, presented a more difficult problem, since the attitude of France was to be of particular significance. In January 1820 Spanish liberals and army officers had combined under Rafael Riego to raise a revolt in Cadiz and had forced Ferdinand VII to re-establish the constitution of 1812. During the following two years the liberals had theoretically made considerable headway. Spain was divided into fifty-two provinces to facilitate the centralizing of administration and the Inquisition had been suppressed. Their lack of unity, however, was clearly demonstrated by the fierce argument in the *Cortes* between moderates and extremists, and the highly conservative attitude of the peasantry, mistrustful of the anti-clericalism of the liberals, gave Ferdinand the hope of popular support in any attempt to restore absolutism. Accordingly, in 1822, Ferdinand made his appeal for assistance to the Powers.

The question of intervention in Spain was the principal subject for discussion at another Congress which met at Verona in October 1822. Who was to intervene? What would be the international repercussions? Metternich was already fully occupied with Germany and Italy and had little liking for Alexander's scheme to send an army across Europe for the purpose. France seemed the obvious choice. Ultra feeling strongly supported such a project and although Villèle, who had by now replaced Richelieu, was doubtful about the financial and military difficulties involved, the French delegates, Chateaubriand and Mathieu de Montmorency, fell in with the general opinion at the Congress that the French army should cross the Pyrenees in support of Ferdinand. The Duke of Wellington, attending the congress in the role of an observer, protested strongly. The State paper of 1820 had already enunciated the British dislike of the Powers' claim to the right to guarantee the governments of 1815 and Castlereagh had accepted intervention in Italy only as an individual action on Austria's part within her own sphere of influence. The thought of a French army once more invading Spain was a very

different proposition; ever since the war of the Spanish succession
at the beginning of the eighteenth century the fear that a weakened
Spain might fall completely under the influence of France had constantly recurred, and Canning, who became British Foreign Secretary on Castlereagh's suicide in 1822, was even more outspoken in
his objections.

Villèle decided to act. Chateaubriand was appointed Foreign
Minister and in 1823 a French army, under the command of the
Duke d'Angoulême, crossed the Pyrenees. In Great Britain Canning
obtained an increase in the personnel of the navy, insisted that there
should be no permanent occupation of Spain, no advance into Portugal, nor any interference with the Spanish American colonies now
in a state of revolt, and expressed his hope in the Commons that the
new régime in Spain would survive the struggle. He was speedily
disappointed. This time, in contrast to Napoleon's attempt to establish his brother Joseph on the Spanish throne, the French army acting on behalf of the legitimate sovereign had the support of the local
population. The Spanish liberal forces were swept aside. With the
capture of the Trocadero fortress at Cadiz absolute rule under Ferdinand was entirely re-established in Spain, and the only consolation for Canning was an agreement with Polignac, the French
ambassador at London, whereby France renounced any intention
of restoring to Spain her South American colonies (see p. 63).

In September 1824 Louis XVIII died. The success of his reign
was largely due to the good sense with which he had appointed
ministers in accord with the swings of opinion reflected in the Chamber, while at the same time managing to avoid the extremes of
political emotion. Already, the assistance to Ferdinand VII, followed by the withdrawal of French forces from Spain, had demonstrated to the Powers that France could be trusted as a defender
of the established order. Thus Louis' brother the Count d'Artois,
who now succeeded him as Charles X, inherited a stable and prosperous country in which the immediate difficulties of the Bourbon
restoration had been effectively weathered.

Unfortunately the new King, typical of the Ultras whose views
he embodied, was one who had learnt nothing from the Revolution.
Divine Right, a great landowning aristocracy, a clergy once more
controlling education—this programme to which he was obstinately
to adhere was bound to arouse the anger of even the mildest liberals
and within six years was to lose him his throne. A magnificent cor-
onation at Reims with all the ceremonial of the ancien régime set the
tone to the whole reign. Then, with Villèle as his chief minister and
an overwhelmingly right-wing Chamber, Charles embarked on his
campaign. Fifty-six lieutenant-generals of the old Imperial army
were placed on the retired list. Émigré landowners who, on their
return in 1814, had failed to regain their estates were to receive

financial compensation. In fact, this was not an unreasonable measure, but since it was financed by reducing the interest on government annuities from 5 per cent to 3 per cent, it infuriated the bourgeois, who denounced it as the *milliard des émigrés*, although the sum involved only amounted to 650,000,000 francs. Another measure attempted to go some way towards re-establishing the system of primogeniture, thereby finally abolishing the Revolutionary law of inheritance—already modified by Napoleon—which had aimed at breaking up the large estates by stipulating that on the death of the father they should be shared equally among all the sons of the family. Here too, there was something to be said for calling a halt to a process of dismemberment of estates which had considerable economic disadvantages, but such a revision at once conjured up visions of the old privileged landed aristocracy and although the measure was passed in the Chamber, it was thrown out by the Peers.

The religious policy of the government was still more reminiscent of the *ancien régime*. The clergy had been active in attempting to suppress the paganism that had spread during recent years, and Villèle was unable to prevent the passing of a law which made sacrilege committed in any place of worship punishable by death. A more insidious change was taking place in the field of education. Under the Empire this had been a secular monopoly of the University of France. At the Restoration modifications had allowed the establishment of Catholic seminaries, often attended by pupils who, without any intention of becoming priests, simply preferred this form of education, and in 1821 Catholic schools, whose headmasters and teachers were chosen by the bishops, were even granted a status equivalent to the secular colleges. The most significant development, however, was the infiltration of the Church into the centralized system of the State. In 1822 a bishop, Frayssinous, became Grand Master of the University and, two years later, Minister of Education and Ecclesiastical Affairs, and the recapture of education by the clergy went on at such a pace that in 1827 sixty-six out of eighty philosophy teachers in the colleges were priests and, by 1830, about one-third of all the teachers.

It was not long before the intensity of this Ultra programme had awoken a growing hum of criticism in the cafés and *salons* of Paris, which was to find ardent expression in an opposition press, *Le Constitutionnel* and *Le Journal des Débats*, now free from censorship as a result of Charles's one liberal gesture at the beginning of his reign. Moderate and extreme liberals, Bonapartists and even discontented Ultras, such as Chateaubriand, smarting from his dismissal from office in 1824, were moving closer together in a new fervour of anticlericalism. Villèle now set about trying to stamp out this opposition, and in December 1826 a new press law, unhappily labelled by its sponsor, Peyronnet, '*une loi de justice et d'amour*', was introduced in the Chamber. Censorship was reimposed, penalties greatly increased and prosecutions were in future to be levelled against the proprietors of newspapers rather than against the editors; once again, as over the law of inheritance, it was the Chamber of Peers that prevented the passing of the bill by voting so many modifications that Charles eventually withdrew it.

By the spring of 1827 feelings had become so enflamed that cries of '*à bas les ministres*' were raised at a royal review of the National Guard, that symbol of the liberties enshrined in the Charter, and Villèle unwisely advised their disbanding. By November it seemed to Villèle that even the Chamber was no longer reliable and Charles accordingly dissolved it. Seventy-six new peers were created in order to swing the balance in the Upper House, but this time the forces of opposition meant to strike back at the influence exercised by the Prefects in the provinces. Their efforts, through the organization of a society, *Aide-toi, le ciel t'aidera*, raised the numbers of those who came to the polls from 67,000 to 80,000 and when the new Chamber was returned in December 1827, the government found itself faced with a liberal majority of sixty. Villèle's resignation followed in January 1828.

For the next eighteen months Charles attempted unwillingly to work through a government of moderate conservatives under the Viscount de Martignac. 'Je le trouve un peu faible', wrote the King to Villèle, and the tragedy for Martignac was that in his attempts to form a majority out of a centre group he only succeeded in creating the same impression among the opposition. In the spring of 1829 he tried to introduce government reforms which would have placed the appointment of local councillors in the provinces on an elective basis. When this failed to satisfy the Chamber, Charles decided that he would make no further compromise; in August 1829 he formed a new government under his friend Prince Jules de Polignac, the most ardent of the Ultras, and in doing so, took a step that was very soon to bring the Bourbon monarchy to an end.

2. Unrest in Italy

At the same time as the excitements in Spain in 1820 Metternich had been confronted with two outbreaks of resistance to the settlement in Italy. In the July of that year, in the Kingdom of Naples, General Pepe, placing himself at the head of forces raised originally to deal with local brigands and including a great number of the *Carbonari* (see p. 47), marched on the capital and extracted from King Ferdinand a constitution on the lines of the Spanish one of 1812. Within a month revolt had spread to Sicily, although this was inspired by thoughts of Sicilian independence and Pepe was only able to retain control with difficulty.

The Powers conferring at Troppau were not in immediate agreement over this particular development. At first Tsar Alexander confirmed Metternich's mistrust of him by supporting the idea of a liberal constitution for the Kingdom of Naples. This may simply have been a scheme for hindering Austria's freedom of action in Italy, but soon the mutiny of Alexander's own old regiment, the Semenovski, and the resistance that he had just encountered from the Polish Diet enabled Metternich's reproachful persuasion to win the Tsar round. The Congress adjourned to Laibach in Carniola, at the beginning of 1821, where Ferdinand of Naples had been invited to meet them. The recently elected Neapolitan chamber had foolishly agreed to his going, on the understanding that he would speak on behalf of the maintenance of constitutional government in Naples, but Ferdinand naturally had other plans. Metternich now knew that he could intervene without fear of Russian objections, and in February an army of Croats and Hungarians marched south through Italy, dispersed Pepe's forces in a few hours of fighting and restored Ferdinand as an absolute monarch.

There followed almost at once, in March 1821, a mutiny of the army at Piedmont. Victor Emmanuel abdicated in favour of his brother Charles Felix, but since the new King was in Modena at the time, a regency was declared under the young Charles Albert, who had been second in the line of succession (see genealogical table p. 487) and was known to have liberal sympathies. Charles Felix, however, had no intention of submitting to the demands for a constitution and appealed to Austria for help. In Turin Charles Albert, who may have been involved in the initial stages of the outbreak, did eventually agree to the granting of a constitution, but he was not prepared to come out openly in revolt, and when Austrian troops entered Piedmont, the rising was rapidly put down. In September Charles Felix entered Turin to take possession of his kingdom. Metternich now followed up this successful operation by establishing large garrisons at Naples, Alessandria, Ancona and Florence and covering the whole country with a network of police spies. From now on, the only hope for the liberals in Piedmont lay in the fact that Charles Albert was the heir to the childless Charles Felix.

The ease with which these two risings in Italy had been crushed is explained principally by the weakness of the rebels. Within each state they had suffered from divided leadership, and, contrary to Metternich's fear of a general conspiracy, there had been no coordination of activity between Naples and Piedmont; neither had been thinking in terms of an Italian movement of liberation. The Neapolitan rising had certainly been a popular one; there had been no time lost in the summoning of a constitutional Chamber and if the Neapolitans had not panicked, the resistance to the Austrian forces, which were not large, might have been far more effective. The rising in Piedmont had made little appeal to the masses; no arrangements for a constitutional Chamber ever materialized and the refusal of Charles Felix to compromise doomed the movement from the start. The fundamental reason for the failures, however, lay not in Italy, but in the attitude of the great Powers to Austrian intervention. Alexander had acquiesced in this, and the natural conservatism of the Bourbon government in France, anxious to prove its freedom from any taint of revolution, had ruled out any possibility of French resistance to Austria.

3. The German states and the Prussian *Zollverein*

In Germany Metternich had been able to exercise a greater authority, yet even here there were tendencies that made him uneasy. Limited constitutions were granted by the rulers in Bavaria and Baden in 1818, and in Württemberg in 1819. In Prussia, although the hopes for a constitutional assembly were dashed, the reform of the educational system, including the creation of a new University at Bonn in the recently acquired Rhineland, seemed unwise to Metternich, since German University professors and students were the driving force behind the criticism of the Vienna settlement. The student societies, the *Burschenschaften*, had spread rapidly from Jena to most of the other Universities, and the violence of their nationalist enthusiasm was most marked at a great festival at Eisenach in 1817, technically in celebration of the tercentenary of Luther's ninety-five theses against Papal Indulgences, but significantly held on the fourth anniversary of the battle of Leipzig. Before long, however, he had found an excuse to act, when in 1819 a German writer in the service of the Tsar, Kotzebue, was murdered by a theological student at Mannheim. On this Metternich summoned a meeting of ministers of the main German principalities at Karlsbad, where he drew up a series of decrees to be imposed throughout the whole of Germany; the press was to be strictly censored, the *Burschenschaften*, as well as other forms of political gathering, were prohibited, and police officials were appointed to watch over activities in the Universities.

Of all the other states only Prussia might have challenged this Austrian ascendancy in Germany, yet few of the German liberals had much faith in her at this time, regarding her as the home of reaction. It was consequently all the more remarkable that Prussia was now to lead the way in a totally different type of movement which challenged the decentralization and consequent weakness of Germany. It has been seen that one of the principal difficulties of the German business man was the continued existence of internal customs barriers between the states (see p. 22), a situation which the Diet at Frankfurt had done nothing to change. Within the Prussian territories themselves, straggling across the north of central Europe, sixty-seven different tariffs hampered the operations of internal trade and made any concerted policy of protection against British manufacturers virtually impossible. 'All states favour home industries by tariffs,' complained a petition of seventy Rhineland manufacturers to Frederick William III in 1818; 'Germany alone fails to protect her children.' A positive answer to their plea was promulgated by the King that same year. Maassen's Prussian Tariff Reform Law, much influenced by the writings of Adam Smith, swept away the variety of internal customs duties within Prussia and established a single unified tariff to be charged at the frontiers. Prussia was not yet sufficiently strong economically to be able to engage in a tariff war, and in any case high tariffs would only have meant a continuation of the smuggling which the law was partly designed to prevent. Import duties were consequently kept low— raw materials to enter free, an average of 10 per cent on manufactured goods, and of 20 per cent on 'colonial' goods such as sugar and tea. Naturally hardships were suffered by small interests when deprived of the protection afforded by local customs, and the industrialists benefited less than the farmers, since the lowness of the tariff on manufactured goods still left them exposed to British competition, but the general advantage derived from the *Zollverein* (Customs Union) was ultimately to be enormous. It was the essential preliminary to economic advance and the process once begun was to affect the whole of Germany. Between 1819 and 1826 the tiny non-Prussian enclaves within Prussian territory, burdened with the expenses of customs collection, found it more attractive to enter the scheme. Then, Prussia's geographical position commanding most of the north-south trade routes enabled her to place heavy taxes on all goods in transit, and through this pressure Hesse-Darmstadt agreed, in 1828, to join the Prussian Union, while in the south and the centre two other Customs Unions were formed in retaliation.

4. The maintenance of autocracy in Russia

In Germany and Italy, at least, Metternich had been able to rely on his own power of intervention. In Russia he was dependent on the attitude of the Tsar and here Alexander's spasms of sympathy with liberal ideas occasionally worried him. The Tsar had been in touch with a group of liberal Russian officers who had formed a 'Society of Salvation' in 1817 to debate the possibility of constitutional government and of vast land reforms including the emancipation of the serfs. Again, at Aix-la-Chapelle in 1818, he had shown a keen desire to include France within the Concert of Europe and in the same year at Warsaw, he had repeated his promise of liberal reform before the Polish Diet.

Before long, however, Metternich's fears were allayed. In his last years Alexander began moving towards a greater mistrust of liberal experiments and after 1820 adopted a far more conservative attitude towards the press and the Universities. In 1822 he forbade the existence of all secret societies, although this did not prevent a revival, a little later, in the form of a Northern and a Southern Society. Alexander died in December 1825 to be succeeded by his younger brother Nicholas I; the new Tsar, in contrast to his predecessor, was a straightforward soldierly character, quite out of sympathy with liberal movements, and, owing to a peculiar episode at the beginning of his reign, was able to carry out a complete suppression of such activities.

The rising of the Decembrists followed on a momentary confusion over the succession. In 1822 Alexander's brother Constantine, Viceroy of Poland, had renounced his right to the throne. Nicholas, the third brother, much younger than the other two, had, however, been left unaware of the official details of the change and on learning of Alexander's death he proclaimed Constantine emperor at St Petersburg, at the same time as Constantine in Warsaw was proclaiming Nicholas—a show of deference highly unusual in the history of the Tsars. The members of the Northern and Southern Societies at once decided to bring forward the date of their intended uprising in order to seize the opportunity offered by a succession apparently in doubt, and when the troops were eventually summoned to St Petersburg to take the oath of allegiance to Nicholas, who by now knew that he was the rightful heir, the conspirators raised the cry for Constantine and a constitution. They had, however, had too little time to prepare the ground; many of the soldiers imagined that Constitution must be the wife of Constantine and within a few hours Nicholas had gained control of the situation. Five of the leaders were hanged, many others were sentenced to forced labour or to exile in Siberia, and although the Decembrist movement created the martyrs whose memory was to inspire many later movements in Russia, this liberal failure at the beginning of Nicholas's long reign was a powerful reinforcement for the principles of the Holy Alliance.

5. Liberal successes

a) *Latin America and Portugal*

Not all the revolts ended in disaster for the liberals. The tie between Spain and Portugal and their colonies in America had been seriously weakened ever since the Napoleonic era, and in 1819 Spain had already cut her losses to the extent of selling to the United States all her territories along the North American coast east of the Mississippi. But in 1821 revolt flared up in her remaining colonies in Central and South America, and in the following year Monroe, the President of the United States, gave official recognition to the new governments of La Plata, Chile, Peru, Columbia, and Mexico. The agreement between Polignac and Canning in October 1823 (see p. 56) made it clear that, despite the restoration of absolutism in Spain, Europe would do nothing to help her in the New World. In December, in his annual message to Congress, President Monroe stated the famous doctrine that, while there would be no American interference in European politics nor with any existing colonies, the United States would not tolerate any future colonization or interference by European Powers in the American continents. Monroe's statement aroused little public excitement at the time; yet it did have an immediate effect on British policy. Canning had been holding back from recognizing the new South American republics, but the protective interest shown in them by the United States now forced his hand and at the end of 1824, to avoid their succumbing completely to North American influence, he consented to their recognition.

In Portugal the story was long and confused. In August 1820 an army rising at Lisbon and Oporto against the despotism of the regency council had brought a demand for a constitution and for the return of King John VI from Brazil. In 1821 King John, in response to this, agreed to come back, but it was his two sons who thereafter dictated the course of events. In 1822, the elder son, Dom Pedro, who had been left behind as Regent in Rio de Janeiro, announced the independence of Brazil under his rule, while in Portugal the victory of the French in Spain encouraged the younger son, Dom Miguel, to enter Lisbon in force in June 1823 and to suppress the constitution. On the death of King John in 1826, Dom Pedro, in Brazil, renounced his own claim in favour of his daughter Donna Maria, who was eight years of age, suggesting a Papal dispensation that would allow her to marry her uncle Dom Miguel. He also promised a restoration of the constitution under his daughter, and when civil war seemed about to break out with Dom Miguel, whose absolutist inclinations were strongly supported by Ferdinand of Spain, the constitutionalist party appealed to Canning. The British Foreign Secretary enjoyed posing as the champion of liberalism, and, invoking the traditional British interest in Portugal, he dispatched 4,000 troops with a fleet to Lisbon to ensure that there should be no Spanish intervention on behalf of Dom Miguel.*

b) The Greek revolt

The most serious outbreaks in those years occurred in the Balkan

* For later events in Portugal, see p. 79.

dominions of the Turks. In March 1821 they were engaged in putting down a local vassal, Ali, Pasha of Janina, when a Greek aide-
de-camp of the Tsar, Alexander Ypsilanti, took the opportunity to
cross the Pruth into Moldavia, occupied Jassy and called on the
inhabitants to rise against their Turkish overlords. At first this
seemed likely to come to nothing; the Moldavians showed little
enthusiasm to join him and after the failure of his appeal to the Tsar
Ypsilanti was forced to flee to Austria in June 1821.

His attempt was none the less significant, since it had encouraged
the Greeks to the south to rise in a great national movement against
the Turks and a savage war broke out in the Morea and soon spread
to the Aegean islands. In 1822 a declaration of independence was
published by an assembly of Greeks, and a constitution adopted.
Moslems and Christians slaughtered each other in great numbers,
but it was the sufferings of the Greeks that were seized on by the
romantics of western Europe, who, filled with hazy ideas of classical
Greece, saw Byron's death at Missolonghi as a martyrdom in a great
cause.

The governments were less emotional. For them the major consideration was whether Russia would take advantage of the situation
to march in to the aid of the Greeks. Metternich worked hard to
persuade Alexander that the principles of the Holy Alliance
demanded that the Turks should be allowed to put down the rebels.
'Nothing appeared more in my interests, in those of my peoples, in
accordance with the opinion of my country than a religious war
against Turkey,' said Alexander afterwards, 'but I thought I
observed the revolutionary mark in the troubles of the Peloponne-
sus', and Metternich could congratulate himself for the moment on
having averted Russian intervention on the side of the rebels.

Before long, however, further developments had made some form
of intervention inescapable. In 1824, when the Greeks appeared to
have gained the upper hand, the Sultan appealed to his powerful
vassal, Mehemet Ali, Pasha of Egypt, who sent his son Ibrahim to
subdue Crete. Early in the next year Egyptian forces established
themselves at Navarino on the mainland of Greece prior to a reduction of the whole of the Morea, where the Greeks were now beginning to fall out among themselves. These events were followed by
the death of Tsar Alexander in December 1825. His successor
Nicholas might lack the liberal instincts that had made Alexander's
policies so hard to gauge, but he had every intention of making full
use of the Greek revolt to embarrass the Sultan, as was at once made
clear by a Russian ultimatum to Turkey in March 1826.

This intervention by the Egyptians and the Russians convinced
the Powers that they could no longer hold back in the hope of a
return to the *status quo* before 1821. Mehemet Ali's rule had already
set Egypt on the road to becoming a well-organized state, and his

plan to follow up his son Ibrahim's victories with an Egyptian colonization of the Morea would create a new Power in the eastern Mediterranean of far greater consequence than Turkey. Alternatively, Russian intervention on the side of the Greeks against the Egyptians could only result in the creation of a Greek state virtually under the suzerainty of the Tsar.

For the other Powers there were two possible courses of action—either to ally with Turkey and Mehemet Ali against Russia, or to act alongside Russia and to impose a compromise settlement over Greek independence through concerted pressure. In London Canning chose the second of these. This was certainly in accord with his own liberal instincts and with public opinion, but the risks involved were considerable, since the expulsion of the Egyptians from the Morea might well open the way to Russian penetration. The Duke of Wellington went at once to St Petersburg and in April 1826 Tsar Nicholas, to avoid the possibility of a European league forming against Russia, signed an agreement providing for joint mediation in establishing Greece as a tributary dependency of Turkey with a reasonable degree of autonomy and freedom of conscience. The Sultan, alarmed at this development, hastily signed the Convention of Akkerman with Russia, settling a recent dispute over the government of the Turkish provinces of Moldavia and Wallachia, but still failed to shift the Tsar from his determination to intervene in Greece. In Paris certain groups favoured the idea of an Egyptian colonization of the Morea as a more reliable bulwark against Russia than a semi-independent Greek state, but the French government, suspicious of any Anglo-Russian agreement, signed the Treaty of London in July 1827, associating itself fully with the new scheme for forceful mediation on behalf of the Greeks.

Canning never lived to see the dramatic consequences of his policy. His death in August 1827 was an immense relief to Metternich, and the Sultan felt sufficiently encouraged to reject the demand for an armistice in Greece, presented by the three Powers. British and French squadrons were already in the eastern Mediterranean and in September they ordered the Turkish and Egyptian fleet at Navarino Bay to return under escort to Egypt. Ibrahim refused and in October, after being joined by a Russian squadron from the Baltic, the allies entered the bay and in the battle that followed the Turkish and Egyptian fleet was utterly destroyed.

This unexpected development, involving the crippling of Turkish sea power, seemed to play into Russia's hands, and when, in April 1828, the Tsar, claiming a breach of the Convention of Akkerman, declared war on Turkey, it was natural that the Duke of Wellington's government in Great Britain should look aghast at this outcome of Canning's policy. The French, acting in accordance with the Treaty of London, dispatched 14,000 troops to the Morea, where

Ibrahim was ousted without difficulty, but the eyes of Europe were on the Russian forces as they moved south through the Danubian Principalities, and when they occupied Adrianople, it seemed that the last hour of the Ottoman empire in Europe had come.

The momentary panic proved, in fact, to be needless. Russia had no wish for the dissolution of the Turkish empire, since she knew that partition, which would be the only possible basis for agreement among the Powers, would have far-reaching consequences (see p. 41). The French, for instance, earlier in the year, had suggested an extensive rearrangement of the Balkans, including, significantly, the creation of a large kingdom of Greece to be given to the King of the Netherlands, after which the Netherlands themselves would be shared between France and Prussia. As a Russian, Nicholas preferred to have a large but weak Turkey as his neighbour, and as a conservative despot he had no wish to bring about a radical revision of the treaties of 1815. He was therefore happy to make peace with Turkey at Adrianople in September 1829 in return for only modest gains that would have no international repercussions—the port of Poti on the east coast of the Black Sea, certain islands at the mouth of the Danube, a protectorate over the local government of Moldavia and Wallachia, where a Russian garrison was to be maintained for five years, the demilitarization of the right bank of the Danube and commercial concessions in Turkey.

At the same time the Sultan granted Greek autonomy as laid down in Canning's original agreement with Russia. The Greeks, however, did not gain all that they had wished. By the settlement that was finally reached in 1830 they were not to have Crete and Samos and the frontier was placed fairly far south between the gulfs of Volo and Arta, since none of the Powers wanted to see the emergence of a large state. The only compensation for the Greeks was that they now received their independence outright from Turkey, and the crown of the new kingdom was eventually accepted by Prince Otto of Bavaria, who thus became the first King of Greece.

In this way the most dangerous international consequences of the Greek revolt had been averted. For Metternich it had been an uneasy period, since he had little liking for the course of events in Portugal and the New World. Now, however, there was worse to come, for at the very moment when an independent Kingdom of Greece had been created, a new wave of revolution elsewhere in Europe seemed momentarily to threaten the whole internal basis of the 1815 settlement.

Chapter 6

The Revolutions of 1830

The outbreaks in the streets of Paris, which at the end of July 1830 forced Charles X to give up his throne, set off a series of risings throughout Europe in a chain reaction similar in many ways to the events of 1820–1. This time, however, although the revolts failed in Poland and the German and Italian states, they were successful in France, Belgium, and Switzerland. These liberal victories in the west meant an important modification of the Vienna settlement, but although the republican democrats supplied much of the initial impetus, it was the richer bourgeois groups who made the principal gains.

The key to the liberal victories was the swift outcome of the revolution in France. The risings in the small states on her borders would have had little prospect of success if the monarchy of Charles X had not collapsed, and their ultimate survival was due to the fact that geographically they lay in areas where Great Britain and France could allow no interference by the central European Powers. On the other hand, the British and French governments had less immediate concern with revolution in Poland and the German and Italian states. Here the revolutionaries had to act on their own, and since neither Prussia in Germany nor Piedmont in Italy was prepared to perform the same protective function as Great Britain or France in the west, the revolts came to nothing. The Poles were unique in having a sizeable army with which to operate, but although this enabled them to put up a heroic struggle for nine months, they were bound ultimately to succumb to the greater strength of the Russian forces.

On the whole, except in Poland and Belgium, nationalism played only a small part in the revolutions of 1830. Even in Germany and Italy the principal feature was a violent protest by liberal groups against authoritarian rule. In the risings east of the Rhine, however, the very lack of any national unity meant that the forces of revolution were too scattered and too parochial in outlook to offer any serious threat to Metternich's system. Even the Swiss movements, which were restricted to agitation *within* the cantons, were only saved from external interference by the international guarantee of Swiss neutrality.

For the successful and the unsuccessful alike there were lessons to be learnt from the events of 1830. The successful had shown that a violent change of government could be achieved without either a major war or a prolonged period of internal upheaval culminating in a Terror; while to the unsuccessful, in Germany and Italy, it was becoming increasingly apparent that a liberal movement could not be realistic until it had come to terms with the problem of national unification.

1. The liberal victories: France, Belgium and Switzerland

The story of the French Revolution of 1830 really begins in the previous year when Charles X dismissed Martignac's government and appointed in its place a group of ministers whose names epitomized the most uncompromising features of the Ultra party. La Bourdonnaye had been responsible for the White Terror of 1815; de Bourmont had deserted Napoleon on the eve of Waterloo; Prince de Polignac, like his king, was an unrepentant *émigré*, whose tendency to allow his policy to be guided by heavenly visions naturally inclined him more to the notion of Throne and Altar rather than to that of constitutional monarchy.

The members of this new government did have sufficient political sense to realize their own unpopularity, and accordingly, during the seven months before the Chamber would have to be recalled to pass the Budget, Polignac made great efforts to achieve a spectacular success in foreign policy. Secret conversations with the Russian Tsar for the regaining of the left bank of the Rhine came to nothing, owing to Prussian objections. Instead, a punitive expedition against the Bey of Algiers was fitted out. The liberals remained unimpressed; *Le Journal des Débats* and *Le Constitutionnel* had been joined in January 1830 by a new opposition publication, *Le National*, edited by Adolphe Thiers, Mignet, and Armand Carrel, and financed by the banker Jacques Laffitte, and when, in March 1830, the Chamber at last assembled, a vote of no confidence was carried by 221 votes to 158. Charles dissolved the Chamber, but in the subsequent election in July, despite governmental pressure on the electors, the opposition was increased from 221 to 274.

So far there was no question of any threat to Charles's throne. The forms of constitutional monarchy would sooner or later demand the dismissal of his ministers, but even if he insisted on retaining them, the deputies had nothing more revolutionary in mind than a refusal to pay taxes. Unfortunately for the future of the Bourbons news of the capture of Algiers had reached Paris on 9 July and Charles fell a dupe to the device with which Polignac had hoped to win general favour. The public remained coolly unmoved; the King, however, imagined that his position was now unassailable and without any attempt to win over the newly elected Chamber resolved upon a royal *coup d'état*.

On 26 July four ordinances were printed in *Le Moniteur*. No newspaper or periodical under twenty pages was to be published without royal permission. The Chamber was dissolved and arrangements for a new election were announced. The most significant change of all was a modification of the franchise which reduced the effective electorate to about 25,000, excluding most of the industrialist and commercial class. It seemed clear that these measures could be nothing less than a preliminary to annulling the Charter, yet at this crucial moment in his reign Charles demonstrated the full extent of his political incompetence. He had chosen to act when the Paris garrison numbered rather less than 11,000, owing to the military operations in Algeria; the Minister of War, de Bourmont, was absent; his deputy minister, Champagny, had received no warning and Marmont, who had been given command of the troops in Paris, knew nothing of the ordinances until he read them in *Le Moniteur*. Charles himself had gone off hunting at Rambouillet.

In fact, not even the publication of the ordinances caused the deputies to turn immediately to violence. It was the republicans— Godefroy Cavaignac, Trélat, and Raspail—who, seeing their chance to end the monarchy and to bring in universal manhood suffrage, were determined to fight, and they were joined almost at once by Lafayette, who was in his own person a somewhat elderly symbol of the early years of the French Revolution. By 27 July they were mobilizing the discontented elements, such as the printers for whom the suspension of the freedom of the press would mean unemployment, and students in the Latin Quarter who were always ready for a revolution, and soon the barricades began to go up in the narrow streets. The gun shops were raided, and on 28 July it became clear that the revolution was in earnest when the Hôtel de Ville was taken by the rebels, recaptured by Marmont's troops and then taken once again on his withdrawal. On 29 July the Louvre and the Tuileries were attacked and occupied, the palace of the Archbishop of Paris was sacked and two regiments of royal troops deserted to the rebels.

In three days of fighting the republicans in Paris had revealed the flimsiness of the King's rule, but in doing so they also forced the hand of the liberal deputies. These, much as they disliked Charles X, had wished to avoid violent revolution, since this might open the door to republicanism, but by 30 July it was clear that they would have to throw in their lot with the insurgents. Early that morning a group of liberals including Mignet and Adolphe Thiers, whose tiny bird-like figure was to be a gift for nineteenth-century cartoonists, met at the house of the banker Laffitte. Certainly Charles would have to go. What alternative, then, could they find to a republic? Quickly the plot was hatched, and while the men at the Hôtel de Ville looked to Lafayette and dreamed of a republic, anonymous posters appeared in Paris declaring that Louis Philippe, Duke of Orleans, would be the most appropriate successor to the Bourbon Charles X.

The hopes of the liberal monarchists now rested on two men. Could Louis Philippe, who had not yet been consulted, be persuaded to pick up the crown? Would Lafayette allow him to do so? It was Thiers who found a way through the difficulties. Riding out to Neuilly he assured Louis Philippe that his moment had come and that he alone could prevent the creation of a republic which, among other things, might well mean the exile of the Duke himself. At the same time Laffitte had organized a meeting of some sixty of the Chamber of Deputies who, together with a few peers, agreed that Louis Philippe should be invited to Paris and appointed Lieutenant General of the Kingdom. That evening, while Lafayette hesitated over accepting the responsibility of becoming President of a new republic, the Duke entered the city, making his way unobtrusively through the barricades to the Palais Royal; on the next morning, after the deputies had duly appointed him Lieutenant General, he proceeded to the Hôtel de Ville for the fateful interview with the republicans. Here the crowd saw him accept the tricolour and publicly embrace Lafayette, and with that 'republican kiss' the Orleanists knew that they had won the day.

After this there were few complications. By now Charles knew that he had lost his crown and was mainly concerned with aiding his ministers' flight. In an effort to keep the succession in his family he nominated Louis Philippe Lieutenant General, instructing him to proclaim the Duke de Bordeaux, the son of the Duchess de Berri, as King Henry V of France. Louis Philippe chose to ignore this and on 3 August the news that a mob was on the march to Rambouillet convinced Charles that it was time to quit his kingdom. The royal party, including the young Duke de Bordeaux, made a stately progress to Cherbourg, from where Charles sailed to his final exile, and on 7 August the Chamber announced that the throne was vacant and offered the crown with the title of King of the French to Louis Philippe.

The amendments to the Charter which the deputies drew up at the same time certainly established the fact that the new king had been granted his throne on terms, but in themselves they were remarkably mild. Extraordinary courts of law and censorship of the press were prohibited. The tricolour was proclaimed once more the national flag of France. The Chambers were to share with the King the right of initiating legislation and the King was deprived of the power to suspend or to dispense with existing laws. The essential question, however, lay in the composition of the Chamber and here the new Charter said extremely little, simply reducing the minimum age of deputies to thirty and their length of tenure to five years. It was not until a year later, in July 1831, that a new electoral law revealed the extent to which the richer bourgeois had triumphed. The tax qualification for deputies was lowered from 1,000 to 500 francs, and for voting from 300 to 200 francs; thus the previous electorate of 100,000 only rose to rather less than 170,000 out of a population of 32 million (see Appendix 4, p. 490).

A republican viewing the final outcome of the hectic days of July might reasonably speak of a great betrayal. The bourgeois, represented by the liberal deputies, had feared in Charles a return to some form of *ancien régime* in France, but it had been the people, as depicted in Delacroix's famous picture of Liberty on the barricades, who had fought the royal troops in the streets at the cost of some five hundred dead; yet at the end they had gained virtually nothing from the revolution of 1830. The fruits of victory had been adroitly seized by the commercial and industrialist classes. This realization was to lead to a growing antagonism between middle and lower classes throughout the reign of Louis Philippe, and when the monarchy succumbed once more in the revolution of 1848, it was to take more than a republican kiss to settle the issue between them.

For the absolutist Powers, the revolution of 1830 in France was not merely an affront, but a threat to the whole system which they had been at such pains to restore in 1815. To the rulers east of the Rhine a rising *bourgeoisie* was as detestable as a lower class movement, and the angry mistrust which the July monarchy inspired appeared almost at once justified by the spate of revolution that followed the events in Paris.

At the end of August the Belgians rose in revolt against the government of the Kingdom of the Netherlands in which they had been incorporated by the diplomats at the Congress of Vienna. Dutch sentiment in the past had sometimes regretted the division of the Netherlands which had been the price of their freedom from Spain in the seventeenth century; but the main purpose of the reunification of the Netherlands in 1815 had been to shut off France from making any encroachment in the north-east. Indeed, by the nineteenth century, their only unity was geographical. They did not share the same mother tongue, while in religion the Dutch were predominantly Calvinist, the south Roman Catholic. This sense of difference was aggravated by the fact that the government of the kingdom was carried on largely in the interest of the Dutch (see p. 30). The Belgian numerical preponderance was not reflected in the States General; Dutch was the official language, and Dutch officials held about four-fifths of the executive posts. Belgians complained bitterly that they had been saddled with too great a share of the Dutch national debt; economic policy, tending towards low tariffs, favoured the commercial classes, and although the Belgian merchants had no wish to lose the market that existed in the Dutch colonial empire, the rapidly growing industry of Belgium (see p. 86) needed protection against British competition.

The chief difficulty that had stood in the way of any Belgian national movement had been the antagonism that existed between the Catholic party, strong in the rural areas, and the liberal bourgeois group, open to French influence and highly anti-clerical. The essential preliminary to any Belgian rising was agreement between these two, and it was only after 1828 that the influence of Lamennais' ideas of Liberal Catholicism (see pp. 93–4) began to make a compromise possible, whereby the liberals would allow the Catholics their schools and the Catholics allow the liberals freedom of the press.

On 25 August, while the Paris rising was still of recent memory, rioting in the Brussels Opera House gave the local bourgeois their opportunity. Their aims did not run as far as national independence; like their counterparts in Paris, they were uneasy over latent republicanism and would have been well content with an administrative separation, while retaining a personal union of the two countries under William I. Unlike the revolution in France, however, resistance spread rapidly through the provinces and William resolved upon taking Brussels by force. Four days of fighting left the Belgians still in possession of their capital, but after such bloodshed there could be no further question of treating with William, and the liberals found themselves committed to the side of the extremists. The recent alliance of Catholics and liberals made it possible to form a provisional government and on 5 October this government proclaimed Belgium independent of the Kingdom of the Netherlands.

By the end of October an armistice had been signed with the Dutch and early in November a National Assembly, chosen by some 30,000 electors, met to draw up a constitution. Monarchy was to be retained, but the House of Orange was excluded for ever. The executive was placed under the control of bi-cameral legislature; all forms of political and social liberty were guaranteed and considerable rights of local government were left to the provinces. The franchise was extended to all who paid a tax of 20 florins—some 46,000 out of a population of four million.

Thus, in a few weeks the Belgians had shaken off Dutch control and devised a form of government that was to be the envy of liberals throughout Europe. The question of their ultimate survival, how-

ever, lay not in their own hands, but in the attitude of the great
Powers confronted by this violation of the 1815 settlement. At the
end of September 1830 William I had appealed to the other governments to assist him in putting down his rebellious subjects. Metternich was too concerned about possible dangers in Italy to act;
Tsar Nicholas I and Frederick William III would have been glad
to intervene, yet dared not, since they knew that if they sent an army
into the Low Countries, Louis Philippe, who was under great pressure from powerful groups in Paris to annex Belgium, would have
no option but to bring assistance to the Belgian liberals. In fact,
neither Louis Philippe nor his government had any wish to embark
upon a new adventure in Europe, and in September Talleyrand,
now making his final return to public life, hastened to England to
convince the British government of the need for a general agreement
on non-intervention. As a result the Duke of Wellington proposed
an immediate conference of the five Powers at London.

It was soon clear that the Dutch could not bring their Belgian
subjects to heel on their own, and on 29 November the likelihood
of intervention by the autocratic Powers on behalf of the Dutch king
was still further diminished when the outbreak of revolt in Warsaw
turned their attention eastwards. In Great Britain the Duke of Wellington's government had fallen while the conference was still in
session and the principal concern of Lord Palmerston, Foreign Secretary in the new Whig administration of Lord Grey, was to forestall
any attempt by the French to annex Belgium. Thus, on 20 December a Protocol was issued by the Powers in conference announcing
the plan to create an independent Belgian state, and this was followed in January 1831 by two further Protocols sharing the national
debt of the United Netherlands between the two countries and
defining a frontier which excluded Maestricht, Dutch Limburg, and
any part of Luxemburg from the new Kingdom of Belgium.

At this point British fears over French intentions appeared to be
suddenly confirmed. William I was prepared to accept the January
Protocols, but the Belgians were furious at the decision over the
frontier and in retaliation precipitated a new crisis by electing, on
3 February, a younger son of Louis Philippe, the Duke de Nemours,
as their King. Fortunately Louis Philippe, feeling that his newly
established régime was hardly ripe for war, wisely took note of Palmerston's anger, rejected the candidature of his son and replaced
Laffitte with the more cautious government of Casimir Périer.

By June the Belgians had been mollified by the promise of further
negotiation over Luxemburg and had agreed to offer the crown to
Leopold of Saxe-Coburg. This choice, however, caused some resentment among the French, since Leopold had a personal link with
Great Britain as the widower of George IV's daughter, Charlotte,
and in August Anglo-French hostility flared up once more, when

William I invaded Belgium again and Louis Philippe, in response to Leopold's appeal, marched in to repel the Dutch attack. Palmerston at once suspected the worst, particularly when Talleyrand spoke of the possibility of partitioning Belgium, and Prussia too began actively to prepare to come to the assistance of William, now that the French had intervened. The French accordingly withdrew their troops, and after this Anglo-French relations improved, although there was to be one further round with William, when a combined British and French force captured Antwerp from him in December 1832.

Haggling over the precise details of the frontier continued until the final agreement was signed in 1839. The province of Limburg was shared between the two countries; the Belgians were allowed the freedom of the navigation of the Scheldt, while the Netherlands retained control over the mouth of the river. Luxemburg presented an intricate problem, since as a separate duchy in the hereditary possession of the House of Orange it was a member of the German Confederation and the capital was a Federal fortress occupied by a Prussian garrison. The local inhabitants had, however, joined with the Belgians in the rising of 1830 and now a part of the duchy was given to Belgium, while the rest, including the city, remained under its Grand Duke William. Lastly, by the treaty of 1839, the neutrality of the new Belgian state was recognized by the five great Powers of Europe.

Meanwhile, the events in France had also stimulated a movement among the Swiss cantons. The growth of Swiss industry had already strengthened the opposition to the cliques of conservatives and in 1819 a student society, *Zofingia*, had been formed after the pattern of the German *Burschenschaften*, aiming at breaking down the particularism of the cantons on which the power of the patrician families depended. In the summer of 1830 the example of France, the return of six Swiss regiments from the French army, and the initiative of local leaders, lawyers, schoolmasters, and business men, resulted in a series of demonstrations which ultimately caused the ruling cliques to make great constitutional concessions.

As elsewhere, the changes were liberal rather than democratic. Equality before the law and the liberty of the press were guaranteed, but the local franchise, although considerably extended, was still left dependent upon a property qualification. The course of the revolutions varied from canton to canton. In Zürich and Geneva the change came peacefully; in Schwyz there was violence and in Basle the clash between the two parties could only be resolved by a division of the canton into two—a rural area, Basselland, dominated by the liberals, and the city of Basle, where the patrician families retained their power. In Neuchâtel (see p. 13) there were to be further complications, since the canton was still a hereditary possession of the King of Prussia. All this activity, however, was confined to the individual cantons and the form of the central federal government remained as yet unaffected.

2. The liberal defeats: Poland and the Italian and German states

Throughout the summer and autumn of 1830 the rulers of the three autocratic Powers had watched the course of events in France and Belgium in an agony of frustration. Metternich and Nesselrode, the Russian Foreign Minister, had both been on holiday in Bohemia when the news from Paris first arrived; they conferred at once and agreed that they should not interfere, provided that no other country was affected. Yet when the Belgians rose, the subsequent diplomatic imbroglio still held them powerless to intervene and in September Metternich was sufficiently depressed to confide to Nesselrode his belief that it meant the beginning of the end for the old order in Europe.

Tsar Nicholas, however, was still determined on action and was pushing ahead with his military preparations, when he was suddenly confronted by a revolt within his own dominions. The major theme of the Polish insurrection, which began in Warsaw on 29 November, was a romantic nationalism coloured by a dislike of being under the rule of a Russian viceroy and by recent disputes between the Tsar and the Diet. The outbreak was principally the work of a handful of junior Army officers who gained control of the garrison of 10,000 in Warsaw. Superficially this was a more promising start than any of the revolts in the west, but it pointed also to the real weakness of the Polish rising, which never succeeded in turning a military *coup* into a social movement. Russian rule during the previous fifteen years had been sufficiently mild to deprive Polish nationalism of any widespread grievances that might have momentarily united the Polish peasantry and their own landed aristocracy. As it was, the peasantry did not join the rising and the middle class was still too small to constitute a significant factor. The rebels suffered also from a fatal cleavage within their own ranks; the moderates under Prince Czartoryski thought mainly of reclaiming the eastern provinces that Russia had taken in 1772 and had little love for any form of social change, while the radicals talked in terms of agrarian reforms and national independence.

At the outset, at least, the rebel army, far stronger than the available Russian troops, was able to drive out the Grand Duke Constantine, and when the Russians counter-attacked early in 1831 under Field Marshal Dybicz, the Polish forces, now 70,000, were able to hold them off in the lands east of Warsaw, until they suffered a defeat at Ostroleka (see map, p. 143) on 26 May. This military disaster brought about the collapse of the moderate government under Czartoryski in Warsaw, but although a new general Kruko-wiecki was able to restore order in the capital, the days of the Polish revolt were numbered. Cholera, making its first appearance in Europe from the east, played havoc with both armies—particularly disastrous for the Poles who had few reinforcements—and on 8 September the Russians entered Warsaw. The radicals were pre-pared to fight on, but separate units of the army were beginning to desert and on 5 October the remnant of 20,000 marched over the frontier and surrendered to the Prussians.*

The possession of an army had enabled the Poles to make a spec-tacular resistance, but without assistance from the west their cause had been hopeless from the start. They had certainly believed that such assistance would come, although they had little reason for thinking this. In a general appeal issued in April 1831 the Polish government had pointed out that Poland had far more historic right to national independence than Belgium or Greece. What they ignored was that Belgium and Greece lay geographically in areas where Great Britain and France could not allow permanent occupa-tion by the great Powers and where the creation of independent states was the only possible compromise that would avoid political gain by either side. The tragedy for the Poles was that they lay out-side the British and French spheres of action.

In Italy the chances of successful revolution had also hinged on the question of intervention. A young lawyer of Modena, Enrico Misley, had devised a scheme for the creation of a constitutional Kingdom of Central Italy under the rule of Duke Francis of Modena whom he had won over to his ideas. The original plan for the rising, whereby tension between Austria and Russia over Greece was to have prevented Metternich from interfering, had been shattered by the Russo-Turkish treaty of 1829 (see p. 66), but the events in France in 1830 helped to revive Misley's hopes, and when Sebas-tiani, the new French Foreign Minister, announced in September that France would oppose any intervention by Austria outside her frontiers in Italy, the leaders decided tò take the risk and, in Feb-ruary 1831, revolt broke out in Bologna. This realization that Italian hopes depended upon the attitude of the French was perfectly sound and pointed to the means whereby success was ultimately to be achieved in 1860. On this occasion, however, the conspirators were to be betrayed by the French King and the Duke of Modena. Louis Philippe had informed Metternich privately that the French procla-mation had only served to satisfy public opinion and that he would not oppose Austrian action in Italy. In the same month Laffitte's belligerent government was dismissed and the cautious adminis-

---

* For the consequences of the revolt in Poland see p. 113.

tration of Casimir Périer which replaced it had no more intention of intervening on the side of the rebels in Italy than it had in Poland. Francis of Modena had by now turned his face against any further plans of revolt, and although he and Marie Louise of Parma had to escape from their duchies, he arrested the local leaders before he left and took them with him to Mantua.

Thus, Metternich had no hesitation in sending his troops south where the revolts were swiftly crushed. It was, nevertheless, a delicate situation and they were withdrawn as soon as their work was done. When a second rising in Bologna brought them back again, Louis Philippe felt that his government was now sufficiently well established to justify a gesture and, in February 1832, French troops proceeded by sea to occupy Ancona. There they remained for six years—as long as the Austrians stayed in Bologna—but this move was merely due to the need to preserve French prestige and it meant little for those who wished to bring revolution to Italy.

In Germany revolt was inspired as much by the Polish example as by the French, but its extent was limited in the main to the confines of particular states, although a meeting of intellectuals at Hambach in the Bavarian Palatinate did go so far as to discuss the question of German unification. Local risings imposed liberal constitutions on the rulers of Brunswick, Hanover, Saxony, and Hesse-Cassel; in others, where elective Chambers already existed, liberal opposition grew more outspoken. All this, however, was short-lived. Prussia and Austria, acting through the Diet of the German Confederation, were able to re-establish the situation in most states, and when, in April 1833, German students, encouraged by Polish *émigrés*, tried to carry out a *coup* at Frankfurt in order to bring pressure to bear on the Diet, they were easily defeated. In June 1834 Metternich was able to put fresh heart into the princes assembled at Vienna with added restrictions on liberal activity, and for the moment he could feel that the threat of further revolution was no longer immediate.

Chapter 7
The Diplomatic Scene 1830–48

The pattern of liberal successes and failures in the revolutions of 1830 might at first suggest the division of Europe into two camps— the constitutional governments of the west and the autocratic Powers of the Holy Alliance—each with their own accepted spheres of influence. From the point of view of economic development and the general tone of domestic affairs this might be a valid distinction; it is seldom, however, that diplomacy can run in accordance with common political ideologies. Indeed, the most striking feature of these years was a growing discord between Great Britain and France, due partly to commercial competition, but mainly to British uneasiness over the increasing independence of French policy in the Mediterranean.

Another factor at this time was a change in Russian policy towards Turkey. The crisis of 1827–9 had shown Tsar Nicholas that there was no slackening in the nervousness of the great Powers over the possibility of Russian expansion at Turkey's expense. Accordingly he began now to wonder whether friendship rather than enmity with Turkey might not offer greater rewards. Metternich and Frederick William III would probably favour this as part of the maintenance of the Vienna settlement, but Nicholas naturally realized that the consequent growth of Russian influence at Constantinople would be bound to create distrust in Great Britain; thus, since British disapproval could really only be effective with French military support, the Tsar was particularly pleased at the poor state of Anglo-French relations. These aims, however, were purely Russian. Nicholas was perfectly ready to move outside the circle of the Holy Alliance to gain the friendship of Great Britain in order to keep her separated from France; equally, when Anglo-French relations had finally collapsed in 1846, Metternich was prepared to open negotiations with France.

The debate over the Belgian frontier was still continuing when a new crisis in the Near East arose out of the settlement of the Greek question. In 1831 Mehemet Ali, angered by the Sultan's decision to give him Crete instead of Syria, as originally promised, in return for his services in Greece, invaded Syria with 30,000 men and after taking the fortress of Acre swiftly overran the whole country. In 1832 he advanced into Asia Minor and when the Turkish army was defeated at Konieh, it seemed once again that nothing could prevent the collapse of the Ottoman empire.

The reaction of the Powers to this new situation varied. France was not unfavourably disposed towards Egypt, but the monarchy of Louis Philippe was too recently established to face with equanimity the complications that the dissolution of Turkey would involve. Great Britain, on the other hand, was definitely opposed to Mehemet Ali, since her lines of communication with India made her anxious, like Russia, to prevent the emergence of any strong Power in the Near East. Neither Great Britain nor France, however, immediately warmed to Metternich's proposal of forceful mediation, until the Sultan in despair appealed to Russia, and Tsar Nicholas, seeing a chance to develop his new policy of friendship towards Turkey, agreed to come to her aid. The arrival of a Russian fleet in the Bosphorus and the occupation of both sides of the Straits by Russian troops in February 1833 naturally made diplomatic intervention by the other Powers of Europe inevitable, and they hastily imposed a settlement whereby Turkey granted Mehemet Ali the pashaliks of Egypt, Crete, Syria, Damascus, and Tripoli for his lifetime.

The withdrawal of Russian forces was at once followed in July by the Treaty of Unkiar Skelessi between the Tsar and the Sultan. The terms of this defensive alliance, which was to last eight years, promised Turkey Russian aid if she were attacked; on the other hand, the only assistance that Russia would demand in the event of war would be the closing of the Straits to her enemies' warships. This was a significant revision of the Anglo-Turkish agreement of 1809, for although it did not allow Russia to enter the Mediterranean, it did enable her to shut off the Black Sea to her enemies in wartime. These clauses, although secret, were soon known everywhere in Europe and caused considerable indignation in London and Paris. Any collective protest, however, seemed to be ruled out after September 1833, when a meeting took place between Tsar Nicholas and the Emperor Francis at Münchengrätz and a convention was signed between Austria and Russia agreeing on collaboration in central Europe and guaranteeing the maintenance of Turkey.

One consequence of this reaffirming of the principles of the Holy Alliance at Münchengrätz was a slacking of tension over the Eastern Question, much assisted in January 1834 by the withdrawal of Russian forces from the Danubian principalities (see p. 66). A second more positive effect was a short-lived *rapprochement* between Great Britain and France. Since 1831 both countries had been sending unofficial aid to the constitutional party of the Portuguese Queen Maria whose throne had been usurped by her uncle Dom Miguel.

In Spain another young Queen, Isabella, succeeded her father, Ferdinand VII, on his death in 1833, but the government under the regency of her mother had been challenged by her uncle, Don Carlos. Thus civil war was now raging in Spain and Portugal between the forces of the rightful Queens who were supported by liberal opinion, and the two wicked uncles whose views were purely autocratic. Palmerston had for long been suspicious of French intrigues in Spain, and when Talleyrand proposed an Anglo-French military alliance for joint action on behalf of the Queens, he converted it in April 1834 into a Quadruple Alliance with Spain and Portugal. This he hoped might restrain the French from acting on their own initiative and 'would serve as a powerful counterpoise to the Holy Alliance of the East'.

Naturally, Palmerston was exaggerating. The Quadruple Alliance did succeed in defeating the uncles and in establishing the Queens on their thrones. On the other hand, the subsequent worsening of Anglo-French relations precluded any chance of an effective league against the autocratic Powers.

The reasons for this latest hostility lay in the strategic and economic implications of an active French policy in the Mediterranean. Palmerston certainly hoped for a lasting friendship and was careful not to make an issue of the establishment of French power in Algeria, where by 1836 they had begun to occupy the interior (see p. 99). This strengthening of France's position in the western Mediterranean did, however, cause a greater sensitiveness over Spain, and the Quadruple Alliance was virtually disrupted by British endeavours to achieve commercial connections there, which might compensate for any political influence that the French hoped to gain south of the Pyrenees.

France's interest in North Africa also brought about a clash over policy in the Near East. The British reaction to the Treaty of Unkiar Skelessi was to offer the Sultan assistance in reforming his navy, but without any positive alliance, since that might have encouraged him to renew the war with Egypt. In return, the British received commercial concessions in 1838, whereby their merchants might trade freely throughout the Turkish dominions—a blow for Mehemet Ali who was attempting to develop Egyptian exports through state monopolies of cotton, tobacco, and indigo. In contrast to this British friendship with Turkey, France had greater sympathy with Egypt who was thus able to make considerable use of French technicians in the modernizing of the Egyptian army and the beginnings of industrialization. This raised something more than questions of commercial rivalry. The Red Sea route to India was of permanent importance to Great Britain, and the growth of French influence in Egypt, coupled with the efforts of the French consul at Basra to interfere with the use of the overland route through Mesopotamia, naturally seemed to the British like a revival of the plans that Napoleon had once entertained for cutting their direct line of communication with the east.

In the circumstances it was not surprising that the next crisis in the Near East should reveal the full extent of British and French antagonism over Egypt. In 1838 Mehemet Ali, encouraged by the French, refused to pay his annual tribute to the Sultan Mahmud, who promptly sent an army against him into Syria. The outcome was disastrous for Turkey. The Egyptians under Ibrahim won a decisive victory at Nezib (see map, p. 11) in June 1839; the Turkish fleet changed sides and sailed for Alexandria, and it seemed that Turkey lay once again open to conquest by Mehemet Ali.

Metternich's hope was to bring about a form of collective mediation by the five Powers—much to the relief of Constantinople, where the sudden death of Mahmud shortly after the battle of Nezib had put the government somewhat at a loss. In August, however, Tsar Nicholas announced that he would have nothing whatever to do with the scheme, and it looked as if Russia was about to make use of the Treaty of Unkiar Skelessi to embark upon an independent course of intervention in aid of the Turks. But this was not Nicholas's intention. He was by now disillusioned over the value of an alliance with Turkey and in the recent events he had seen an opportunity to aggravate the ill feeling that already existed between Great Britain and France. Accordingly, in the autumn of 1839, knowing full well that the French would prefer to give their support to Egypt, he opened negotiations with Palmerston for imposing a settlement in the Near East which would check Mehemet Ali's ambitions.

His policy was highly successful. Whereas the Austrian and Prussian ambassadors in London joined in the new scheme, the French hung back and in March 1840 a new government under Thiers attempted to bring about a direct settlement between Turkey and Egypt on its own. This convinced Palmerston that the Powers must go ahead without France and in July the four of them signed a treaty at London imposing their own settlement in the Near East. Mehemet Ali was presented with an ultimatum promising him the hereditary possession of Egypt and the pashalik of Acre for his lifetime, in return for the restoration of the Turkish fleet and the evacuation of northern Syria. Mehemet Ali, still putting his faith in French support, made no reply and in the autumn of 1840 a combined naval and military force of the Allies landed near Beirut. Mehemet Ali was already faced with a revolt of the Christians in the Lebanon; Ibrahim was defeated in the mountains above Junieh, Beirut surrendered to the Allies and, farther south, Acre was bombarded and taken. Despairing of any assistance from France, Mehemet Ali now agreed to terms, restored Syria, Crete, and Arabia, as well as the

Turkish fleet, and agreed to pay annual tribute to the Sultan in return for his recognition as hereditary Pasha of Egypt.

In France the treaty of the four Powers in July 1840, from which she had been excluded, awoke a tremendous patriotic fury in the boulevards and Thiers' government was at one with public opinion in denouncing a pact so reminiscent of the Quadruple Alliance of 1814. 'Si l'Europe veut avoir affaire à nous, elle n'a qu'à essayer,' Thiers had said in April, and when it was apparent that the Powers intended to act against Egypt, hotheads spoke of challenging Europe with a revision of the treaties of 1815. 'La France doit se souvenir que, même étant seule, elle a tenu tête à l'Europe,' declared the *Revue des Deux Mondes*, and the government now embarked on military preparations, including the fortification of Paris.

In fact, neither Louis Philippe nor Thiers was keen to thrust France into a general European war. A corresponding surge of German nationalism throughout the states of the Confederation seized on the memories of the war of liberation against France in 1813; the songs *Die Wacht am Rhein* and *Deutschland über alles* and the hope which King Ludwig of Bavaria expressed that Strasbourg might again be a German city, all suggested that another form of revision of the treaties of 1815 might involve the loss of Alsace, and clearly pointed to the need for caution. Palmerston was convinced that France was bluffing, and in October 1840 Louis Philippe decided to hold out no longer and secured the resignation of Thiers. With this France rejoined the Concert of Powers, and took her part in the final agreements with Mehemet Ali. In July 1841 the settlement of the Near East was rounded off with the signing of the Straits Convention whereby Russia gave up the special terms that she had gained from the Treaty of Unkiar Skelessi, and the situation reverted to the ruling laid down in the Anglo-Turkish arrangement of 1809.

Nicholas had certainly been successful in his attempt to use the Egyptian crisis as a means of finally breaking up the alliance of 1834 between Great Britain and France, but it was Palmerston who could claim to have scored the greatest success in this episode. Realizing that Russia was bound to oppose the capture of the Ottoman empire by such a powerful ruler as Mehemet Ali, he had been able to rely on her support for his policy, and sensing the anxiety of the French over the resurgence of German nationalism, he had known that he could call their bluff. Thus he had cut short Egyptian expansion, undermined the extension of French influence in the eastern Mediterranean, and with the Straits Convention of 1841 had seen Russia abandon the policy of Unkiar Skelessi in favour of continuing friendly relations with Great Britain.

Many of these features of the international scene were to hold good until the revolutions of 1848. Nicholas continued to nurse his

new friendship with Great Britain, and in 1844, when he feared that
Anglo-French relations were on the mend, he came to England to
warn Lord Aberdeen, Foreign Secretary in Sir Robert Peel's administration, that the collapse of Turkey would offer France the chance
of gains which only close Anglo-Russian collaboration could prevent. No positive alliance resulted from these conversations, but
relations between Russia and Great Britain remained favourable
and there was little indication that within ten years the two countries would be at war.

Nicholas, however, had been right to suspect the renewal of some
sort of *entente* between Great Britain and France. New personalities,
Guizot in Paris and Aberdeen in London, were convinced of its
importance and worked hard to heal the rift between the two countries—a policy in which Queen Victoria played her part with two
visits to France in 1843 and 1845.

There were, however, still too many bones of contention for their
efforts to achieve much more than an uneasy truce. In the policing
of the Atlantic against the slave trade, the French suspected the
British of attempting to increase their control of the sea. There was,
too, considerable tension over the opening up of the Pacific at this
time, and it had been mainly due to fears of the possibility of
annexation by France that the British government had placed New
Zealand under British sovereignty in 1840. This decided the French,
in 1844, to take possession of the island of Tahiti, where an English
missionary, Mr Pritchard, had been carrying on a lonely struggle
to persuade Queen Pomare to put herself under the protection of
the British Crown, and although Aberdeen was determined to leave
well alone, the arrest of Pritchard by Admiral Dupetit-Thouars
caused a minor sensation, which Louis Philippe finally settled by
a personal payment of £1,000 to the missionary.

As before, however, the key to continued Anglo-French discord
lay in the Mediterranean. In Athens the ambassadors of the two
countries intrigued against each other. In Tunis the British hoped
to see Turkey re-establish firm rule as a bulwark against French
expansion from Algeria, and when the French intended, in 1844, to
march on Fez in Morocco, where the local potentate had been
assisting the Algerians against them, it was only strong British
objections that held Louis Philippe back. The final breakdown in
their relations occurred over Spain. By 1840 Queen Isabella was ten
years of age and a long wrangle ensued when Louis Philippe put
forward a scheme for her marriage to one of his sons. The British
government, reacting strongly against this, suggested a Coburg husband for the Queen, but Guizot regarded this with equal suspicion
owing to Coburg connections with Great Britain and Belgium. The
two governments, anxious to preserve the somewhat battered *entente*,
handled the problem as tactfully as possible and were moving

towards a compromise involving a double marriage—the Queen to a Spanish cousin and her sister to one of Louis Philippe's sons—when Peel's government fell and Palmerston replaced Aberdeen as Foreign Secretary. Palmerston at once took up the Coburg candidature again in no uncertain terms, whereupon Louis Philippe refused to negotiate any longer. In September 1846 he declared the Queen of Spain betrothed to her cousin and her sister to his son, the Duke de Montpensier, and the fury of indignation to which this announcement gave rise in Great Britain marked the end of any further attempt to keep up even the pretence of an Anglo-French *entente*.

It may seem odd that a simple dynastic issue should bulk so large in nineteenth-century diplomacy. Yet when the dispute is placed in the wider context of rivalry in the Mediterranean, the question of French or British influence at the Court of Madrid naturally assumes a greater significance. It is possible that France was moving towards a new and enterprising foreign policy linking her with the two Bourbon kingdoms of Spain and Naples in a league that could have freed her from any dependence on Great Britain and might even eventually have enabled her to challenge Austrian power in Italy—as the earlier expedition to Ancona in 1832 had suggested (see p. 77). The full extent of Guizot's possible aims must remain a matter for speculation. The immediate outcome of the breakdown of the *entente* was the beginning of a friendship between France and Austria—France, because she feared isolation, Austria, because Metternich wished to present a united front to Palmerston whom he suspected of favouring the gathering forces of liberalism and nationalism. Contacts between the two remained purely tentative; Louis Philippe, mindful of the left wing in the Chamber, hesitated to announce a definite *entente* with a country that stood for the maintenance of the settlement of 1815, and Metternich had little confidence in the stability of any parliamentary government. As it turned out, their doubts were not unfounded; within a year the revolutions of 1848 had driven them both from power and the scheme for a Franco-Austrian alignment had ceased to have any practical relevance.

Chapter 8

Forces of Change

1. The economic transformation of Europe

In their outcome the revolutions of 1830 had shown that, although its original aim had been European-wide, the system of Metternich was really only effective in central and eastern Europe. Great Britain had always fought shy of it; France had been suspect as the home of revolution. But the west in these years was to offer something more than an example of political nonconformity; it was the point of origin of an economic revolution which was to be fundamentally more destructive of the old order than any local insurrection and which in its later developments has continued to transform the European scene to this day.

The first factor in this period of change was a remarkable growth in population, (see Appendix 7, p. 492). In 1800 the population of Europe as a whole stood approximately at 188 million; by 1850 it had reached 267 million. This sharp increase was reflected variously in different countries, most marked in the British Isles and in Germany, more gradual in France, who by 1850 had already been surpassed by Germany. The immediate significance lay, however, in distribution rather than in total size. In Great Britain and France industrialism caused towns to grow out of all proportion to the general increase in population; in the first half of the century Paris and Lyons were doubled, Toulouse and Marseilles rose by 75 per cent, and in the industrial regions of the north-east a small town such as St Étienne expanded from 16,000 to 56,000. East of France this urban development was much less striking. Thus, in Germany, the 73.5 per cent of the population classed as rural in 1816 had only dropped to 72 per cent by 1846; in Prussia, as late as 1850, the factory workers amounted to no more than 4 per cent of the total population, and in Hungary, out of 11 million people, there were by 1839 only 117,000 engaged in any form of industry. Nevertheless, the pressure of a growing population in the countryside was causing the peasantry to move into the towns. Berlin and Vienna each doubled their size between 1815 and 1848, and in central and eastern Europe, although the numbers of middle class and proletariat were still small, the advent, in many of the towns, of peasants speaking their own dialects was to be an important factor in the awakening consciousness of national loyalties.

The far greater urban development in the west is largely explained by the second characteristic of economic change at this time. By 1815 the new industrial processes affecting the production of iron and textiles, the manufacture of machinery and the application of steam power had given Great Britain an enormous lead over all other European countries. With the return of peace it was unlikely that her principal economic competitors would allow one country to remain the workshop of the world; an effective response to the British challenge, however, could only be made in the west, where capital was available and small forms of industry were already in existence. Even here the type of industrialism which developed in the years following the war and which began to accelerate after 1830 was distinctly dependent upon the technical experience of British engineers and workers who played a considerable part in this first phase of the Industrial Revolution on the Continent.

The major economic difficulty for France in 1815 was the loss of the Belgian coalfields which, until the tapping of the fields of northern France after 1850, left her with only those of the Upper Loire and the edge of the Belgian fields around Valenciennes. This meant that in 1815 her coal output was little more than that of 1789, although by 1847 it had been raised from 914,400 to 5,235,448 tonnes. The use of coke in the smelting of pig-iron was only seriously developed after 1815 through the aid of English experts and capital, and although output rose from 224,536 tonnes in 1821 to 600,456 in 1847, the enormous demands made by the building of railways in the 1840s could only be met by considerable imports of coal and iron from Great Britain. Cotton-spinning mills, which had begun to appear during the Napoleonic period, grew throughout the first part of the century until by 1847 there were in Mulhouse in Alsace 1,150,000 spindles and another 550,000 in the cotton areas of Lille, Roubaix, Tourcoing, and Armentières. The power-loom developed much more quickly and by 1846 there were 10,000 in operation in France. Other textile industries made less use of steam power, but machinery was gradually affecting many trades such as riveting, leather-cutting, and nail-making, and since chemical science was advanced in France, Paris could boast its gas burners for street illumination by 1844.

Compared with the fairly slow pace in France the industrialization of Belgium advanced with astonishing speed, both under Napoleon and during the period of Dutch rule. Rich in coalfields, the Belgians were working some 300 collieries and raising more than 6 million tonnes of coal a year by the time they struck out for independence in 1830. They had long been skilled in metal work—Liège had been one of Napoleon's great munitions centres—and a considerable immigration of British engineers and workmen after the war helped them to build up a great industry of machinemaking with a market in Holland, Russia, and Germany. In 1817, for example, John Cockerill founded the famous iron and machine works at Seraing which within twenty years was employing 2,000 workers—a very large labour force for those times. In these years Belgium was second only to Great Britain, and in the words of the report of an English commission: 'Belgium surpasses in proportion to her size and population every nation in the world.'

The only other part of Europe seriously affected by industrial development was Germany. Like Belgium, she was rich in coal resources and the existence of thousands of tiny establishments gave her a long tradition and experience in the working of metals from the Harz mountains. There was, however, not much attempt made to exploit the coalfields in the Ruhr and the Saar until after 1815, nor in Silesia until about 1840, and by 1846 the total output of coal in Prussia was barely more than 3,251,200 tonnes, a figure which compares unfavourably with Belgium. The Prussian government was certainly alive to the need to industrialize and in 1821 the *Gewerbe Institut*—an institute of trades—was set up to encourage industrial enterprise. This, together with the services of British technicians, helped to foster the development of machines in factories, but in Berlin itself the lack of any coal nearby made progress slow, and in the rest of the Confederation insufficiency of capital and the confusion of frontiers and local laws hampered any speedy development. In the Rhine provinces the firms of Krupp at Essen and Haniel, Huyssen and Jacobi at Ruhrort and Oberhausen were indications of a greater power to come, but these were very early days for German industry and in the 1840s Belgium was still producing more iron than the whole of the *Zollverein*.

The greatly increased volume of goods circulating within Europe naturally demanded sound communications and the third characteristic of this period of economic transformation was a revolution in transport. Even before the railway age striking improvements had been made in the use of roads, canals, and rivers. In France the restored Bourbons and Louis Philippe continued to develop an invaluable heritage of good highways, as well as undertaking a great programme of canal building. Similarly, the Prussian government benefited greatly from its acquisition of the Rhineland roads, although communications in the eastern provinces of Prussia remained poor. River transport in Europe had always been problematical, since waters were often shallow or rocky or dangerously swift, and in Germany the local river tolls continued to be a hindrance to trade until 1834. The invention of the steam-boat, however, overcame some of the physical difficulties, making it possible as early as the 1820s to run services on the Rhine, the Weser and the Elbe, as well as across the Danish Belt and the Sound to Sweden, and farther north from Stockholm to St Petersburg. In 1830 the Austrian Danube Steam Navigation Company was formed with the intention of opening up a great waterway which until then had been little used, but the reefs and rapids of the Danube and the sand-bars at the delta were always to prevent it from becoming a great economic artery.

It was, of course, the railways that were to bring about the real revolution in European communications. Much of the initial impetus and knowledge came from Great Britain, where independent companies had been experimenting with various forms of steam locomotion in the 1820s, and among Continental countries it was once again Belgium that jumped into the lead. With their thriving industry and geographical situation, the Belgian Parliament quickly recognized the potential value of a well planned railway system and in 1834 voted in favour of entrusting the whole project to the State— in contrast to the British pattern of authorizing individual companies by Act of Parliament. In the next thirteen years, as a result of the work of Lebeau and Charles Rogier (see p. 124), a network of railways connected Belgium with Holland, Germany, and France; they proved expensive—an average of £16,500 a mile—but the indirect gain in terms of increased export of coal and pig-iron made it an investment of incalculable national profit.

In France the approach to the whole question was far more cautious. Torn between systems of State control and private enterprise, the French Chamber spent most of the 1830s in discussion over fundamental principles. In fact, a few concessions to private companies did result in the laying of 564 kilometres of track in this decade, but it was not until 1842 that a compromise solution was reached whereby private companies could build the railways according to a national pattern, on the understanding that they would eventually become State property and that in the meantime the State would supervise rates and safety precautions. After this there followed a great boom in railway building, attracting British capital through the banker Edward Blount and bringing to France a whole army of British engineers and railway workers, and by 1848 over 1,932 kilometres of track had been laid in France.

The enthusiasm for railway building was spreading fast in the 1840s. In Germany the southern and western states tended to rely upon governmental direction, while Prussia, after at first hanging back, began to work in cooperation with private companies, and by 1848 the completion of 4,830 kilometres of track had brought Germany within reach of a national network. By the same date Vienna was linked with Prague and Warsaw, and Amsterdam with the Hague and Rotterdam. The Swiss made little progress with railways at this time; a mountainous countryside created great engineering difficulties, the conservative element foresaw a dangerous threat to the independence of the cantons, and farmers anticipated a fall in local prices with the increase of foreign competition. In the industrial north their development was seen in a more favourable light, but was hampered by the rival railway schemes of Zürich and Basle, and it was not until 1847 that the first Swiss line was opened between Zürich and Baden.

In north Italy small local lines were completed between Venice and Milan, Turin and Genoa, and Pisa and Leghorn, but it was the Kingdom of Naples, always decried as the most backward state in the peninsula, that actually produced the first railway in Italy. In 1839 a line between Naples and Portici was officially opened by King Ferdinand, who had stipulated that there should be a chapel at every station and no tunnels, which he regarded as conducive to immorality.

The enormous demands made on capital to finance these developments helped to create a fourth characteristic of the economic revolution—the enhanced position of banking on an international scale. The tendency in each country was for the government to rely upon one bank as an agent for its own financial transactions and as a means of controlling the fiscal economy of the country. The difficulty of performing the second function was greatly increased by the existence of many private note-issuing banks, and it was the struggle to restrict the right of issue that marked banking history in England, France, and Prussia during these years. In Holland the Netherlands Bank had enjoyed a monopoly of note issue from the time of its establishment in 1814, while in Belgium the rivalry between two houses—the Société Générale and the Banque de Belgique—ended in the government granting each the right to issue notes. Another problem was the standardization of currency. The uniform French franc system was introduced in Belgium in 1832 and, later, in Switzerland, but in Germany a variety of local currencies was still in circulation at the end of the 1830s.

The most striking feature of all was the growth of international financial operations. The notes of the Bank of England enjoyed an unrivalled position in Europe after the Napoleonic war and the immense amount of capital available in England, due to her earlier industrialization, combined with a long experience in the handling of credit, the development of cheques, and the clearing-house system, made London the financial centre of the world. Merchant bankers in the City, the great houses of Rothschild and Baring Brothers, were the sources to which governments and business men all over the Continent and in North and South America increasingly turned for the floating of loans to finance new industrial developments and the building of railways. The activities of these London bankers, together with others such as the Hopes of Amsterdam and the Parishes of Hamburg, spun across the political frontiers a delicate web of international credit so sensitive to the rise and fall of public confidence that the economy of one country became inextricably involved in the economy of the others.

Two periods of distress were to illustrate this new interdependence. In 1833 President Jackson deprived the Bank of the United States of its function as a central financial agency for the government, and the investment of Federal funds in a number of state-chartered banks led to a period of speculation, followed by a panic in 1837 in which the failure of many banks involved a loss of European capital in America. The consequent shock to credit in Europe meant bankruptcy for many firms, unemployment for the workers, and a frantic search for capital as Belgian financiers fell back on the Bank of England, which in its turn had to rely on the Bank of France. Prosperity returned in the 1840s with the era of railway building, but the potato blight and bad harvests of 1845–7 caused a draining away of capital on imported foodstuffs from south Russia and America and the sudden drop in available money brought a fresh collapse of confidence with its usual accompaniment of bankruptcies and unemployment (see pp. 119–20). Great Britain, as the most highly industrialized country in Europe at this time, suffered the greatest dislocation in these two slumps, but as industrialism grew, so subsequent crises in the century were to reveal the new closeness of economic relationship throughout the entire Continent.

These four principal characteristics of the economic transformation of Europe suggest a great variety of consequences of growing significance during the rest of the century. National commercial policies were directly influenced by the strengthened position of the commercial and industrial classes after the revolutions of 1830 in France and Belgium and the Reform Act of 1832 in Great Britain and were all based on the assumption that in open competition the British industrialist had an enormous advantage over his counterpart on the Continent. Free Trade, as Bismarck once said, was the weapon of the strongest nation. Thus, whereas in Great Britain the tendency was to continue to lower or to remove import duties, a policy of protection for the new industries prevailed on the Continent.

In this respect there was little difference in France between the policy of the Bourbons and that of Louis Philippe's government. In the years following the Restoration duties on imported cotton and iron as well as on corn had constantly mounted. Louis Philippe, who would have liked to lower them, did succeed to some extent at the beginning of his reign, but in 1841 he had to pander to the interests in the bourgeois Chamber with an increased tariff and it was the resistance of French manufacturers, coupled with strong British objections, that forced him to abandon the scheme for a Customs Union with Belgium.

In Germany the most significant change was the merging of the Prussian *Zollverein* with the Unions of the centre and the south, which took effect on 1 January 1834.* The establishment of a general protective tariff for German industry, the abolition of internal customs enormously facilitating local trade, the beginnings of a uniform currency, and the rapid growth of a network of railways, all formed part of the theme constantly reiterated by the economist Frederick List, that Germany might one day accomplish the economic conquest of the world; and although List committed suicide in 1846, the foundations of a great German national economy had in fact been laid before his death. In Switzerland Berne strongly supported the demand of the liberals to follow the example of Germany and, in 1835, cantonal customs were abolished, although a complete economic union did not come until the victory of the federalists in 1848 (see p. 133).

Unlike the bourgeois liberals of western Europe who gained state legislation in their own interest, the new working class was left unprotected by any governmental action. In the industrial towns France was beset with the same ills as in England—child labour, long hours, starvation wages and appalling living conditions in slums lacking all means of sanitation, where the great cholera epidemics of 1832 and 1848 spread like wildfire. In England the efforts of Lord Ashley and other humanitarians had succeeded in restricting child labour in the mines and factories and in establishing a ten-and-a-half-hour day in certain forms of industry by 1850. In France a Factory Act of 1841 also restricted the use of child labour in concerns employing more than twenty persons, and in Prussia, after complaints from the army that physical defects were having a serious effect on the intake of recruits, Frederick William III, in 1839, forbade the employment of children under nine years of age and decreed a ten-hour day for those under sixteen. These French and Prussian measures, however, were largely vitiated by the absence of an adequate system of inspection.

Among the workers themselves there was little success in organization. In France the penal code forbade any association larger than twenty, striking and picketing were criminal offences, and the workman's *livret*, instituted by Napoleon, gave the employer a considerable hold over his labour force. The harshness with which this control was exercised varied, but an average of two hundred workmen a year were sentenced to imprisonment between 1825 and 1847,

* Oldenburg, Brunswick, Hanover, and the Hanse cities still remained outside the scheme, but most of them had joined the *Zollverein* within the next twenty years.

and two attempts to establish the right of association—in 1831 and 1834 among the silk workers at Lyons (see p. 100)—frightened the government of Louis Philippe into treating them as armed rebellion which was put down by military force after bitter fighting. Two fundamental weaknesses hampered the French proletariat in these years. First, there were still too few of them—only a million by 1846 throughout France; second, large forms of industrial enterprise had not yet developed on the Continent even in the west. The scene was one of thousands of tiny workshops. In 1848, for example, there were 64,000 private concerns in Paris—50 per cent of them consisting of no more than the proprietor either on his own or aided by one workman—and in these circumstances the organization of workers was difficult to achieve.

Thus, by 1848, the full implications of the economic revolution were far from being completely worked out; yet they were ultimately to create a situation that would utterly shatter the assumptions of the *ancien régime* so carefully pieced together again at the Congress of Vienna. Industrialism, finance, the growth of railways, the improvement of postal services and the development of the electric telegraph were all to bring various regions into far greater closeness of contact and within the countries themselves to exert a strong centralizing influence. The size and armament of military forces and their systems of mobilization were to be transformed, and areas of Europe, rich in minerals, were to acquire a new strategic significance. In the east, a growing urban population in greater touch with the provinces was to hasten the awakening of nationalism; in the west, a proletariat was eventually to become capable of organization, and throughout the whole Continent, even as early as the 1840s, there was evidence of a new pressure of social and political aspiration bearing inexorably against the foundations of the Holy Alliance.

2. Early forms of Socialism

There were many who were conscious of the possible repercussions of these various forces of change. 'Europe is racing towards democracy', wrote Chateaubriand in 1834, '. . . the most audacious doctrines concerning property, equality and liberty are proclaimed night and morning in the face of monarchs trembling behind a triple guard of unreliable soldiers.' If the language was exaggerated and the monarchs trembled slightly less than Chateaubriand imagined, the 1830s and 1840s were none the less a time of audacious doctrines. Their very diversity almost precludes any coherent systemization, yet one feature they shared in common; an intoxicating air of romanticism blows through these Utopian schemes, the delight of poets, philosophical visionaries and university students, impatient of piecemeal legislation and compromise, envisaging not simply reform, but a total regeneration of society.

'The name of Paris', wrote Alexander Herzen on his arrival from Russia in 1847, 'was closely bound up with all the noblest enthusiasms of contemporary humanity. I entered it with reverence, as men used to enter Jerusalem and Rome.' It was not long before he was recording his disillusionment—'death in literature, death in the theatre, death in politics, death in the Chamber'—yet despite the heavily bourgeois instincts that sheltered beneath the umbrella of Louis Philippe, his original comment was not inappropriate. Paris at this time was the centre of a literary scene as brilliant, perhaps, as France has ever known, one in which romantic novelists and poets made a colourful, if somewhat uncoordinated contribution to political and social ideas through their warm sympathy with the working class. 'The proletarian question,' said Lamartine, who became a member of the Chamber in 1833, 'is one that will cause the most terrible explosion in present day society, if society and government decline to fathom and resolve it.' In Great Britain poets were more wary of becoming directly involved in political life than they were in France, yet an interesting parallel exists between the writers of the two countries in these years of social adjustment. The conventional picture of George Sand as a pipe-smoking Bohemian, the maternal guardian of Chopin on Majorca, might not immediately suggest a parallel with a West Country vicar like Charles Kingsley; yet, just as Kingsley expressed the indignation of the Christian Socialists in *The Water Babies* and *Yeast*, so the ideas of Pierre Leroux were proclaimed in the Socialist novels of George Sand, who was a close friend of Michel de Bourges, the lawyer who had defended the leaders of the Lyons riots of 1834 (see p. 100).

There was thus no lack of revolutionary sentiment in the periodicals and literary circles of Paris, they provided an atmosphere of romantic enthusiasm and they were passionately sincere. 'Le poète aujourd'hui,' wrote Victor Hugo in 1824, 'doit marcher devant les peuples comme une lumière et leur montrer le chemin.' Yet it is important not to rate them too highly, for even in France they were to some extent a class apart. A more significant movement is to be found in Liberal Catholicism, since it affected an infinitely wider range of the French public. Amid the tumult of the nineteenth century the Church of Rome stood as a guarantor of the established order of society. Throne and Altar remained its ideal and as a consequence the sense of a great cleavage between the Catholic right and the republican left, which had torn France asunder in the French Revolution, persisted. This was a simplification, however, that not all Catholics could accept. In Ireland Daniel O'Connell had worked furiously against Protestant rule from Westminster; in Belgium Catholics and liberals had combined to expel the Dutch (see p. 72), and these efforts were now to inspire a Breton priest, the Abbé de Lamennais, to lead a movement that combined Catholicism with liberal reform. In a series of writings culminating in his *Paroles d'un croyant* in 1834, he demanded that the Church should separate itself from the State, that the press and education should be free from secular control and that elections should be more frequent and the franchise extended. Gradually Lamennais fell away from the Church, partly because it condemned his ideas, partly because it would give no support to Polish nationalism, one of the great emotional cries of the French romantics. Liberal Catholicism, however, was to have important consequences not only in France, but also in Germany and Italy. Firstly, it opened up an alternative road for those who, while remaining devout Catholics, believed in the need for change; secondly, those who supported it fell back on the direct authority of the Pope and thus greatly strengthened the cause of Ultramontanism.

This was not all. As well as the writers, poets, and religious controversialists there was, mainly in Paris, a hard core of dedicated professional revolutionaries. Of these it is indeed strange that the man whose ideas were in the end to come closest to the European scene of the mid-twentieth century should have been a direct descendant of the memorialist of Louis XIV's Versailles. The central problem that puzzled the Count de Saint-Simon was how to find a new spiritual unity in an industrial age which he sensed was to transform the world. In his view these changed circumstances must mean a society organized 'in the manner most advantageous to the largest number'. This, however, did not imply egalitarianism; Saint-Simon, as an aristocrat, naturally thought in terms of a graded society, but for him the aristocracy of the future, based not on privilege but on ability, would consist of scientists, technicians, and bureaucrats, a class dedicated to improving the lot of the poor. It is this understanding of the extraordinary increase in *technical* means at the disposal of the State that gives Saint-Simon his astonishingly modern note. Others certainly reflected upon the possible consequences of the new power in the hands of a government; Herzen wrote gloomily of 'Genghiz Khan equipped with telegraphs, steamships and railways'; de Vigny in his *Servitude et grandeur militaire*, published in 1835, speculated on the dangers of 'quelques aventuriers parvenus à la Dictature' taking over the machinery of State at a stroke—a method later adopted by Louis Napoleon and Adolf Hitler. Yet it was the remarkable quality of Saint-Simon's thought that in acknowledging the fact he went on to conceive the totally different pattern of a technological society that must result.

Saint-Simonianism spread rapidly through France, Belgium, and Germany, but the movement was not greatly helped by the antics of his disciples after his death. Perhaps this was partly his own fault.

His last advice to them on his death-bed was: 'il faut être passionné', and they certainly took it to heart. There had been a strong religious element in Saint-Simon's writing which the new leaders Bazard and Prosper Enfantin now stressed. Before long, however, the leaders had fallen out, since Enfantin, seizing on Saint-Simon's belief in the equality of the sexes, decided that the movement could not be complete without a Woman Messiah, an idea which Bazard, a married man, found unacceptable. Styling himself as 'le Père', Enfantin established a community of about forty of the disciples, where amid hymn-singing and the tilling of the soil they were to await the arrival of 'la Mère'. 'La Mère' did not arrive and after a year's imprisonment for organizing an illegal society, the Saint-Simonians set out east to look for her, but the nearest that they ever came to their goal was a meeting with Lady Hester Stanhope at Beirut. Fortunately this phase of silliness did not last, for in Egypt their natural technical interests caused them to divert their energies to the possible construction of a Suez canal and of a Nile dam. Neither scheme came to anything for the moment, but on their return to France the Saint-Simonians reverted to a more normal social life and many of them were later to play a leading part in the development of French railways and banking.

Thus the Saint-Simonians, standing for a creed which was to prove a most acute prognostication of mid-twentieth century society, ended by coming to terms with the nineteenth. There remained, however, a strange variety of professional revolutionaries whose whole lives were dedicated to an attack on the existing system. Of these the most colourful was the Russian Michael Bakunin, a colossus of mob oratory, who castigated every form of injustice and indeed every form of restraint or government. 'This Columbus without America and without a ship' Herzen called him, an appropriate epithet, since Bakunin in his passion for destruction was less interested in any constructive alternative; for him all systems were equally oppressive.* Something rather more positive lay behind the aims of Auguste Blanqui who demanded the abolition of private property, but he, too, was essentially a man of the barricades. A *Carbonaro* in his youth, he gained a medal from the government of Louis Philippe for his part in the revolution of 1830, but from then on Blanqui was always on the losing side. With Barbès he organized the *Société des Saisons* in Paris which, in 1839, attempted an armed rising that was put down by the National Guard, and after this he was to spend a large part of his life in prison, only to emerge as the unrepentant apostle of revolution in 1848 and in the Paris Commune of 1871.

Others were more constructive in their views. The ideas of

* For the later development of Anarchism see pp. 244–6.

Charles Fourier were motivated by a revulsion against the competi-
tiveness of unrestricted capitalism, a state of economic war in which
the casualties were always suffered by the working class. Cooperation was the doctrine that he preached, but because he was deeply
suspicious of all central authority, he conceived a whole series of
small communities whose members would share the produce of their
work. Like Saint-Simon, he was obsessed with the possibilities of
the technological application of scientific knowledge, envisaging a
society that would offer both congenial work and a great deal of
leisure. Much of this thought was wrapped up in fantasy, and to the
world Fourier appeared as a strange old man wending his way each
morning to feed his cats in the garden of the Palais Royal, before
returning to his room at midday to await the arrival of the imaginary
millionaire who was to finance his schemes. Yet something of his
ideas found expression in the English Cooperative movement that
began with the small store opened at Rochdale in 1844; his writings
spread as far afield as Russia, and in America several experimental
Fourierist communities were established, just as Robert Owen had
attempted to create his own model society at New Harmony in
Indiana.

This need to strike out on virgin soil and to create a totally new
form of ideal community was a natural consequence of the more far-
fetched schemes of Utopian Socialism. Yet even those that were
rooted in the immediate surroundings of industrial Europe sometimes ended on a note of vague hopefulness. In 1839 Louis Blanc
published his *Organisation du travail*, a short book which grew steadily
longer as successive editions included the comments of his critics
and his answers to them. Blanc regarded the State as the 'supreme
regulator of production', responsible for organizing all branches of
industry in *ateliers sociaux*, in which workers, grouped by trades,
would govern themselves democratically and share their wages
according to an agreed proportion. There is, however, a touch of
Utopianism ever in Blanc, for he believed that capitalists too would
be prepared to join the *ateliers sociaux*, although he denied that he
was envisaging the State as the owner of all property and the
controller of all enterprise. In fact, Blanc never really thought
out the later stages of his scheme: 'la machine une fois montée, elle
marcherait d'elle-même.'

In contrast to all these, the revolutionary theory of Karl Marx
was striking in its completeness, springing from an analytical appreciation of the contemporary scene and based not on a new religion
of humanity, but on a philosophy of history in which romantic
aspiration was replaced by a cold sense of logical inevitability.
Marx, a German Jew, the son of a lawyer in Trier, had studied at
the Universities of Bonn and Berlin, where he had been profoundly
influenced by the teaching of Hegel. For a short while he was editor

of the *Rheinische Zeitung* in Cologne, in which he criticized the Prussian government and the German landowning class to such effect that the paper was suppressed in 1843, and after this he moved to Paris. Here he met and quarrelled with most of the leading Socialists. 'His voice was disagreeably harsh,' wrote an acquaintance at this time, 'and he spoke of men and things in the tone of one who would tolerate no contradiction and which seemed to express his own firm conviction in his mission to sway men's minds and dictate the laws of their being.'

There are innumerable echoes of his predecessors and contemporaries in Marx's writing. Trier had been a centre of Saint-Simonianism; his own father as well as his professors at Berlin had been influenced by it, and ideas of social regeneration, of association replacing antagonism, had all been common parlance long before Marx. Yet for Marx these similarities were superficial and irrelevant, since the whole basis of his thought was utterly different. To him it was a waste of time to draw up a blue-print for a perfect society or to argue that the present society was unjust or unpleasant. All that mattered was to discover the laws of historical change and then to direct a revolutionary movement so that it ran in accordance with those laws. Throughout the past the principal feature of society, as Marx saw it, had been the domination of one class over the rest through its control of the means of production, until the circumstances of that domination eventually produced an economic situation out of which a new class rose to replace the old. Thus the medieval aristocracy based on a system of feudal land tenure had been ousted by a commercial *bourgeoisie*. But the process did not end there, for the competition to produce had led to an industrial revolution bringing in its wake the growth of a vast factory-worker population. The continued competition of capitalism would cause the economy to oscillate between boom and slump, would bring war between nations in the search for markets and raw materials, and eventually create the circumstances in which the working class would rise against their masters and establish a new ruling class of the proletariat. Thus for Marx a capitalist society was not merely unpleasant. It was doomed. To compromise, to bring in humanitarian reforms, to incorporate the capitalist in a moderately Socialist state, all this was simply to attempt to prolong a moment in history that was already passing and for this reason he had nothing but furious contempt for most of his fellow revolutionaries.

Chapter 9

The Constitutional Monarchies 1830–48

1. France under Louis Philippe

The growing sense of dissatisfaction through Europe, aggravated by the inevitable tensions of a period of economic transition, was naturally reflected in the problems that confronted all governments in the years following the revolutions of 1830. In France it might well have seemed that no royal prince could have been more suitable for the role of constitutional sovereign than Louis Philippe at this particular moment in French history. The testimonial which Thiers and his companions had produced for their candidate in July 1830, and which was at least partly true, had already indicated this. A son of Philippe Égalité, he had fought for the Revolution at Jemappes in November 1792. After the Revolution he had shown little interest in the extravagance of the Ultras, preferring to devote his energy to regaining the Orleans estates until, by 1830, through tireless litigation and highly skilful investment, he had become one of the richest men in France. His orderly domestic life, his large family to which he was devoted, the umbrella which he carried under his arm, were all symbols of bourgeois virtue. Daumier in his cartoons might mock the fleshy pear-shaped face, but there was no escaping the fact that in many ways Louis Philippe was a monarch ideally of his time.

The leading political figures of his reign—bankers, journalists, and university teachers—were also symbolic of the victory of 1830. There were in the main two groups—a party of resistance which regarded the Revolution as no more than a change of king and, beyond that, wished for law and order within France and peace with the rest of Europe; and a party of movement which contemplated further social reforms and wished to give active assistance to the revolutionaries outside France's boundaries. Throughout most of his reign Louis Philippe was to rely on governments drawn from the party of resistance, few of which lasted long until his appointment of Guizot, a university professor, who after 1840 remained his principal counsellor. Only on three occasions did he entrust himself to more venturesome spirits and each time he secured their resignation within a few months, when a serious international crisis seemed to be developing—Laffitte in 1831 over the Belgian question, (see p. 73), Thiers in 1836 when he wished to intervene more forcefully in Spain, and again in 1840, when war over the Near East appeared imminent (see p. 82).

Caution and common sense were thus the hallmark of the reign of Louis Philippe, its principal monument in the Place de la Concorde an Egyptian obelisk of an epoch sufficiently remote to avoid controversy. The membership of the National Guard was restricted to the middle class, and the Chamber was one in which the business man could successfully resist Louis Philippe's schemes for the lowering of tariffs, or a Customs Union with Belgium. In education, at least, the government did make some headway, with Guizot's law of 1833 setting up primary schools in every commune of more than 6,000 inhabitants, as well as *écoles normales* for the training of teachers. Schooling was to be free, but not compulsory, and by 1847 the number of primary schools had increased from 33,000 to 43,000. Clergy were not prohibited from teaching in these schools and since no State monopoly was imposed, the Church enjoyed reasonable freedom of education at the primary level. The King was, however, disappointed in his hopes of being able to extend this freedom to secondary levels, which for the moment remained purely secular and strongly anti-clerical in outlook.

Only in one field did Louis Philippe make a bid for *la gloire*—the colonization of Algeria; thus Charles X's expedition against the Bey of Algiers was prolonged throughout the entire reign in a bitter campaign of conquest which constantly demanded more and more troops—64,000 by 1840, 101,000 by 1847. In 1841 27,000 French immigrants were settled there as a conscious means of consolidating France's hold and by 1845 their numbers had grown to 75,000. Yet the acquisition of Algeria failed to awaken any patriotic pride. Rather, the expense of the war, the viciousness of the fighting, and the appalling ravages of disease became objects of criticism, and the part played by five of Louis Philippe's sons in Algeria, instead of adding honour to the royal family, only associated them personally with an unpopular military adventure.

It was, however, within France that the principal discontents were to grow. At a parliamentary level an obvious grievance was the smallness of the electorate, for the paradox of the bourgeois monarchy of Louis Philippe was that its electoral regulations left so many of the bourgeois unrepresented. The pressure increased, but the government would not budge. 'I cannot find among us today,' said Guizot in 1842, 'in the actual state of society, any real and serious motive, any motive worthy of a free and sensible country, to justify the proposed electoral reform.' There was, too, among the deputies themselves, a dissatisfaction at the degree of control which Louis Philippe attempted to exercise over the Chamber; between

1830 and 1847 the number of officials who sat as deputies rose from 142 to 193 out of a total of 459 seats, and although this cultivation of a Court party had been a time-honoured practice during the development of constitutional monarchy in Great Britain, it hardly accorded with the axiom that Thiers had stated in 1830: 'le roi règne et ne gouverne pas.'

The King and his bourgeois allies might quarrel over powers of government; they remained united in the face of a restless working class. Two outbreaks in Lyons towards the beginning of the reign appeared to underline this second danger. In 1831 a period of unrest during the summer, due to a slump in the silk trade, led to a series of strikes and lock-outs in November, after the workers had attempted to establish a minimum wage scale, and in the subsequent fighting, during which some six hundred casualties were suffered, the city was for a short time in the hands of the workers. In April 1834 another slump, together with disputes over a new law restricting the right of association, caused a further outbreak of fighting in Lyons, and at the same time the *Société des Droits de l'Homme* attempted to stimulate a sympathetic rising in the east of Paris. This time the repression was sterner. At Lyons the rioting was crushed after three days of battle, and eighteen of the leaders were sentenced to transportation; in Paris the troops played havoc in the working-class districts with a ferocity which Daumier recorded in his gruesome lithograph of the massacre of the rue Transnonain.

In fact, despite all the moderation to which Louis Philippe aspired, there was an undercurrent of violence throughout his reign. No less than six attempts were made on his life—the most spectacular being in 1835, when an infernal machine killed forty-one people but only slightly wounded the King. The police had to watch constantly for conspiracy by republicans or by Bourbon legitimists, and in addition to all other revolutionary activity there always remained the shadow of Bonapartism.

It could be argued that Napoleon Bonaparte's most effective work was accomplished after his exile at St Helena. The Napoleonic legend, inspired by his memoirs and the record of his conversations on the island, wafted through the Continent during the following decades, creating an entirely imaginary picture of what might have been—a constitutional government for France, which would have given full rein to national aspirations in other parts of Europe. Napoleon himself died in 1821; there remained his son, the Duke de Reichstadt, a frail figure hemmed in by the aura of his father and the fearful suspicion of his father's enemies, who kept him in a form of decorous imprisonment in Vienna until his death in 1832. The Emperor's family, however, had been Italianate in its proportions and there was always to be a Bonaparte Pretender. Napoleon's brother, Louis, had married Hortense, Josephine's daughter by her first marriage, and of their two sons the elder had died during a *Carbonaro* escapade in the Italian revolt of 1831, leaving to his younger brother the somewhat insubstantial inheritance of the Bonaparte clan. An upbringing in exile, tinged with the excitement of romantic conspiracy, set its mark on the early activities of young Louis Napoleon. From Switzerland, where he served for a time as an artillery officer in Canton Berne, he embarked in 1836 on a forlorn attempt to rally revolutionary sympathies in Strasbourg. The *coup* failed, but the government of Louis Philippe thought it wiser not to give him the publicity of a public trial and dispatched him instead to the United States. In 1838 he settled in England and in the following year gave practical form to the legend in a little book, *Des idées napoléoniennes*, at the same time as Disraeli found him a useful model for one of the characters in his novel *Endymion*. In 1840 his next attempt at greatness, however, far outran the imagination of the novelist—a Channel crossing by paddle-boat with a few companions and an eagle in a cage, an unsuccessful effort to inflame the Boulogne garrison with the memory of his uncle's name, ending in a desperate swim from the shore and an ignominious arrest. This time the French government did risk putting him on trial and he was sentenced to perpetual imprisonment in the fortress of Ham in the north-east of France, where he busied himself with another book, *L'extinction du paupérisme*, before he finally made his escape to England in 1846.

On the whole, Louis Philippe had dealt lightly with Bonapartism; indeed, in terms of symbols he had been positively favourable. In 1833 Napoleon's statue had been placed once more at the top of its column in the Place Vendôme; in 1840 the French king had secured agreement with the British government whereby Napoleon's body might be brought back from St Helena to lie eventually in the church of the Invalides. Yet symbols were not enough 'If you reject peaceful reform, then you will have reform by violence,' Victor Hugo warned the King. A welter of newspapers preached the same message, appealing to different sections of the population; *Le National* had by now grown more moderate, advocating only a gradual extension of the franchise, but a more radical group under Ledru-Rollin founded *La Réforme* in 1843, while Louis Blanc's short-lived *Revue de progrès* and its successor the *Revue indépendante* under George Sand and Pierre Leroux helped to spread ideas of Socialism. 'In God's name,' cried de Tocqueville in a debate on electoral reform in January 1848, 'change the spirit of the government; for, I repeat, that spirit will lead you to the abyss.' But the Chamber, as blind as its King, rejected the proposals for an extension of the franchise by 228 votes to 189, and disaster now lay only a few weeks away.

2. The Low Countries

Meanwhile, Belgium had become the model liberal constitutional state of its time. King Leopold retained a personal control over foreign policy, carrying on a considerable correspondence with his niece Queen Victoria as well as with Metternich and the King of Prussia, and fostering the dynastic interests of the Saxe-Coburg family through the arrangement of marriages with the ruling houses of Great Britain, France, and Portugal. In home affairs, however, he kept meticulously to the ideal of constitutional monarchy. Unlike Louis Philippe, he made no attempt to engineer a submissive majority in the Chamber, worked mainly through coalition ministries and on one occasion horrified the autocratic Powers by accepting in the Belgian army a Polish general who had taken part in the Warsaw rising of 1830. His happy relations with his subjects were assisted by a thriving economy (see p. 86) and by the continuation of that compromise between the liberal and Catholic parties which had facilitated the movement for independence in the 1830 rising—a harmony that survived even the establishment of State schools and did not begin to break up until 1847.

In the Netherlands the constitution of 1814 (see p. 30) gave the Dutch considerably less share in the government of their country and King William showed little inclination for any change. The example of the Belgians, however, after gaining their independence, brought increasing pressure on the King and in 1840 he was forced to give way. In response to the demands of the second Chamber a limited form of ministerial responsibility was granted; in future each department was to submit its own financial requirements every two years and the legislature was to have the right to alter the franchise, although, in fact, no alteration was made. These changes were hardly revolutionary, but King William was too much of an autocrat to relish this new situation and since he had already shocked his subjects by his proposal to marry a Belgian Catholic, he decided to abdicate in favour of his son in 1841. William II was perfectly prepared to work with the revised constitution and a cautious liberalism began now to weaken the hold both of a rigid Calvinist orthodoxy and of the old conservative classes.

3. Scandinavia

The same tendencies were to be found in Scandinavia. In Sweden the representative assembly still met in the old form of the four Estates, but although the middle class pressed for the establishment of a unified Parliament, constitutional revision was successfully resisted by the clergy and the nobility. By 1840 however Bernadotte, reigning as Charles XIV, had been forced to pay some attention to the wishes of the *Riksdag* in selecting his ministers, and the general economic improvement of the country did much to mollify liberal ambitions. In 1834 the Göta Canal created a shorter link by water from the North Sea to the Baltic; centres of technical education were established, mining and forestry developed, and the agricultural yield of Sweden was so increased that despite a rising population no further importation of grain was necessary after 1850. In 1842 primary schools were established in every parish. On Bernadotte's death, in 1844, his son succeeded as Oscar I and the new king, Swedish-speaking unlike his Gascon father, was more popular with the Swedes and had stronger liberal instincts. In 1846 the trade guilds which had hampered the new business classes were abolished and in the following year the first Poor Law was established.

Sweden's recent acquisition of Norway (see p. 12) presented a slightly different problem. The Union of 1815 had come about with the consent of the Norwegian constitutional assembly, the *Storting*, established the year before, but its subsequent history was marred by recurring disagreements. The Swedes tended to regard Norway merely as a possession granted to them in compensation for the loss of Finland, a view which was not accepted by the Norwegians who insisted upon equality within the Union. There were, too, social differences, since the Swedish society was headed by an aristocracy, whereas in Norway a population of a million, mainly farmers and seafarers, was far more egalitarian and in 1821 the *Storting* formally abolished hereditary nobility. As elsewhere in Europe, the sense of a separate national identity found expression through language and in the early 1840s Jörgen Moe and Peter Asbjörnsen worked together to edit a series of Norwegian fairy tales and poems, while Ivar Aasen began collating and combining the local Norwegian dialects to produce a national language which might oust the predominantly Danish tongue spoken by the urban and bureaucratic classes. This growth of Norwegian national consciousness was naturally exacerbated by Bernadotte's eventual proposal that the royal veto on the *Storting* proceedings should become absolute rather than suspensive and in 1836 the relations between the two peoples had reached a point of crisis. In the last years of his reign, however, Bernadotte modified his attitude towards Norway; his son, Oscar I went still further with concessions over the coinage, flags to be flown at sea and the juxtaposition of Swedish and Norwegian on official Norwegian documents, and for the moment Norwegian nationalism continued to develop within the framework of the Union.

Chapter 10

Nationalism and the Autocracies
1830–48

For the constitutional monarchs there must have seemed an enviable simplicity about the autocratic rule which other sovereigns could exercise elsewhere. And yet that apparent simplicity was to some extent belied by the problems which many of these autocrats faced. In Germany and Italy the hopes of the new middle class for constitutional government and economic liberty fused with the longing for national unification; among the peoples of the Austrian Empire the aims were almost entirely national. Everywhere these aspirations were to become increasingly insistent against the changing economic background of Europe and were eventually to explode in the year of revolutions in 1848.

1. Conflicting aspects of national unification

a) The German states and Denmark
In Germany, where a working-class movement was only just beginning to develop, the atmosphere of growing discontent and agitation was centred mainly on questions of liberalism and nationalism. A numerous middle class, impatient of a system in which the landed class was still socially and politically predominant, continued to demand constitutional forms of government, but the regional and historical differences between the German states, made any united effort almost impossible. In 1837, for example, it was easy for the new King of Hanover, Ernest Augustus, Duke of Cumberland and uncle of Queen Victoria, to suppress the Hanoverian constitution, and when seven professors of the University of Göttingen, including the Grimm brothers and Dahlmann, published their protest and were dismissed, there was nothing that the liberals could do; the Federal Diet refused to intervene and the only consolation for the professors was the offer of chairs at other German Universities.

This powerlessness against a system which rested on Austrian control led to an overlapping of thought between German liberals and nationalists, since the successful experiment of the *Zollverein* naturally seemed to lend the force of practical argument to the emotions of nationalism; '... we have instead of one Germany thirty-eight German states, wrote the *Düsseldorfer Zeitung*, 'an equal number of governments, almost the same number of courts, as many representative bodies, thirty-eight distinct legal codes and administrations, embassies and consulates. What an enormous saving it would be, if all of that were taken care of by one central government.'

Yet within the span of these aspirations there remained many difficulties. The general mistrust of Prussia, and the sense of rivalry between the Lutheran states and the Catholic south and Rhineland were still strong. The precise definition of a unified Germany's frontiers was highly debatable (see p. 136). Many of the liberals, suspicious of the social implications of democratic republicanism, thought in terms simply of a stronger federal state (a *Bundesstaat* (see Glossary of Technical Terms, p. 497) rather than the *Staatenbund* of 1815), or if a unitary state were to be created, hoped for the retention of monarchy and looked with some misgiving at the more radical sentiments suggested in a verse of Ferdinand Freiligrath:

> Dass Deutschland frei und einig sei,
> Das ist auch unser Dürsten,
> Doch einig wird es, nur wenn frei,
> Und frei nur ohne Fürsten!*

These complications, however, did little to check the ardour of German nationalism which derived much of its emotional force from the manifold aspects of the Romantic movement, (see p. 46) considerably aided by the intellectual leadership of the Universities. A great flowering of poetry, philosophy, history, and philology combined to demonstrate the unique character of the German people and to create in the imagination a sense of spiritual unity, *der Volksgeist*. 'Venerable Barbarossa,' wrote Geibel in 1835, referring to the legend of the medieval Emperor Frederick I, 'when will the eagle disperse the ravens that hover round the summit of the Kyffhäuser and thus herald your return to earth?' The publications and lectures of the historians in particular helped to build up a highly coloured version of Germany's role in Europe. Her historic mission was to check the Slav onrush from the east and, by conquest, to civilize them; her undoing had been due to the machinations of the French who had undermined her unity in the Thirty Years' War, robbed her of Alsace under Louis XIV, and of still more under Napoleon. Thus, while Metternich's system was the immediate obstacle to unification, extreme German nationalism looked far beyond Austria for its ultimate fulfilment. Its greatest hatred was for France, 'the

---

* 'It is also our desire that Germany should be free and united; she can be united only when she is free, and only free when she is without princes.'

hereditary foe, the eternal, tireless, destructive enemy', as Stein wrote in 1815, and the flaming of German patriotism in the war of liberation in 1813 was to find continued expression in Fallersleben's *Deutschland über alles*, Becker's *Sie sollen ihn nicht haben, den freien deutschen Rhein*, and Schneckenburger's *Die Wacht am Rhein*. In the east it was a question not of frontiers, but of peoples, and here no river marked the goal of German nationalism—only a mystic sense of destiny, whereby the racial purity of the *Volk* might be preserved.

Naturally, it was difficult to translate these vague dreams into an immediate programme. For the moment liberals restricted themselves to the more mundane aim of parliamentary government and it was eventually in Prussia that there seemed to be some chance of success. Here the government had relied on an efficient bureaucracy and a good army, and Frederick William III had, on the whole, been prepared to follow Metternich's advice. In 1840, however, a new King ascended the throne. Like Tsar Alexander I and Charles Albert in Piedmont, Frederick William IV was one of those sovereigns of the first half of the nineteenth century who were torn between conservatism and a romantic desire to be accepted as a liberal monarch. On his accession he released many of the political prisoners of the previous reign, abolished the censorship and appointed to the Council of State Boyen, who was one of the leaders of the party for reform. Disliking the more modern type of constitutional Parliament, he granted greater power to the provincial Diets which met on the basis of Estates, allowing them the right to publish their debates. These concessions at once ended the period of relative quiet that Prussia had known since 1815. Middle-class liberals in the Rhineland, the most industrialized region of the Prussian dominions, began to agitate for a constitution of the Belgian type; in 1841, at Cologne, Karl Marx opened his attack on the existing governmental and social system in the *Rheinische Zeitung*; handcraftsmen seriously affected by the new industrialism, and peasantry often unable to keep up the payments on their commutation of feudal dues, became more openly restive. The conservative Junker class watched the activities of the King with growing doubt and at Berlin found spokesmen in a pietistic Court circle led by Leopold and Ludwig von Gerlach, who turned to the heir to the throne, the King's brother William. Frederick William IV wavered, and then swung towards the conservatives. The *Rheinische Zeitung* was suppressed in 1843. Freiligrath, to whom he had given a pension, was banished, and by 1845 he was requesting the French government to expel German writers from France. His vacillation was finally exemplified by the summoning of the United Diet at Berlin in 1847. Liberal hopes were raised since the declared purpose of the Diet was to vote a loan for the building of a railway to link East Prussia with Berlin. Yet they were simultaneously dashed by the realization that the United Diet was to be no more than a combination of all the provincial Diets of Prussia, based on the division into social Orders, and in his opening speech Frederick William made it clear that he would go no further in the direction of constitutional government. 'Never will I permit a written sheet of paper to come between our God in Heaven and this land, as if it were a second Providence, to rule us with its paragraphs and supplant the old sacred loyalty.' As a result the United Diet came to nothing. The liberals demanded a national legislative assembly, as had been promised after the Napoleonic war, and when this was refused, rejected the loan. The Diet dispersed in June 1847 and within a few months Frederick William was to find himself confronted with a far more dangerous situation.

In Denmark the liberal movement had gained no more than the establishment of consultative provincial Estates in 1831— on the Prussian model of 1823 (see p. 27)—but social and political antagonism here was less bitter owing to the enlightened despotism of the Danish kings. Liberal feelings were concentrated far more on the question of Slesvig. Since the Middle Ages the King of Denmark had ruled over the duchies of Slesvig and Holstein as their Duke. The Union was a purely personal one and its significance in the nineteenth century rested on the fact that while the population of Slesvig was partly Danish- and partly German-speaking, the Holsteiners were almost entirely German. By now German nationalism in Holstein was becoming outspoken, supported by the local nobility who resented the absolutism of the Danish kings, and by the students of the University of Kiel where Dahlmann was teaching after his expulsion from Göttingen in Hanover. The immediate complication was that the Salic law, excluding succession through a female line, applied in the duchies, but not in Denmark; thus if a Danish king was actually to succeed through a female line, the way would be open for German interests to establish a duke of their own in the duchies. Such a possibility was now not far distant, since Christian VIII, who ascended the Danish throne in 1839, had only one son Frederick, who was childless, and beyond him the Danish succession would have to pass through a female line (see genealogical table p. 486). Foreseeing this eventuality, German nationalists insisted on the indivisibility of the two duchies and began to look to the Duke of Augustenburg as their future candidate. The Danes, determined that they should at least not lose both duchies, began to emphasize the distinctness of Slesvig from Holstein. This policy was finally stated in 1846, when Christian VIII published an open letter in which he declared that Slesvig was governed by the same laws of succession as in Denmark. This clearly suggested an intention ultimately to absorb Slesvig within the kingdom and awoke a storm of indignation among the Germans in the duchies and throughout most of Germany. The full significance of the dispute is that it illustrates the fatal confusion of liberal and nationalist ideals that was to bedevil the revolutionary movements of central Europe. For it was the German liberals who maintained most fervently the indivisibility of the duchies which might one day be under a German prince, while the liberals at Copenhagen, who hoped to extract a constitution from their king, fell in whole-heartedly behind Christian VIII with their demand for Denmark up to the Eider, the southern boundary of Slesvig.

This excitement over the future of the duchies was indicative of the heightened emotions everywhere in Germany. Working-class unrest in the new industries of Saxony, a mounting antagonism between Protestant and Catholic in the Rhineland, a new wave of anti-Semitism among the radicals of the southern states, all formed a background of latent violence to such political developments as the forcing of a liberal ministry on Grand Duke Leopold of Baden at the end of 1846 or the unsuccessful attempt on the part of the Elector of Hesse-Cassel to restrict the local constitution in 1847. At the same time, in Bavaria, old King Ludwig had become completely captivated by the charms of a dancer of partly British extraction, who, after assuming the name of Lola Montez, had already enjoyed an exotic career throughout most of the Continent, and her inter-ference in the work of government led to an outcry that was later to lose Ludwig his throne.

b) Italy

There are several striking parallels between German and Italian nationalism at this time. In Italy Napoleonic rule had carried through a highly beneficial rationalizing of the old system, at the same time awakening a strong sense of Italian national feeling in opposition to foreign interference; and resentment at the reimpo-sition of Austrian influence throughout the peninsula after 1815 had found thinly veiled expression in the historical novels of Manzoni and the early operas of Verdi. As in Germany, resistance to the Vienna settlement had been hamstrung by the particularism of the Italian states, jealous of each other and especially nervous of the ambitions of Piedmont. There was one further problem that was peculiar to Italy in that the existence of the Papal States remained the supreme obstacle to unification that Machiavelli had deplored centuries before. For the Italian nationalist Rome was the only poss-ible capital of Italy; for the Popes the Temporal Power was inviol-able and any interference with it was certain to incur the wrath of Catholic opinion throughout Europe. On the other hand, geography which provided the nationalists with one of their principal argu-ments left little doubt where the general line of an Italian frontier would lie, and in the Italian *risorgimento* there was much less of the mystique of the *Volk* with which the Germans challenged the various forms of Slav nationalism.

Amid the constant discussion and literary activity in Italy during these years three main streams of thought may be discerned, two of them moderate and liberal in their social programme, the third radical and democratic. The first was embodied in *Il Primato*, the work of the Abbé Gioberti, a Piedmontese priest, who had been banished in 1833 and who published his great scheme ten years later from Brussels. The essence of Gioberti's plan was that the predominance of Piedmont and the antagonizing of Catholic opinion might both be avoided by the creation of an Italian federation out of the existing states under the presidency of the Pope. The second group, in which Massimo D'Azeglio and Cesare Balbo were significant personalities, turned instead to the leadership of Piedmont, reckoning to establish a North Italian Kingdom as a beginning. Both movements hoped for the usual liberal reforms of constitutional government and freedom of the press; neither of them had very much idea of how the blow was to be struck.

In contrast to these sane, cautious schemes, 'Young Italy', the movement of Giuseppe Mazzini, the son of a university professor at Genoa, had all the fire of a crusade. For Mazzini there could be no compromise with Rome or Piedmont; the only solution for Italy lay in a unitary republic. An early flirtation with the *Carbonari* had led to his exile from Piedmont in 1831, and after two unsuccessful attempts to stir up revolt in Piedmont from France and Switzerland he eventually came to England in 1837 to work ceaselessly for the great day. 'Religion and politics are inseparable,' he wrote, and Mazzini, solemn-eyed, clothed always in black and consumed with a sense of personal dedication, was indeed like some high priest of a new religion of humanity in which all national sentiment must find expression and in which all social ills would be solved by the brotherhood of man.

It was hardly likely that Mazzini would be seen as anything other than a dangerous revolutionary by the established classes. For the moderate liberals there seemed to be a more promising outlook when Charles Albert ascended the throne in Piedmont in 1831. The new king could not respond to them at once. After his experiences in 1821 (see p. 59) he knew that he must disarm the suspicions of Metternich and this he attempted, first by a military alliance with Austria, and then by the ostentatious severity with which he crushed Mazzini's conspiracies to raise a mutiny in the Piedmontese army in 1833 and to invade Savoy in 1834. In the second part of his reign, however, Charles Albert began to win back a little of the sympathy of the liberals, who by now had come to regard him as a creature of Metternich's. A noble of liberal tendencies, Count Pes di Villamarina, was appointed Minister of War in 1835 and in the ten years following 1837 a series of codes of a Napoleonic type, abolishing feudal practices in Sardinia and encouraging commerce, were introduced. Tariffs were considerably reduced, guilds abolished, and the University of Turin expanded. A new short-service system for the army enabled Piedmont to put 70,000 troops in the field in 1848 and plans went ahead for the development of railways. This modernizing of the kingdom was naturally in tune with liberal aspirations and at the same time it was noticeable that good relations with Austria were deteriorating in the 1840s through a number of disputes over the sale of salt to Canton Ticino and the plan for a railway line which would link Genoa with Lake Maggiore—in conflict with the Austrian scheme for a line bypassing Piedmont from Leghorn to the Brenner pass via Florence and Trieste. Yet to the end Charles Albert remained an enigmatic figure—the Hamlet of Savoy, as Mazzini called him; the weakness of Piedmont against Austria forced him to dissemble and, in any case, he never entirely knew his own mind.

2. Tension within the Austrian Empire

In eastern Europe the principal motive force was literary. The Romantic enthusiasm for salvaging local *patois* and bringing to light remote heroic epochs gave rise to the publication of a host of grammars, dictionaries, and histories of literature, striving to create formed languages out of what for centuries had been no more than peasant dialects. In this medley of submerged peoples language was the only means of individual identification and swiftly became a political symbol, since the conscious cultivation of a national tongue was an essential step in establishing the unity of a national group. The effect of this linguistic movement was mostly confined to the towns, where it was to prove a powerful instrument of national pride, raising questions of the language to be used in the law courts and taught in the schools, and exacerbating local antagonisms where difference of class coincided with difference of racial origin (see p. 24).

This growing sense of national identity was bound to pose special problems within the Austrian Empire, yet at Vienna there was little indication of any attempt to come to terms with them. The succession of the Emperor Ferdinand on his father's death in 1835 brought no change in the stagnant atmosphere of repression. The new Emperor was so utterly incapable of rising to his responsibilities that the work of government was managed by a State council over which Ferdinand's uncle Archduke Ludwig presided; here Metternich had to contend with his rival Kollowrat, a Bohemian nobleman whose skill in financial matters had added enormously to his influence since his entry into the administration in 1826. Such a group was hardly likely to hammer out a positive solution to the problems of serfdom and tariff reform which were becoming insistent, and proposals for reform from any other source were made unlikely by a vigilant police supervision.

In the 1840s, however, the provincial Diets did begin to give some expression to discontent. The Bohemian Diet raised a demand for the right to vote taxes; the Estates of Lower Austria agitated for agrarian reform, and since they met in Vienna, began to find support in the *salons* of the capital. In Hungary two movements were at work. One group under Count Szechenyi, an extremely wealthy member of the Magyar aristocracy, recommended the end of immunity from taxation which the nobility enjoyed, together with an improvement in the position of the peasantry and agricultural reforms which might increase the economic output of the country. The second group, led by Louis Kossuth, one of the lesser nobility, embraced most of these suggestions, but went further in demanding a greater economic independence for Hungary. Before long, social jealousies had created a considerable cleavage between the two, and at the same time both were regarded with profound mistrust by the non-Magyar people within Hungary, as, for example, when the Croat deputies refused to accept the innovation of Magyar as the official language of the Hungarian Diet of 1844. It was a situation symbolic of the incompatibility of all the great aims quickening into life in central and eastern Europe, a mutual intolerance that was eventually to undermine the hopes of the revolutionaries in 1848.

3. Russia under Nicholas I

In Russia there were very broadly two groups of thinkers and writers which were beginning to emerge in the 1830s, each drawing a different conclusion from their common realization of the peculiar nature of Russian history. To the westernizers it seemed that Russia had been too long cut off from the rest of Europe. 'Isolated from the European family, we sought our moral code in miserable Byzantium,' wrote Peter Chaadayev in a letter first published in 1836, 'and while the world was being built anew, we remained as before cowering in our hovels of mud and straw, cut off from the universal movement in which the social idea of Christianity was formed and developed.' Thus the westernizers drew their inspiration from European sources, particularly from German philosophy, and it was not surprising that several of their leaders such as V. S. Pecherin, Nicholas Ogarev, and Alexander Herzen should eventually leave Russia to spend their lives in the west.

In contrast to them the Slavophils saw the future in terms of the individual character of Russian society. They did not hate the west; they were conscious that much was wrong in Russia, but they believed that the solutions must be worked out in accordance with her own particular destiny. 'These native foundations which we previously ignored on account of our blind partiality for western civilization, our reckless neglect of our own past history (regarding it as barbarous),' wrote Kireyevsky, 'are quite distinct from those elements which compose the civilization of western European peoples.' The Slavophils based their faith on the Orthodox Church and the small decentralized social unit of the *mir*, the village commune; it was out of these, they argued, that a new Russian society must be shaped. This sense of isolation from the rest of Europe did not in itself create an organized movement, but as a general attitude it was to lend added impetus to the ideas of the Populists (see p. 245) in the 1870s, and in the twentieth century a strong Slavophil thread was to run through the development of Russian Communism.

At the time the atmosphere of political repression tended to make movements of reform a matter of purely intellectual discussion. Certainly under the rule of Nicholas I, there could be no question of constitutional development. The new Tsar, who liked to refer to his empire as his 'command', had soon subordinated the existing central organs of government to a system of secret committees and police agents, but despite his militarist approach, Nicholas was not averse to reform, provided that it was imposed from above. Speransky carried out a great codification of existing laws and a new department was established under Kisilev through whom the position of the Crown peasants was considerably improved. Nicholas himself was particularly concerned with exerting a greater control over the nobility and gentry and did make some progress in regulating their relations with their serfs. He restricted the punishments that they could inflict, introduced measures whereby it would be possible for serfs to acquire property, and, in 1845, prohibited night work for children under twelve years of age in the factories which some landowners had set up on their estates; but the full effects of all these decrees were largely nullified by the passive resistance of the proprietors.

For Nicholas, however, a·benevolent interest in the serfs was not to be confused with any sympathy with the wider movements in favour of pan-Slavism or constitutional reform, and the Tsar who could not even accept the idea of Louis Philippe as King of the French, naturally imposed the sternest censorship on all forms of liberal writing. Gogol did manage to gain permission to perform his play *The Inspector General*, which mocked Russian officialdom, but a little later he felt so stifled by the atmosphere of repression that he emigrated to Rome, and in 1852 Turgenev was arrested and confined to his country residence simply for calling Gogol 'great' in an article on his death.

If this was Nicholas' attitude towards his Russian subjects, it was hardly likely to be more liberal towards any national aspirations in

Poland and Finland within the western borders of his empire. In Poland the rising of 1830 had confirmed all Nicholas' worst suspicions of Alexander's experiment in liberalism and in 1832 an Organic Statute abolished the Diet and the constitutional liberties that had been granted to the kingdom. Technically Poland retained governmental autonomy, but the period of repression that followed involved an intensive process of russification. Tribunals confiscated about one-tenth of Polish property and distributed it to Russians. The sons of the rebels were sent to Russian military schools; the Russian language was established in all institutions of primary and secondary education, the Universities of Warsaw and Vilna were closed and in the Russo-Polish border districts the new policy included the transportation of thousands of suspects to the east and a fierce persecution of Jews and Uniates (see p. 37).

In Finland all had remained quiet since Russia had taken possession in 1808 and a considerable programme of building had been carried out in Helsinki which was now the administrative capital of the Grand Duchy. As elsewhere in central Europe, however, a growing sense of national identity among the Finns was expressed through the literary development of their language. Elias Lönnrot, a Karelian doctor, had compiled a written version of the Finnish saga *Kalevala* and Johann Snellman was voicing the demand for the use of Finnish in educational institutions. 'The bulk of the nation', he said in 1840, 'can never be raised so long as Swedish remains the language of administration.' This last illustrates the greater complexity of the situation in Finland, for whereas Polish patriotism was predominant among the landed classes, mindful of an independence that had only recently been lost, the resentment of the Finns towards the local Swedish-speaking upper class only confused the issue of independence from Russia, and Tsar Alexander II was later able to make use of this in attempting to reconcile the Finns to Russian rule (see p. 206).

4. The eve of 1848

Thus, both under the constitutional monarchies and the autocracies there had been a steady growth of the factors which had already momentarily threatened the Vienna settlement in 1820 and 1830, and before long a series of events suggested that Metternich's defence of the establishment was about to face its most serious challenge.

In June 1846 Pope Gregory XVI died and a wave of excitement swept through the liberals at the election of Cardinal Giovanni Mastai-Ferretti, who assumed the title of Pius IX. For it was known that the new Pope, a man of great personal charm, was favourably disposed towards liberal ideas and was familiar with the writings of Count Balbo and particularly Gioberti's *Primato*. They were not disappointed. Pius at once embarked on a much needed plan of reform in the Papal States; an amnesty for political prisoners was declared, the press was to enjoy a greater freedom, and a Civic Guard and an advisory body, the *Consulta*, each consisting of laymen, were established. A liberal Pope was the one thing that Metternich had never anticipated, and his fears of the possible consequences soon appeared to be not entirely unfounded. Pius IX's liberalism was essentially cautious, but in the secret societies the republicans saw their chance to foment public excitement and the agitation for reform began to spread. In 1847, in Tuscany, Grand Duke Leopold II was impelled to abolish the secret police, and in Lucca a Civic Guard was formed. Hastily Metternich ordered the reinforcing of the garrison at Ferrara. On this Pius appealed to the Powers of Europe, and when Charles Albert placed the Piedmontese army at the Pope's disposal and began to speak in terms of a war for the independence of Italy, this dangerous situation, coupled with the persuasion of Lord Palmerston, the British Foreign Secretary, caused Metternich to withdraw his troops from Ferrara.

Meanwhile, in 1846, there had been an outbreak of Polish national-ism within Prussia. The milder rule of Frederick William IV at the beginning of his reign had encouraged Polish patriots in the province of Posen, to the south of West Prussia, to prepare an insur-rection under the leadership of Mieroslavski, but in February 1846 the Prussian police got wind of the scheme and imprisoned the lead-ers, so that the insurrection never came to anything more than an unsuccessful attack within the city of Posen itself. The movement, however, did spark off a republican rising in the Free City of Cra-cow, and it appeared to the Habsburg government that the unrest was about to spread to their own Polish province of Galicia. Polish nationalism in these regions, however, was a sentiment largely con-fined to the landowning class. To deal with this threat, therefore, the Habsburg authorities decided to exploit the hatred that the local Ruthenian peasantry felt for their Polish landlords and actually urged them on to a great mass rising in which the gentry were mas-sacred and their mansions destroyed. In Western Galicia alone it was reckoned that about two thousand were killed. At the same time the rising in Cracow had been suppressed within ten days by Rus-sian and Austrian troops, and in the following year the city was annexed by Austria. The entire episode had been hopeless for the Poles from the start, but these events do have a bearing on the rev-olutions that followed in 1848. The Polish nationalists were to enjoy a short-lived alliance with the Prussian liberals, who saw them as a possible ally against the conservatism of Russia, and when revol-ution finally broke out in Berlin in March 1848 (see p. 127), one of the first acts of the crowd was to release Mieroslavski and the other Polish leaders from the Moabit prison. Another aspect, more sinister for the liberals, was the skill with which the Habsburgs had been able to make use of the antagonism which existed between the subject peoples and their immediate overlords.

There was to be further disorder within Metternich's sphere of interest before the end of 1847—the outbreak of civil war in Switzerland. Political dispute here had recently centred itself not merely on the cleavage between liberals desirous of a stronger federal authority and conservatives who took their stand by the independence of the cantons, but also on a more bitter struggle between a Catholic Ultramontane party and a group of free-thinking radicals. The decision in Argau to dissolve the monasteries, two unsuccessful attempts by radical forces in 1844 and 1845 to march on Catholic Lucerne, and the installation of the Jesuits at Lucerne on November 1845, were all stages in a civic strife that culminated in the formation of the *Sonderbund*, a league of seven Catholic cantons—Lucerne, Schwyz, Uri, Unterwalden, Zug, Fribourg, and Valais. The Protestant liberals held ten cantons, and the gaining of Geneva and St Gallen by May 1847 gave them the majority that they needed in the Diet. Berne had already appointed as President of the Confederation Ulrich Ochsenbein, who had led the 1845 expedition against Lucerne, and in July the radicals used their majority in the Diet to set up a committee for a revision of the federal pact and to demand the expulsion of the Jesuits from all cantons as well as the dissolution of the *Sonderbund*. On the refusal of the Catholic cantons the Diet declared war on them in the name of the Confederation. The war lasted twenty-five days, at the end of which the *Sonderbund* forces surrendered, completely out-manoevured by General Dufour who commanded the troops of the Diet.

Metternich had fully understood that defeat for the *Sonderbund* would mean an open challenge to the conservative principle in Europe, but the swiftness of the liberal victory, together with Palmerston's refusal to countenance intervention, stopped him from taking effective action. 'Today,' said Metternich in December, 'the Powers are faced with radicalism in control.' He was not alone in realizing the significance of the Swiss Diet's victory. The news was greeted with wild enthusiasm in Rome, Florence, and Prague. 'May Europe be inspired by your great example', wrote Michelet and Quinet from France to the Swiss Diet, and they had not long to wait. Within a couple of months Switzerland was to be saved from any further threat of foreign intervention by a series of revolutions throughout the whole of Europe, in which the Swiss have always considered that they led the way.

Part 3

The Failure of Liberal Revolution 1848–51

Chapter 11

The Outbreak of Revolution in 1848

1. The immediate causes

In 1848 all the smouldering grievances of the Continent suddenly flamed up in the greatest conflagration of revolt that Europe has ever known. The 'year of revolutions', more violent and widespread in its effect than those earlier outbreaks of 1820–1 and 1830, marks the climax of that period of constant unrest which characterized Metternich's Europe. Nearly all the risings failed. The governmental pattern of Europe, which in the spring of 1848 seemed everywhere in dissolution, had within eighteen months been almost completely restored. Yet all was not entirely fruitless. The movements of 1848, unsuccessful as they were, provided lessons both for the governments and for their opponents, and through that new experience a period of change was to ensue in the middle decades of the nineteenth century as revolutionary as the events of 1848, although utterly different to what the revolutionaries themselves had anticipated.

The complicated history of the years since 1815 might well suggest the possibility of a revolutionary outbreak almost anywhere in Europe, but the mere existence of general unrest does not explain why the 'year of revolutions' should happen as and when it did. The ruling classes were convinced at first that they were faced with a European-wide conspiracy and this fear lies behind much of the initial success of the risings. 'Je ne puis pas monter à cheval contre les idées', said William of Württemberg to Prince Gortchakov, the Russian minister at Stuttgart. In fact, there was no general conspiracy at all. 'Le 24 février', said Proudhon speaking of the revolution in Paris, 'a été fait sans idée', and his remark could be applied to the whole of the European scene, for the revolutions of 1848 were utterly confused and lacking in any preconceived plan, a series of spontaneous explosions which often took the leaders of revolutionary thought completely by surprise. Karl Marx and Bakunin were both in Brussels when the Paris revolution broke out; Mazzini was in London; and even after they had hurried to the centres of action, they had little success in gaining control. In June

Bakunin in Prague only heard by chance that a new insurrection was just about to break out in the city, and in May 1849 he was on the point of leaving Dresden when he found the barricades up in the streets. This helplessness of the so-called leaders was best summed up by Ledru-Rollin during a fruitless rising in Paris in May 1849: 'Je suis leur chef, il faut que je les suive.'

Most striking of all is the lack of any organized Socialist movement at this time. The masses in the towns manned the barricades, but most of their leaders are unknown and in some cases were non-existent. By chance the *Manifesto of the Communist Party*, drawn up at the request of the London centre of the Communist League, had been published in January 1848. This remarkable document, based on Marx's theory of history and couched in language that makes it one of the world's greatest masterpieces of propaganda, closed with its ringing challenge: 'The workers have nothing to lose but their chains. They have a world to win. Workers of all lands, unite!' Yet the only immediate effect of its publication was the expulsion of Marx from Belgium. It is true that in Paris and, later, in Frankfurt he hoped that a momentary alliance between bourgeois and workers would enable the workers ultimately to gain the upper hand, but everywhere in Europe the fear of Socialism was to drive the bourgeois back into the arms of their rulers. Marx denounced them furiously in his newspaper, the *Neue Rheinische Zeitung*; this led to his being charged with incitement to treason, and although his impassioned speech before a Cologne jury secured his acquittal, he found, by August 1849, that England was one of the very few countries that was still open to him.

Thus, personal leadership does little to explain the revolutions of 1848. The most important cause lies in an agricultural and economic crisis that affected every region of Europe. Poor corn harvests in the years 1845 and 1846 coinciding with a blight that ruined the potato crop from Silesia to Ireland sent the price of food soaring, and soon hunger had led to violence in France, Belgium, the Rhineland, Württemberg, and northern Italy. Then typhus broke out—to be followed, in 1848, by the second terrible visitation of cholera. All this misery was soon to be increased by mass unemployment, when shortage of capital brought a sharp curtailing of credit that turned the boom of the mid-1840s into a slump (see p. 90). In France and Belgium, on the railways alone, 750,000 men found themselves without work; in many of the larger towns of southern Germany almost one-third of the inhabitants became dependent upon charity, and the general despair in central Europe was reflected in the figures for emigration which leaped up from 34,000 in 1840 to 93,000 in 1846 and 100,000 in 1847 (see Appendix 9, p. 494). This dislocation of everyday life was felt most keenly in the cities—a significant factor, since the revolutions of 1848 were essentially urban movements—

and although the worst aspects of the crisis were passing by 1848, the hunger, the hopelessness of the unemployed who turned to machine-breaking, and the innumerable bankruptcies of the smaller business concerns, all formed a more compelling motive for rebellion than the watchword of any revolutionary theorist.

2. The succession of outbreaks

The basis of any study of the year 1848 must be the chronological sequence of events. In many ways it might seem simpler to consider each country or region in turn. This method, however, would obscure the most significant element in the whole imbroglio. The revolutions did not happen in the neat isolation of local history. They happened within days of each other and the news of revolt in one city after another was the greatest general motive force in the story of this tumultuous year. Another important factor is the order in which the risings occurred. The chances of successful revolution in small states depended ultimately upon the attitude of the governments of France and Austria; thus, the abdication of Louis Philippe on 24 February and the dismissal of Metternich on 13 March are crucial dates in the early months, since they were at once followed by fresh outbreaks, or by more drastic action in states where revolt had already taken place.

The sequence begins in the first days of January 1848, when the citizens of Milan suddenly gave up smoking. This was not simply a New Year's resolution. It was a concerted attempt to be a nuisance to the Austrian authorities in Lombardy who enjoyed a monopoly of tobacco, and the situation quickly became explosive. On the one side were Radetzky's troops, who had been taunted mercilessly since clashes in the previous autumn, on the other the Milanese pining for a smoke, and a series of incidents in the city, the 'tobacco riots', culminated a cavalry charge in which several people lost their lives.

Then, on 12 January, in Sicily, an attack by the crowd on the garrison of Palermo ultimately forced King Ferdinand II to offer the islanders an independent administration, but when the Sicilians would only accept a fully constitutional government the fighting continued until, by the end of January, the Neapolitan army had been driven out of most of the island and the rebels had re-established the constitution of 1812, declaring Sicily's independence. Within a few days Ferdinand, unsure of his position on the mainland, hastily proclaimed a constitution for the whole of his kingdom, including an Assembly with two Chambers, one of which was to be elective. These events in Naples naturally gave rise to fresh demands on the rulers farther north. On 8 February Charles Albert appointed a commission to draw up a constitution, while three days later the

Grand Duke of Tuscany yielded to revolutionary pressure centred on Leghorn and agreed to allow representative government.

Few of these changes in Italy could have survived long if the major capitals of Europe had remained untouched by the movement towards revolution. Within a couple of weeks, however, the whole outlook was changed by a sudden rising in Paris. The fall of the July monarchy in February 1848 was as much a surprise to the opponents of the King as it was to Louis Philippe himself. A growing opposition in the Chamber, reinforced by attacks in the press, had been demanding a slight extension of the franchise, but the middle-class liberals were not seriously thinking of ending the monarchy. Left-wing propagandists had been active advocating social changes in the interest of the working class, and the mass unemployment had lent strength to the cry 'le droit au travail'; yet even here there is little evidence of any concerted plan of attack at this moment. 'On ne renversait pas le gouvernement,' wrote Alexis de Tocqueville two years later, 'on le laissait tomber.'

A reform banquet had been prohibited by the government; a protest march through Paris on 22 February and the appearance of a few barricades on the next morning persuaded Louis Philippe that the time had come to dismiss Guizot. Count Molé took his place, but that evening another procession had an encounter with royal troops cordoning off the Foreign Office, which resulted in the death of sixteen of the crowd, and by the morning of 24 February Paris was once again in the throes of revolution. Molé, unable to form a ministry, resigned. Louis Philippe turned to Thiers and at the same time gave Marshal Bugeaud the task of subduing the city by military force. The troops might have succeeded, but Thiers, not wishing to involve his new administration in further bloodshed, ordered a ceasefire; the barricades remained untaken and many of the soldiers, sensing the weakness of higher authority, began to go over to the rebels. Thiers' own scheme was for the King to leave Paris without further resistance and to wait at St Cloud until the middle-class opposition fell out with the working-class element. His instinct was sound, but Louis Philippe rejected the advice. He preferred to rely upon the National Guard, but when later it seemed that the Tuileries were about to be attacked, their cries of 'à bas le système' revealed a wavering loyalty that robbed him of any further intention to resist. He seemed unmindful of the army of 80,000 regular troops at his disposal. For Louis Philippe the National Guard was a symbol of the bourgeois on whose support his monarchy had rested; with that support apparently lost, he yielded to the persuasion of the Duke de Montpensier to abdicate in favour of his grandson, and a little later the monarch who had entered his capital on foot on a July night in 1830 took his leave of it in a brougham—ahead of him the road to exile in England, behind him the Tuileries abandoned to a fury of looting and destruction by the mob, which Flaubert was to describe in his *l'Éducation sentimentale.*

The fall of Louis Philippe was in many ways similar to that of Charles X. 'Comme un autre en trois jours,' wrote de Vigny, 'il tombait en trois heures.' Both had lost the support of a significant element of the middle class. Both had been caught off guard by the strength of the outburst of opposition, although Charles X had less excuse since he, at least, had attempted a *coup d'état*, whereas Guizot had only forbidden a banquet. Both had sought escape in abdication in favour of a grandchild, neither of whom was destined to rule. Two points of difference, however, were to give the events of 1848 a more radical twist. First, the working class of Paris were more powerful and articulate than they had been in 1830; second, there were no further branches of the royal family to whom the bourgeois could turn in order to avoid the extremes of republicanism. These two factors explain the far greater caution exercised by the bourgeois in the weeks immediately following Louis Philippe's abdication and their apparent readiness to work in some sort of accord with the extreme left-wing leaders.

The Chamber would probably have been prepared to accept the accession of the Count de Paris with his mother as Regent, but a mob broke in on them and insisted on the proclamation of a republic, thus extinguishing the last flicker of hope for the survival of kingship in France. Armand Marrast, the editor of *Le National*, who had hurried to the Chamber as soon as he had heard the news of the abdication, persuaded Lamartine to announce the establishment of a republic. There and then, before the mob had dispersed, seven republican deputies were nominated to form a provisional government—Lamartine, Marrast, Ledru-Rollin, Arago, Crémieux, Marie, and Garnier-Pagès. These seven were at once swept off to the Hôtel de Ville in accordance with revolutionary tradition, but here they were met by a crowd from *La Réforme* who were only prepared to accept them if three others were added—Louis Blanc, Flocon, the editor of *La Réforme*, and Martin, a mechanic, better known as Albert, all of them spokesmen of the left-wing movement.

Thus from the beginning the provisional government consisted of an indigestible amalgam of two utterly different political groups. For a short time this ill-assorted team jogged along together, each group too unsure of the strength of its own position in the turbulent capital to risk attempting to dispense with the other. It was part of the irony of the situation that Bakunin, who had rushed to Paris on hearing the news, soon appeared almost embarrassingly revolutionary even for the extremist section. 'On the first day of a revolution,' remarked Caussidière, the new left-wing Prefect of Police, 'he is a perfect treasure; on the second he ought to be shot.' Before long, however, Bakunin had scented greater excitement farther east and Flocon was only too happy to grant him a loan for a journey to Posen. Meanwhile, on 26 February, Lamartine, in an impassioned speech in favour of the tricolour had managed to avoid the adoption of the red flag—to Blanqui's disgust. At the beginning of March, the various political and financial restrictions on the press were removed, and between March and June well over two hundred journals entered upon a brief and uncertain life; on 5 March the government announced that elections to a Constituent Assembly would take place on 9 April, in which every adult Frenchman should have the right to vote—a gigantic leap in the size of the electorate from 241,000 to about 8,000,000 (see Appendix 4, p. 490).

The left-wing members of the government were naturally not slow in pressing on with their own programme of social reform, and as early as 28 February the government almost fell apart over the question of reducing the length of the working day. A compromise was eventually arranged whereby a *Commission du gouvernement pour les travailleurs* consisting of 242 workers and 231 employers under the presidency of Louis Blanc was to meet in the Luxembourg Palace. Through the efforts of the *Commission* hours of work were reduced to ten hours in Paris and eleven in the provinces. A more significant achievement was the establishment of the *ateliers nationaux* whereby the unemployed were organized in a whole hierarchy of military-sounding formations under Émile Thomas, a young engineer, to be given work at 2 francs a day or to be paid a dole of $1\frac{1}{2}$ francs. The general dislocation of economic life consequent on the recent revolution had added enormously to the number of unemployed in Paris, and by April 70,000 had enrolled in the *ateliers nationaux*. They were not entirely ineffectual; they did produce some constructive work—including the preparation of the hall in which the Constituent Assembly was to sit—but the main object of Marie, the right-wing Minister of Public Works, was simply to keep this large body of men away from political activity, and the final form that was given to the scheme was a far cry from Louis Blanc's original plan of workers organized in a vast federation of trades.

For the moment both sides, liberal parliamentarians and republicans, were simply manoeuvring so as not to lose the unexpected opportunity that the fall of the monarchy had given them. The crucial issue remained the elections to the Constituent Assembly. How would the provinces of France view the recent events in Paris? It was the left wing who were most worried about this, for, as Blanqui realized, they needed time in which to spread their propaganda among the peasantry. Accordingly, the Minister of the Interior, Ledru-Rollin, who stood closer to the left than many of his colleagues in the provisional government, dispatched carefully chosen *commissaires* to the provinces to give impetus to the left-wing movement, while two demonstrations in Paris on 17 March and 16 April attempted to force the government to postpone the elections. The first of these did succeed in getting the date of the elections shifted to the end of April; the second failed, mainly because Ledru-Rollin chose to support the bourgeois and called out the National Guard against the imminent insurrection.

If anything, these efforts on the part of the left wing proved harmful to their cause. In 1830 it had been a small group of bourgeois in Paris who had defeated the extreme republicans. In 1848 it was almost the whole of France that spoke against them. The French peasant, mistrusting any Socialist schemes that might rob him of his land, showed himself once again to be the most conservative element in nineteenth-century French politics, and the news of mob violence in Paris only confirmed him in his fears. When the elections did finally take place in April, 84 per cent of the vast new electorate went to the polls to return an Assembly of 900 deputies, overwhelmingly right wing in outlook—lawyers, teachers, landowners, and army officers, middle-class men of established position, four-fifths of them over forty years of age—and with the emergence of this new factor in the French revolution of 1848 a fresh stage in the struggle between right and left was about to open.

Meanwhile, as in 1830, the news from Paris had sent a wave of revolutionary fervour throughout Europe. In Belgium the economic crisis during the two preceding years had resulted in the formation of a liberal ministry under Charles Rogier in June 1847. On 28 February, four days after Louis Philippe's abdication, Rogier proposed a lowering of the property qualification for voters, thereby increasing the parliamentary electorate from 46,000 to 79,000, and this measure, coupled with the suppression of the stamp tax on newspapers, the exclusion of government officials from the Chambers, and the regulating of the King's power to nominate burgomasters, ended the likelihood of any continued discontent among the middle classes. A Belgian Legion, formed in Paris, on which the extremists relied, was easily defeated in March by government troops, and by June the country was sufficiently quiet for the government to hold an election in which the moderate liberals were completely successful. Three factors help to explain this controlled liberal victory in Belgium at a time of rampant revolution. First, the Catholics and liberals, in the face of radical republicanism, had recreated the union which had been the essential preliminary to national independence in 1830. Second, many of the working classes in Belgium still lived in rural districts where the Roman Church was powerful and Socialist ideas had not spread at all. Third, the wisdom of Charles Rogier in granting a wider suffrage—in contrast to Guizot's obstinacy in France—had robbed the extremists of any chance of an alliance with the middle class.

A similar policy of concession was to enable the Dutch to make an appreciable step in the direction of constitutional monarchy. Warned by the news of Louis Philippe's fall, William II attempted, first of all, to impose reform from above by a series of suggested revisions of the Fundamental Law, but when these had met with little response, William set up a Royal Commission which included several of the liberal leaders, and in the course of the year a new scheme of government involving many radical alterations was worked out and eventually put into operation. The Second Chamber was no longer to be elected by the provincial States, but by direct suffrage, the right to vote being dependent upon a certain level of taxation—a franchise that was also to apply in the elections to provincial States. Ministerial responsibility was acknowledged and annual budgets were to be presented to the States General, whose powers were also to include some control over colonial affairs, education, and provincial administration. These measures opened the way to later constitutional development, such as the growth of political parties and further extensions of the franchise, but for the moment they still left considerable power with the sovereign and, in any case, the modifications were mainly in the interest of the richer middle class.

The same unrest now threatened the position of the princes in the German Confederation. As in the Netherlands, the demands were mostly middle class in character and except in the Rhineland, where industrialism had already gone some way, any Socialist tendencies were weak. Nevertheless, the pressure was such that the rulers of Baden, Württemberg, and Brunswick, and the patrician families of Lübeck, Bremen, Hamburg, and Frankfurt all found themselves assailed and were forced to give ground.

These movements in the German states, however, were as local as they had been in earlier decades. The hope for the creation of German national unity which might overcome this particularism found expression in a scheme put forward by Heinrich von Gagern, the minister of Hesse-Darmstadt. He was responsible for a meeting of fifty liberals, mostly from the south-west, on 5 March at Heidelberg, where it was decided that invitations should be sent to all past and present members of state legislatures in Germany to confer at Frankfurt at the end of March. When it met, this preliminary gathering, the *Vorparlament*, 600 in number, worked in conjunction with the Federal Diet and set about organizing elections throughout Germany for a National Constituent Assembly in which representation was to be on the basis of one deputy per 50,000 inhabitants, although the extent of the franchise varied from state to state.

Thus, by the middle of March, the fall of the monarchy in France had had repercussions far outside her frontiers, and it was natural that an enthusiast like Bakunin should imagine that a new world was dawning throughout Europe. Already, before leaving France in March, he had written in *La Réforme*: 'Soon, perhaps in less than a year, the monstrous Austrian empire will be destroyed. The liberated Italians will proclaim an Italian republic. The Germans, united into a single great nation, will proclaim a German republic. The Polish democrats after seventy years of exile will return to their homes. The revolutionary movement will stop only when Europe, the whole of Europe, not excluding Russia, is turned into a federal democratic republic.' In fact, the pattern so far seemed little different from that of 1830, and it is difficult to assess what might have been the course of events, if Metternich had been free to act. But this time Metternich himself was to succumb, for on the very day that Bakunin threw out his great prophecy, revolution burst in the heart of the Habsburg dominions themselves.

On 3 March, in the Hungarian Diet at Pressburg, Louis Kossuth had demanded the abolition of serfdom, the end of absolute rule from Vienna and the establishment of virtual independence for Hungary, a speech so violent that it had seriously alarmed the party of the nobility led by Széchényi. Within a week it had been echoed in similar demands by the Lower Austrian Estates and, a little later, by the Bohemians in Prague. Vienna itself was in an uproar of excitement and, on 12 March, after two professors had presented a petition from the University, the State council agreed to summon a meeting of delegates from the provincial Estates.

The storm broke on 13 March. Students and workers swarmed into the Ballhausplatz to hurl abuse at Metternich standing with his family at the windows of the Chancellery. They swept on to the Hofburg and when, amid the usual confusion, the troops opened fire, a new fury led to further outbreaks of fighting and destruction throughout the city. Now at last, at the very centre of his government, Metternich was face to face with those forces of popular violence which he had hated and dreaded ever since he had watched the pillage of the Hôtel de Ville at Strasbourg in 1789. To the end he refused to make terms. Immaculate in his green top coat and light grey trousers, contemptuous of the mob and indifferent to his colleagues, the Chancellor came to give his last advice at a Council of State. The troops must disperse the crowd; to avoid the fate of Louis Philippe, the Emperor had only to stand firm. But Metternich had his enemies inside as well as outside the Hofburg. Amid the whispering of archdukes and ministers throughout the rest of that day the notion predominated that the monarchy might be saved by the sacrifice of the Chancellor himself, and in the evening, when Metternich returned, he was informed that the answer to the crowd was to be his own resignation. 'Tell the people that I agree to everything', said the Emperor Ferdinand. With those words the career dedicated to the service of the Habsburg monarchy came to a close, and under cover of darkness the Chancellor of Europe made his escape as best he could from the city that had rejected him.

The fall of Metternich was to bring the revolutions in Europe to their climax. A manifestation at Budapest encouraged the Diet of Pressburg in March to pass measures, ending serfdom and establishing parliamentary rule with an electoral property qualification, and henceforth the only link with the Habsburg empire was to be a purely personal one in the King-Emperor himself. Louis Batthyány became the head of the government in Hungary, Deák Minister of Justice and Kossuth Minister of Finance, and in the following month Ferdinand gave the royal assent to all these changes, accordingly known as the April Laws.

In Vienna, on 15 March, he had already promised to grant a constitution, but the lack of leadership among the Viennese rebels made it possible for the initiative to remain in the hands of a succession of elderly Court officials, first Kollowrat, Metternich's great rival, then Ficquelmont, and after him Pillersdorf. The Imperial ministers delayed taking action and eventually drew up a constitution on their own, in which there were to be two Chambers, one of which would be elective, the vote being severely restricted by a high property qualification. Then further revolt in May forced them to agree to the summoning of a single-chamber Constituent Assembly, elected by universal suffrage, and a little later this body, predominantly middle class, met in Vienna. Long before this, however, on 20 May, the Court had fled to Innsbruck, from where it might be free to stem the tide of revolution.

As in Hungary, so in Germany and Italy Metternich's fall was to bring the national question out into the open. In Prussia Frederick William IV, who in a confused way had always regarded himself as a liberal monarch, was confronted with a rising in Berlin on 18 March and within twenty-four hours, after one engagement in which 230 of the crowd were shot down by his troops, he ordered a cease-fire and promised the summoning of a Constituent Assembly, thus attempting to place himself at the head of the revolutionary movement in Prussia. But by now revolution in Germany was turning towards something more than local revolt; German deputies were already being elected to the *Vorparlament* that was to meet at Frankfurt, and Frederick William impulsively coming to terms with the situation rode through the streets of Berlin beneath the new German flag of black, red, and gold. 'Henceforth,' he announced in a proclamation, 'Prussia will be merged in Germany.' With Metternich gone, even the monarchs of Europe could speak differently.

The same acceleration of events was to be seen in Italy. In Rome,

on 15 March, Pius IX granted a constitution for the Papal States—
the accepted pattern of two Chambers, one of which would be elective, the vote dependent upon a property qualification. In Venice
a Civic Guard was formed which at once gained control of the
arsenal, and on the withdrawal of the Austrian troops the Republic
of Venice was proclaimed under the presidency of Daniele Manin.
In Milan street fighting broke out, and after five days Radetzky, the
commander of the Austrian garrison, withdrew his troops to
Verona. The climax came on 24 March, when Charles Albert took
his great decision at last and declared war on Austria. Four days
later the Piedmontese army crossed the frontier to join forces with
the Milanese rebels and made a swift advance over the Lombard
plain towards the Austrian army, which had fallen back east of Lake
Garda.

Chapter 12

The Clash of Aims

Metternich dismissed; Prussia to be merged in a new Germany; Piedmont at open war with Austria in the struggle for Italian independence. It looked indeed as if the early months of 1848 were to be 'the springtime of nations'. Yet the upsurge of revolution had been so spectacular that it was easy to overestimate its significance. 'Oui, ma chère,' said Metternich to his wife on the night of his dismissal, 'nous sommes morts.' In fact, very few of the rulers in Europe had lost their thrones. Louis Philippe and Ludwig I of Bavaria had been compelled to abdicate; the Dukes of Modena and Parma had fled. Otherwise, the rulers had wisely given way to the demands that had been presented with such sudden violence; they still retained command of their military forces and they had only to wait to see whether the revolutionaries could maintain the united front with which they had won the first concessions.

It was precisely here that the weakness of the revolutions of 1848 lay, for the clash of aims made any constructive achievement virtually impossible. Middle-class liberals desiring consitutional monarchy and a restricted parliamentary franchise came into conflict at once with the egalitarianism of the radical republicans. In France, where there could be no turning back to monarchy for the moment, this was to mean a pitched battle between the two. In Italy and Germany, the same question, complicated still further by regional jealousies, bedevilled all efforts to achieve national unification. Was there to be a unitary republic, or a compromise with the existing duchies and kingdoms within a federal government? In central Europe there was the additional problem of the geographical definition of national frontiers. The claims of language and history were so confused that it was self-evidently impossible for any frontier to be drawn on which all would agree, and the larger national groups—Germans and Magyars—energetically pressing their claims, had no patience with the aspirations of smaller groups such as Bohemians, Slovaks, Croats, Serbs, and Roumans, whom they firmly intended to include within their new frontiers. It is consequently not surprising that these smaller groups should soon deplore the apparent break-up of the Habsburg dominions, preferring to remain within the old non-national structure of central Europe rather than to become subject peoples of new nation states.

In France it was with considerable relief that the moderate element in the provisional government found that the Constituent Assembly, which first met on 4 May, represented such a triumph for the right wing. Their nervousness until this moment was highly understandable. Since the fall of the monarchy almost 450 clubs had been formed in Paris, and a flood of newspapers had spread ideas of Socialism; the National Guard had been thrown open to those who could not afford to buy their own arms and equipment, and although the *ateliers nationaux*, which by now had absorbed well over 100,000 unemployed, had mostly remained uncommitted during the demonstrations of March and April, their very existence represented a potential weapon of mass power of which the extremists might yet gain control.

Both sides knew at once that the election of such an Assembly meant an end to the uneasy truce between the bourgeois and the left wing. The first action of the Assembly was to replace the provisional government by an executive commission of five—Arago, Garnier-Pagès, Marie, Lamartine, and Ledru-Rollin—all of them moderates except Ledru-Rollin, whose action against the demonstrators on 16 April (see p. 124) had nevertheless won him the trust of the bourgeois. On 12 May it prohibited the direct presentation of petitions, thereby depriving a crowd of its main excuse to invade the hall of the Assembly, and this stimulated the left wing to make one further desperate move. On 15 May the crowd burst in on the Assembly, declared it dissolved, and then marched off to the Hôtel de Ville to proclaim a new government. But it was too late for a Paris mob to influence the course of the 1848 revolution. The existing government stood firm and the National Guard dispersed the crowd. The leaders, Blanqui and Barbès, were placed under arrest, and the executive commission took the opportunity to close the revolutionary clubs, purge the National Guard, and remove Caussidière, the radical Prefect of Police.

The next step in the right-wing reaction concerned the *ateliers nationaux*. They were expensive and it had been noticed that the workers enrolled in them had taken some part in the activities of 15 May. The main problem was that their abolition would almost certainly have violent consequences. On 26 May, however, the government took the risk of dispatching Émile Thomas to Bordeaux and on 21 June a decree was issued giving all enrolled workers who were unmarried and under twenty-five years of age the option of joining the army, and warning the rest that they were to be sent out into the provinces—where, of course, they could easily be dispersed.

The outcome was as Émile Thomas had predicted. Once again,

on 22 June, barricades began to go up in the narrow streets of Paris—mainly in the eastern districts between the Place de la Concorde and the Hotel de Ville. Lamartine, who had opposed the abolition of the *ateliers*, hastened round the city appealing to the rebels in a vain attempt to avoid bloodshed, but only succeeded in earning the mistrust of both sides; poetic romanticism had no further part to play in the French revolution of 1848. Fighting had already begun on 23 June and the Assembly, by now frightened that it was about to suffer the same fate as Charles X and Louis Philippe, hastily vested supreme power in General Eugene Cavaignac, a veteran of North Africa. Troops were rushed in by train—a new factor in governmental action—and for three days a savage war raged in Paris. The workers fought virtually without leaders, since Blanqui and Barbès were already under arrest and Louis Blanc and Ledru-Rollin refused to become involved: and the pathetic hopelessness of the whole insurrection is perfectly captured in some of the short stories of Turgenev, who was living in Paris at the time. At the end, when the rising had been utterly crushed and Cavaignac had received the thanks of the Assembly, it was reckoned that 1,460 of the insurgents had been killed, but this figure ignores the numbers of those who were shot in summary executions.

The June days finally enabled the right wing to consolidate their position; 15,000 suspects were arrested, 4,000 deported, and Louis Blanc fled to England. Many of the clubs were closed and the press laws reimposed. *Le droit au travail* as a fundamental principle of society came increasingly under attack until it had been whittled away almost to nothing, and in September the length of the working day was increased to twelve hours in Paris.

By November the Assembly had completed the constitution of the Second Republic. The legislature, a single Chamber of 750 deputies, elected by universal male suffrage, was to sit for three years, but was not to include any minister or public officials. Executive power was to be vested in a President, also elected by universal suffrage to hold office for four years, but not eligible for re-election. The whole scheme was based on a separation of powers, which in the minds of the theorists was still the accepted formula for the avoidance of despotism. In fact, they should have known by this time that such a separation made it impossible to overcome a deadlock between the legislature and the executive. The President was forbidden to dissolve the Assembly before the three years had expired; nor could the Chamber dissolve itself. If a deadlock did arise, neither side would be able to refer to the electorate. On the other hand, while both could claim to have been elected by the country, it would obviously be easier for a President to mobilize public opinion and to act decisively than for an Assembly of 750 consisting of many shades of opinion; thus, a skilful politician, once installed as President, might be able to use his executive power to overthrow the legislature with all the justification of public support.

Clearly a great deal would depend upon the personality of the first President, and it was here that the memory of the June days proved highly significant. The working-class movement had been defeated, but there were many among the bourgeois and peasantry who wondered whether any parliamentary republic could effectively resist another left-wing rising. By now all faith had been lost in the men of the centre such as Lamartine, and no leader had yet emerged on the right to capture the popular imagination. It was at this moment that there appeared on the scene a new figure, quite unassociated with the preceding events of the year. Prince Louis Napoleon (see p. 101) had been allowed to return to France in the summer. At first sight he would not have seemed the man who was eventually to rise to supreme power in France. The heavy moustache, the dull expressionless eyes, the shy clumsiness on public occasions, the French spoken with a German accent, all convinced the deputies of the Constituent Assembly at least that there was no danger in allowing this head of the house of Bonaparte to stand as a candidate in the approaching presidential election. And yet, as a number of by-elections to the Constituent Assembly had already shown, at this precise moment in the revolution of 1848 Louis Napoleon was in the remarkable position of appealing to almost every class. His uncle's name suggested *la gloire*; for the peasantry he seemed to stand for strong orderly government; to the workers, deprived of any other leadership, his essay on *L'extinction du paupérisme*, written in 1844, offered a hope that seemed to exist nowhere else; to the bourgeois of the extreme right he seemed a useful stopgap to enable them to prepare the ground for a restoration of monarchy. On 10 December the presidential election took place and 'Poléon' was swept to victory with $5\frac{1}{2}$ million votes, a majority that utterly overwhelmed the other four republican candidates. The elections to the Chamber of the new constitution had yet to be held, but the French had already chosen the man who was to destroy the republic in which most of them had already lost faith.

The basis of the struggle in France had remained purely social. In Switzerland the fundamental problem was the establishment of a stronger central government, although this too implied a social readjustment, since it meant a surrender of power by the local patrician families. The success of the Swiss in reaching a solution was due partly to the speed with which the liberals had overcome their opponents in the *Sonderbund* war of 1847, partly to the common sense, willingness to compromise and experience in local government of the victorious group.

At first, the commission set up by the Diet in August 1847 to revise the federal constitution was bound to proceed cautiously owing to the possibility of foreign intervention. The revolutions in Paris and Vienna released them from this fear; a successful rising in Neuchâtel ended the existence of a Prussian enclave within Swiss territory (see p. 74), and the way was now open for the reconstruction of a unified Federal State. The new scheme was drafted in the early months of 1848, and debated in the Diet in May and June. It was accepted by a considerable majority of the cantons and by the autumn the new constitution was already in operation.

Under the new system a Federal legislature was to consist of two Chambers, a Council of States, with one deputy from each canton, and a National Council, elected by universal manhood suffrage, with seats allotted in proportion to the population of the cantons. The arrangement naturally satisfied the larger cantons, which had previously never had a representation relative to their size. The two Councils were together to elect the seven members of a permanent Federal executive. The Federal government, now with a revenue of its own, became responsible for diplomacy and national defence, public works and the maintenance of a postal service. It had the right to approve cantonal constitutions, prohibited political treaties between cantons, and established a Customs Union, together with a uniform currency, throughout the country. On the other hand, local forms of government, provided that they respected civil rights, were left entirely in the hands of the cantons. Thus the Swiss, despite the existence of three different languages within their frontiers and a deeply rooted local patriotism among the cantons, succeeded in finding a permanent solution to their difficulties out of the turmoil of 1848.

In comparison with the Swiss the problems that faced Charles Albert were infinitely more complex. The Habsburg dominions were in uproar and Radetzky had fallen back east of the Mincio. The Austrian force, however, now firmly based on the four fortresses of the Quadrilateral—Peschiera, Mantua, Verona, and Legnago—the key to the valley of the Po, had still to be defeated in the field, while the precise relationship of Piedmont, Lombardy, and Venetia in any new system was a problem fraught with local jealousies and conflicting aspirations and greatly complicated by the attitude of Great Britain and France.

At first the general weakness of the Habsburgs forced Radetzky to remain on the defensive and by the end of April Charles Albert, reinforced by Piedmontese reservists and about 5,000 Tuscans and Modenese, had laid siege to Peschiera and actually defeated an Austrian army under General D'Aspre at Pastrengo ten miles farther east. This promising beginning, however, was deceptive and was immediately followed by three major setbacks. First, on 29 April,

Pius IX issued a Papal Allocution in which he stated that it was impossible for the Papacy to lend itself to a military operation, thus robbing Charles Albert of vital moral support and of the Papal forces that had been on their way northwards. Next, on I May, urged on by his ministers at Turin, who stressed the political necessity for a rapid victory, Charles Albert made a hasty attack at Santa Lucia, but was repulsed—only a slight defeat, but one which caused a storm of criticism at the military leadership among the radical elements in Turin. Third, in the middle of May, King Ferdinand of Naples felt sufficiently sure of his army's loyalty to revoke the promises that had been extracted from him in February; the constitution was quietly ignored and the Neapolitan troops—of whom 40,000 had originally been promised—were recalled southwards.

These ominous signs did little to check the activity of the politicians. In Turin Count Cesare Balbo, the Premier, was presiding over a fury of constitution-making which depended both on the defeat of Austria and the suppression of any Mazzinian democratic movement. The future state of North Italy still remained a political unknown, since Lombardy and Venetia, having each declared their independence, were doubtful about surrendering it at once to a new kingdom of North Italy centred on Turin, but by the beginning of July something tangible had emerged, when all the duchies, including Lombardy and Venetia, did agree to union with Piedmont.

This agreement had a considerable bearing on the attitude of the western Powers, since, although Great Britain and France would have been glad to see the Habsburgs removed from Italy, any mediation on their part was governed by the distrust that each had for the other over the gain that might be made out of the changed situation. Palmerston's aim was to negotiate a settlement with Austria before the French could march to the assistance of Charles Albert as a means of revising the frontiers of 1815, and since a North Italian kingdom would act as a bulwark against France, proposed the union of Lombardy and Venetia with Piedmont. Pillersdorf in Vienna was also fearful of possible French intervention, and in May an Austrian under-secretary, Hummelauer, was sent to London to discuss the terms of a pacification. Hummelauer, however, would not go beyond an offer of independence for Lombardy and autonomous rule for Venetia under an Austrian archduke. 'The Emperor cannot surrender Venetia without virtually giving up the Italian Tyrol,' he pointed out to Palmerston, and there for the moment the matter rested. In Paris, however, the notion of intervention was really only supported by the left-wing element; Lamartine had no wish to start a general revolutionary war, still less to launch the French army against the Austrians. 'La France,' he said, 'interviendra seulement si l'Italie l'appelle,' a safe promise, since he knew that Piedmont had no wish for French intrusion. 'Italia farà da sé,'* Charles Albert had said. The principal aim of the French government was to avoid the aggrandisement of Piedmont and this could only mean the creation of Lombardy and Venetia as independent republics—which, by July, seemed to be ruled out by the decision of the two provinces to fuse with Piedmont.

The common assumption behind all these negotiations was military victory for Charles Albert. In July, however, this assumption was abruptly shattered. The loss of Papal and Neapolitan reinforcements, coupled with the notable absence of Lombard troops, had seriously affected Charles Albert's prospects. At the same time the hard-pressed Austrian government was able to dispatch 20,000 men under Count Thurn and another 15,000 under General Welden, and on 22 July Radetzky launched a great attack on Charles Albert's forces, 30,000 of whom had been engaged in besieging Mantua. For the next five days there raged the highly fluid battle which takes its name from the nearby village of Custoza, ending with the retreat of the Piedmontese army. Charles Albert hoped at least to make a stand before Milan, but when this project appeared hopeless, he agreed to an armistice which would allow him twenty-four hours to withdraw his troops into Piedmont, and by the end of the first week of August Lombardy was once more under Austrian rule.

In central Europe the social struggle between liberal bourgeois and radical republicans was complicated by the further question of defining national frontiers. The German National Constituent Assembly, elected through the efforts of the *Vorparlament*, had met in the Pauluskirche, the church of St Paul, at Frankfurt on 18 May, but the weakness of this body soon became apparent. Its members were drawn almost entirely from the upper ranks of the professional middle classes—university professors, school teachers, lawyers, and civil servants—and they spent most of this exciting year under the presidency of von Gagern debating the general principles, the *Grundrechte*, on which a constitution for a united Germany should be based. The main division of opinion was between moderates who wished for some sort of compromise with the existing states of Germany, and extremists who demanded a centralized republic. The practical problem which they could hardly hope to solve was the immediate creation of an armed force with which to defend their newly-found freedom, and in due course, when confronted with the outbreaks of left-wing extremists and with the requirements of their own nationalist policy, they were to become dependent upon the armies of Austria and Prussia.

* 'Italy will do it on her own.'

Actually, left-wing activities in Germany were more noisy than dangerous. A German Legion formed in Paris by the poet Georg Herwegh, envious of Lamartine's prominence in the revolutionary scene, set out to march on Baden in April, in order to establish a republic, but on encountering the forces of the princes, scampered to safety over the Swiss border. Karl Marx had moved to Cologne early in the year, but he took no active part in any of the risings, since he believed that from a working-class point of view they were premature. Nevertheless, in the larger cities of Germany workers' movements were sufficiently in evidence to cause alarm to the bourgeois, particularly in Frankfurt itself.

It was the national question that really occupied the deputies sitting in their pews in the Pauluskirche. The definition of the frontiers of the new Germany gave rise to a controversy that was to recur throughout all subsequent German history. One group favoured the conception of *Grossdeutschland* (Great Germany), maintaining that wherever German was spoken was German territory and thus demanding that a large part of the Habsburg dominions, excluding Hungary, should come within the frontiers of the new state. This would mean the inclusion of a number of Slav minorities under German rule, and the resistance of the Bohemians to such an idea was made clear at the very beginning when Palacky, a professor at the University of Prague, refused the invitation of the Germans to attend the *Vorparlament* at Frankfurt. It would also mean the partition of Habsburg territories, which was hardly likely to be acceptable to Vienna, once order had been restored. The other group, headed by Professor Dahlmann, advocated a *Kleindeutschland* (Little Germany),which would exclude the whole of the Habsburg lands. The weakness here was that it would leave Prussia by far the strongest element within Germany and few of the liberals from the south had much confidence in Frederick William's assertion that Prussia would be merged in Germany. The idea was equally unacceptable to Austria who could not allow her own permanent exclusion from German affairs.

This concern with frontiers was to give the German liberal movement an intensely nationalist flavour lacking in English and French liberalism, and two issues, the Polish provinces and Slesvig-Holstein, came increasingly to occupy the time of the Frankfurt Parliament. After the demonstrations in Berlin Frederick William had agreed to Polish autonomy in Prussian Poland, but the resident German population had objected so violently that by April local German domination had been re-established. In Denmark the new King Frederick VII had lent full support to the nationalist claim to Slesvig and the Germans in the duchies had declared their independence and appealed to the Frankfurt Parliament. In both these issues an ambitious nationalism among the Frankfurt liberals triumphed over counsels of moderation. In Slesvig-Holstein the claims of the German language were said to over-ride the historic rights of the Danish King; in Posen precisely the reverse argument was used to reject the appeal of the Poles.

The Danish question revealed the fundamental weakness of the Frankfurt Parliament, which, lacking any military power, could only rely on the armies of others. It was the Prussians who, on behalf of the Frankfurt deputies, marched into the duchies to the assistance of the Germans there against the Danish forces, and the full ineffectualness of the Frankfurt liberals was revealed when Prussia, alarmed at the possible international consequences of this invasion, signed a truce with Denmark at Malmö on 26 August without any reference to them. Worse was to follow. The recently established ministry at Frankfurt fell during the subsequent debate in the Parliament, but when the truce of Malmö was finally accepted by a narrow majority, a left-wing revolt broke out, on 16 September, in the city itself and the Parliament was only saved by the intervention of Prussian and Austrian troops from the federal fortress of Mainz.

Thus, by the end of the summer of 1848, the hopes of the German liberals had been shown to depend not upon any great movement of the people throughout Germany but upon the governments of Berlin and Vienna. Yet by this time the revolutionary force that had momentarily threatened these centres was already waning, and although Frederick William had not yet finally made up his mind to break with the movement, the position of the Habsburgs had changed noticeably for the better. In Prague any alliance between Germans and Bohemians had been short-lived. On 2 June the Bohemian leaders had opened a Slav Congress in retaliation to the German Parliament at Frankfurt at which their allegiance to the Habsburg dynasty was reaffirmed. *Grossdeutschland* seemed a greater menace than Vienna, and the smaller Slav groups had realized that complete national independence for them would be meaningless, since they would never be strong enough to defend themselves against an independent Germany or Hungary. 'If the Austrian Empire did not exist,' Palacky had said, 'it would be necessary to create it,' and the aim of the leading Bohemian politicians was no more than a greater independence within the framework of Habsburg rule. Farther east, other minorities were also growing aware of the need for Habsburg support. Magyar nationalism under the influence of Kossuth had led to the attempted absorption of Croats and Serbs to the south, and of Roumans in Transylvania. The Croat Diet at Zagreb consequently looked to the governor of Croatia, Jellačić, appointed by the Emperor and extremely pro-

Austrian, while the Rumanians declared at a meeting in Blaj Cathedral that the Rumanian nation would always remain faithful to the Emperor of Austria.

All these divisions naturally pointed the way to Habsburg recovery—Bohemians to be played off against Germans; Croats and Roumans against Magyars; liberals against social extremists. In June, a nationalist revolt broke out in Prague, strongly disliked by the moderate Bohemians, and this gave Windischgrätz, the Imperial general who had withdrawn there from Vienna, the opportunity to subdue the Bohemian movement with military force—a suppression which was actually viewed with approval by the Frankfurt deputies. In July, the news of Radetzky's victory at Custoza gave the Court sufficient confidence to return to Vienna. Here the Pillersdorf administration had been replaced by Wessenburg, and Schwarzer, the Minister for Public Works, decided that the moment had come for the reduction of the industrial wages of women and children. This was at once followed by the Viennese equivalent of the June days in Paris, and on 23 August, after a pitched battle with the police and the National Guard, the working-class movement in Vienna was crushed. The only other major force that the extremists might have used was the peasantry, but when, on 7 September, the Austrian Constituent Assembly granted them their one serious demand—the abolition of feudal tenure—they lost all further interest in revolutionary action.

Meanwhile, the situation had been deteriorating for the Hungarians. Elections in June had produced a National Assembly consisting mainly of nobility, interspersed with a certain number of professional men, but by this time relations with the Serbs and Croats had become so bad that within eight hours of its first meeting on 4 July Kossuth had to proclaim 'the country in danger'. In Croatia Jellačić, first dismissed at the request of Hungary, was reinstated in September by the Imperial government. He immediately declared war on Hungary, and on 11 September his troops crossed the Drave river in an advance on Budapest.

Hungary at once appealed to Vienna and a momentous debate took place in the Austrian Constituent Assembly. The extremists and the Germans supported Hungarian independence, since this was the surest way of undermining the Habsburg power; the conservatives and Bohemian deputies, each conscious of their need to maintain the Habsburg dynasty, formed a majority and the appeal of Hungary against the Croat invasion was thus rejected. The government consequently felt that it was unlikely to be hampered by any pro-Hungarian movement in Vienna and, on the assassination of Count Lamberg who had gone to Budapest as an Imperial intermediary, Latour, the Minister of War, actually sent reinforcements to Jellačić's Croats. In Hungary Batthyány, who had genuinely tried to reconcile the Croats, had already tendered his resignation as head of the government and on 3 October Ferdinand appointed Jellačić—of all men—in his place and dissolved the Hungarian Parliament. This was an ultimatum. The Hungarians, in reply, rejected the royal decree and set up a National Defence Committee under the chairmanship of Kossuth, who thus became virtual ruler of Hungary

The troubles in Vienna, however, were not yet over. On 6 October the extremists who considered rightly that Hungary's fate was bound up with their own, fomented a great revolt in the city, determined to prevent the dispatch of any more troops to the Croats. Latour was hanged from a lamp-post, and when, on the next day, it seemed that the city was completely out of hand, the Court fled once again, this time to Olmütz. With them went many of the conservatives and Bohemians of the Austrian Constituent Assembly, and this second rising in Vienna was supported mainly by workers and university students. They were able to muster a force of about 40,000, but after the Hungarian army had made a half-hearted attempt to come to their assistance, the Viennese rebels were left to their fate. Jellačić, repulsed in Hungary, marched westwards against them, but the main counter-attack was carried out by Windischgrätz, and by 31 October, after a series of violent encounters, his army had broken the resistance and the city was given over to an orgy of looting and slaughter.

In November a new government under Prince Schwarzenberg, Windischgrätz's brother-in-law, was set up in Vienna. An abdication was arranged in order to get rid of Ferdinand, whose personal acceptance of the April Laws would be an embarrassment in any further action against Hungary, and on 2 December his nephew, the young Francis Joseph, was proclaimed Emperor in his place (see genealogical table, p. 484). Thus, by the end of the year, although there was still to be trouble in Hungary and Italy, the ruling classes of Habsburg Europe surveying their battered dominions might reckon that they had weathered the worst part of the storm that had burst upon them only ten months before.

Chapter 13

Varieties of Liberal Defeat
1848–51

1. The struggle in central Europe

With these recent changes in the situation in central Europe the rulers of Prussia and Austria now felt sufficiently encouraged to impose their own solution within their dominions. In Berlin the conservative Junker party finally gained the ear of Frederick William and after the city had been occupied by General von Wrangel and a new Prime Minister, Count Brandenburg, had dissolved the Prussian National Assembly, the King simply proclaimed a new constitution, the *octroyierte Verfassung*, on 5 December. There was a shadow of consolation for the liberals, since the most startling aspect of this constitution was the manner of its birth; in content it came close to the aims of the Prussian National Assembly and even included the election of a Lower Chamber by universal manhood suffrage.

In Austria the government of Schwarzenberg under the new Emperor Francis Joseph had, in November, already drawn up a new programme for establishing strong centralized rule from Vienna, and on 19 December an army under Jellačić entered Hungary, where the abdication of Ferdinand had naturally not been accepted. Budapest fell on 4 January 1849 and after an Imperial victory at Kápolna on 27 February, Schwarzenberg decided that it was time to follow the example of Prussia. The Constituent Assembly, which had been dispatched to Kremsier to complete its labours, was dissolved and on 4 March a new constitution, drawn up principally by Count Stadion, the Minister of the Interior, was proclaimed. As in Prussia, some account was taken of the aspirations of the constitutionalists; a Parliament of two houses as well as elective local councils had the correct revolutionary ring, but their rights were carefully circumscribed and the essence of this dictated constitution was the establishment of a unitary state cutting across the historic divisions of the provinces and thus ending the hopes for the federal solution which the deputies at Kremsier had devised at the beginning of the year.

For the Austrians, however, the struggle was not yet at an end. In North Italy Charles Albert reopened hostilities with Radetzky in

March, but was crushed almost at once in the disastrous Novara campaign (see p. 147). The Hungarians, who knew that all was lost if the Stadion constitution should triumph, fought back with greater success. An army equipped under a Polish general, Bem, in Transylvania repulsed the Austrian troops at every point and regained Budapest, while, on 14 April at Debrecen, the Hungarian Parliament, shaking off its earlier restraint, declared the complete independence of Hungary from Habsburg rule, and elected Kossuth as governor of the new state.

It was this turn of events in Hungary that decided the Austrian government to look for assistance outside their dominions, and on 21 April 1849 Francis Joseph made his personal appeal to Nicholas I of Russia. Ever since the beginning of 1848 the Tsar had been an agonized spectator of events throughout Europe, fearful lest the excitement of revolution would spread to Russian Poland, and now the Austrian Emperor's invitation to him to intervene released him from his frustration. Louis Napoleon's expedition to Rome (see p. 149) removed any remaining need for caution, and on 1 May Nicholas announced his intention of coming to the aid of his fellow sovereign. From this moment the fate of the Hungarians was sealed. Like the Poles in 1830, they could only hope for assistance from the west, but once again geography and the dictates of diplomacy ruled out this possibility. In vain Kossuth offered Palmerston markets for British goods in an independent Hungary, including even free ports on the Adriatic and the Danube. For Palmerston, much as he might admire the Hungarian efforts and abhor the Russian intervention, the maintenance of the Habsburg empire seemed of greater importance to British interests, and his views were echoed by Louis Napoleon whose Foreign Minister, de Tocqueville, made it clear to the French ambassador at St Petersburg that France was not to be drawn into a contest alongside Hungary. As a consequence the new state of Hungary did not survive the summer. Eighty thousand Russians under Paskevich crossed the Carpathians at the same time as General Haynau penetrated along the Danube and Jellačić drove through in the south. The Hungarians were surrounded, outnumbered and torn by internal rivalries, despite Kossuth's desperate sacrifice in surrendering political as well as military power to the Hungarian commander-in-chief, Görgey, and three days after a defeat at Temesvar on 10 August, Görgey surrendered his army of 30,000 to the Russians at Világos.

The Tsar, desirous only of the restoration of the *status quo* in central Europe, had no interest in any territorial acquisition as a reward for his intervention. The concentration of the Austrians on Italy and Hungary in 1848 had, however, left them open to a new threat to their position in Germany. The Frankfurt Assembly under von Gagern had, by the end of 1848, drawn up a list of fundamental rights on which the new German constitution would be based, and which the parliaments of the various states seemed prepared to accept. The constitution itself, which was completed by 27 March 1849, established a central Federal government with a Parliament of two Chambers, one representing the states, the other a House of Representatives elected by universal manhood suffrage on a secret ballot. Executive power was to be vested in a hereditary German emperor with command of the military forces, a suspensive veto and the right to dissolve the Lower House for new elections.

It is easy to mock the lack of realism of the deputies at Frankfurt; they had, in fact, seized their opportunity when it came, and although they were to be robbed almost immediately of their constitution, to whose general principles they devoted so much thought, they had, nevertheless, laid a foundation of ideas on which later generations in the twentieth century might hope to build. In fact, a federal scheme was not unrealistic—the solution which Bismarck was later to adopt under a different guise. This represented a victory for the more cautious right-wing groups. They had, too, faced up to the problem of whether to include Austria—*Grossdeutschland*—or to exclude her—*Kleindeutschland*—and here the temporary setbacks suffered by Austria at this time in Italy and Hungary played their part in events. The Frankfurt deputies settled for the exclusion of Austria, and it was Frederick William IV of Prussia whom they elected as emperor on 28 March. Twenty-eight of the German states accepted these proposals and for the moment it seemed as if Austria, despite her denunciation of this new step and the withdrawal of her delegates from the Frankfurt Assembly, was to have no part in the new government of Germany.

Salvation, however came from an unexpected quarter. At Berlin Frederick William, mistrustful of the democratic nature of the new Federal constitution and now strongly in sympathy with the conservative elements, looked askance at a crown granted to him by the people. On 27 April he refused the Assembly's offer. At the same time he dissolved his own Parliament who had appealed to him to accept, and by a decree divided the electors into three classes, based on a tax qualification that would ensure the predominance of the richest section of society in any future Prussian Parliament.

Shortly after this the Frankfurt Assembly, powerless as ever, disintegrated, as the delegates were summoned home by their various governments. The struggle between Austria and Prussia, however, continued. Frederick William might have rejected a crown offered by the people, but he was not averse to a new federal arrangement in Germany which might allow Prussia to enjoy what had previously been Austria's position of influence. On 26 May 1849 in a 'Union of the Three Kings'—Prussia, Saxony, and Hanover—he accepted a new proposal put forward by a Prussian Catholic conservative,

CENTRAL EUROPE AND ITALY 1848–71

General von Radowitz. This was similar in many respects to the Frankfurt scheme, but with one highly significant difference. Prussia, instead of being merged in Germany, was to establish her own leadership over all the states of *Kleindeutschland*. The moment was certainly propitious; Austria was still tied down in Hungary, and a series of radical republican outbreaks in Saxony, the Palatinate and Baden forced the German princes to turn to the protection of the Prussian army, which by the end of July had restored order in their territories. By the beginning of September, although mistrust of Prussia caused Bavaria and Württemberg to hold themselves aloof, twenty-eight states had agreed to accept the new Union and in March 1850 a German Parliament assembled at Erfurt to discuss the final details of the Prussian scheme.

By now, however, Schwarzenberg had his hands free from trouble in Italy and Hungary and was determined to wreck this Prussian bid to usurp Austria's position in Germany. Accordingly he put forward a scheme of his own—a *Grossdeutschland* including the *whole* of the Habsburg dominions, in which the government of Germany would be entrusted to a Directory consisting of delegates from Austria, Prussia, and the larger states. Before long the tide was running fast against Prussian ambitions. In May 1850, at a meeting with Frederick William and Schwarzenberg at Warsaw, Tsar Nicholas insisted on friendly relations between Prussia and Austria, and when he remarked that 'the aggressor is not always the one who attacks, but the one who causes the quarrel', Frederick William realized that in any continuation of the dispute Russian sympathies would be with Austria. In July this desire for a restoration of the *status quo* was underlined by an agreement between Great Britain, France, and Russia confirming the position of the Danish king for the future as Duke of Slesvig-Holstein (see p. 191): Hanover and Saxony had by now begun to move away from dependence on Prussia, and in October Schwarzenberg formed a military alliance with Bavaria and Württemberg.

The immediate crisis which was to test the strength of the two groups occurred in Hesse-Cassel, where the Elector was threatened with internal disorder. The Prussian army prepared to intervene; Schwarzenberg replied with an ultimatum, insisting that intervention should only come from the forces of the old German Federal Diet. In the first week of November there was a little skirmishing between Austrian and Prussian troops in Hesse, but the new Prussian Prime Minister, Otto von Manteuffel, was anxious to avoid the development of hostilities, and von Radowitz who had become Foreign Minister in September had already resigned. The Minister of War, General Stockhausen, had no faith in Prussia's chances in a war with Austria, and in the diplomatic field Great Britain and France had both made it clear that they would remain neutral. As a consequence, Manteuffel agreed to a personal meeting with Schwarzenberg at Olmütz and here, on 29 November, Prussia agreed to abandon the Erfurt scheme. This victory for Austria, however, did not mean that the way was open for Schwarzenberg's own proposals. The smaller German princes were aware that their survival must depend upon the maintenance of a balance between Prussia and Austria in central Europe and at a conference held at Dresden in 1851 Prussia was now able to put herself on the side of those who wanted a return to the *status quo*. Schwarzenberg, somewhat disgruntled, had to accept a revival of the German Confederation of 1815, and on 16 May an alliance between Austria and

Prussia rounded off a settlement which appeared to nullify the efforts made on all sides in Germany during the past three years.

2. The collapse of Italian hopes

The defeat of Charles Albert at Custoza, followed by the armistice of Salasco in August 1848, had not meant the immediate end of the movements in Italy. It did, however, bring them to a new period of crisis in which the spirit of optimism and of common purpose faded before the old local jealousies and divergence of aim among the revolutionaries. To the radicals it seemed that the Piedmontese armistice simply marked the defection of Charles Albert from the revolutionary cause, in line with Ferdinand of Naples' recall of his troops and Pius IX's Allocution. In Naples, Ferdinand, sure of his army, was able to crush a Sicilian rising, during which his bombardment of Messina in September earned him the nickname of King Bomba, and by 1849 there was little left of the Neapolitan constitutional experiment. In Piedmont, Tuscany, and the Papal States, however, the rulers still remained uneasily at the head of liberal governments which had increasingly to come to terms with the angry vehemence of the radical element. Venice under Manin was unsubdued; the Piedmontese army remained fully mobilized, and while the Habsburgs still had to give much of their attention to central Europe, it was not impossible to hope that some reshaping of Italy might yet emerge from the confusion.

In Turin the news of the retreat through Lombardy had brought down the government of Count Casati, and between August and December the new cabinet in which Count Revel and Dionigi Pinelli were the dominant personalities was assailed by a growing demand from the left for a renewal of war, which the government knew to be impossible owing to the condition of the Piedmontese army. Struggling to find a way out of the dilemma in which a negotiated peace could only bring about their own downfall, while a continuation of the war must mean military disaster, the cabinet was assisted at first by the new difficulties that confronted the Habsburgs in Vienna. At no time, however, would the Austrian government offer anything more than Home Rule for Lombardy and Venetia— unacceptable to the Piedmontese radicals—and after Windischgrätz had crushed the October rising in Vienna (see p. 139) and Prince Schwarzenberg had assumed control, determined on the full restoration of Habsburg power, there was little chance of any further delaying tactics. In December the government, in a last effort to restrain the war party, revealed the true state of the army at a secret session of the Chamber, but the only consequence of this was to bring about their fall. Gioberti now accepted office as premier.

Meanwhile, to the south of Piedmont, extremist pressure had also become more marked. In Tuscany the Ridolfi government fell after the news of Custoza, and its successor collapsed in October when Montanelli and Guerrazzi took over as the only leaders acceptable to Leghorn, where radical sentiment was so strong that the city appeared to be on the verge of seceding from Tuscany. In Rome Pius was faced with a similar scene of mounting violence. His Allocution of 29 April had already robbed him of much of his popularity with the masses, and he had by now lost confidence in his own liberal Premier who seemed to wish to deprive him of temporal power in the Papal States. In September he appointed Count Rossi, a liberal who, but for his sudden death, might have played a great part in this phase of Italian history. Rossi not only reckoned to stabilize the situation in Rome; he had a plan for Italy, the Gioberti scheme of federation under the presidency of the Pope. Negotiations were opened up with Turin, but the delicate position of the Pinelli–Revel government made it impossible for them to abandon the idea of a North Italian kingdom. It will never be known what Rossi might still have achieved. The radicals in Rome had already seen that here was a man who might be strong enough to capture the revolution for the moderates and on 15 November, on his way to attend the opening of the Chamber, he was stabbed to death by the guard of honour that lined the steps to the entrance.

For Pius this murder of his premier meant the end. He stayed long enough to accept a new cabinet including Dr Sterbini, who was afterwards suspected of having had a hand in Rossi's assassination, but he had by now made up his mind to flee from Rome and on 24 November he slipped out of the Quirinal and was driven by coach to Gaeta in Neapolitan territory. This flight of the Pope was the final blow for any moderate movement south of Piedmont. In itself it was an appeal to all Catholic opinion in Europe and it shattered the hopes of the liberals as effectively as his election in 1846 had awoken them.

In Rome the road was now open to the Mazzinian republicans, and after elections in January 1849 the Chamber proclaimed a Roman Republic, declaring the abolition of the Temporal Power, but guaranteeing the Pope his spiritual prerogatives. There had already been a hope at this time that Tuscany and Piedmont would send deputies to Rome so that a Constituent Assembly might be created for a new united Italy. In Tuscany Guerrazzi yielded to the pressure of public opinion and for a short time even managed to persuade Grand Duke Leopold to agree. Leopold, however, could not side against the Pope, who had already denounced these latest developments, and in the first week of February he fled to Siena and thence to Gaeta. This was naturally followed by further excitement, but strong action by Guerrazzi, supported by the moderate deputies in the Assembly at Florence, prevented the extremists in Tuscany from gaining power, and for the moment the duchy remained only half committed to the republican movement in Rome. In Turin, Gioberti, who might have been prepared to collaborate with the scheme of Rossi, turned his face against the Mazzinian republicanism of Rome, and believing that Piedmont must keep Tuscany by her side before the war with Austria was renewed, he actually prepared an expedition to restore Grand Duke Leopold to power. Neither Charles Albert nor the cabinet would support him in this and since his refusal to recognize the Constituent Assembly in Rome had already lost him the left-wing deputies in the Chamber, he was forced to resign on 21 February.

After Gioberti, Charles Albert could hold off the extreme nationalists no longer; a new cabinet was formed, dominated by Urbano Rattazzi, and on 12 March the truce with Austria was denounced. It is easy to understand the determination of the war party; the repression of the Lombards by Radetzky's troops after the Piedmontese withdrawal the previous summer had caused considerable emotion; Schwarzenberg seemed unlikely to accept any compromise, and the overwhelming cost of keeping an army inactive in the field meant that Piedmont must either demobilize or seek a final decision in war. Yet the renewal of hostilities was a hopeless project from the start. The failure of the Italian states to come to any agreement among themselves condemned Piedmont to fight entirely alone, and there was little likelihood of any assistance from Great Britain or France, both of whom wanted only a peaceful settlement in Italy. Nothing daunted, however, the Piedmontese government placed the army under the command of a Polish general, Chrzanowski, and staked everything on a last throw.

The war lasted less than a week. On 20 March Radetzky crossed the Ticino and advanced on Mortara. Chrzanowski seemed at first to attempt a direct advance on Milan, but then had to pull back to meet Radetzky's thrust. On 21 March Mortara was taken by the Austrians and by 23 March Chrzanowski had fallen back to a position in front of Novara. Here Radetzky attacked and after a day of fierce fighting Charles Albert's generals confessed that they could not continue the action and that a surrender must be negotiated. Radetzky's terms, however, were so heavy that Charles Albert preferred to abdicate rather than to accept them. 'Since today I have failed to find death on the battlefield, I make my last sacrifice for my country: I lay down my crown and abdicate in favour of my son, the Duke of Savoy.' He set off at once, escaped undetected through the Austrian lines, and travelled through France and Spain to Oporto, where he died the following July—a Hamlet who, having cast aside his doubts, had still failed to find a solution to his problems in resolute action.

The revolutionary movement in Italy did not long survive

Novara. Piedmont suffered no territorial loss in the final peace treaty, since Schwarzenberg was anxious not to antagonize Great Britain and France, and the principal demand was an indemnity of 75 million lire to Austria. Within Piedmont, Victor Emmanuel duly succeeded to the throne and agreed to retain the constitution which his father had granted. In April the moderates in Florence managed to overthrow Guerrazzi's government and declared for the return of the Grand Duke. Leopold had, meanwhile, appealed to the Emperor Francis Joseph, and in May the Austrian army, advancing south to occupy Modena, Parma, and Lucca, moved on into Tuscany, forced its way into Leghorn against the resistance of the populace, and on 25 May occupied Florence. Venice continued to hold out, but the withdrawal of the Piedmontese fleet made the end inevitable and in August the city surrendered, although Manin and Pepe were able to make good their escape

In Rome, too, the revolution went down fighting. In March, Mazzini, shortly after his arrival, had been elected by the Assembly as one of the Triumvirs with full power to defend the Republic. During his short period of rule he did his best to preserve law and order, only confiscated some of the land of the religious houses, which was shared out among farmers at nominal rents, and in his treatment of the clergy tried to give substance to the claim that the new republic would not interfere with the Pope's spiritual authority. There was a wilder note in the presence of the Italian patriot, Guiseppe Garibaldi, whom the news of the events in Europe had brought back from an adventurous career in South America, and Mazzini was careful to keep his red-shirted Legion away from the city of Rome. But the Roman Republic had not long in which to demonstrate to the world that its republicanism was an orderly form of government that respected private property. On 25 April a French expeditionary force under Oudinot landed at Civita Vecchia and within a few days began its march on Rome.

Louis Napoleon's decision to intervene in Italy—apparently so contrary to the ideals of the new French Republic—was dictated by domestic and diplomatic considerations (see p. 150). At home he had become increasingly aware of the general sympathy with the Pope, a feeling by no means restricted to the right-wing deputies of the French Assembly; and in Italy itself he dared not allow the Habsburgs to use the flight of Pius as an excuse for an advance as far south as Rome. Similarly, Mazzini's decision to fight to the last was purely political. There could be no hope of a successful resistance for long, but he believed that the mere fact that their enemies would have to crush them by force would be a proclamation to the world that the Republic of Rome, the only possible capital for a united Italy, had lived and suffered and one day would rise again.

In fact, the French were hoping not to fight at all, but when on

30 April they were bloodily repulsed at the western gates of the city, military self-esteem made it essential that Rome should be. taken. If Mazzini wanted glory for his doomed Republic, surely he had it now. The Austrians were approaching from the north, the Neapolitans from the south, and there was a Spanish army at Gaeta. Garibaldi, who had brought his Legion back into Rome in time to drive off the French on 30 April, dominated the military scene. In May, while a French envoy, de Lesseps, negotiated with Mazzini—a lull during which Oudinot was able to build up his reinforcements at Civita Vecchia—Garibaldi turned south to check the Neapolitan advance. Then, on 3 June, the French, now 20,000 strong, began their assault and for the rest of that month the fighting raged as Garibaldi's troops were gradually driven back from the Villa Corsini, then to the western gate, then to the Aurelian wall; they were amateurs, hopelessly outnumbered, fighting without any chance of success, and on the last day of the month Garibaldi, battle-stained but still defiant, had to report to the Triumvirs that no further defence was possible.

With the surrender the French occupied Rome. The Assembly was dissolved and the keys of the city were sent to Pius, who appointed three cardinals to rule until his return in April 1850. Mazzini escaped and made his way to London. Garibaldi in an epic journey northwards, during which his wife Anita died, eventually reached the coast of Tuscany, from where he sailed to Tangier and later to the United States.

Thus, by the summer of 1849, the great hope of Italian unification seemed utterly crushed. It could be argued that the Italians had never deserved to succeed, for they had remained a prey to local jealousies which even their hatred for the Austrians could not overcome. Yet two other factors lie at the root of their failure. First, the military effort of Piedmont had shown that Charles Albert had been wrong to believe that *Italia farà da sé*; the Quadrilateral was too strong a bastion for the Italians to act without a powerful military ally. Second, the Pope's refusal to give his support had ruled out any possibility of a compromise solution that might have had the blessing of Catholic Europe. Yet with that refusal a further emotional factor had emerged, which until this time the extremists had lacked. The Mazzinian republicans had lost their city of Rome, but they had created a legend and in history legends often count for more than hard realistic facts.

3. The life and death of the Second Republic in France

In attempting to assess the French revolution of 1848 it is easy to assume that a republic which lasted for less than four years was doomed from the beginning. Certainly among the right wing and even the moderates there was little belief in a form of government which only the unexpected fall of Louis Philippe had forced upon them. The Spanish ambassador described France at this time as a country 'filled with monarchists who cannot establish a monarchy and who groan under the weight of a republic which has no republicans to defend it'. In the circumstances it might seem simple, indeed inevitable, that the newly elected President should soon establish himself in a more permanent and resplendent position, and the enigmatic melancholy of Louis Napoleon lends strength to the notion of the conspirator about to take his final step to absolute power. He was inscrutable. 'Les paroles qu'on lui adressait étaient comme les pierres qu'on jette dans un puits,' wrote de Tocqueville in his *Souvenirs*; 'on en entendait le bruit, mais on ne savait jamais ce qu'elles devenaient.'

Yet a republic, which, in Thiers' famous phrase *nous divise le moins*, was not an inappropriate *modus vivendi* for nineteenth-century France. Even during its short lifetime there was very little likelihood of the monarchists or the Socialists gaining their ends, and although there is not much doubt over Napoleon's intentions, it would be wrong to underestimate the difficulties that confronted him at this decisive stage in his career. He had constantly to walk a tightrope. His greatest strength lay in the fact that he could claim to represent the choice of the French people. He dared not alienate that support, yet at the same time he needed the goodwill of an influential section of the upper and middle classes who had only accepted him as a temporary expedient against some left-wing form of government.

This state of dilemma was well illustrated by his action over the Roman Republic in 1849. After Charles Albert's defeat outside Novara in March 1849, the prospect of Austrian influence becoming established in Piedmont was naturally abhorrent to France, and it was out of consideration for this that the Austrians imposed only the mildest terms. Within a month, however, the restoration of Habsburg rule in Tuscany pointed clearly to an impending attack by the Austrian forces on the Roman Republic. Traditional French interests in Italy and Louis Napoleon's own instincts as a former *Carbanaro* were in accord at this point in the orders to Oudinot to sail for Civita Vecchia on 21 April with 7,000 men. The Austrians were to be forestalled, but the problem of the expedition's ultimate role remained unresolved. Was it to be a reinforcement for Mazzini's Republic? Or was the Republic to be crushed and Pope Pius IX restored? The answer was provided by the energetic repulse of Oudinot's troops by Garibaldi when they attempted to enter the city, and by the election in France, on 13 May, of a new Assembly in which Bonapartists collaborating with monarchists created a right-wing majority of 500 out of 750 seats. The clericals were to have their Pope restored, and the hopeless failure of Ledru-Rollin's rising in Paris on 13 June meant the end of Mazzini's last hope.

During the following twelve months the conservatives in the Chamber continued to make good their position. In March 1850 *la loi Falloux*, named after the minister who introduced it, established liberty of teaching for any person or institution, thereby allowing complete freedom for the religious orders to establish their own secondary schools and institutions of advanced education.* In the same month some thirty by-elections to fill the place of those deputies who had been arrested for their part in the rising of the previous June resulted in the return of twenty candidates of Socialist or extreme republican views. To the bourgeois this awoke all the fears of a new left-wing insurrection, and in May they made use of a loophole in the constitution to decree a three-years residential qualification for all voters—a refinement which had the effect of disfranchising about three million of the poorer classes.

In the summer of 1850 all sides were thinking in terms of a régime which would supersede the Second Republic. The extreme left, contrary to expectation, disregarded any possibility of insurrection and centred their energies on preparations for the election of a new President and Assembly, due in 1852; monarchists paid visits to their respective sovereigns, Orleanists to Louis Philippe at Claremont in Surrey, Legitimists to the Bourbon Count de Chambord, 'Henry V', at Wiesbaden. It was, however, the President who embarked upon the most significant campaign. The developments of the last eighteen months had been something of an embarrassment to Louis Napoleon, who could never be sure that public opinion would not associate him exclusively with a right-wing movement, and in August and September he made two journeys throughout France stopping at many of the larger cities to preach the Bonapartist gospel.

On his return he felt sufficiently sure of his position to challenge the Assembly; yet he did attempt at first to gain his ends in cooperation with the deputies. Between May and July 1851 he struggled to pass an amendment to the constitution which would have prolonged his tenure of office, but failed to win the necessary majority of three-quarters. By the autumn of 1851, however, when the expiry of his term of office was not far distant, he was already thinking in terms of a *coup d' état*. In November his attempt to gain the repeal of the electoral law of May 1850 was defeated by the Assembly— possibly a cunning means of enhancing his own popularity at the expense of the Assembly, although there are indications that he genuinely wished the measure to be passed. In the same month an

* These schools were, nevertheless, to be under the supervision of the University of France—a fact which angered the extreme Ultramontanes.

attempt by the right wing, by now highly mistrustful of their President, to secure control over the military forces of the country, was
defeated by the republicans in the Assembly, who saw the measure
simply as a monarchist manoeuvre. And then in the early hours of
2 December—the anniversary of his uncle's proclamation of the first
Empire and of the victory at Austerlitz—Louis Napoleon struck.
The announcement of a conspiracy against the State, his opponents
divided and surprised, the control of the necessary military forces
at the disposal of the President, all made the outcome a foregone
conclusion; and within forty-eight hours Louis Napoleon had no
need to trouble himself any further with the restrictions imposed by
the constitution of the Second Republic.

Part 4

The Destruction of the Vienna Settlement 1851–71

Chapter 14

The Changing Background

The practical outcome of the revolutions of 1848 might well seem depressing to liberals throughout most of the Continent. The national movements had failed utterly; after the collapse of the Second Republic the character of Louis Napoleon's government remained as yet an unknown quantity, and outside France the advance of constitutional rule was restricted to only a few small regions of Europe. In Belgium and the Netherlands the powers of the existing legislatures and the size of the electorates had been increased. The Danish king had bowed to the demands of a popular Convention which tempered the royal despotism with a two-chamber Assembly elected on a limited franchise. In Prussia and Piedmont, although the forms of parliamentary government recently granted by Frederick William IV and Charles Albert had survived, the Prussian system, after the modifications of April 1849 (see p. 142), weighted representation heavily in the interest of the richest class, while the Piedmontese rested on an extremely narrow franchise. Beyond this, only the Swiss could claim a fundamental revision of their whole constitutional pattern—the establishment of a strong federal authority based on universal manhood suffrage.

To the north and the east nothing had been challenged. Sweden had been relatively untouched by the revolutions and despite a gradual trend towards a greater liberalism it was not until 1866 that the four Estates of the *Riksdag* were transformed into an elective bicameral Parliament. In Russia there had been no chance of any outbreak. Tsar Nicholas's police had even pounced upon what was little more than a politically-minded literary society and twenty-two of the suspected rebels—Dostoevsky among them—had reached the scaffold on a winter's morning in 1849 before the news of their reprieve was announced and they were dispatched instead to Siberia.

In Italy and central Europe much indeed had been challenged, but to little avail. 'From Rome, which fell before a people which betrayed humanity, to Hungary sold to the enemy by a general who betrayed his fatherland, everything in 1849 has been sinful, gruesome and vile,' wrote Alexander Herzen. In Italy, Lombardy and Venetia remained under military rule until 1857 and the lands of *émigrés* were confiscated. Austrian garrisons in the northern duchies and legations ensured the suppression of all forms of constitution, while in the Kingdom of Naples absolutism had already been restored. French troops continued to occupy Rome until 1870* and although Pius IX did retain the *Consulta*, he had no wish to attempt any further experiments in constitutional government.

In Germany all traces of the Frankfurt Parliament were quickly swept away; the German flag of black, red, and gold was removed from the hall of the Federal Diet, and the ships of the national fleet which the liberals had begun to create were sold by public auction. Among the states themselves recent constitutional changes were virtually wiped out in Mecklemburg, Saxony, Hanover, and Hesse-Cassel, and throughout Germany leading liberals were executed, imprisoned or forced to escape abroad. Even in Prussia, where the constitution survived, local self-government was strictly curtailed, the power of police surveillance greatly increased, and in 1854 the Upper Chamber was transformed into a House of Peers.

In Hungary there were over a hundred executions including thirteen generals and Count Batthyány; the separate identity of the Kingdom was smothered in a new policy of centralized absolutism, whereby Schwarzenberg and Alexander Bach gave full expression to the tendencies already suggested in the constitution of 1849 (see p. 140), which was itself revoked in December 1851. Everywhere throughout the Habsburg dominions German was to be the official language, and in 1855 a Concordat restored to the Roman Catholic Church its old power of supervision over education, a privilege of which it had been deprived by Joseph II in the 1780s and which had not even been revived in the settlement of 1815.

It has been seen how the liberals had only known success in the 1848 revolutions where they had been able to gain their ends without becoming dependent upon the forces of the urban masses, and how failure had inevitably followed when their fears that the working class might gain too great a control over the revolutionary movement had quelled the liberal attack on the old order. To the governments it seemed that there was a further lesson to be learnt; they were confirmed in their determination to make use of the natural conservatism of the peasantry. In France it had been the small farmer on whom Louis Napoleon had been able to rely for his strongest support; in Austria, the peasant, once he had gained the abolition of feudal tenure in September 1848, had lost all interest in the later efforts of the revolutionaries, and in the Hungarian revolt the mobilizing of the Croat peasantry against their Magyar overlords had merely been a repetition of the Habsburg stratagem of 1846 in Galicia (see p. 114).

---

* Except for a short interval in 1867 (see p. 209).

The idea had already been formulated before the revolutions. 'Our princes have not yet exhausted the resources with which they may survive the struggle against triumphant mediocrity,' commented Radowitz in 1846. 'Let them but have the courage to turn to the masses.' Thus, throughout central Europe in the 1850s the governments did not rest content with the suppression of liberal activity; they embarked upon a deliberate policy of encouraging the peasantry and the handcraftsmen in the face of a growing industrialism. In those parts of Germany where the process of rural emancipation from feudal obligations had not yet been completed, it was greatly accelerated. In Prussia government measures passed in 1850 entitled *all* peasants to commute their manorial dues and established special banks offering credit facilities to farmers. Thus, whereas by 1848 only 70,000 Prussian peasants in the regions east of the Elbe had obtained their freedom, a further 640,000 were to do so between 1850 and 1865.

Similarly the governments attempted to bolster up the craftsmen's guilds whose intricate regulation of labour might act as a brake on *laissez-faire* capitalism. 'Handcraftsmen,' wrote Bismarck in October 1849 at the beginning of his political career, '. . . constitute the backbone of the burgher class, of an element whose survival is essential to a healthy national life and whose maintenance seems to me to be fully as important as was the creation of a free peasantry at the beginning of this century, for the sake of which the authorities did not boggle at serious infringements of law and property.' Nassau and Saxe-Gotha in 1849, Frankfurt in 1850, and Bavaria in 1853 all decreed greater control over the practice of crafts. In Prussia guilds were restored as early as February 1849; in the following years some 4,600 craft corporations were re-established and after 1854 they came more directly under State supervision. In Prussia another stroke in the governmental campaign against the new capitalist class was to benefit the industrial worker. In 1853 a Factory Act prohibited the employment of children under the age of twelve in factories and mines; those between twelve and fourteen were not to work more than seven hours a day, were to be free from night work and were to continue their education in factory schools. Such a measure, reinforced by a system of inspection, gave far greater protection than had yet been extended to the young in Great Britain, France, or in most other parts of Germany.

Benefit there might be for many, yet the assumptions behind these measures remained utterly impracticable. This conservative trend throughout central Europe in the 1850s was the last stand of a social order which, although it had survived the assaults of 1848, could not hope to resist the cumulative forces of economic change with which it was sooner or later bound to come to terms.

The statistics of the production of coal and iron (see Appendix 10, p. 495) show clearly how the tide of industrialism was moving progressively eastwards across the Continent in the years between 1850 and 1870. In Great Britain the increase in the annual output of coal from 57 to 112 million tonnes still kept her economy comfortably in a class of its own; the most significant change on the Continent was to be seen in Germany, where the annual output rose from 6 to 34 million tonnes, whereas in France, although trebled, it stood only at 13 million tonnes in 1870. Similarly, in the manufacture of pig-iron Great Britain still remained well ahead with an output of slightly less than 6 million tonnes in 1870, while Germany in these two decades raised hers by 1,185,000 to 1,300,000 tonnes as against France's increase of 78,000 to 1,180,000. In 1856 Great Britain was to be the home of another fundamental discovery, the Bessemer process for the manufacture of modern steel, and by 1870 she was turning out 700,000 tonnes—more than double the production of either France or Germany.

Equally striking was the continuing revolution in communications. The 22,540 kilometres of railway track that had been laid in Europe by 1850 had grown by 1870 to 104,650 kilometres, and the international network across the whole Continent encouraged the development of a cheap postal service. At sea the development of the steamship had halved the time for the crossing of the Atlantic as early as 1838, and the general bulk of world freight had risen from 10 million nautical tonnes in 1840 to 25 million in 1870. The most startling conquest of the ocean, however, was represented by the electric telegraph; a cable from Dover to Calais was laid in 1851, and Europe had been linked with the United States by 1866 and with India and Australia by 1871.

All this astonishing increase in the tempo of economic life naturally stimulated a greater borrowing of capital. Banks for the promoting of companies sprang up in profusion—*Crédit Lyonnais, Crédit Industriel*, and the *Société Générale* in France, *Kreditanstalt* in Austria, and many others in the German states; the international ramifications of banking were well illustrated by the French *Crédit Mobilier* under the Péreire brothers, one-third of whose shares in the 1850s were held by British investors and whose promotion of industrial joint-stock enterprises eventually led to the acquisition of considerable interests in Austrian and Russian railways. Governments, too, availed themselves of the new facilities and between 1848 and 1872 the total public debt of European states rose from £1,730 million to £4,605 million—much of it raised from outside the frontiers of each state.

Another aspect of the economic scene was the general growth of the population of Europe (see Appendix 7, p. 492) which rose steadily in the 1850s and 1860s from 266 to 296 million. This increase is all the more remarkable in that some five million emigrants left the Continent during these years—predominantly central European and Irish peasantry moving to the United States (see Appendix 9, p. 494)—the annual average reaching 350,000 in the early 1850s, dropping to 200,000 and then rising to 400,000 a year by 1870.

The rate of increase within the various regions of Europe differed enormously. In 1850 France and Germany had each numbered slightly less than 36 million, yet the French, even after the acquisition of Savoy and Nice in 1860 (see p. 181), were only 37 million by 1870, in contrast to 41 million Germans; thus in population, as well as in industrial output, these were the years when Germany clearly began to outstrip her rival across the Rhine. The most startling change, however, was to be seen in Russia where an additional 20 million had brought her to a total of 77 million in 1870. Another feature, common to most regions of Europe was the growth in the size of the urban population. The eighteenth-century streets and squares were becoming a historic core about which new residential areas sprawled out over the surrounding countryside, and as the old walls and fortifications were swallowed up by the towns that they had once defended, they were gradually demolished to make way for broad encircling boulevards—such as the Ringstrasse in Vienna, the great thoroughfares of Napoleon III's Paris, and similar roadways in Florence and Turin.

The general economic pattern of the period was one of rising prices, due to the greater volume of trade, and particularly to the enormous increase in the world's output of gold after the discoveries in California and Australia. This tendency was interrupted by two great slumps in 1857 and 1866 which illustrated the growing closeness of economic relationship throughout the whole world, already suggested by the earlier crashes of 1837 and 1846 (see p. 90). Prosperity seeped down only very slowly to improve the condition of the poor, and the fine new façades of the towns often served to mask the appalling slums that lay behind. Still, the position of the working class *was* changing slightly for the better in these years, since wages did rather more than keep pace with prices and continued to rise until 1873.

Another aspect of the economic pattern was a movement towards free trade. Great Britain had long espoused this policy; the Netherlands and the *Zollverein* slowly lowered their tariffs; in 1850 Belgium repealed her Corn Laws, and in 1857 Denmark's agreement to abolish her Sound dues was another step in the same direction. Unlike their counterpart in Great Britain, however, continental industrialists were seriously divided over the question of protection, and the governments accordingly approached Free Trade with considerable caution, preferring to make private trade agreements with individual countries, rather than to adopt a general principle. Thus, as early as 1851, Cavour (see p. 174) as Piedmontese Minister of Agriculture, Commerce, and Marine had completed Free Trade treaties with Great Britain, France, and Belgium, while France's famous treaty with Great Britain, as a result of Richard Cobden's visit to Paris in 1860, was paralleled by others with Belgium, Turkey, the *Zollverein*, Italy, the Netherlands, and Austria.

The full consequences of industrialism were far more than purely economic. The growing concentration of the working classes in the factories was soon to facilitate their political organization, while in central and eastern Europe the drift of the peasantry into the towns lent strength to the development of nationalism. For the governments, new techniques were to bring greater powers and wider problems. French engineering skill, for example, which had accomplished the cutting of the Suez canal by 1869, not merely shortened the commercial route to the east; it opened up political issues over the future control of the canal, which had originally caused the British to oppose its construction. Military and naval forces, too, were to be revolutionized as muskets were gradually replaced by rifles, muzzle-loading cannon by breech-loaders, and wooden sailing ships of the line by screw-driven ironclads. 'To move an army now is to move a great city', commented *The Times* in 1861, and on the Continent General Staffs were growing increasingly aware of the strategic significance of railways. Troop movements by rail had played some part in the suppression of the revolt in Cracow in 1846 and in Hungary in 1849, and in the 1860s the varying speeds with which countries could mobilize their armies were not merely to alter decisively the balance of military power, but were also to become a factor in diplomacy of which Bismarck was to make devastating use.

All these changes pointed to an eventual alliance between the rulers and the new forces of industry and commerce. In the west and in Scandinavia this alliance had been slowly forcing itself on the governments since 1815, gradually weakening the chances of survival for Metternich's Europe. In Piedmont Cavour was to seize on it from the beginning of his political career. In central Europe the change came late and then with a dramatic suddenness, as the realization dawned on the governments that an obstinate determination to resist the advance of the new capitalist classes by encouraging the peasantry and the handcraft guilds was not only useless but positively harmful.

In Prussia the anti-liberal reaction lasted until 1858, when the insanity of Frederick William IV could no longer be disguised and his brother William took over as Prince Regent. The conservative government of Manteuffel and the Gerlachs, already discredited by the failure of an attempt in 1857 to regain control of the Swiss canton of Neuchâtel (see p. 133), had been weakened still further by the economic slump of the same year and was now replaced by a more liberal ministry under Prince Karl Anton von Hohenzollern-Sigmaringen. In the following years Prussian parliamentary elections lent impetus to this swing away from the right, and the subsequent tendency to ease restrictions on industry in Prussia was reflected almost immediately afterwards in the legislation of more than a third of the other German states—as well as in Austria after the shock of the Italian war of 1859 (see p. 178).

Nor was this change limited to the attitude of the governments. The awareness of their economic strength had enabled the Italian and German middle class to recover from their recent disillusionment and to dream once again of the commercial advantages that they would derive from national unification. Yet they, too, had learnt their lesson from 1848. This time they did not intend to succumb to the romance of political idealism divorced from the hard facts of power; with a new realism they began to look to Piedmont and Prussia as the only possible leaders who might accomplish their aim through a process of diplomacy and war, without at the same time letting loose the radicalism of the masses. The year 1859 marked not only the beginning of Cavour's great venture to form with French help a North Italian Kingdom, but also the organization of the *Deutscher Nationalverein* (German National Association) which aimed at the creation of a united Germany under Prussian leadership. A new social alliance was in the making, and events to which it soon gave rise in Italy and Germany were finally to destroy the pattern of central Europe devised at the Congress of Vienna.

Chapter 15

The French Second Empire 1852–70

1. The domestic scene in France

In France the Second Republic had succumbed almost without a blow to Napoleon's *coup d'état* of 2 December 1851. In Paris the only serious street fighting two days later had been crushed in an afternoon; in the provinces left-wing republicans had held out for a while in the south-east, but the major cities remained firmly under control. Thus, within three weeks Louis Napoleon could gamble on a plebiscite, and although some of the 7,481,000 votes approving his action and accepting the need to redraw the constitution may have been due to official pressure, the bulk of them were no more than a confirmation of the election that had carried him to the presidency three years before.

The new constitution was completed in January 1852. It opened with a resounding guarantee of the principles of 1789 and then proceeded to name Louis Napoleon as President for ten years. This office was entrusted with the fullest executive powers, including command of the armed forces, the initiation of all legislation and the appointment of ministers and officials. There were to be two Chambers—a Senate of 150 selected by the President and with its functions limited to a right of veto on all laws that might violate the constitution; and a *Corps Législatif*, elected by universal suffrage every six years and only able to vote on new laws without discussion. This representative Chamber was not to contain any ministers and the chairmen of both were to be appointed by the President.

It might well seem that Louis Napoleon had provided himself with an instrument admirably suited to the establishment of autocracy. Certainly he envisaged a form of strong personal rule; the deliberations of the Senate were not to be public, while those of the *Corps Législatif* were only to be published in an official summary. For the elections the constituencies were carefully arranged in the conservative interest, and the Prefects and mayors received instructions for the promotion of official candidates. On the other hand, Louis Napoleon's system clearly depended upon much more than a mere power of repression. The members of the Senate were irremovable and after the initial creation there would be no further possibility of his packing the House. The *Corps Législatif* might not be able to discuss the laws and the budget, but they did at least have the right of voting on them. Furthermore, they were elected by universal manhood suffrage on a secret ballot, and later political developments were to prove this to be much more than an empty form. Had Louis Napoleon stood at the head of a highly organized Bonapartist party, this would not have been so. In fact, Bonapartism was more of a mood than a party and he had instead to rely upon that general appeal which had already taken him so far. 'When one bears our name and when one is at the head of the government', he wrote, 'there are two things one must do: satisfy the interests of the most numerous classes and attach to oneself the upper classes.' Thus, in the first elections the official candidates were not selected by those Bonapartist committees that did exist, but by the Prefects, and were drawn from a wide range of political views including a number of Legitimists, Orleanists, and men of recent wealth. In the outcome, over six million voters went to the polls, five-sixths of the official candidates were returned and only six opposition candidates were successful, four of whom were republican. For the moment, at least, Louis Napoleon had the situation that he needed, but the broad base for which he hoped could never be entirely stable, and the authoritarian nature of his government remained very much at the mercy of public opinion in an age when the technical means of controlling it were still comparatively weak.

It was typical of Louis Napoleon's whole conception of his rule that he should revert once again to a plebiscite before taking the final step in his venture. In November 1852 seven million voters agreed to the restoration of hereditary rule, and on 2 December the Prince President became the Emperor Napoleon III—a style that took a leaf out of the royalist book in emphasizing the myth that Napoleon I's son, the Duke de Reichstadt, had reigned after his father's abdication. The Emperor now had only to find an Empress, and there followed in January 1853 Napoleon's marriage to Eugénie de Montijo, a Spanish noblewoman, who in 1856 gave birth to a son and thus provided an heir to the Imperial throne. Yet for all his efforts to acquire respectability Napoleon never quite succeeded in living down the origins of the Second Empire. As a monarch he remained to the end a *parvenu*, a conspirator who had made good; always there was a touch of theatre about this reappearance of a Napoleonic court at the Tuileries and in the popular imagination the memory of the Second Empire is essentially a romantic one, a world of petticoat influence and elegant licence amid the flickering gas-lamps of Paris.

None of this, however, should obscure the fact that Napoleon's reign marks a time of immense energy and activity for the domestic economy,* a time when Saint-Simonian influences found their most powerful practical expression. A new institution, *Crédit Mobilier*, under the Péreire brothers undertook the financing of a variety of industrial concerns, while *Crédit Foncier* provided much of the capital needed for urban development. The government was particularly concerned to extend the railway system, and by 1870 the length of track in service had grown to 17,710 kilometres. The value of French imports and exports rose from 2,615 million francs in 1851 to 8,008 million in 1869, and the Paris Exhibition of 1867 proclaimed French industrial advance to the world. Paris itself was the greatest advertisement of Napoleon III's rule. Under the masterful direction of Baron Haussmann, the Prefect of the Seine, great broad boulevards cut through the tangle of narrow streets which had earlier resounded with the excitements of the revolutionary years, and across which the barricades had been thrown up in 1830 and 1848. Twenty thousand houses were demolished; more than double that number were erected, and the great shopping centres, the new Opera, the market of Les Halles and the development of the Parc Monceau, the Buttes de Chaumont, and the Bois de Boulogne, all date from this period. The city which the twentieth-century tourist sees today is largely the Paris of Napoleon III.

Authoritarian rule proved not only efficient; it was also mild. The laws controlling the press had in principle been inherited from the Second Republic, but did at least allow an editor two indiscretions, and although tribunals had had to deal with 26,000 persons arrested after the *coup d'état*, 10,000 of these were acquitted or simply placed under police surveillance. Of the rest who were imprisoned or transported to Algeria, only 6,153 were still unpardoned by 1853, while in 1856 all who were prepared to accept the existing government were allowed to return.

Nevertheless, by 1860 there were signs that the general popularity on which Napoleon based his government was beginning to be seriously weakened. He had always hoped to retain the support of the clericals, but the Ultramontane group was becoming increasingly impatient of the Concordat, and the growth of Church schools, consequent on *la loi Falloux* of 1850 (see p. 151), added fuel to the conflict with the secular state system of education. It was, however, over Napoleon's foreign policy that the issue really came to a head. In the Crimean War clerical interests and national aims went hand in hand, but in 1859 Napoleon embarked upon an Italian adventure in which his support of Cavour seemed to threaten the whole basis of the Temporal Power of the Papacy; the liberal sentiments of the Emperor and the conservatism of the clericals had clearly become irreconcilable. Then again, Napoleon's desire for greater freedom

* For comparative figures see pp. 157–8 and Appendix 10, p. 495.

of trade had aroused the hostility of many business interests, particularly the smaller ones who still depended upon a system of protection, and the Anglo-French commercial treaty of 1860, which reduced import duties on British coal and manufactured goods and on French wines and brandy, proved to be the forerunner of similar treaties involving reciprocal reductions with Belgium in 1861, the *Zollverein* in 1862, Italy in 1863, Switzerland in 1864, Spain and the Netherlands in 1865, and Austria and Portugal in 1866. Lastly, the expansion of industry had naturally led to the considerable growth of a proletariat concentrated in large towns where republicanism began actively to revive.

Napoleon's response to these dangers was to veer towards the left. In 1859 the remaining exiles were allowed to return without the imposition of any condition, although a few, such as Victor Hugo in the Channel Islands, still refused to live under Bonapartist rule. By a decree of 24 November 1860 liberal changes were introduced into the constitution, permitting the Senate and the *Corps Législatif* to vote a reply to the Emperor's address at the beginning of each session and to publish the record of their debates. In 1864 the working class were granted the right to strike. In 1867 both Houses were allowed to interrogate ministers, and the Senate acquired a more parliamentary role when it was given a suspensive veto over legislation passed by the *Corps Législatif*. In 1868 a relaxation of the press laws resulted in the appearance of an additional 150 newspapers, the vast majority of which were hostile to the government.

This tendency towards a greater liberalism was a calculated risk which, although it inevitably offered greater scope for the forces of opposition, might have gone far to preserve the Second Empire. Unfortunately it was accompanied by other factors. Napoleon's health was failing fast in the 1860s and his own personal control over events at home and abroad during these years was gravely weakened. The system of official candidates was no longer so effective; the mayors were becoming more independent and a pamphlet published in 1868 commented: 'the Prefect is no longer the dazzling star who alone spreads his light on the *département*.' More disastrous still, the Emperor's foreign policy encountered one check after another; for a Napoleonic régime this meant a serious loss of prestige.

The consequence of this decline was to be seen in the elections of 1863 and 1869. The republicans who had only gained five seats in 1857 were able to add to their numbers, capturing many of the larger cities, and were strengthened by the appearance of such personalities as Léon Gambetta, Jules Ferry, and Henri de Rochefort. To the right of the republicans a new Third Party under Thiers demanded greater concessions in the direction of parliamentary government—winning 35 seats in 1863 and 116 in 1869. At no time did the government positively lose an election, but the voting in 1869 convinced Napoleon that the moment had come to take a further step towards constitutional rule.

The outcome was that short-lived period known as the 'Liberal Empire'. The changes decreed in the autumn of 1869 granted the *Corps Législatif* the right to initiate legislation, completed the transformation of the Senate into an upper House and allowed ministers to be drawn from the members of either Chamber. As his Prime Minister, Napoleon selected Émile Ollivier, one of the five republican deputies of 1857, a superb orator, who had by now become less extreme in his political outlook. In January 1870 Ollivier formed a ministry from official candidates and moderates, and after the right of confirming any constitutional revision had been transferred from the Senate to the people, a plebiscite was held in May in which the electorate were asked to accept all the changes that had been introduced since 1860. Once again the government gained the approval that it sought with an overwhelming vote of seven million, although the two million abstentions suggested some doubts and the one and a half million who opposed reflected the republican hold on the cities.

It can never be known whether these concessions would have given a new lease of life to the Empire. Certainly they had not yet satisfied all political aspirations, for the ministers remained responsible primarily to the Emperor—a situation more reminiscent of eighteenth-century England than of a modern parliamentary democracy—yet the responsiveness of the Empire to political forces does suggest an elasticity that might have been equal to further domestic tensions. As it turned out, Napoleon's fate was sealed ultimately by defeat in war. 'More than ever before,' he said in May, 'can we look forward to the future without fear', but before the summer was out, his country had been overrun by the Prussian army and in September the abdication of the Emperor brought this colourful epoch of French history to a close.

2. The Crimean War 1854–6

Little more than a year after the establishment of the Second Empire France found herself once again at war with Russia, this time with Great Britain as her ally. The seige and capture of Sebastopol, the great Russian naval base in the Crimea, did not perhaps wipe out the memory of the retreat from Moscow; yet the eventual surrender of Russia followed by the imposition of terms at the Congress of Paris in 1856 marked a restoration of political prestige for France that she had not known since the days of the first Napoleon.

The initial circumstances of the quarrel had already been developing in the last years of Louis Philippe. The French supported the claims of the Latin Catholics, and the Russians those of the Greek

Orthodox over the Holy Places in Jerusalem and Bethlehem, and after the accession of Napoleon III the Turkish government was subjected to mounting pressure from both sides. Concessions were made to the Latins and then revoked in a secret agreement with the Greeks, whereupon the French ambassador, La Valette, coming back to Constantinople in April 1852, insisted on his ninety-gun screw-driven battleship, the *Charlemagne*, sailing through the Dardanelles, and in July a threatened bombardment of Tripoli by a French naval squadron forced the Turks to give way.

As usual, however, these details had little to do with the fundamental issues at stake. Religious disputes in the nineteenth century did not in themselves lead to international hostilities. Nor, for that matter, was the Crimean War simply the continuation of a vendetta between a Bonaparte and the Russian Tsar; it arose out of a question of far wider import—the extent to which the Powers should allow the extension of Russian influence in the Balkans. In January 1853 Tsar Nicholas began to sound British reactions to proposals for a partition of Turkey, but these came to very little and in any case he did not push them too hard. His real interest was in the special mission of Prince Menshikov to Constantinople, who after some preliminary negotiation virtually presented the Turks with an ultimatum in May. Control of the Holy Places was to be granted to the Greeks and a Russian protectorate was to be recognized over all Greek Christians under Turkish rule. It was this second demand that revealed the full extent of the Tsar's ambitions, since this would enormously increase Russia's influence over the whole of Turkey without the embarrassment of a partition among the Powers. In Great Britain Palmerston had been dismissed from the Foreign Office in December 1851 after his over-hasty acceptance of Louis Napoleon's *coup d'état* and the coalition government formed under Aberdeen in December 1852 seemed unlikely to intervene. From Austria Nicholas expected positive support; the Habsburgs were already indebted for Russian assistance in Hungary in 1849, and as recently as February 1853 they had had a dispute of their own with Turkey whom they had forced to abandon a projected invasion of Montenegro. Thus, Nicholas was convinced that he was now well placed to impose his demand for a protectorate with the threat of an occupation of the Danubian Principalities.

It was a serious miscalculation. In March 1853 Napoleon had already dispatched the French fleet from Toulon to Salamis, and Stratford Canning, the British ambassador at Constantinople, encouraged the Turks to reject the proposal for a protectorate, although he still hoped for negotiations to continue. The British government was certainly more cautious than the French, but when on the departure of Menshikov Nicholas repeated his threat, the Malta fleet was ordered on 2 June to Besika Bay outside the Dardanelles. Nicholas, however, still felt sufficiently confident to send Russian forces across the Pruth on 2 July, and the occupation of Jassy and Bucharest, the capitals of Moldavia and Wallachia, followed at once.

Now at last, the Tsar learnt that he had really overplayed his hand. Both Vienna and Berlin reacted strongly against this invasion. In Austria Count Buol, who had become Foreign Minister on Schwarzenberg's death in 1852, made it clear that no moral obligation to Russia would allow his government to countenance such an alarming outcome of the Menshikov mission, and turned at once to Great Britain and France. Nicholas, faced with this disappointment, began a diplomatic retreat in accepting the Note which the other four Powers drew up at Vienna in July, whereby Turkey was simply to be asked to guarantee no change in her rule over her Christian subjects 'without previous understanding with the Governments of France and Russia'. This agreement was partly the work of Napoleon and it naturally enhanced his own position both in Europe and among the clericals in France. It was, however, doomed to failure; the Turks refused to accept it and in September a 'violent interpretation' of the Vienna Note by Nesselrode, the Russian Foreign Minister, still maintaining the original aims of the Tsar, suggested that they had been wise to do so.

Throughout the autumn the crisis slowly mounted. On 22 September the French proposed to the British cabinet that their combined fleets should sail through the Dardanelles, and although Stratford Canning resisted this for as long as he could, he had eventually to summon the British fleet to Constantinople in October. Meanwhile, Nicholas was painfully conferring with Francis Joseph and Frederick William IV, but could draw neither of them from a policy of neutrality. In Constantinople the belligerence of Mehemet Ali,* the Turkish Minister of War, was strongly supported by the anti-Russian feeling that had been growing steadily and on 4 October the Sultan declared that there would be war unless the Principalities were evacuated within two weeks. The Russians did not move and by the last week of October Russo-Turkish hostilities had opened north of the Danube. Stratford Canning was still able to hold the Turks back from sending their fleet into the Black Sea, but on 30 November a light flotilla was destroyed by the Russians at Sinope. Although this was a perfectly legitimate operation of war, it had a startling effect upon public opinion in the west—particularly in Great Britain— and in France a £2 million loan was immediately raised for Turkey, while Napoleon declared that if the British fleet would not enter the Black Sea with the French, he would act alone. In January 1854 the British gave way to this pressure, the

---

* He is not to be confused with Mehemet Ali of Egypt who had died in 1849.

two fleets passed through the Bosphorus and after Nicholas had been presented with a demand that his fleet should take no further action against the Turks, the Russian ambassadors were withdrawn from London and Paris. War was officially declared on 31 March, but although Great Britain and France had already signed a treaty with Turkey a fortnight before, they did not actually become allies themselves until 10 April.

None of the participants had seriously expected the outbreak of a major war. Diplomatic miscalculation and the pressure of public opinion had combined to create a situation in which neither side had been able to pull back. Yet behind all the concern for prestige there had been a very real issue in the proposed Russian protectorate over the Balkan Christians, and the occupation of the Principalities, followed by the outbreak of a Russo-Turkish war, had confronted the western Powers with the old threat of a Russian advance on to Constantinople.

It was in order to meet this threat that by the beginning of June 1854 the first British and French contingents were being landed at Varna, a Bulgarian town on the coast of the Black Sea. The key to the situation, however, lay not in the military action of Great Britain and France, but in the attitude of the Central Powers. 'If Prussia and Austria go with us,' commented Prince Albert, 'matters are different and the war becomes impossible for Russia.' By now Nicholas was only too aware of such a danger. On 20 April Austria had formed an alliance with Prussia, in May her army on the Turco-Hungarian frontier was mobilized, and in June the two Powers demanded that Russia should evacuate the Principalities. More ominous still, by July the Austrians were in consultation with the French in drawing up the Four Points on which peace might be negotiated. These were finally established early in August, stipulating a European guarantee of the Principalities, the freedom of the navigation of the Danube, the revision of the Straits Convention of 1841 'in the interests of the Balance of Power in Europe', and the abandonment of the Russian claim to a protectorate over the Christian subjects of Turkey.

Russian policy was inevitably governed by this fickleness on the part of the Austrians. Nicholas dared not allow them to move any closer to the west and accordingly by August his troops were already evacuating the Principalities, which were occupied by Austria during the remainder of the war. The danger, however, was not yet past. In November the Austrians seemed about to join with the Allies in insisting on the Four Points and Nicholas had once again to give way, instructing Gortchakov, the Russian ambassador at Vienna, to open negotiations on them while the war continued. Fortunately for Nicholas, Buol, the Austrian Foreign Minister, intended to do no more than to fish in troubled waters. It was only after the

Russians had made it known that they were prepared to negotiate that he made Austrian military intervention dependent upon their refusal to do so, and then duly collected his reward from Napoleon III in the form of a convention signed on 22 December guaranteeing the territorial *status quo* in Italy. This convention, however, did not prevent the Allies from turning to Piedmont where King Victor Emmanuel, aided by the French ambassador, compelled his Prime Minister Cavour against his own judgement to join the western allies in January 1855, and a small Piedmontese army of 15,000 was dispatched to the Crimea in return for which Cavour was only able to gain a promise of a place at the subsequent congress. In fact, this Piedmontese alliance represented the principal achievement of the diplomats, since Austria would not be drawn any further, and despite two Allied naval expeditions to the Baltic when the fortifications of the Åland Isles were destroyed and Sveaborg, the island fortress outside Helsinki, bombarded, Sweden refused to be enticed out of a cautious neutrality.

Meanwhile, by the autumn of 1854 the revision of the Straits Convention of 1841, the third of the Four Points, implying an Allied aim to neutralize the Black Sea, had become the main issue of the war. This had not played any part in the circumstances of the outbreak, but it was indirectly relevant, since the removal of a Russian fleet from the Black Sea would obviously greatly strengthen Turkey's security. Thus, when the Russian evacuation of the Principalities deprived the Allied forces at Varna of any immediate objective, they were dispatched in September to the Crimea across the Black Sea, preparatory to an assault on Sebastopol. The British and French armies, commanded respectively by Lord Raglan and St Arnaud, numbered together over 50,000. Marching south they imposed a retreat on the Russians at the battle of the Alma, but then instead of making at once for Sebastopol moved inland round the port and eventually took up siege positions on the south side. There followed the appalling winter of the Crimean war; the British drove off the Russian attacks at Balaclava on 25 October and at Inkerman on 5 November, but the troops suffered frightfully on the exposed plateau. Military leadership was hopelessly incompetent on both sides, but it was clear that of the Allies the French army was better supplied and administered than the British. In May 1855 the Kerch peninsula was captured, but it was not until 9 September that the final assault on Sebastopol was successful.

Tsar Nicholas had died earlier that year and his son, who succeeded as Alexander II, was determined to bring the war to an end. An armistice was signed in February 1856 and in the same month a peace congress assembled in Paris. By the terms of the treaty signed in March Russia lost southern Bessarabia, and Kars, which she had taken from Turkey in the Caucasus, was restored to the

Sultan. The Black Sea was to be neutralized and the Straits were to remain closed to warships while Turkey was at peace. The Danube was placed under international control, and Europe, instead of Russia alone, assumed a protectorate over the Principalities and the Christian subjects of the Turks. Finally, by a separate treaty with Great Britain, the Åland Isles in the Baltic were to remain unfortified. Only Piedmont failed to gain any positive advantage, and although it was doubtless pleasant to hear the British Foreign Secretary attack Austria's rule over her subject peoples at the peace congress, Cavour was unable to acquire the duchies of Modena and Parma whose rulers he had suggested might be compensated with Moldavia and Wallachia.

The war had cost the combatants dear. The British lost nearly 33,000 men, and the French 32,000, the vast majority of these through sickness. The Russian losses were heavier, although the figure of 500,000 given by their medical department seems excessive. Both Great Britain and Russia attempted to remedy some of the deficiencies that the war had revealed; the medical and administrative services of the British army were overhauled, and in Russia Tsar Alexander II embarked upon a great programme of general reform (see p. 202). These were perhaps the most lasting results of the war, since the neutralization of the Black Sea which was the most significant change engineered by the victors was only to hold good until 1871 (see p. 218).

Nevertheless, it was precisely in these next fifteen years that the Vienna settlement was finally to be destroyed and the circumstances that made this possible sprang directly from the diplomatic consequences of the Crimean war. First, the Holy Alliance which, if it had any meaning at all, must rest on friendship between Austria and Russia, was utterly shattered, and as a result of Buol's policy of playing off one side against the other Austria was condemned to a fateful isolation. Second, Russia, exhausted by the war, temporarily abandoned any forceful intervention on the European scene and began to look for an ally in France and then later in Prussia. Third, the Congress of Paris marks the opening of a period of French predominance which until 1863 appeared to make Napoleon III the diplomatic arbiter of Europe.

3. The foreign policy of Napoleon III

In the period between the two empires French foreign policy had been fundamentally conservative. The expeditions to Spain in 1823, to Ancona in 1832 and to Rome in 1849 had all been in defence of the established order; caution had prevailed in the crises over Belgium in 1831 and Egypt in 1840, and although there had been an extension of French influence in the Mediterranean during the reign of Louis Philippe, this policy had been developed largely within the limits of the Restoration settlement. The essential factor in the momentous changes of the mid-century decades was Napoleon III's desire to make use of the short-lived pre-eminence of France after 1856 to attempt a radical revision of that settlement. The irony of the story is that he was not equal to such a task and it was Cavour and Bismarck who seized the opportunities with which the Emperor's revolutionary foreign policy provided them.

The habits of of the conspirator died hard and historians share the same uncertainty as his contemporaries over the precise aims of Napoleon's diplomacy, which was always a highly personal matter, *un secret de l'empereur.* Indeed, it has been suggested that he was none too sure of them himself—a sphinx without a riddle, as Bismarck called him. There were, in fact, a variety of motives that inspired the cloudy workings of Napoleon's political imagination. Not all of them were entirely compatible and it was never certain which of them would predominate in the Emperor's mind at any one moment. No Bonaparte could be indifferent to *la gloire*; no ruler in France dependent to some extent upon conservative support could ignore the French clerical concern for Rome and the survival of the Temporal Power. His old interest in nationalism was perfectly genuine, yet it did at times blend with a more practical aim to cause embarrassment for other Powers and to create a series of client states. 'On est plus grand par l'influence morale qu'on exerce,' he said in 1859, 'que par des conquêtes stériles.' Most of all, he longed to revise the treaties of 1815—hence his passion for European congresses and his determination to remain on good terms with Great Britain.

It was unfortunate that his greatest successes in the realm of *la gloire* were overseas where they excited little interest in France. By 1860 Algeria, whose conquest was now complete, had a European settler population of 290,000 and the native areas were largely under military rule. To the south the coast of Guinea and Dahomey was occupied and under the governorship of Faidherbe the interior of Senegal was opened up and the port of Dakar founded. The greatest French achievement in Africa was the building of the Suez canal, begun in 1859 and completed ten years later under the direction of Ferdinand de Lesseps, a fitting expression of the Saint-Simonianism which had earlier influenced him. In the Far East Saigon was captured in 1859 and France later assumed sovereign rule over parts of Indo-China and a protectorate over Cambodia, while in 1860 she joined forces with the British in an expedition to Pekin to gain greater trading privileges in China. In 1861 another French expedition intervened in Syria after a massacre of Christians, but withdrew shortly afterwards to avoid offending British susceptibilities.

Napoleon's most grandiose performance overseas was in Mexico.

Here French forces, which had been sent out in 1861 together with British and Spanish on a debt-collecting expedition, remained behind at Vera Cruz in an attempt to oust the anti-clerical reforming Mexican leader Juarez and to establish in his place the Habsburg Archduke Maximilian. This was certainly contrary to any nationalist principle, but naturally it pleased the clericals in France. A puppet French empire in Central America might well act as a bulwark against the growing penetration by the United States and offered a prospect of *la gloire* which did capture the imagination of French public opinion. This was unfortunate, since the Mexican venture turned out to be an appalling fiasco. By 1863 the French commander, Bazaine, who was sufficiently enamoured of the project to acquire a Mexican wife, had established Maximilian on a somewhat unstable throne, but the long resistance put up by Juarez eventually involved over 38,000 French troops, of whom 6,000 died. In 1865, with the end of the American Civil war, the United States government was at last in a position to object strongly to this serious infringement of the Monroe Doctrine, and Napoleon, already worried by the course of events in central Europe, had to cut his losses. In 1867 his troops were withdrawn and Maximilian paid the price of the French Emperor's ambition before a Mexican firing squad.

In Europe, however, it was the encouragement of suppressed nationalities that seemed most likely to produce a practical reward in the form of French satellite states and a revision of the treaties of 1815. During the Crimean war Napoleon had toyed with ideas of fostering Finnish independence and at the Congress of Paris had wanted to hasten the emergence of a Rumanian state out of the Danubian Principalities, which were actually placed under a single governor three years later. This duality of purpose was particularly marked in his attitude towards Italy, for although his belief in the need for Italian independence had romantic undertones, his support of Cavour in 1859 was motivated by a desire to create a federation dependent on France.

In fact, Napoleon's determination to alter the *status quo* was ultimately to enable others to bring about changes seriously to the detriment of France. The united kingdom of Italy that had emerged by the end of 1860 was a far cry from what he had originally intended; the predominance that France enjoyed after 1856, followed by her acquisition of Savoy and Nice—the price of her assistance to Covour—only aroused suspicions which thrust her into isolation. And in the 1860s Napoleon's dream of gaining Belgium as a puppet state in the Rhineland led him constantly to play into the hands of Bismarck who was thus aided in his own work of national unification and the eventual defeat of France.

Chapter 16
The Unification of Italy
1859–60

Personalities are easier to visualize than social tendencies, and when in the middle decades of the nineteenth-century political developments are seen to centre round three such fascinating individuals as Napoleon III, Cavour, and Bismarck, it is tempting to oversimplify the course of European history at this time. The historian often finds the attraction of success irresistible; thus, while the ultimate failure of Napoleon merely reinforces his charm as the romantic conspirator, the remarkable achievements of Cavour and Bismarck have too easily encouraged the cult of the master-mind shaping the destiny of modern Europe. In recent years, however, this conception has been attacked from two points of view. First, their personal success has been set in the context of a growing economy and technological development; second, the interpretation of their efforts has been brought down to a more human level at which it is possible to see that they sometimes made miscalculations and, unlike the historians, were quite unable to anticipate what was going to happen next. Despite this, the fact remains that the map of central Europe was utterly changed in less than a dozen years; economic and technical developments alone do not create a nation state in the face of opposition, and the triumphs of Cavour and Bismarck may appear the greater when viewed, not as the inevitable workings of a master plan, but as the outcome of the day-to-day perplexities that govern political action.

Count Camillo Benso di Cavour was born in 1810 of an old and distinguished Piedmontese family. The full rounded line of the face encircled by the short fringe of beard, revealed in the photographs taken in later life, appears at first sight benign and paternal; it is the features, the strong set of the mouth, the eyes shrewd and narrowed behind the spectacles that suggest the sharp mind of the *Realpolitiker*. As a younger son he was educated at the Military Academy of Turin and later served for a few years as an officer in the engineers. He did not remain in the army long, but his interests remained technological and scientific in the development of his estates and soon brought him into contact with the business world. He became a director of the railway laid between Turin and Genoa, and of the Bank of Turin, and was an active member of the National Agricultural Society founded in 1842. One of the great formative influences on his outlook was a visit to England in 1835; the growth of the first railways, the sense of commercial and industrial expansion encouraged by the emergence of Free Trade, the atmosphere of the debates in the House of Commons which he attended, the common assumption of political liberty under a constitutional monarchy, all helped to shape the policies that he was later to advocate in his own newspaper *Il Risorgimento*, which he started in 1847.

In the summer of 1848 he was elected to the Chamber of Deputies. His opposition to a renewal of the war with Austria led to his failure to be returned in January 1849, but in the elections of the following July, after the final defeat, he won a seat for Turin which he was to hold for the rest of his life. Under the premiership of D'Azeglio he rapidly made his mark as a shrewd debater and an excellent administrator, and in October 1850 he entered the cabinet as Minister of Agriculture, Commerce and Marine, to which he added the post of Minister of Finance in April 1851. Early in the next year, however, a protest from Louis Napoleon at Piedmontese press comments on the *coup d'état* of December 1851 led the government to bring in the Deforesta Press Law making the press liable to trial without jury in actions involving foreign Powers. Cavour supported the government on this measure, but realizing the need to retain the sympathy of the liberals, came to a working agreement on his own initiative with the centre left group under Rattazzi, an agreement that became known as the *connubio* (marriage). Shortly after this, D'Azeglio and Cavour fell out; Cavour, lacking the King's support, had to resign in April 1852, but by October D'Azeglio, confronted by the forces of the *connubio*, could carry on no longer and at the beginning of November Victor Emmanuel found that he had no option but to nominate Cavour as premier at the head of a coalition of centre parties, a post that he was to hold until his death in June 1861, except for one short break in 1859.

Much of the later Cavour can be seen in his behaviour during this astonishingly rapid rise to power—his refusal to support the renewal of war by Piedmont alone against Austria in 1849, his series of Free Trade treaties with Great Britain, France, Belgium, the *Zollverein* and Holland, and his determination to build a strong centre liberal group, even to the point of undermining the Prime Minister in whose cabinet he was serving. His fundamental ambition was the creation of an Italian Kingdom through the extension of Piedmont's frontiers, but it is probable that for the moment he did not conceive anything more than the incorporation of all the provinces to the north of the Papal States. This would create a compact area geographically well placed to exploit the opportunities of European economic expansion. It would, of course, mean the expulsion of Austria from Lombardy and Venetia, but at least it would avoid the complicated question of the Papal territory, and he did not have much interest in the poverty-stricken Kingdom of Naples until Garibaldi's efforts in 1860 made its acquisition inescapable.

For the moment the first essential was the transformation of Piedmont into a modern state, and here he owed a great deal to his business experience and his knowledge of western Europe. He seized upon the importance of railways, hoping to make Piedmont part of an international network, initiating a scheme for the piercing of Mont Cenis by a railway tunnel, and turning Genoa into a great commercial port. This, of course, necessitated heavier taxes, but although much of this revenue was being used on capital expenditure, prosperity was such that the national deficit had been reduced to 25 million by 1854. At the same time a considerable reform of the army and of the state administration was carried out, and the Civil Code reorganized. The boldest stroke of all was the considerable reduction of the Church's secular power. The Siccardi laws of 1850 had already openly defied the authority of Rome by ending the existence of ecclesiastical courts, and in 1855 all religious orders were declared abolished except those concerned with teaching, preaching, or helping the sick. It was natural that such a policy should earn for Cavour the lasting mistrust of Pius IX, who watched events in Piedmont with increasing wariness, but Cavour was far from being an enemy of the Church; his attitude was merely that of liberal Catholicism maintaining that the Church's role should be confined to the purely spiritual side of life.

This policy of modernizing Piedmont while avoiding any suggestion of revolution or republicanism was simply a preliminary to the greater aim of some form of Italian independence. Yet Cavour never fell into the error that Italy could achieve this on her own. War with Austria would be inevitable. For this he must have the active assistance of a great military Power, and from the beginning he knew that such assistance could only come from France.

The hope was not vain, since Napoleon's need for glory and his inclinations as an old *Carbonaro* would both be satisfied by assisting in the realization of Italian liberty; at the same time the expulsion of Austria from Italy, together with the French acquisition of Savoy and Nice as a reward, would form an attractive revision of the treaties of 1815. On the other hand, although Napoleon had said in 1852: 'Je suis résolu à faire quelque chose pour l'Italie que j'aime comme une seconde patrie', he was well aware of the dangers that would attend such a policy. Clerical opinion in France demanded that Rome should remain inviolate; a coalition of the central Powers might lead to an attack on France's north-eastern frontier, and even if the issue was brought to a successful conclusion, he had no desire to see a strong united Italy on France's borders. It was these considerations that governed the whole of Napoleon's vacillating policy throughout the Italian adventure.

Piedmont's participation in the Crimean War on the side of the Allies was certainly a step in the right direction, but Cavour was unable to obtain any territorial concession in return for her services (see p. 170) and the really decisive change came about in a totally unexpected manner. In January 1858 an Italian revolutionary, Felice Orsini, made an attempt on the life of Napoleon as he was about to enter the Opera in Paris. The bomb killed many of the bystanders, but left untouched the man whom Orsini blamed for the Oudinot expedition against the Roman Republic in 1849. There was understandably a strong French diplomatic reaction against Great Britain, where Orsini had prepared his plot, and against Piedmont, his country of origin. In Great Britain Palmerston cooperated to the extent of introducing a new Conspiracy Bill; in Piedmont Cavour, although resisting the immediate French demands, passed a measure for the prosecution of journals that attacked foreign states, and ostentatiously threw the blame on the Mazzinians. Surrender to pressure from a foreign state at a time of heightened national feeling could be a hazardous matter for a constitutional government. Palmerston actually fell from power over his Conspiracy Bill owing to the fervent public sympathy for the Italians; Cavour dared not risk losing the support of Piedmontese liberals, as D'Azeglio had done over the Deforesta Press Law in 1852, although at the same time he knew that he had to retain the friendship of France. The final outcome was a complete surprise. Napoleon was deeply impressed by Victor Emmanuel's letter to him rejecting any French dictation to Piedmont, and his entourage began to reflect that there might be further attempts on the Emperor's life unless he took a more positive lead in Italian affairs. Whatever the reason—and there is a point beyond which Napoleon's thoughts defy analysis—the scales now tipped definitely in favour of supporting the Italians. Orsini's appeal to the Emperor to assist Italy in gaining her liberty was read out at his trial and later published, and when Victor Emmanuel's emissary was leaving Paris for Turin, Napoleon assured him that in case of war with Austria France would stand beside Piedmont.

There followed a meeting between Napoleon and Cavour at Plombières in the Vosges on 20 July 1858. As one might expect from these two conspirators, nothing was signed, but a great deal was agreed. France was to supply 200,000 men and Italy 100,000 to fight in a combined effort against Austria, who was to be driven out of Italy. Cavour was to engineer the outbreak of hostilities in such a way that Austria would appear to be the aggressor, and after the victory Italy was to become a federation of four states under the presidency of the Pope—a kingdom of Upper Italy under Victor

Emmanuel including Piedmont, Lombardy, Venetia, Modena, Parma, and the Romagna; a kingdom of Central Italy including Tuscany and a large part of the Papal States, all under the Duchess of Parma; Rome and the Patrimony of St Peter; and the Kingdom of Naples. In return, Napoleon was promised Savoy and, rather more vaguely, the hand of Victor Emmanuel's daughter Clothilde for his uncle Jerome's son.

Cavour naturally left Plombières highly delighted. Napoleon, too, returned to Paris satisfied with the terms of the bargain. A marriage alliance with one of the oldest reigning houses in Europe was in accord with the *arriviste* tendencies of a Bonaparte; the gaining of Savoy would be a moral blow at the Vienna settlement and the re-emergence of the federalist solution to the Italian problem might mollify the French Catholics, at the same time ensuring that a new great Power did not suddenly emerge on the French frontier. In January 1859 an ominous remark by Napoleon to the Austrian ambassador was followed some ten days later by a warlike speech from Victor Emmanuel in the Piedmontese Chamber, in which he announced that 'we cannot remain insensible to the *cris de douleur* that reach us from so many parts of Italy'. In the same month a definite treaty was signed between France and Piedmont, adding Nice to the territory that France was to gain, but making no mention of the proposed Italian federation, after which the projected wedding of Jerome's son and Princess Clothilde took place in the Chapel Royal in Turin.

Yet there were anxious months ahead for Cavour. Rumours and speculation on this latest intrigue in European diplomacy ran from chancellery to chancellery, and Napoleon began to have serious doubts over the acquiescence of the Powers. Lord Derby's ministry in London was openly pro Austrian, but public opinion, strongly supporting the Italians, made any effective British intervention unlikely. Napoleon had hoped that Russia might have been prepared at least to threaten the Habsburg eastern frontier, but in a secret treaty of March 1859 Alexander II would promise no more than benevolent neutrality. The attitude of Prussia gave the least satisfaction of all, since the Regent Prince William, suspicious of Napoleon's desire to revise the 1815 treaties, held firmly to friendship with Austria. This inability to gain a promise of support or even of neutrality awoke all Napoleon's fears of a Prussian attack from the Rhineland, and his ministers were by this time strongly encouraging him to drop the whole scheme.

At the same time as the Emperor was reflecting on these diplomatic difficulties, Cavour was struggling to find some means of provoking Austria into an aggressive act. In fact, no independent issue ever existed—merely a growing tension in the north Italian plain, particularly after the publication of Napoleon's article 'Napoléon

III et l'Italie'; Piedmont and Austria piled up their military preparations, and it was only through the attempts of the Powers to
mediate that Cavour found his excuse. By April the question of a
congress had been raised; Cavour, almost at his wit's end, found
that his partner was growing increasingly lukewarm and when
Napoleon agreed to a proposal made by the British government that
both sides should demobilize simultaneously as a preliminary to a
congress, Cavour had no option but to accept such a reasonable
suggestion. But for Buol it was all too reasonable; needing a diplomatic and if possible a military humiliation of Piedmont before
any congress assembled, the Austrian government dispatched an
ultimatum to Piedmont on 19 April demanding that Piedmont
should demobilize immediately and unconditionally. Thus, at the
last moment the Austrians had played into Cavour's hands. He had
only to point out the intransigence of Vienna in the Chamber—and
hence to the world—reject the ultimatum and await the Austrian
attack. On 29 April Austrian forces under Gyulai crossed the Ticino
into Piedmont and on 3 May Napoleon, satisfied that Austria could
be stigmatized as the aggressor, declared his intention of coming to
the defence of his Piedmontese ally.

The war of 1859 lasted little more than two months. The Austrian
forces available in Italy numbered only about 90,000, since the
government in Vienna fully expected a French attack through south
Germany, and Gyulai decided on a speedy advance against the
50,000 Piedmontese before they could be reinforced by the French.
Napoleon's troops, however, had been on the move since the last
week of April and by the beginning of May almost 10,000 a day
were entering Piedmont either across the Mont Cenis pass or by sea
to Genoa. The Austrians acted too slowly and by the middle of May
the allies were ready to advance on the northern front, thereby turning the Austrian right flank. On 4 June the first major encounter
took place outside Magenta to the east of the Ticino and after heavy
fighting the Austrians withdrew to the south of Lake Garda. This
left most of Lombardy open to the allied advance, and Napoleon
III and Victor Emmanuel riding together through the streets of
Milan received an ecstatic welcome from the crowds. Sterner fighting, however, lay ahead, and on 24 June a long bloody battle among
the hills around the village of Solferino cost the French 17,000 men
against Austrian losses of 22,000. At the end Count Schlick, who
had replaced Gyulai a few days before, fell back on the Quadrilateral and by 2 July the French had crossed the Mincio.

Then suddenly all Cavour's hopes were dashed. On 5 July, without any previous consultation, Napoleon proposed an armistice, and
a week later at Villafranca met Francis Joseph to discuss the terms
whereby France would withdraw from the war. Lombardy was

given to Piedmont, but Venetia and the fortresses of Mantua and Peschiera were to remain in Austrian possession; the hereditary rulers of Tuscany, Parma, and Modena, all of whom had fled to the Habsburg camp after the news of Magenta, were to be restored to their duchies, and all parts of Italy were to be included in a new Confederation under the presidency of the Pope. Cavour had not been present at Villafranca, and when late at night Victor Emmanuel brought the terms to him, it was hardly surprising that he should give way to a passion of vituperative rage. For him the war had been pointless; Lombardy alone meant nothing, with Austria still in possession of Venetia and the Quadrilateral and Habsburg influence re-established in Tuscany and Modena. He stormed at his king, offered his resignation, which was accepted on the spot, and returned in despair to Turin. A few days later Napoleon set off for France, agreeing to let the question of Savoy and Nice drop in return for Piedmont paying the expenses of the war.

Francis Joseph, whose dislike of the war had been reflected in the appointment of Rechberg in place of Buol as Foreign Minister in May, had been only too glad to accept the terms of Villafranca. Magenta and Solferino had revealed the weak state of his army and the significance of this affected more than Italy. The draining of any further reinforcements into the Lombard plain would have made Austria utterly dependent on the Prussian army in Germany, and the arrival of Kossuth at Napoleon's headquarters suggested a recurrence of trouble in Hungary. As Cavour had seen, the loss of Lombardy was a relatively small price for Francis Joseph to pay for retaining Habsburg power in Italy—a better bargain, probably, than any congress would have given him.

Why had Napoleon deserted Cavour at this moment? One reason was that swift military victory was an essential requirement of mid-nineteenth century *Realpolitik*; Europe had to be presented with a *fait accompli*. One may see Bismarck urging his generals on to bombard Paris in January 1871 for precisely the same reason. To Napoleon, shocked at the toll which the Austrians had taken of the French army at Solferino and alarmed at the thought of diplomatic reactions to his latest adventure, the prospect of a long siege of the Quadrilateral fortresses was unthinkable. The decisive factor was the reappearance of the original difficulties that he had recognized before entering into the compact with Cavour. The failure to gain a promise of Prussian neutrality meant that the diplomatic preparation had been incomplete. It is true that Bismarck was using all his influence to let 'Austria's war against France eat deeply into her substance' as a means of substituting Prussian for Austrian hegemony in Germany, but Bismarck was only ambassador at St Petersburg and the Prince Regent was determined to support Austria. On 24 June the Prussians mobilized six army corps in the Rhineland and this threat to his north-eastern frontier meant the realization of Napoleon's worst fears.

Then, again, there was the question of the future state of Italy. Did Cavour really mean to rest content with a federation under the Pope? Napoleon had begun to doubt it. After the flight of the hereditary rulers Cavour had been quick to dispatch Count Pallieri to Parma, and Farini to Modena, where they were to act as royal commissioners to organize pro-Piedmontese governments; similarly, the withdrawal of the Austrian garrisons from Bologna and Ancona after Magenta had opened the door to the Romagna. None of this was contrary to the agreement of Plombières, but when the Piedmontese ambassador at Florence engineered Ricasoli into the position of dictator, Napoleon began to see that Cavour had hopes of incorporating Tuscany also into the kingdom of Upper Italy— thus undermining the federal scheme of Plombières, which had earmarked Tuscany for inclusion in a Central Kingdom. 'Je ne veux pas l'unité,' remarked Napoleon after Villafranca, 'mais l'indépendence. L'unité me procurerait des difficultés en France à cause de la question romaine; et la France ne verrait pas avec plaisir surgir à son flanc une grande nation qui pourrait diminuer sa prépondérance.' Napoleon was right in suspecting Cavour's plans which were really as great a breach of Plombières as Villafranca where Napoleon, even if he deprived Piedmont of the hope of Venetia, did at least reaffirm the federal plan to which Cavour had originally agreed.

But Villafranca only affected the major actors in the drama. France had withdrawn, Cavour had resigned, and Piedmont was at peace with Austria. It was the question of the duchies that remained unsettled, and here Ricasoli and Farini were to play a great part in the story of Italian unification. Although it had been agreed at Villafranca by France and Austria that the hereditary rulers should be restored, the royal commissioners there refused to stand down, and since Napoleon had stipulated that there should be no military intervention on Austria's part, they remained in control of the duchies. Farini united Modena, Parma, and the Romagna under the title of Emilia, but was dissuaded from a scheme of union with Tuscany by Ricasoli who pointed out that this would be tantamount to creating a possible kingdom of Central Italy as envisaged in the federal scheme. Instead, each organized their governments to petition for annexation by Piedmont; yet without the consent of the Powers Piedmont could make no move. The result was deadlock.

Two factors enabled Piedmont to gain her end. In Great Britain a general election in 1859 had brought Palmerston back into power with Lord John Russell as Foreign Secretary. These 'two dreadful old men', as Victoria called them, strongly favoured the creation of a unitary state in Italy and in January 1860 Russell put before Napoleon four points which would allow the duchies to vote on annexation through elected assemblies. The second factor was Napoleon's own change of mind. His failure to gain any territorial acquisition appeared to make the war of 1859 a senseless adventure; at home he had lost rather than gained prestige, at the same time infuriating Italian nationalist sentiment. To forestall the British in gaining influence at Turin; to annex Savoy and Nice after all; these now became his new objectives.

Cavour returned to power in January 1860 and it was typical of his skill to use the British offer to tempt Napoleon to a new bargain—Savoy and Nice against Tuscany and Emilia. There were dangers involved for both of them. Austria might be angry at this change of front by Napoleon; the British were particularly anxious to prevent France from gaining Savoy and Nice—hence Russell's four points. However, a careful sounding of Habsburg opinion showed that Austria would be prepared to acquiesce in such a rearrangement, provided that Venetia and the Quadrilateral remained untouched, and Cavour was prepared to brave the displeasure of the British government, knowing that in the last resort the support of France was the decisive factor. On 24 March a treaty between France and Piedmont settled the bargain. Plebiscites in all the affected territories followed—not a great obstacle to two such realists as Cavour and Napoleon—and thus only ten months after Villafranca, Victor Emmanuel found himself king of the whole of north Italy, except for Venetia, while the French frontier had moved eastwards into the Alps.

The most colourful episode in the history of the Risorgimento was yet to come. Garibaldi had taken a typically hazardous but successful part in the extreme north in the war of 1859, and had later been responsible for holding the southern frontier of the duchies, causing constant alarm in official circles that he was about to invade the Papal States. To Garibaldi it seemed that the great moment of Italian liberation had arrived; he had little patience with parliamentary practices, mistrusted Cavour's reliance on France, and hated the cession of Savoy and Nice to Napoleon, particularly since Nice was his own birthplace. Then in April the chance of further action came with the news of revolt in Palermo, and Garibaldi at once began to collect arms and volunteers, until in May he had a force of a thousand with which he set off in a couple of paddle-steamers from Genoa. The outcome was beyond the wildest romantic dream. The landing at Marsala was unopposed; Neapolitan troops sent out to meet them were defeated in an untidy soldiers' battle at Calatafimi, and with his forces now raised to three thousand by local recruiting Garibaldi advanced through pouring rain on the army of 20,000 holding Palermo. Through cunning feints and the aid of the local population he fought his way into the centre of the town and by the end of May negotiation with General Lanza had resulted in the withdrawal of the Neapolitan garrison to Naples, thus leaving Garibaldi free to mop up the rest of Sicily.

Cavour, however, was not a romantic. Historians are divided over his precise attitude towards the embarkation of the expedition. One view is that he publicly disowned it, while secretly allowing it to go forward. 'The argument was—', wrote Hudson, the British ambassador at Turin, at Russell in June, 'if he fails, we are rid of a troublesome fellow, and if he succeeds, Italy will derive some profit from his success.' A more recent view is that he genuinely tried to stop the expedition while it was at sea, but could not act openly, since he dared not offend both the King and public opinion in the new North Italian Kingdom. Whatever he thought, there is no doubt that Cavour was seriously worried. There had been no diplomatic preparation for this latest development in the south; he could not be certain yet of the possible political repercussions of the cession of Savoy and Nice to France, and Garibaldi's activities might well convince the Powers that the changes in the Italian peninsula were assuming such proportions that they must intervene. Events in Rome in 1849 had linked Garibaldi's name with that of Mazzini in the public imagination, and whereas the revolutionary movements in the central duchies had been under Cavour's control, those in the south owed their inspiration to Mazzini; Garibaldi's anger over Nice might well incline him towards the establishment of a republic, thus making foreign intervention highly probable, followed by a congress at which Piedmont might lose some of her recent gains.

By the beginning of June Cavour's mind was more at ease. Garibaldi had adopted the cry of 'Italy and Victor Emmanuel' and the capture of Sicily was a hard fact that appealed to realist and romantic alike. The problem now was to hold the ring. For this he had simply to play on the mutual suspicions of the great Powers. Palmerston and Napoleon were each convinced that the other intended to make capital out of events in southern Italy, and when Napoleon proposed in June that a separate independent Kingdom of Sicily should be created, the British government rejected the suggestion, fearing that it might become a satellite of Napoleonic France, endangering British naval bases at Gibraltar, Malta, and Corfu. For the same reason Napoleon's plan for an Anglo-French naval force to prevent Garibaldi reaching the mainland was rejected and on 18 August Garibaldi set off unopposed across the Straits of Messina.

So far, so good; but it was clear now that Garibaldi would stop at nothing, and Cavour knew that no diplomacy could prevent Austrian and French intervention if Garibaldi marched on Rome—as he had every intention of doing. How was that to be avoided? Cavour's first plan was to forestall him by stirring up a revolution of his own in Naples, but the scheme failed, since the Neapolitans were content to await the arrival of Garibaldi. The only other possibility was for the Piedmontese army to march south through the Papal States and to interpose itself between Garibaldi and Rome. This would also enable Cavour to recapture the initiative; but for Napoleon the essential element in the enterprise was that it would relieve him of the unpleasant necessity of sending more French forces to the rescue of the Pope in Rome, and he secretly assured Cavour that it would be safe to proceed. It was not a moment too soon. Garibaldi had swept up through Calabria before the crumbling resistance of the Neapolitan troops and by 7 September he was in Naples. Four days later the Piedmontese army, coming nominally to the assistance of revolts in the Papal States, crossed the frontier. It defeated the small Papal army at Castelfidardo, rapidly occupied Umbria and crossed the Garigiliano into the Kingdom of Naples just after Garibaldi had fought his first serious engagement with the Neapolitans on the Volturno on 1 October. Other fears were soon silenced. Cavour was able to convince the British that French acquiescence had not been bought with the promise of the cession of Genoa, while at Warsaw Francis Joseph found it impossible to reach agreement over concerted action with Prussia and Russia, without which he was not prepared to act. Plebiscites in Naples, Sicily, Umbria, and the Papal marches brought an overwhelming vote for union with Piedmont, and the disapproval which the Powers had been swift to express was soon shown to be without substance, when Russell took the lead in a famous dispatch at the end of October in which he spoke of 'the gratifying spectacle of a people building up the edifice of their liberties and consolidating the work of their independence' Early in November Garibaldi officially handed over his conquests to Victor Emmanuel and on the day after the King and he had made a state entry into Naples, he set off for his home on the rocky island of Caprera, after refusing all honours and rewards. In January 1861 the first national Parliament met at Turin.

Thus only a dozen years after the collapse of Italian hopes in the risings of 1848-9 a united kingdom of Italy had been created, lacking only Venetia and the Patrimony of St Peter, the enclave of territory round Rome. The key to success had been careful diplomatic preparation based on a realization of the need for military assistance from France, rather than reliance upon a general revolutionary situation. What revolutionary feeling there had been in the north had been carefully controlled by Cavour and his agents--almost as artificial as the circumstances of the outbreak of the 1859 war—and he had been determined to avoid any public association with the Mazzinians, although he had found them a useful diplomatic threat as the grisly alternative if he did not get his way. Two other advantages Cavour had had over the leaders of the 1848–9 movements. There was no question this time of the leadership of the Pope; the only essential was that Rome should be left unmolested—here lay the difference between *Realpolitik* and romantic nationalism. The second advantage was that a system of parliamentary government had already been firmly established at Turin and there was no need for the furore of constitution-making that had crippled the activities of 1848–9.

Yet however great may have been the part that Cavour played in the unification of Italy, he was undoubtedly aided by extraordinary good luck. 'How many times', he wrote afterwards, 'have I not exclaimed: Blessed be the peace of Villafranca.' Napoleon still lacking Savoy and Nice, Ricasoli's and Farini's efforts in the central duchies—these factors gave him a North Italian kingdom as a continuation of the war might have failed to do. Nor did he ever imagine the possibility of Garibaldi's swift success in the south, for that desperate venture of a thousand men might do well enough in South America where Garibaldi had served his apprenticeship, but could hardly seem a worthwhile gamble under the nose of the chancelleries of Europe. On the other hand, the way in which Cavour seized his opportunity, when it seemed that the impossible had happened, is a supreme testimony to his diplomatic skill, and it is on the whole a just verdict that links the names of these two men in the last act of the Risorgimento.

Chapter 17

The Defeat of Austria 1862–6

1. Bismarck's rise to power

From the moment when, in November 1852, Cavour had become premier in Piedmont, it had taken him little more than eight years to accomplish the unification of Italy; almost exactly the same length of time was to elapse between Bismarck's appointment as Minister President of Prussia in September 1862 and the proclamation of the German Empire in the Hall of Mirrors at Versailles in January 1871. Both men made a calculated use of war to attain an end which the liberals of 1848 had hoped to achieve in a different form by different methods; both were enabled by the mistakes of their enemies, in Bismarck's phrase, 'to assume the role of the injured'. One cannot, however, press the parallel too far. Whereas Cavour saw his work completed with a dramatic suddenness and then died within a few months of his success, the road for Bismarck ran through a whole series of short wars—with Denmark in 1864, with Austria in 1866 and with France in 1870. Although more fortunate than Cavour in that the excellence of the Prussian army gave him greater independence of action, he still had to ensure that his enemy of the moment fought alone; the implications of his policy raised infinitely wider diplomatic complications, and the ultimate emergence of the German Empire so transformed the balance of power in Europe that for the subsequent twenty years it needed all his skill to control the situation which he had created.

The personality of Count Otto von Bismarck was far more complex than the popular conception of the 'Iron Chancellor' would allow. Outwardly he might seem a typical son of the old Junker family from which he sprang; as a university student at Göttingen he had duelled, drunk, and run into debt; all his life he loved good food and wine, and his military bearing, thick moustache and stern heavy-lidded eyes might well suggest a Prussian officer whose life was bounded by his regiment and the management of his estates. Yet the appearance and the myth both, to some extent, belie the inner character of the man. He had the temperament of an artist—although without any interest in art—quick-thinking, infinitely flexible, and so highly strung that in moments of tension he could find relief only in tears or the smashing of china. An authoritarian himself, he could not endure to be under the authority of others; thus he hated his year of military service at Potsdam; he resigned from the Prussian civil service, because, as he said, he could not 'put up with superiors', and later as a diplomatic representative his dispatches read like general statements of higher policy. During his early manhood he spent long periods on his family estates, first in Pomerania, later at Schönhausen in Brandenburg, but the peace of the countryside only bored him to distraction, driving him into escapades that earned him the name of 'the wild Bismarck'; and until the age of thirty-two, his tremendous energies still unharnessed, he seemed no more than a neurotic failure. Then, in 1847, two events changed the whole course of his life. His marriage to Johanna von Puttkamer brought him a new background of personal happiness and encouragement; and with his election to the Prussian United Diet (see p. 106) a new ever-absorbing interest awoke within him.

Bismarck's politics at this time were those of a staunch Prussian conservative, strongly hostile to any change in the existing situation. In the United Diet he constantly attacked the liberals, and in the spring of 1848 he rushed to Berlin to put heart into the Court to resist the revolutionaries. Naturally he gained no place in the Prussian National Assembly, elected by universal suffrage in that year, but under the terms of the constitution which Frederick William promulgated in December he was able to find a seat in the new Chamber by a narrow majority, and here he poured scorn on the proposed Frankfurt constitution of 1849 and welcomed the defeat of Radowitz's scheme at Olmutz (see p. 144).

It was this apparent belief in the maintenance of the old system of the German Confederation, based on Prussian cooperation with Austria, that led to his being selected as the Prussian representative at the Federal Diet in 1851. The beginning of his diplomatic career, however, was to bring about a fundamental change in his outlook. The Austrian assumption of superiority at the Diet naturally irked his own arrogant individualism, and before long he was moving towards the attitude that had prompted Radowitz's attempt in 1849—the conception of a Prussian-dominated *Kleindeutschland* from which Austria would be excluded. 'Germany is too small for both of us,' he was writing by 1856, 'both plough the same contested field.'

This new attitude was reflected in his personal reactions to all the diplomatic moves in the 1850s. During the Crimean War he advocated neutrality, noting how Austria's wavering was antagonizing all her possible friends (see p. 168), and deploring the idea of 'tying our trim and seaworthy frigate to the worm-eaten and old-fashioned

Austrian man-of-war'. In 1859 he was dispatched as ambassador to St Petersburg, and from there he watched impotently as the Prussians mobilized on the Rhineland in support of Francis Joseph against Napoleon III, instead of taking advantage of Austria's embarrassment to end her control over the German Confederation (see p. 180).

In fact, as it turned out, the indirect consequences of this policy were eventually to serve Bismarck well. The mobilization in the Rhineland in 1859 had revealed certain weaknesses in the Prussian military machine. The reforms at the beginning of the century had established a system of compulsory military service including three years with the colours and two in the reserve, after which the citizen passed into the *Landwehr*, a form of militia. The size of each year's intake of recruits had, however, remained fixed, despite Prussia's rising population, and the three years active service was in practice no more than two. The Regent, Prince William, a keen soldier, strongly supported by von Roon, the Minister of War, and von Moltke, the Chief of the General Staff, now proposed that, in order to exploit the full military potential of the country, all young men should serve for the full three years, and that the reserve should be greatly increased at the expense of the *Landwehr*. These changes, raising Prussia's war establishment from 230,000 men to 450,000 and involving the creation of forty-nine new regiments, would have to be financed out of additional taxation, and when the scheme was put before the Prussian Parliament, it encountered considerable opposition from the liberals—not simply because of the cost, but because they mistrusted the whittling away of the *Landwehr* which, as a citizen's army with its own non-aristocratic officers, represented a military force remote from the conservative instincts of the Prussian Officer Corps. The debates in the Chamber soon exposed the deeper social and political implications that lay behind a simple reorganization of the army, and after two years of unsatisfactory bargaining the crisis was reached in 1862 when it became clear that the Chamber was not prepared to accept the budget.

For some time the conservative elements had known that Bismarck was the man to handle this situation, but William, who in 1861 had finally succeeded to the throne on the death of his brother (see p. 159), mistrusted Bismarck's outspoken views on Prussia's relations with Austria and held back as long as he could. Recalled from St Petersburg in March 1862, Bismarck was dispatched to the embassy at Paris. Here he awaited the call of destiny and when, in September, he received a telegram from von Roon—'Periculum in mora. Dépêchez-vous'—he knew that the moment had come. He hastened to Berlin and on 22 September he emerged from an interview with the King which gave him at last the power for which his imperious nature longed—a Prime Minister whose appointment depended upon his ability to overrule a constitutional Assembly, a conservative now able to give free rein to a revolutionary foreign policy. It was a situation completely in harmony with the contradictions of his own character.

2. The Slesvig-Holstein question

The crisis was reached almost at once, for on the day after Bismarck's appointment the Prussian Lower House finally rejected the budget. As soon as he had formed an extremely conservative Cabinet, he made some attempt at negotiation, insisting, nevertheless, on a reform of the army as a vital necessity for Prussia. 'Nicht durch Reden und Majoritätsbeschlüsse,' he lectured the deputies on 29 September, 'werden die grossen Fragen der Zeit entschieden—das ist der grosse Fehler von 1848 und 1849 gewesen—sondern durch Eisen und Blut.' ('The great questions of the day are not decided by speeches and resolutions of majorities—that was the blunder of 1848 and 1849—but by iron and blood.') The statement has echoed down the years in every assessment of Bismarck's career, and, whatever cynicism it may seem to imply, it was perhaps the most honest thing that he ever said, and despite the shock that it may have caused the deputies in 1862, they were more than willing to accept the fruits of its application in 1866 and 1871. It was indeed a simple statement of fact, as Cavour had already shown.

But for the moment it had no persuasive appeal, and when deadlock had been reached over the budget Bismarck fell back on a demonstration of the flimsiness of parliamentary institutions in Prussia at this time. There was no problem over the actual collection of taxes, since the government's right to this was part of the existing constitution; the budget was only concerned with the control of expenditure. Technically this should have been an effective safeguard, but Bismarck argued that a profound disagreement between King and Parliament could not be allowed to prevent the government from continuing to run the country. In other words, he proposed to ignore the opposition of the Chamber, and during the next four years taxes were collected and the army reorganized as if the Prussian Parliament did not exist. William I watched with considerable alarm at first, convinced that he and his minister would meet the same fate as Charles I and the Earl of Strafford. The fact that they did not is one of the many differences between the pattern of English and German history, and with the apparent success of the policy the King found himself increasingly dependent upon his remarkable Minister President.

Even for Bismarck such a course could only be a temporary expedient, but at least it kept him in power. Within a few months, early in 1863, there had occurred three developments in Germany,

Poland and Denmark, each of which threatened to modify the structure of the 1815 settlement, and although none were originally of
his making, his response to them suggested a new authority in the
handling of Prussian policy.

The first move was initiated by Austria when Anton von Schmerling (see p. 201) decided on a remodelling of the German Confederation. Despite the resistance of the Austrian Foreign Minister,
Rechberg, whose conservatism favoured the maintenance of the
Metternich system, he was able to gain the ear of Francis Joseph,
and a meeting of the German princes was summoned at Frankfurt
in August 1863. The essence of the new scheme was the creation of
a *Grossdeutschland*, reminiscent of Schwarzenberg's abortive proposal
at Dresden in 1851 (see p. 144). An executive Directory of six states,
including Austria, Prussia, Bavaria, and three others chosen in
rotation, was to be set up under the presidency of Austria, while a
Federal Assembly was to consist of 302 delegates elected indirectly
by the representative bodies of the German states.

Such a plan was really no more than a device on Austria's part
to win over liberal sentiment, now greatly excited by the recent success of Cavour and Garibaldi in Italy. It is doubtful whether it
would ever have amounted to much, and in any case Bismarck was
determined that it should not succeed. The key to the whole problem
was the attitude of King William. Twice Francis Joseph attempted
to persuade William to attend the meeting of the princes at Frankfurt—once in personal conversation with him at Gastein, and again
in August, when the King of Saxony approached him at Baden as
an emissary from the congress. Each time it was the passionate
opposition of Bismarck that held him back, and when the princes
realized that Prussia would not enter the proposed scheme, they too
refused to go any further, since they feared that the absence of Prussia in the reshaping of central Europe would entail their own submission to Austria. As at the Dresden Conference of 1851 (see
p. 144), they saw rightly that their survival depended upon a balance between the two great Powers of Germany. This failure of the
congress at Frankfurt not only marks the last positive attempt of
Austria to gain the initiative in preserving her own position; it gave
Bismarck a chance to outbid her in winning liberal support for Prussia, for on 15 September a Prussian envoy to the congress justified
the absence of King William by demanding that in any new scheme
a Federal Assembly must be based on *direct* elections by the German
people.

At the same time as this debate in Germany, the Powers of Europe
had been closely concerned with the diplomatic repercussions of a
very different issue—the great Polish rising against Russian rule
(see p. 207), which broke out in January 1863. Bismarck had long
made it clear that he had little sympathy with the Poles; Prussia's

own Polish territories gave her a common bond of interest with Russia in this respect and at the beginning of March General von Alvensleben was dispatched to St Petersburg to conclude a convention with the Tsar, whereby it was agreed that the military forces of the two countries would cooperate within their own territories in putting down the Polish rebels.

Until now the Powers had on the whole been prepared to let the Polish question rest; in 1856, for instance, Prince Czartoryski had tried in vain to have the matter discussed at the Congress of Paris. The liberation of Poland, however, had remained a great cry of the liberals throughout Europe, and the deliberate assistance which Bismarck was lending the Russian government fired the western Powers to make a positive attempt at intervention. A joint note from Great Britain, France, and Austria contained proposals which would have given the moderate Polish party much of what they wanted, but when the Tsar showed no inclination to accept this as a basis for negotiation, the mutual suspicions among the mediating Powers prevented them from continuing to insist upon a settlement. Napoleon offered an alliance to Austria, but Rechberg was too mistrustful of his sympathy with the submerged national groups of Europe to allow Austria to be bound to France; similarly, the British, much of their attention taken up with the economic and maritime complications of the American Civil War, regarded Napoleon's acquisition of Savoy and Nice as a warning of further designs that he might have on the Rhineland; and when Napoleon bolstered up his proposal for a European congress in the autumn with a public statement that the treaties of 1815 were no longer in effect, the British government made it clear that this was not their view and the negotiations went no further. Thus, whereas the failure among the great Powers to agree on intervention had been an essential factor in the success of the Italians in 1860, a similar lack of agreement sealed the fate of the Poles, who were now condemned to the isolation that had wrecked their hopes in 1831, and by the beginning of 1864 the Russians had crushed the rising.

Nor was this all. The diplomatic exchanges of these months had revealed the dangerous lack of cohesion among the Powers that was to be an essential element in Bismarck's success. Austria had repeated her blunders of the Crimean War—antagonizing Russia without finding a partner elsewhere. An alliance with France might have saved her from her later defeat by Prussia, but Napoleon's schemes for Venetia and the Balkans put this out of reach. Equally significant, France's attempts to organize intervention in the Polish crisis brought to a close the *entente* with Russia which had made French assistance to Cavour possible in 1859 (see p. 177). The Alvensleben convention has sometimes been depicted as a subtle stroke of policy by Bismarck who reckoned to make Russia more dependent on Prussia in this way. This theory, however, may be an echo of the old cult of the master-mind. Not everything happened entirely as Bismarck wished, and the worsened relations between France and Russia could very well have been a setback for him, since it is possible that he had been hoping to align himself with the two of them against Austria.

There seems less doubt about his intentions in the third issue that arose in this troubled year—the reopening of the Slesvig-Holstein question. The earlier attempt of the Danes in 1848 to incorporate Slesvig within their kingdom (see p. 137) had come to nothing in the general restoration of the *status quo* after the year of revolutions. In an act of mediation between Denmark and the German Confederation a settlement of the Danish problem had been signed at London in 1852 by the great Powers, when it had been agreed that Christian of Glücksburg (see genealogical table p. 486) should eventually succeed the childless Frederick VII as King of Denmark and, despite the complications of the Salic Law, should also inherit the duchies to which Christian of Augustenburg would give up his family's claim in return for financial compensation. The Danes, on the other hand, agreed that the duchies should remain indivisible, promising 'not to incorporate Slesvig within the kingdom' and not to take any steps 'tending towards that end'.

There were two weaknesses in the Treaty of London. First, Christian of Augustenburg's renunciation of his claim had not been explicit, since the Danish government had never admitted that he had any rights to renounce; and through a legal quibble his eldest son, Frederick, who had not been of age in 1852, was later able to revive the claim for himself—with the additional justification that the Estates of the duchies had never actually ratified the eventual succession of the Glücksburg Danish King as their Duke. Second, the treaty had disappointed both Danish and German nationalists. The German Confederation had not been a signatory to it, and the Danes soon showed that they had little intention of keeping their part of the bargain.

By a number of governmental measures, including a new constitution in 1855, Frederick VII strove to divide the two duchies, constantly stressing the closeness of Slesvig to the kingdom. The final step came in March 1863 when Frederick decided to take advantage of the general uproar over the Polish rising to propose a further constitutional revision. The March Patent substituted a bi-cameral Parliament for a single representative Chamber, but its principal significance lay in the fact that although the Estates of Holstein would be able to exercise control over legislation within their own duchy, their opposition would have no effect upon measures passed in Denmark and Slesvig. German feeling in the Confederation, still determined on the indivisibility of the duchies, was at once violently outspoken, but the Danish government, encouraged by a treaty of defence with Sweden in August, refused to retract. Then, in November 1863, Frederick died before he had actually signed the new constitution and the final decision was left to his Glücksburg successor. Christian IX knew that the Patent was bound to be considered a breach of the Treaty of London of 1852 to which he owed his title as Duke of Slesvig-Holstein, but the force of Danish public opinion left him little option and he accordingly gave his consent to the new constitution.

No sooner had this been announced than angry voices in the Diet of the German Confederation demanded the immediate occupation of Holstein, and Frederick, the son of the Duke of Augustenburg, took up his claim to the duchies. The events of 1848 were not, however, to be repeated in their entirety, since this time Prussia was not to lend her assistance to the Confederation. Bismarck had to insist upon this decision against the strongest opposition. 'Sind Sie denn nicht auch ein Deutscher?' cried William in fury, but being still dependent upon his minister, the King had to accept his policy. The Danes had put themselves in the wrong, as the British Foreign Secretary, Lord Russell, pointed out to his ambassador at Copenhagen in December; on the other hand, Frederick of Augustenburg's claim, in contravention of the Treaty of London of 1852, was an equally aggressive step, and Bismarck did not intend throwing away this diplomatic advantage. Certainly he meant to resist the Danes, but not on behalf of Frederick or the German Confederation. Instead, he took his stand on the Treaty of London and turned to Vienna for cooperation. In fact, this was a moment when Austria might very well have strengthened her position by placing herself at the head of German nationalist feeling in support of Augustenburg, but after the failure of the Frankfurt meeting of princes Francis Joseph had lost faith in the ambitious schemes of Schmerling and preferred to listen to his Foreign Minister. Rechberg, as a conservative, was only too anxious to preserve the existing map of Europe and, conscious of Austria's isolation, responded gladly to Bismarck's proposals, which seemed to represent a far more respectable policy than what he had feared from Prussia.

On 16 January 1864 a treaty was signed between Austria and Prussia providing for joint military intervention if Denmark would not retract. Bismarck was careful to exclude from its terms any mention of the Treaty of London, claiming that his King's sympathies with German nationalism would not allow this, and it was simply stated that the future of the duchies would only be settled by mutual agreement between the two countries. This gave Bismarck precisely what he wanted, although the Austrian *Reichsrat* (see p. 201) showed itself to be considerably more alert to Prussian ambitions than Rechberg. 'Prussia has scarcely digested Silesia,'* argued one of its speakers, 'and now she is getting her claws into the duchies, while we are leading her into them with drum and trumpet. But what music will get her out again?'

Forces of the German Confederation had already moved into Holstein, where the Danes withdrew without resistance. The independent ultimatum presented jointly by Berlin and Vienna was, however, rejected at Copenhagen; on 1 February a combined Prussian and Austrian army entered Slesvig and by the middle of April had driven the Danes back into Jutland. Naturally these events were watched with some alarm by the Powers, but there was little that they were prepared to do by way of concerted action. Russia still felt in need of friendship with Prussia during the last stages of her suppression of the Polish rising. The attention of Great Britain was still partly distracted by the havoc which British suspicions of Napoleon's designs on the Rhineland had wrought on Anglo-French relations during the Polish crisis, and this made any cooperation unlikely. Sweden, too, hung back, since the attack by Austria and Prussia suggested a greater commitment than she had envisaged at the time of her treaty with Denmark in 1863.

The only contribution made by the Powers was the summoning of an international conference at London in April. For Bismarck it was essential that the conference should break down through the apparent intransigence of the Danes. Accordingly he changed his ground, maintaining that since a state of war existed with Denmark, the treaty of 1852, of which she, Prussia, and Austria had all been signatories, was no longer valid, and Prussia and Austria were therefore free to impose new conditions. By these means he was to ensure that Denmark would continue the fight, and he was assisted in this by the hopes that the Danes still entertained of foreign aid. Originally they had had some grounds for imagining this. In the summer of 1863 only a few months after the marriage of Christian IX's daughter Alexandra to Edward, Prince of Wales, Lord Palmerston had uttered a rash threat in the British House of Commons to the effect that Denmark would not fight alone; in Paris there had been rumours that Napoleon intended an attack on Austria over Venetia early in 1864. 'It is quite possible', the Italian minister had told the Danish ambassador, 'that we will be able to make a diversion in your favour next spring.' But no treaties of alliance existed with either Great Britain or France and by April 1864 the Danish government should have been able to read the signs.

They did not read them, and Bismarck was able to attach so many qualifications to a suggested personal union of the duchies with the kingdom of Denmark that the Danes rejected such a compromise. Only now did Bismarck take up the cry of the German nationalists,

* Annexed by Frederick II.

proposing independence for the duchies under Frederick of Augustenburg. 'We must let the whole pack howl,' he said, and howl they did, as the war continued and the Prusso-Austrian forces thrust on through Jutland. Augustenburg's hopes naturally lifted, but they soon fell again when Bismarck made it plain to him in conversation that he would be little more than a puppet of the Prussian government. In fact, Bismarck had no intention that he should become even that. 'At the London conference,' he said to Beust, the Saxon Prime Minister, a year later, 'I hitched the Prince to the plough as an ox to get it moving. Once the plough was in motion, I unhitched the ox.'

For the moment the renewal of the war was all that he needed. By the end of June the army had completed the overrunning of the. mainland and the Prussians had crossed to the island of Alsen off the east coast of Slesvig. Diplomacy could do nothing to save the Danes. A mild Russian attempt at mediation came to nothing. The British toyed with the idea of gaining French support, but still could not quieten their fears of Napoleon: '. . . what will France require as the price of her alliance with England?' wrote Lord Russell to Queen Victoria on 23 June, 'and is it in the interest of England to pay that price?' As a consequence the British cabinet decided two days later not to intervene. With its last hope gone, the Danish government resigned on 8 July, and on 1 August preliminary peace terms were signed whereby the two duchies were surrendered to Prussia and Austria.

3. The war of 1866

Thus far, Bismarck's skill had lain in strengthening his position while acting within the framework of what was superficially a conservative foreign policy. For although his outbidding of Austria at Frankfurt in 1863 with a demand for a German Parliament elected by universal suffrage and his momentary support of Augustenburg after the failure of the London conference were calculated appeals to liberal feeling, his actual diplomatic moves—the defeat of the Austrian attempt to create a *Grossdeutschland*, the Alvensleben convention with Russia, and the treaty of January 1864 with Austria against Denmark's rejection of the existing settlement of the Slesvig-Holstein question—could all claim to represent the attitude of a Metternich rather than a Cavour.

In the following two years, however, this apparent conservatism was sharply modified as he manoeuvred for the position from which he might effect the transference of power in Germany from Vienna to Berlin. In the joint occupation of the duchies he had an excellent situation in which to pick a quarrel with Austria; with the Prussian expulsion of the troops of the German Confederation and the grad-

ual conversion of Kiel into a Prussian naval station, he showed scant
regard for his ally, and in May 1865, at a meeting of the Crown
Council, he openly stated his intention of annexing both duchies
and of reorganizing the German Confederation. By the summer of
that year Prussian activity in the duchies had become so overbearing
and the dispatches from Berlin to Vienna so violent that the Austrians began to anticipate the severance of relations between the two
countries. In an endeavour to avoid this Count Mensdorf, who had
replaced Rechberg after the Danish war, arranged a meeting of an
Austrian envoy with King William and Bismarck while they were
taking the waters at Gastein, and by the convention that was signed
in August it was agreed that the condominium in the duchies should
end. Instead, Austria would administer Holstein, and Prussia
Slesvig. This 'papering over the cracks', as Bismarck called it,
was simply one step nearer to annexation, as most foreign governments realized; it did not render Austria any more secure in her
relations with Prussia, and by dividing the duchies it confirmed the
impression among the states of the German Confederation that
Francis Joseph was the accomplice of Bismarck in destroying the
cause of Frederick of Augustenburg.

It was not enough, however, simply to prepare the way for a
breach with Austria. 'If war in alliance with France against Austria
is banned,' Bismarck had declared at the Crown Council·in May,
'then a Prussian policy is no longer possible.' In fact, what he
wanted from France was not a firm alliance—that might be dangerous and costly—but simply neutrality in the event of an Austro-
Prussian war. On the other hand, an alliance with Italy—less
dangerous and costly only to Austria—would serve him well. In both
these aims he had the extraordinary good fortune to be assisted by
the mistakes of the Emperor of the French himself.

As has been seen, Napoleon III had not been content to follow
the foreign policy of his predecessors. His encouragement of foreign
nationalism and his hopes of revising the French frontier of 1815
had caused him to develop a policy in striking contrast to that which
had shaped the French government's attitude towards Germany in
the crisis of 1840 and towards Italy in 1848. Amid a confusion of
hesitancy and rashness he had at least acquired Savoy and Nice for
France in 1860, but only at the price of developments in Italy far
beyond what he had originally intended, and in France there were
already many voices raised in dissent. Thiers pointed out that by
assisting Italian and German unification France was only creating
a rod for her own back, and added the prophecy that one day the
two of them would combine against France. It was the folly of
Napoleon that he did not realize that, for France too, the Vienna
settlement represented a guarantee.

In October 1865 Bismarck visited Napoleon at Biarritz. Exactly what they discussed is unknown, but before he left Berlin, Bismarck had hinted to the French *Chargé d'affaires* at the possible acquisition of Belgium by France. Nothing positive emerged from their meeting; Napoleon, whose powers of decision were declining as his health deteriorated, remained uncommitted, but Bismarck could feel that he had forestalled the likelihood of any immediate French alliance with Austria.

So far Napoleon had been cautious. Over the negotiation of the Prusso-Italian treaty, however, he revealed both the extent of his hopes and the serious misconceptions on which his policy was based. The Italian government had recently failed in a bid to purchase Venetia from Austria and at the beginning of 1866 began to respond to Prussian suggestions of an alliance. They were at first extremely mistrustful over the use to which Bismarck might put this, but their doubts were eventually overcome by Napoleon's persuasion. 'Italy will get Venice,' he remarked to Nigra, the Italian ambassador in Paris, 'and France will benefit by the conflict of the two Powers whose alliance hems her in. Once the struggle has begun, France can throw her weight into the balance and must obviously become the arbitrator and master of the situation.' Here in a nutshell lay his two fundamental mistakes. He believed that the gaining of Venetia would take Italy's eyes off Rome, to whose defence the Catholic interest in France committed him. More particularly, he believed that in any Austro-Prussian war the two sides would be so evenly matched that there would be time for him to bring off a diplomatic *coup*.

The secret military alliance between Prussia and Italy was finally signed on 8 April 1866. Italy promised to declare war on Austria as soon as hostilities between Prussia and Austria had begun, and as a reward was to receive Venetia without the Trentina district. The agreement was to be valid for only three months and Bismarck lost no time in attempting to goad Austria into violent action by a proposal at Frankfurt on 9 April that a German Parliament should be elected by universal suffrage. He had already played this card before in September 1863, but his own treatment of the Prussian Parliament had by now made German liberals highly suspicious of the honesty of his intentions. 'Universal and equal suffrage, direct election and a German Parliament are fine words,' commented the *Nationalzeitung*, 'but what have they to do with Count Bismarck or the Diet?'

Despite this disappointment, however, two factors gave Bismarck the whip-hand in drawing Austria into what Prussia could claim was a defensive war. First, the speed with which Prussia could mobilize on her southern frontier was so much greater that, as the tension between the two steadily mounted, Austria had to take the apparently aggressive step of mobilizing before Prussia. Second, her diplomatic position was so weak that she dared not rely upon a proposal for international mediation which Prussia, in order to keep herself in the right, would not have been able to reject. Thus it was Austria who refused the suggestion for a congress put forward by Great Britain, France, and Russia—to the wild relief of Bismarck who had unwillingly had to accept it. Similarly, Bismarck did not obstruct the efforts of a Prussian deputy, Anton von Gablenz, whose mission of pacification to Vienna also came to nothing. The only positive diplomatic move that Austria did make at this time was a treaty with France, whereby French neutrality was purchased in return for the surrender of Venetia and a promise of the creation of a new Rhineland state. This was naturally in accordance with Napoleon's schemes at this time, while Austria hoped to gain Silesia from Prussia in compensation for her loss of Venetia.

The Franco-Austrian treaty was signed on 12 June. Relations between Austria and Prussia had already collapsed at the beginning of the month when Austria had referred the question of the duchies to the German Diet—an open breach of her treaty of January 1864 with Prussia. Bismarck had replied with the occupation of Holstein. To his disappointment this did not lead to immediate conflict. He followed it up with an amplified version of the Prussian proposal for a new German constitution and then, on 14 June, when the Federal Diet passed a Bavarian amendment of an Austrian proposal for a Federal mobilization, the Prussian representative announced Prussia's withdrawal from the German Confederation. On the following day Prussian troops marched into Hanover, Hesse-Cassel, and Saxony, all of whom had sided with Austria, and without any more formal declaration the war began.

The die was cast, and the whole future of Bismarck now rested in the hands of the Prussian generals. 'If we are beaten', he said to the British ambassador, 'I shall not return. I can die only once and it befits the vanquished to die.' He was not left long in suspense. The defeat of the Italians at Custoza on 24 June made little difference to the course of hostilities in the north. To prevent the Austrians from gaining time to organize their defence, Moltke took the deliberate risk of crossing the Bohemian frontier on 23 June with three separate armies; on 3 July the centre army under Prince Frederick of Prussia encountered the main forces of the Austrian commander Benedek outside Königgrätz, and with the arrival of the Crown Prince's army on the Prussian left wing the Austrians suffered a staggering defeat with a loss of 44,000 men—almost five times as many as the Prussian casualties.

'Excellency,' said a Prussian general to Bismarck afterwards, 'you are now a great man. But if the Crown Prince had come too late, you would now be a great villain.' This was certainly true. Yet the victory at Königgrätz was not entirely complete, since Benedek had still been able to withdraw a large part of his forces. It was Bismarck's statesmanship that now ensured that Königgrätz alone should be the decisive battle. All that he wanted from Austria was freedom of action for Prussia in north Germany. 'We need Austria's strength in future for ourselves,' he said, and the chances of a revived friendship for which he looked, once Prussia had the upper hand, would only be damaged by territorial annexation. In any case, a quick peace was essential if he was to forestall any attempt on the part of Napoleon to make some profitable form of mediation.

To achieve this he had to fight on a good many fronts. His appeals to Czech and Magyar nationalists, coupled with the prospect of moderate terms, soon had their effect on Vienna. Almost more difficult was the resistance of King William, who had now tasted military triumph and saw himself as 'the conqueror at the gate of Vienna'. Eventually Bismarck had his way and on 26 July a preliminary peace was signed at Nikolsburg, to be followed a month later by a final settlement at Prague. The terms were primarily concerned with the remodelling of Germany along Prussian lines. Prussia herself was to absorb Slesvig and Holstein as well as Hesse-Cassel, Hanover, Nassau, and Frankfurt. All the other states north of the Main—including the kingdom of Saxony whose autonomy Austria did at least manage to preserve—were to become members of a new North German Confederation under Prussian leadership. The states south of the Main were to form a vague union of their own—a political expression of no significance, since Prussia immediately signed secret treaties of military alliance with Bavaria, Württemberg, and Baden. Paradoxically Austria's only territorial loss was in the theatre of operations where she had enjoyed complete success. Her military victory over the Italians was followed on 20 July by the annihilation of the Italian fleet in the Adriatic, but despite these disasters, Bismarck kept his word and Venetia was surrendered indirectly through France to Italy. It was, however, the territories that she did not lose which pointed to the full significance of the Austrian defeat, for her exclusion from the new North German Confederation meant that the point of control in German affairs had shifted from Vienna to Berlin, and the way was open for the creation of that *Kleindeutschland* which the Habsburgs had previously been able to resist.

Chapter 18

The Fruits of Victory and Defeat

1. The North German Confederation

Königgrätz was not the only victory that Bismarck could claim on 3 July 1866. On the very same day elections held in Prussia reflected the patriotic excitement of war in a great increase of conservative seats from 38 to 142. The most significant aspect of the Prussian political scene, however, was a change in the attitude of the liberals. A policy of 'blood and iron' seemed about to achieve the unification which they had sought to no avail in 1848 and many now found themselves unable to resist the attraction of Bismarck's success. The issue was put clearly before them when, in September, Bismarck introduced in the new Chamber an Indemnity Bill excusing the government for having ruled without a constitutional budget since 1862. Only seven votes were cast against it and in the subsequent split among the Progressives a new National Liberal Party was to emerge, including leading members of the former opposition who were prepared to support the Prussian government over foreign policy.

This abdication by the liberals was to bring about a new harmony between Bismarck and the Prussian Chamber. Gratuities were voted for the victorious generals and Bismarck himself received 400,000 thalers—approximately £60,000—with which he purchased Varzin, a large estate in Pomerania. All parties agreed to the annexation of Hanover, Hesse-Cassel, Nassau, Frankfurt, and Slesvig-Holstein by Prussia. The deposition of King George of Hanover aroused objections among the right wing of the conservatives, but there could be little effective resistance, even when in 1868 the government confiscated the King's personal income, thereby creating a useful private source of financial supply known as the *Welfen-Fonds*.

By the autumn of 1866 Bismarck was completely worn out, but in December he had recovered sufficiently to return to Berlin to begin work on the drafting of the constitution of the North German Confederation (the *Norddeutscher Bund*), which was promulgated in July 1867. The President, who was the King of Prussia, had the right of concluding all treaties and declaring war and was commander-in-chief of the Federal forces. A Federal Council (the *Bundesrat*) consisted of delegates voting on instructions from the governments of the member states who had appointed them. Here Prussia, owing to her now greatly increased size, enjoyed seventeen votes, while twenty-six votes were shared among the other twenty-one states in the Confederation. The Lower House (the *Reichstag*) was a single representative Chamber elected by direct universal manhood suffrage, and with the right to veto the budget and all legislation. The sole Federal minister was the Chancellor, Bismarck, who, since he was only directly responsible to the President, could not be dismissed through a parliamentary vote.

The new constitution thus differed significantly from that of the old German Confederation of 1815 since, within the limits of north Germany, it had created a far stronger federal executive. It was equally remote from the proposals of the liberals at Frankfurt in 1849; the predominance of Prussia was barely disguised at all and, as Napoleon III had already shown, universal suffrage by itself was no serious obstacle to authoritarian rule, so long as the powers of the representative Chamber were carefully restricted. 'Let us put Germany into the saddle,' Bismarck had said during the debate on the constitution; 'she will know how to ride.' It was a memorable figure of speech, but hardly exact, for in reality it was German political sentiment that had been placed in harness and Bismarck who sat in the saddle.

2. The *Ausgleich*: the creation of Austria-Hungary 1867

If the Prussian victory had opened the way to the remodelling of Germany, the two Austrian defeats of 1859 and 1866 had had an equally profound effect upon the government of the Habsburg Empire. The loss of Lombardy had forced Francis Joseph to realize that it would be dangerous to refuse to come to terms with the political and social forces that had been suppressed since 1849, and the system of centralized autocracy (see p. 155) which Bach had continued to administer after Schwarzenberg's death in 1852 had accordingly been modified in a succession of constitutional experiments.

Bach was replaced by Count Goluchowski, a Polish aristocrat, and in 1860 the March Patent increased the membership of the *Reichsrat* (the Lower House), with an additional thirty-eight representatives from the *Landtage*. This simply gave rise to demands for greater regional autonomy which were then hurriedly granted in the October Diploma of that year, since Francis Joseph wished to strengthen his position at home while he was in consultation with the Russian Tsar and the Prince Regent of Prussia at Warsaw (see

p. 183). The Diploma, together with a number of rescripts, re-established the position in Hungary as it was before 1848 and reinstated institutions of local government including the Diets of Transylvania and Croatia. It met, however, with little success, since the Magyar leaders insisted upon the validity of the April Laws of 1848 (see p. 127) and German and Magyar opinion objected generally to the concessions which had been made at the same time to the other nationalities. Goluchowski was dismissed in December and succeeded by Anton von Schmerling, who had earlier testified to his liberal instincts by resigning from the post of Minister of Justice at Vienna when the Austrian constitution of 1849 had been abolished in 1851. His attempted solution, the February Patent of 1861, simply revised the October Diploma in the direction of slightly greater central control. The *Reichsrat* was to consist of 343 deputies elected by the various Diets, but with the balance heavily weighted in the favour of the Germans. This, too, proved unacceptable and Schmerling eventually dissolved the Hungarian Diet which had refused to send its delegates to the *Reichsrat*. The Croat Diet, which objected to the exclusion of Dalmatia from Croatia, was also recalcitrant and was dissolved in the following November.

Nevertheless, during the next few years Francis Joseph's negotiations with Hungary did make some progress and would have made still more but for his appointment of a Bohemian aristocrat, Count Belcredi, in place of Schmerling. Belcredi still hankered after a federal scheme which would include other national groups as well as the Magyars, but it was at this point that Austria suffered her great defeat by Prussia in 1866 and to the Hungarian extremists it seemed that the moment for independence had come. Francis Joseph was fortunate, however, in that Deák and Count Andrássy both recognized the need to retain a connection with Austria in order to stand firm against the Slav elements within the Empire, and the negotiations between these two on the Hungarian side and the Saxon Count Ferdinand von Beust, who had now entered the Austrian government, eventually led to a settlement in 1867.

The *Ausgleich*, sometimes known as the Compromise, divided the Habsburg Empire into two halves, a dual monarchy in which Francis Joseph was to rule in two separate capacities—as Austrian Emperor and as King of Hungary. The territories within which Hungary was to enjoy a considerable autonomy included not only those of the old historic kingdom, but also Croatia-Slavonia on the Turkish border to the south (see map p. 143). The remainder of the Habsburg dominions centered on the original territories of upper and lower Austria, Bohemia and Moravia, and Polish Galicia, all now to be known loosely as Austria. In this new arrangement Austria and Hungary were to have independent governments of their own, each headed by a premier with subordinate ministers, each responsible through budgetary control to biennual parliaments meeting in Vienna and Budapest. The upper houses of both were made up of great magnates and Crown nominees, and the lower houses were elective, but there were differences here in that the Austrian deputies were chosen by the seventeen provincial assemblies, while the Hungarians were elected directly on a narrow and complicated franchise.

The union between Austria and Hungary, however, entailed more than the sharing of the same sovereign. Above the two separate Austrian and Hungarian governments there was established a small executive and consultative structure that still served the whole extent of the Habsburg Empire. Foreign policy and military and naval affairs were to be regulated to joint ministries responsible purely to the Crown, and decisions taken at this level would involve the raising of taxes and of contingents of men. These had to be approved by two delegations, each of sixty members nominated respectively by the Austrian and Hungarian parliaments, and once this approval had been gained, the two parliaments were bound to raise the necessary money and men. This considerable vestige of central control meant that the *Ausgleich* was not quite as sweeping as the April laws of 1848 and was thus still something of a compromise with the Hungarian nationalists.

Nevertheless, it did mark the abandonment of the old Habsburg principle of playing off the master races against the subject peoples; autonomy gave the Magyars almost total control over large minorities of Transylvanians, Ruthenians, Slovaks, Jews and Germans, and although in Croatia-Slavonia the preponderance of Croats did at first produce a miniature *Ausgleich* with the Croat Diet at Zagreb in 1868, the moderation of the older leaders, Deák and Andrássy was soon replaced by the far more intransigent attitude of a new generation of Magyars towards the suppressed nationalities.

3. The reforms of Tsar Alexander II 1855–81

In March 1855 death brought the long reign of Nicholas I of Russia to a close. 'I hand over to you my command,' said the dying Tsar to his son Alexander, 'but unfortunately not in such order as I should wish.' There was good reason for his sense of despair. The despotism which for thirty years he had exercised through secret committees and the agents of the Third Section had proved itself unequal to the tasks of government. At home the constant risings of the peasantry pointed to the fact that the great problem of serfdom had still to be solved; in the realm of foreign affairs a dangerous isolation had forced Russia to fight alone in the Crimea and at the moment of Nicholas's death Sebastopol lay invested by British and French troops.

With this uneasy inheritance Tsar Alexander II was to embark on a vast programme of reform that involved the greatest transformation of Russian society and government since the days of Peter the Great. When, in April 1856, Alexander announced to a gathering of the Moscow nobility: 'better to abolish serfdom from above than to wait till it begins to abolish itself from below', he put in a nutshell the two assumptions on which he was to govern. Reforms must come in order to anticipate revolution; yet he knew that they *could* only come if they were imposed by Imperial decree. The backwardness and conservatism of the peasantry, the smallness of the middle class, Tsardom's mistrust of a nobility gaining greater power, and the problems of control over such an enormous land mass, are all constant factors which explain the despotic character of the great periods of cataclysmic change that punctuate Russian history. Thus the paradox of Alexander's reforms was that although they moved towards greater social freedom and constitutional development, they could never be allowed to interfere with the authority of the Tsar, and the reign which began on a high note of optimism was to grow increasingly conservative and was to end with an assassin's bomb.

For Alexander the memory of the revolutions of 1848 appeared less ominous than the deficiencies revealed in Russia's system of government by her fortunes in the Crimean War. So pressing did this need for internal reform seem to him that he was prepared to cut his losses and to accept the terms of the Treaty of Paris in March 1856 (see p. 169). This left him free to concentrate on the emancipation of the privately owned serfs. He was not entirely without support in this. Some of the larger landowners in the south were beginning to prefer wage labour, and it was clearly essential in the gradually developing factories; among the liberals and writers emancipation had long been an accepted aim and the Tsar himself may have been influenced by the publication of Turgenev's *Sportsman's Sketches* in 1855. Yet among the bulk of the nobility and gentry and even many of the peasantry the idea awoke a suspicious hostility, and it took all of Alexander's determination to keep the project alive through four years of discussion in the various committees and provincial commissions. There were in fact many practical difficulties. The experience of emancipation in the Baltic provinces under Alexander I (see p. 21) suggested that freedom without land might well reduce the peasantry to an even worse position than before; if, on the other hand, the peasantry were to be given some of the land, the landowners would require compensation which could only come in the first place from the government.

Eventually, however, Alexander achieved his object and in March 1861 the emancipation of the serfs was proclaimed by Imperial decree. The legal position of serfdom was declared abolished without compensation to the owners. The peasantry were to receive a portion of the estates of their landlords at an agreed price, four-fifths of which was to be advanced by the government, who would recover this outlay through redemption payments by the peasantry during the next forty-nine years. The peasantry gained about three-fifths of the land in all, but the actual division of the estates and the amounts to be paid in compensation varied greatly from province to province, being settled by Arbitrators of the Peace, drawn mostly from the nobility and gentry. Thus compensation was everywhere fixed at a far higher level than the existing land-prices; this discrepancy was particularly marked in the central and northern regions where the soil was almost exhausted, while in the fertile black-soil regions, where the rate of compensation came closer to the real value, the landowners retained a far larger share of their estates.

The emancipation of the Russian serf was probably as fair a compromise as could be imposed from above, but like most compromises it was highly unsatisfactory to both sides. Many of the 262,000 landlords had been in debt, with a high proportion of their serfs mortgaged to State credit institutions; hence, much of the financial compensation due from the State was retained to pay off these debts, and even the government bonds that they did receive were found to depreciate in value in the course of time.

For the majority of the 20 million privately owned serfs the economic consequences of emancipation came as a considerable shock. Household serfs received no land whatsoever and were forced to look for employment elsewhere. The partitioning of the estates gave the farming serf less land than what he had actually been able to cultivate before 1861; on average, this loss has been calculated as much as one-fifth, and in the more fertile southern districts it was even higher. The redemption payments to the State were another source of resentment among the peasantry, who in a confused way had always regarded the land as theirs and now found themselves compelled to pay for it. In fact, it was the *mir*, the village commune to which the peasant belonged, that became financially responsible to the government and would ultimately possess the land. The *mir* had always played a large part in Russian peasant society in allotting the strips of serf-land. Now this conception of collective ownership gave it a further hold over the peasant, since it decided what each individual's share of the *mir's* redemption payment should be, and through the system of passports it could prevent the peasant from leaving the district or from separating himself economically from the community, unless he was able to guarantee his share of the whole of the outstanding debt. Thus, although the peasant was now legally free from his old master, this dependence had been largely replaced by the *mir*.

The full consequences of emancipation, however, did not end

here, since the change in the legal relationship between landlord and peasant was bound to involve modifications in local government and the judiciary. In January 1864 Alexander decreed the establishment of representative assemblies at two levels in local government—district and provincial. By a method not unlike the Prussian electoral system landowners, townsmen, and peasantry chose their deputies for the district *Zemstvo* separately—the peasantry by a system of indirect election—but the distribution of seats was so arranged that no single class had an absolute majority, although in the higher assembly, the provincial *Zemstvo*, whose members were elected by the district *Zemstva* from their own deputies, the landed class did tend to predominate. Within three years this new type of institution had been established in twenty-seven provinces and soon brought about striking local improvements in medical and veterinary services, hospitals, asylums, and various forms of fire insurance. Their most remarkable achievement lay in encouraging the growth of elementary schools which, between 1856 and 1880, increased in number from 8,000 to 23,000. In 1870 a similar system of self-government in the towns established municipal councils whose functions corresponded roughly to those of the *Zemstva*. From the point of view of their immediate practical consequences these governmental reforms were more beneficial than the emancipation of the serfs, yet the restrictions that constantly hampered the activity of the assemblies pointed to the caution with which a Tsarist régime was bound to regard all such experiments.

Meanwhile, another edict in 1864 had proclaimed a totally new system of judicial procedure whereby petty cases were to be heard by the equivalent of Justices of the Peace elected through the *Zemstva*, while criminal cases were to be tried in regional courts by appointed judges before juries chosen from lists prepared by the *Zemstva*. Trials were to be in public and the provision of salaries for the judges made them less liable to bribery. The Third Section still retained its powers of 'administrative arrest', enabling it to exile any suspect to Siberia without trial, but the general improvement in the tone of judicial proceedings after this time was clearly observed by impartial observers. At the same time Golovnin at the Ministry of Education was working to improve the quality and number of secondary schools, and the relaxing of the censorship created a new sense of freedom in the Universities. At the Ministry of War Miliutin abolished the most brutal forms of punishment in the army, equipment was brought up to date, and the education of army cadets improved. His greatest struggle was to introduce a system of universal conscription, a burden which until then had been borne almost exclusively by the peasantry, and it was not until 1874, after the warning of Prussia's victories over Austria and France, that the measure was actually proclaimed. All men of twenty years of age were to be liable to perform six years with the colours, but the actual selection was to be by ballot—with considerable reductions in length of service according to the level of education which the recruit had attained before joining the army.

It was perhaps in Finland that Alexander was to see the most successful aspect of his rule. At the beginning of his reign his official visit to Helsinki, where he was Chancellor of the University, and the re-establishment of the Finnish committee at St Petersburg through the efforts of the Finnish Secretary of State, Count Armfeldt, indicated the Tsar's interest in the Grand Duchy. In 1863 the first Diet to be summoned in Finland since 1809 was opened by Alexander himself at Helsinki, and by 1867 had drawn up a Fundamental Law which meant nothing less than the restoration of constitutional rule in Finland. There was a highly conservative note in the preservation of the old form of the four Estates, instead of a modern parliamentary assembly, but the franchise was extended, the agreement of three of the Estates was needed for the passing of any new law, and the Diet was to meet at least once every five years. Liberal ambitions were encouraged by currency reform, the weakening of the guilds and the ending, in 1869, of the Church's control over schools; and plans were made for a railway line linking Helsinki with the inland provinces. All these reforms in the economy and administration of the country were naturally facilitated by a long tradition of local self-government and the absence of any serfdom. Alexander's principal aim, however, was to reconcile the Finns to Russian rule, and here the social antagonism between Finns and Swedo-Finns suggested that the fostering of a growing Finnish national spirit might be an effective means of quelling those who still looked to Sweden. In 1863 the Finnish language was granted equality with Swedish in the law courts and government offices, and in 1865 notice was given that by 1872 it would be compulsory for all officials throughout the Grand Duchy. Despite the greater conservatism of the later half of his reign, Alexander never went back on his word to the Finns and it is a remarkable fact that even today, long after the gaining of Finnish independence and two desperate wars with Russia in the twentieth century, the statue of Alexander II still stands in the Great Square in Helsinki.

In Poland the same liberal policy led to disaster, in striking contrast to its success in Finland. This was partly because the more recent memory of Polish independence encouraged the Poles to take advantage of the general relaxation of control to make more violent demands; also partly because the upper classes were the leaders of national feeling. Alexander began in 1857 by authorizing the establishment of an Agricultural Society for the consideration of agrarian reforms, and in 1861 a Polish magnate, Alexander Wielopolski, was given ministerial powers to introduce a number of measures includ-

ing the recognition of Polish as the official language, the establishment of new schools, and the emancipation of the Jews. A growing
national excitement in Warsaw, however, led to violent demonstrations on the anniversary of Kosciuszko's death; Wielopolski resigned
and Russian military rule was established until June 1862, when
Wielopolski was reinstated. The situation continued to deteriorate,
however, when an attempt on the life of the new Governor-General,
Alexander's brother Constantine, was followed by public executions, and a new levy of army recruits finally provided the spark for
the great Polish rising of 1863.

'This much is certain,' wrote Marx to Engels in February, 'that
the era of revolutions is now once more fairly opened.' He was completely wrong. The Polish revolt did not spread and was doomed by
almost exactly the same factors as in the rising of 1830 (see p. 75).
First, the peasantry, hating their masters, refused to take much part
in the struggle. Second, the rebels were still divided among themselves. Even in exile there had been two centres of resistance; the
moderates under Prince Czartoryski, living in his splendid seven-
teenth-century mansion on the Ile St Louis in Paris, concentrated
on the frontiers of 1772 and the constitution of 1791, while the radicals, who demanded the emancipation of the peasantry and the
Jews, were led by Mieroslavski, who in 1861 had established a training school for his movement at Cuneo in Piedmont and was in touch
with a Polish society organized by Joseph Conrad's father at Kiev.
Each party accordingly established its own military dictator
throughout the fighting in Poland and Lithuania. Third, the rebels
were not only divided, but also outnumbered—10,000 Poles against
80,000 Russians—and the refusal of the western Powers to do more
than protest, coupled with Prussia's active assistance to Russia (see
p. 190), sealed the fate of the revolt.

By the spring of 1864 resistance had been crushed and the inevitable executions, deportations, and heavy fines for the rebels followed. From now on Alexander decided that the conciliation of
Polish national sentiment was an unworkable policy. Instead, he
would revert to his father's plan of 'russification', and in the hope
of winning over the peasantry, complete emancipation granting
them about one-third of the land was proclaimed in March 1864;
redemption payments were made considerably lower than in Russia
and were to be financed by a general land tax, which meant that
the Polish landowner actually had to contribute to his own compensation. Polish institutions soon disappeared. Russian became the
official language in all schools, and in 1866 the Kingdom of Poland
was renamed the Vistula Region. It was a sad end to the hopes of
the Polish patriots; yet it is hard to escape the conclusion that by
antagonizing Alexander's initial goodwill they had thrown away a
splendid opportunity and brought disaster on themselves.

Chapter 19

The Defeat of France 1870–1

1. The Franco-Prussian War

Significant though the constitutional changes in Germany and Austria-Hungary may have been, the diplomatic consequences of Bismarck's success in 1866 were still greater. Only the southern states remained to be brought within a new Germany from which Austria had been excluded; in Italy only Rome and the patrimony of St Peter still lay outside the frontiers of Victor Emmanuel's kingdom. For Napoleon III it was now vital that he should regain the initiative in the revision of the Vienna settlement; on the other hand, the clerical interest at home forbade him to abandon Rome, and the realization that Königgrätz implied a defeat for France made it essential to resist any further step towards German unification. Thus the years immediately following the Peace of Prague saw a duel between Napoleon III and Bismarck, in which the Emperor of the French, weakened by failing health and still torn between conflicting policies, was simply no match for the Chancellor of the North German Confederation.

For Napoleon the need to regain prestige was an overriding consideration. He sought first some territorial gain which might make less obvious the contrast between Bismarck's recent success and his own failure in Mexico (see p. 172). A bid to purchase the Grand Duchy of Luxemburg from the King of the Netherlands came to nothing; through Benedetti, the French ambassador at Berlin, he opened fruitless negotiations over the possibility of acquiring a part of the Palatinate, and a proposal whereby France should absorb Belgium achieved no more than to place in Bismarck's hands a highly incriminating document of which he was to make good use in 1870.

A second more sensible aspect of his policy in these years was an attempt in 1868 to create an active alliance with Austria-Hungary and Italy against Prussia. It was not unreasonable to assume that Francis Joseph might have been ready to seize an opportunity to reverse the decision of 1866, but here again Napoleon was to be disappointed. The mildness of the terms which Bismarck had imposed on Austria made her unwilling to embark upon a hostile policy. 'What our monarchy wants', wrote Beust, 'is the maintenance of peace.' And over Italy the problem of Rome remained insuperable. Napoleon had actually withdrawn the French garrison there in December 1866, but the subsequent raids into Papal territory had forced him to send it back in November 1867 and the principal condition on which Victor Emmanuel insisted—the evacuation of Rome by the French—was a price that Napoleon knew he could not pay.

These hopes that Napoleon entertained of creating an alliance against Prussia naturally have a bearing on the outbreak of the Franco-Prussian War in 1870, since they might suggest some justification for Bismarck getting his blow in first. Indeed, the causes of the war still remain a matter of controversy. The story begins in Spain in 1868 when a military junta headed by General Prim drove Queen Isabella from her throne and the *Cortes* in the following year agreed upon the establishment of a liberal form of government under a constitutional monarchy. This presented an immediate problem. 'Finding a democratic king in Europe,' remarked Prim, 'is like looking for an atheist in Heaven.' In the event it proved to be not only difficult but also highly dangerous, for the choice of a sovereign for the Spanish throne was of particular concern to France, who had been well satisfied with the pro-French policy of Queen Isabella. The danger became still more apparent when the choice of the Spanish government eventually fell on Leopold, a son of Prince Karl Anton of Hohenzollern-Sigmaringen—highly suitable from the Spanish point of view, since his family was Roman Catholic. It was hardly likely, however, that the thought of a Hohenzollern on the throne of Spain would commend itself to the French. For this reason Prim was anxious to keep the negotiations secret, but when by March 1870 Leopold had twice refused the offer, it seemed that Prim and his agent Salazar would have to look elsewhere.

For long after the Franco-Prussian War the Prussians always maintained that the negotiations had only concerned King William in his capacity as head of the Hohenzollern family. Towards the end of the century, however, evidence emerged to show that Bismarck, while remaining quietly in the background, had fostered the Hohenzollern candidature even to the extent of using the *Welfen-Fonds*, the confiscated income of the King of Hanover, to bribe the Spanish *Cortes*, and had worked hard to persuade both Leopold and King William to fall in with the idea. But even if this is established, there remains the question of his motive. Napoleon III had informed him that he would never tolerate a Hohenzollern on the Spanish throne, and in view of later events it would be tempting to assume that Bismarck intended to use the issue to provoke war between the two countries, after which France would be unable to prevent the incorporation of the south German states within Germany. Certainly he must have seen this as one possibility. On the other hand, a Hohenzollern candidature was not a good emotional cause with which to rally the south German states, among whom considerable antagonism existed towards Bismarck, and it may well have been that he would have been satisfied simply to see a peaceful solution with Leopold on the Spanish throne. The presence of an ally on France's southern frontier would be useful for the future and a diplomatic success here might well have the effect of further undermining Napoleon's prestige at home. In any case, at the end of 1869 Napoleon had embarked upon the experiment of parliamentary government and Bismarck could well afford to wait to see whether this would improve his chances of including the south German states within the Confederation.

In May 1870, however, a strongly anti-Prussian Foreign Minister, de Gramont, took office in France and Bismarck at once revived the question of the candidature. Leopold was persuaded to accept and King William agreed 'mit schwerem, sehr schwerem Herz'. The essential for Bismarck now was speed, but when on 21 June Salazar sent the news by telegraph to Madrid, a mistake in the deciphering of the message led Prim to believe that Salazar's return was not imminent and he accordingly prorogued the *Cortes*. This fatal error played havoc with the plans of Bismarck and Prim, since on Salazar's return to Madrid, the *Cortes* had to be summoned again to carry out the election of Leopold to the throne, and in the general delay and excitement the secret leaked out to the French. Thus, before the election could take place, there was time for France to protest and for King William to have second thoughts.

In Paris there was at once a fierce reaction in the press and de Gramont's speech before the *Corps Législatif* made it clear that France could never allow 'a foreign power, by placing one of its princes on the throne of Charles V, to disturb to our detriment the present equilibrium of Europe'. Instead of remonstrating with Prim the French government resolved to cut through any subterfuge by negotiating directly with King William at Ems. William at once responded to this approach by Benedetti, the French ambassador, and it was mainly due to his efforts that on 12 July Prince Karl Anton agreed to withdraw the candidature on his son's behalf. This decision was communicated from Sigmaringen to King William at Ems, Prim at Madrid, and the Spanish ambassador at Paris. Thus by two o'clock in the afternoon the French government could relax, while Bismarck, who arrived at Berlin from Varzin a few hours later that day, found that he was faced with a major diplomatic reverse.

Then, at the very moment when Bismarck claimed afterwards that he was contemplating resignation, the French threw away their moral advantage by overreaching themselves. Not content with the withdrawal, Napoleon and de Gramont sent instructions to Benedetti that he should demand of King William that the Hohenzollern candidature would never be renewed. Benedetti's fateful interview with William took place on 13 July on the Brunnenpromenade at Ems and resulted simply in an emphatic refusal by the Prussian king to acquiesce in this attempt to bind his actions for the future. A telegram describing this new turn of events was at once dispatched to Bismarck who was authorized to publish it. Bismarck later made much of the historic scene when the telegram reached him that evening as he was dining with Moltke and Roon; a rapid editing of the text made the incident at Ems appear like a heated argument ending with a direct snub to the French ambassador, and its publication in the press and in the foreign courts worked official and public opinion up to a fever pitch in France and Germany, culminating in a French declaration of war on 19 July. Whatever Bismarck's intentions may have been previously, war had certainly been his aim at the end as the only way out of a diplomatic crisis in which the stakes had become too high for either side to surrender, and the sensitiveness of the French to possible Prussian schemes had ultimately played into his hands.

Like Bismarck's earlier opponents, France soon learnt that she must fight this war without allies. In March 1868 Russia had already promised that she would intervene on Prussia's side if Austria-Hungary joined France, and the knowledge of this was sufficient to keep Francis Joseph neutral; in any case, the Germans and Magyars of the Dual Monarchy were strongly opposed to going to the assistance of the French. Danish public opinion favoured war against Prussia in the hope of regaining Slesvig, but the government wisely waited to see how militarily effective France would be as an ally. In Italy Victor Emmanuel put up his price, demanding not merely the evacuation of Rome by the French, but also freedom for Italy to modify the position of the Papal territory, and once again Napoleon dared not accept. 'France', said de Gramont, 'cannot defend her honour on the Rhine and sacrifice it on the Tiber.' British mistrust of France was still considerable and was greatly heightened when, on 25 July, Bismarck published in *The Times* the text of Benedetti's earlier proposal that Belgium should be annexed by France.

Once again Bismarck's diplomacy was aided by the immediate success of the Prussian army. Napoleon himself had had an inkling that the French army was in need of reform and had struggled unsuccessfully to establish universal military service, although he did at least secure the adoption of a new rifle, the *chasse-pot*, by the infantry. Yet not even he could have anticipated the appalling confusion of the French mobilization which produced only 200,000 troops, in contrast to the Prussian staff work which transported

380,000 men to the front in eighteen days. With this numerical superiority Moltke thrust into Lorraine and defeated the French right wing at Wörth on 6 August. The rest of the German forces swept on to the south of Metz and after two indecisive battles at Vionville and Gravelotte in the middle of August, Bazaine withdrew into the fortress of Metz. A fresh army which had been organized under Marshal MacMahon at Châlons had now to advance to the aid of Bazaine, but when it encountered the German Third Army at Sedan near the Belgian border, three days fighting ended in the surrender of the French army on 1 September. Among the 82,000 prisoners was Napoleon III himself who had hoped in vain for death on the battlefield. He now had one last conversation with Bismarck at a wayside cottage before his ensuing internment at Wilhelmshöhe. Here he remained for six months, after which he crossed the Channel to exile once again in England where he died in January 1873.

Indeed, Sedan was to mean more than the end of any serious chance of victory for France; the official publication of the news in Paris on 4 September brought about the fall of the Second Empire. Crowds invaded the Chamber, and in response to their demands the opposition deputies under Jules Favre and Gambetta agreed that a Republic should be proclaimed at the Hôtel de Ville; by now revolution had its own well-established traditions. An American dentist engineered the escape of the Empress Eugénie, whom Napoleon had appointed as Regent during his absence, and a provisional government of National Defence was formed by the deputies of Paris under the presidency of General Trochu.

The new government was determined to continue the fight. 'We shall yield neither an inch of our territory, nor a stone of our fortresses,' announced Jules Favre, now Foreign Minister, but by 19 September the German army was besieging Paris and the conduct of the war rested almost entirely with a few of the deputies who had been sent to Tours before the capital was invested. They were greatly strengthened by the arrival of Gambetta, who escaped from Paris by balloon in October, but the hastily organized Army of the Loire attempting to relieve Paris was thrust back by the Germans and in December the delegates had to leave Tours for Bordeaux. A second effort failed to strike effectively at the German communications across northern France and the army had eventually to seek refuge in Switzerland. Meanwhile, at the end of October, Bazaine had surrendered at Metz with 173,000 men and on 28 January 1871 Paris, which had been bombarded and was near to starvation, finally capitulated. The government of National Defence now negotiated a three weeks armistice during which national elections were to be held throughout France, and when the new Assembly had met on 12 February at Bordeaux, it became clear that a peace settlement would not be long delayed.

2. The consequences of the war

a) The creation of the German Empire

On 18 January 1871 Bismarck finally brought his work to its triumphant climax, when in the Hall of Mirrors at the palace of Versailles he proclaimed William I German Emperor. The date was in a sense the Hohenzollern counterpart to the Napoleonic 2 December, for it had been on 18 January 1701 that Frederick III, Elector of Brandenburg, had assumed the title of King-in-Prussia; the place, too, was significant, for the proclamation of the German Empire in the palace of the *roi soleil* appeared to mark the final victory of Prussia in her long struggle over the years with France.

There was also much that was symbolic in the actual negotiations which had led up to this moment. At the beginning of the war the fear of invasion by France had caused the south German states to turn to Prussia, and as popular opinion swung round in favour of their inclusion within the victorious German Confederation, it was soon apparent that the only issue was to be their actual method of entry. Bismarck was determined that the offer of the Imperial crown should not, as in 1849, emanate from the people of Germany; it must come from the German princes, and in October 1870 he opened discussions along these lines with the representatives of the four south German states who had arrived at the army headquarters at Versailles. By playing off one against the other he brought Württemberg, Baden, and Hesse to agreement with his terms and a little later Bavaria was won over with a few meaningless concessions. Then Ludwig II of Bavaria was prevailed upon to invite King William of Prussia to become German Emperor. Ludwig had little respect for the Hohenzollerns, but the orgy of building with which he attempted to enhance the glory of the Wittelsbachs and which later in the twentieth century was to be a godsend for the Bavarian tourist industry, had put him in such debt that he was glad to accept an income of £15,000 a year from the *Welfen-Fonds* and allowed himself to be deluded into imagining that the Imperial throne would be occupied alternately by a Hohenzollern and a Wittelsbach.

It was only after his fellow princes had joined with Ludwig in his proposal, that William consented to receive a deputation from the German *Reichstag* who made the same request on 19 December. Strangely enough, their President, Eduard Simson, had been the spokesman of the Frankfurt Assembly which had originally offered the Crown to Frederick William IV in 1849, but there the similarity with the epoch of liberal revolution ended. The entry of the south German states had been negotiated by Bismarck alone; the constitution of the new Empire was to be little different from that of the North German Confederation, an autocracy only slightly held in check by democratic forms, and the Imperial crown had been granted, as William II claimed in 1910, 'by God's grace alone and not by Parliaments, popular assemblies and popular decision'.

b) The Paris Commune
France's settlement of her affairs was to be rather less tidy. Initially the speed with which the deputies had acted in Paris on 4 September had forestalled any immediate threat of social revolution, and the government of National Defence under Trochu was far more homogeneous than the executive committee that had been set up in February 1848. Within Paris the tension was nevertheless considerable; the working-class clubs and societies were highly suspicious that the middle-class republicans were half-hearted in their resistance to the Germans, and on two occasions during the siege the new government almost succumbed to an assault on the Hôtel de Ville—first, at the end of October, when the failure of an attempt to break out from Paris coincided with the news of the surrender of Metz and the arrival of Thiers who, after the failure of his diplomatic mission to London, Vienna, and St Petersburg, wished to arrange an armistice with Bismarck; then again on 22 January after a further *sortie en masse* had come to nothing.

In fact, the extreme left wing were proved correct in their doubts. The propertied classes had by now lost all faith in the continuation of the war, and when elections had been held during the three weeks armistice following the surrender of Paris, the attitude of the National Assembly which met at Bordeaux on 12 February 1871 made it clear that the provinces were determined on peace. This time the pattern of 1848 *had* been repeated, since the Assembly was predominantly right wing with some 400 monarchists and conservatives against 200 republicans, many of whom were moderate; Gambetta, who had demanded a continuation of the war, had to admit defeat and Thiers, who at the age of seventy-three had enjoyed an overwhelming electoral triumph, was nominated as 'Chief of the Executive Power of the Republic of France'.

Thiers lost no time in carrying out his policy of making peace with the Germans. The preliminaries which had been completed by the end of February included the surrender of Alsace and Lorraine, an area rich in iron ore and agricultural land, although Bismarck's motives were largely governed by strategic considerations. In addition to this, France was to pay a war indemnity of five milliard francs in the next three years, during which various *départements* were to remain under German occupation. Despite all his arguments

Thiers could gain no more in concessions than a slight reduction of the indemnity and the retention of the fortress of Belfort in return for a ceremonial entry of the German Army into Paris. These were hard terms, and the annexation of Alsace and Lorraine was to rankle for many years afterwards, but the National Assembly had no choice; on 1 March the preliminaries were duly accepted and formed the basis of the Treaty of Frankfurt signed later that year.

For France, however, the end of the conflict was to be followed almost at once by the horrors of civil war. The extreme left-wing elements in Paris had never accepted the decision for peace which had been imposed upon them; Thiers himself was regarded as an enemy of the working class and the parade of German troops on 1 March brought emotions in the capital to boiling point. Furthermore, the National Assembly's decision to end the moratorium which had been declared on commercial bills and house rents appeared as a new move on the part of the bourgeois, and at the same time a decree stopping the payment of one-and-a-half francs a day to the National Guardsmen deprived many of the poor of their principal means of support.

On 18 March Thiers, who had established his government at Versailles, gave orders for the guns of the Paris National Guard at Montmartre and Belleville to be seized. It is uncertain whether he intended this as a deliberate provocation, but when the attempt led to violent local resistance, he followed the course which he had originally suggested to Louis Philippe in 1848 and ordered the government authorities to evacuate the city. This abandonment of Paris gave the left-wing elements their chance to organize, on 26 March, a municipal government known as the Commune, and to prepare a desperate resistance to Thiers' forces at Versailles. Although the rebellion has all the characteristics of class conflict, heightened by the bitterness of defeat in war, it would, however, be wrong to consider it a manifestation of organized Socialism. There was a diversity of political groups within the Commune, and the haziness of their attitude towards capitalism is exemplified by the orthodox way in which they financed their activities by raising loans from the Bank of France, which at the same time was making similar advances to the government of Versailles. The Paris Commune represented no more than an explosion of anger, an echo of the June days rather than an anticipation of Marxist conspiracy.

It was, nevertheless, an appalling episode of bloodshed and cruelty. At Versailles Thiers built up his forces, negotiating with Bismarck for the release of prisoners of war, while the German army forming an outer ring looked on at this object lesson in the working of French democracy. Already in April government troops were shooting prisoners captured in the clashes and the Commune seized hostages preparatory to retaliation. On 8 May the main attack on the city was launched under MacMahon and by the middle of the month his forces were fighting within Paris. For a week the battle raged through the streets; prisoners were massacred on both sides, and eventually the Commune ordered the shooting of fifty-six hostages, including the archbishop of Paris. By the last week of May the government forces had conquered—after a final stand by the Communards in the cemetery of Père-Lachaise, where on the following day 147 of them were executed. In the whole course of the struggle some 20,000 had perished, although the precise figure will never be known, and subsequent trials condemned 13,450 to terms of imprisonment and 7,500 to deportation. Only at this fearful cost did the National Assembly once more become master of Paris, a city devastated and shocked by the ferocity of a holocaust in which the Tuileries and the Hôtel de Ville—twin symbols of French political antagonism—had both gone up in flames.

c) The question of the Spanish monarchy
The continued search for a new monarch was to bring almost as much tribulation to Spain herself as it had already done to France. With the events of July 1870 Prim turned from the Hohenzollerns and the Crown was eventually accepted by Amadeus, the second son of Victor Emmanuel of Italy (see genealogical table, p. 487). The short reign of King Amadeus, however, was hardly a success. Prim, on whom he depended, was assassinated at the end of 1870 and to the majority of Spaniards their new King was simply a foreigner whose father had just shocked Catholic sentiment with his occupation of Rome (see p. 217). Within a year the republicans, excited by the Paris Commune, had greatly strengthened their hold on the municipalities, while at the same time the supporters of Don Carlos, the grandson of the original claimant (see p. 80), seized their opportunity to raise Catalonia and the Basque provinces in rebellion. Amadeus tried for a time to work in conjunction with the liberal and republican elements, but eventually gave up the struggle, abdicated, and returned to Italy in February 1873.

The republic which the *Cortes* now attempted to establish was no more successful. The Carlists were still holding out in the north and the introduction of a federalist system, coupled with a rapid succession of presidents in a single year, so weakened the authority of the Spanish government that in January 1874 General Pavia overthrew the *Cortes*, which was replaced by a group of generals. The new administration did not immediately succeed in crushing the Carlists, but it did at least bring an end to the republican period. The deposed Queen Isabella had eventually abdicated in favour of her son Alfonso, who was now sixteen years of age, a cadet at Sandhurst, and in December 1874 General Martinez Campos proclaimed him king to his troops at Saguntum. This restoration was supported by

Primo de Rivera at Madrid and in 1875 the reign of Alfonso XII duly began. By February 1876 the Carlists had been driven back across the Pyrenees and in the same year a constituent Assembly devised the system under which Alfonso was to rule. The legislature was to consist of a bi-cameral Assembly, the Upper House being partly elected, partly nominated by the King, the Lower elected on a franchise based on a property qualification. By this means the Bourbons in alliance with the upper classes continued to govern Spain until 1923, when Primo de Rivera, nephew of the general who had assisted in the restoration in 1874, carried out the *coup* which was to reduce the King of Spain to a mere figurehead.

d) Rome and the Black Sea

The year 1870 was to be of profound significance also for the Roman Catholic Church. Already in 1864 Pius IX had issued the Syllabus of Errors which had formally defined the Papal attitude towards the growth of modern secular systems of government. It condemned Socialism, Communism, and the subordination of the Church to the State; it denied the validity of public opinion as the fundamental sanction of civil society and insisted upon the exclusive right of the clergy to control the education of the young. Then, in 1867, Pius announced his intention to summon a General Council and in the autumn of 1869 there began to assemble at Rome some 700 bishops from all over the world. One purpose of the Vatican Council was to consider the precise nature of the Pope's authority and on 18 July 1870, as a thunderstorm raged outside, there took place the final vote and promulgation of the constitution *Pastor Aeternus*. The controversial doctrine of Papal Infallibility was now explicitly stated, and the Pope speaking *ex cathedra* on matters of faith and morals was held to be 'possessed of that infallibility bestowed by Christ on his Church and therefore such definitions of the Roman Pontiff are irreformable of themselves and not from the consent of the Church'.

The Franco-Prussian War broke out on the next day and although Napoleon III would enter into no positive political agreement with Victor Emmanuel, military requirements necessitated the withdrawal of the French garrison from Rome at the beginning of August. With the news of Sedan and the capture of Napoleon, Victor Emmanuel had nothing more to fear from France. His troops entered the Papal enclave and on 20 September the bombardment of Rome began. Pius, however, insisted that there should only be a token show of resistance and with the occupation of the city Rome had at last become the capital of the kingdom of Italy. In November the Law of Guarantees accorded the Pope all the attributes of sovereignty, allowed him to retain the Vatican, the Lateran, Castel Gondolfo, and his Swiss Guard, and granted him an annual income of 3,225,000 lire. Catholic opinion throughout Europe did at least secure this much for the Pope; it could not prevent the loss of all his territories together with the final separation of secular and ecclesiastical affairs in Italy, and although Pius refused to accept the Law and placed the King and his government under the ban of the Church, this only served to exacerbate their relations until the signing of the Lateran Treaty with Mussolini in 1929.

One other European Power was able to take advantage of the French disaster. Russia was at once aware of her opportunity to denounce the neutralization of the Black Sea which had been imposed on her by the Treaty of Paris in 1856, and her decision to do so was communicated to the other governments at the beginning of November 1870. France was not in a position to object and Bismarck regarded such a concession as a small price to pay for continued Russian friendship and acquiescence in the intended German annexation of Alsace and Lorraine. Great Britain was more concerned about the possibility of a secret agreement between Russia and Germany, and Gladstone's government merely took a stand against the denunciation of an international treaty by one of the signatories. A compromise was reached at a conference held in London from January to March 1871, when the Russians accepted the general principle that international agreements could not be revised by unilateral action, and were then granted their wish with a formal abrogation of the Black Sea clauses of the Treaty of Paris. For the Russians the victory was largely theoretical, since they could not yet contemplate the creation of a great naval power on the Black Sea, and it was Bismarck who made the greatest capital out of the conference. The British were by now considering a friendly alignment with the new power of Germany on the Continent, and although Bismarck avoided any positive alliance with them, he was able to profit by their attitude when Great Britain and Russia, who was naturally satisfied with the outcome of the London negotiations, agreed that the peace settlement with France should not be a matter for general European negotiation. Thus the French were left in isolation to the end, and the revision of the Treaty of Paris and the Italian occupation of Rome formed an appropriate accompaniment to the downfall of the empire of Napoleon III.

Part 5

The Armed Peace
1871–1914

Chapter 20

Forces of Expansion

1. Social and economic change

Between 1815 and 1870 the course of European history might be summed up as the impact of forces of social and economic change upon the settlement of Vienna. The new situation which had been emerging in the 1850s and 1860s implied more than a radical alteration in the balance of power in Europe; it was a consequence of the fact that the governments had been prepared to take into partnership the rising *bourgeoisie* whom Metternich had stigmatized as the 'presumptuous' men. In the outcome it was not unnatural that during the forty-three years which elapsed before the outbreak of the first World War the middle-class liberal whose discontent had lain behind so much of the unrest of the earlier part of the century should imagine that the fruits of the earth were now his to inherit.

Indeed, to some extent they were. The aristocracy of central and eastern Europe might still be socially predominant; yet optimism and materialism were to be the predominating themes of a great period of middle-class affluence—'the world of security' Stefan Zweig called it, when from the middle of the twentieth century he looked back wistfully on the years of his youth in Austria. In Germany the new sense of power and wealth was reflected in the rapid expansion of Berlin, now becoming one of the great cities of Europe. In Paris it consolidated the position of the sophisticated upper stratum of new rich mingling with old aristocracy that Proust depicted in *A la recherche du temps perdu*, and at the same time it helped to create the *petit bourgeois* society of Georges Duhamel's chronicle of the Pasquier family; over them all loomed the Eiffel Tower, constructed in the Champ-de-Mars for the industrial fair of 1889, a symbol of the new engineering skills whose social and economic implications were changing the face of Europe.

Secure and benevolent the world might seem to those who did not live at the lowest economic level; yet the paradox of the liberal victory for greater personal freedom was that the continued development of the very forces that had given rise to it were seriously to curtail the individual's liberty of action. In diplomacy a new balance had to be found against a background of sharpened mistrust and more specialized techniques of warfare. On the domestic scene the requirements of social organization in an age of the masses and the tentacular complexity of growing industry imposed new forms of collectivism with which every government had to come to terms whatever its political complexion.

This collectivism was the cumulative effect of a number of social and economic factors which had already been at work throughout most of the century. First, the population of Europe (see Appendix 7, p. 492), aided by improvements in medical science and public sanitation, mounted extraordinarily in the last three decades of the nineteenth century, despite the emigration of 21 million overseas. Although this rate of increase was not maintained, the 293 million inhabitants in 1871 had risen to 490 million by 1914. Between 1870 and 1910 Great Britain rose from 31 million to 45 million, and Germany from 41 million to 65 million; France, on the other hand, was not only surpassed, but lagged still further behind with a relatively slight increase to 39 million, a figure which put her only slightly ahead of Italy's 35 million. The most prodigious increase was in Russia who over the same period rose from 77 to 111 million. In an age when men were becoming more and more conscious of statistics, numbers implied strength; thus it was natural that France should appear to be in decline, and that while the west kept a watchful eye on the growing population of Germany, the Germans themselves should look eastwards with still greater apprehension at the rising manpower of their Russian neighbour. In fact, a balanced population in terms of age groups may be more advantageous than a rapidly rising one which is bound to be unbalanced, and in Russia, where the change was most marked, the increase from 50 million peasantry in 1861 to 100 million by 1917 played havoc with the successful working of Tsar Alexander II's division of the estates.

The effects of the general rise in population were accentuated by the drift towards the towns. This tendency, which had already long been a feature of western development, became far more noticeable throughout central Europe after 1871 and was particularly striking in Germany, where the enormous growth of her industry raised her urban population to 60 per cent in 1910. The concentration of so many thousands of people in the cities involved something of a social revolution in itself. When Elizabeth of Bavaria married the Emperor Francis Joseph in 1854, she found not a single bathroom in the Imperial Palace of the Hofburg; yet in the last decades of the century local civic authorities were everywhere interesting themselves in the problems of plumbing and main drainage and attempting to safeguard the health and welfare of town-dwellers through a host of local regulations which, twenty years earlier, would have seemed an intolerable infringement of the rights of property. Where the architect had previously been employed to build palaces and churches, he now turned his attention to main thorough-fares, municipal buildings and railway stations, many of them designed in a heavily ornamented neo-classical style. The effect was not only local; improvement in communications through the invention of the telephone and the growth of the railway network throughout Europe from 225,400 kilometres in 1890 to 342,930 in 1913 added enormously to the closeness of control from the capital city and enabled all forms of association to work with greater discipline and strength.

The general consequence of this collectivism in the organization of social life was to create far greater uniformity on a national scale. This was assisted by two additional factors—schools and newspapers. Before the outbreak of the first World War almost every country in Europe had established its own system of primary education, compulsory and free, while the curricula of secondary schools were beginning now to include the study of modern languages and science. The growth of literacy and the prospect of a wide circulation in the cities encouraged the development of a national popular press. In 1896 Alfred Harmsworth founded the *Daily Mail* in Great Britain; in the same year the prices of *Le Petit Parisien* and *Le Matin* were lowered to appeal to a larger public in France, and 1898 saw the launching of the Ullstein venture of the *Berlinermorgenpost*. Naturally all these influences represented a tremendous challenge to the parochialism which had always been the very essence of European life, and the local barriers of tradition and dialect were to be still further weakened in the twentieth century by the development of radio and the cinema. Yet at the time, startling though they must have seemed to contemporaries, they only marked the beginning of a process of change which was inevitably slow. In his novel *Buddenbrooks* Thomas Mann made much of the gulf that still existed between a north German and a Bavarian, while Daudet's *Lettres de mon moulin* and *Tartarin de Tarascon* and Pierre Loti's study of Breton fishermen in *Pêcheur d'Islande* suggest that in many parts of the Continent life was still relatively unchanged.

A fundamental factor in this new pattern of European life was a remarkable acceleration in the industrial revolution. The development of coal mines, iron foundries, and textile factories which had formed the basis of the transformation of western Europe in the first half of the century (see pp. 86–90) was now spreading fast eastwards. Germany, which by 1870 had already surpassed France, was by 1914 seriously challenging Great Britain as the principal industrial Power in Europe. More striking still was the rapid industrialization of Russia, particularly after 1890. The 1,610 kilometres of railway track, which was all that she could claim in 1860, had grown to 70,840 kilometres by 1914, and it was not inappropriate that Sergei Witte, who became Russian Minister of Finance in 1892, should earlier in his career have been a provincial stationmaster.

Between 1870 and 1914 coal production (see Appendix 10, p. 495) in France rose from 13.3 million tonnes to 40 million, in Austria-Hungary from 8.6 million to 47 million and in Russia from 750,000 to 36.2 million. The French were still hampered by a comparative poverty of coal deposits and these figures for Austria–Hungary and Russia indicate how previously non-industrial countries were beginning to catch up with her. In the whole of Europe Great Britain remained in the lead, rising from 112 million tonnes to 292, but German production from 34 million tonnes in 1870 came close to equalling Great Britain with 277 million in 1914. In 1913 12 million tonnes were raised in the Saar alone and 43 million in Silesia, and by 1906 more than half a million men were employed in the mining of German coal and lignite.

The same tendency is to be observed in the manufacture of pig iron. France rising from 1.2 million tonnes to 4.6 million was being challenged by Russia whose output of half a million in 1870 had increased to 3.6 million in 1914, although Austria-Hungary had attained no more than 2 million by this date. Great Britain had risen from 6 million to 11 million, yet despite this advance she was by 1914 no longer the leading producer in Europe, owing to a prodigious increase in Germany from 1.3 million to 14.7 million, aided by the geographical proximity of her coal and iron ore. Similarly, the British went ahead with the production of steel with the new Bessemer process, which depended upon the use of non-phosphoric ores not easily available in Germany, but after the work of Gilchrist and Thomas in 1879 had shown how this limitation might be overcome, the phosphoric ores of Lorraine enabled Germany to produce 14 million tonnes of steel in 1914 as against the British 6.5 million.

In shipbuilding Great Britain still remained in the lead; in 1910 her steam tonnage was more than four times as great as Germany's. None the less, the German advance was significant and opened up many avenues for the future. Naval rivalry between the two countries was to be an important political factor from the beginning of the twentieth century, and by 1913 the Hamburg-Amerika line had 172 steamships operating in competition for the new passenger services. The general increase was staggering, for between 1893 and 1913 the world tonnage of merchant fleets was actually doubled.

All this growing production, together with an enormous expansion of textile factories, was simply due to the development and refinement of the techniques which had first launched the industrial revolution on the world. There were, however, at this time a number of discoveries and inventions which gave a further impetus to the transformation of the economy. The generation of electricity, facilitated by Siemens's invention of the dynamo, provided a new source of power for the factories. In 1882 the first generating station was operating in New York, and in the following year in Germany Emil Rathenau laid the foundations of what was to become the AEG (*Allgemeine Elektrizitäts Gesellschaft*). Electric cable linking the continents multiplied, and before 1900 wireless communication, pioneered by Marconi, was already an established fact. Another sphere in which there was a tremendous advance at this time, particularly in Germany, was the chemical processes which were to have an astonishing effect on commercial life with the production of synthetic dyes, fertilizers, margarine, and soap, and whose new drugs were to be an important ally for medical research, leading to a better understanding of malaria, cholera, and tuberculosis and the development of antiseptic methods in hospitals. Most striking of all was the invention of the internal-combustion engine which was to be followed by the diesel engine in 1895. The motor car had made its appearance before the end of the century and in 1903 the Wright brothers in America made their first successful flight in a propeller-driven aeroplane.

Such a profusion of industrial activity combined with the development of technical means of control and communication was bound to have consequences that were entirely in keeping with the general tendency towards collectivism. The concentration of thousands of workers in the factory and mining towns facilitated the organization of trade union movements on a scale that had been impossible before. In the incessant economic struggle small industrial firms were absorbed into bigger concerns, local shops succumbed to the mammoth store, provincial banks became amalgamated and everywhere larger and larger units appeared to dominate the scene. Soon, both in the United States and Europe, these large units themselves began to merge with others. Sometimes the method was to develop what was known as a vertical combine, where the various stages of production from the ownership of the raw materials to the distribution and retailing of the finished article were all brought under the control of a single authority. Another type was the horizontal combine known as a cartel, which consisted of a working agreement between large industries dealing with the same commodity. By this means the amount of production might be regulated, the market shared on a rational basis and a common selling price fixed—very often at two levels, one for home consumption, the other much lower for selling abroad. In France a metal industries trust, the *Comité des Forges*, was virtually controlled by six major firms; in Germany the Rhenish-Westphalian Coal Syndicate, created in 1893, controlled half the coal production of the whole country, and the *Stahlwerkverband* almost the entire steel industry in 1904. By 1900 there were 275 German cartels, and in 1906 the Austrian consul at Berlin commented in a report: 'never before was economic Germany so entirely under the absolute rule of a group of men barely fifty in number.'

These concentrations were largely on a national basis. A further consequence of the industrial and technical advances, however, was to draw the whole world into a single economic unit. Everywhere the demand for capital added to the ramifications of international finance. In this field Great Britain retained a position which sheltered her for the moment from the full consequences of German industrial advance; thus, although in 1895 her imports exceeded her exports by £130 million, this difference was more than compensated by the interest from enormous overseas investments. France and, to a lesser extent, Germany were the other principal creditor nations, and the rapid growth of industrialization outside western Europe meant enormous loans to the Balkan countries, Turkey, Japan, and the South American states. Within Europe the most significant feature was the immense investments in Russia, where by 1897 48 per cent of her national debt and by 1914 one-third of the stock of her joint-stock companies were in the hands of foreigners—predominantly French.

This growing closeness of relationship was bound to exercise a unifying influence upon the economic pattern throughout the world. In the mid-century prices had been rising, but between 1870 and 1893 they tended to fall. There were two main reasons for this. First, the amount of precious metal in the world had not kept pace with the vastly increased quantity of commodities on sale; this shortage was bound to have a deflating effect, and after 1871 Germany, the Scandinavian countries, the Netherlands, Portugal, and the United States all abandoned the gold standard. Second, there was a relative glut on the European market, since the use of farming machinery had enormously increased American production of corn, which could now be distributed by railways and steamships, while refrigerator ships could bring frozen meat from South America. The subsequent drop in the European farmers' selling prices naturally reduced their own purchasing power, which in turn had its repercussions on industry; this helps to explain three particularly bad periods of depression—in 1873, in the early 1880s, and in 1893—when bankruptcies were followed by widespread unemployment, although the actual moment of impact varied slightly from country to country.

In the twenty years before the outbreak of the first World War, prices began to rise again. This was due partly to the discovery of the deposits of gold in South Africa, Western Australia, British Columbia, and Alaska, partly to a return to a policy of Protection in Europe. There was, however, no escape from the cycle of boom and slump and further depressions in the periods 1900–1, 1907–8,

and 1912–13, all added to the militancy of the working-class movements which were making an increasingly effective use of the strike
weapon. The violence of these economic oscillations pointed to the
great paradox of the modern industrial world—that the more the
inventiveness of the human mind opened up the resources which
might raise the general standard of living, the more the life of the
ordinary individual was placed at the mercy of economic forces that
he did not understand and could not control. The world might be
becoming a single economic unit; yet the principle by which the men
of Europe still governed their affairs was increasingly one of national
survival in a state of haphazard competition, and within Europe the
conflict of national commercial policies led to the growth of tariff
walls, thereby creating new obstacles for the interflow of goods, just
when railways and steamships had broken down the old.

In fact, the governments did not lightly abandon the old ideal of
moving towards Free Trade. In France, after an initial period of
wavering at the end of the Franco-Prussian war, these was a short-
lived return to the policy of the Second Empire; in Germany von
Delbruck, the Minister of Finance, worked for the continued reduction of tariffs, and in 1873 duties on the importation of iron and
shipbuilding materials were abolished. Gradually, however, the governments were won over by the appeals of farmers and industrialists,
made more insistent by the crash of 1873 and the general fall in
prices throughout the 1870s, and as each country retaliated against
the others, so the tariffs began to rise.

In Germany duties on corn and manufactures were reimposed in
1880 and in France a tariff law of 1881 established mild Protection
for industry, although not for the farmer. Russian tariffs rose sharply
in the 1880s, and by 1887 they had become extremely high in Italy.
In 1891 a referendum in Switzerland produced a vote of 220,000
against 159,000 in favour of heavier duties, and in 1894 the return
of an agriculturalist majority in the Swedish *Riksdag* ensured a
return to Protection. The principal method of adjustment was still
by treaty with individual countries, but in 1892 the French Chamber
placed restrictions on this by establishing a minimum rate for commercial friends and maximum rates for others. In 1902 a new German law decreed a high minimum rate on agricultural goods, and
although raw materials were still to enter free, the rate was gradually to increase on manufactured articles according to the degree
to which they were finished.

By 1914 only Great Britain and a few of the smaller countries
such as Belgium and the Netherlands still clung to Free Trade. It
is true that ideas were at work for bringing an end to these tariff
walls that threaded their way across the Continent. Bismarck had
once discussed with the French ambassador the possibility of a central European Customs Union which might include France, and in

1897 the German Emperor William II suggested to Tsar Nicholas II the formation of a general European union against American competition. But nothing came of these schemes and the continuing economic conflict was often bitter. The trade treaty between Germany and Russia in 1894 was almost like a peace settlement after a period of keen tariff war. The passing of the Italian tariff law in 1887 involved the denunciation of a French commercial treaty, and the sharp drop in trade between the two countries was translated into terms of political animosity. 'France must now forget the history of the supremacy and influence which she once possessed on this side of the Alps,' declared the Italian premier Crispi,* and the French *Charge d'affaires* at Rome discovered that Italian children believed firmly that the Italians had defeated the French at the battle of Solferino in 1859! Thus a general tendency towards collectivism did not necessarily unify; if anything, it created a more highly charged atmosphere of rivalry in which the issues became ever more dangerously complex.

2. Imperialism

Until the 1870s there were only five countries in Europe which held overseas possessions of any significant size—Great Britain, France, the Netherlands, Spain, and Portugal—and of these only two had made any substantial gains in the nineteenth century. France had fostered a considerable colonization of Algeria as a means of consolidating her hold there; in the 1840s she had laid claim to Tahiti and the Marquesas in the Pacific, and under Napoleon III had established interests in Africa and Indo-China (see p. 171). British acquisitions had been far more extensive; in addition to the empire which had already been hers in 1815, Natal, Singapore, New Zealand, and Hong Kong had all been settled during subsequent decades, while imperial rule had been established over parts of Burma and large regions of the north-west of India. Of the other three, the Dutch, after losing the Cape to the British in the course of the Napoleonic wars, now simply retained their possessions in the East Indies. Spain and Portugal had suffered great losses in South America (see p. 63) and now held only a fraction of their former empires—Spain in the Philippines, Cuba, San Domingo, and Porto Rico; Portugal in the African colonies of Angola and Mozambique, where her actual settlements did not reach far beyond the coast.

Although, as has been seen, these developments had had some bearing on international relations, their significance for European diplomacy had been largely peripheral. In contrast to this, the last decades of the nineteenth century saw an extraordinary intensifi-

---

* Quoted from D. Mack Smith: *Italy 1860–1960*.

cation of national concern over the acquisition of colonies, which now came to occupy a central position in political negotiation. The most dramatic feature of this new period of expansion was the opening up of Africa, whose enormous territories were almost entirely shared out among European states in the space of about twenty years. A second feature was that the old colonial Powers were now joined by several new competitors—Germany, Italy, and Belgium in Africa, the United States and Germany in the race for the Pacific Islands, Russia and Japan in the demands for territorial and commercial concessions from the decadent Chinese empire—while the presence of oil in the Turkish dominions of the Middle East created a new source of rivalry among British, American, German, and Russian interests.

Few of these gains would have been possible or even desirable, had it not been for the recent advances in science and industry. Improved medical knowledge now enabled white men to spend prolonged spells in the tropics; with the development of light weapons, such as the machine gun, comparatively small numbers of Europeans could shatter the resistance of local native peoples, and the new techniques of engineering and railway construction facilitated the exploitation of raw materials which would otherwise have been out of reach. All these factors were essential prerequisites, but they do not in themselves explain this remarkable acceleration in imperial enterprise.

The causes were extremely varied. Much of the exploration of Africa had been inspired by genuine scientific interest, coupled with missionary and humanitarian zeal to spread the Gospel and to stamp out the Arab slave trade. In an age in which colonialism has grown unpopular it is fashionable to treat these disinterested motives with a certain cynicism; yet it is a fact that in Africa, Madagascar, and the Pacific explorers and missionaries were active long before the diplomats had any interest in their whereabouts, and far from being political agents were sometimes a source of embarrassment to their own governments—as in the episode of Mr Pritchard on the island of Tahiti (see p. 83).

A more commonly accepted explanation is that the scramble for territory was stimulated by the mounting economic competition between the countries of Europe, since a growing industrialism had created a demand for the rarer types of raw material that were not available in Europe. It has also been suggested that colonies would supply new markets and greater scope for emigration at a time when populations were rising sharply. None of these arguments, however, are decisive. The gaining of raw materials did not necessitate the acquisition of such vast territories; the tropical climate was unlikely to attract a large number of immigrant settlers; and if there were any hopes of developing new markets they were soon to be disappointed; even by 1913 Germany's trade with all her colonies amounted to no more than 0.5 per cent of her total foreign commerce.

A more persuasive economic thesis was put forward in 1902 by J. A. Hobson in his book *Imperialism*, in which he claimed that the expansion of empire was due to the need of financiers to find a new outlet for the investment of their surplus capital. British investments overseas, for example, rose from £785 million in 1871 to £3,500 million in 1911, and it was natural that an apparent link between capitalism and imperialism should be seized upon by Lenin whose pamphlet *Imperialism, the Highest Stage of Capitalism*, published in 1916, was largely based upon Hobson's book. Yet this argument, too, is fundamentally unsatisfactory.

A more detailed analysis of the figures for these years shows that the bulk of overseas investment was attracted to regions other than those seized by the Powers after 1870. The enormous increase already cited for Great Britain is largely explained by mounting investments in the United States, Canada, Australasia, India, and the South American countries. Similarly, although South African gold and Rhodesian copper offered good prospects, the total public and private investment in the whole of British, French, German, and Belgian territories between the Sahara and the frontier of northern Rhodesia amounted to no more than £237 million by the end of 1913. Naturally there were considerable economic advantages to be gained from certain imperial developments; yet the facts would not seem to suggest that they operated as a decisive influence in the shaping of this remarkable expansion of Europe throughout the world.

Indeed, the political moves of the governments in negotiating territorial frontiers and spheres of influence appear to have been based on a series of *ad hoc* decisions rather than any general principle. The regions of Africa, Asia, and the Pacific under debate offered a field for diplomatic manoeuvring which was no longer possible on the Continent, entangled as it was towards the end of the century in a network of alliance and counter-alliance. Strategic considerations tended to predominate. The opening of the Suez canal and her concern for the route to India drew Great Britain into Egypt and East Africa despite the greater economic significance of West Africa, while France hoped that the recruiting of native troops might bolster up her failing manpower; eventually, once the race was on, ambitions were often governed simply by the desire to prevent a rival from gaining an advantage. In fact, the most striking motive was irrational—the desire for prestige in which the new mass electorates and the popular press entered with enthusiasm. Sir John Seeley's lectures on *The Expansion of England* and the writings of Rudyard Kipling, the hunger of the French for *la gloire* after the humiliation of 1871, and the aspirations of the German Colonial League were all indications of this new fever; all were in accord with Treitschke's remark in 1879 that 'every virile people had established colonial power'.

Bismarck himself had little interest in colonies and saw the race for empire purely from the point of view of its impact on continental politics. 'My map of Africa lies in Europe,' he said. 'Here lies Russia and here lies France and we are in the middle. That is my map of Africa.' Nowhere was this attitude more clearly demonstrated than in the African territories north of the Sahara. It was his encouragement that led France to annex Tunis in 1881, for by this means he hoped to lull the French into forgetting their loss of Alsace and Lorraine, and to create a lasting division between them and the Italians, who had hoped to gain Tunis for themselves. The French did not forget Alsace and Lorraine, but at least he was able to profit from the anger of the Italians with the Triple Alliance of Germany, Austria-Hungary, and Italy which was concluded in 1882.

At the same time Bismarck had been urging Great Britain on to the annexation of Egypt, which would certainly create bad feeling between the British and the French. The opening of the Suez canal—a French engineering project—in 1869 had introduced a new factor in the international significance of Egypt. Throughout the century the British had been extremely suspicious of possible French designs on their route to India. This had partly governed their attitude towards Mehemet Ali in the 1830s (see p. 79), and in 1875 it had been in order to forestall French financiers that Disraeli had bought up from the Egyptian Khedive Ismail seven-sixteenths of the shares in the Canal Company. The two countries, however, did cooperate in the following years in setting up a dual control of Egyptian finances. Ismail, who had announced virtual bankruptcy, was deposed to be succeeded by his son Tewfik, and in 1882 a rising Egyptian nationalist movement under Arabi Pasha, determined to oust European influence, prompted the dispatch of an Anglo-French naval force to Alexandria. In the event, however, the British acted alone. The French premier, Freycinet, was defeated in the Chamber, fearful lest French forces should become too deeply involved far from home, and while the French fleet steamed away, the British bombarded Alexandria and after landing an army which defeated the Egyptians at Tel el Kebir on 13 September, occupied Cairo. Initially the British had had no intention of staying in Egypt, which never became formally a part of their empire; yet once they were in occupation, concern over the control of the canal which had brought them in prevented them from leaving. This new acquisition naturally aroused the animosity of both France and Russia, and thus in the realm of diplomacy it was Bismarck who had made the principal gain.

South of the Sahara the penetration of the vast territories of the interior by British, French, and German explorers in the 1850s and 1860s was followed by the growth of claims to possession. In the 1870s the French were pushing inland through Senegal towards the upper Niger; de Brazza was exploring the regions to the north of the mouth of the Congo, and in 1883 French forces undertook the conquest of Madagascar. At the same time private British interests were developing on the lower Niger and in East Africa. In addition to this, there were three newcomers in the colonial field. In 1876 King Leopold of the Belgians formed an International African Association and employed H. M. Stanley to act for him in exploring the Congo basin, which Leopold hoped to develop as a personal concern, an aim which soon brought him into collision with the French and the Portuguese. In 1883 Italy took possession of Eritrea and in 1884 Germany suddenly embarked upon a bid for German colonies in South-West Africa, Togoland, the Cameroons, and East Africa. This startling change on Bismarck's part was still motivated by European considerations, since his aim was to furnish himself with grounds for a quarrel with Great Britain. He had two reasons for this. The first was based on the hope of forming a friendship with France, who bitterly resented the British occupation of Egypt. The second was due to his fear that on the death of William I, which could not be far distant, his son Frederick who was married to Queen Victoria's daughter would embark on a liberal pro-British policy. 'When we entered upon a colonial policy,' he explained years later, 'we had to reckon with a long reign of the Crown Prince. During this reign English influence would have been dominant. To prevent this we had to embark upon a colonial policy because it was popular and conveniently adapted to bring us into conflict with England at any given moment.'

The outcome of this new period of competing imperial aims was a Congress held at Berlin in December 1884. Here agreement was reached over the general area of expansion, the suppression of the slave trade; and a rather vague formula for free trade in the Congo basin until various regions had been definitely annexed. The Berlin conference, however, only set the stage for the next act in the scramble for empire. By now the central regions were gaining a significance of their own in that their acquisition might enable one country to develop a band of territories right through the continent, either north-south or east-west, at the same time foiling similar designs of others.

Thus, in 1885 Great Britain annexed Southern Bechuanaland in order to prevent a possible link-up between the Boer Transvaal and German South-West Africa which would have blocked the way to her own expansion northwards. The road was thus open for Cecil Rhodes's South Africa Company, formed in 1889, to found two colonies—North and South Rhodesia—beyond the Transvaal. All political aims were now converging on these central regions. In 1888 Sir Donald Mackinnon founded the British East Africa Company in an attempt to counter the growth of German interests there, and the British government, now saddled with the problem of Egypt, was anxious to prevent the headwaters of the Nile falling into foreign hands.* At the same time a quarrel had developed between Great Britain and Portugal, who feared that British infiltration into Mashonaland and Nyasaland would prevent any eventual link between Angola and Mozambique.

Most of these disputes were satisfactorily settled in 1890. In Germany the Emperor Frederick III had died a few months after his succession in 1888 and Bismarck had by now swung round to the idea of friendship with Great Britain. Accordingly it was agreed that the British should safeguard the Nile by holding Kenya and Uganda and should assume a protectorate over Zanzibar; in return they ceded the island of Heligoland in the North Sea which they had held since 1815 and recognized Germany's possession of Tanganyika. At the same time the British made two other treaties—with France recognizing her seizure of Madagascar and certain of her West African boundaries, and with Portugal who gave way over the establishment of Nyasaland and Mashonaland.

The race between Great Britain and France, however, was not yet over. In March 1896 the Italians suffered a great defeat at Adowa at the hands of the Abyssinians from whom the French hoped for cooperation, and the British government decided that the moment had come for the conquest of the Sudan. In September 1898 Kitchener occupied Khartoum after having defeated the dervishes under their Khalifa at Omdurman, and a few days later encountered Captain Marchand who had just reached Fashoda with a small French force at the end of an epic journey through the heart of Africa from the west in an effort to cut off the British from further expansion southwards. Marchand, however, was too far from his base to present any effective resistance and in March 1899 the two governments agreed upon a dividing line between the basins of the Nile and the Congo.

Meanwhile, there had been considerable activity in the Pacific, where, apart from Australia and New Zealand, colonial claims had been limited to a few islands held by Great Britain, France, and Spain. In 1884 Germany had annexed the Bismarck archipelago and the north-eastern segment of New Guinea, to which the British responded by taking the south-eastern segment of the island. Then

* The same anxiety affected the British government's attitude towards Italy's invasion of Abyssinia in 1935—although not sufficiently to bring about any intervention. See p. 408.

at the end of the century the United States began to move into the Pacific. In 1898 Hawaii was finally annexed, in 1899 the Samoan group was shared with Germany, and on the conclusion of the Spanish American war of 1898 the former Spanish colonies of the Philippines, as well as Cuba and Porto Rico, were established as American dependencies.

In most parts of Africa and the Pacific the absence of any highly developed systems of government had resulted in direct territorial acquisition by the Powers. In Asia the struggle took a different form. Here the goal was to establish terms of preferential treatment from the existing local governments which would protect national, economic, and strategic interests. Along the northern frontier of India the British and the Russians intrigued for influence over Afghanistan and Tibet, while in the Turkish dominions of Mesopotamia and in Persia Great Britain, Germany, Russia, and the United States competed for concessions which would enable them to develop the rich deposits of oil.

In the Far East the weakness of China had already been demonstrated in the wars of 1839–42 and 1857–60, which, although fought primarily by Great Britain, had enabled several other European Powers and the United States to obtain considerable concessions for their own economic interests. Shortly after this the Chinese government attempted to carry out some sort of modernization of its military and naval forces, but was still unable to prevent further encroachments, including the French acquisition of Annam in 1885. The challenge to the position of the western Powers came ultimately not from China, but from the emergence of a new Power. In 1894 Japan gave sudden proof of the efficacy of her own programme of modernization on which she had embarked in the 1860s, when she fought a short successful war with China who by the Treaty of Shimonoseki in 1895 was forced to recognize the independence of Korea and to surrender Formosa, the Pescadores, and the Liao-tang peninsula, which included the harbour of Port Arthur. This victory for the Japanese was naturally an affront to the other rivals for power in the Far East, and almost at once France, Germany, and Russia imposed their own revision of the treaty insisting that Japan should at least relinquish the Liao-tang peninsula in return for a heavier indemnity.

The emergence of Japan was of particular significance for Russia, since it was an immediate challenge to the political and economic hopes centred on the Trans-Siberian railway which had been under construction since 1891, and the Russian foreign ministry took a sufficiently serious view of it to suggest a policy of cooperation with her over the partition of Manchuria. Nicholas II, who had succeeded as Tsar in 1894, preferred, however, to cultivate friendship with China, and in 1896 his government concluded an agreement with her whereby Russian warships could use the ports of the Liao-tang peninsula, a port in Shantung was leased for fifteen years, and the Trans-Siberian railway was to take a short cut through Man-churia to Vladivostok. These Russian gains at once stimulated fur-ther demands from the other Powers for corresponding concessions. In 1897 Germany used the excuse of the murder of two German missionaries to extract a ninety-nine year lease of Kiao-chow, whereupon Russia obtained in 1898 a twenty-five year lease of Port Arthur, which was to be linked by a branch line with the Trans-Siberian railway. In the south France gained Kwang-chow-wan, while the British government yielded to the pressure of public opin-ion and accordingly secured Wei-hai-wei. 'It will not be useful and it will be expensive,' commented the British Prime Minister, Lord Salisbury, 'but as a matter of pure sentiment we shall have to do it.' It would be an over-simplification to say that his remark sums up the whole of the great Powers' race for empire, but it does cer-tainly stress one very compelling motive.

Chapter 21

The Intensifying of Aspirations

1. The new realism

'Facts, not emotional pleas,' wrote Émile Zola, when he was making the preliminary notes for his novel *Germinal*, published in 1885. These words sum up a remarkable change of outlook in the last half of the nineteenth century, a change undoubtedly stimulated by the emergence of a modern technological society; in place of the roman-tic imagination which had inspired both art and revolution, the new trend was set by a clear sense of scientific realism and there were few sides of life that were not to be deeply affected by it.

Germinal itself was one of a series of twenty novels in which Zola traced the influence of heredity and environment on two branches of a family, the Rougons and the Macquarts, observing the effects of corruption, poverty, and disease with a dispassionate ruthless-ness. This was something more than a photographic technique; it was an attempt to turn the writer's desk into a sociological labo-ratory. The same desire for a careful documentation of life is to be found in Flaubert's *Madame Bovary*, published as early as 1857, and was the basis, later, of the novels of the de Goncourt brothers and the short stories of Guy de Maupassant. It was as a consequence of this new mood that the translation of the great Russian novelists made such an impact on France in the 1880s. 'Quel peintre et quel psychologue!' wrote Flaubert to Turgenev in thanking him for a copy of Tolstoy's *War and Peace*, and although the Russian novels were less harsh in tone than the French, the delicacy of human observation in the great works of Tolstoy, Turgenev, and Dostoev-sky certainly made them part of this new school.

On the stage the predominating influence came from Scandina-via. *A Doll's House, Ghosts, The Wild Duck*, and *An Enemy of the People*, written by the Norwegian Henrik Ibsen in the 1870s and 1880s, were set against a modern bourgeois background and eschewed such artificial devices as the soliloquy. Neither he nor the Swede August Strindberg, however, was content to remain a detached spectator, Ibsen constantly attacking the complacency and hypocrisy of mid-dle-class respectability, Strindberg obsessed with the tensions of family life. In contrast to this, the plays of the Russian Anton Chek-hov—*The Seagull, Uncle Vanya,* and *The Cherry Orchard,* all written at about the turn of the century—simply suggest an overwhelming sense of acceptance and resignation, although as drama they too depend on a power of wry observation. All three writers were linked by a common attitude towards their art and it is significant that Tchekov had been trained as a doctor and that Strindberg should devote a good deal of his time to chemical research.

The same swing away from romanticism was to be discerned in other spheres. In France a new school of poets who called them-selves the Parnassiens shunned all forms of high-flown phraseology, insisting on simple concrete images. In painting, a new technique known after 1874 as Impressionism attempted a scientific approach to the problem of conveying a sense of light. Like the playwrights, these painters—Manet, Monet, Renoir, Pissarro, Degas, and Sis-ley—tended to use everyday scenes as their subject matter, and were to create one of the great periods of French art, although their work was recognized abroad, particularly in Germany, long before it was accepted in France.

This attitude, which at a popular level found expression in the vogue for the science fiction of Jules Verne and, later, H. G. Wells, was also reflected in various forms of intellectual activity. The study of history was becoming more and more dependent upon the exam-ination of the archives; the *Cambridge Modern History* edited by Lord Acton, the *Dictionary of National Biography* edited by Leslie Stephen, and the massive works of Ernest Lavisse, Alfred Rambaud, and Gabriel Hanotaux pointed to a growing professionalism, while Jacob Burckhardt's *Civilization of the Renaissance in Italy,* published in 1860, suggested a new comprehensiveness of approach. At the same time there were serious attempts to promote economics and sociology to the level of exact sciences—as, for example, in the work of the Germans Max Weber and Werner Sombart on the develop-ment of capitalism, in Fréderic Le Play's analysis of family life in Europe, in Charles Booth's survey of living conditions in London, and in Sidney and Beatrice Webb's research into the history of the working class.

This awareness of the potentiality of scientific method in its application to the arts and society was only one aspect of the change. It was the actual message of the scientists that had the greatest con-sequences. The new theories of the time seemed to place the whole conception of mankind in an utterly changed perspective. For many years the researches of the geologists had clearly suggested that the earth had been in existence for millions of years, contrary to the literal interpretation of the Old Testament already coming under the critical scrutiny of German Biblical scholarship, and with the publication of Darwin's *Origin of Species* in 1859, followed by his

Descent of Man in 1871, the biologists finally brought the whole issue out into the open. Darwin in attempting to explain the diversity and development of species propounded a theory in which the emergence of man in the world was not due to a cataclysmic act of divine creation, but simply to a process of selection through a relentless struggle for survival. This sense of the haphazard was strengthened—among the experts, at least—by the revolutionary notions of the mathematicians and the physicists when, early in the twentieth century, Albert Einstein's theory of relativity added a fourth dimension of time to matter and energy, suggesting a continuous process of change.

Of all these intellectual developments it was Darwin's theories with their implication that man was simply the product of the law of the jungle that really fired the public imagination and led to the long dispute between the scientists and the theologians. But this was not all. It so happened that at about the same time the archaeologists were beginning to publish their discoveries of substantial traces of hitherto unknown civilizations. Throughout the nineteenth century work had continued on the Egypt of the Pharaohs, assisted by the deciphering of the hieroglyphics on the Rosetta stone. Then in Mesopotamia in the 1840s Henry Layard uncovered the cities of Nineveh and Nimrud, and the deciphering of cuneiform opened the door to a knowledge of the Assyrians, which in turn established that there had been a still earlier Sumerian civilization at the mouths of the Tigris and the Euphrates. In 1872 a German businessman, Heinrich Schliemann, discovered not merely the site of Troy, but a whole series of cities one upon another, and his later excavations at Mycenae were afterwards to lead Sir Arthur Evans on to the discovery of the Minoan civilization with its centre at Knossos in Crete. At the same time there was hazier evidence of others—the Hittites, the Ceylonese, the Incas west of the Andes, the Maya in Yucatan, and the ruins of Angkor lost in the forests of Indo-China.

The glimpse which these discoveries gave of a history of mankind far richer and more complex than had previously been imagined naturally suggested that forms of human society developed, flourished, and decayed in accordance with the Darwinian theories of the struggle for survival. This did not deter several thinkers from continuing to discern a sense of purpose in the history of the world. In Great Britain, now at the height of her prosperity, Herbert Spencer considered that the theory of evolution in its application to society encouraged a belief in progress, while the Russian Kropotkin in a series of articles in the 1890s stressed the essential element of cooperation and mutual aid in humanity's successful survival. Alternatively, it was natural that Darwin's hypothesis should appeal to Karl Marx, who had been living in the direst poverty in London since 1849, working on his interpretation of history as a class struggle (see pp. 96–7), and when the first volume of *Das Kapital* was completed in 1867 he proposed to dedicate it to Darwin who, however, was careful to refuse.

Utterly different though the social aims and assumptions of these three men may have been, they did all nevertheless share a certain optimism in envisaging a positive goal towards which mankind was evolving. For others, however, the conclusions to be drawn were pessimistic. Among the most significant of these was the son of a German pastor, Friedrich Nietzsche, who at an early age became Professor of Classical Philology at the University of Basle. The basis of his philosophy, gradually developed in a series of works published in the 1870s and 1880s, was a feeling of despair at the meaningless process of change in the universe. To Nietzsche it seemed that the only hope for man was to impose his will upon this chaos by violence, and in place of Christianity whose doctrine of humility and love he despised as inculcating a 'slave-morality', he postulated the rule of certain individuals whose ruthless strength qualified them to govern the rest. 'Formerly one spoke of God when contemplating distant seas. But today I enjoin you to say: superman. . . .'

A similar note of despair was to be heard much later in Oswald Spengler's *Der Untergang des Abendlandes* (*The Decline of the West*) which, although completed in 1914, was not published until after the first World War, when its pessimism was entirely in tune with the disillusionment of German intellectuals. 'Man is a beast of prey,' wrote Spengler. 'For me humanity is a zoological quantity. I see no progress, no goal, no way of humanity—except in the heads of western philistines who believe in progress.' The only pattern that he observed was a cycle of world cultures, each passing through a series of phases from spring to winter, and the conclusion which he drew was that the western democracies had reached the final stage of their decline and that the time was ripe for the emergence of a new Caesarism.

This rejection of any idea of rational progress was matched by other aspects of scientific advance. The beginnings of the study of psychology, the behaviourist theories of William McDougall, the work on conditioned reflexes by Ivan Pavlov in Russia, the new techniques of psychoanalysis developed by Sigmund Freud, Karl Jung, and Alfred Adler, the experiments in hypnotism carried out by Charcot in Paris, all threw a new light on the extent to which human action was dependent upon the emotional and the irrational.

Thus scientific realism had almost come full circle. Like early nineteenth-century romanticism, this stress on instinct and intuition manifested itself in a variety of forms. It encouraged the concentration on the self, as in the excesses of the Decadents in their exploration of every kind of sensation during the *fin de siècle* period, and it played its part in inspiring the elusive hints and emotive images of the Symbolists, the school of writers who succeeded the Parnassiens. It lent an extraordinary significance to Raskolnikoff, the character whom Dostoevsky created in his novel *Crime and Punishment*— the student who commits a murder to prove to himself that he is great enough to be above the rules of conventional morality. It encouraged the growth of the philosophy of the absurd and the unpredictable within the general systems of thought known as existentialism. The desire to plumb the depths of the subconscious led to the development of Surrealism, a new movement in art and writing, which the originators described as 'the dictation of thought in the absence of all control exercised by the reason and outside all aesthetic and moral preoccupations', and although their pictures sometimes appeared almost light-hearted, they suggested more often a delving into the darker sides of the mind, the stirring of a muddy pool.

2. Nationalism in central and eastern Europe

'The wars of peoples will be more terrible than those of kings,' said Winston Churchill in the House of Commons in 1901, and indeed the cult of the irrational was to lend itself to something far more sinister than the encouragement of an erratic individualism. A new ferocity of emotion took possession of extreme racial and national movements, playing some part in the ultimate disaster of 1914 and opening the way for the new Caesarism of the inter-war years with its shrill emphasis on the power of the group and on the weakness of liberalism and intellectualism.

In 1894 a French army officer, Captain Dreyfus, was charged with selling military secrets to Germany and the debate over his guilt, complicated by the fact that he was the only Jew on the General Staff, raged throughout France for more than ten years (see p. 254). In 1912 Leonardo da Vinci's *Mona Lisa* was stolen from the Louvre by an Italian determined that the picture should be returned to its country of origin. These are only two instances that point to the heightened sense of pride and antagonism in the years before the first World War, but it was essentially in central and eastern Europe that the theory of the struggle for survival now gave the most ambitious turn to these emotions. The effect was to be seen on subject and dominant peoples alike. On the one hand, it lent force to the small groups still partly submerged under Habsburg, Hohenzollern, and Romanov rule, and in the Balkan countries whose national evolution was not yet complete; on the other, it led the governments to impose a far greater uniformity within their frontiers, while at the same time the conflicting doctrines of pan-Germanism and pan-Slavism aimed at a radical revision of those frontiers which far outran the more cautious aspirations of the professional diplomats.

Some four years before the publication of Darwin's *Origin of Species*, a Frenchman, Arthur de Gobineau, had published his *Essai sur l'inégalité des races humaines*, in which he gave a precise formulation to racialist ideas that had previously been no more than a vague Romantic notion. Gobineau's fundamental assumption was the superiority of the white over the black races and of the Aryan people among the whites. The yellow races Gobineau explained away as an unfortunate attempt on God's part to create the white. 'Évidemment le Créateur n'a voulu faire qu'une ébauche.' This superiority of the Aryan involved among other things a new interpretation of history, for Gobineau saw the decline of the Roman Empire as the collapse of an unworthy Latin world before the revitalizing onrush of the Nordic tribes—a conception which was implicit in many German history books.

The natural right of a group to express its will to power, a mystical patriotism and a racial pride encouraging a contempt for the Slavs and a hatred for the Jews—these were the principal themes of German nationalist writing in the years before the first World War. In 1874 Heinrich von Treitschke became professor of history at the University of Berlin and, although a Saxon himself, never ceased to proclaim the glory of the Prussian hegemony over the rest of Germany and the right of the State to demand the sacrifice of the individual in war. 'He must renounce his whole ego for the sake of the great patriotic idea. Therein lies the moral sublimity of war.' The series of operas that Richard Wagner composed around the *Nibelungenlied* was a musical panegyric to the German race, and when Wagner wished to explain how the descendants of Siegfried had until recently been surpassed by the peoples of the west, he wrote: 'we should seek to take earnest account of this [degeneration] if we wish to explain the decay of the German folk which is now exposed without defence to the penetration of the Jews.' The same anti-Semitism is to be found in the writings of Houston Stewart Chamberlain, an Englishman who adopted Germany as his country and married Wagner's daughter Eva. His *Foundations of the Nineteenth Century* was devoted to inveighing against the mixing of blood and to exalting German greatness. 'And because the German soul is indissolubly bound up with the German tongue,' he wrote in a letter to the Emperor William II in 1901, 'the higher development of mankind is bound up with Germany, a mighty Germany spreading far across the earth the sacred heritage of her language, affirming herself everywhere and imposing herself on others.' With Eugen Dühring the argument is even more strongly anti-Semitic, but concentrating on Germany's need 'to free herself from the curse of English economic theory under the firm of Adam Smith, Ricardo,

Malthus, Stuart Mill, Cobden' by the establishment of Protection and State control.

The outcome of this more fanatical form of nationalism was two-fold. At a governmental level it encouraged the imposition of a policy of germanization on the non-German people within the Reich. In Slesvig, and in Alsace and Lorraine, known as the Reichsland directly under the authority of the Emperor, this was largely a matter of the acquisition of business interests and the use of the German language in schools and law courts. In the Polish provinces an official commission for colonization—the *Ansiedlungskommission*—first established by Bismarck in 1886 and later assisted by the *Deutscher Ostmarkverein*, stimulated an influx of German settlers. This had the effect of reinforcing the position of the German upper class who held some 59 per cent of the great estates in Posen, West Prussia, and Upper Silesia, although the total Polish population of the provinces remained a growing challenge, rising from 67 per cent in 1867 to 71 per cent in 1910.

Various other patriotic associations operated at an unofficial level, although not without influence on the government. The Colonial League, founded in 1887, the Navy League, the All-German Association, which later became the Pan-German League, the writings of Friedrich Lange and Karl Lamprecht, all preached the same fundamental doctrine of German greatness and of the need for all peoples of Germanic origin to be included within the frontiers of the Reich. Pan-Germanism with its racial assumptions went far beyond the claims of *Grossdeutschland*, and in the years immediately preceding the first World War became far more specific in its demands, as in the work of Otto Tannenberg and Friedrich von Gerhardi. 'Our aim is the creation of a powerful, world-embracing German empire,' wrote Eduard Weber in 1913, '. . . if England stands in the way, then let the cannon speak!'

This intensified sense of nationalism was by no means restricted to Germany. It was becoming increasingly active among the subject peoples on the periphery of the Russian dominions, at first largely cultural, then more political in its expression, as the Tsarist government attempted to counter it with a policy of russification.

In Finland this meant a sharp break from the policy of Alexander II who had attempted to cultivate Finnish national feeling (see p. 206). The growing influence from St Petersburg was already being felt in the last years of his son Alexander III, and later, when in 1898 the appointment of General Bobrikov as Governor General was followed by the drafting of Finnish recruits into the Russian army and of Russian officers into the forces of the Grand Duchy, Finnish local authorities refused to comply. By 1903 Bobrikov had taken over most of the administration of the country and the constitution had been suspended. Bobrikov was assassinated in 1904 and the short-lived revolution in Russia in 1905 (see p. 265) did bring Finland some relief, when in the following year the old Diet of four Estates was replaced by a single-chamber Assembly elected on a wide franchise for both sexes, the first instance of votes for women in any country in Europe. The Tsarist government, however, continued to press on with its policy of russification. This only served to encourage the growth of Finnish nationalism, which had been still further excited by the success of the Norwegians, when in 1905 the Swedish *Riksdag* agreed to the repeal of the union and a separate Kingdom of Norway was created under Haakon VII, a prince of the Danish house (see genealogical table p. 486).

In the lands on the south coast of the Baltic there had been a considerable revival of local Estonian, Latvian, and Lithuanian cultures. Here, however, the domination of the German upper class over Estonians and Latvians and of the Polish over the Lithuanians inspired as much antagonism as the fact of Russian rule. The implications of these grievances were thus social as well as political, and local Social Democrat parties took the lead in the various separatist movements. But the German and Polish upper classes too were hit by the policy of russification. Russian became the official language in the schools, which in 1886 were placed under the Russian Ministry of Education; the German university of Dorpat became a Russian University renamed Yuryev, and at the same time the Orthodox Church embarked on a great campaign for expansion in the Baltic lands.

In Poland the Russian government had hoped to blanket national feeling by means of industrial development, but the effect of this was lost through the recurrent slumps and the decline of agricultural prosperity (see p. 225). To the south there were growing demands for autonomy among the Georgians, the Volga Tartars, and the Rumanians of Bessarabia, while in the Caucasus Russia found herself actually working in cooperation with the Turkish Sultan in repressing the Armenians. This was also a period of fierce anti-Semitic legislation by the Russian government. The local *pogroms* which followed the assassination of Alexander II in 1881 were succeeded by a series of enactments against the five million Jews who lived with Russia, excluding them from many professions, restricting their attendance at secondary schools and universities, and often expelling them from their place of residence; and it was hardly surprising, in view of the growing anti-Semitism throughout Europe at this time, that the Jews, under the leadership of an Austrian Jew, Theodor Herzl, whose *Der Judenstaat* was published in 1896, should themselves contrive to form the movement known as Zionism which dreamed of a national home in the region of Palestine.

Nationalism in its most uninhibited form was to be seen in the Balkans, where the newly-formed states were free to indulge in all their patriotic rivalry. The creation of Bulgaria after the Congress of Berlin in 1878 (see p. 277) awoke a fierce animosity among the neighbouring peoples, since both Serbia and Greece feared Bulgarian expansion into regions still Turkish which they hoped eventually to gain for themselves. Among the Serbs there was, too, the desire to acquire Bosnia, and although their dislike of the Catholic Croats made this difficult of realization, a movement of reconciliation aiming at a federal southern Slav state—Yugoslavia—had been initiated as early as 1861 by the Catholic bishop of Zagreb, Strossmayer.

This growth of national aspirations in the Balkans naturally exercised an enormous attraction for the subject peoples under Habsburg rule, and here there was to be a marked difference of governmental attitude between the two sections of the Dual Monarchy. When in 1868 autonomy was granted to the Croats, including the use of the Croatian language in the Diet at Zagreb, it seemed as if the Magyars might be prepared to grant their subjects terms as good as they had themselves received from Vienna, but in the following years they began to impose an overwhelming policy of magyarization in political, economic, and cultural spheres on Poles, Slovaks, Transylvanians, and even on Croats, despite the agreement of 1868. In contrast to this enforced uniformity the Austrian government was moving towards greater liberal reforms extending the franchise and offering wider representation to its subject peoples (see p. 263). 'Only by cultivating the Slavs can Russian influence be paralyzed,' wrote the Crown Prince Rudolph a few years before his death at Mayerling in 1889, and Austrian mildness was a conscious attempt to find some answer to the attraction of Russian pan-Slavism.

This movement in Russia was parallel in some ways to pan-Germanism, but whereas the pan-Germans thought in terms of conquest, the Russian pan-Slavs saw themselves as the liberators of subject Slav peoples. Like the pan-Germans in Germany, they did not actually represent official Russian policy, but their view was akin to the claim to a protectorate over Orthodox Christians under Turkish rule which had contributed to the outbreak of the Crimean War, and thus had a bearing on the Tsarist government's rivalry with the Habsburgs in the Balkans. Many of the Slavs themselves, however, had doubts about succumbing to the embrace of Russian protection, and in the years immediately preceding 1914 Russian pan-Slavs had developed a modified scheme known as Neo-Slavism, aiming at no more than close friendship between all Slav countries, including Austria-Hungary.

To the end, the future of the Habsburg Empire remained at the mercy of its own complexity, and amid the mounting tensions of eastern Europe it seems improbable that any lasting Habsburg solution would have been feasible. Ironically, it was the circumstances of

Francis Ferdinand's death that precipitated the final collapse, for his assassination at Sarajevo in June 1914 led indirectly to the outbreak of the first World War, and although the eventual destruction of the Russian, German, and Austrian empires could not automatically solve the problems of eastern Europe, it did mean that a solution to them must be sought along totally different lines.

3. The world of Socialism

'Liberalism is but the accomplice of demagogy and serves, very often unconsciously, to drive a road for it and often to level it most conveniently. Liberalism shares the fate of all forerunners. Once the true lord appears, it is almost impossible to find any traces of the forerunner. Nothing is further from liberalism than demagogy; this latter is categorical, tyrannical in its ends as in its choice of means.' Naturally these remarks made by Metternich earlier in the century were uttered from a very different standpoint from that of Karl Marx; yet in their belief that the victory of liberalism would only mark a temporary stage on the road to the rule of the masses Metternich and Marx were in striking agreement. The decades preceding the outbreak of the first World War confronted the established society with a threat far more serious than anything before, since the multiplication in the numbers of industrial workers greatly increased their power of collective resistance, and there developed a considerable corpus of Socialist philosophy imbued with a keen sense of political realism and intellectual analysis quite remote from the Utopian excitement of the barricades of 1830 and 1848. For the Socialists there was, however, one weakness in this new precision in the definition of revolutionary aims in that it tended to sharpen the points of difference between the various groups.

The two major forces at work at this time were Anarchism and Marxism. The essence of Anarchism was a hatred for the State as a political organization; the Anarchist ideal was a loose federation of small communities in which the natural goodness of man would allow the individual to enjoy a full personal development. 'All exercise of power perverts and all submission to authority humiliates,' wrote Bakunin, who had taken up the leadership of the movement again after his escape from Siberia in 1861. Anarchism, in fact, despite its more modern and extensive organization, still retained a good deal of an out-moded Utopianism, and the terrorist methods of its more extreme supporters were reminiscent of the individual acts of violence of earlier revolutionaries. Indeed, between 1881 and 1901, they singled out the political Heads of State with a remarkable pertinacity; a Russian Tsar, a President of the French Republic, an Empress of Austria, a King of Italy, and a President of the United States, all figured in their record of assassination, which could hardly fail to impress the crowned heads of Europe.

One of the more positive features of Anarchism was that it had its attractions for a rural as well as an industrial society. In Russia the Populist movement appealed strongly to the Slavophil outlook (see p. 112), since it seized on the collective unit of the village community, the *mir*, as an essentially Russian phenomenon on which future society could be based. 'History is fond of her grandchildren,' said Chernyshevsky, one of the great exponents of the movement, 'for it offers them the marrow of the bones which the previous generation had hurt its hand in breaking,' and to the Populists it seemed that the development of the *mir* as a local unit of industry and agriculture might enable Russia to by-pass both the horrible living conditions of mass industrialism and the dictatorship of a new technical bureaucracy. Their propaganda was successful in recruiting a large number of enthusiasts who set out in 1873–4 on a great mission to the provinces to educate the peasantry for their new role, but these *narodniki*—men of the people—soon encountered the same mistrust and lack of comprehension among the peasants that the earlier reforming landowners had experienced, and this, coupled with the hostility of the government, who regarded the whole thing as highly subversive, led the more extreme members to fall back on a policy of sporadic violence.

In France the memory of the June days in 1848 and the Paris Commune of 1871 lent considerable emotional support to Anarchism and its impatient insistence on direct action, but with the growth of industry the movement was to become affiliated with a new doctrine of Syndicalism. First inspired by Fernand Pelloutier, then developed into a positive philosophy by Georges Sorel in his *Réflexions sur la violence*, published in 1905, Syndicalism desired a pluralist type of industrial organization in which federations of trade unions would replace the bourgeois parliamentary system. The Syndicalists were consistent in refusing to fight for their aim through the existing organs of government, and their principal weapon in the class struggle was to be the general strike through which the whole community could be brought to heel.

In Spain both the peasantry and the industrial workers were strongly influenced by Anarchism. It was particularly active during the unrest of 1873 and although General Pavia temporarily banned all working-class organizations when he seized power in the following year, the movement continued to grow in the rural districts and gained a hold on the trade unions of Catalonia, later to be reinforced by Syndicalist theory. In 1892 peasantry marched into Jerez and had to be dispersed by cavalry, and in 1909 the proclamation of a general strike in the north led to a week of civil war in which there was fierce street fighting in Barcelona. The working-class movement in Spain remained strongly Anarchist long after the movement had faded away in the rest of Europe; it was dominant in the *Confederacion Nacional del Trabajo*, which by 1919 had 700,000 members, and although it never made its peace with other left-wing movements it was to play a considerable part in the resistance of the Spanish government to the advance of General Franco in the Spanish Civil War of 1936–9 (see pp. 411–13).

The gulf between the aims and methods of Anarchism and Marxism was one of the most significant aspects of the Socialist movement in the 1880s and 1890s. Anarchism wished to destroy the State at once; Marxism accepted the State as a necessary evil until the final stage of social development had been reached. Anarchism believed in a policy of terroristic violence; Marxism regarded this as futile, a last sputter of revolutionary romanticism. Anarchism was prepared to accept the peasantry as a fundamental force of revolution; Marxism looked unequivocally to the workers who would take over the development of a bourgeois economy—although Marx himself towards the end of his life was beginning to wonder about the role of the peasantry in a Russian uprising.*

The argument between the two sides raged throughout the remainder of the nineteenth century. This was a time when the improved communications and the involuntary closeness of relations throughout the world had encouraged the growth of a whole range of organizations devoted to international cooperation; the Red Cross Convention had been signed in 1864; a Postal Union was formed ten years later, and an Inter-Parliamentary Union in 1889, as well as various pacifist associations, and in 1899 and 1907 the Powers themselves held conferences at The Hague, where it was agreed that a Court of International Arbitration should be established, although efforts to achieve an all-round reduction in armaments were unsuccessful. It was consequently hardly surprising that a Socialist organization should develop along the same lines; in 1864 Marx was largely responsible for the founding of the International Working Men's Association, the First International, whose congresses continued to meet until it was finally dissolved in 1876 at Philadelphia. In 1889 this was succeeded by the Second International which remained a significant Socialist organization until 1914.

The seriousness of the split between the Anarchists and the Marxists was naturally emphasized in the congresses of both the First and the Second International. Indeed, the First was virtually destroyed by it, but although the meetings of the Second in the 1890s were often hampered by the virulence of the dispute, the Marxist element predominated largely through the discipline of the German party—the *Sozialdemokratische Partei Deutschlands* (SPD)—under Wilhelm Liebknecht and August Bebel.

There were, however, other issues of disagreement that were eventually to shatter the effective political strength of the Second Inter-

---

* For the general doctrine of Marxism, see pp. 96–7.

national. The Marxists rejected the theories and tactics of the Anarchists; on the other hand, although they were for the moment prepared to accept the continued existence of the State, they could not countenance any form of gradualism. This was the hope of moderate Socialists, who believed that their ends could be attained by a policy of cooperation with liberals through parliaments and negotiation by trade unions, an idea that was naturally anathema to the Marxists who saw that it would win the working class over to the acceptance of a society which would still be fundamentally bourgeois. The hopes of the gradualists were greatly strengthened by the growth of social and industrial legislation improving working and living conditions throughout most of the Continent. In Germany Bismarck's laws for social insurance in the 1880s (see p. 257), in France the limitation of the working day to ten hours in 1900 and the enforcement of a six-day week in 1906, in Austria the establishment of factory inspection in 1883 and the general regulation of industry in 1907, and in Great Britain the extension of earlier Factory Acts followed by the Liberal administration of 1906, all had their counterpart in smaller countries such as Switzerland, Belgium, and the Netherlands. Many of the concessions by the governments were grudgingly made, and the alternation of boom and slump continued to stimulate the class antagonism in the labour disputes of these years and lent strength to the Marxist thesis; yet the Social Democrats remained deeply concerned over the growing attraction of gradualism. 'The idea of a social democrat must not be a trade union secretary, but a tribune of the people,' warned Lenin in his pamphlet *What is to be done?* in 1902. 'A trade union policy of the working class is simply a bourgeois policy for the working class.'

It was in those countries where parliamentary practice was strongly established that gradualism made its greatest appeal. The English trade unionists were incorrigibly bourgeois in Marxist eyes, an idea epitomized by an occasion at the London congress of the International in 1896 when the English president threatened to end an Anarchist disturbance by summoning the police. In France there were inevitably a whole variety of political sects, and while the Marxist element stood firm under Jules Guesde, there were many such as Paul Brousse and later Jean Jaurès and Viviani, who were prepared to work through the party machinery in the Chamber, and in 1898 a French Socialist, Alexandre Millerand, actually became Minister of Commerce under Waldeck-Rousseau. Similarly, at the beginning of the twentieth century Socialists and liberals were cooperating in the Italian Parliament as well as in Belgium over the establishment of universal suffrage. In Germany the tendency was less marked, partly because the deputies in the *Reichstag* had little control over the actions of their government, partly because, in contrast to France, the German Socialist movement was monolithic in its structure and predominantly Marxist. Nevertheless, it was a German, Eduard Bernstein, who in 1899 produced a positive doctrine of gradualism in a formal criticism of Marx's arguments. This attempt to revise the basic tenets of the faith was strongly resisted by Karl Kautsky and its rejection by the German Social Democrats was duly ratified at the Amsterdam congress of the International in 1904.

Another issue which exercised the minds of the International during these years was the question of their attitude towards a European war. Fundamentally they were in agreement that the idea of such a conflict in which the working classes of different nations would be forced to slaughter each other was utterly abhorrent; yet, when the extremists urged that the governments of the Powers should all be immobilized at the moment of outbreak by a general strike and by a unanimous refusal to vote war credits and to serve in the armed forces, various nationalities found that under certain circumstances they would have to align themselves with their governments. 'If Russia, the champion of cruelty and barbarity, the enemy of all human culture were to attack Germany,' said the German Bebel in 1891 '. . . we are as much and more interested than those who stand at the head of Germany, and we would resist Russia, for a Russian victory means the defeat of social democracy.' The conflict with the submerged nationalities was also reflected in his remark in 1897: 'A good comrade who only knows German is more use than an incompetent Polish-speaking one.' Similarly, at an Austrian Social Democrat congress in 1899, a German Austrian remarked: 'German will remain a language of culture and communication whether we like it or not and regardless of the likes and dislikes of our Czech comrades.' And in the countries where gradualism was an active force, Socialists who were fighting to win the votes of a parliamentary electorate had to be even more outspoken in their patriotism. 'We shall at no moment forget', announced Millerand in France, 'that at the same time as being internationalists we are Frenchmen and patriots.'*

National emotions were one serious obstacle in the preparations for averting the outbreak of war, but there was another in the very doctrine of Marxism itself. Marx and Engels had declared categorically that the whole course of historical development made a vast capitalist war inevitable, indeed essential, for it was through this catastrophe that the bourgeois governments would topple and the dictatorship of the proletariat emerge. Yet for the men who would have to endure the horror of general war on the Continent the prospect was so appalling that despite their national differences they

* This selection of quotations is taken from *The Second International 1889–1914* by James Joll.

continued to think in terms of the impossibility of such a contravention of the brotherhood of the working class, and at the congress of 1913 at Basle, amid a frenzy of wishful thinking, they made a solemn affirmation of faith at a great gathering in the old cathedral of the city.

Many of the divisions within the International had consisted of a struggle between the Marxists and their opponents. There was, however, at the same time a considerable debate within the Marxist party itself over revolutionary methods. This finally came to a head in 1903 at a Russian Social Democrat congress which began in Brussels and then, owing to the attentions of the Belgian police, had to be transferred to the Tottenham Court Road in London. Under the presidency of George Plekhanov, a former Russian Populist who had turned to Marxism, the meeting was to debate the statutes of the party and at once issue was joined between Lenin and Martov.

Lenin whose real name was Vladimir Ilyich Ulyanov was the son of a school inspector at Simbirsk. His work as a student of law at the University of Kazan had been interrupted owing to the mistrust of the authorities after the execution of his elder brother for participating in a plot to assassinate Tsar Alexander III. He turned, instead, to reading Karl Marx, whose first volume of *Das Kapital* had been translated into Russian as early as 1868—to Marx's surprise—and when he was eventually allowed to qualify in 1891, he devoted the next four years to the dissemination of Socialist propaganda. This led to his arrest and a spell of exile in Siberia, where he was able to continue his studies, and shortly after his release in 1900 he left Russia for the greater freedom of the west. By the time of the Brussels congress Lenin, as he now called himself, was thirty-three years of age, a persuasive speaker, a skilful antagonist in argument, and utterly dedicated to revolutionary Socialism.

The clash over the first clause of the party statutes was due to Lenin's insistence on the restriction of membership to those who accepted the party programme and who supported it 'both materially and by personal participation in one of its organizations'. His conception of the party, in fact, was of a disciplined *élite* whose authority was essential for the accomplishment of the revolution in Russia—an attitude which possibly owed something to his training as a lawyer and to the hereditary influence of his Volga German mother. Martov, on the other hand, wished to frame the clause so as to include the milder liberal elements who merely sympathized, and it was his motion that won the day. Later, however, some of Martov's supporters left the congress, and Lenin's group, who were thus able to secure the election of their candidates to leading positions in the party, became known as the *Bolsheviki* (the men of the majority).

Despite this temporary victory Martov had considerable backing in the Socialist world from Axelrod and Trotsky, as well as Kautsky and Rosa Luxemburg among the Germans, while Plekhanov, although he had supported Lenin at the congress, could not agree with him entirely. Indeed, the *Mensheviki* (the so-called men of the minority) felt themselves sufficiently strong to denounce the Bolshevik Central Committee, and as other issues arose, so the split widened. The Mensheviks were absolutely orthodox Marxists in that Russia's peculiar difficulty in their eyes was that the bourgeois revolution which must, according to their theory of history, precede the proletarian, had not yet taken place. Thus they believed that since the historical process was inexorable, their immediate role must be to facilitate this bourgeois revolution—hence Martov's wider definition of party membership; then a long interval of time must elapse during which the victory of the bourgeois would create the conditions from which their own downfall would automatically follow. The emergence of a large proletariat was the essential factor for the Mensheviks and they did not envisage the peasantry playing an effective part at any stage of the revolutionary process.

To Lenin, however, the very peculiarity of the situation in Russia demanded a different technique which he outlined in *Two Tactics of Sound Democracy in the Democratic Revolution* in 1905. First, he recognized the existence of a revolutionary element among some, at least, of the peasants. Second, he felt that this possible reinforcement for the proletariat might be lost if the bourgeois revolution were allowed to consolidate itself, and although he clearly emphasized the distinction between the two revolutions, he declared that the second must follow upon the first almost at once. As soon as the Russian *bourgeoisie* had embarked upon their revolution against Tsarist absolutism, the proletariat, aided by some of the peasantry, must capture it for themselves. 'We stand for uninterrupted revolution,' he wrote in an article in 1905. 'We shall not stop half-way.'

Thus, in a sense, the doctrine of the Bolsheviks was as much a revision of Marxism in the direction of accelerating the revolutionary process as Eduard Bernstein's proposals had been in the direction of gradualism. Yet, of all the schools of thought that divided the Socialist world, the emergence of Bolshevism was to have the most startling effect—and this mainly because of the original issue that had split the Russian congress of 1903. For, unlike any of the other sects, Lenin's creation of a disciplined *élite* gave them a striking power in 1917 out of all proportion to their numbers, which was to enable them to accomplish the second revolution within eight months of the outbreak of the first.

Chapter 22

Stages of Parliamentary Democracy

In the decades before the outbreak of the first World War the new social and economic power of the middle classes was reflected in varying degrees in the growth of parliamentary institutions throughout the Continent. The most striking aspect of this development was the extension of the franchise. Universal male suffrage was established in the German Empire and the French Third Republic and was later granted in Bulgaria, Greece, and Norway. In 1874 the Swiss even introduced a system of direct democracy by referendum, which in 1891 came to include proposals for individual legislative changes. Other countries proceeded more cautiously in lowering tax and property qualifications. In Austria there were extensions of the franchise in 1882 and 1896 and it was finally made universal in 1907, although remaining severely restricted in Hungary. In Belgium an electorate of 116,000 out of a population of five and a half million was increased in 1893 to 1,370,000 half of whom were to enjoy two or three votes, while in 1913 the franchise was made universal--each concession being prompted by the threat of a general strike. In Italy the quadrupling of the electorate in 1882 only enfranchised 7 per cent of the population, but in 1913 most adult males were granted the right to vote. In Russia, after the revolution of 1905, a national Parliament, the *Duma*, was to be elected on a system that nominally came close to universal suffrage.

At first sight it might seem that the age of democracy had dawned. For conservatives this only justified the gloomy comment of Jacob Burckhardt in 1842: 'This frightening accentuation of the rights of the individual consists in this: *cogito* (whether correctly or falsely doesn't matter) *ergo regno*.' And for many liberals now safely ensconced among the established classes it revived the old dread of 1848 that their own success would open the way to the working-class masses among whom Socialist ideas were now rife.

In fact, these concessions were not as startling as they might appear. The franchise in itself was only one element in the full exercise of democratic power; what mattered was the extent to which the distribution of seats represented the balance of political opinion among the electorate, and, more important still, the degree of control which the elected assembly could exert over the government of the country. The practice of democracy rests not simply on the granting of votes, but on the general evolution of a parliamentary tradition at a local as well as a national level. In this respect the study of the franchise alone is misleading. In central and eastern Europe, where executive power had been virtually absolute, the development of parliamentary assemblies made only a minor impact upon the authority of the State. In Germany, Austria-Hungary, Russia and the Balkan countries, government remained largely in the hands of the ruling few, and only in the west and in Scandinavia, where constitutional limitations had already been imposed before the days of universal suffrage, did these considerable extensions of the franchise have any great meaning.

1. The French Third Republic

In France the debate over the future form of government continued for some four years after the Franco-Prussian War. At first all the indications suggested a restoration of the monarchy. The National Assembly elected in 1871 was strongly royalist; in 1873 Thiers was replaced by the devoutly Catholic and conservative Marshal MacMahon as President of the Republic, and when Bismarck embarked upon his campaign against the Catholic party in Germany, (see p. 256), the French clericals were able to strengthen their cause with a patriotic antagonism towards the Imperial Chancellor. Monarchy, however, was not to be restored. Paris had been worth a Mass for Henry IV, but for the Bourbon claimant, 'Henry V', Count de Chambord, it was not worth a tricolour. He insisted on the adoption of the white Bourbon flag, and MacMahon himself, conscious of the revival of republican ardour reflected in recent by-elections, knew this to be an impossible condition. Nor would the disappointed Legitimists join forces with the Orleanists, and in 1875 a series of 'Organic Laws' established the Third Republic for lack of any other solution.

There were to be two Houses, a Chamber of Deputies elected by universal male suffrage, and a Senate of 300, a quarter of whom were elected for life by the National Assembly, the remainder for nine years by the *départements* and colonies. The most that the conservatives could do was to gain equal legislative powers for the Senate and to hope to strengthen the position of the President, who was to be elected by the two Houses and to hold office for seven years. Over this second point they were to be defeated, for a new Chamber elected in 1877 forced MacMahon to dismiss the government which he had formed under the Duke de Broglie, and the constitutional predominance of the Lower House was confirmed two years later when MacMahon resigned and was replaced by Jules Grévy under whom the presidency was reduced to a more nominal position.

This victory for the republicans was followed by a renewed assault upon the position of the Church. Since the middle of the century religious orders had greatly increased in numbers, authorized communities held property worth a total of 421 million francs –nearly £17 million–and as a consequence of the *Loi Falloux* of 1850 (see p. 151) two-fifths of all French school children now attended Catholic schools. To the anti-clericals the Syllabus of Errors and the doctrine of Papal Infallibility (see p. 217) appeared to represent a declaration of war, and although the Senate rejected a law forbidding members of unauthorized congregations to teach anywhere in France, a precise interpretation of the existing Concordat did enable the government to dissolve a certain number of unauthorized communities. In 1882 Jules Ferry made primary education compulsory, free, and secular, thereby prohibiting religious instruction in State schools; *écoles normales* were instituted for girls, and Catholic universities were deprived of the right to confer degrees.

By the end of the 1880s, however, the republicans were once again in danger of falling between two stools. They had based their power on the support of the *petite bourgeoisie*, ending the system of life-membership of the Senate in 1884 and loosening the central government's power to the extent of allowing all mayors except those in Paris to be elected by local councils. By now, however, the radical forces of the industrial proletariat were becoming far more coherent, and the death of Napoleon's son, the Prince Imperial, in Zululand in 1879 and that of the Count de Chambord in 1883 might have made it possible for all monarchists to fall in with the Orleanists. In fact, the right wing—Catholic, anti-parliamentary and strongly represented in the army—were by this time ceasing to be royalist and were developing a more sinister tendency to look simply for a strong man who might seize power. In the years 1887–9 it seemed as if they might have found him in General Boulanger, the Minister of War, who won tremendous popularity both with the right and with a section of the radicals in one of those instances, common in French history, when the two extremes join forces against the centre. Boulanger, however, was not the man for a *coup d'état* and his loss of nerve and eventual flight to Belgium in 1889 discredited both sides and enabled the Third Republic to enjoy a new lease of life.

Indeed, despite the rapid changes of government and the general sense of mediocrity in political life the new Republic had shown a remarkable resilience. It demonstrated the total recovery of France from the war with the great Paris Exhibition of 1889; it survived the financial scandal of the Panama scheme in which several members of the government were found to be involved, and remained unshaken by the assassination of one of its Presidents, Sadi Carnot, in 1894. After the Boulanger incident greater harmony between the moderates of the left and right suggested that the Republic might be moving into calmer waters, but these hopes were to be wrecked by the storm of the Dreyfus *affaire*. In 1894 Alfred Dreyfus, a young Jewish staff officer, was court-martialled for selling military information to Germany and was later sentenced to imprisonment on Devil's Island. Dreyfus's family continued to fight to establish his innocence, and when the authorities refused to accept new evidence that seemed to clear him, political opponents of the government began to take up the case. The controversy reached its height when in 1898 Émile Zola published in Clemenceau's newspaper *L'Aurore* an open letter to the President of the Republic, '*J'accuse*', and eventually after fresh developments Dreyfus was brought back to France, retried by court-martial at Rennes, found guilty again and then granted a pardon from the President.

The *affaire* had torn France apart with all the passions of conservative anti-Semitism and republican hatred of the Catholic military high command, and the possibility of a coalition of moderates faded amid a new governmental onslaught on the Church. In 1903 Pope Leo XIII had been succeeded by Pius X, less prone to compromise with the forces of secularism, and after the new Pope's denunciation of President Loubet's visit to the King of Italy, the French government passed legislation in 1905 that brought the Concordat to an end. The State was now to be entirely separate from all forms of religion, and consequently the Catholic Church was no longer to be subsidized and lost practically all its property by confiscation. Thus although the impact of the Franco-Prussian War had been relatively brief, the wounds which France had inflicted upon herself more than a hundred years before still remained unhealed.

2. Imperial Germany

Not surprisingly the constitution of the federal German Empire in 1871 merely consolidated the position that Prussia had enjoyed since 1866. The Prussian army remained the principal military force; the federal civil service was largely manned by Prussians, and the few concessions made to particularist sentiment on the entry of the south German states were almost entirely meaningless; the King of Württemberg could appoint the officers of his army; the King of Bavaria commanded his army in peacetime, ran his own railway system and issued his own postage stamps. Apart from this, they had all been accommodated in that strange unwieldy contraption that Bismarck had devised in 1867 as a means of making German unification compatible with the pre-eminence of Prussia.

Of the federal legislature, the Upper House, the *Bundesrat*, now had 58 delegates appointed by the member states—seventeen of them for Prussia. The Lower House, the *Reichstag*, numbered some 400 deputies, who were elected by universal suffrage every three years, but their powers were fairly limited, since the Chancellor was not responsible to them. They could only vote on matters that he or the *Bundesrat* had initiated and although their consent was needed for the federal budget, this only concerned indirect taxes; the right of imposing direct taxes belonged to the individual states who made their own contribution to the imperial treasury from this revenue.

Nevertheless, the federal budget could create difficulties. Indirect taxes were often controversial, since the commodities chosen might not be acceptable to some of the sectional interests on whom the Chancellor was relying within the *Reichstag*. There was a further complication in that once a tax had been voted, it could only be rescinded by a constitutional amendment. This required a two-thirds majority in the *Bundesrat*, and there Bismarck could almost certainly block it. As a consequence, deputies were rather wary of voting a tax which would very probably become permanent. Thus, William and the generals were never able to get a permanent vote for a standing army of 400,000 men and had instead to be content with the system of the *Septennat*, whereby the necessary tax was only voted for seven years at a time.

At least, while Bismarck remained in office, the system worked reasonably well, mainly because nobody else was allowed to play much part in it. Until 1878 there was to be no appointment of any other federal ministries and, even after that, the secretaries of state who were to deputise for him remained strictly subordinate. He was also minister president and foreign minister of Prussia, and William I, who did not die until 1888, was unlikely to challenge anything that his Chancellor said. It was a position in total accord with Bismark's neurotic obsession with power, but it should be added that he did combine this with a certain skill in handling the groups in the *Reichstag*.

At first Bismarck relied principally on the Free Conservatives, two-thirds of whom were landowners, and on the National Liberals under a Hanoverian, Rudolf von Bennigsen. The latter had supported him since the victory of 1866 (see p. 199), and the alliance with these two groups, which ensured him a firm bloc of about 160 seats, also allowed him to give vent to his mistrust of the Catholic Centre party, which under Ludwig Windthorst had about seventy seats in the *Reichstag*. There were a number of reasons for these doubts over the political reliability of the Catholics. The Syllabus of Errors and the declaration of Papal Infallibility was to create considerable tension between Church and State in Germany, but in addition to this the Catholic party was sympathetic towards the Poles in West Prussia and Posen and towards the French in

Lorraine, while the Catholics of south Germany still supported the notion of *Grossdeutschland* on which Bismark had turned his back.

This period of alliance with the National Liberals, which lasted until 1879, was marked by a great onslaught by the government on the Catholic Church in Germany—the *Kulturkampf*. In 1872 the Jesuits were expelled from the Reich; in 1873 the May laws brought all ecclesiastical education and appointments under State control; in 1875 civil marriage became compulsory and, later, Catholic rights of assembly were restricted and their publications severely censored. Bismarck had been determined to win; 'we shall not go to Canossa', he had boasted, but the passive resistance of the Catholics eventually forced him to submit to his first political defeat; bishops and priests went to prison rather than obey, and by 1876 nine Prussian sees were unoccupied and 1,400 parishes had no legally appointed priest.

In many ways this was an entirely unnecessary problem that Bismarck had simply created for himself. At the same time, however, there was another development over which he had less control and this was eventually to cause him to consider a fundamental realignment of his forces. In 1875 a Marxist Social Democrat party (SPD) had been formed in Germany and was already showing signs of gathering mass support. For Bismarck this was the greatest of all dangers and in 1878 he managed to rush through law whereby the Social Democrats were deprived of their rights of assembly and publication, and individual leaders could be expelled from their place of residence. The National Liberals, however, had not been at ease over the authoritarian nature of the law, and Lasker, the leader of their left wing, managed to ensure that it was only to last for two and a half years at a time.

It was now clear that the National Liberals were not an absolutely reliable ally against the Social Democrats. They were in any case losing some of their electoral support and it seemed that some of the conservative groups might have more to offer. This was to be the beginning of a major shift in Bismarck's political alignments. Conservative landowners who were by now suffering seriously from the effects of overseas competition, were sure to demand higher tariffs and this must mean the end of any alliance with the National Liberals, since they still believed in free trade. The Social Democrats would be still more incensed over tariffs, because protection for the farmer would mean dearer food for the worker. Hence, to be absolutely secure against this new pattern of opposition, Bismarck needed the Catholic Centre party as well. Their price was bound to be a relaxation of the *Kulturkampf*, but by now Bismarck could almost welcome some escape from that deadlock and in 1878 the pacific tendencies of the new Pope Leo XIII opened a way to a settlement with the Catholics, although this was not finally achieved until 1887.

The arrangement with conservative groups was to be the principal means whereby Bismarck managed the *Reichstag* during the last eleven years of his chancellorship. It enabled him to get the military budget passed for seven years in 1880, and again, with a 10 per cent increase, in 1886. He was also able to put through laws for social insurance—against sickness in 1883, accidents in 1884, and old age and disability in 1889. The principal purpose of this was to steal the thunder of the Social Democrats, and indeed for many years these measures were regarded as a model by radicals elsewhere and were to be the inspiration of Lloyd George's Liberal scheme in Great Britain in 1911. Yet neither repression by means of the anti-Social Democrat laws, nor paternalism through welfare legislation could entirely achieve the effect that he wanted and by 1890 the popular vote of the Social Democrats had reached nearly one and a half million.

The old Emperor William I died at last in 1888 and was succeeded first by his son Frederick III, who only survived him for three months, and then by his grandson William II, usually known as the Kaiser (see genealogical table p. 485). Unstable, conceited and struggling with a deep inferiority complex, the young Emperor was determined to assume a personal control of government which Bismarck had kept so long to himself, and in 1890 the Imperial Chancellor was virtually dismissed.

For subsequent Chancellors the principal aim was to continue with a broad conservative bloc which might keep the Social Democrats at bay. Bismarck had often been able to use the tensions of foreign policy to assist him at crucial moments in his dealings with the *Reichstag*, but none of his successors had the necessary skill or control in that sphere and the occasional intrusions of William II only added to their difficulties. The most that they could do in this respect was to make a massive patriotic appeal at the time of elections. This sometimes strengthened the parties on whom the Chancellor was relying in the *Reichstag*, but it did nothing to reduce the horse-trading among them, once the election was over. Paradoxically the power of the executive was actually a hindrance. The Chancellor had no responsibility to the deputies; they consequently had none to him and the resultant groupings were always likely to be short-lived. Indeed, the inescapable impression during these years is that the position of the Chancellor was growing less significant. Yet this did nothing to strengthen the influence of the *Reichstag*; it merely made it more probable that the exercise of executive power would drift away to other quarters, such as the military or the court, where there were many voices urging the Kaiser to think of restoring direct personal rule through the army—an emergency action known as the *Staatsstreich*.

The sharpest break with Bismark's methods came immediately after his departure, when General Caprivi took over and tried to please everyone. He allowed the anti-Social Democrat laws to lapse; to win back the National Liberals, he reduced duties on imported wheat and rye; and to keep the Centre with him, he introduced a Prussian school bill allowing greater freedom for Polish Catholics— which promptly outraged the National Liberals and had to be withdrawn. He also greatly reduced the concentration of power on himself; the position of Prussian Foreign Minister was abolished, that of Prussian Minister President was passed on, and in future the Federal Secretaries of State were to be allowed to pursue their own policies. Yet none of this increased the constitutional responsibility of the executive; it simply became more difficult for the Chancellor to control, and Caprivi eventually sickened of the ensuing intrigues and resigned in 1894.

His successor, Prince Hohenlohe-Schillingsfürst, was an elderly Bavarian politician. Conservative circles around the Kaiser were now pressing for renewal of the anti-Social Democrat laws; the Prussian Minister of Commerce and groups in the *Reichstag* opposed this and the various bills were thrown out, but throughout the battle the Chancellor appeared to be an increasingly weary figure in the middle. Similarly, it was Admiral von Tirpitz, Secretary of State for the Navy since 1897, who took the initiative in gaining the Kaiser's support for a vast naval expansion (see p. 289) and in March 1898 the *Reichstag* was persuaded to vote 400 million RM as a first instalment of the cost. Yet, while Hohenlohe described the new venture as purely defensive, Tirpitz was already making it clear that he hoped eventually to challenge the British navy, and a supplementary bill in 1900 doubling the number of proposed battleships put that ambition beyond doubt. Once again, it was extra-parliamentary interests that were calling the tune—industrialists eager for shipbuilding orders, bankers eager to make loans, patriots extolling the glory of a navy and of the colonies that it would protect (see p. 241), and a working class whose patriotic emotion was encouraged by the prospects of full employment.

Bernhard von Bülow took over in 1900. He was the son of one of Bismarck's Secretaries of State and was a man of considerable diplomatic experience. Yet it is a sign of the triviality of German political life that he owed his appointment to his friendship with the Kaiser's favourite Philip von Eulenburg, and he eventually fell in 1909 because he was somewhat lukewarm in his defence of the Kaiser before the *Reichstag*, after William had given a tactless interview to the *Daily Telegraph*. He was succeeded by Theobald von Bethmann-

Hollweg whose experience was limited to provincial administration and who had little knowledge of foreign or military affairs.
Both were faced with a mounting debt, which doubled during
Bülow's chancellorship, owing to the increasing cost of the new
navy; both had to try to keep together a conservative bloc of industrialist and agrarian interests in the *Reichstag*, who supported the
navy, but who could easily become divided over the type of indirect
tax needed to finance it. And so for much of their time they were
distracted by incessant niggling over the various proposals—an
inheritance tax, a federal income tax, the raising of duties on spirits
and tobacco, or a tax on mobile stock—and occasionally falling back
on patriotic appeals, as Bülow attempted in the election of 1907.

All this might suggest some semblance of parliamentary life, yet
in reality it was very slight, as was illustrated in the Zabern affair
in November 1913. In Alsace a Lieutenant Zabern had insulted the
local population in a speech and the subsequent disorders led to
arrests by the military. The Kaiser fully supported Zabern, but
when the *Reichstag* took the matter up, Bethmann Hollweg, attempting to defend the Kaiser, was unable to prevent the passing of a vote
of no confidence by an enormous majority. In any parliamentary
form of government such a vote should have signified something. In
fact, the charges against all the officers in the affair were dismissed
by the military courts and nothing more was heard of it. Thus by
1914 it seemed that the *Reichstag* had not acquired any decisive
power, and the position of Chancellor had become that of an uneasy
go-between, while small cliques of industrialists and high ranking
service personnel formed the major decision-making centres, all
competing for influence around Kaiser William II.

9. Italy after unification

'Italy is made,' remarked D'Azeglio in 1860. 'Now we must make
Italians.' This proved to be a rather more difficult task; the sense
of particularism was strong and many of the other regions of Italy
regarded unification with suspicion as a piece of Piedmontese
aggrandizement. Indeed, this was how many of the Piedmontese
saw it; the new King retained his original title of Victor Emmanuel
II, and in 1864 there was fury in Turin when the capital was shifted
to Florence, and again fury in Florence, when it finally shifted to
Rome in 1870.

It was consequently quite natural that the constitution of the
Kingdom of Italy should simply be an extension of the one that the
Piedmontese had devised in 1848. The King had considerable
executive powers, but they had to be exercised in conjunction with
a bi-cameral Parliament. The Upper House, the Senate, however,
was appointed by the Crown and although the Lower House, the

Chamber of Deputies, was elective, a high property qualification made the franchise extremely narrow—in 1870 about half a million adult males, although in 1882 this was increased to about two million and in 1913 the introduction of universal male suffrage raised it to eight and a half million. At the time of elections the prefects who ruled the provinces could usually influence their small local electorate through bribes or coercion. The deputies themselves were untrammelled by any national party organizations and simply gave their support to a premier who was prepared to satisfy their personal demands or those of their constituents. It was Agostino Depretis who first mastered this system of bribery, known as *transformismo*, and thus ensured that, except for two short intervals, he was to be premier from 1876 to 1887. His successor, Francesco Crispi, one of the Thousand who had sailed with Garibaldi to Sicily, stood for a more high-minded interpretation of Italian government; yet he too had to operate the system in order to enjoy two periods of rule between 1887 and 1896. Probably the most skilful operator of all was Giovanni Giolitti, who between 1903 and 1914 was able to take himself in and out of power almost at will.

In some ways the prospects of the country which these men attempted to govern improved greatly in the last half of the nineteenth century. A population of 26 million had risen to more than 35 million by 1911. There was an immense expansion of railway and road building, a vast extension of the telegraph service and enlargement of the ports of Genoa, Leghorn and Naples. Industrialization in the north began seriously to develop after 1880, principally in steel, textiles and mechanical engineering, and between 1881 and 1889 alone the national output of steel rose from 4,064 to 160,528 tonnes.

The fruits of this economic growth, however, were not shared equally. For the bulk of the population income per family was a great deal lower than in England or France, and taxes were levied on almost all commodities of everyday life. The agricultural labourer was paid barely a subsistence wage; even a country doctor earned no more than the equivalent of £2 a week, and one minister of finance calculated that only 0·13 per cent of the population enjoyed an annual income of more than £400. There was also a geographical divide, since much of Italy's wealth lay in the north; an intensive cultivation of the coastal regions of the south seemed to offer a possible solution, but by the end of the 1870s Italy had been affected by the general fall in agricultural prices throughout Europe (see p. 225) and the south reverted to its customary condition of poverty. Here the share of national wealth was the smallest, the burden of taxation relatively the largest, and despite the establishment of State schools, the level of illiteracy the highest and the rate of improvement the slowest.

Extreme poverty in many parts of Italy naturally provided a fertile soil for various Marxist and Anarchist organizations. In 1893 a growing Socialist movement in Sicily got out of control in a wave of violence, and eventually Crispi had to send in 40,000 troops to restore order; Socialist activities were dissolved and the eight Socialist deputies in the Chamber placed under arrest. Within a few years his successor Rudini had to face still worse, when a concentration of unemployment and high prices resulting from the Spanish-American War (see p. 233) stimulated outbreaks of violence throughout many cities in the spring of 1898, and in Milan open fighting in the streets caused the loss of eighty-two lives. This was sufficiently horrifying to bring down Rudini's administration, but it was perhaps understandable that King Humbert, the son of Victor Emmanuel, should choose a general as his next premier. In fact, it was principally economic recovery after the turn of the century that helped to quieten the scene, apart from further outbreaks in Sardinia and Sicily in 1904.

This type of popular unrest was common in many parts of Europe at this time. There was, however, one problem that was peculiar to Italy. Pope Pius IX had utterly rejected the Law of Guarantees with which the secular power had attempted to reconcile the Church to the taking of Rome in 1870 (see p. 217); Catholics were instructed to abstain from all aspects of political life including voting in elections, and the Pope remained a voluntary prisoner in the Vatican. Throughout the pontificate of Leo XIII, who succeeded him in 1878, the two sides remained unreconciled, but although some issues such as religious teaching in State schools or civil marriage were insoluble, the fear of Socialism eventually caused the Church to relax the ban on entering into political life, and in the elections of 1904 Catholics were allowed to vote and to stand as candidates.

Against this rather unpromising background there was not much kudos to be gained by Italian politicians at home. Consequently their hope was to be able to strengthen their position by some success abroad. European diplomacy offered very little. Italy came back empty-handed from the Congress of Berlin in 1878, and her joining the Triple Alliance with Germany and Austria-Hungary in 1882 was merely an angry reaction to France's annexation of Tunis the previous year (see pp. 230, 279). It seemed, however, that colonial adventures in Africa might promise more prestige and by 1890 Italian settlers were being established in Eritrea and Somaliland. Yet even this had its dangers and in 1896 a serious defeat inflicted on the Italians by the Abyssinians at Adowa brought down Crispi's second administration. Even so, the lure of colonialism remained. For years Italian governments dreamed of seizing Libya from Turkey and eventually did so in 1911 (see p. 296). By this time, however, colonialism was not simply a political gambit for politicians;

it had become part of a fierce mood of Italian nationalism, encouraged by the writings of the poet Gabriele D'Annunzio and imbued with a heady atmosphere of patriotism which continued to be an important political factor in the years after the Great War.

4. Austria-Hungary

At five o'clock in the morning the Emperor Francis Joseph would rise and toil at his desk throughout the day on the minutiae of Habsburg administration. He was a man of simple tastes, totally uninterested in the luxury and comfort that were his to command. In the Schönbrunn palace the Emperor slept on an ordinary iron bedstead and in an age of gas and electricity preferred his oil lamp. He was a devout Catholic and every Maundy Thursday would solemnly wash the feet of a dozen old men brought to the Hofburg from a local almshouse. No ruler could have been more dedicated to the government of his dominions than Francis Joseph; no man more unfortunate in the tragedies of his personal life.

The unflinching sense of duty and decorum that sustained him played havoc with his relationship with his family. His wife, Elizabeth of Bavaria, rebelling against the strictness of court formality, was drawn towards the greater flamboyance of the Hungarians and spent much of her later years in travel around Europe. His son, the Crown Prince Rudolph, was opposed to him on political grounds; his nephew Francis Ferdinand, had offended him by marrying Countess Sophia Chotek, a Czech lady whom the Emperor did not consider sufficiently high-born for such an honour, and even after Francis Ferdinand had become heir to the throne on Rudolph's death, the couple were constantly on their guard against real or imagined slights.

The end was violent for all of them. There had been signs of mental instability in Rudolph, whose relative on his mother's side, King Ludwig II of Bavaria (see genealogical table p. 484), had eventually gone mad and drowned himself with his attendant, and although Rudolph's death at the hunting lodge at Mayerling in 1889 remains something of a mystery, it seems probable that he and his mistress died in a suicide pact; the Empress Elizabeth was stabbed to death in 1898 by an Anarchist on the shore of the Lake of Geneva, and in 1914 Francis Ferdinand and his wife were shot down in the fateful assassination at Sarajevo. Thus in the end Francis Joseph outlived them all, a bearded patriarch symbolizing the past, an old man burying himself in the details of a riddle to which neither the nineteenth nor the twentieth century could find a satisfactory answer.

At least the *Ausgleich* of 1867 (see p. 200) had reduced the extent of the riddle. The Magyars were content for the moment to enjoy their relative independence in the Hungarian half of the Dual Monarchy. In the Austrian half, however, this success of the Magyars was only too likely to stimulate the ambitions of other national groups. The Poles of Galicia, who had been granted a good many concessions including the official use of their own language, remained extremely loyal to the régime, but in Bohemia and Moravia the Czechs increasingly resented the privileged position of the German Austrians. As elsewhere in the struggle between ethnic groups, this predominance was reflected in the fact that German was the sole official language, even though the population in Bohemia was roughly two thirds Czech to one-third German, while in Moravia the Czech element was still larger.

It was with these grievances in mind that Count Taaffe, who became premier in 1879, attempted to gain Slav support. As well as giving them the benefit of a wide franchise, his principal reforms divided the University of Prague into a Czech and a German section, insisted on the use of Czech in the law courts, and required civil servants to speak German and Czech at the levels at which they had dealings with the public. This last was particularly advantageous to the Czech officials, since they were usually bilingual, whereas the Germans would not deign to learn Czech.

Like most attempts at reconciliation these measures aroused opposition from the two extremes. The German Austrians expressed anger at what they regarded as their abandonment by Vienna. In 1882 at Linz they produced a programme which included the headier aspects of pan-Germanism laced with anti-Semitism and hatred of the Slavs, and one of their more radical spokesmen, Georg von Schönerer, demanded the shedding of the non-German regions of Dalmatia and Galicia and the direct inclusion of the remainder within Germany. This fanatical longing for the German fatherland was characteristic of a minority increasingly conscious of the national spirit growing among the other minorities, and it is significant that Adolf Hitler, the greatest exponent of German patriotism in the twentieth century, was a German Austrian, born in 1889, and most appropriate that he should have grown up in Linz.

There was also resistance from the more radical 'Young Czechs'. The 'Old Czechs' had been satisfied with the Taaffe reforms and hoped to move gradually towards a greater autonomy. The 'Young Czechs' disliked the common sense and moderation of Taaffe; they objected to a plan of his that Bohemia should be divided into German- and Czech-speaking zones, since they hoped eventually to exclude German altogether from Bohemia and Moravia, and they wanted independence from Vienna which they regarded as an instrument of German oppression of the Slavs. This last ignored the fears expressed by Palacky in 1848 (see p. 137), of which an 'Old Czech' Prince Karl von Schwarzenberg now reminded them. ' . . .

what will you do with your country which is too small to stand alone? Will you give it to Germany or to Russia, for you have no other choice if you abandon the Austrian union.'

The 'Young Czech' representation in the Austrian Lower House, the *Reichsrat*, had become so great after the elections of 1891 that Taaffe decided to break the middle-class support on which they relied by introducing universal male suffrage, but this proposal was too adventurous for his ministerial colleagues and for the Emperor and he was forced to resign in 1893. The government of his successor, Prince Alfred Windischgrätz, was soon wrecked over another nationalist squabble about a Slovene secondary school, and in 1896 Francis Joseph turned to a former Polish governor of Galicia, Count Badeni. He embarked on a bold course of electoral reform and the extension of the use of Czech at all levels in the Bohemian civil service, but in 1897 the protests of German deputies reduced the *Reichsrat* to a shambles, and Badeni was dismissed. Then two years later, when the language ordinance was withdrawn and German was restored as the sole language of the inner civil service, the *Reichsrat* became a shambles again as a result of Czech protests. Wearily Francis Joseph struggled on. During subsequent years elections continued to be held and the *Reichsrat* continued to meet; there was even the establishment of universal suffrage in 1907, yet government itself seemed to depend increasingly upon nominated premiers ruling through emergency regulations.

The problem in Austria was that the Imperial government had been genuinely trying to find a solution which treated all parties fairly. The Magyars in the Hungarian half of the empire had not been hampered by such considerations. Their policy was to impose a general magyarization. This gave them a virtual monopoly of entry into State service or the professions; it enforced the use of Magyar in non-Magyar schools and ensured that the parliamentary electorate, some 6 per cent of the whole population, and only 2 per cent in Croatia, was restricted almost entirely to Magyars.

So long as relations between Vienna and Budapest remained reasonably good, there was very little that the subject nationalities could do. In 1902, however, the Emperor attempted to gain an increase in the size of the Hungarian contingent in the common Habsburg army, and this was countered by demands in Budapest that Magyar should be the language of command in Hungarian units. Such interference was utterly unacceptable to Francis Joseph, and for two years a new Hungarian premier Stephen Tisza, who feared that the demands of the extremists might destroy the Dual Monarchy, struggled to find some compromise solution, but eventually resigned after the election of 1905 had produced a chamber determined not to vote the necessary money for the army.

The quarrel between Vienna and Budapest now caused the

Magyars to look for support from their own national minorities, and in October 1905 they managed to persuade the Croats to join with them against the Emperor. Even more remarkable, the Serbs within the Empire, who normally detested the Croats, were also prepared to enter this alliance. In fact, the Magyar stand soon crumbled. In 1906, after evicting the Hungarian parliament with his troops, Francis Joseph suspended the Hungarian constitution and threatened to undermine the position of the Magyars by introducing universal male suffrage. That was sufficient to get the Magyars to abandon their military demands in return for a restoration of the old constitution and from then on their interest in the alliance with the south Slavs waned. Yet the league between Catholic Croats and Orthodox Serbs persisted and in the absence of Magyar support they turned increasingly to the Kingdom of Serbia just outside their borders. Thus the stage was set for the final conflagration. Only concessions to the Slavs within the Empire could have eased the mounting tensions; yet these were made impossible by the attitude of the German Austrians in the west and the Magyars in the east, and instead the monarchy, drifting on, could only look with growing alarm at the prospect of Serbia as a new Piedmont who might one day march to the rescue of the south Slavs.

5. Russia and the revolution of 1905

It might well have seemed that the reforms of Tsar Alexander II would at last set Russia on the road to western constitutional development; yet this was not to be. The bomb which was flung at Alexander on 13 March 1881 as he was driving in his carriage through the streets of St Petersburg, not only killed the Tsar; it confirmed all the conservative tendencies of his son who now succeeded as Alexander III.

The old note of unrestricted autocracy sounded unmistakably in the accession manifesto drawn up by Alexander III's tutor, Pobedonostsev, who regarded western liberalism as alien to the spirit of Russia; and the late Tsar's most recent scheme for elective commissions working in consultation with the government was never put into operation. In 1884 the universities were deprived of their autonomy. In 1889 changes in the electoral system gave the landed gentry complete control over the *Zemstva*, and in 1890 the administration of the peasantry was placed under the supervision of Land Captains who were appointed by the Ministry of the Interior from among the poorer gentry and who took over the functions of the local justices previously elected by the district *Zemstva*. In 1892 similar amendments brought the municipal councils under the control of the central executive. Thus, the whole delicate relationship between the bureaucracy and regional interests which Alexander II

had hoped to foster was abruptly shattered, and a policy of russification in the outlying provinces (see p. 241) and a persecution of
the Jews emphasized the return to an uncompromising centralized
autocracy. This tendency seemed unlikely to change after the accession of Nicholas II in 1894, when the new Tsar denied any intention
of allowing a greater participation by the *Zemstva* in internal
government.

At the same time as the cause of liberal reform was suffering this
setback, Russia was passing through the extraordinary period of
economic change already noted (see p. 223). Railway construction,
including the beginning of the Trans-Siberian railway in 1891, proceeded at a remarkable pace under Sergei Witte, the Minister of
Communications, and there was also a startling development of textiles, metallurgy, shipbuilding on the coast of the Black Sea and oil
in Baku. A good deal of encouragement was given to this by the
State through the establishing of tariffs, government investment and
the floating of domestic loans, and in 1897, while he was Minister
of Finance, Witte put the rouble on the gold standard with the result
that some 2,000 million roubles of foreign investment had been
attracted to Russia by 1914.

Such a rapid economic development was bound to have considerable social consequences. Peasantry working in the factories soon
became permanent city dwellers with little contact with their *mir*
and by 1914 formed a proletariat numbering about three million.
Living and working conditions were often appalling, although
Bunge, who was Minister of Finance in the early years of Alexander
III's reign, introduced factory laws protecting women and children,
which were to be enforced by inspectors. Bunge's liberal tendencies
also led him to abolish the poll tax on the peasantry, and it was
perhaps not surprising that the more conservative elements in the
government secured his dismissal in 1887. After this the factory laws
were simply evaded, until industrial unrest led to a decree in 1897
imposing a working day of no more than eleven-and-a-half hours,
or of ten if it included night work.

Meanwhile, bitterness was growing in the countryside, where the
rapid increase in population (see p. 221) was reducing the average
size of holdings for the majority of peasants, on whom the bad harvests of the 1880s and the famine conditions of 1891–3 weighed
heavily; this was further accentuated by a new division between rich
and poor peasantry, since a minority were beginning to prosper,
renting the land of the gentry and purchasing more of their own
through a peasants' bank founded by Bunge in 1884. Conscious of
these pressures Witte attempted in 1902 to make use of the *Zemstva*
to bring about agricultural reforms, but his efforts simply enabled
Plehve, the Minister of the Interior, to oust him from office and the
policy of reaction continued unchecked.

Naturally this background of discontent offered opportunities for various secret revolutionary organizations. Of these the Social Revolutionaries had the closest connection with the peasantry, since they were the spiritual heirs of the Russian Populist movement; they believed that a great spontaneous outbreak across the countryside would sweep away the landlords' estates and replace them with the old Anarchist dream of thousands of small autonomous communities (see p. 244). In contrast to this the Russian Social Democrats were purely Marxist and hence concentrated mostly on the growth of the proletariat. Both parties were developing their underground organizations, but the attentions of the police, who were fairly skilful at infiltrating them, forced the leaders to operate principally from outside Russia. Thus it was from Geneva and London that a group of Russian Social Democrats published a newspaper *Iskra* (The Spark) under an editorial board including Plekhanov, Lenin and Martov. It was not, however, only the police who hampered their work. Social Revolutionaries and Social Democrats were irreconcilable; within the Social Democrat party itself the divide between Bolshevik and Menshevik (see pp. 249–50) was a further distraction, and they were still all squabbling when they suddenly heard the news of revolution in Russia in 1905.

The new course of events had been preceded by the outbreak of war between Russia and Japan in February 1904 (see p. 291). Throughout that year while Russian forces in the Far East held out in Port Arthur under siege, the strain that this imposed on the government had seemed to offer the liberals an opportunity to press for constitutional concessions. Plehve was assassinated in July and his successor Prince Svyatopolk-Mirsky consented to the holding of a *Zemstva* conference in November, where a unanimous demand was made for greater personal and political liberty.

In January 1905, however, the fall of Port Arthur to the Japanese saddled the government with all the odium of military defeat and the cautious efforts of the liberals were now suddenly reinforced by other classes of society in an upsurge of violence inspired by land hunger and industrial conditions. In January Father Gapon, who had been organizing a workers' movement under police supervision in St Petersburg, led a great deputation to the Winter Palace, where the troops opened fire, killing a great number of the crowd. This was followed by a wave of strikes and the murder of police officials throughout Russia, and in February the Grand Duke Sergei, the Tsar's uncle, was assassinated. Nicholas II now declared himself ready to consult representatives on the government of the country, although still insisting on the maintenance of autocracy, and a series of conferences were held among the reformers during the summer to discuss the demands which should be put to the Tsar. These hopes were to be quickly disappointed, however, when the constitutional concessions which the government announced in August proved to be purely nominal; a national Parliament, a *Duma*, was to be set up, but its consultative functions were to be so hedged about and the franchise so narrow that it proved quite unacceptable.

By now more extreme elements were beginning to seize their chance. In June the crew of the battleship *Potemkin* mutinied and conducted a short campaign on the Black Sea before seeking refuge in a Rumanian port; at the same time the Social Revolutionaries had stirred up the peasantry with the cry: 'all the land for the peasants', and there had ensued a great rising in the provinces in which landowners were expelled and their estates taken over. In October a general strike virtually paralyzed all civic life in St Petersburg, where a little later in the same month Trotsky, who had hurried back from Switzerland, was elected vice-president of a workers' Soviet (council) whose executive included Mensheviks, Bolsheviks, and Social Revolutionaries.

Witte had just returned from the United States after the conclusion of the peace treaty with Japan, and was convinced by these developments in Russia that the Tsar must offer further concessions which would divide the liberals from the extremists. The outcome was the issue of the October Manifesto. A *Duma* with the right to veto legislation was to be elected on a wide franchise, and the committee of ministers under their president was to acquire something of the character of a cabinet, although remaining independent of the *Duma*. In November the St Petersburg Soviet called an end to the strike, Finland's old rights were restored to her, and preparations were made for the general election. This, however, was followed by demands in Warsaw for Polish autonomy, and when Witte, who was now head of the government, imposed martial law in Poland, the St Petersburg Soviet ordered a fresh strike in sympathy with the Poles.

This activity on the part of the Soviet might well seem to foreshadow the revolutions of 1917. In fact, the revolution of 1905 has far more in common with those of 1848. In spite of mutinies at Kronstadt and Sebastopol, the monarchy still retained control over the bulk of its armed forces and the clash of aims between the various political and social groups gave Witte his opportunity to restore the situation. He attempted to conciliate the peasantry by promising the reduction and eventual abolition of their redemption dues, and in December he made a gesture towards the liberals by decreeing a further extension of the franchise so that it became virtually universal. Simultaneously martial law was declared in St Petersburg, most of the members of the Soviet were placed under arrest, and a fierce campaign in the countryside put down the peasant rising, culminating in a savage social war in the Baltic provinces. Thus, the extreme elements were crushed and the liberals were fobbed off with a constitution which was not the work of a constituent Assembly, but had simply been decreed from above; this was apparent from the details of the new system, which not only left the Tsar absolute control over the armed forces but even allowed him to raise loans on his own initiative, so that it was perfectly possible for him to escape from the *Duma's* control of the budget. Even so, the conservatives found it highly alarming; Witte's efforts to win over the liberals had created many enemies for him at court, and as soon as he had raised an enormous loan from France he was dismissed.

Once order had been restored, the original form of the constitution did not survive long. The first *Duma* which met in May 1906 in the Tauride Palace was dominated by the Constitutional Democrats (Kadets) who hoped for further concessions, and was dissolved in July after they had led a great attack on the government. Official pressure during the elections to the second *Duma* succeeded in reducing the number of liberal deputies, but the left-wing representation was increased and the session, which only lasted from March until June 1907, was disrupted by an incessant struggle between the conservatives and the Social Democrats. By now the government felt sufficiently strong to introduce a modification of the franchise which greatly favoured the interest of the country gentry and reduced the representation of the non-Russian peoples, so that when the third *Duma* met in November 1907, the Octobrists—so called because they were content with the provisions of the October Manifesto—held a commanding position. This third *Duma* and its successor in 1912, which was almost identical in personnel, were consequently both far more acquiescent; yet they did voice criticism, encouraged a good many minor measures of administrative reform and, within their limitations, did suggest the beginnings of parliamentary life in Russia.

Meanwhile, under Peter Stolypin, who became President of the Council of Ministers in 1906, the process of restoring the Tsar's authority had been completed; revolutionary elements in the cities were rounded up, fifteen members of the St Petersburg Soviet, including Trotsky, were sent to Siberia for life, although Trotsky succeeded in escaping almost immediately afterwards, and in the provinces a series of field court-martials imposed hundreds of death sentences. Stolypin, hated though he was for these measures, was not simply a senseless reactionary. Industry and commerce were encouraged through contact with a federation of leading industrialists and businessmen. The *Zemstva* were to participate in an extension of systems of health services and insurance, and by 1914 50,000 additional primary schools had been established. The most significant feature of Stolypin's work was his policy for the peasantry. His aim here was to create greater support for the existing régime through a system of peasant proprietorship. 'The natural counterweight to the communal principle is individual ownership', he said; 'it is also a guarantee of order, since the small-owner is the cell on which rests all stable order in the State.' Thus he set out to break the hold of the *mir* over the individual peasant which Alexander II's reforms had actually strengthened, and before the end of 1906 decrees had been issued allowing the peasant to leave the *mir* when he wished, or, if he remained, to consolidate his strips of land in one place and to hold them permanently. Communal responsibility for taxation was ended and this general weakening of the position of the *mir*, coupled with a more extensive use of the peasants' bank, hastened the development of a richer class of peasant farmers, the *kulaks*, so that by 1917 some 1,300,000 peasant households had been established with their own consolidated farmlands.

Social tensions and political agitation continued to trouble the Russian scene and in 1911 Stolypin himself was assassinated. It is not impossible to imagine that with these governmental and economic changes Russia might have been able to find her way towards the modern western type of constitutional state, but the roots of this transformation were still all too shallow; what was needed was time, and when by 1917 the pressure of war, as in 1856 and 1905, seemed to threaten the whole basis of Russian government, the changes had not gone far enough to create a powerful alternative to the extremes of revolutionary Socialism.

Chapter 23

Bismarck's Europe 1871–90

'The worst of all this is not the present war,' wrote Jacob Burckhardt in 1870, 'but the era of wars upon which we have entered.' From a long-term point of view this was a remarkable prophecy; in fact, the subsequent forty-four years were to be a period not of war, but of armed peace, as each great Power, mindful of the efficiency of the Prussian army on which Bismarck's success had ultimately rested, sought to improve and expand its own military forces. Ironically, Bismarck himself reckoned that the creation of the German empire marked the limit of his ambitions in Europe, and after 1871 his diplomacy was aimed almost entirely at preventing the outbreak of further wars from which Germany could have nothing to gain. 'We have no further demands to make,' he said in 1890. 'Germany does not need the three million Dutchmen who have no desire to be absorbed by us, nor the Baltic countries, nor Poland, nor any other territory. We have enough annexed populations.'

The new policy of defensiveness presented him two fundamental problems. First, he had to ensure that France should remain without an ally so that she might be discouraged from attempting a war of revenge. The British certainly looked with some anxiety at the change in the balance of power on the Continent; 'Napoleon III', remarked Odo Russell in 1872, 'was not more powerful than Bismarck is in this moment.' Yet their traditional suspicion of France, aggravated by colonial rivalry, made an Anglo-French alliance highly unlikely, particularly at a time when the British government wished to avoid any continental commitments.

Second, it was essential that he should preserve good relations between Austria-Hungary and Russia, because if war broke out between them, Germany would almost certainly find herself drawn into it. This would not only be disastrous in itself, but would also have a direct bearing on the French question, since in the inevitable scramble for alliances France would be able to escape from the isolation that Bismarck was determined to impose on her. The principal danger here lay in the heightened significance of the Eastern Question. Austria-Hungary, excluded from Italy and Germany, could not remain indifferent to Russian ambitions in the Balkans.

The possible creation of Russian satellite states out of the territories of Turkey-in-Europe affected more than Austrian foreign policy; the emergence of a strong independent Slav state would represent a considerable domestic danger, since it would act as a focal point of resistance for all the subject Slav peoples of the Habsburg Empire. Thus, the Austrian government remained ever mindful of Gentz's prediction in 1815 (see p. 41) and the growing menace of nationalism in the Balkans gave a new urgency to her fears of Russian pan-Slavism. Until 1879 Bismarck's method of dealing with these problems was based on the avoidance of any system of international alliance. Instead, he attempted to create a league of friendship between Germany, Austria-Hungary and Russia, and several meetings between the sovereigns in 1872 and 1873 helped to consolidate this *Dreikaiserbund*. After the revision of the Black Sea clauses in the Treaty of Paris in 1871 Russia was satisfied for the moment; Francis Joseph had abandoned any thoughts of undoing the results of the war of 1866 by alliance with France, and Count Andrássy, a Magyar aristocrat who had replaced Beust as Foreign Minister, wished to base his policy on friendship with Germany. Naturally the League of the Three Emperors, reminiscent of the earlier Holy Alliance and prompted by the same motive of conservatism, did not attempt to settle any of the deeper issues, since that would only have invited its disruption; it merely fostered a deceptive sense of unity, and its flimsiness was soon made apparent in two successive crises.

The first—the French war scare of 1875—was mainly the consequence of the speed with which France seemed to be recovering from her recent defeat. As early as 1873 the indemnity of five milliards of francs had been paid off and the German occupation force had accordingly been withdrawn. In the same year relations between France and Germany became cool when a right-wing pro-clerical government was formed in Paris at the very time when Bismarck had begun to mount his *Kulturkampf* (see p. 256). The crisis came to a head in January 1875 when the French Chamber began to discuss a bill for the reorganization of the French army, including the addition of a fourth battalion to each regiment, and when the bill was passed in March, the German press—largely through Bismarck's encouragement—embarked upon a great campaign, accusing France of preparing for war. In fact, William I was adamant that all talk of military hostilities was absurd, but the French government, keen to seize the opportunity for a diplomatic success, flung back the charge of chauvinism, declaring that Bismarck was determined on a preventive war against France and giving full publicity to some indiscreet remarks made by one of his political agents to the French ambassador at Berlin. The whole incident was really only a war of nerves, a technique which was to become highly familiar in the twentieth century, but it had the effect of bringing

Tsar Alexander and his Foreign Minister, Gortchakov, to Berlin in May to warn the German government to go no further. After this the German press campaign was called off and the excitement very soon died down.

Artificial though it was, the crisis was nevertheless not without its significance. Probably Bismarck had intended no more than to frighten the French into dropping their plans for military reform. It is idle to speculate on how far he would have gone, if he had been able to gain the acquiescence of the great Powers. The fact was that he had failed to do so. Both Great Britain and Russia had made it clear that they objected strongly to any suggestion of the waging of a preventive war by Germany against France; only on Austria, apparently, could Bismarck safely rely. The alignment was momentary, yet it demonstrated how easily Bismarck's hopes for the *Dreikaiserbund* and the isolation of France could be shattered. He was in a sense the victim of his own success; the pattern of events whereby the German empire had been created had awoken a deep mistrust among the governments of Europe, and not even Bismarck's skill could avoid the instinctive workings of the balance of power.

There was nothing artificial about the second crisis, which at its height seemed likely to bring about a major war between Austria and Russia. In 1875 the Christian Slavs of Bosnia and Herzegovina rose in revolt against their Turkish masters, and as unrest continued to spread, all the old problems implicit in the Eastern Question came to the fore once again. Would Russia take advantage of the situation to carve a new Slav state out of the Balkans?

Fortunately for Bismarck Gortchakov, the Russian Foreign Minister, was equally aware of the delicacy of the situation; Alexander II did not allow himself to be impelled by pan-Slav enthusiasm within Russia, and to Bismarck's relief the Powers of the *Dreikaiserbund* did at first act in some degree of unison.

Mediation was attempted unsuccessfully in the summer of 1875; in December Andrássy's Note put forward a scheme for the reform of Turkish rule in the Balkans, which the Turks accepted, but failed to apply. In May 1876 the three Foreign Ministers agreed on a fresh proposal of reforms, the Berlin Memorandum, and offered to include France, Italy, and Great Britain in their negotiations. France and Italy accepted, but Disraeli, suspicious that some plan for a general partition of Turkish territories in Europe was in the making, refused.

By now Ottoman fortunes had taken a turn for the worse; the Sultan had been deposed, the Bulgarians had joined in the revolt, and at the end of June Serbia and Montenegro declared war on Turkey. Yet even this did not bring about the threatened split between Russia and Austria-Hungary. In July Gortchakov and Andrássy met at Reichstadt and agreed that there should be no intervention, but that if Turkey did fail to re-establish control over her Slav subjects, Austria-Hungary was to take Bosnia, while Russia should regain that southern part of Bessarabia which she had lost in 1856.

By the autumn of 1876, however, Turkey had recovered. The Bulgarian Christians were put down with a murderous brutality that inspired Gladstone to publish his pamphlet, *The Bulgarian Horrors and the Question of the East*, a fierce indictment of Turkish rule in the Balkans. More significant from Russia's point of view was the defeat of the Serbian and Montenegran armies, which seemed to presage a revival of Turkish power throughout the Balkans, and before the end of the year Tsar Alexander had swung round to the pan-Slav view that Russia must take military action against Turkey.

This Russian decision to intervene presented her diplomats with a new set of problems, since it was essential that, once the attack had been launched, Turkey should not find an ally in Great Britain or Austria-Hungary. With the British they felt that they could take a chance; in January 1877 at a conference at Constantinople Lord Salisbury and Ignatiev, the Russian ambassador, had been in accord over further proposals of reforms which the Turks had once again blocked, and the effect of Gladstone's pamphlet on the British public had created a storm of anti-Turkish feeling that Disraeli could not ignore. With Austria-Hungary the difficulty was overcome by secret military and political treaties—the Budapest conventions—signed early in 1877. In return for observing benevolent neutrality in the forthcoming Russo-Turkish war, she was to receive Bosnia and Herzegovina, the continued existence of Serbia and Montenegro was guaranteed, and, most important of all, no large Slav state was to be set up in the Balkans. Both sides could be satisfied with this. Russia had ensured that an Anglo-Austrian alliance would not be formed against her; Austria-Hungary had been able to exact compensation and a guarantee as the price of her acquiescence in a course of events which Andrássy in any case did not feel he could prevent.

Thus far, Bismarck, who had refused to commit himself, could feel that the worst had been avoided, since Austro-Russian relations had survived even this latest development. In the last weeks of April 1877 Russia declared war on Turkey and with Rumania as an ally advanced into Bulgaria. The Russian diplomats, like Bismarck in his earlier days, now depended upon the generals for a swift victory. In this they were disappointed through the stubborn resistance of the Turkish fortress of Plevna under Osman Pasha, who did not surrender until December. The Russian advance was swift after this; at the end of January 1878 Adrianople fell to their forces and once more—as in 1828—it seemed that nothing could save Constantinople. But the long siege of Plevna had taken its toll; the Russian army was by now not in good shape, and during the nine months that the war had lasted British public opinion, alarmed by the Russian advance, had had time to swing round to the side of the Turks. At this point the Russians wisely decided to call a halt and an armistice was signed.

Continued doubts over Russian intentions led to the dispatch of the British fleet through the Dardanelles into the Sea of Marmora in the middle of February, and the crisis came to a head at the beginning of March with the signing of the Treaty of San Stefano between Russia and Turkey. This was not the work of Gortchakov, who had favoured a moderate peace settlement, but of Ignatiev who was a pan-Slav enthusiast. By its terms the independence of Serbia, Montenegro, and Rumania was recognized by Turkey and all three were allowed to extend their frontiers, although Rumania's acquisition of the Dobruja was a poor compensation for the loss of Southern Bessarabia, which Russia now regained as well as making an extension of her frontier in the Caucasus. There was no mention of Austria-Hungary's right to annex Bosnia and Herzegovina—only the imposition of governmental reforms within Turkey-in-Europe that had been agreed upon at the Constantinople conference; worst of all, Bulgaria was to become a large autonomous principality under a Christian governor, while paying tribute to Turkey, and her frontiers were to run west into the Balkan mountains and as far south as the coast of the Aegean.

Thus the Treaty of San Stefano awoke all the worst fears of Great Britain and Austria-Hungary; it completely ignored the Budapest conventions, and through the creation of a large Bulgarian state almost certainly under Tsarist influence appeared to be the fulfilment of Russia's hopes of gaining substantial control over the Balkans without the embarrassment of a partition among the Powers. This was naturally unacceptable to Austria-Hungary, and for Great Britain the advance of the Russian frontier in the Caucasus represented a threat to British communications with India.

During the next three months anxious negotiations, culminating in the Congress of Berlin, led to a complete revision of the Treaty of San Stefano. This diplomatic retreat by Russia is explained by a number of factors. Gortchakov was furious at Ignatiev's clumsiness in overreaching himself, and in the last resort Tsar Alexander II was not prepared to go to war for the maintenance of the treaty. There was no hope of military support from Germany. Bismarck's concern throughout the crisis was to maintain a complete neutrality, and in December 1876 he had announced in the *Reichstag* that the issues contained 'no German interest worth the bones of a Pomeranian musketeer'. There was no immediate cooperation between Great Britain and Austria-Hungary, since Andrássy would have preferred to reach a private agreement with Russia, but his negotiations with Ignatiev at Vienna came to nothing, simply because

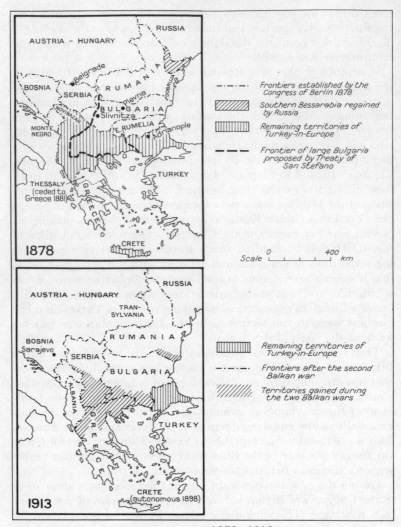

THE BALKANS 1878–1913

it was impossible to devise any formula that would be adequate to
compensate Austria-Hungary for the creation of a large Bulgaria.
It was the British government who forced the pace. Disraeli, now
Lord Beaconsfield, summoned 7,000 Indian troops to Malta; Lord
Salisbury, who was determined on a firm stand, replaced Lord
Derby as Foreign Secretary and on 30 May signed an agreement
with the Russians who abandoned the project of a large Bulgaria.
This was followed on 4 June by an Anglo-Turkish treaty whereby

Great Britain agreed to defend Turkey-in-Asia against Russia in return for the purchase of Cyprus as a military and naval base, and on 6 June by an understanding with Austria-Hungary over her right to annex Bosnia.

The Congress of Berlin in June was thus largely concerned with tidying up the details of these fundamental decisions. It was the first time that Berlin had been the scene of an international settlement and Bismarck, who presided in his capacity as 'the honest broker', plainly delighted in the glamour of a great diplomatic occasion amid a round of receptions and gargantuan meals. Even so, there was a bizarre note in this evocation of the great days of Vienna and Paris. Lord Beaconsfield, who headed the British delegation, had to be persuaded to address the Congress in the Radziwill Palace in English, and in a letter he described how 'Prince Bismarck, with one hand full of cherries and the other of shrimps, eaten alternately, complains he cannot sleep and must go to Kissingen.'

The details were eventually settled, although not without considerable negotiation. The autonomous principality of Bulgaria was to consist of no more than the area immediately to the south of the Danube; below this, Eastern Roumelia was to be a Turkish province under a Christian governor, while the southernmost regions were to remain directly under Turkish rule. As Bismarck said, the diplomats were not there 'to consider the happiness of the Bulgarians, but to secure the peace of Europe'. Austria was to be allowed to occupy Bosnia and Herzegovina and to garrison the Sanjak of Novibazar which separated the frontiers of Serbia and Montenegro. Russia was to retain southern Bessarabia and Batum, but agreed to concessions along the Caucasian frontier. In addition to this, in accordance with the terms of the Cyprus Convention, Great Britain supported her guarantee of Turkey's Asiatic frontier with a scheme for posting British military consuls in Armenia, and declared her freedom to send a fleet through the Straits virtually whenever it suited her.

On the face of it the Treaty of Berlin was a resounding diplomatic defeat for Russia. The Treaty of San Stefano had been wiped out and during the Congress the Russians had even been unable to prohibit the Turkish military occupation of Eastern Roumelia owing to Beaconsfield's stubborn insistence. Yet the gains with which they were ultimately left were very similar to the claims which Gortchakov had originally envisaged. Great Britain and Austria-Hungary could feel that they had preserved Turkey-in-Europe, even though she had suffered certain losses, and each had to some extent strengthened their own position for the future—the British by increasing their power in the eastern Mediterranean, the Austrians by opening the road to a far greater influence over the western Balkans.

Bismarck himself was content that a highly explosive situation had not led to an Austro-Russian war, even though the outcome was little more than a process of what Gortchakov called 'replastering'. The Balkan crisis, nevertheless, made a turning point in the shaping of his policy. The significance of the negotiations at Berlin was that although to outward appearances Bismarck had maintained his neutrality, he had by his very refusal to uphold the Russian claim to a large Bulgaria revealed that, if forced to decide, Germany would favour Austria-Hungary. This attitude was finally confirmed in October 1879 by the Dual Alliance, a treaty signed between Germany and Austria-Hungary promising mutual aid if either of them were attacked by Russia and benevolent neutrality in the case of an attack by any other Power.

From Austria-Hungary's point of view the creation of the Dual Alliance is simple to understand; it meant that she had at last escaped from the isolation which had been so disastrous for her since the Crimean War, and for Andrássy, who had always hoped for such an agreement with Germany, it was the culminating triumph of his career. For Germany there is rather more to explain, since the treaty meant the abandonment of her policy of freedom from diplomatic alliance; Bismarck had now openly committed her to the defence of the Habsburg Empire—the very system which he had fervently denounced during his years at Frankfurt in the 1850s. It is clear that he feared that the Balkan crisis had seriously prejudiced the continued working of the *Dreikaiserbund*; an anxious Austria-Hungary might turn to France, and he hastened to offer a firm promise of support, in order, as he said, to 'dig a ditch between her and the western Powers'. There was, too, the chance that the Russians, who now blamed Bismarck for the failure of their plans in 1878, might be sufficiently alarmed at this new development to forget their resentment and to bid once again for friendship with Germany. Nevertheless, the Austro-Germany treaty was something of a gamble for Bismarck. It might equally well wreck the whole of his policy by driving Russia into alliance with France. It could also encourage Austria-Hungary to embark on a much more venturesome course in the Balkans, and indeed after his departure in 1890 the weakness of German foreign policy did later allow Germany to become harnessed to Austrian requirements.

From this first step much was to follow; for the next eleven years Bismarck strove to strengthen Germany's position in Europe through a web of written treaties of which Berlin was the central point, while at the same time doing his best to frustrate the creation of any counter system of alliances. In this last he was assisted greatly by the anti-Austrian attitude of the Gladstone administration formed in Great Britain in 1880, and by British anxiety over Russian expansion southward in Central Asia. He was, too, in a strong position to exploit the colonial rivalries of the other Powers, since he had had no intention of involving Germany in Africa or Asia. The only interest that he ever expressed in colonial acquisitions was due mainly to his domestic policy in 1884–5 (see p. 231). Thus, he was delighted when in 1881 the French, to the anger of the Italians, occupied Tunis; and he was perfectly prepared to encourage Great Britain to take Egypt in 1882, since this might exacerbate her relations with Russia and France.

This mutual antagonism of others enabled him to develop his own system. In June 1881, despite the objections of Austria-Hungary, he managed to renew the *Dreikaiserbund*, which guaranteed a benevolent neutrality if any of the three should find themselves at war with a fourth great Power, including as well a vague understanding over both the annexation of Bosnia by Austria-Hungary and the union of Bulgaria and Eastern Roumelia under Russian influence, both at an unspecified date in the future. By this means he had undone some of the harm that Russo-German relations had suffered through the Congress of Berlin, and could now rely on Russian neutrality in a Franco-German war in return for German neutrality in an Anglo-Russian war.

In May 1882 a Triple Alliance was formed between Germany, Austria-Hungary, and Italy. The Italian government, conscious of Italy's isolation and piqued by the French annexation of Tunis, was only too keen to make a treaty with Germany and hoped that an alliance with Austria-Hungary might assist them in their domestic difficulties with the Pope. Austria-Hungary wanted to silence Italian propaganda attacking her rule over Italians in the South Tyrol and was glad of the promise of Italian neutrality in the event of a war with Russia. Germany, anxious at the momentary improvement in Franco-Russian relations, reckoned to enlist a possible ally against France. The treaties that were signed were to last for five years and were essentially defensive in character. Italy and Germany were each to help the other in the event of one of them being attacked by France. Austria-Hungary was also to help Italy defend herself against France, but here the agreement was not entirely reciprocal, since Italy's assistance to Austria-Hungary against Russia would depend upon Russia's being joined by France.

Although the implications of the Triple Alliance looked both east and west, it did not seriously involve Germany in new commitments. It was the separate agreement of the Dual Alliance of 1879 that continued to draw her into the Balkans. Already in 1881 Austria-Hungary had signed a secret treaty with Prince Milan of Serbia, whereby Serbia became bound to her economically and politically, and in return the prince was allowed in 1882 to assume the title of King. Then in October 1883 Rumania, soured by the loss of southern Bessarabia after her support of Russia in the Turkish war of

1877, signed a secret treaty of mutual defence with Austria-Hungary and Germany. For Austria-Hungary this was a diplomatic *coup*, for not merely had she weaned Rumania from Russia, but also Germany had by this last agreement guaranteed the defence of Austrian interests in the Balkans.

The development of a new crisis in the Balkans soon put this intricate network of German commitments to the test. The trouble began in September 1885, when a revolt against Turkish rule broke out in Eastern Roumelia and the inhabitants declared their intention to be included within the frontiers of Bulgaria. This might well have seemed to be in accordance with Russian ambitions, but by now the attitude of the Powers had changed. Prince Alexander of Battenberg, who had been established as the ruler of Bulgaria, had resisted Russian attempts to make his country a satellite state, and as a consequence in 1885 it was Russia who objected to the enlarging of Bulgaria, while Austria-Hungary and eventually Great Britain— after some hesitation on Lord Salisbury's part—supported it. The situation grew more tense in the autumn, when King Milan of Serbia, determined on compensation for the increase in the size of his neighbour, invaded Bulgaria and was decisively defeated at Slivnitza. At this point Austrian intervention prevented the overrunning of Serbia and in the spring of 1886 the Powers agreed on a personal union of Bulgaria and Eastern Roumelia.

But the crisis was not yet over. In August 1886 the Russians organized the kidnapping of Prince Alexander, who abdicated a few days after his return. Despite considerable pressure, however, it seemed unlikely that Bulgarian nationalists would submit to a Russian nominee on their throne and the powers began hastily to prepare for a new contest over the Balkans.

In February 1887 Great Britain and Italy signed a treaty in which they were joined by Austria-Hungary in March. This was a purely defensive agreement, no more than a vague promise to cooperate over the maintenance of the *status quo* in the Mediterranean. On the other hand, the renewal of the Central Powers' Triple Alliance, also in February, included additional treaties which went much further than the original arrangements of 1882. Austria-Hungary had hoped to gain a definite promise of Italian assistance in the event of an Austro-Russian war; Bismarck, anxious lest such an agreement would encourage Austria-Hungary to embark on a warlike course, was able to avoid this, and the Austro-Italian treaty simply provided for Italian compensation in the Balkans in the event of any Austrian gains. The Italian treaty with Germany was more positive, for it was agreed that if Italy went to war with France as a result of any further French expansion along the north coast of Africa east of Tunis, she would receive military support from Germany and would be entitled at the end to annex Corsica and Nice.

Naturally this treaty with Italy suggested a far more dangerous involvement for Germany, but it was Bismarck's hope that the recent Mediterranean agreement between Great Britain and Italy could hold France back from making any move along the north Africa shore. He had wanted to strengthen the position of the Central Powers, if possible without antagonizing Russia, who might otherwise turn to France. It was consequently with Russia that he now embarked upon the most delicate negotiation of all. The terms of the Reinsurance Treaty signed between Germany and Russia in June 1887 had to be woven carefully around all other existing German obligations. It stated that each would remain neutral if the other went to war with a third Power, but the agreement would not become operative if Germany attacked France or if Russia attacked Austria-Hungary. Bismarck had no intention of attacking France and he hoped that the treaty might discourage aggressive action by Russia against Austria-Hungary. Thus the Reinsurance Treaty was not strictly a contravention of the Dual Alliance, which was purely defensive, but it was nevertheless a slightly dubious transaction in that the distinction rested simply on Germany's power to decide whether Austria-Hungary or Russia was the aggressor, if war did break out between them—and the history of Bismarck's own wars had shown how debatable such a definition of aggression could be.

The crisis in the Balkans finally came to a head in July 1887 when the Bulgarians elected Ferdinand of Saxe-Coburg as their prince. Ferdinand, who was a grandson of Louis Philippe and had served as an officer in the Hungarian army, was naturally acceptable to Vienna and it seemed as if Russian intervention was bound to follow. In December a second Mediterranean agreement between Great Britain, Austria-Hungary, and Italy provided for limited support of Turkey against Russia, but when the Austrians requested the assistance of Germany, Bismarck warned them that he could not agree to an Austrian attack on Russia unless they were 'absolutely certain of English cooperation'. His final step to preserve peace in February 1888 was the publication of the Dual Alliance. This was a warning both to Russia if she should attack Austria-Hungary, and to Austria-Hungary, since it revealed to the world that the Dual Alliance was purely defensive and that Austria-Hungary would fight alone if she took the initiative in attacking Russia herself.

After this the tension relaxed. The Russians contented themselves with asking the Sultan to declare the election of Ferdinand illegal. In this they were supported by France and Germany and opposed by Great Britain, Austria-Hungary, and Italy. The Sultan acquiesced in the Russian demand, the Bulgarians ignored the declaration, and since none of the Powers intended to take the matter any further, the crisis could be considered safely past. 'Bulgaria, that little country between the Danube and the Balkans,' declared

Bismarck in the *Reichstag*, 'is not by any means a matter of sufficient importance to justify an all-European war from Moscow to the Pyrenees and from the North Sea to Palermo; at the end after such a war nobody would know just what he had fought for.' His words have a prophetic note; they are a tribute to his common sense, and at the same time a warning against the dangers that his own efforts had helped to create.

Chapter 24

The End of the Armed Peace
1890–1914

1. The breakdown of the Bismarckian system
1890–1907

In 1890, within a year and a half of the accession of the Emperor
William II, the long career of Bismarck came abruptly to an end.
The fundamental reason for this was that the young emperor and
the elderly statesman who had created his empire were tempera-
mentally incompatible. The practical issue over which they split was
Bismarck's desire to attack the growing forces of Syndicalism and
Socialism within Germany, but it so happened that their clash
coincided with a further development in foreign policy—the expiry
of the three-year Reinsurance Treaty signed with Russia in 1887.

The treaty had admittedly been a somewhat desperate attempt
on Bismarck's part to preserve friendship with Russia alongside the
alliance with Austria-Hungary and among the inner circles of the
German government there had developed a considerable opposition
to it. Baron Fritz von Holstein, the most significant figure at the
German Foreign Office from 1890 until 1906, believed that it
actually contradicted the terms of the Dual Alliance of 1879, and
that in any case it was unlikely to ensure Russian neutrality in the
event of a Franco-German war. The German General Staff merely
reckoned that in any future war they would have to contend with
both Russia and France and were therefore keen to strike at Russia
before she became any stronger. With the resignation of Bismarck
in March 1890 the government of his successor, General von
Caprivi, came markedly under the influence of Holstein, and when
shortly afterwards the Russians proposed a renewal of the Reinsurance Treaty for six years, the offer was rejected.

The new German government was thinking of turning from
friendship with Russia to alliance with Great Britain and in July
1890 the Anglo-German agreement over Heligoland and East Africa
(see p. 232) gave some encouragement to these hopes. Unfortunately for the heirs of Bismarck the Russian government drew the
same conclusion; 'the *entente* with Germany has virtually been
accomplished', the Russian ambassador in London warned St

Petersburg, and it was natural that Russia should begin to look in the very direction which Bismarck had always attempted to block. There was already considerable French investment in Russia; (see p. 225); France was only too anxious to escape from her own isolation and in August 1890 General de Boisdeffre was invited to attend Russian army manoeuvres.

The formation of a positive Franco-Russian alliance was not yet, however, the immediate aim of either side. The French, like the Russians, would in many ways have welcomed an agreement with Germany, but the somewhat tactless behaviour of William II's mother on a visit to Paris at this time turned public opinion firmly against such an idea; other French groups would have preferred a British alliance, but rivalry over Africa put this out of reach. The Russians themselves still thought wistfully of the Reinsurance Treaty, but when in June 1891 the Triple Alliance of Germany, Austria-Hungary, and Italy was renewed and the Italian premier, Rudini, went out of his way to stress his country's good relations with Great Britain, the Russians and the French finally became convinced that the British were about to join the Central Powers. This was enough to send a French naval squadron on a courtesy visit to Kronstadt, where it was officially welcomed by Alexander III who actually stood up for the playing of the *Marseillaise*. Tsardom could make no greater gesture, and yet military conversations had advanced so little beyond the expression of good intentions during the next twelve months that by July 1892 *Figaro* was demanding 'alliance ou flirt?'

Eventually, in August 1892, a positive military agreement was signed between the two countries. In future, if France were attacked by Germany or by Italy supported by Germany, Russia would attack Germany; alternatively, if Russia were attacked by Germany or by Austria-Hungary supported by Germany, France would attack Germany. If any member of the Triple Alliance mobilized, then France and Russia would both automatically mobilize without further consultation, the French force to number some 1,300,000, the Russian between 700,000 and 800,000. In October 1893 a Russian naval squadron paid a return visit to Toulon and in January 1894 the French government gave its approval of the alliance which had already been officially accepted by Alexander III the previous month. Since it was technically a military agreement, it did not have to be presented to the French Chamber, and thus, although its existence was soon common knowledge, the actual terms of the treaty remained secret.

On the face of it the Franco-Russian alliance was not offensive; it mentioned no positive aims such as the return of Alsace and Lorraine and was really little more than an escape for both countries from isolation. As a military agreement, however, it was particularly concerned with the question of mobilization which both sides recognized as a highly significant step. 'Mobilization is declaration of war', remarked General de Boisdeffre. 'To mobilize is to oblige one's neighbour to do the same,' and although the two systems of alliance balanced fairly well during the next twenty years, the obligations that they involved, coupled with the requirements of a speedy mobilization, were to be an essential link in the chain reaction that led to the outbreak of war in 1914.

The immediate consequence of the Franco-Russian alliance was to confirm the recent calculations of the military in Germany and of the naval experts in Great Britain. The German General Staff had long been resigned to the thought of war on two fronts, but their plans for meeting this threat had recently undergone considerable changes. Moltke had reckoned that the repetition of an invasion of France as in 1870 was out of the question and had accordingly planned to hold a defensive position in the west, while making for limited objectives in the east. In 1891, however, Count Alfred von Schlieffen took over as Chief of the General Staff and the whole plan of battle was reversed. Schlieffen disliked the idea of possibly having to give ground in Lorraine and turned instead to the preparation of an attack on France through the Vosges. Much later, however, he devised a new scheme for a great out-flanking movement through Belgium and northern France eventually wheeling south to the west of Paris and enveloping the French forces. This would entail placing so much strength on the German right wing that the French might be able to make some advance in the south and thus the whole line would pivot. In six weeks, however, Schlieffen believed, all would be over in the west and then the German armies could be rushed across Germany by railway to deal with the Russians whose mobilization would have been considerably slower.

The Schlieffen plan, based on the current theory of the sudden 'knock-out blow', has all the completeness of an essentially academic theory, and provides an interesting insight into the totally unpolitical cast of Schlieffen's mind. As a professional soldier it was unthinkable to him that the resistance of the French could continue after they had suffered defeat in the field, although the experience of the *francs-tireurs* during the Franco-Prussian War ought to have taught him caution here. He was indifferent to the diplomatic consequences of the violation of Belgian neutrality which was certain to involve British intervention. More surprising, he seems to have utterly ignored the possibility that the Russians might be able to launch a diversionary attack in the east—as indeed they did in August 1914. Schlieffen remained at the head of the German General Staff until 1906; under his successor, von Moltke, the nephew of William I's Chief of Staff, his plan continued to dominate all German military thought and preparation until 1914, and this was to affect far more than the opening moves in the first World War, for it created a strange diplomatic complication in that, although the most dangerous crises were likely to arise to the east of Germany, any full-scale mobilization would be bound at once to threaten France.

For Great Britain her lack of a large conscript army and the sense of detachment with which she could view events on the Continent were luxuries dependent upon a naval supremacy that had not been challenged since Trafalgar. The problem for the British admirals was whether that supremacy could be maintained in the face of the growing fleets of France, Italy, and Russia. The French construction of ironclads had been a particular source of alarm in the naval scare of 1888 and in the following year Parliament passed a Naval Defence Act which authorized the expenditure of £21,500,000 for the construction of ten new battleships and many smaller craft. It was the near certainty of a Franco-Russian alliance, advertised by the Russian naval visit to Toulon in 1893 that brought the next scare to a head. France and Russia had been Great Britain's two most likely opponents throughout the nineteenth century. Would her naval forces be able to maintain themselves in the Mediterranean and to hold the Straits against their combined fleets? Joseph Chamberlain, for one, had serious doubts. 'The British navy', he remarked, 'would have to cut and run—if it could run,' and in December 1893 Lord George Hamilton formulated the two-Power principal that 'our fleet should be equal to the combination of the two next strongest navies in Europe'. In fact, this was the minimum requirement of the admirals; what they would have liked was a five to three superiority, but this might be difficult to get even under the Conservative government that was formed in 1895.

It was this same sense of insecurity that now caused the British to concentrate on some means of escape from their diplomatic isolation. Alliance with France was for the moment ruled out by continued antagonism over Egypt and Central Africa. On the other hand, the British were quite open at this time to the thought of an alliance with Germany. Indeed, so far as diplomatic issues were concerned, nothing stood in the way of the two countries becoming firm friends—just as the Russians themselves had imagined at the time when they had retaliated by turning to France. The German government, however, believed that the British were becoming increasingly dependent upon gaining an alliance with them and accordingly made their terms high, insisting that Great Britain should join the Triple Alliance.

Certainly British isolation was to be greatly emphasized by several diplomatic moves in the next few years. In 1895 the pressure which was brought to bear on Japan to make her surrender her mainland gains from China (see p. 233) was due to a Continental group formed by France, Germany, and Russia, from which Great Britain was pointedly excluded. In January 1896 she suffered a far greater affront. In South Africa Dr Jameson, a close associate of Cecil Rhodes, had just failed ignominiously in a raid from Southern Bechuanaland into Transvaal territory and William II now sent a famous telegram to the Boer President Kruger congratulating him on having overcome this danger 'without appealing for the help of friendly Powers'. William's intention with this heavy hint was to convince the British government of their isolation and to force them to accept Germany's terms for an alliance. In fact, like most of William's excursions into *la haute politique*, it was based on a misconception of the situation. All that he achieved was to anger public opinion in Great Britain, where a flying squadron was hastily prepared in case of active German intervention, and when he turned to the other Powers for moral support, he found that none of them had the slightest interest in involving themselves in a quarrel with the British over the Transvaal. On two further occasions William strove to bring home her isolation to Great Britain—in August 1897, when he suggested to Tsar Nicholas II that they should act in unison against her, and in June 1898, when he made a similar unsuccessful proposal to the French.

Meanwhile, other significant events were taking place within the Ottoman empire. Between 1893 and 1898 Sultan Abdul Hamid set about crushing a growing nationalist movement among the Armenians, and when the numbers slaughtered appeared to be approaching 200,000, Great Britain, France, and Russia all sent official protests. The Sultan did not have to pay much attention to this, since he knew that there was little likelihood of unity among the Powers; Russia herself had little love for the Armenians and in any case would never have agreed to Lord Salisbury's suggestion that a British naval force should be sent through the Straits to the Armenian shore of the Black Sea. The episode, however, was important in two ways. First, it created considerable anti-Turkish feeling in Great Britain; second, the fact that Germany did not send a protest opened the way to closer diplomatic relations between Berlin and Constantinople.

The next event in this part of Europe was the outbreak of war, in 1897, between Turkey and Greece over a revolt of the Greeks under Turkish rule in Crete. At first the Powers had reckoned simply to hold the ring, but a Turkish advance across the plain of Thessaly in April made intervention inevitable and in June an armistice was imposed. By 1898 it had been agreed that Crete should have autonomy, although still technically under the Turkish flag, but the most important outcome of these negotiations lay elsewhere. It sprang from the fact that Russia was by now wanting to concentrate on her Far Eastern policy without being hampered by any complications in the Balkans. France, however, refusing to go beyond the letter of the treaty of 1894, was not prepared to stand guard for Russia. She 'would not regard herself as at all committed in a conflict which sprang from the question of the Black Sea and the Straits', the Russian ambassador was informed in December 1896, and on this Russia turned instead to her most likely opponent. Negotiations during the Cretan war in 1897 revealed that Austria-Hungary was only too anxious to preserve the *status quo* in the Balkans, and in April Russia reached a firm agreement with her over this, fully accepting the situation created by the Treaty of Berlin in 1878, including the Austrian occupation of Bosnia and Herzegovina. Thus the Russians were free to concentrate entirely on the Far East and from now until 1905 there was to be a diplomatic truce in the Balkans.

This change of direction in Russian interests had a marked effect upon Great Britain. Until now, although no longer so confident over her isolation, she had not tried very hard to escape from it, but the growth of Russian influence in the Far East, coupled with the granting of territorial concessions to France and Germany on the Chinese coast (see p. 234), made it important for her to find an ally who would safeguard her own interests in these regions.

There followed as a consequence two serious attempts by Great Britain to gain a positive alliance with Germany. The first was mainly the work of Joseph Chamberlain in 1898. It failed because William II believed rightly that Germany had no fundamental interests to defend in Africa or the Far East. 'The Niger and the Gulf of Pechili concern us less than Alsace-Lorraine.' And for this reason, knowing that Russia was Great Britain's principal opponent, he was anxious not to become a cat's-paw for the British. 'Chamberlain must not forget', he remarked, 'that in East Prussia I have one Prussian army corps against three Russian armies and nine cavalry divisions from which no Chinese wall divides me and which no English ironclads hold at arm's length.' And so although they reached a minor agreement over British control of the Portuguese Delagoa Bay railway, the first attempt came to nothing.

Further developments in the intervening years before the second attempt made its success extremely unlikely. It is true that the Fashoda episode (see p. 234) had heightened Anglo-French antagonism and had been followed by a reaffirmation of the Franco-Russian alliance which was now slightly extended in its stated aims to include 'the maintenance of the balance of power'. In every other respect, however, the likelihood of an Anglo-German alliance receded. Germany herself was continuing to cultivate her friendship with Turkey. In 1898 William II paid a second visit to Constantinople and plans were discussed for the building of a Berlin-Baghdad railway. Long afterwards this scheme was often quoted as an instance of German economic imperialism stretching out a tentacle into the Middle East. At the time it was only Russia who made serious objections, since such a line seemed likely to cut her off from the Balkans, whereas the British and French governments were, on the whole, not displeased to see German interest diverted from Africa. A further incident was the outbreak of the Boer War which made Great Britain intensely unpopular on the Continent, although the other Powers had to swallow their indignation when they found themselves in need of cooperation with Great Britain over the quelling of the Boxer rising against foreign influence in China.

More decisive than all these events, however, was the German decision to build a navy. The policy of adopting a somewhat distant attitude towards Great Britain, which the politicians had mistakenly imagined would drive her into a German alliance on their terms, had begun to create a sense of rivalry between the two countries and the dispatch of a British naval squadron in 1896 in response to William's telegram to Kruger had naturally lent force to the demands of the German naval enthusiasts. In 1897 Bülow replaced Marschall as German Foreign Minister and Admiral von Tirpitz became Secretary of State for the Navy; there followed in 1898 the first German Navy Law which laid the foundations of a large battle fleet, and the excited approval with which this was greeted may be gauged from the creation of the German Navy League financed by the industrialist Krupp and gaining 240,000 members within three years. For the British it was understandable that such a step should seem a considerable challenge. Their army, although reformed, was tiny by Continental standards; the building of a German navy naturally seemed like a direct threat to their own security, and William II's personal attitude certainly gave some justification for alarm in Great Britain. 'I am not in a position to go beyond the strictest neutrality,' he said at the time of the Boer War, 'and I must first get for myself a fleet. In twenty years' time, when the fleet is ready, I can use another language.'

The passing of the second German Navy Law in 1900, making provision for a still larger fleet, did not in itself prevent Lord Lansdowne from attempting a new approach to Germany in 1901. As in 1898, however, this came to nothing. The British government was still primarily concerned with the Far East, and the Germans, convinced that a war between Great Britain and Russia was imminent, had no intention of being drawn into it. They still believed that if they waited long enough the British would be bound to turn to them and they ignored the warnings of the German ambassador in London who suggested that the British might look elsewhere—a threat which Holstein dismissed as 'an absolute swindle'. As it turned out, this second rejection was to prove the crucial miscalculation of German foreign policy. The loss of the chance of an alliance with Great

Britain was to deprive Germany of room for diplomatic manoeuvre and to throw her back on to entire dependence upon Austria-Hungary. Thus Great Britain moved into the orbit of her opponents, and the growing excitement of public opinion in both countries over the naval question, coupled with William II's almost pathological mistrust of Edward VII made any reversal of this situation extremely unlikely.

Eventually, in 1902, Great Britain found in Japan the partner that her particular interests required. Both of them had reason to mistrust the growth of Russian influence in Manchuria, particularly after the suppression of the Boxer rising; both had recently failed to reach agreement with Russia, and a treaty was duly signed between them on 30 January 1902. Each recognized the other's interest in China; if either were involved in war with a third Power, the other would observe strict neutrality; if either were involved in war with *two* Powers, then the other would lend active assistance. For the British this treaty simply forestalled any Russo-Japanese alliance aimed at a partition of economic interests in China, and it fortified the Japanese sufficiently to contemplate an attack on Russia. The terms of the treaty were published at once, thus making French support of Russia in such a war much less likely, since this, according to the Anglo-Japanese treaty, would bring France into direct conflict with Great Britain—over an issue in which no French interests were seriously at stake.

This last factor was to play an important part in the next development in European diplomacy, since the French, anxious to avoid being dragged into a Russo-Japanese war, began to look for an alignment that would help to keep them out. This clearly pointed to some sort of agreement with Great Britain. There was a further motive for the French in that Delcassé, the Foreign Minister, was aiming to establish direct control over Morocco; he had already gained Italian acceptance of such a move in 1902 by promising French acquiescence over the future annexation of Tripoli by Italy, but Spain was not prepared to agree without the assent of Great Britain, who was bound to be concerned about the security of Gibraltar.

British motives were rather less precise. They were still hoping to find a European ally without entangling themselves in excessive commitments, and the growth of German naval rivalry now naturally inclined them a little more towards France. Even so the process was a slow one. Shortly after King Edward VII had paid a famous State visit to Paris in May 1903, private negotiations were opened, but it was not until a year later that agreement was reached on a number of specific points. As well as a settlement over the frontier of Gambia and over spheres of influence in Siam, this included a mutual recognition of British interests in Egypt and French interests in Morocco, although over this last the British were careful to stipulate that they should enjoy commercial equality with the French and that the Mediterranean coastline opposite Gibraltar should remain unfortified. Thus, the Anglo-French *entente cordiale* of 1904 involved no treaty of alliance between the two countries; yet these highly limited political agreements between them were to form the basis of a remarkable psychological reconciliation which subsequent events were to strengthen.

Before the agreements had been signed, it suddenly seemed to the French that the worst had happened. The Japanese, despairing of ever being able to persuade the Russians to evacuate Manchuria, launched a naval attack on Port Arthur on 8 February 1904 without any official declaration of war. The course of the fighting was governed by the fact that the Russians failed to gain control of the sea, and the Japanese were thus able to build up their reinforcements; in January 1905 Port Arthur fell to them and, as they advanced northwards, General Nogi succeeded in outmanoeuvring the Russian forces drawn up in defence of Mukden. There is an element of fantasy in the last act of this drama when the Russian Baltic fleet, having sailed all the way round the Cape of Good Hope to come to grips with the enemy, duly did so on 27 May 1905 and was annihilated in the Straits of Tshushima. American mediation now led to the signing of the Treaty of Portsmouth in September 1905. Inevitably this meant considerable cessions to Japan—Port Arthur, the southern half of the island of Sakhalin, part of the railway in Manchuria and Russian recognition of Japanese supremacy in Korea. On the other hand, hardly any indemnity was charged and no lasting bitterness created, so that in the next few years Russia and Japan were able to draw closer together over the division of Manchuria into spheres of influence.

The most striking aspect of the war had been the effectiveness of the Japanese forces against a major European Power, and at a technical level naval experts had duly noted the psychological effect of the torpedo and the mine, even if the practical efficiency of both still left a good deal to be desired. But although it was fought on the other side of the earth, it also had considerable political repercussions in Europe. Germany regarded the situation with some satisfaction, since she was convinced that the long anticipated war between Great Britain and Russia was now about to break out. Indeed, there had been a moment of great tension in October 1904 when the Russian Baltic fleet at the beginning of its fateful voyage to the east opened fire on British fishing boats off the Dogger Bank in the North Sea under the impression that they were Japanese torpedo boats. However, the Germans' hope that the Russians would now turn hastily to them for an alliance was shattered by the determination of the French to prevent a war in which they would have to choose between their alliance with Russia and their new friendship with Great Britain. The crisis came to nothing. The Russians were too occupied in the Far East, and for the British there was by now not the slightest need for war with Russia; their Japanese alliance gave them the support that they needed in China and the Anglo-French *entente* had helped to quieten their fears of the combined French and Russian navies—particularly after the Japanese had dealt so effectively with the Russian fleet at Tshushima.

Thus, despite the fears of the French, the Russo-Japanese war did not seriously endanger the new alignment. There were, however, other trials ahead. The German government, conscious of having lost their immediate chance of a British alliance, began to take positive steps towards both weakening the Anglo-French *entente* and working towards some sort of agreement with Russia. The obvious trouble spot that might still split Great Britain and France was Morocco, and on 31 March 1905 William I I landed at Tangier and made a public statement that Germany would regard Morocco as an independent country. The purpose of this artificially stimulated crisis was to cause an international conference to be convened, where the Germans hoped that the weakness of the Anglo-French *entente* would be revealed to the whole world. A little later, in July, William I I sailing in his yacht in the Gulf of Finland had a consultation with Tsar Nicholas I I at Björkö, where the two sovereigns agreed on a treaty of defensive alliance against attack by any European Power in Europe.

In the event each of these schemes failed. The Björkö agreement was ratified by neither government, Bülow in Germany fearing that it would be too great a liability, the Russian ministers apprehensive of offending France on whose support they now felt far more dependent after Russia's poor showing in the war with Japan. Over Morocco the Germans did get their conference. It was held at Algeciras in January 1906, but it failed conspicuously to strengthen Germany's hand. The *entente* Powers remained undivided, whereas Germany found herself supported only by Austria-Hungary. Thus, with the defection of Italy the Powers of the Triple Alliance had themselves been revealed as the weaker group; on the other hand, Germany's initiative in provoking this conference now led the British and the French to begin a series of purely informal military conversations which were later to be of considerable significance.

The failure of the German emperor's diplomacy was to be followed by another remarkable development—the formation of the Anglo-Russian *entente* of 1907. Russia's weakness as revealed by her war with Japan made her anxious to find another friend, and her fears of German influence in Persia through the building of the Berlin-Baghdad railway suggested that it would be as well to end her differences with Great Britain. On the British side there was the desire to prevent Russia from drifting back to her policy of a Rein-surance Treaty with Germany, and when Sir Edward Grey became Foreign Secretary in the 1906 Liberal administration in Great Britain, negotiations began almost at once.

The convention between the two countries was finally signed in August 1907. Like the Anglo-French *entente*, it simply took the form of the settlement of a number of disputes without the creation of a positive alliance. A striking feature of the negotiations was the new freedom with which the British, now firmly based on Egypt, felt they could discuss the opening of the Straits, and although Grey did not intend to throw in such a concession immediately, he did suggest a vague promise for the future. This was sufficient to give the British the best of the deal in Central Asia, where it was agreed that Tibet should be a neutral state, while Russia renounced her interests in Afghanistan. In Persia the spoil was to be shared—a northern zone including the capital, Teheran, to be a Russian sphere of influence, a southern zone on the north side of the Gulf to be a British one, while the area in the middle was to be neutral.

The news of the *entente* was not well received in Great Britain, where public opinion was strongly anti-Russian; liberals and radicals disliked the *pogroms* of the Jews and the crushing of the revolution of 1905 (see p. 268), and the cry went up that Russia had gained too much from the bargain. In fact, the agreements represented a reasonably fair settlement of a number of outstanding disputes and in the area in which Russia seemed to have done best—in Persia—it was no more than a recognition of the existing situation. In Germany reactions were still stronger. In 1885 Bismarck, commenting on the possibility of an Anglo-French-Russian alliance, had remarked: 'it would provide the basis for a coalition against us more dangerous for Germany than any other she might have to face'. The terms of the Anglo-Russian *entente* make it clear that there was no conscious attempt at the encirclement of the Central Powers here; yet it was perhaps understandable that many Germans should think so, and there could be no denying that Germany's diplomatic position had deteriorated greatly since the departure of Bismarck in 1890.

2. The approach of war 1907–14

From now until the outbreak of the first World War European relations were dominated by two general factors—the renewal of rivalry between Russia and Austria-Hungary over the Balkans, and the growing naval competition between Great Britain and Germany.

There were in the main two reasons for the end of the diplomatic truce between Russia and Austria-Hungary. First, Russia's defeat by Japan and the settlement of many of her disputes with Great

Britain along her Asian frontiers turned her attention back once again to the Balkans. Second, there had recently been a radical change of policy in Serbia. Until 1903 under the rule of King Alexander Obrenović this had been pro-Austrian, but in that year a group of officers carried out a palace revolution in Belgrade, assassinated the King and his Queen Draga and established a new king, Peter Karageorgović. This meant much more than simply another bloody chapter in the story of a Balkan feud, since King Peter introduced parliamentary government and embarked upon a pro-Russian policy, at the same time drawing money and munitions from France.

At first, Austrian reactions to this change in Serbia were only mild, but in 1906 with the appointment of Aehrenthal as Foreign Minister and Conrad von Hötzendorff as Chief of the General Staff a far stiffer attitude was adopted. For the moment relations with Russia were not upset; in September 1908 Aehrenthal and the Russian Foreign Minister Izvolski met at Buchlau, where they agreed that Austria-Hungary should proclaim the annexation of Bosnia and Herzegovina, which had in fact been under Austrian military occupation since 1878 (see p. 277); thus, without moving a single soldier, an effective blow would be dealt to the pride of the Serbs who had long hoped to gain these provinces for themselves. In return, Aehrenthal agreed that Izvolski should canvass the governments of Europe on the opening of the Straits.

Unfortunately for their future relations Austria-Hungary allowed Russia very little time in which to make sure of her side of the bargain. Izvolski had just come up against objections to the Russian proposals at London and Paris, when he heard on 6 October that Aehrenthal had openly proclaimed the annexation of Bosnia and Herzegovina. Taken by surprise, Izvolski swung round and supported the Serbs in their indignation. The crisis lasted several months, but this time—unlike Algeciras—it was the Central Powers who won the day. Great Britain condemned the annexation, but had no military commitment; France, who had ultimately, was hesitant in her support of Russia, whereas Germany took her stand positively by Austria-Hungary. 'The moment Russia mobilizes,' wrote Moltke to Conrad in January 1909, 'Germany also will mobilize and will unquestionably mobilize her whole army.' Thus, in March 1909 Russia decided to accept the situation and the only remaining formality was for Turkey to receive an indemnity of £2,400,000.

The Bosnian crisis was, on the face of it, a victory for the Central Powers—an outcome that was to have a significant effect on Russia's attitude in 1914. Yet it was a victory that entailed certain disadvantages, since the very realization of the fact soon brought the *entente* Powers closer together. Nor from Germany's point of view was the new turn in diplomacy an entirely happy one, since the

Moltke-Conrad correspondence, supported by William II, seemed to bind Germany to underwriting the whole of Austria-Hungary's activities in the Balkans—an interpretation of the Dual Alliance of 1879 of which Bismarck would never have approved. 'There exist specifically Austrian interests which we cannot undertake to defend,' he had said in the *Reichstag* in 1887, 'and there are specifically German interests which Austria cannot undertake to defend. We cannot each adopt the other's special interests.'

A further outcome of the Bosnian crisis was the stimulation of anti-Austrian feeling in Serbia. A new society for national defence, *Narodna Obrana*, was founded to encourage the training of spies and saboteurs and the dissemination of anti-Habsburg propaganda in Bosnia. In 1909, after Austrian objections to its activities, this had to be turned into a purely cultural organization, which, however, could still act as a screen for a secret society—the Black Hand— continuing to work at the original objectives. One of the leaders of this secret organization, Colonel Dragutin Dimitriević, who acted under the code name of Apis, was chief of the Intelligence Department of the Serbian General Staff and had earlier participated in the assassination of King Alexander in 1903. The Black Hand, which received a good deal of support in high places, while remaining essentially unofficial, was extremely successful in establishing contact with Serb and Croat students from Croatia; in 1910 and 1913 it was responsible for two abortive attempts to assassinate the Austrian Governor of Bosnia, and in 1914 was to accomplish the most resounding political murder of its career.

At the same time as this reawakening of hostility in the Balkans the British and the Germans were continuing to compete over the size of their respective navies. In Great Britain Sir John Fisher, First Sea Lord from 1904, was realigning the whole disposition of British naval forces, basing them on Malta, Gibraltar, and the home ports, particularly in the north of Scotland, and despite the desire of the Liberal government to limit naval rearmament, the development of long-range gunnery and the torpedo necessitated the laying down of a new design of all-big-gun ship—the *Dreadnought*. In Germany, in 1908, an amendment to the Navy Law raised the number of capital ships to be constructed from three to four a year, but it was not until 1909 that the Liberal government in Great Britain was prepared to retaliate, alarmed by the rumours of shipbuilding in Austria-Hungary and Italy.

The next crisis in Germany's relations with the west came in 1911—once again over Morocco. A local rebellion had driven the Sultan out of his capital at Fez, which French troops proceeded to occupy in order to restore order, and Germany, determined on compensation for any French gains in this area, declared that France's action nullified the Algeciras agreement and on 1 July sent a German gunboat, the *Panther*, to Agadir as a token of her interest in the affair. The German demand for the French Congo was rejected by France, but the Prime Minister Caillaux was known to be friendly towards Germany and the British government was alarmed lest France and Germany might strike a private bargain which might include the cession of Agadir to Germany as a naval base on the Atlantic coast. Thus, when the British Chancellor of the Exchequer, Lloyd George, announced in a speech at the Mansion House on 21 July that Great Britain could not be indifferent to these possible changes, the warning may have been addressed as much to France as to Germany. The war scare mounted throughout August, but in September there was a financial panic in Germany and by the beginning of November a new agreement had been negotiated, whereby Germany recognized France's right to establish a protectorate over Morocco in return for a small part of the French Congo with access to the sea.

War for the moment had been averted, yet the second Morocco crisis was followed by a succession of developments that continued to threaten the peace of Europe. Italy, regarding the establishment of French power in Morocco as imminent, now resolved to seize Tripoli from Turkey. She had already gained the assent of the French (see p. 290) and the British over this and at the end of September 1911 embarked upon a war with Turkey in which the Italian fleet bombarded Beirut and carried out the occupation of some of the Aegean islands. By the spring of 1912 her activity in these waters had so alarmed the British that they intervened diplomatically, and in October 1912 the Treaty of Lausanne was signed between the belligerents, whereby Italy gained Tripoli and Cyrenaica, but not the Aegean islands, which were to be evacuated—although the Italians never actually complied with this last condition.

A further consequence of the second Morocco crisis was the dissatisfaction of the naval enthusiasts in Germany. Tirpitz considered that they had 'suffered a diplomatic check and we must solve it by a supplementary naval bill'; he was thinking now of attaining naval parity with Great Britain by 1920 and he did succeed in gaining increases in plans for construction. All this, however, was in conflict with the advice of the German ambassador in London, Count Metternich: 'if we now state bluntly to the British government the alternatives: either you remain neutral or we increase our fleet, the result will be an even closer attachment to France—if the relations between England and France could be closer than they are at present.' Indeed, the politicians of Germany and Great Britain were by no means happy about this growing naval competition; Bethmann Hollweg, the Chancellor, did not care greatly for Tirpitz's programme and as a matter of principle Asquith's Liberal government objected to an armaments race. It was this attitude that led to the

visit of Lord Haldane to Germany in 1912, but although negotiations continued over colonial questions and a Mesopotamian railway agreement, Germany's price still remained far too high for any
definite political alliance to be achieved.

The news of the Haldane visit did, however, have a marked effect
upon French diplomatic activity. Military conversations between
the British and French General Staffs had concentrated on the dispatch of a British military force to the Continent in the event of war
and now a coordination of naval strategy led to a revolutionary
change in British dispositions in that the French in future were to
be responsible for the Mediterranean, thus leaving the British free
to concentrate on their home waters and the Channel.

At the same time France was anxious to strengthen her ties with
Russia, which had not shown themselves to be particularly effective
during the crises of 1908 and 1911. The Russians, too, were conscious of the need to reinforce their position, since they were anticipating further complications in the Balkans. The tension here was
due to the formation of a Balkan league. In March 1912 Serbia and
Bulgaria had signed a treaty for the partition of Macedonia and in
May this had been joined by Greece and Montenegro. Russia herself
had become involved in these negotiations, since Turkey's performance in the recent war with Italy suggested that she was now no
longer strong enough to guard the Straits, which were a vital trade
route for Russia's economy. The Tsar's government did not care
greatly for the projected partition; yet they did not wish to offend
the Balkan bloc on whom the security of the Straits might soon
depend.

In August, shortly after these developments in the Balkans, the
French Prime Minister, Poincaré, visited Russia, and the subsequent conversations were to be of immense significance in attaching
a far wider interpretation to their existing agreements. According
to the military treaty of 1892 French aid to Russia would only follow
an attack on Russia by Germany or Austria-Hungary supported by
Germany. The Bosnian crisis of 1908, however, had made it clear
that the problem was hardly likely to be so clear-cut. If Serbia were
threatened by Austria-Hungary, Russia might well find herself
attacking Austria-Hungary in Serbia's defence, and if a German
attack on Russia then followed in accordance with the Dual Alliance
of 1879, whose terms had been made public by Bismarck in 1888,
it might have been possible for France to argue that Russia had
brought this upon herself by her own action and that the Franco-
Russian alliance therefore did not become militarily operative. The
Poincaré visit now established the fact that if such circumstances
should arise, France would regard herself as bound to support Russia. Thus the agreement supplied a fatal link in the chain of diplomatic commitments; for, when it is taken in conjunction with the

Moltke-Conrad correspondence of January 1909 (see p. 294), it is clear that the situation had been finally created whereby a Balkan crisis could lead automatically to a general war. This was certainly not intentional. It is true that certain historians of the postwar period seized on the agreement as a dastardly plot by French and Russian politicians, but it is by now generally accepted by German as well as French historians that it did not represent a warlike policy. It sprang simply from a desire to bolster up the Franco-Russian alliance which without this further interpretation would have been virtually meaningless in the circumstances of 1912.

Within a couple of months the Russians were proved correct in their anticipation of a new Balkan crisis, when in October Montenegro, swiftly followed by Bulgaria, Greece, and Serbia, declared war on Turkey. They were everywhere successful. The Bulgarians attacked through Thrace and were only checked before Constantinople, while the Serbs drove south and the Greeks north into what was left of Turkish territory in Europe. This was a crisis entirely of the Balkan states' own making—a novel situation for the great Powers, who found themselves watching a radical alteration in the *status quo* contrary to their own interests. Russia had no intention of letting Constantinople fall to Bulgaria, while Austria-Hungary was determined to prevent Serbia from gaining a part of the Adriatic coast, and on 3 December 1912 the Powers cooperated to impose an armistice which was followed by a peace conference at London. Here they were able to agree to the creation of a new state, Albania, which effectively prevented Serbia from extending her frontiers to the Adriatic and a peace treaty was finally signed on 30 May 1913.

Once again, however, the Balkan states showed that a mere agreement among the great Powers was now no longer sufficient to decide their fate. Serbia, demanding compensation for the loss of the territories involved in the creation of Albania, insisted on retaining areas of Macedonia that were to have been part of Bulgaria's share of the spoil. Bulgaria, confident of her own military powers, declared war on Greece and Serbia and at once encountered disaster. Rumania joined her two opponents; Turkey was able to recapture Adrianople, and in August 1913 the Treaty of Bucharest robbed Bulgaria of some of her recent gains as well as the region of the Dobruja, which was taken by Rumania.

The Powers accepted the Treaty of Bucharest, but the emergence of a greatly enlarged Serbia suggested to the government at Vienna that the hour might not be far distant when she would attempt to adopt the role of Piedmont in 1859 or of Prussia in 1866. From now on, Conrad, the Chief of Staff, and Count Leopold von Berchtold, who had become Austrian Prime Minister in February 1912, thought to seek a solution in a short war, followed by the partition of Serbia. Italy seemed unreliable, but William II made it clear that

Austria-Hungary could count on German support. 'You can be certain I stand behind you and am ready to draw the sword whenever your action makes it necessary,' William told him in October, '... whatever comes from Vienna is to me a command.'

This subservience of German policy to Austrian requirements was all the more dangerous because of the mounting armaments race between the Powers. Already in January 1913 a new German Army Law had increased the annual intake of conscripts from 280,000 to 343,000; in March the German government had ignored Winston Churchill's proposal for a short truce in naval construction, and the widening of the Kiel Canal for the larger German battleships was proceeding with all speed. In August 1913 France extended her period of military service to three years—the only way in which she could compete with Germany's greater population. Russia, too, was planning an expansion of her military forces, and in Great Britain measures were taken for the defence of the new naval bases at Cromarty and Scapa Flow.

Even so, it was not impossible for the Powers to reach agreement over some of their difficulties. When Russia protested at the appointment of a German general, Liman von Sanders, as head of a military mission at Constantinople with command of a Turkish army corps, Germany was prepared in January 1914 to make his post purely advisory. And even later in 1914 relations between Great Britain and Germany actually seemed to be improving with conversations about Africa and an agreement over the south of Persia.

Everything rested on the situation in the Balkans and it was here that the Black Hand organization in Serbia brought about the last fatal crisis. For some time Colonel Dimitriević —Apis—had been determined on a fresh assassination attempt; a plan to strike down General Potiorek, the Austrian Governor of Bosnia, came to nothing, but when in the late summer of 1913 Potiorek invited Francis Ferdinand, the heir to the Habsburg throne, to attend army manoeuvres in Bosnia in June 1914, Apis decided that here was a more illustrious victim. In April 1914 he had selected three of the youths who were to take part in the attempt and by the end of May they had already secretly crossed the frontier from Serbia into Bosnia. At this point in the drama Pašić, the Prime Minister of Serbia, seems to have heard something of the plot and was consequently faced with a highly unpleasant dilemma. To denounce it might lead to his own assassination by the Black Hand and would in any case place Serbia in a difficult diplomatic position; on the other hand, to let it go forward might have the most appalling consequences. His reaction to the problem was to send a guarded warning to Vienna— so guarded that it never penetrated to the relevant authorities. As it was, Francis Ferdinand duly attended the manoeuvres in June 1914 and on the last day of his visit proceeded with his wife to pay a formal visit to Sarajevo. On the way to the City Hall the bomb that was thrown at their car did not harm them, but on the return journey, owing to a remarkable series of mischances, their car actually came to a halt within a few yards of the spot where Gavrilo Princip, one of the young conspirators, was standing on the pavement. Princip shot them both with his revolver and at such close range it was inevitable that their wounds should be mortal.

Nearly all those involved in the plot were captured by the police. Their Serbian origin was undeniable and although they declared that they were not acting on orders, Berchtold and Conrad at once believed that fate had presented them with a justification for the war which would enable them to crush Serbia. The German government supported them, simply envisaging a local war between the two countries, and on 23 July Austria-Hungary presented Serbia with an overwhelming ultimatum. A few minutes before its expiry Serbia accepted almost all its conditions, but the Austrians were determined not to hold back. They were still unable to prove conclusively a positive link between the Sarajevo conspirators and the Serbian government, and diplomatic intervention by the other powers might rob them of what seemed a golden opportunity. On 28 July Austria-Hungary, insisting that she was simply engaging in local hostilities in self-defence, declared war on Serbia.

For Russia this new crisis was too reminiscent of the Bosnian episode of 1908. She had failed Serbia then, and if she failed her again, her influence at Belgrade would finally be lost. On 26 July the Tsar had already reassured the Serbian Crown Prince that 'Russia will in no case be indifferent to the fate of Serbia,' and on 28 July Russia began a partial mobilization against Austria-Hungary. On the following day Germany warned Russia that if she did not desist, German mobilization would be bound to follow. But by now technical considerations were beginning to predominate. The Russian General Staff could not carry out their plans properly without a general mobilization, and on 30 July the Tsar, convinced that the only alternative was the abandonment of Serbia, consented to this.

In Berlin Bethmann Hollweg, highly alarmed at the course that events were taking, was beginning to urge caution on Vienna; yet at the same time Moltke was demanding more positive action. On 31 July Germany began general mobilization and when Russia refused a further request to check her own measures, Germany declared war on her on 1 August. The problem here was that German mobilization automatically involved the Schlieffen plan which was based on the assumption of war against France. The French were accordingly asked to promise their neutrality in a Russo-German war; this was known to be extremely unlikely and even if they had agreed, the Germans intended to force the issue by asking for the surrender of Verdun and Toul. In reply, the French Prime Minister, Viviani, stated simply that 'France will act in accordance with her interests'; a German declaration of war followed on 3 August, and when the opening stages of the Schlieffen plan led on naturally to the invasion of Belgium by Germany, Great Britain declared war on 4 August.

Few historical issues have been the subject of such detailed analysis and controversy as the outbreak of the first World War. Viewed narrowly from the point of view of professional diplomacy, it may be summed up as the consequence of a moment when two major Powers each believed that they were faced with a crisis of existence. A failure of nerve brought the Austrians to the conclusion that the multi-national Habsburg state could no longer endure the continuing threat from Serb nationalism, and resolved to crush Serbia while they had the support of Germany. This decision confronted the Russians with a crisis of their own. The brief closure of the Straits during the Turco–Italian war had had a severe effect on the Russian economy and this could easily lead to serious internal disorders. Thus they knew that they dare not allow the control of the Straits to fall into hostile hands and it was therefore vital for Russia to retain the friendship of Serbia whose position had been greatly strengthened in the Balkan wars.

The repercussions of these fears at once made themselves felt through the diplomatic machinery of rival alliances. Local war could only be prevented from becoming general if one of the two groups was prepared to give way and this time neither would do so. A consequence of Germany's diplomatic arrogance in the previous years had been to leave her utterly dependent on her alliance with Austria-Hungary, a crucial factor, since the policy of Berchtold and Conrad might well have been different, had they not had the unqualified support of Germany. For France the principal fear remained the armed might of Germany, hence Poincaré, now President of the Third Republic, on a visit to St Petersburg in July reaffirmed the Franco–Russian alliance, although it is true that on 30 July the French government was urging caution on her Russian partner.

Great Britain was not directly involved in this tangle of diplomatic retaliation and it has sometimes been suggested that war might have been averted, if Sir Edward Grey, the British Foreign Secretary, had made it clear to the Central Powers that Great Britain would come to the aid of France. This criticism ignores Grey's difficulty that, whatever his personal views, he could not hope to convince the Liberal cabinet of the need to intervene in a continental war over Serbia; only the invasion of Belgium would stir British public opinion sufficiently to accept this step. In fact, an earlier British intervention would have made no difference at all. The German cry of encirclement presupposed British enmity, and in any case Germany had little interest in the tiny British army; when the

British expeditionary force did cross the Channel to France in August, Moltke told the German navy not to stop it, since he wished to destroy it on land. Furthermore, while an announcement of British intervention would have had no effect upon the Central Powers, it might well have encouraged the French and the Russians to take an even firmer line at a time when Grey was hoping that negotiation might still be possible.

It was, however, not diplomacy alone that was responsible for the final stages in the story. The most significant factor in these last fateful days was the surrender of the diplomats to the needs of the General Staffs. The final moves in Austria-Hungary, Germany, and Russia were dictated by the technical requirements of military programmes all constructed round the launching or the parrying of the vital 'knock-out blow'. Long ago Bismarck had foreseen the danger when he had advised the Austrian government: 'we must both take care that the privilege of giving political advice to our monarchs does not in fact slip out of our hands and pass over to the General Staffs.'

Diplomacy had failed and the military staffs had had their way. Yet the outcome was so catastrophic that it is natural to wonder whether these factors alone can supply an adequate explanation, or whether there were not more deeply rooted causes. It has been suggested, for example, that colonial and economic rivalries were the fundamental issue, of which diplomacy was merely the reflection. All these had certainly added greatly to the air of tension, yet none of them can be seen to have been particularly decisive in 1914. Indeed, the settlement of colonial disputes by peaceful means had been one of the most remarkable achievements of the period; nor can economic factors be simplified sufficiently to account for the military conflict.

In recent years, however, a new line of thought has been opened up by a school of German historians. This postulates a connection between home and foreign policy, in that diplomatic moves are seen to have been inspired by the search for a solution to domestic problems. In Germany these problems arose out of a tension between the new classes created by an immense economic expansion, and the older society which Bismarck's form of unification had been designed to preserve. At the top of the social scale the old and the new were beginning to merge with the intermarriage of Prussian landowning families and those of the great industrial magnates of the Rhineland. Further down, however, a growing working class was more difficult to assimilate within the original pattern and might offer great opportunities for the S.P.D., which despite its revisionist tendencies was still nominally Marxist (see p. 248). From this point of view Tirpitz's naval policy can be seen as a patriotic focus for all classes; a navy had the added advantage that it could be more selective in its recruiting and was therefore preferable to a great conscript army which was bound to include politically unreliable elements. The process, however, was circular, since it imposed a financial strain that could eventually only be overcome by further patriotic appeal.

Nevertheless, if the aim was to counter the attraction of Socialism, it can be said to have had some success—although it was not only in Germany that nationalism proved stronger than Socialism. It had been the hope of the Second International that at the moment of the outbreak a general strike and a refusal to join the colours would cause the machinery of war to break in the hands of the belligerent governments (see p. 248). Yet to the chagrin of the leading Socialists they found that the rank and file of the Socialist parties only echoed the cries of their governments. 'We will not have our women and children sacrificed to the brutality of the Cossacks,' remarked the editor of *Vorwärts*, the German Social Democrat newspaper, and when Hermann Müller, a member of the central executive, rushed frantically to Paris on 1 August, he found that the French Socialists were prepared to vote in favour of war credits against German attack. Only in Serbia did two Social Democrat members of parliament have the courage to vote against war credits, while in Russia Mensheviks and Bolsheviks abstained. Otherwise, although the summer of 1914 had been a time of considerable industrial unrest, the governments found that Socialists were prepared to fall in obediently behind them.

The question of patriotic appeal, however, leads to a further aspect of the debate which relates particularly to Germany. The danger of a belligerent foreign policy was that it might strengthen the wilder demands of the pan-German groups and this in turn has thrown a new light on the acquisitions made by Germany in the first year of the Great War (see p. 336), and on the terms imposed on Russia in March 1918 (see p. 330). It has been suggested that the hope for such gains played a part in her policy before 1914 and was not merely the fortuitous outcome, once the war had started; in other words, that her support for Austria was not simply the result of a blind dependence, but was encouraged also by the thought of a new thrust eastwards.

The whole controversy over German war aims rests on a variety of distinctions—between formal policies and informal pressures, between statements made before or after the outbreak of war. It does not seem that either of the Central Powers had any specific plans for making vast annexations; even Austria's over Serbia were vague and makeshift. The handful of men who at the end took the crucial decisions must have been aware of the demands of the pan-Germans. Yet there is almost no evidence that they were governed by these demands, when the decisions were taken. The military were largely consumed with the race over mobilization. The diplomats were simply wrapped up in the technicalities of what they regarded as their own specialist activity and certainly do not appear to have been influenced by any abstruse intellectual theory about resolving domestic problems by plunging into war. Indeed, Tirpitz was strongly opposed to such a course, since he did not believe that his navy was yet ready. Levity rather than a grand design is how one British historian characterized their efforts—the folly of imagining that a war to crush Serbia could remain local. On the other hand, that levity may well have been encouraged by a broad sense of patriotic support or by the feeling that a confrontation with Russia was sooner or later inevitable. Thus the new theories do at least illustrate the volatile and unbalanced atmosphere of the years before 1914 and may help to explain why it proved impossible to check that escalation of threat and counter-threat which eventually unleashed the armies in an orgy of mutual destruction.

Part 6

The Eclipse of Nineteenth-Century Europe 1914–21

Chapter 25

The Great War 1914–18

1. The failure of the offensives 1914

Few wars have been so terrible in their course or so dramatic in their consequences as the war of 1914–18. In the savage pattern of the twentieth century it now has its place simply as 'the first World War'—the forerunner of the second; but for the generation that grew up after 1918 it was 'the Great War', an event of unparalleled horror that seemed to have left the participants numbed by the very memory of it. For four years millions of men faced each other in trenches across a shattered No-man's-land; they were smashed by shell-fire, shot, burnt, and gassed; wounded men hung for days on the barbed wire between the lines until they died, and hundreds of thousands were mown down in long murderous offensives that achieved virtually nothing. The Great War was the war of the unknown civilian soldier, and the thunder of the artillery barrages and the rattle of the machine-guns were like some requiem for the civilization of the nineteenth century.

One man, at least, had foreseen the type of war that would come. 'Everybody will be entrenched in the next war. It will be a great war of entrenchment. The spade will be as indispensable to the soldier as his rifle. . . . Your soldiers may fight as they please, the ultimate decision is in the hands of famine.' But the author of this remarkable prophecy made in 1899 was a civilian, a banker of Warsaw, and certainly no professional soldier would have envisaged such a turn of events in August 1914. The prevailing belief was in the swift 'knock-out blow' and in the eyes of the professional the whole issue would be resolved in a race to launch the various plans of operations. All these schemes, however, were upset by one miscalculation. The period of armed peace since 1871 had deprived any single country of that overwhelming superiority which the 'knock-out blow' demanded. The Dual Alliance and the Entente Powers had created something of a balance and, even after this had failed to preserve the peace, the crude military balance remained. The contending forces were too equally matched, the 'knock-out blows' were inconclusive, and the outcome was to be a long desperate war of attrition.

Purely in terms of statistics the Entente Powers with their combined population of 238 million had a considerable preponderance; on the other hand, the 120 million of Germany and Austria-Hungary were centrally placed and their forces could thus enjoy closer coordination and greater flexibility of movement between the eastern and western fronts. The German army, probably the best in Europe, mustered 87 infantry divisions and 10 divisions of cavalry, while the *Landwehr* provided approximately a further 22 divisions. Austria-Hungary's army was sizeable—49 infantry divisions and 11 divisions of cavalry—but hampered by the usual Habsburg difficulties in that orders had to be given in eight or nine languages and the political reliability of some of the troops—Czechs and Serbo-Croats—was uncertain. On 2 August 1914 Turkey had signed an alliance with Germany, but although she gave shelter to the two German cruisers, the *Goeben* and the *Breslau*, and closed the Straits to commercial shipping on 26 September, it was not until the end of October that she took definite action against Russia with the bombardment of Odessa. The Young Turk party in Constantinople was convinced that Germany would win the war and reckoned that Turkey could make a useful contribution, since her 36 divisions could harass Russia in the south, while the closing of the Straits severed an important Russian line of communication with the west.

Of the Entente Powers France had what was probably the most effective army with 62 infantry divisions and 20 divisions of cavalry; Russia certainly had the largest—114 infantry divisions and 40 divisions of cavalry—although there were doubts about their quality; the British Expeditionary Force of 6 divisions was certainly the most highly trained of all, a purely professional army, but far too small for the coming struggle. Indeed, Belgium could muster as many divisions, and Serbia almost double, not all well armed but with the advantage of the recent experience of the Balkan wars. In naval strength, however, Great Britain had a fair lead over Germany in modern battleships and a far greater one in the older types of ship, although German submarine strength was later to be a considerable threat.

The campaigns of 1914 were to be the most fluid and significant of the whole war; none of the initial offensives succeeded and out of their failure the pattern of the next four years of hostilities was established. In the west all depended upon the great German sweep through Belgium and France in accordance with a modified version of the Schlieffen plan. Could France be knocked out of the war in six weeks before Germany had to turn back to the east? In fact, there had already been considerable activity in the east long before the issue had been settled in the west. The first clash between the Russians and Germans took place in the middle of August, when two Russian armies began to advance through the pine forests and marshes of East Prussia—a gallant effort on the part of the Russians, since they undertook this move before their mobilization was completed simply in response to a plea from the French.

This Russian thrust into East Prussia was begun by General Rennenkampf's First Army, which routed the German forces at Gumbinnen on 20 August. At the same time General Samsonov's Second Army, which the Masurian lakes separated from Rennenkampf by some forty miles, began to move north towards Tannenberg. At this point the German commander Prittwitz expressed such alarm on the telephone to Supreme Headquarters at Coblenz that Moltke decided to replace him by Hindenburg and his Chief of Staff Ludendorff. Afterwards Hindenburg always enjoyed the credit for the victory over the Russian forces, yet before he and Ludendorff had arrived, a new plan drawn up by a local staff officer, Max Hoffmann, had already been set in motion. It was certainly daring. The bulk of the German forces facing Rennenkampf were to be switched away to the south-west in the hope that they might inflict a decisive defeat on Samsonov's Second Army before Rennenkampf realized that he could advance unopposed. The manoeuvre, carried out partly by train and partly on foot, was successfully completed, and after several days of fighting near Tannenberg the Germans had shattered Samsonov's army and taken 90,000 prisoners. Hindenburg now had to rush his forces north again to meet Rennenkampf and during the first fortnight of September the battle of the Masurian lakes, although not as overwhelming a victory as Tannenberg, resulted in the retreat of the Russians, of whom some 30,000 were taken prisoner. 'Up to now, with our inferior numbers,' wrote Hoffmann, 'we have defeated about fifteen Russian army corps and eight divisions, and we are not finished yet.'

The Austrians had been rather less successful. On 12 August Potiorek had launched a great invasion of Serbia—retribution for Sarajevo—but during several months of ferocious fighting the Serbs under Marshal Putnik threw the Austrians back, invaded Bosnia themselves, fell back before a new onslaught, and finally recovered to drive the Austrians north of the Danube by the middle of December. In August the other group of Austrian armies under Conrad von Hötzendorff advanced north towards Lublin and then after several weeks of mobile warfare were gradually pushed back into Galicia. By 10 September the Russian Grand Duke Nicholas was poised for a great enveloping movement on the right wing which would probably have destroyed the Austrian forces, had not Conrad heard of the plan in advance owing to the remarkable Russian habit of sending important messages by wireless uncoded. As it was, he was able to retire in time, but he could not rest free from the threat of

encirclement until he had withdrawn as far west as the river Duna-
jec which he reached by the beginning of October.

Meanwhile, in the west, the most decisive drama of all had been
played out. Here a million and a half German troops were committed to that great wheeling operation through Belgium and
France which had obsessed their General Staff for so long. The German Second Army under von Bülow captured Liège, the essential
preliminary to the advance of the northernmost First Army under
von Kluck, who occupied Brussels on 20 August, while the Belgian
forces fell back on Antwerp.

As the great line of German armies moved towards the Franco-
Belgian frontier, the French produced their reply in the form of the
famous Plan XVII. This was to meet attack with attack, to thrust
into the north of Lorraine at the hinge of the German swing, but
although the French assault which began on 14 August was serious,
the German Fourth and Fifth armies had succeeded in repulsing it
after a week's hard fighting. By the end of the month French forces
facing the First and Second Armies were falling back towards Paris
and the British Expeditionary Force under Sir John French had to
retire with them, although the effectiveness of British fire power
enabled them to give a good account of themselves at Mons.

It was now that the campaign reached a crucial stage. The plan
that von Schlieffen had devised (see p. 285) had always assumed
that the extreme right wing of the German sweep would swing south
only when it was well to the west of Paris, whose defending forces
would then be swiftly enveloped. In the last days of August, however, three decisions changed the whole character of the attack on
France. First, four divisions were detached from the western front
and sent to the eastern, despite the fact that the Tannenberg operation was already launched. Second, the German centre and left
began an advance on Verdun with the result that the German line
now seemed to be attempting a gigantic pincer operation. Third,
and most significant of all, on 30 August, von Kluck, finding that
a serious gap was already developing between his First Army and
von Bülow's Second, decided to wheel south while he was still east
of Paris.

The apparent abandonment of the Schlieffen plan by Moltke was
afterwards blamed for the eventual failure of the German attack.
Certainly Moltke had departed from it by sending away four divisions and strengthening the left sufficiently for the attack on Verdun
at a time when he needed every possible reinforcement on the right;
yet it would be wrong to blame Moltke for the inherent weaknesses
in the plan itself, since even with total concentration of all forces on
the right wing it had always been very doubtful whether the German
Army could be strong enough to sustain a sweep of so wide a radius

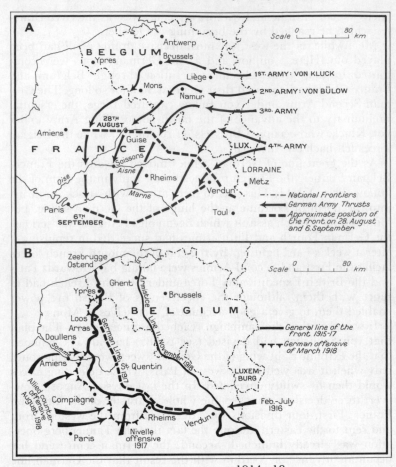

THE WESTERN FRONT 1914–18

as to pass to the west of Paris; the Schlieffen plan was in reality a
staff officer's pipe dream to which time had given an almost religious
air of inviolability.

Whatever was to blame, von Kluck had no option. The need to
regain contact with von Bülow, already badly shaken at Guise on
29 August, forced him to turn south towards the Marne with Paris
on his right. This might mean that he could roll up the retreating
French forces from the flank; equally, his own flank was now
exposed to attack from Paris. It was Galliéni, Military Governor of
Paris, who first saw this opportunity and on 4 September flung the
French Sixth Army into the assault on von Kluck's flank; and
although Joffre, the French Commander-in-Chief, took a little time

to digest the implications of this new situation, a French counter-attack soon developed against the German Second and Third Armies which had already crossed the Marne. Joffre's hope was to isolate von Kluck, and on 7 September the British Expeditionary Force and the left wing of the French Fifth Army began to advance into the gap that was widening between the German First and Second Armies. By now Moltke, far back at Luxemburg and only in fitful wireless communication with his commanders, was desperately anxious at the thought of an Allied breakthrough, and after a rapid tour of the various army headquarters had been made by one of his staff officers on 8 and 9 September, the German forces began to pull back to the river Aisne.

On 14 September Erich von Falkenhayn, the Prussian Minister of War, replaced Moltke as supreme commander, and there now followed a series of attempts by each side to outflank the other to the north until the sea was reached. At the end of October and in the first weeks of November German forces made tremendous efforts to break through to the Channel ports, but failed to do so despite the appalling losses inflicted on the British and French at the first battle of Ypres. Gradually the opposing lines of armies settled down to digging themselves in, and the separate lengths of trench began to link up in an elaborate system of dugouts, reserve lines, and communication trenches running intermittently from the Channel to the Swiss frontier.

Thus in Europe no attack was successful, yet no repulse was final. Overseas the results were more decisive. In South Africa, Botha, the Prime Minister, was able to contain and then to crush German forces in German South-West Africa; Togoland was overrun by British, French, and Belgian troops and only in Tanganyika did the Germans manage to put up a sustained resistance. In the Pacific, Japan, Australia, and New Zealand helped themselves to the German island colonies, while on the shores of the Persian Gulf Indian Army troops established themselves around Basra. At sea, the sinking of two British cruisers at the battle of Coronel off the Chilean coast in November was followed a month later by the destruction of almost the entire German naval force in those waters, near the Falkland Isles, and by the end of the year, with German cargo boats taking refuge in neutral ports, the British could at least feel that they still ruled the waves.

2. The deadlock 1915–17

For the next three years trench warfare predominated on the eastern and the western fronts. In the east, however, there was room for manoeuvre and the lines oscillated over considerable distances, whereas in the west only frontal assault was possible and advances costing tens of thousands of lives were to be measured in hundreds of metres. The Germans were for the most part content to hold a defensive position on French and Belgian territory. In April 1915 their attack on the British salient east of Ypres was simply an experiment in the use of poison gas, since Falkenhayn was already committed to a major offensive on his eastern front in that year. Even so, the second battle of Ypres was sufficiently fierce for the total casualties on both sides to amount to more than a hundred thousand, and enabled the Germans to flatten out most of the salient, thereby gaining the high ground from which they were to observe the British positions outside Ypres for the next two-and-a-half years. Apart from this the only other major assault by the Germans in the west was the attempt to take Verdun between February and July 1916; the concentration of so much artillery on a narrow front made this a hellish struggle, as the Germans fought to gain the outlying forts and the French under General Pétain put up a resistance of extraordinary tenacity which cost them 315,000 casualties as against the Germans' 281,000.

The other major assaults on the western front in these years were launched by the French and the British, and with minor variations there is an appalling similarity about them all. For the attackers it meant an immense artillery bombardment which was supposed to shatter the opposing artillery and machine-gun posts, break a gap through the barbed wire entanglements, and cow the enemy manning the opposite trenches. Under such conditions no surprise was possible; the preliminary bombardment and the cutting of the gaps in the wire made the precise point of the intended attack all too obvious, and when the extended lines of infantry climbed out of their trenches, weighed down with every form of weapon and equipment, and plodded, very often knee deep in mud, towards their objective, they were simply mown down by the enemy machine-gun posts in concrete pill-boxes which had usually survived the bombardment.

In 1915 Joffre attempted to break in on either side of the German bulge—from Champagne in the south and Artois in the north—and by the end of the summer the French had lost 190,000, the Germans 178,000, and the British 60,000 after being committed at Festubert in May and at Loos in September. In 1916, when Sir Douglas Haig had taken over from Sir John French and Pétain was badly in need of relief at Verdun, an assault along the line of the Somme by fourteen British divisions and five French on 1 July resulted in the most appalling slaughter, in which the British lost in a single day over 57,000 men, including 19,000 dead—the flower of a generation that had volunteered in the early months of the war—and even by the middle of November the greatest advance was no more than eight kilometres on a front of thirty-two kilometres.

There was worse to follow in 1917. In April General Nivelle, who had now replaced Joffre, launched a great offensive in the region of Reims, hoping for a quick breakthrough northwards. He was to be assisted by a British attack east from Arras during which the Canadians captured Vimy Ridge. The French army fought hard and effectively, but no breakthrough was achieved and the loss of 187,000 men, coupled with the mistrust of the French politicians, resulted in Nivelle's dismissal. Pétain now took over, while Foch became Chief of the General Staff. The collapse of the Nivelle offensive had given Haig his chance to press for his own scheme of a British assault east of Ypres aiming at a breakthrough north-east to Ostend and Zeebrugge, and between 1 July and 10 November the British forces edged their way forward a distance of eight kilometres along the ridge that commanded their positions outside Ypres; the weather always broke for each attack, and the low-lying Flanders soil, soaked with rain and pulverized by millions of shells, became a quagmire in which, during the last stages of the advance on Passchendaele, movement was almost impossible without duckboards. Men actually drowned in the mud and the total cost of the advance, all of which was lost the following spring, was 240,000 men according to Haig's supporters, 400,000 according to his critics.

The real wonder of the first World War is that men could stand so much. It is true that after the Nivelle offensive the French army was partially incapacitated by a mutiny which Pétain had rapidly to stamp out—a period of weakness which Haig was able to use as an added justification for the continuation of the third battle of Ypres—but in the main men continued to walk forward to certain death throughout this terrible deadlock. The debate over the generalship on the western front has raged ever since. The principal defence of the generals has been that since the line was continuous, no other form of attack was possible, and that since the German positions were of such strength and depth, a breakthrough soon became impossible and the only aim left was to kill as many of the enemy as possible in a war of attrition. Within these limits it has been suggested that they developed new tactical methods from experience of the enemy, and with the invention of the tank introduced a totally new feature of modern war. Yet when all this is allowed, the great storm of criticism that broke upon the generals in the inter-war years, when the ex-servicemen were free to speak their minds, remains essentially unanswered. A war of attrition on such a scale was no less than an abandonment of military art, a senseless massacre in which men continued to be sent forward to their deaths in thousands long after it was clear that the offensive had failed. Indeed, towards the end of 1917 Lloyd George was holding reserves in England for fear that Haig would fling them away in one more blood bath. And whatever the difficulties of the situation may have been, there was little excuse for the gulf that existed between the soldiers in the trenches and the General Staff launching their attacks from their desks. 'Did we really send men to fight in that?' cried one general who first saw the swamp at Passchendaele the day after the battle had ended. And he burst into tears.

In fact, the general's defence lends force to a second school of thought that Great Britain as a maritime power should never have allowed her armies to become sucked into the Flanders mud simply to form part of the French defence, and that she should have retained mobility for her forces by mounting a series of amphibious operations. Before 1914 there had been little thought along these lines; the military conversations with the French after Algeciras had been purely concerned with shipping the expeditionary force to France, and although the French, as early as 1906, had agreed that the British should command at sea, a naval Staff was not created at the Admiralty until Winston Churchill had become First Lord. In any case, the initial German attack and the continuing threat to Paris robbed the British of any chance to take the initiative in combined operations, binding them increasingly to the side of their French allies, who naturally saw the presence of German armies on their soil in a more simple light.

There was only one serious strategic attempt made by the British to open up a new flank—the Gallipoli expedition of 1915 inspired primarily by Winston Churchill—and this failed largely through the constant demand for troops on the western front. The object of the attack was grandiose; Turkey was to be knocked out of the war; with the opening of the Straits more direct contact with Russia would be established, and Bulgaria, still hanging back from commitment in a wavering neutrality, would probably join the Allies. The method, however, was unfortunate in that it envisaged an attempt by a naval force to penetrate the narrow mine-strewn waters of the Dardanelles unsupported by military forces, and to cross the Sea of Marmora to Constantinople whose bombardment was to bring about the collapse of the Turkish government. When this attempt failed on 18 March, a military force was landed a month later on the Gallipoli peninsula, but the loss of surprise and the fanatical defence by the Turkish army, recently reorganized by the German military mission under Liman von Sanders, made it impossible to advance and all forces were withdrawn at the end of the year. It had been a daring and imaginative campaign and, but for certain errors in command, might have succeeded; as it was, 500,000 Allied forces had been involved, of whom half had become casualties—all apparently to no purpose—and for many years afterwards the Gallipoli expedition was to give a bad name to those who had been associated with the planning of it.

On the eastern front (see map, p. 331) the struggle remained for some time indecisive, but never so static as in the west. In 1915, while Joffre battered unavailingly against the bulge in the west, Falkenhayn was forced to turn to the aid of the Austrians. In May Mackensen, on a plan suggested by Conrad von Hötzendorff, broke through the Russian line at Gorlice in Galicia, taking over 100,000 prisoners, and there developed a stupendous advance all along the front. On 5 August Warsaw fell to the Central Powers, much of Lithuania was taken and by December the line ran from Riga due south to the Carpathians—an advance of 300 miles in eight months with the capture of 300,000 prisoners and more than 3,000 guns.

Nor was this the only achievement of the Central Powers on the eastern front that year. Both sides had been hoping to win over Bulgaria; the Entente Powers had offered her Macedonia, but the Central Powers were prepared to raise the bid with Greek and Rumanian territory as well, and in September King Ferdinand, drawing his own conclusions from a comparison of the success of the eastern offensive with the deadlock in Gallipoli, threw in his lot with the Central Powers. The principal significance of his decision was that in the second week of October German and Austrian forces were able to invade Serbia from Bulgarian territory in the east as well as from across the Danube in the north, and despite skilful manoeuvring Putnik, the Serbian Commander-in-Chief, was inevitably forced to retreat. The Allies sent one British and one French division to Salonica from the Gallipoli force, but the difficulty of the terrain and the equivocal attitude of Greece, whose King Constantine was pro-German, made it unlikely that they would be able to do much to assist the Serbs, who eventually made their escape to the coast of Albania where Allied ships conveyed them to Corfu.

The Entente Powers thus had no military success in 1915 with which they could match these achievements of their opponents, but in the diplomatic field they did at least gain Italy. As over their ultimately unsuccessful negotiations with Bulgaria, the problem for the Entente statesmen was the incompatibility of Serbian and Italian aims. The Russian minister Sazanov's earlier offer of Macedonia to Bulgaria was bound to mean heavy compensation for Serbia on the Adriatic coast and that in turn clashed with the aims of the Italians, who were making control of the eastern coast of the Adriatic the price of their alliance. Eventually, however, Sazanov demanded no more than southern Dalmatia for Serbia. Fortunately for the Entente Powers all this took place before the battle of Gorlice had broken the Russian front; thus the Italian government was still in a hurry to join in the war, in case it should end before they had established a claim to a share of the spoil. The treaty that was finally signed in April 1915 promised them Trieste, the Istrian peninsula and northern Dalmatia, as well as more hypothetical regions in Asia Minor and among the German colonies in Africa. On 23 May Italy declared war on Austria-Hungary and the Italian army embarked upon a long unsuccessful assault on the Austrian positions in the mountainous region to the east of the Venetian plateau.

In 1916 there was another spectacular swing in the fortunes of the military. In March a Russian attack in the north, made in response to an appeal by the French, now hard pressed at Verdun, was a disastrous failure causing them 110,000 casualties. In May it was the Italians who appealed for help when they were pushed back by the Austrians, and on 4 June General Brusilov, commanding the south-western sector, launched a great offensive before which the Austrian Fourth and Seventh Armies began to break up. Other Russian generals to the north were unable to support him, but Brusilov pushed on magnificently on his own for 150 miles as he thrust into the Bukovina and by October he had captured 400,000 prisoners and some 500 guns. This was a highly significant achievement, for the Germans had to rush forces from the western front and the Austrians halted their offensive against the Italians.

Yet even this good news for the Entente Powers was to be clouded over by another disastrous development. In October 1914 Rumania, in return for the promise of gaining Transylvania from Hungary after the war, had come to an agreement with Russia whereby she would observe benevolent neutrality. The effect of the Brusilov offensive, however, was to fire her ambition still further, and in August 1916 she signed a treaty with Russia and France which gave her the Bukovina and the Banat as well as Transylvania, on the understanding that the Allies would keep the Bulgarian army engaged—the British and French from Salonica, the Russians through the Dobruja—so that the Rumanians would be free to concentrate on invading Transylvania. In fact, they had left it too late, for the full strength of the Brusilov offensive was by now almost spent. In September a force of Germans, Bulgarians, and Turks under Mackensen thrust north into the Dobruja, and the Rumanian army itself which had triumphantly invaded Transylvania was flung back by German and Austrian divisions under Falkenhayn, who had just been replaced as Chief of the General Staff by Hindenburg. By the end of the year the Rumanians had lost over 300,000 men—half of them prisoners—and retained no more of their country than the northern province of Moldavia.

The Entente Powers had certainly been unfortunate in their satellites—Serbia overrun in 1915, Rumania virtually knocked out in 1916, Italy clearly in danger of becoming a liability—and now in 1917, the year of the Nivelle offensive and the third battle of Ypres in the west, Russia herself was to succumb to revolution and defeat. The first revolution in March brought about the abdication of the Tsar, but not Russia's immediate withdrawal from the war (see p. 322). A July offensive under Brusilov, in which the Rumanians joined, met with some initial success, but by the beginning of August the Germans were beginning to counter-attack effectively and even before the revolution of the Bolsheviks in November paralyzed any further war effort, it was clear that the Russian forces would be incapable of much more. And with this realization there came the news of a great Italian rout at Caporetto on 24 October, when the Austrians, strengthened with German reinforcements, broke through and put the Italians into a flight which could only be checked at the Piave river.

The war at sea in these years was less spectacular than the land battles, yet highly significant for the combatants. It demonstrated in particular the ability of the British navy to maintain an effective blockade of the Central Powers, at the same time keeping open the sea lanes through which the newly devised convoys of merchant shipping were able to pass despite the ferocious German submarine campaign. The one major action between the enemy fleets took place on 31 May 1916—the battle of Jutland—when the German High Seas Fleet under von Scheer tried to lure Jellicoe's battleships into torpedo range and then returned to port—after which the caution of both admirals made any further serious encounter unlikely.

In the Near and Middle East the Allied forces met with gradual success against the Turks. The British advance on Baghdad in 1915 was unsuccessful and ended in the recapture of Kut el Amara by the Turks in April 1916. In June, however, a revolt of the Arabs against their Turkish overlords clearly offered a great opportunity which was seized by a young peace-time archaeologist, Colonel T. E. Lawrence, one of the very few figures in this war to fire the popular imagination. In March 1917 Baghdad was occupied by the British. In Palestine General Allenby finally broke through the defences of Beersheba and Gaza and on 9 December took Jerusalem. To the pious and the romantic this might seem to lend an air of crusade to the efforts of the Allies; it did not disguise the fact that by the end of 1917 the Allied cause was still not in particularly good shape.

3. The climax of the war 1917–18

Four principal factors combined to bring the war to a climax in 1918. First, the entry of the United States in April 1917 began to bring about an appreciable increase of fresh troops on the western front. Second, the Bolshevik revolution in Russia in November 1917 was followed in March 1918 by the Treaty of Brest Litovsk, whereby the new Russian government conceded complete victory to the Central Powers. Third, this success on the eastern front enabled Germany to swing all her forces into a great western offensive in March 1918. Fourth, when this offensive had spent itself by the middle of the summer, the Allied armies, now greatly reinforced, were able to take advantage of the loosening of the whole front, and in August, after the assault had been contained, began to drive the Germans back in a retreat that ended with the armistice in November.

The Germans really had only themselves to blame for the entry of the United States into the war. It is true that American objections to the thought of fighting on the side of Russian autocracy were ended by the outbreak of the March revolution, but this in itself would not have drawn the United States in, since anti-interventionist feeling was strong and President Wilson had been re-elected to a second term of office in 1916 on the understanding that his government would continue to follow a policy of neutrality. Two events at the beginning of 1917 brought about the rapid reversal of this attitude. In January the German Foreign Minister, Zimmermann, dispatched a telegram in code to the German minister in Mexico City in which he described his plans for stimulating a Mexican invasion across the Rio Grande in the event of the United States entering the war; this message was intercepted by the British, decoded, and after being passed on to Washington, actually appeared in the American press. Then on 1 February the German government, after having given due warning, embarked upon an unrestricted submarine campaign in which their U-boats were prepared to sink the merchant ships of any country which approached the shores of the western Allies. The Germans had previously been cautious over offending American opinion—particularly after American lives had been lost on board the British liner *Lusitania* sunk in the Atlantic in 1915—and until now the Americans had been more irritated by the inconvenience caused to their shipping by the British search for contraband in the imposition of the Allied blockade. The ferocity of the new German campaign, however, involving the sinking of 600,000 tonnes in March alone, very rapidly swung American opinion round to accepting a decision that Wilson knew was inevitable, and on 2 April 1917 the United States formally declared war on Germany.

If Great Britain and France had gained an ally in the west, it was nevertheless some time before her contribution could be effective and meanwhile they were to lose their principal ally in the east. The Bolshevik party, which seized power in St Petersburg in November 1917 (see p. 328), had sworn to take Russia out of the war. 'This government', announced Lenin, 'solemnly declares its resolution to conclude at once a peace ... equally just to all nations and nationalities without exception.' By the second week of December the Bolsheviks were already in negotiation with the Germans and Austrians at Brest Litovsk and after some delay due to the harshness of the demands made by the Central Powers peace was formally signed on 3 March 1918. Thus Russia, whose support of Serbia in 1914 had brought France and then Great Britain into this appalling struggle, passed out of the war. Still, until this moment she had certainly been a good ally. Her threat to Germany's eastern frontier had helped to save France in 1914 and in the following years her millions of peasant soldiery had held down as many enemy divisions as the French, British, and Belgian forces were containing in the west.

For Ludendorff this cessation of hostilities in the east released a vast number of troops whom the German railway system could now switch to the west for an all-out offensive before the Allies had been too strongly reinforced by the new American contingents. This was launched on 21 March against the British section of the line between Arras and St Quentin, and although the British had attempted to copy the extremely flexible German method of defence in depth, fog assisted the Germans in pressing through* and within a few days the situation seemed so desperate that a conference was summoned under the French President, Poincaré, at Doullens on 26 March. Pétain expressed a gloomy belief that the British would be broken 'in the open field'—an interesting anticipation of his pessimism in 1940 (see p. 435)—but on Haig's initiative Foch was given a unified command as *Général-en-Chef des Armées Alliées en France*.

By now Bapaume and Peronne had been given up, but although the Allies had suffered some 240,000 casualties, the Germans had already lost as many and the railway junction of Amiens had not yet been reached. Ludendorff turned next to the valley of the Lys south of Ypres and on 9 April a new thrust drove the line back as far as Armentières—an advance which imposed a withdrawal from the Passchendaele ridge whose capture had cost the British so many thousands of lives in 1917. By 11 April the situation had become so grim that Haig, a man to whom memorable phrases did not normally come easily, issued his famous order of the day: 'With our backs to the wall and believing in the Justice of our cause each one must fight on to the end.' This was, in fact, the last battle in the war for the Channel ports and by the end of April after the most furious fighting the Flanders line still held.

Ludendorff now turned to the south, and in May attacked between Soissons and Reims. By 3 June German forces had crossed the Marne and Paris lay only eighty-nine kilometres distant. Ludendorff's real aim was to draw off the Allied reserves southwards, so that he might then renew the Flanders attack, and in July he thrust forward once more on either side of Reims, but once again the French line, although pushed back, did not break. Furthermore, Ludendorff had struck so heavily in making this feint that he had to pause before turning to the Armentières front again; thus the

* In the west the Germans seem constantly to have had the advantage of the weather—as, for example, during the third battle of Ypres.

Allies gained the time to seize the initiative and to justify an Intelligence commentary of January 1918: 'The German accession of morale is not of a permanent character and is not likely to stand the strain of an unsuccessful attack with consequent losses. . . . If Germany attacks and fails, she will be ruined.'

Already in May, at the height of the German onslaught, Haig had given instructions for the preliminary study for an offensive in the area of Amiens, and on 8 August an assault whose preparation had been carefully kept secret was launched by the British Fourth and the French First Armies. It met with overwhelming success; on that one day—which Ludendorff described as 'the black day of the German army in the history of the war'—the Germans suffered some 26,000 casualties, and from this time on, as the French and the Americans joined in the attack to the south, the German line was constantly in retreat. 'We have nearly reached the limit of our powers of resistance,' said William II at a meeting with the military leaders on 11 August; 'the war must be ended.' The struggle was still to continue, however, with appallingly heavy casualties as the Allies continued to press the line back towards the frontier.

By the end of September Bulgaria had surrendered and Allenby, now north of Damascus, had routed the Turks, while the Italians having successfully resisted an Austrian offensive in June made a great thrust in October aimed at Vittorio Veneto. Meanwhile, negotiations with Germany had begun; Foch received the German delegates in his train in the forest of Compiègne and after a little argument the armistice was finally signed early on 11 November. At eleven o'clock that morning the fire of artillery and machine-guns gradually died away across the battlefields of western Europe. In four years the civilization of the nineteenth century had been blown to shreds; a whole generation of young men had been massacred in anonymous millions, and although the ordinary soldier on that November morning might listen in unbelieving relief to the first silence of peace, the British and the French now found themselves victorious after a struggle which had gone on too long for victory to have any sweetness.

Chapter 26
The Internal Consequences of War

1. The acceleration of collectivism

'Sein oder Nichtsein, das ist hier die Frage.'* Thus William II addressed the German nation in August 1914. The quotation may have a self-conscious exaggerated ring; yet it was not in itself inappropriate. For this was not simply the outbreak of a war with precise limited objectives—like most of those of the nineteenth century; it was nothing less than a crisis of national existence.

It was consequently hardly surprising that in such a war demands should accelerate the general tendency towards collectivism. On both sides it involved the granting of emergency powers to the governments, and in Germany and Austria-Hungary this greater authority was concentrated more and more in the hands of the army. By 1917 the German military chiefs could virtually make and break a Chancellor at will. In Vienna the *Reichsrat*, prorogued in March 1914, did not meet again until May 1917, and considerable administrative powers were given to the Habsburg military authorities in regions such as Bohemia and Moravia, even though they were a very great distance from the front. Among the western Allies parliamentary institutions remained actively critical. In France, after his assumption of power in November 1917, Georges Clemenceau wielded enormous power in the last desperate year of the war, but at least the politicians did not succumb to the generals, as they did in Germany, although the long feud between Lloyd George, who became British Prime Minister in 1916, and Field Marshal Haig illustrated the peculiar limitations that the circumstances of a major war imposed upon the civil authority.

On both sides there was an intensive organization of social and economic life. The Allied blockade, the German U-boat campaign, and all the requirements for maintaining vast armies in the field necessitated an extraordinary degree of State control of industry. In May 1915 Albert Thomas in France and Lloyd George at the Ministry of Munitions in Great Britain were put in charge of the supply

* 'To be, or not to be—that is the question.

of shells which were in such demand on the western front. In Germany Walter Rathenau was responsible for a vast mobilizing of German industry and labour to overcome with various forms of *ersatz* (substitute) material the deficiencies created by the blockade. In November 1916 all this activity was brought under the control of the *Kriegsamt*, a department of the Ministry of War, and in December a National Service Law made men between the ages of seventeen and sixty liable to be directed into the forces or the factories.

All these developments were the work of governments determined to employ every possible means in the struggle for victory, and in so far as they accustomed the individual to a further surrender of his freedom of action to the needs of the community, they were to be of lasting significance. The more dramatic aspects of the internal consequences of war, however, were to be seen towards the end, as the three great dynasties of Romanov, Habsburg, and Hohenzollern collapsed amid the ruin of the political and social framework of central and eastern Europe.

2. Two revolutions in Russia:
March and November 1917

Twice during the recent past Russia's defeat in war had been followed by revolutionary domestic change. The tragedy of these reforms was that, although remarkable in themselves at the time of their inauguration, they never developed sufficiently to create a basis for a new social stability. A rapidly rising population had undone much of the benefits of the emancipation of the serfs after the Crimean War and there had not yet been time for the more recent land reforms of Stolypin (see p. 270) to give the peasantry a vested interest in the existing structure of government and society. Similarly, the national *Duma*, granted by the Tsar after Russia's defeat by Japan and the revolution of 1905, had been carefully relegated to acting in an advisory capacity and there had been little opportunity for middle-class liberals to gain experience in government.

The royal couple, Nicholas and Alexandra, presented one more unfortunate example of a devoted husband married to a narrow-minded dominating woman whose determination that he should be a king was to bring disaster to them both. In September 1915 Nicholas took over as Commander-in-Chief and during his absence at his headquarters at Mogilev Alexandra was really able to enjoy power herself in Petrograd, the new name for St Petersburg since the beginning of the war. The *Duma*, in which a Progressive bloc of Octobrists and Kadets had appealed in vain for constitutional reform, was prorogued. Governmental decisions came increasingly under the influence of an unsavoury monk, Rasputin, who managed to combine a reputation of mystical piety with a life of utter immorality and who had convinced Alexandra that he could exercise some guardian power over her son Alexis when his life was endangered by haemophilia. In February 1916 Rasputin virtually nominated his own Prime Minister, Stürmer, who also took over the Ministry of Foreign Affairs on Sazanov's dismissal in the following July.

Eventually, when there were distinct signs of unrest among the soldiers and the workers, the *Duma* was recalled in November; here the liberals denounced the utter inadequacy of the government, but it was the court aristocracy who took the most dramatic step with their assassination of Rasputin in December. This was an appropriately dramatic episode, yet typically inconclusive. Rasputin was poisoned, then shot, and his body finally thrust beneath the ice of the Neva, but although there were rumours of an impending palace revolution, nothing ever happened and within a couple of months the power of taking the initiative had passed to forces outside the palace.

Already in January and February 1916 there had been working-class unrest which had led to widespread strikes. This does seem to have been a positive attempt at subversion and owed something to the recent supply of funds from Germany. The outbreak in March 1917, however, appears much more haphazard, reminiscent of the revolution of 1848, and the protracted debate over its origins has not yet identified any positive leadership.

On 8 March* there was rioting at the bakers' shops in Petrograd and later, when the police opened fire on the crowds, this was followed by a general strike. At first it seemed that the disturbance could be contained and there was little sense of alarm among the authorities until 12 March when the regiments, on which they relied, began to mutiny. That afternoon the *Duma*, which had recently reassembled, was prorogued once more, but decided to ignore this and instead set up a provisional committee representing all parties; at the same time a Soviet of factory workers was being formed in another part of the same building. By the evening the government's loss of control was so plain that the Grand Duke Cyril sent a telephone message to the *Duma*'s provincial committee suggesting that they should assume power. Accordingly, by 14 March the committee had established a new government under Prince Lvov and on the following day Tsar Nicholas II agreed to abdicate.

Naturally, this extraordinarily rapid sequence of events has been the subject of considerable analysis. For a long time the most popu-

---

* On 23 February, according to the Russian calendar, which was still based on the Julian or Old Style, by now thirteen days behind the rest of Europe. After their accession to power the Bolsheviks modernized the Russian system in February 1918.

lar explanation assumed that such a collapse was largely inevitable. It depicted a country overwhelmed by a great sense of war weariness, a defeated army reduced to a point of despair because Russian industry had been unable to provide arms and ammunition, and appalling food shortages in the cities resulting from the lack of agricultural labour after peasants had been conscripted into the army.

In fact, almost all these views are now considered incorrect. In 1917 there was still a great determination to win the war and the criticism of Tsar Nicholas had mostly questioned his competence and his zeal. During the riots in Petrograd banners demanding an end to the war had brought great protests from the crowd and even a year later, after Lenin had seized power, the peace terms which he accepted at Brest Litovsk in March 1918 created grave political danger for him. Russian industry may still have been far less developed than that of most western Powers, but there had been an astonishing transformation during the last decades of the nineteenth century (see p. 222) and although administrative confusion had at first jeopardized the supply of rifles and equipment in the army, this had eventually been resolved and by September 1916 Russia was producing four and a half million shells a month. The Russian army itself had mobilized far more quickly in 1914 than the Germans had anticipated; there had been the remarkable Brusilov offensive (see p. 316) in 1916, and although the Germans had pushed back on to Russian soil, the line was still intact by the beginning of 1917. The morale of Russian troops at the front does not yet seem to have been affected, and the mutinies in Petrograd had merely been a local reaction on the part of the motley collection of garrison troops who had sickened of shooting civilians and who, once they had mutinied, could not retreat from a revolutionary course of action.

Certainly food shortages played a large part in the initial outbreak, but this was not due to any failure in agricultural output, since the wartime harvests had been better than those before 1914. The main difficulty was economic, a mounting inflation which resulted from the government's printing of paper money to finance the war, and which had brought the value of the rouble to a quarter of what it had been in 1914. This not merely made food expensive; it affected the peasantry who had to pay higher prices for seed and fodder, but who did not make an equivalent gain from the sale of their corn, since this was largely taken by middlemen. As a consequence, many of the peasantry had reverted to subsistence farming, consuming the harvest themselves or feeding it to their cattle.

Food shortages in Petrograd, however, are hardly a convincing explanation for the fall of the monarchy within a week of the outbreak. This merely created the background against which other factors came into play. First, the liberal politicians had by now lost all faith in the Tsar; in 1915 they had appealed in vain for the establishing of constitutional government; in 1916 there had been a couple of plots to replace him, and another in 1917 was only forestalled by the events in Petrograd, when on 12 March the politicians decided to ignore the order for the proroguing of the *Duma*. Second, the collaboration of the railwaymen's trade union was a vital element, since they controlled the telegraph system and the movement of troops by train; they were even able to obstruct the Tsar when he attempted to return to Petrograd on 13 March and eventually caused him to be shunted into a station at Pskof. Third, the generals, particularly General Ruzsky, the commander of the northern armies, whose headquarters was at Pskof, had also lost faith in the Tsar and a telephone conversation between him and the president of the *Duma* persuaded Ruzsky that if the monarchy was to be saved, then Nicholas must abdicate. The fourth factor was Nicholas himself, locked away in a fatalistic dream of a God-given autocracy, and deciding in the end that if the autocracy could not survive, he would prefer to abdicate. He did this in favour of his brother, Grand Duke Michael, but on the next day Michael declared that he could accept nothing until a Constituent Assembly had expressed its will. In this way the reign of Nicholas II came to an end in a railway station in Pskof, although it does not seem that either the *Duma* or the generals had originally intended that this should also mean the extinction of the monarchy itself.

The form of government which emerged from this turmoil rested on a strange kind of dualism. On one side of the Tauride palace in Petrograd the Provisional government set up by the *Duma* deputies consisted of aristocrats and liberal bourgeois, while on the other side the Petrograd Soviet and then later a central executive committee of workers' and soldiers' Soviets controlled the main means of supply and communication. For the moment neither body felt that it could dispense with the other and until 5 May the central executive committee cooperated with the provisional government and, after that, actively participated in a series of coalitions.

The only uncompromising opponents of the new government were the Bolsheviks. These, however, only numbered some 26,000 and at the time of the outbreak the majority of the leaders had been far from Petrograd, where the young Molotov, a member of the Russian bureau of the central committee, had simply issued a party manifesto and resumed the publication of the Bolshevik newspaper *Pravda*. It was not until the end of March that Stalin and Kamenev returned from Siberia, not until May that Trotsky arrived from the United States. The most spectacular event of all was the journey of Lenin in April with a small party of Bolsheviks including Zinoviev, Radek, and Lunacharsky from neutral Switzerland across Germany and thence by ship to Sweden. The motive of the German government in allowing this was simple, since the Bolsheviks were sworn to take Russia out of the war. 'Since we are interested that influence of radical wing gains the upper hand in Russia,' commented the Foreign Minister, Zimmermann, 'I consider travel permission through Germany perhaps appropriate.' And so this group of Russian revolutionaries was hurriedly transported across Germany in two sealed railway carriages like dangerous germs to be injected into the body politic of the enemy, although it is doubtful whether even the Germans imagined that they would so quickly take effect.

Lenin himself wasted no time. At the Finland station at Petrograd he was met by members of the Bolshevik party as well as the President of the Soviet and on the following day proclaimed the 'April theses'—'not a parliamentary republic—return to that from the Soviet of Workers' deputies would be a step backward—but a republic of Soviets of Workers, Poor Peasants and Peasants' Deputies throughout the country, growing from below upwards.' Thus Lenin totally rejected any working relationship with the *Duma* government, advocating instead the doctrine of the uninterrupted revolution which he had developed after the split with the Mensheviks in 1903 (see p. 250).

As with the fall of the monarchy, it is very easy after the event to regard the Bolshevik seizure of power in November as inevitable. Yet in the spring of 1917 the prospects of the provisional government were by no means hopeless. They had responded almost at once to the various telegrams and petitions with which they had been deluged. Civil liberty was proclaimed for all; provincial governors were removed, the summoning of a Constituent Assembly was announced and a number of committees were created for the collection of information on which land reform could be based. And in the first All-Russian Congress of Soviets, which met in Petrograd in June, 105 Bolsheviks were still greatly outnumbered by 248 Mensheviks and 285 Social Revolutionaries, both of whom were represented in the coalition government.

The fundamental factor which wrecked the hopes of the non-Bolshevik groups was the continuation of the war. This was virtually inescapable if the new régime was to gain recognition from the western Allies, and in any case the foreign minister Milyukov had no wish to lose the possession of the Straits and Constantinople promised to Russia in a secret treaty in 1915. The problem was that the war distracted the government from all its immediate domestic concerns. The committee set up to devise land reforms failed to arrive at any concrete conclusion. The election of the Constituent Assembly was constantly postponed. Inflation accelerated and by November 1917 the rouble was worth a tenth of what it had been in 1914. With this came wage demands and strikes, more aggressive activity by trade unions and factory committees, and growing hunger in the cities as the peasantry ceased to deliver food to them. In its efforts to retain control the government attempted to hold wages down and by the end of the summer was sending out Cossacks on punitive raids against peasantry who, tiring of waiting for land reform, were taking Lenin's advice and beginning to help themselves to the land-owners' estates.

The consequent unpopularity of the government naturally suited Lenin well, since it also helped to discredit the Socialist groups who were participating in the coalitions. The numbers of Bolsheviks had grown to about 200,000 by August; money from Germany was financing over 40 Bolshevik newspapers and at the same time as he was building up his own force of Red Guards, Bolshevik propaganda advocating peace and the distribution of land to the peasantry was undermining the morale of the army at the front and may have played some part in the immediate failure of a new offensive in July.

The increasingly precarious position of the government was soon to be emphasized by two successive crises. On 16 July an abortive rising of workers and sailors in Petrograd swung the government back towards dependence on right wing elements. Order was restored after forces had been recalled from the front, but the occasion had been serious enough to bring about the fall of Prince Lvov's administration. His place as premier was taken by Alexander Kerensky, a Social Revolutionary, who at the beginning of the revolution was both a member of the *Duma* and Vice-President of the Petrograd Soviet and who had been appointed Minister of Justice and later Minister of War in the provisional government. Although it seems that the Bolshevik leaders may not have been responsible for the July rising, Kerensky was determined to take no chances. *Pravda* was banned, Trotsky and others were arrested and Lenin went into hiding in Finland.

Yet no sooner had Kerensky shown that he intended to stand firm against the Bolsheviks than he was confronted with the threat of a counter-revolutionary action, when, after the fall of Riga to the Germans on 3 September, the Russian Commander-in-Chief, General Kornilov, decided to attempt a march on Petrograd. To meet the threat Kerensky had to fall back on the Bolsheviks; their Red Guards were now mobilized and their political agitation had the most decisive effect on Kornilov's troops, who melted away. Kornilov himself was placed under arrest.

Kerensky continued to rule, yet the two incidents of July and September had revealed the utter weakness of his position. To check the forces of the extreme left he had to rely upon the right, while to resist the attempts at counter-revolution he was driven back to dependence upon the Bolsheviks. At the same time the careful work of preparation carried on by the Bolsheviks since the outbreak in March was greatly assisted by the disastrous continuation of the war and Kornilov's unsuccessful *coup*. By the middle of September they had a majority in the Moscow Soviet, while Trotsky, now released from prison on bail, had been elected President of the Petrograd Soviet.

To Lenin it seemed clear that the moment to act had come. He spurned the idea put forward by Zinoviev and Kamenev that the central committee of the Bolshevik party should wait for the long promised Constituent Assembly, which by now was almost certain to be a fairly radical body. Instead, he wished the party to strike immediately. This time, unlike most revolutions of the previous hundred years, the rising was not simply a spontaneous outbreak without leadership. It was a carefully planned *coup* timed by Lenin to coincide with the greatest likelihood of acquiescence on the part of the populace. It could be argued that such a *coup* would be premature according to the Marxist philosophy, but Lenin insisted that this would not matter, provided that it was accompanied by similar risings in other parts of Europe, which he believed were imminent. In fact, the detailed timing was eventually in accordance with Trotsky's proposal that it should come on the eve of the second All-Russian Congress of Soviets due to meet on 7 November.

The operation was organized by Trotsky from the Smolny Institute, the headquarters of the Bolshevik party, and carried out by the Red Guards and regular regiments who on the night of 6 November rapidly occupied strategic points in Petrograd. Lenin emerged from hiding to find the battle virtually won, and on the morning of 7 November Kerensky fled from the city. In the same month as the British were dying in their thousands to gain the swamp and ruins of Passchendaele, the Bolsheviks had captured control of the government of Russia at the cost of a handful of casualties.

That evening the Congress of Soviets met in the hall of the Institute. The Winter Palace was still holding out and the delegates could hear the guns of the cruiser *Aurora* and of the fortress of Peter and Paul bombarding it—with blanks—as the Bolshevik leaders announced what they had accomplished. With a majority of almost two-thirds they had little to fear from this gathering. Lenin declared that peace would be negotiated with the Central Powers at once and that 'landlord property is abolished forthwith without compensation'. A Council of People's Commissars was set up on the next day including Lenin at the head, Trotsky as Commissar for Foreign Affairs and Stalin as Commissar for Nationalities. Thus, the Bolsheviks had little intention of sharing the power that they had won; they would not form a coalition with Mensheviks and Social Revolutionaries, who accordingly walked out of the Congress. 'You are bankrupt,' cried Trotsky after them; 'you have played out your role. Go where you belong: to the dust heap of history.' Still less did the

Bolsheviks mean to surrender to the democratically elected Constituent Assembly, which met at last on 18 January 1918. When it became clear that the Bolshevik party was in a minority, a sailor commanding the military guard informed the president that he had been told to close the meeting 'because the guard is tired'. The instructions actually came from Lenin and the Constituent Assembly did not meet again.

There is a tendency for left-wing historians to use such phrases as 'the logic of history' when speaking of Lenin's extraordinary success in 1917. In fact, history is profoundly illogical and the victory of the Bolsheviks is more easily explained in simple practical terms. The absence of a widespread liberal bourgeois class with some experience of government made a left-wing success more likely in Russia than elsewhere, once the circumstances of March 1917 had shattered the royal autocracy. And among the left wing it was Lenin's disciplined group who could act with confidence at a time when there was a power vacuum at the heart of the government of Russia. There was, however, a price to be paid, if so small a group was to maintain its position. 'This intricate task cannot be solved by placing above the proletariat a few well-picked people,' Trotsky had written in 1904, '... or one person invested with power to liquidate or degrade.' Yet by 1917 Trotsky was a Bolshevik and the dictatorship of the party was soon to become consolidated under the stress of civil war.

The Bolsheviks were now free to open their attack on capitalism with a doctrinaire programme that was pushed to impracticable extremes. Banks were abolished; all forms of private trading were prohibited, and the management of factories was handed over to councils of workers. But the most startling aspect of their rule was their attitude towards the non-Russian nationalities to whom they intended to give independence. Their hope was that these emancipated peoples would then carry out their own Socialist revolutions and a new link be established with Russia through a community of political outlook. In fact, they were to be disappointed in this, owing partly to the resistance of local anti-Bolshevik interests, and partly to the presence of the German army to whom they had to surrender enormous areas of the Russian western borderland.

In Finland Stalin announced the attitude of the new Russian government at a Finnish Social Democrat congress held at Helsinki some three weeks after the November revolution, and on 6 December 1917, a newly elected Parliament took him at his word by declaring Finnish independence, which was accepted by the Russian Bolsheviks early in 1918. The real struggle was still to come. Would this new republic under the presidency of P. E. Svinhufvud survive in the face of the efforts of Finnish Bolsheviks supported by the Russian government from across the frontier? Towards the end of January 1918 Bolshevik groups had gained control of Helsinki, and for the next five weeks the most that the right-wing forces could do under General Mannerheim, who had recently returned from the Rumanian front, was to consolidate their position in the western province of Ostrobothnia. In March, however, they began to advance; at the same time a German Baltic Division under General von der Goltz landed at Hanko in the extreme south-west of Finland and moved along the coast towards Helsinki, and by the middle of May the Bolshevik threat to the new republic of Finland had been ended.

It was naturally the terms of the peace with Germany that involved Russia in the most striking concessions of territory. Before the end of the year the Bolsheviks had opened negotiations with the Germans and in the bleak fortress of Brest Litovsk Trotsky, representing the new masters of Russia, faced the representatives of the old order in central Europe—Prince Leopold of Bavaria, the Commander-in-Chief, General Hoffmann, his Chief of Staff, Kühlmann and Count Czernin, the German and Austrian Foreign Ministers. The terms demanded were so heavy that not even Trotsky as a Bolshevik sworn to make peace could accept them, and he left the conference with the meaningless formula 'no peace, no war'. The Germans simply continued their advance unopposed—'the most comic war I have ever experienced', wrote Hoffmann—and on 19 February, after an agonized debate in the Central Committee, the Russians decided to sue for peace.

The Germans could now put up their price, and the result was a *Diktat* more overwhelming than anything which the Allies in the west were to impose on Germany in just over a year's time. This was the high watermark of the dreams of the pan-Germans. Russia was to demobilize entirely, and in addition to the surrender of Poland, the Ukraine, and Courland which had been in the original terms, Estonia, Latvia,* and Finland were to be evacuated by Russian troops and Russia was to guarantee 'a speedy and orderly return' of eastern Anatolia to Turkey. To all this the Bolsheviks finally gave their consent and the Treaty of Brest Litovsk was signed on 3 March 1918. Before this the Germans had already been working to undermine the establishment of Bolshevik influence in the Ukraine. Here in 1917 a nationalist government had been set up under Hrushevsky, but as with Svinhufvud's government in Finland there was soon a serious clash with Bolshevik elements and the Central Powers were quick to seize their chance in February 1918. At the same time as the Bolsheviks were setting up a Ukrainian Soviet government, national delegates were signing a separate peace treaty

* By the supplementary treaty of 27 August Russia agreed to relinquish Estonia and Latvia entirely.

THE TREATY OF BREST LITOVSK, MARCH 1918

at Brest Litovsk, and within a few weeks German forces had overrun the Ukraine and a pro-German Ukrainian government had been established under the Hetman Skoropadsky.

The German victory in the east was now rounded off with a peace treaty with Rumania. The eastern slopes of the Transylvanian mountains were to be given to Hungary, the Dobruja to Bulgaria, Bessarabia to Russia. Thus Rumania was deprived of the Black Sea coast and Germany's lease of her oil wells for ninety years pointed to the confidence with which the Central Powers could now turn to the great western offensive of 1918.

For the Bolsheviks, however, peace with Germany only rid them of one of their opponents. General Kornilov had managed to escape from arrest and now moved to the south of Russia where he took command of a White Russian (i.e. anti-Bolshevik) force, until he was killed in action and General Denikin took over. Farther east, Social Revolutionary members of the Constituent Assembly, indignant at their dismissal by the Bolsheviks, organized themselves under Chernov on the lower Volga. They had a considerable hold also on Siberia and Vladivostok, while in Manchuria General Horvat had established a conservative government. In the summer of 1918 the Allies, highly dubious of Bolshevism, landed a combined military force at Murmansk and authorized Admiral Kolchak to coordinate the various forces of resistance in Siberia. The most remarkable feature of the whole scene was the Czech army corps organized by Professor Masaryk from the prisoner-of-war camps in Russia and now on its way to France via Vladivostok (see p. 334). Strung out across Siberia they held much of the Trans-Siberian railway and they were so effective in their attacks that in July 1918 Ekaterinburg seemed likely to fall to them. Here the Tsar and his family were interned and the Bolsheviks afterwards claimed that they had no time to organize a swift evacuation; on the other hand, they dare not let their opponents rescue Nicholas, whose presence would rally many waverers to the side of the anti-Bolshevik forces. Thus the entire royal family was done to death in a cellar. Yet even without this rallying point the resistance to Bolshevism was to continue for long and it was ironical that the Bolsheviks who had claimed to bring an end to war should continue to be deeply engaged in a ferocious struggle for survival long after the ceasefire had sounded in the west.

3. The last of the Habsburg Empire

In eastern Europe the beginning of the war appeared to suggest one more phase in the old struggle between German and Slav. This naturally raised the question of the dependability of the various nationalities under Habsburg rule, but although the Austrian army did not enjoy any great military triumphs—except for the rout of the Italians at Caporetto—there was little sign of any political disintegration during the first two-and-a-half years of the war.

The south Slavs within the Empire might certainly have represented a considerable danger on the Serbian front, but for the fact that the Croats had a considerable mistrust of the Serbs and disliked the Italians still more. What was even more striking was that the Poles, whose independence had been one of the great lost causes of nineteenth-century Europe, continued to support their existing political masters. Thus in Russian Poland a National Democrat party under Dmowski still looked towards St Petersburg in the hope of gaining local autonomy, while in Austrian Galicia Josef Pilsudski, who also stood for Polish independence, actually raised forces to fight on behalf of the Habsburgs. Not even when the Central Powers had overrun Warsaw and eastern Poland in the offensive of 1915 was this division healed. Only the promise of a united independent Poland would have won the Poles of Russian Poland over to the side of the Central Powers, and on this Germany and Austria-Hungary did not see entirely eye to eye. At first the Germans held back because they were still hoping for a separate peace with Russia, who would hardly be agreeable to such a territorial loss. There was, too, the question whether the new Poland would be orientated towards Germany or Austria-Hungary. The Habsburg proposal—sometimes known as the Austro-Polish solution—was to incorporate Galicia and Russian Poland in one political territory whose inhabitants would have their own parliament. This would, in fact, have amounted to a new form of 'trialism' within the Empire. It suited the German Austrians, who saw that the existence of a Polish parliament would draw off the Polish element in the *Reichsrat* and leave them in greater control in Vienna; it did not suit the Magyars, who saw it as a modification of their own special position within the Dual Monarchy. The German government, however, preferred a solution which would turn Poland rather more towards them, and since Austria's military dependence on Germany had soon become undeniable, a manifesto issued by the two Powers in November 1916 virtually established the German plan; a Polish Council of State included Pilsudski as head of the ministry of war, but real power lay with the German Governor-General in Warsaw.

The danger from the south Slavs and the Poles had been that they might turn to compatriots outside the Empire. The weakness of the Czechs was that they had no one to whom they might look across the frontiers, and since their territories lay much closer to the heart of the Habsburg dominions—unlike Galicia or Croatia—their only hope of obtaining independence lay in the total disintegration of the Empire. At first, the majority of Czech politicians did not regard this as remotely possible, since they anticipated either an Austrian victory or, at the most, a compromise peace; besides, among many of them there remained the old fear of 1848 that complete freedom from Habsburg rule would simply lay them open to German domination. Indeed, the German parties within the Empire—except for the Social Democrats—were already repeating by Easter 1915 their earlier proposals whereby Galicia and Dalmatia should be given up and the rest of Austria including the Czech territories became a unitary germanized State. Czech radicals, however, did not allow themselves to be restrained by these factors. Thomas Masaryk, a professor of philosophy at Prague University moved to Italy in December 1914, and nine months later Eduard Beneš, his former pupil, who had been placed under police surveillance, managed to leave the country on a forged passport. From now on, communication between the Czech exiles and their former colleagues at home was extremely fitful, but to radicals like Masaryk and Beneš it seemed essential that there should be spokesmen for the Czechs among the western Allies.

For the first two years of the war, however, nationalist aspirations seemed unlikely to hinder seriously the war effort of the multi-national Empire—the obverse of the failure of the international ideals of the Socialists to prevent the opening of hostilities in 1914. Thus the Emperor Francis Joseph, who died in November 1916 at the age of eighty-six, was at least spared the final disruption. He had come to the throne at a time when the Empire had seemed on the verge of collapse; his life ended with the incompatibilities of the Habsburg inheritance still unresolved, with the entire Continent drawn into an appalling war on account of them; and under his successor Karl, the nephew of Francis Ferdinand (see genealogical table, p. 484) the Empire was only to survive a further two years.

It was the news of the Russian revolution in March 1917 that awoke a fresh excitement among the Habsburg peoples. The *Reichsrat*, which the Emperor had reopened as a liberal gesture in May 1917, became the forum for renewed nationalist claims—Ruthenes demanding a Ukrainian state separate from the Polish territories, Slovenes demanding an autonomous state of Serbs, Croats, and Slovenes, Czechs demanding 'the transformation of the Habsburg monarchy into a federal state consisting of free and equal national states'. At the same time, outside the Empire, Masaryk had made contact with the provisional government in Russia and in May arrived in St Petersburg to organize the creation of a Czech army corps from among the Czech prisoners-of-war, of whom the Russians had taken some 210,000. In August Brusilov agreed to its formation, and as a result of Masaryk's visits to the camps about 39,000 volunteers were raised. The advent of the Bolsheviks to power, however, made it impossible for these troops to be used on an eastern front which had almost ceased to exist, and it was agreed that they should now proceed to France to continue the fight there. By March 1918 they were sufficiently organized to begin the long journey across Siberia to Vladivostok, which was the only possible route open to them, but by May they had come into conflict with local Russian Bolsheviks and before long Czech units had taken possession of much of the Trans-Siberian railway (see p. 332).

Meanwhile, the Central Powers' treaty with the Ukraine in February 1918 (see p. 330) had infuriated the Poles, since it was clear that they were being sacrificed to German interests. Kholm was surrendered to the Ukraine, Eastern Galicia and the Bukovina were to form a separate crownland with its own administration, Lithuania was to be recreated and the Prussian frontier to be extended farther east. To the Poles this was simply another partition; whole military units deserted to Russia and there seemed little likelihood of any further cooperation between the Poles and the Central Powers. Pilsudski himself had already been interned in July 1917 for refusing an oath which would have made his troops part of the German forces.

Thus the various interests which had believed it best to acquiesce during the first two years of the war were everywhere becoming more restless, aggravated by the poor food situation due to the Allied blockade. Prisoners returning from Russia were infected with ideas of revolution, and in January 1918 there were mass strikes and a naval mutiny in the Adriatic. Furthermore, the Allies were by now beginning to see that they could make the same use of the discontent of the Habsburg peoples as the Germans had made of Lenin, with the added advantage that the nationalist leaders were middle-class men strongly antagonistic to Bolshevism. In April a congress of 'suppressed nationalities' was held at Rome; agreements between Italian and Yugoslav representatives were published; on 3 June the British, French, and Italian premiers at the Supreme War Council at Versailles issued a declaration that 'a united and independent Polish state with free access to the sea would be an essential condition of peace. On 29 June the French government accepted the Czechs' National Council as the 'first basis of the future government' and on 14 August the British recognized the Czechs as an Allied nation.

Thus, as the German army wore itself out in its last great offensive in France, the Allies had already committed themselves to policies which were bound to mean the break-up of the Habsburg dominions, and by the autumn the various peoples of the Empire were taking the law into their own hands. On 28 October the Czech National Council assumed powers of government in Prague; on 29 October the Slovaks declared their readiness to be part of a Czechoslovak state; on the same day in the south, Serbs, Croats, and Slovenes proclaimed their new state Yugoslavia. On 31 October the

Emperor Karl appointed by telephone Count Károlyi, a liberal aristocrat, as Prime Minister of Hungary and on 3 November Károlyi announced the complete independence of Hungary. And so, while the armies of the Allies were still many miles distant, the Habsburg Empire, rehabilitated at the Congress of Vienna in 1815, jarred yet not shattered by the emergence of Italy and Germany some fifty years later, finally fell to pieces at the end of a war which had destroyed so much else of Europe, and the last of the Emperors crossed the Swiss frontier by train into exile.

4. The German revolution 1918–19

As so often happens in war, the immediate circumstances which gave rise to the outbreak in 1914 were soon swallowed up by new issues which arose after hostilities had begun. It was not the fate of Serbia which caused the war to drag on for more than four murderous years; the major stumbling block to negotiation was the question of annexations consequent on the success enjoyed by the German armies during the opening months. This placed large areas of territory under German control and whereas the Entente Powers insisted on German withdrawal as an essential condition for any peace talks, many interests in Germany regarded such a withdrawal as unthinkable.

These early advances seemed to offer the fulfilment of the greatest hopes of pan-Germanism (see p. 241), a vast annexationist programme of expansion along the Baltic coast and into Belgium and north-eastern France, the creation of a system of client states stretching as far east as the Urals, and the development of a German Mittelafrica. It was not only the military who warmed to this radical transformation of frontiers. The kings of Bavaria, Württemberg and Saxony all imagined some splendid acquisition for their kingdoms. In May 1915 groups of industrialists petitioned the Chancellor with pan-German demands, and three months later a so-called petition of the intellectuals, including over 350 university professors, made an almost identical plea. The political parties varied a little. The Conservatives and the National Liberals were hotly in favour of annexation; as early as September 1914 Erzberger, the leader of the Centre, envisaged an almost totally pan-German programme, although by July 1917 he had swung round to demanding a negotiated peace. Even the Progressives were tempted by the thought of some form of *Grossdeutschland*. The Social Democrats became divided on the issue; one section of the party known as Majority Socialists had been prepared to support the government from the beginning and had voted war credits; as a consequence two other sections eventually broke away—the Independent Socialists who wanted to end the war, and a Marxist revolutionary body known as Spartakists led by Karl Liebknecht and Rosa Luxemburg.

In fact, this ferocious sense of territorial ambition which the war had unleashed was not absolutely universal. In all areas of society there were those who were sceptical of the dreams of pan-Germanism, but amid the current excitements their voice was not often heard. Even the Chancellor Bethmann Hollweg was extremely doubtful about the wisdom of the enthusiasts, yet the circumstances of wartime had by now brought the position of the Chancellor to its lowest point in the history of imperial Germany.

After the appointment of Hindenburg as Chief of the General Staff with Ludendorff as his Quarter-Master-General in August 1916, the influence of the military over the government of Germany increased markedly. Their determination to create a satellite Polish state in the declaration of 5 November 1916 (see p. 333) ended the chances of any negotiated peace with Tsarist Russia; their insistence on embarking on unrestricted submarine warfare in January 1917 was to bring the United States rapidly on to the side of the Allies, and in July 1917 they were able to secure the dismissal of Bethmann Hollweg, who was replaced first by Georg Michaelis, and then by Count von Hertling. Most striking of all, their power was to be seen in the negotiation of the Treaty of Brest Litovsk and the separate agreement with the Ukraine.

Naturally, these ambitions all assumed victory in war. In the offensive of March 1918, however, Ludendorff had only enough strength for tactical success, not enough for a strategic break-through, and since the annexationist policy of Germany's military rulers precluded any possibility of a negotiated peace, the Allies fought on with their backs to the wall. With the Allied assault near Amiens on 8 August Ludendorff knew that the last gamble had failed. The retreat went on across the eastern territories of France and through Belgium, until at the beginning of October he was forced to acknowledge that an armistice could no longer be delayed.

There then followed during the last month of the war a most remarkable transformation of the system of government in Germany. Prince Max of Baden, who was appointed Chancellor on 3 October, opened negotiations with the Allies on the same day and formed a government out of conservative and liberal groups including the Majority Socialists. He had, however, to convince the Americans as well as the left wing of his own supporters that the rule of the war-lords was now a thing of the past, and a 'revolution from above' was speedily organized. In future, German governments were to be fully responsible to the *Reichstag*; deputies were to be eligible as ministers, and the military were to be subordinated to the civil authority. Within Prussia the system of three classes of electorate which had existed since 1849 (see p. 142) was abolished. In short, Germany was to become a parliamentary democracy, and if only William II had been prepared to abdicate—as Prince Max begged him to do—the Hohenzollern monarchy might still have survived.

Throughout October, as the German line was pressed back towards the frontier, notes continued to be exchanged between Prince Max and President Wilson over the Fourteen Points which Wilson had issued in January 1918 as the basis for a peace settlement. On 26 October Prince Max dismissed Ludendorff and three days later William II, still clinging to his crown, turned to Spa where the army headquarters was now established. But by this time the news that Germany was suing for peace had begun to awaken more revolutionary forces, which the politicians with their eyes on the Russian scene had been hoping to forestall with the 'revolution from above'. At the beginning of November the German navy at Kiel mutinied on being ordered out for one last hopeless battle against the British. On 6 November Cuxhaven, Bremen, and Hamburg were partly under the control of workers' and soldiers' councils, and on the same day Kurt Eisner, an Independent Socialist, led a demonstration in Munich which resulted in the occupation of public buildings and the proclamation of a Bavarian republic. Soon there were similar scenes of excitement in Cologne, Frankfurt, Stuttgart, and Leipzig, and on 7 November the Majority Socialists declared that they would not continue to support Prince Max's government unless William II announced his abdication within forty-eight hours.

The struggle reached its climax on 9 November. Prince Max in despair proclaimed the abdication of William II, before the German Emperor had actually given his consent, but when, despite this, the Majority Socialists withdrew from the government and joined forces with the Independent Socialists, he handed over the Chancellorship to Friedrich Ebert, the leader of the Majority Socialists, who had little liking for extreme revolution. The situation was already tense in Berlin; Karl Liebknecht on the steps of the Imperial Palace was proclaiming a Soviet régime, and it was in order to preserve the shaky existence of the constitutional government that Philip Scheidemann, another Majority Socialist, until recently a member of Prince Max's cabinet, hastily countered Liebknecht with the proclamation of a German republic from a window of the *Reichstag* building.

With this the rule of the Hohenzollerns had finally come to an end in Germany, although it was not until the next day that the Emperor William II agreed to abdicate and travelled into exile in Holland. What was less clear was the nature of the régime that was to succeed him and Ebert might well wonder how long his government with its mixture of Independent and Majority Socialists could survive in the face of a Communist onslaught. At this moment, however, help arrived from an unexpected quarter. On the night of 9 November, as Ebert sat in the chancellery listening to the noise of the street demonstrations, the telephone rang. It was General Gröner, Ludendorff's successor, speaking from Spa. In a short dramatic conversation these two men—Gröner, the son of an N.C.O., and Ebert, the son of a tailor—made their pact designed to save from Bolshevism the Empire still technically ruled by a Hohenzollern. The government would support the maintenance of military discipline and guarantee the means of supply for the army; the army would support the existence of the government and suppress the forces of Bolshevism. It was almost as if General Kornilov and Kerensky had joined forces against the Russian Bolsheviks in 1917.

That Ebert, a Socialist, should take this chance of alliance with a military clique who in the last years of the war had come close to gaining control over the government of Germany, is the measure of his dislike of the extreme left. For Gröner the agreement is more easily understandable. He knew that the Majority Socialists at least were hardly a revolutionary force; the General Staff badly needed some sort of national authority to which they could turn against the soldiers' councils; furthermore, at this very moment the armistice delegation was in contact with the Allies at Compiègne and to the military it was vital that some sort of civil government should be in existence to shoulder the responsibility for the defeat.

The immediate question was the means whereby a new constitution was to be created. Ebert favoured the traditional method of a national constituent assembly elected by universal male suffrage. As Lenin had already shown in January 1918 in Russia, the extreme left regarded such a gathering as a bourgeois device and wanted all power to be centred on the soldiers' and workers' councils. Thus, when a congress of these councils meeting in Berlin on 16 December demanded the dismissal of Hindenburg and the surrender of the organization and discipline of the army to the soldiers' councils, it seemed that the Communists might get their way. This particular measure, however, was inspired more by a general sense of antimilitarism than by adherence to extreme political views, and in other aspects the congress proved to be a good deal more moderate than had been feared. The German Communists—the Spartakists—were consistently out-voted. The Majority Socialists captured all the seats on the executive elected by the congress and gave full support to Ebert over the election of a national constituent assembly.

Nevertheless, the threat from the left-wing groups remained sufficiently powerful to leave the government dependent on the armed forces and even that was not always decisive. On 23 December Ebert and his cabinet were actually besieged in the chancellery by sailors demanding arrears of pay, and although a frantic telephone call from Ebert brought a military force from Potsdam to their rescue, these troops proved very unreliable and the sailors eventually had to be persuaded to leave in return for a promise that they would be paid.

Inglorious though it was, the episode did clarify the situation. The attempted use of troops against the sailors prompted the three Independent Socialists to resign from the cabinet and with their replacement by Majority Socialists the government achieved a greater homogeneity. At the same time the apparent unreliability of the ordinary rank and file made it very unlikely that the demand of the congress for the transference of military control to the soldiers' councils would be implemented. Instead, the army command had been organizing units of volunteers and in January 1919 a few days after the Spartakists had attempted a *coup* in Berlin, these *Freikorps* went into action under General von Lüttwitz. The Spartakists were put down in a series of bloody engagements during which the leaders Karl Liebnecht and Rosa Luxemburg were killed. In the next two months similar repression took place in Bremen, Cuxhaven, Düsseldorf and Halle. In March the left lost some 1500 dead during further outbreaks in Berlin, and in April the *Freikorps* continued their work in Brunswick, Magdeburg, Dresden and Leipzig.

Meanwhile, in Bavaria parliamentary elections in January had brought about a victory for the Majority Socialists against Kurt Eisner, who was assassinated a month later. The new government under Johannes Hoffmann, however, was unable to resist the growth of the extreme left against a background of unrest and unemployment and eventually moved to Bamberg, while a Soviet republic was proclaimed in Munich. On this Noske, the Minister of Defence in Berlin, sent in regular army forces who in May, assisted by troops of the local *Freikorps*, put down the Communists in an action that involved the deaths of several hundreds, and re-established the Hoffmann government.

With this it could be reckoned that the immediate possibility of a Communist takeover in Germany had been averted. In fact, although there had been moments since November 1918 when events might have seemed to be swinging towards the extreme left, there were several reasons why the emergence of a Bolshevik dictatorship had been highly unlikely. First, the development of commerce and industry had naturally greatly increased the strength of the German middle class, who, since the 1830s, had been endeavouring to cultivate a political life of their own. When on 14 November the leaders of the workers' and soldiers' councils in Dresden and Leipzig announced the collapse of bourgeois capitalism, they were really guilty of wishful thinking. Capitalism had not collapsed, and

the widespread discontent was aimed chiefly at the military hierarchy, officialdom, and the stringent conditions of wartime—not at
a capitalist form of society. A second factor was the absence of
anarchy in Germany; the country had not been overrun, the civil
service was still functioning, and the army was falling back on its
own frontier in reasonable order. Thirdly, the armistice had been
signed at the moment of the fall of the monarchy and thus the
Majority Socialists, unlike the provisional government in Russia
1917, did not have to cope with the strain of fighting a war at a time
when they were struggling with the political uncertainties. Lastly,
the common sense of Groner and Ebert had enabled the General
Staff and the new government to strike a bargain that ensured that
they would both survive.

Chapter 27

The Aftermath of War 1919–21

1. Peace-making with the Central Powers

On 18 January 1919 the Peace Conference was officially opened at Paris. This was essentially a meeting of the victors, including some thirty-two separate delegations, but none representing either the neutrals or the defeated Powers. Originally it had been intended to follow the pattern of peace-making in 1814—a swift conclusion of terms with the enemy countries, followed by a general European Congress to redraw the political map of the Continent; it soon became apparent, however, that nothing so clear-cut was going to emerge from the confusion of what Arthur Balfour described as 'a rough and tumble affair'.

It would perhaps be unjust to stress the unfavourable comparison between Vienna and Versailles. Unlike their predecessors of 1814, the principal statesmen of 1919 were committed to satisfying the demands of the nationalist movements rampant in eastern Europe, whose spokesmen were quick to assert their claims in the absence of any German or Austrian representatives. Nor could the peace-makers ignore the forces of democracy, dependent as they were on their own electorates whose fury was constantly stimulated by a virulent press. It was also highly significant that for the first time the United States was to play a leading part in a European settle-ment, and the scope of the treaty with Germany was inevitably widened by President Wilson's determination that it should include his great scheme for a League of Nations. Lloyd George and Clemen-ceau might differ over the details of the peace; they were as one in their acceptance of the cynical workings of European diplomacy. But for President Wilson this was to be the opening of a new era of sweetness and light in international relations. With all the New World's suspicion of the trickery of the Old, he was determined to set right the complexities of central and eastern Europe at a stroke. He saw himself, said Lloyd George, as 'a missionary whose function it was to rescue the poor European heathen from their age-long worship of false and fiery gods'. The French press, which lampooned him mercilessly, did not even allow him the credit of his idealism.

'He speaks like Jesus Christ,' remarked Clemenceau, 'but he acts like Lloyd George.'

Democratic procedures were responsible for some delay in the assembling of the conference after the armistice of November 1918. In Great Britain the issues raised by the ending of hostilities, heightened by the light-headedness of war exhaustion, threatened to wreck the uneasy coalition government which Lloyd George had led since 1916, and as war-time conditions had kept the existing House of Commons unchanged for over eight years, the Prime Minister decided on a general election in December. There was certainly time for this, since President Wilson, whose personal representative at Paris, Colonel House, had failed to dissuade him from attending the conference, could not sail from the United States until he had delivered the annual presidential address to Congress on 2 December, and after his arrival on 14 December there followed a month of informal conversations in London, Paris, and Rome. Delay was perhaps not undesirable; it might allow a little time for the angry bitterness of war to subside and as Clemenceau pointed out to Lloyd George, 'it is not a bad plan to let the German revolution settle down for a while in order that we may know before proceeding what we have before us.'

Indeed, as has been seen (pp. 336–41), the whole form of future government in Germany still hung in the balance. By January 1919, however, it had been possible to hold elections for a constituent assembly and on 6 February this had met at Weimar under the presidency of Ebert with Philip Scheidemann as Chancellor. Naturally the new government had a great deal to cope with and its task was not made any easier when it learnt with a sudden shock the terms drawn up by the Allies.

At Paris the major decisions had been taken by an inner council of the five major belligerent Powers—the United States, Great Britain, France, Italy, and Japan. Clemenceau presided and had the advantage of being able to speak English, whereas neither Wilson nor Lloyd George could speak French. Japan soon dropped out, and Orlando, the Italian premier, withdrew his delegation in April in protest at Wilson's direct appeal to the Italians over his head to accept a frontier line which would exclude Fiume on the Adriatic coast. Lloyd George was particularly concerned with the question of the German colonies, since many of these had already been taken in possession by the Dominions. For Clemenceau, who as a young man had watched the Prussian army besieging Paris and whose country had now been ravaged by four years of war, the sole aim of victory was to ensure that Germany might never again invade France. French demands for an autonomous republic to be carved out of German territory on the left bank of the Rhine and for a permanent Allied control of the four Rhine bridgeheads brought about

EUROPE IN 1921

the major crisis of the conference; the resistance of both Wilson and Lloyd George, however, eventually forced a compromise, and on 7 May the German delegates who had arrived at Versailles could be presented with the statement of the terms that the Allies had agreed to impose on Germany.

Both the refusal to negotiate and the nature of the terms themselves were profoundly abhorrent to the Germans. Alsace and Lorraine, including all State property therein, were to be ceded to France, and the districts of Eupen and Malmédy to Belgium; in Slesvig a plebiscite was to decide the position of the Danish-German frontier. In the east the new state of Poland was granted the provinces of Posen and West Prussia, thus giving her access to the sea—the controversial Polish corridor—although Danzig was to have the separate status of a Free City. Memel and the surrounding region was to be detached from East Prussia to provide a port for Lithuania, and a small strip of territory was to be given up to Czechoslovakia. The German colonies were simply shared out among the Allies. South Africa gained South-West Africa, Australia German New Guinea, New Zealand Samoa, and Japan the northern Pacific islands, while Great Britain, France, and Belgium received the remainder of German possessions in Africa—all these territories being held technically under a mandate from the League of Nations (see p. 352).

There were also stern measures to ensure against the revival of German military power. The army was to be reduced to 100,000 men, based on voluntary enlistment for a period of service of twelve years; it was to have no tanks, heavy artillery, or aircraft, and the fortifications of Heligoland were to be dismantled. The General Staff was to be dissolved. The navy was to have no U-boats, and its heaviest vessels were to consist of six battleships of 10,000 tonnes In addition to this, French fears were quietened by an Allied occupation of the Rhineland for fifteen years after which it was to remain permanently demilitarized.

Debatable though they may be, the fears of the French and the requirements of the new states in eastern Europe go far to explain these terms of the settlement. The justification of the economic clauses, however, rested almost entirely on the assumption of Germany's war guilt, which actually formed Article 231 of the treaty. It was argued that in causing the war Germany had wrought appalling havoc on the other Powers and that now she must pay. In compensation for the destruction of her own coal mines France was to administer the Saar district with its annual output of 17,272,000 tonnes of coal under a League of Nations commission for the next fifteen years. All the victors, however, were each determined to press their account until the final figure to be demanded seemed likely to be so large that it was left to later negotiation—a festering sore which would jeopardize international relations and European economy for years to come.

During the next six weeks the German government struggled to escape its fate. It was useless. Beyond agreeing to a plebiscite in Upper Silesia the Allies were adamant. Scheidemann and his cabinet resigned rather than accept such terms, but Ebert in consultation with Hindenburg and Groner knew that a continuation of the war in the west could only end in defeat and that the subsequent domestic turmoil would deliver Germany into the hands of either a Communist government or a right-wing dictatorship of army officers. Scheidemann was replaced as Chancellor by a Social Democrat, Gustav Bauer, and eventually the Assembly agreed by a large majority to accept the treaty.

On 28 June—five years to the day after the assassination of Francis Ferdinand at Sarajevo—the ceremony of signing took place in the Hall of Mirrors in Louis XIV's palace of Versailles, where forty-eight years previously the German Empire had been proclaimed. 'Faites entrer les Allemands,' came Clemenceau's command, when the representatives of the victorious Powers were duly assembled. The two German delegates were led in; they signed, and shortly afterwards with hardly a word spoken were escorted out again. 'Oui,' said Clemenceau with tears in his eyes, 'c'est une belle journée.' It was perhaps understandable that for the French this was the supreme moment of triumph, but there were many that day who had doubts about its wisdom.

For the next two decades the Treaty of Versailles was to be a source of deep anger for the Germans. They spoke of it as a *Diktat* through which they had been deprived of any chance of negotiation, and they resented the heaviness of its terms which they claimed went far beyond the original Fourteen Points. They could certainly argue that the partition of the German colonies by the victors was inconsistent with 'a free open-minded and absolutely impartial adjustment of colonial claims'. The principle of national self-determination had deprived them of some seven million inhabitants; yet the treaty had positively forbidden the inclusion of German Austria within the frontiers of Germany. The general disarmament which had been proposed seemed to apply only to Germany, and the admission of war guilt appeared to lay them open to absurdly heavy reparations.

In fact, any defeated country, whether it negotiates or not, has to accept the conditions that the victor demands. Great Britain and France had both made reservations over the Fourteen Points, and in any case the terms which Germany had imposed on Russia at Brest Litovsk in March 1918 deprived her of any moral right to complain of Versailles; indeed, in comparison with her allies, Austria-Hungary and Turkey, Germany had kept the bulk of her territory intact and those regions which had been removed from her were of mixed population and had mostly been the fruit of conquest. She had lost roughly 13 per cent of her lands and economic potential, but the revival of German power in the 1930s would hardly suggest that these territorial changes had permanently maimed her.

The fundamental significance of Versailles, however, was emotional rather than rational. Allied statesmen, urged on by the pressure of public opinion, had made peace in a spirit of revenge. The cries of 'il faut en finir', 'hang the Kaiser', and 'squeezing the German lemon until the pips squeak' were indicative of the desire not merely for a guarantee of future security, but for the national humiliation of Germany. Similarly, the Germans, confronted with disaster less than a year after their overwhelming victory in the east, accepted the inevitable in a spirit of sullen resentment. The actual thought of military defeat, the loss of overseas colonies, and the surrender of land to the Poles and the Czechs were a constant hurt to national pride; four years of war followed by the upheaval of social revolution were bound to mean a long painful period of recovery and readjustment for the entire Continent; yet the Germans saw every difficulty in subsequent years as a further indignity that they alone must suffer as a result of the hated Treaty of Versailles.

Two other treaties were concluded by the Allies in 1919. With the signing of the Treaty of Saint-Germain on 10 September, Austria was reduced to a tiny rump in the German-speaking Alpine lands. Trieste, Istria, and the southern half of the Tyrol were surrendered to Italy; she was severed from Hungary, and the subject peoples of the rest of the old Habsburg dominions were free to go their own way. Vienna, the only reminder of her past Imperial greatness, had become the capital of a small European republic, its industry hampered by the loss of the minerals and raw materials on which it had formerly drawn, its frontiers harassed by the ambitions of new nation states. Two months later, on 27 November, Bulgaria made her peace with the Allies by the Treaty of Neuilly, which simply confirmed the territorial losses which she had suffered at the end of the second Balkan war in 1913.

2. The emergence of the new nation states in central Europe

Of the enemy countries there remained Hungary and Turkey. Before settlement could be reached with them, however, the Allies had had to grapple with the countless problems created by the collapse of four empires, whose existence had been the mainstay of an entire political and social system. When Bismarck commented in 1878 that the duty of the Powers was to consider the peace of Europe rather than the happiness of the Bulgarians, he had spoken with the voice of the nineteenth century. Now, in 1919, the assumptions on which central and eastern Europe had previously been governed were no longer valid. This time legitimacy was to be based not on dynastic right, but on national self-determination; the Allies were to supervise a new 'springtime of the nations', an 1848 in which the emancipated peoples would be free to pursue their conflicting national aims without the fear of any immediate retribution.

This was an appallingly difficult task. It involved problems of securing strategically defensible frontiers and a workable economy within each of the new states, and was complicated by one further consideration that the statesmen of 1919 did share with their predecessors of 1814. Both were haunted by the fear of social revolution; thus, just as the men of the Congress of Vienna were prompted by a desire to shore up an aristocratic social system against the ambitions of a middle class inspired by the doctrines of the French Revolution, so the victors of 1919 attempted to contain the Communism of Russia through the establishment of liberal parliamentary democracies in the new states that were emerging from the ruin of eastern Europe.

Over the creation of Czechoslovakia the main difficulty had been for Czechs and Slovaks to reach agreement, but when the Slovaks were at last persuaded that they would enjoy full national autonomy within a federal state, Dr Beneš and Professor Masaryk, the Czech leaders, were able to present a powerful case to the western Allies. At the end of the war the Czechs were accordingly granted the right to occupy Bohemia and Moravia, until the Peace Conference assembled. The Hungarians were determined to resist the loss of Slovakia, and a week after an armistice had been signed at Padua on 3 November, they invaded Slovakia and drove out the Czechs. In March 1919, however, the Allies forced them to withdraw, and by the treaty that was finally signed in September 1919 a Czechoslovak State was brought into existence including the whole of Slovakia, as well as several purely Magyar districts, and Ruthenia, whose people had elected to join the new state on the basis of local autonomy.

Rumania's conclusion of a separate peace with the Central European Powers in January 1918 had released the western Allies from their secret treaty of 1916, whereby she had been due to receive a considerable area of Hungarian territory, but despite the unpopularity of the Rumanian Prime Minister, Bratianu, at the Peace Conference, they agreed in response to the wishes of a majority of the population that Bessarabia, the districts of the Dobruja and the Bukovina, as well as the whole of Transylvania, should be included within the frontiers of Rumania.

In Hungary, however, Count Károlyi's government had lost support after the enforced withdrawal from Slovakia in March 1919, and in the hope of gaining the friendship of Russia the Socialists combined with the Communists under Bela Kun, who proclaimed a Soviet republic. The Allies' demand for the surrender of Transylvania to Rumania was rejected and in the early summer Hungarian forces reoccupied Slovakia and checked the advance of the Rumanian army westwards. Their resistance did not last long. Russia was not in a position to help and the attempt of the Communists to turn the great estates into cooperative farms disappointed the Hungarian peasantry, whose hopes had been raised by an earlier Social Democrat decree that the land would be divided among them. In June Slovakia had to be evacuated again and in August—to the relief of the western Powers—Bela Kun fled before the Rumanian army, which proceeded to occupy Budapest until November, when it finally withdrew behind the frontiers laid down by the treaty.

It has sometimes been said that no one was the victor in the first World War. This may well have been true of the Powers who were brought into it indirectly, but for Serbia, who saw the whole struggle as one between herself and Austria-Hungary, the issue was more simple. Austria-Hungary had lost and paid the price in disruption, and in the Balkans there emerged an 'enlarged Serb-Croat-Slovene state, the Kingdom of Yugoslavia, including some 250,000 Magyars along its northern frontier, many Albanians living in Montenegro, and the Italians of Fiume on the Adriatic coast.

Thus the successes of Czechoslovakia, Rumania, and Yugoslavia in pressing their claims before the Allies all involved Hungary in serious losses, and only a plebiscite held in December 1920 saved her from having also to surrender the Burgenland on her western frontier to Austria.

3. The establishment of the Russian frontier

The settlement of the lands that had lain under Tsarist rule was complicated by the course of the Soviet government's struggle in Russia. Only in Finland was the situation relatively straightforward. Finnish independence had already been recognized by the Bolshevik government in January 1918; under General Mannerheim the Finnish Whites had overcome the Reds in the civil war of that spring, and her constitutional form of government gave her a firm basis on which to put her affairs in order. Finland's principal need at this time was to re-establish friendly relations with the west, which had been jeopardized by her use of a German expeditionary force against the Bolsheviks (see p. 330) and, in October 1918, by the Finnish Diet's election of Prince Frederick Charles of Hesse, William II's brother-in-law, as King of Finland. By the end of the year, however, these western suspicions had been quietened by the appointment of Mannerheim as Regent, since he had strongly opposed the German election, and after the establishment of a new republican government and a general election in the spring of 1919, Finland's international situation seemed to be satisfactorily stabilized. The balance of forces on the south coast of the Baltic naturally concerned her, but she took no part in any direct attack on Russia, since the White Russians, who were pressing for her support, would give no guarantee of confirming the independence which she had already gained.

South of the Gulf of Finland the turmoil was inevitably greater. The position of the German Baltic barons was naturally challenged alike by Estonian and Latvian nationalists and by Bolsheviks, and both had been savagely suppressed by the German army advancing eastwards in the first months of 1918. Then on the collapse of Germany in the west, Bolshevik forces returned and in December 1918 Estonian and Latvian Soviet republics were officially recognized by Russia. There were, however, a great many German troops still in the field and units of these, organized in *Freikorps* under General von der Goltz, combined with the local national militia to continue the resistance to the Bolsheviks. As a consequence of their efforts and of the appearance of British ships in the Baltic, the whole region was under the control of non-Communist governments by the spring of 1919. These now began to clash with the Germans who seemed to be attempting to establish an occupation, and eventually Allied intervention caused von der Goltz to withdraw to East Prussia.

In Poland the problem of independence was confused at the end of the war by the existence of two separate governments, one under Pilsudski at the head of the Polish Regency Council which the Central Powers had set up in 1916, the other under the pro-Russian Dmowski whose National Committee had been recognized by the Allies in Paris. It was the great pianist Paderewski who managed to weld the two into a workable organization, and in January 1919 a Polish parliament was elected by universal suffrage. Poland's western frontier was largely defined by the terms of the Treaty of Versailles, leaving only the disputed area of Upper Silesia to be settled by a plebiscite. To the north and east, however, Pilsudski was determined to establish Poland's claims by force of arms. In April 1919 Vilna, which the Lithuanians had established as their own capital, was seized, and throughout the rest of the year Polish forces thrust into Eastern Galicia where the Ukrainians put up a fierce but unavailing resistance to them.

These Polish successes on the eastern front in 1919 are partly explained by the presence of the anti-Bolshevik forces that were occupying the attention of the Red Army in Russia during this year. In March Kolchak (see p. 332) had made a fresh attempt to strike towards the Volga, but by the end of April had been pushed back by General Kamenev in the direction of the Urals. No sooner had this threat been met than Denikin began a great thrust north and west through the Ukraine, captured Kiev, Kursk, Voronezh, and Orel, and by October appeared to be coming within striking distance of Moscow. At the same time General Judenich launched an assault through Estonia on St Petersburg. For the Bolsheviks it was the supreme crisis of their struggle for survival, but in Trotsky they had the man to rise to the challenge. He organized his reinforcements, prepared a plan for the defence of St Petersburg street by street, argued the Politbureau into accepting it, and fired his commanders with such determination that by November the armies of Judenich and Denikin, whose lines of communication had become seriously over-extended, were in full retreat.

After this the survival of the Soviet government in Russia was no longer in question. Denikin was driven out of his base in the Crimea: in February 1920 Kolchak, who had by now fallen back east of the Urals, was surrendered to the Bolsheviks and executed, and the Allied expeditionary forces at Archangel and Vladivostok were withdrawn. The new non-Communist governments of Estonia and Latvia still held firm; on the other hand, they had given little support to the White Russians and the Bolsheviks decided to accept the situation, as they had done over Finland, by concluding peace treaties with them in 1920.

There remained the problem of Poland. Like the Finns and the Baltic peoples the Poles had been cautious over giving direct assistance to the White Russians, whom they did not trust to recognize their independence. Pilsudski, however, had no wish to accept the eastern frontier suggested by the Allies—known later as the Curzon line (see map p. 344), after the British Foreign Secretary who had proposed it—which came close to that of 1815, and in April 1920 he embarked upon a new attack in the hope of gaining the old 1772 frontier. For six months the fortune of war swung to and fro. The Poles reached Kiev, but the Red Army, now able to concentrate all its forces on a single front, pushed them back until it stood before Warsaw, and the Poles now declared their acceptance of the Curzon line. This time, however, it was the Russians who rejected it, but on 16 August Pilsudski won a great victory by the Vistula. A second Polish advance began, and on 12 October Lenin decided to cut his losses with an armistice, followed in March 1921 by the Treaty of Riga which established the frontier some two hundred miles to the east of the Curzon line. For the Lithuanians this Polish success was disastrous, since Vilna and the region around it, known as the Suwalki triangle, was placed under a Polish military occupation which was able to ensure that in the subsequent plebiscite the territory became part of Poland.

4. Turkey

In the extreme south-east of Europe it had been agreed at Paris that Albania should receive a part of Epirus on her southern frontier, and after a little difficulty with the occupying forces of Italy and Yugoslavia an independent government was established under Ahmed Zogu as Prime Minister. Concessions to Greece, which included most of Thrace and a large area of Smyrna in Asia Minor, where there was a considerable Greek population, were all part of the Allies' settlement with Turkey—the Treaty of Sèvres signed in August 1920—whereby the Ottoman Empire suffered a fate similar to that of Austria-Hungary. She was to lose all her Arab territories in Africa and Asia; some, such as Arabia, were to receive outright independence; others were to be governed under a type of mandate which left them considerable control over their domestic affairs, Syria being entrusted to France, Transjordania, Iraq, and the Sheikhdoms of the Persian Gulf to Great Britain.

The effect of these terms was to add tremendous support to a Turkish nationalist movement under Mustapha Kemal, which had already so threatened the Sultan's position that the Allies had had to occupy Constantinople in March 1920. Kemal's reply to the publication of the Treaty of Sèvres was a military attack on British and Greek forces in Asia Minor, and the Allies agreed with the Greek Prime Minister, Venizelos, that Greek reinforcements should be sent in. At this point, however, the whole course of political and military events was changed by a most remarkable chance. In June 1917 the Allies had forced through the deposition of Constantine, the pro-German King of Greece (see genealogical table, p. 486), who was succeeded by his son Alexander. In October 1920, however, Alexander died as a result of a bite by his pet monkey. In the general election that followed, Venizelos was defeated and the pro-German Constantine was restored to the Greek throne. The outcome was to be disastrous for Greece. The Allies at once withdrew their support. By November 1922 the forces of Mustapha Kemal had taken over the government of Turkey and driven the Greeks from Smyrna, and in the final settlement by the Treaty of Lausanne in August 1923 the Allies made their peace with Turkey, confirming the expulsion of the Greeks from Asia Minor and restoring to her the eastern half of Thrace and several islands near the entrance to the Dardanelles.

5. The League of Nations

'It is not done well,' remarked Dr Johnson of a dog walking on its hind legs, 'but you are surprised to find it done at all.' The same judgement might be made of the settlement of central and eastern Europe after the war. There could be no fundamental solution to the problems of the nineteenth century; the new frontiers had simply been superimposed upon them, and at best the Allies had managed to tidy up a chaotic map. Some of the new states were composite creations out of different national groups—Czechs, Slovaks, and Ruthenians in Czechoslovakia; Serbs, Croats, and Slovenes in Yugoslavia. Class divisions aggravated by differences of language complicated the national unity of others—Swedes in southern Finland, German-speaking landowners in the Baltic states. Many were dissatisfied with the frontiers that had been allotted to them; most included national minorities under their rule—German Sudetenlanders and Magyars within Czechoslovakia, Austrians of the southern Tyrol within Italy, Ukrainians, Germans, and Lithuanians within Poland, Magyars, Germans, and Albanians within Yugoslavia—all resentful of their new condition and determined to preserve their own identity (see Appendix 8, p. 493).

Of these it was the German problem which was to be the most significant for the future. 'I cannot conceive any greater cause of future war,' Lloyd George had written in a memorandum in March 1919, 'than that the German people, who have certainly proved themselves one of the most vigorous and powerful races in the world, should be surrounded by a number of small states, many of them consisting of people who have never previously set up a stable government for themselves, but each of them containing large masses of Germans clamouring for reunion with their native land.'

There was, nevertheless—in the west, at least—a strange sense of hopeful idealism which must have produced a sardonic smile from the ghost of Metternich. There were two reasons for this optimism. The first was purely wishful thinking; the World War had been so appalling that it must never, and therefore could never, happen again. The second was slightly more practical in that the Allies believed that through the establishment of a League of Nations all future disagreements could be settled by negotiation. The congresses of nineteenth-century Europe have sometimes been regarded as an anticipation of such a scheme, but in fact these had been no more than occasional gatherings of the great Powers to safeguard their own interests; the happiness of the Bulgarians had played no part in them. The conception of the League of Nations was totally different; it aimed at a concert of governments of the whole world, in which all the member States were pledged to apply economic and, if necessary, military sanctions against any apparent aggressor, thus ensuring a system of collective security for great and small alike. The preservation of peace was no longer to depend upon the *ad hoc* arrangements of the Powers concerned, but upon a permanent assembly at Geneva with an International Court of Justice at The Hague. The League was to supervise the protection of national minorities, the government of the mandated territories, the Saar and the Free City of Danzig, and through a variety of subordinate bodies, such as the International Labour Organization, was to develop organs of international cooperation to deal with questions of health, working conditions, and white slavery.

So much scorn has been poured on the ultimate failure of the League that it would be as well to suggest some of the points in its favour. It was certainly a positive and gallant attempt, strongly supported by many high-minded Europeans, to move away from the anarchy of power politics, and if as a pioneering attempt it did suffer from many inadequacies, it nevertheless provided a body of experience from which it was possible to design a more effective international organization after the second World War. For a few years, at least, it was able to adjudicate over minor frontier disputes, and in the less spectacular non-political spheres its achievement was quite considerable.

The efficacy of an international political organization, however, must depend upon the extent to which each State is prepared to surrender some part at least of its national sovereignty, and the weakness of the League lay in the fact that it was entirely based upon the rights and existence of independent nation States. Despite the insistence of the French, it did not even possess an international force of its own, relying simply upon the voluntary cooperation of its members. Small issues it might be able to resolve, but in any major crisis involving the great Powers it was eventually to find itself ignored. The dream of the idealists had been of an international parliament. But the League was never a parliament; it was not even a confederation. Worse still, even its impartiality was in some doubt. Seeing Germany and Russia excluded from membership and the Covenant of the League written into the peace treaties, many countries regarded the League as little more than an instrument of policy for the western Powers. And after March 1920 this meant only Great Britain, France, and Italy, for in that month the United States Senate, shrinking from any further commitment in Europe, refused to ratify the Treaty of Versailles and thereby rejected American participation in the President's own scheme.

Part 7

The Crisis of Liberal Democracy
1921–45

Chapter 28

The 1920s: (1) The struggle for internal stability

1. Communists and Fascists

Before 1914 it could be assumed that any new State would naturally become a principality or a kingdom, and Greece, Belgium, Rumania, Bulgaria, Norway and Albania had each in their turn added to the number of crowned heads in Europe. It is the measure of the upheavals brought about by the end of the war that every State created after 1918 should declare itself a republic. The sole exception was Yugoslavia which the Serbs regarded as an extension of the Kingdom of Serbia, while of the defeated Powers Hungary did remain a kingdom, but had no king. Forms of parliamentary democracy now prevailed and although the extent of the franchise varied greatly, the new republics established elected presidents as heads of state and reigning kings became constitutional monarchs.

The nature of the political parties that competed for power in the new States depended upon the ethnic and social peculiarities of each country and in the main reflected the sectional interests that had been recognizable before the war. The recent turmoil, however, had brought about significant changes at each end of the political spectrum. For the left the new factor was the existence of a Communist government in Russia. This might have been expected to be a source of inspiration, but the manner in which Lenin had concentrated all power in the hands of the Bolshevik party aroused a sense of unease among many Social Democrats outside Russia. Even a leading Spartakist Rosa Luxemburg (see p. 337) had written in 1918: 'let the German government Socialists cry that the rule of the Bolsheviks in Russia is a distorted expression of the dictatorship of the proletariat,' and more moderate Social Democrats were confirmed in the view that their party must work for a policy of reform through accepted parliamentary processes. Thus the Austrian Social Democrats adopted an extremely cool attitude towards the workers' and soldiers' councils that emerged at the end of the war, and in Germany Ebert's Majority Socialists collaborated with right-wing *Freikorps* in putting them down (see p. 340). Within a couple of years most extreme Socialists had broken away to form separate Communist parties and the Social Democrats had moved relatively closer to the centre—an uncomfortable position, since conservatives still regarded them as reds, while the Communists denounced them as bourgeois renegades.

A more startling phenomenon affecting most parts of Europe was to be seen on the right. The rise of Fascism was largely an emotional response to the shattering of the old political framework, coupled with a fear of Bolshevism. Its essence was an intensely militant nationalism, scornful of parliamentary systems and imbued with a belief in a party élite headed by a leader whose word was law; its aim was totalitarian rule and its instrument private armies with their own uniform and insignia. So far as it had any philosophical basis, this was little more than a eulogizing of strength derived from a crude interpretation of social Darwinism (see p. 237). 'He who would live must fight,' wrote Adolf Hitler, the leader of the German Nazi party, in 1924. 'War alone,' declared Mussolini some years after he had come to power in Italy, 'brings all human energies to their highest tension and stamps with the seal of nobility the nations who dare to face it.' Mussolini's régime showed little interest in racialism, but in central Europe this was a marked feature of the Fascist movements. Here a strident patriotism was accompanied by a demand for a purification of the race and particularly by a hatred of the Jews, and Hitler was able to combine two strands of his message by denouncing Bolshevism as a Jewish conspiracy. Fascism itself did lay claim to an element of Socialism in that it declared that the condition of the workers woud be improved more effectively by State decree rather than by the slow methods of parliamentary legislation, although once in power Fascist régimes tended to disband trade unions and to work in conjunction with the major capitalists.

It was understandable that Communists should regard Fascism as the last desperate defence put up by the propertied classes against the eventual collapse of the bourgeois world. And indeed there were many landowners and industrialists who did see the Fascist parties as a potential ally. Yet this alone would not be enough to explain their eventual success in Germany and Italy. Nationalists hankering for what seemed a glorious past, ex-soldiers unable to reconcile themselves to the frustration of peacetime, small farmers, professional men and shopkeepers fearing their own social decline into the ranks of the working class amid the economic uncertainties of the post-war period, all these represented a source of support. The motives, however, were not always selfish, since there were others who genuinely warmed to the notion of national regeneration and a dynamic sense of purpose. Throughout Europe the leaders came from a variety of classes, but in Germany and Italy the relatively humble origins of Hitler and Mussolini did help to carry some conviction with a working-class audience and there could never be any doubt about Hitler's genuine dislike of the frock-coated world of German respectability.

Thus amid this amalgam of emotions there was plenty for the leaders to play upon. 'Whoever wishes to win over the masses,' wrote Hitler in 1924, 'must know the key that will open the door to their hearts. It is not objectivity which is a feckless attitude, but a determined will backed up by force when necessary.' This was the challenge that faced the new shaky parliamentary régimes still struggling into existence and it remained to be seen whether they would find that key before others did.

2. Italy: the rise of Mussolini

It might seem that Fascism was more likely to emerge in states which had suffered the political and social disruption of defeat in war. Yet Italy, where the change first came, had been on the winning side and had had a parliamentary constitution since her unification in 1860. None of this made the problems facing the Italian government any easier during the year immediately following the war. Peasantry were impatient to get the farm land which had been promised them when they were in the forces; by 1920 they were helping themselves to the landowners' estates, while workers, angered by rising prices and unemployment, were taking over many of the factories in the cities of the north. For the property-owning classes the situation was all too reminiscent of Russia in 1917 and they now turned to organising their own security forces with bands of armed men. At the same time the inclusion of Fiume within the frontiers of Yugoslavia roused the anger of the nationalists, and in September the Italian poet D'Annunzio, who saw himself as a latter-day Garibaldi, launched a private expedition to take Fiume, where he established his own régime, and it was over a year before the Italian government under Giolitti had the courage to bring about his withdrawal.

The real strength of extreme right-wing nationalism, however, found expression not in D'Annunzio's romantic crusade, but in the rapidly developing Fascist party. The leader of this movement, Benito Mussolini, unlike Lenin, Trotsky, and Hitler, really was of working-class origin. The son of a blacksmith, he had been educated in a Catholic seminary, from which he was expelled after stabbing another pupil; after a short spell as a schoolmaster, he had drifted into politics, and in the years before the war was editor of a Marxist newspaper. During the war he swung round in favour of intense nationalism, and when in the elections of 1919 he failed to gain any success against the great party machines of the Christian Democrats and the Socialists, he began to build up his own private army of

blackshirted hooligans who were soon much in demand from industrialists and wealthy farmers.

The most telling factor in Mussolini's rise to power was the weakness of the successive governments in dealing with Fascist excesses.
They had at their disposal a reasonably reliable military force, but
they were loathe to make use of it because, like the property owners,
they too feared a Communist revolution. In fact, the threat from the
left was largely illusory. The Italian Socialist party had taken little
advantage of the lawlessness in the cities and the countryside, and
in any case was in a state of some confusion after the Communists
had seceded in September 1920 in protest at the decision taken by
the bulk of the party to continue to work through parliamentary
processes. Yet the fear of the left remained and in the election of
May 1921 Giolitti decided to include Fascists in the government list,
with the result that they gained thirty-five seats.

Even so, this was a tiny representation in a Chamber of 535 and
Mussolini tended to demonstrate his power principally outside Parliament. By 1922 the north Italian cities and countryside had
become a scene of ferocious gang warfare; in August Fascist squads
virtually took control of Milan and ejected the local Socialist administration, and soon they had established themselves in Ferrara,
Cremona, Ravenna, Parma, and Leghorn. In Rome one government
after another had failed to come to grips with this open lawlessness,
but in October 1922 decisive action could be postponed no longer,
when it became known that the Fascists were planning a march on
Rome. There seemed good reason to suppose that the army would
support the constitutional government in this time of crisis and the
premier, Facta, resolved upon a proclamation of martial law. At this
point King Victor Emmanuel III made a fateful intervention. He
refused to sign the decree. He, too, had lost all faith in the existing
system of government; reckoning that the Fascists could at least
establish strong rule in the defence of property, he sent an invitation
by telegram to Mussolini to form an administration, and only on
this was Mussolini prepared to give the word for action; the march
on Rome duly took place after the real battle had already been
won—nothing more than a rather unnecessary piece of theatre—
and Mussolini himself travelled comfortably from Milan by train.

Once in power he still had to work in conjunction with other
right-wing groups, while he strengthened his position for the next
step. There were deals with the Catholic party and the industrialists;
Fascists were moved into positions of control in the police and local
administration, and at the end of 1923 a new electoral law gave two-
thirds of the seats in the Chamber to the largest party, provided that
it gained 25 per cent of the votes cast. When the election of April
1924 won him 65 per cent of the vote, the way was now clear for
the extinction of democratic government and in the following June

not even the murder of Matteotti, a leading Italian Socialist, could shake Mussolini's hold, even though he eventually admitted responsibility for it. Most of the dissident deputies were excluded from the Chamber; within a few months opposition newspapers had been suppressed or taken over, and from now on any other opposition could be dealt with by the police and the Fascist squads. In this way the half-heartedness of previous liberal administrations, a general lack of faith in the parliamentary system and the fear of Communism had made possible the first Fascist dictatorship.

Mussolini set about his task with some energy. Since the blackshirts had been the principal law-breakers, his advent to power did ensure a restoration of order and the new authoritarianism of government was reflected in the philosophy of the corporate state which placed all industry and trade in a hierarchical framework. The actual record of his achievement is less impressive. Production of electricity, automobiles and war materials increased considerably and there were schemes for public works such as the building of canals and the draining of the Pontine marshes. In the main, however, Italy's economic position was not transformed. She was still dependent on foreign imports of coal, oil, cotton and many metals. Businessmen, who had at first welcomed the prohibition of strikes and the appointment of trade union officials from above, found that the corporate state also meant bureaucracy, corruption and high taxes for themselves, while for the working classes conditions and pay simply deteriorated and there was still no cure for unemployment. The principal characteristic of Mussolini's Fascism was a theatricality which ultimately failed to convince, perhaps best summed up by the incongruity of the short, corpulent, heavily-jowled figure who throughout the 1920s and 1930s proclaimed a new Caesarism from the balcony of the Palazzo Venezia and who was eventually to lead his country into the fiasco of the disastrous Italian campaigns of the second World War.

3. The Weimar Republic

On 6 February 1919 the German Constituent Assembly finally met at Weimar, after the elections in the previous month had given the Majority Socialists 163 seats out of 421. The next largest representation was for the Centre party with 91 seats, and then the German Democratic party (D.D.P.), the old Progressives, with 75 seats; it was out of a coalition of these three that a government was set up under the chancellorship of Philip Scheidemann. For the time being the Constituent Assembly was also to act as a parliament, but its principal task was completed on 11 August, when the constitution of the new republic was finally adopted.

On paper, at least, this offered Germany a strikingly democratic system of government, in marked contrast to the subterfuge of the Empire of 1871. The legislature was to be bi-cameral—the Lower House, the *Reichstag*, elected every four years on a basis of proportional representation by universal suffrage for men and women who had reached the age of twenty; the Upper House, the *Reichsrat*, consisting of representatives of the regional governments. All legislation was to be introduced in the *Reichstag*, whose control over finance included direct, as well as indirect, taxes. The head of the State was to be a President elected on a popular vote to hold office for seven years, although a referendum proposed by a two-thirds majority in each House could bring about his removal. On the other hand, the President, too, had the right of appeal to the electorate, since he could dissolve the *Reichstag*, provided that the government concurred, and he could temporarily veto legislation, while the issue was decided by a national referendum. The Chancellor was appointed by the President to form a government, but these ministers remained responsible to the *Reichstag*. The position of the army within this system was of fundamental significance, since under the Empire the Officer Corps had been bound by a personal allegiance to the Emperor quite apart from the normal ties of citizenship. The President was now technically Supreme Commander of the armed forces, but the oath of allegiance was simply taken to the constitution, and the *Reichstag* had secured the sole right of declaring war.

This new system of government for Germany, drawn largely from the experience of other constitutional states, might well seem like the long-awaited realization of the hopes of the German liberals of 1848. Not merely had Germany at last a democratic government with as many safeguards for its preservation as a legal document could devise; she had, too, established a stronger central control over the various regions—now known as *Länder*—than either the men of 1848 had envisaged or Bismarck had achieved in 1871; the new constitution marked a further stage in the unification of Germany.

There were a few weak points. Proportional representation was to encourage the growth of a multiplicity of small political parties and that was bound to create difficulties for parliamentary government. As a consequence, it was decided that in the event of a political deadlock the President was to have a discretionary right by Article 48 to impose the Chancellor's measures by presidential decree. Thus paradoxically through their determination to make democratic representation as exact as possible, the framers of the constitution had been forced to envisage certain circumstances in which parliamentary sovereignty could be suspended. In this they were obviously influenced by the unsettled conditions existing in 1919, and certainly in the early years of the Weimar Republic it was sometimes found necessary to invoke these emergency powers.

Nevertheless, it was a dangerous feature and was to play its part in the eventual downfall of the Weimar Republic in 1933.

The true weakness of the new constitution, however, did not result from the technicalities of its wording; it lay in a much deeper psychological handicap. There could be no doubt that in the late summer of 1918 the German Army had sustained a crushing defeat, and the fact that the General Staff accepted this is plainly indicated by their refusal to contemplate a resumption of hostilities in the spring of 1919, when the terms of the Treaty of Versailles were made known. Yet the army had nevertheless withdrawn to the frontier in reasonable order and since no fighting had taken place on German soil, it was easy for the civilian to accept the myth that the army itself had never been defeated, only betrayed by revolution at home—the *Dolchstoss*, the stab in the back. The General Staff were naturally only too anxious to propagate this myth and unfortunately gained considerable support from Friedrich Ebert himself, when he reviewed German troops at the Brandenburger Tor in Berlin in December 1918: 'I salute you who return unvanquished from the field of battle.' Thus, since the army claimed to be blameless, the Assembly of the new Republic which had accepted the terms of the treaty was burdened with all the odium of national surrender. This meant more than an unhappy start for democracy in Germany; for certain individuals closely associated in the public mind with events at the end of the war it meant personal danger. Extreme nationalists never forgave them. In 1921 an attempt was made on the life of Philip Scheidemann; in the same year Erzberger, the president of the German armistice commission, was murdered, and in 1922 Walter Rathenau, the Foreign Minister, was shot down in Berlin.

The invidious position of the German government had already been made clear in the summer of 1919. Not only did they have to accept terms of Versailles, but in August the Allies demanded the withdrawal of all *Freikorps* and other military units which under General von der Goltz had been combatting Bolshevik forces in the Baltic states (see p. 350). By now the Bolsheviks were mostly on the defensive and the Allies simply wanted to end an anomalous situation in which the Germans still had large numbers of troops in action. It was, however, questionable whether the Weimar government had sufficient authority to bring about this withdrawal and in March 1920 the matter was put to the test, when the proposed disbanding of two Baltic brigades inspired an attempted right-wing *coup*.

This was led by a Prussian politician, Dr Wolfgang Kapp, and General von Lüttwitz. It never seriously threatened the government; yet it did reveal one disconcerting feature of relations between the army and the civil power. There had never been any question of the army failing to honour the agreement made between Gröner and Ebert in November 1918 (see p. 339), so long as the threat had come from the left; hence the severity with which the Spartakists had been crushed early in 1919. The significance of the Kapp *putsch* was that when a march on Berlin by Luttwitz's forces seemed imminent, Noske, the Minister of Defence, found that the army chiefs were not prepared to involve their forces in the clash. 'Would you force a battle at the Brandenburger Tor,' demanded General von Seeckt, 'between troops who a year and a half ago were fighting shoulder to shoulder against the enemy?' Faced with the withdrawal of the army into neutrality, the President, the Chancellor and his cabinet fled to Dresden and thence to Stuttgart, where they proclaimed a general strike. Thus it was not the power of the military, but of the trade unions, coupled with the political ineptitude of Dr Kapp, that brought to an end within four days the régime which he and von Lüttwitz attempted to set up in Berlin.

For some time the government had been aware that public opinion was swinging to the right and it was with this in mind that the Majority Socialists had decided not to risk any popular election in the summer of 1919. Instead, the Constituent Assembly itself elected Ebert President in the August of that year, even though this was contrary to the provisions of the Weimar constitution. Eventually, however, the general election of a *Reichstag* could be postponed no longer and in June 1920 the country went to the polls. The outcome suggested that the Kapp *putsch* had helped to bring about a dangerous polarization of views. On the left the Independent Socialists rose from twenty-two to eighty-four seats, and even the Communists won four. On the right, middle-class and nationalist parties made considerable gains, including the Bavarian People's party and Gustav Stresemann's German People's party (D.V.P.), while the parties that formed the coalition government—the Majority Socialists, the Centre and the Democrat—all lost heavily. The most significant consequence of this was the decision of the Majority Socialists to withdraw from the government, where their place was taken by Stresemann's party; thus, for much of the following decade the one party that believed fervently in the Weimar Republic was to spend its energies in opposition.

A series of short-lived administrations followed. Divided views over the fulfilment of Versailles were bound to make them insecure, and there were recurring crises over the payment of reparations. This particular tension came to a head at the beginning of 1923 after the Germans had defaulted and France and Belgium decided to retaliate by occupying the Ruhr and taking reparations in kind (see pp. 377–8). At first the German counter-measures of non-cooperation did put the whole nation behind the government at Berlin, but in

August 1923 when Stresemann became Chancellor, his decision to bring the resistance to an end awoke a fury among the extremists which seemed once again to threaten the life of the Republic.

Prussian nationalists plotted the occupation of Berlin. In Saxony, Thuringia, Hamburg, and the Ruhr, Communists appeared about to gain the upper hand. In Bavaria the Hoffmann government, which had fallen at the time of the Kapp *putsch*, had been succeeded by a series of right-wing administrations giving protection to many extreme nationalist movements which now came to the fore. The Bavarian situation was complicated, however, in that the local authorities under the influence of Gustav von Kahr were thinking in terms of separatism with a restoration of the Wittelsbach monarchy, while the National Socialist German Workers' Party, with whom they were closely associated, was aiming at an authoritarian régime which would unite the whole of Germany.

The leader of this Nazi party, as it came to be known, was Adolf Hitler. Contrary to later propaganda which always stressed his rise from utter poverty, Hitler, the son of an Austrian customs official, had grown up in modest lower middle-class surroundings. After his father's death he left school without passing his final exams and spent an idle three years, supported by his mother at Linz, while he made unsuccessful attempts to enter the Academy of Fine Arts and the School of Architecture at Vienna. His mother died at the end of 1908 and Hitler settled in Vienna, which had completely captivated him, but he still managed to avoid any regular employment, eking out an existence with odd jobs and selling little sketches of the city. During the next four years he certainly sank to the lowest level of society, dependent on doss-houses and soup kitchens, an odd remote individual, reading voraciously, brooding over a world that had rejected him, and nursing a growing sense of German nationalism and a hatred for the Slavs and the Jews, who peopled the polyglot capital of the Habsburg Empire.

In 1913 he went to Munich, where on the outbreak of war he volunteered for service in a Bavarian regiment. The violence of war suited the melancholy nihilism of his nature; during four years on the western front he rose to the rank of corporal, was twice wounded and twice decorated for bravery—on the second occasion with the Iron Cross, First Class, an award seldom given to uncommissioned ranks. In November 1918 he was discharged from hospital, where he had been recovering from temporary blindness after a gas attack, and in 1919 was posted to a regiment in Munich as an educational officer, after a violent speech against the Jews had attracted the attention of his military superiors.

It was through this new work that Hitler came to realize his own powers of demogogy and to see in political life an outlet for the hatred and megalomania that consumed him. When in the course of his activities he came across a small German Workers' Party which had been founded by Anton Drexler, a locksmith, he decided to join in order to take it over for his own ends, and within two or three years this strange figure with his lank black hair, his tooth-brush moustache, and his burning compelling eyes had imposed himself upon the political life of Bavaria. He preached against the monstrosity of Versailles, the corruption and weakness of the Wei-mar Republic, the threat of Communist Russia, the folly of democ-racy, and the wickedness of the Jews; he demanded a new strong united Germany. No politician ever made such a clean breast of all his intentions; none ever came so close ultimately to achieving them. He collected around him a number of post-war misfits who surren-dered to the driving will of this new leader—Rudolph Hess, a stu-dent of economics at Munich, Hermann Goering, a war hero of the German Air Force, Alfred Rosenberg, who had grown up in Tsarist Russia, and Joseph Goebbels, an unsuccessful novelist. He began to amass funds through the army, manufacturers, Goering's wife, and Putzi Hanfstaengel, who financed the party's newspaper the *Völkische Beobachter*; he raised a private army, the *Sturmabteilung*, the S.A., who with their brown-shirt uniform and their insignia of the swastika kept order at his own meetings and broke up the meetings of others. And in 1923 he gained the support of General Ludendorff, who had been living near Munich in disgruntled retirement since the failure of the Kapp *putsch* and whose name might add strength to a movement that aimed at nothing less than the overthrow of the Republic.

In fact, the government weathered the storm in the autumn of 1923 with greater ease than in 1920. 'Will the army stick to us, General?' President Ebert had asked before announcing the end of passive resistance in the Ruhr. 'The army, Mr President,' replied von Seeckt, 'will stick to me.' His answer, although not entirely reassuring for the head of a constitutional government, was strictly in the tradition of Prussian history and at least this time the army did not hold back. The threatened revolt in Berlin was crushed on von Seeckt's orders and in Saxony army commanders arrested the Communist and Socialist members of the government and dis-banded the militia.

In Bavaria von Kahr, who had taken over as State Commissioner, and General von Lossow, the local military commander, were still prepared to ignore the orders of Berlin and in November were actually planning a restoration of the Wittelsbach monarchy. Their hands, however, were forced, when in a famous scene at a meeting in the Bürgerbräu cellar, Hitler, who was determined to wreck any separatist movement, forced them to participate in his proclamation of a new nationalist government for Germany. Hitler, however, was relying on bluff; as soon as they were out of the cellar, von Kahr

and von Lossow hastened to put themselves on the side of the legitimate government, and when on the next day the Nazis attempted
a march through Munich led by Hitler and Ludendorff, their column was broken up by rifle fire from the police, and Hitler and
Ludendorff were placed under arrest.

The Munich *putsch* had been a hasty and ill-prepared affair and
Hitler had acted contrary to his own principle of working alongside
rather than against the major forces in power—mainly because of
his desire to forestall the separatists. He was, however, able to take
advantage of his trial to make one speech after another, all reported
in the national press, denouncing the government from the dock and
offering an eventual alliance with the army. 'The *Reichswehr* remains
as untarnished as before. One day the hour will come when the
Reichswehr will stand at our side, officers and men.' Even when confronted with this open declaration of war on the Republic, the judges
remained true to the Weimar policy of leniency towards those who
had erred in the direction of right-wing nationalism. There were too
many Germans who believed in their hearts at least some of the
accusations that Hitler voiced; even von Seeckt himself had said
after a meeting with Hitler six months before the events in Munich:
'We were one in our aim; only our paths were different.' Hitler thus
received the mildest sentence that the court could give—five years
of fortress detention, from which he was to be released on parole
after six months.

All these upsets in the course of 1923 had been accompanied by
an appalling inflation which virtually wiped out the German Mark.
This had already begun during the war years, when the value of the
Mark against the American dollar had dropped from four to nine,
but the deterioration had later become much sharper, and between
the beginning of 1921 and the middle of 1922 it fell from 64 to 493
to the dollar. The explanations put forward for this reflect all the
animosities of the post-war period. In German opinion the payment
of reparations was preventing Germany from meeting the cost of her
imports with her exports and when the difference was made up by
the issue of paper money, the inflationary spiral ensured that the price
of her imports became still greater. The Allies, on the other hand,
preferred to believe that Germany had simply failed to balance her
budget and should be filling the gap between expenditure and
income by attempting to increase taxation and to curb government
spending. There was even a theory that the Germans were ruining
their currency as a means of evading reparations, although there is
little evidence that this was a deliberate policy. Once the French
and Belgians had occupied the Ruhr, however, the German government had had no inhibitions about printing off millions of Marks
to finance the general strike with which they were retaliating, and
the consequences made any earlier inflation seem trivial by com-

parison. By August 1923 the Mark had sunk to four and a half million to the dollar and by November it had reached 4,200,000.

All this was eventually put right with the revaluation of the Mark (see p. 379) and the implementing of the Dawes plan, but that could not entirely undo the damage which had been caused. The effects varied greatly for different sections of the community. There was positive gain for financiers who had access to foreign currency and for industrialists who could pay off their debts in worthless Marks; landowners and small businessmen could on the whole manage to keep afloat. Wage-earners, poor before, became still poorer, but the greatest revolution was suffered by that section of the middle class who depended for their place in society on their salaries and the income from the investment of their private savings, which were now virtually wiped out. It was a most appalling blow for the most stable element of society and it was eventually to cost the Weimar Republic dear. Thousands became destitute, and from their despair the Communist and Nazi parties were later to draw a powerful reinforcement.

The last years of the decade showed something of an economic recovery. Between 1924 and 1929 investment from abroad, attracted by high rates of interest, amounted to 25.5 billion Marks—rather more than the total paid by Germany in reparations—and after 1927 German industrial production was rising beyond its pre-war level. There were, nevertheless, hidden dangers within this apparent return to prosperity. The reliance on foreign loans was bound to form a precarious basis, the rationalization of older industries occasionally created high levels of unemployment, and the small farmer, disappointed over any major land reform, was finding that his prices were rising more slowly than those in the industrial market. Politically governments became less dependent on presidential decree, but here, too, the greater stability was largely superficial, since they still rested on uneasy coalitions—mostly of the Centre, the Democrats and Stresemann's German People's Party—and while this was adequate for the time being, they might prove a doubtful bulwark in any new period of crisis amid the stresses inherent in post-war German society.

4. Eastern Europe

Meanwhile, the successor states which had emerged from the collapse of the old empires had been coping with the problems of their new identity. As the confusion of the post-war period died down, they all devised forms of parliamentary democracy, but the working of these constitutions was often bedeviled by the great number of political parties and by the competing aspirations of different national groups. They had also to undertake considerable land reforms. In some areas these were simply aimed at dispossessing an alien landlord class, but everywhere the proximity of Communist Russia made it important to satisfy the demands of the peasantry. Naturally, the consequent multiplicity of small holdings hardly made for efficient agriculture and this, together with primitive methods of farming and a steadily rising population, created some doubt whether the new states could survive as viable economic units. Indeed, the early years of their existence were harassed by inflation and unemployment, but gradually they began to attract the investment of foreign capital and as the European economy slowly recovered in the last part of the decade, they were able to develop some industry of their own, although, contrary to the hopes expressed at the time of the peace settlement, this depended upon protection behind high tariff barriers.

In the north, Finland's constitution as a parliamentary republic was established by the middle of 1919, the subsequent governments consisting of a series of moderately conservative coalitions in which the agrarians predominated. The only ethnic problem, represented by the fairly small but long settled Swedish section of society, was amicably resolved. A relatively large land mass for a population of about four million freed her from some of the economic difficulties that beset many eastern European states, and Finland's growing export of timber provided an economic base from which other industries began to grow.

The problems confronting the Baltic states south of the gulf were more complex since the turbulence had lasted longer here and national independence involved a greater social readjustment. By the beginning of 1920 Estonia, Latvia and Lithuania had each set up parliamentary régimes which broke up the estates of the old German, Russian and Polish landlord class, largely without compensation, and replaced them with small peasant holdings. As in Finland, agrarian parties tended to be the most powerful, but the variety of political views was so great that these governments were never particularly stable, and although Estonia and Latvia managed to maintain their parliamentary systems, Lithuania had by 1926 fallen back on a right-wing dictatorship under Voldemaras.

The immediate difficulties of the new Polish State were all brought to a conclusion in March 1921. In that month the treaty of Riga defined her eastern frontier with Russia (see p. 351), the plebiscite in Upper Silesia gave Poland two-fifths of the disputed area, and a democratic constitution established a bi-cameral Parliament whose Lower House was to be elected on a wide franchise. This, however, did not bring an end to Poland's problems. The presence of fifteen political parties created great instability, strikes and riots, and eventually in May 1926 Pilsudski marched on Warsaw with three regiments and set up a right-wing dictatorship behind a façade of constitutional rule. Pilsudski's *coup* was followed almost at once by the Locarno agreements (see p. 381) and in the subsequent atmosphere of recovery Poland's industrial production increased sharply and her foreign trade was expanded by the building of a new port Gdynia which relieved her of dependence on Danzig. Land reform came slowly and less wholeheartedly than in the Baltic states. There was an annual distribution of some 130,000 hectares which might eventually have allowed a third of the population about five hectares each, but by 1931 the rising population in Poland had reduced the average size of these holdings to considerably less.

In Czechoslovakia the presence of Bohemians, Slovaks and Ruthenians as well as the non-Slav minorities of Germans and Magyars had naturally suggested the need for some kind of federal organization, and indeed it had only been on that assumption that the Slovaks had consented to incorporation within Czechoslovakia. The efforts of the Czechs, however, ensured that their parliamentary democracy was placed on a unitary basis, whereby Slovakia was virtually merged with Bohemia, while Ruthenia, which was originally to have been granted autonomy, was largely under the rule of Czech officials. Some linguistic concessions were made to Germans and Magyars, but there was clearly considerable potential for discontent, quietened for the moment by the introduction of a greater decentralization in 1927 and by the eventual growth of an economic prosperity that was less dependent on foreign loans than elsewhere in eastern Europe.

Yugoslavia was similarly composite, a kingdom of Serbs, Croats and Slovenes, also including German and Magyar minorities. Here a parliamentary system was set up with a single chamber elected by universal male suffrage, but like the Czechs in Czechoslovakia the Serbs organized a highly centralized system in which they occupied most positions of responsibility. The Croats fared worst in this, since they paid higher taxes and were excluded from all the higher administrative posts, whereas the Slovenes did slowly gain a greater autonomy. Economically Yugoslavia was able to achieve a reasonable prosperity through the export of agricultural goods and attracted an increasing amount of foreign investment, but the political tensions precluded any lasting stability in government. In June 1928 a Montenegran deputy actually shot dead two other deputies in the Chamber and as the Croat demand for autonomy grew fierce, King Alexander brought the existing system to an end by proclaiming a royal dictatorship in January 1929.

In Rumania Bratianu, dissatisfied with the gains made at the peace conference (see p. 348) resigned in September 1919 and after King Ferdinand had appointed Marshal Averescu as premier, a considerable land reform distributed three and a half million hectares to 1,350,000 peasants. Proposals for a tax on property, however, brought about Averescu's dismissal and it was under a liberal administration that the constitution of 1923 was promulgated, establishing the usual pattern of a centralized parliamentary democracy. During the subsequent years there were efforts to revise the fiscal system and to raise foreign loans, but it was only the oil interest that flourished and other industries developed very slowly despite the protection provided by tariffs.

The most radical land policy was to be seen in Bulgaria where Stambolisky, the leader of the agrarian party, introduced a redistribution which made 30 hectares the maximum size of holding, at the same time as he encouraged rural education and relieved the peasantry of most taxation. Stambolisky hoped also to reach an understanding with Yugoslavia, but this proved too much for right-wing nationalist groups such as the Internal Macedonian Revolutionary Organization (I.M.R.O.). In June 1923 they carried out a *coup* in Sofia, murdered Stambolisky and fought a bitter war with the agrarians and the Communists, in which some ten thousand died. Forms of parliamentary government did continue after this, but they were largely a façade behind which I.M.R.O. ran their own régime of private vendettas, arbitrary arrests and torture.

For most of these states problems of government had arisen from digesting the territories that they had gained. For Austria and Hungary they consisted of coming to terms with their territorial losses. Austria's frontier now enclosed only the purely German area of the old Habsburg Empire. Consequently her application in 1919 to be included within Germany was entirely in accordance with the doctrine of national self-determination, but this was prohibited by the Allies who had no desire to enlarge Germany's frontiers. Thus Austria remained a separate state and although this could have been organized on a unitary basis, the federal constitution of September 1920 granted extensive rights for the provincial administrations. The early days of the new republic were harassed by an inflation in which money fell to one-fifteen-thousandth of its original value, but in October 1922 the Chancellor Ignaz Seipel managed to negotiate a large foreign loan and the budget was balanced by making a considerable reduction in the size of the civil service. This did bring some recovery, but a high level of unemployment still persisted and the struggle between the right and the left created a continuing instability. The Social Democrats (S.D.) were the most powerful single group and although right-wing coalitions were able to exclude them from the federal government, they did control the local administration of Vienna where a programme of municipal housing and welfare was financed out of taxes on the property-owning class. The danger of the situation was heightened by the existence of two private armies—the S.D.'s *Schutzbund* and the right-wing *Heimwehr*—and after an outbreak of fighting in Vienna in July 1927 the government turned increasingly to the *Heimwehr*, until in December 1929 the President had to be given greater emergency powers in order to avert the likelihood of civil war.

There might seem even less prospect of stability in Hungary— smarting from the loss of Slovakia and Transylvania and plagued with the upheavals of the short-lived Bela Kun régime (see p. 349) and the White Terror which followed its collapse. Even the devising of the constitution was hampered by the two attempts of the last Emperor Karl to reclaim his kingdom in 1921. Eventually a parliamentary system was set up, but since this was based on a limited franchise and was largely dominated by the Magyar landowning classes, it was hardly suprising that there should be little land reform. One third of Hungary still consisted of vast estates, and some 60 per cent of the rural population had only tiny holdings or none at all. Economic life was at first at the mercy of the usual difficulties of inflation and lack of capital and of raw materials, as well as the burden of reparations, but Stephen Bethlen, the conservative premier throughout this decade, was able to negotiate foreign loans which did assist a general recovery including a marked industrial growth, although Hungary was still principally agricultural.

Thus in many ways the problems taxing the relics of the Habsburg Empire were as great as they were for Germany, and throughout eastern Europe the new states that had won their national independence through the Versailles agreement were to find this an uneasy inheritance.

5. Russia after Lenin: the struggle for power

By the end of 1920 the last of the White Russian forces had been driven out of the Crimea, an armistice had ended the fighting on the Polish front (see p. 351) and the Bolsheviks could reckon that they had survived the immediate threat to their régime. The demands of civil war had greatly consolidated the hold of their party over the state and in contrast to the limited forces at their disposal in 1917 Trotsky's Red Army now numbered five million.

In almost every other respect, however, their position was deplorable. Russia lay in ruin. Industrial output was minimal, railway rolling stock was worn out and much of the population of the cities had fled to the countryside in a desperate search for food. Economic life had been reduced to a primitive system of barter, since the government had printed millions of paper notes in order to finance the war and the consequent inflation had reduced the value of the rouble to one per cent of what it had been in October 1917. The emergency had also brought about a marked revision of the ideals which the Bolsheviks had originally proclaimed. Most industrial concerns had been nationalized, but their factory committees had proved to be so inefficient that they had largely been replaced by former managers and technicians earning high rates of pay, just as Trotsky had had to draw on Tsarist officers for the Red Army. And when the peasantry, who had been granted all the land by Lenin's decree of October 1917, became reluctant to accept worthless roubles for their crops on which the cities and the army depended, armed detachments of workers descended on them and carried out a ruthless requisitioning of anything beyond immediate local requirements. As a result, the peasantry confined themselves to subsistence farming or cultivated the land secretly in scattered strips—concealed sowings, which by 1920, it was reckoned, occupied some twenty million acres.

While the civil war raged, these hardships were endured, but once victory seemed certain, protests began to mount against the dictatorship of the Bolshevik party and its policy of terror exercized through the secret police, the Cheka. The retreat of the White armies was followed by peasant revolts. Already in 1920 support for the Mensheviks had been growing in the Soviets and the trade unions in the larger cities, and in February 1921 strikes broke out in Petrograd. The climax of this discontent came in March with a rising in Kronstadt, the island naval base off Petrograd, once the very centre of Bolshevik support, where a full programme of political and economic freedom was demanded.

The Kronstadt rising did not last long. Trotsky mounted a major military operation; an attacking force stormed the island across the frozen sea and the rebels were massacred. It may, however, have played some part in the opening of a new phase of Bolshevik rule. Lenin had already been moving in his own mind towards the acceptance of a controlled form of private enterprise as the quickest means of bringing about economic recovery in Russia and at a party congress, which met while the fighting was still in progress, he was able to use the rising as a lesson which pointed to the need for a greater relaxation.

The New Economic Policy (N.E.P.), which was now introduced, allowed the peasant to trade freely in produce that was surplus to his own requirements. And since there would be no incentive for him to do this unless he could use his profits to purchase goods from the cities, it followed that there must also be a greater freedom for industry to cater for this new demand. The doctrinal objections to such a course were obvious; laissez faire would allow the rise of a new rich class—prosperous peasants (the Kulaks) and traders acting as middlemen between factories and the countryside (the Nepmen)— and according to Marx this economic power should eventually lead to political power. Lenin, however, proposed to avert this in two ways. First, the government would retain its control of the commanding heights of heavy industry, banking and foreign trade. Second, the Bolsheviks must close their ranks; they could not allow any dissident factions within the party, and the central committee was to have the power to expel any member; this was even to include members of the central committee itself, provided that there was a two-thirds majority in favour. In these circumstances there could hardly be toleration for other Socialist groups outside the party. The Mensheviks were persuaded to leave Russia, and the Social Revolutionaries, who proved more obdurate, found thirty-four of their leaders placed on trial in the summer of 1922.Thus while allowing a temporary return towards economic freedom, N.E.P. finally established the position of the central committee as the potential instrument for a personal dictatorship.

Lenin did not live to see the full working of his new scheme. In May 1922 he suffered the first of a series of strokes that finally killed him in January 1924, and the following years were occupied with a long struggle over the leadership of the party. The flamboyant role which Trotsky had played in recent events seemed to make him a likely candidate, but there were many of the Bolshevik old guard who were jealous of this former rival of Lenin, who had only joined the party in 1917. They were so obsessed with their doubts about his autocratic tendencies that they did not notice another figure in the contest. Stalin's antecedents were unimpeachable—a peasant, an original party member who had served his time in Siberia, and since then, a diligent committee man working tirelessly in the background; 'a grey man', Trotsky had called him and only learnt later to his cost how dangerous grey men can be. Already in 1918 Stalin belonged to both the Politbureau and the Organization Bureau on the central committee, and in 1922, when he became General Secretary of the committee, he had achieved a position from which he could appoint provincial party leaders and keep an eye on all the 400,000 members of the party. Lenin himself had become profoundly mistrustful of Stalin and stated his objections in a political testament dictated a year before he died, but so much did his colleagues underestimate Stalin's ambition that the central committee decided not to publish the document.

The issue did not rest on personalities alone. It also involved two major questions which directly affected the future course of the government. First, what was to be the attitude of Soviet Russia to other parts of Europe, which, contrary to Lenin's hopes, had failed to turn Communist? This was fundamental to the original decision to seize power in October 1917, since it had been a generally accepted Marxist belief that a proletarian revolution in Russia could only succeed if it was accompanied by revolution elsewhere in more advanced industrial countries. It was with the purpose of fostering this that the Third International had been set up in 1919 and Trotsky with his doctrine of 'permanent revolution' was convinced that it must remain a principal objective. This was opposed by a trium-

virate of Stalin, Zinoviev and Kamenev, who insisted that Russia
should now concentrate her effort on achieving 'Socialism in one
country'. For many this sounded a more peaceful and constructive
aim and as Stalin tightened his grasp on the party organization,
Trotsky, always a lone wolf, found himself slowly being pushed into
isolation and in January 1925 was forced to resign as commissar for
war.

Meanwhile, the second question had created a different division
of views. How long should the government continue with N.E.P.,
before taking a more Socialist turn in time to frustrate the emergence
of new wealthy classes? The left wing, which on this issue included
Zinoviev and Kamenev, wished to abandon the N.E.P. and to shift
the peasants towards a greater collectivization of farm land. Against
them a group under Bukharin believed that the continuing prosperity of the *Kulaks* would be an essential element in the growth of
Russian industry. With the threat from Trotsky apparently fading,
Stalin now decided to take his stand with Bukharin so as to dislodge
his former allies Zinoviev and Kamenev. Their position in the central committtee was undermined and when they looked frantically
for reconciliation with Trotsky, Stalin used his control of the party
machine to bring about their temporary expulsion from the party.
In October 1927 Trotsky was deported to Alma Ata and a year later
was exiled from Russia.

This turn of events did nothing to save the N.E.P. By 1927 agricultural and industrial production had roughly recovered its pre-
war level. The price being demanded by the *Kulaks* for their grain,
however, was placing some strain on the feeding of the cities and
Stalin himself was coming to think that it was time to enter a new
Socialist phase. He had merely been determined that this should not
be the work of others and now that the Trotsky-Zinoviev bloc had
been broken, his former alliance with the Bukharin group was
hardly likely to hold him back from an attack on the N.E.P. The
first Five Year plan, which included the beginning of the collectivization of peasant land, was approved in April 1929 and by the
autumn Bukharin and his supporters had been removed from their
position of influence. In this way the struggle over the succession
had finally been resolved and there were many old Bolsheviks who
were later to regret that for once they had not acted on Lenin's
advice.

Chapter 29

The 1920s: (2) Reparations and Revisionism

Very gradually the grass grew back over the tortured land of the battlefields amid the deserted pill boxes and the rusting barbed wire, but on the minds of men the wounds inflicted by the First World War took longer to heal. For all belligerents the cost had been appalling—for Great Britain and the Empire a million dead, France well over a million, Germany perhaps two million, Austria-Hungary a million, the United States 81,000 and for Russia, who had probably suffered worst of all, the final figure cannot be established. The memory of that horror was like some great divide cutting off one epoch from another and the break was matched politically by the emergence of a new map of Europe. The doctrine of national self-determination had created a multiplicity of frontiers in the east, yet at the same time there had come about a remarkable simplification of the position of the great Powers. Austria-Hungary had disintegrated. Germany could hardly play an independent role, and Russia, ostracised by non-Communist countries, wished merely to barricade herself against interference, while she set her domestic affairs in order. Thus with the withdrawal of the United States into isolationism, Great Britain and France remained the two Powers who could take the initiative on the Continent.

This simplification, however, did not produce any great unity of purpose between them. The French, whose north-eastern province had been utterly devastated in four years of war and whose population was markedly smaller than Germany's were haunted by the fear of eventual German recovery. This explained their insistance on the reparations and disarmament clauses of the treaty, their encouragement of the Poles to take the whole of Upper Silesia, and their original plan to create a separate Rhineland state which would have made the Rhine the western border of Germany (see p. 343). The attitude of the British was quite different. The eclipse of Germany as a naval and colonial Power ended any immediate threat from her and although the general election of 1918 had expressed a mood of revenge, this had been a relatively short-lived emotion and the French soon became suspicious that they were not going to have full British support in their schemes for the containment of Germany. This nervousness was not entirely without foundation. The British were wary of making any general Continental commitment, particularly after the American Senate had refused to ratify the Treaty of Versailles.

Faced with the danger of isolation, the most obvious step for the French would have been a return to the 1894 alliance with Russia, had it not been for the changed situation in eastern Europe. One of the aims of the western statesmen in 1919 had been to devise a *cordon sanitaire* of small states that would bar the way to any expansion westwards by Soviet Russia, and the disadvantage of such a scheme for France was that it also precluded any direct intervention by Russia against Germany. As early as 1916 Arthur Balfour had predicted that if Poland were to be recreated, 'France would be at the mercy of Germany in the next war, for this reason that Russia could not come to her aid without violating the neutrality of Poland.' Thus France was now forced to look elsewhere. In 1920 a military alliance was concluded with Belgium, but her main efforts were directed towards signing a series of treaties with countries immediately to the east of Germany—with Poland in 1921, with Czechoslovakia in 1924, with Rumania in 1926, and with Yugoslavia in 1927. This was far from creating a unified system of defence against Germany, whereby each would act on behalf of the others. It is true that after the war Czechoslovakia, Rumania, and Yugoslavia had formed a 'little *entente*', but this was mainly to guard against any attempt by Hungary to regain her lost territories, while Yugoslavia was concerned with her quarrel with Italy over Fiume. Poland did share French fears of a German national revival, but she was equally suspicious of Russian and Lithuanian designs upon her frontier. This diversity of aims naturally militated against the likelihood of any concerted action against Germany, whose great bulk in the centre of Europe separating France from her allies was at the same time the *raison d'être* and the fundamental weakness of the French system.

A number of reasons have been given for the reluctance of the British to give full backing to the French. They may have felt that too great a pressure on a German government so recently established might open the way to Communist gains. There was even a theory that in accordance with the balance of power they were actively turning towards Germany against French preponderance in Europe, but this is hardly convincing, since there was at this time little likelihood of a French hegemony. The simplest explanation lies in a desire to avoid Continental entanglements, which would certainly be consistent with earlier British attitudes. Beyond that, their principal concern as a trading nation was the re-establishment of peace-time markets and for this a speedy restoration of the German economy was essential.

A general recovery from the strain and expense of war, however, was made more difficult by the question of a settlement of accounts among the belligerents. Great Britain and France had lent large sums to their European allies, but the situation was complicated by the fact that both had also incurred considerable debts of their own. From the United States and Great Britain France had borrowed almost three times as much as she had lent, while Great Britain had borrowed from the United States slightly less than half. Shortly after the war the British proposed an all-round cancellation of debts with a direct payment of German reparations to the United States, but the suggestion was acceptable to neither the French who were determined not to lose their share of German reparations, nor to the Americans who were the principal creditor nation. 'They hired the money, didn't they!' remarked President Coolidge, and the most that could be achieved in this direction was a general reduction in the total amounts to be repaid. Thus, an acrimonious situation was prolonged, adding a sense of urgency to the demand for reparations from Germany, so that the western Powers might be able in turn to meet their own liabilities. Only the Russians managed to escape from this imbroglio by the simple means of disowning all debts of the Tsarist government.

A decision over the total amount of reparations had not been reached at the time of the peace-making, Germany simply being required to make an interim payment of £1,000 million. In March 1921, when Germany had defaulted over this, the Allies occupied Düsseldorf, Duisburg, and Ruhrort on the east side of the Rhine, and on 27 April the Reparations Commission followed up by announcing the total figure that would be exacted from Germany— £6,600 million in gold to be paid off in annual instalments. Not surprisingly this brought about the downfall of a German government already deep in domestic difficulties, but in May its successor had to accept the demand.

The wisdom of the Allies' policy over reparations has often been seriously questioned. Certainly there was nothing unusual in the payment of an indemnity by a defeated nation, and the appalling devastation that France and Belgium had suffered gave them a perfectly good case for compensation. Yet the very size of the payment demanded was without precedent and was to have disastrous political and economic consequences for victors and vanquished alike. As Bernard Shaw pointed out in a later broadcast, there were no gold mines in Germany; all payment must depend ultimately upon the sale of goods and services abroad and this could only be achieved by the stimulation of German foreign trade; the financial profit that

Germany might thereby gain would then be drained off in the form of reparations. Thus, foreign rivals would be faced with a far greater German competition without any corresponding increase in consuming power on the German home market, where they might have been able to retaliate. This aspect of reparations was of particular significance for the British, whereas foreign trade mattered less to the French, whose economy was more self-contained and who were concerned with the immediate question of repairing the material damage of the war.

Consequently, reparations were to be a further source of division between Great Britain and France and this became apparent almost at once when, in 1922, the German government requested a moratorium on cash payments. The British were prepared to grant this, but the French refused and in January 1923, when Germany defaulted once more, French and Belgium troops crossed the Rhine to occupy the Ruhr, the heart of German industry, to undertake the direct supervision of continued payment. The German government replied by proclaiming a policy of non-cooperation throughout the occupied area, giving financial aid to strikers and indefinitely suspending all further reparations payments to France and Belgium. Casualties were suffered in many clashes between French soldiers and Germans, and ill feeling became still further inflamed, when in the course of the year French generals attempted to foster in the Rhineland a local separatist movement whose supporters eventually expelled the officials of the Weimar Republic. The British had already refused to participate in the occupation of the Ruhr, and their disagreements with the French came to a head in January 1924, when they were outvoted in the Allied High Commission, which proceeded to recognize an autonomous government for the Rhineland. In fact, strong British pressure led to the abandonment of the separatist movement and the German government, recently harassed by an unsuccessful *coup* in Bavaria, (see p. 366) was assisted in its suppression by the Rhinelanders themselves, most of whom had seen the movement as no more than a French strategem.

Meanwhile, a defiant German government had proceeded to finance its policy of non-cooperation by recklessly printing paper money to an extent that eventually made the Mark worthless (see p. 366). Thus when Gustav Stresemann took office as German Chancellor in August 1923, he was faced with an appalling inflation, hunger and the industry of the country at a standstill. Although a monarchist and a conservative at heart, he believed that for the moment the only hope of German recovery lay in the survival of the Republic, and in September he abandoned the policy of non-cooperation in the Ruhr and resumed payment of reparations. The Allies, who had become seriously alarmed at the situation in Germany, responded at once to this first step by Stresemann; the British

Prime Minister, Stanley Baldwin, appealed to the United States to collaborate in a new settlement, and in January 1924 a committee under an American general, Charles G. Dawes, was set up in Paris to examine ways of setting German finances aright and to devise a more sensible approach to the problem of reparations.

The Dawes Committee presented its report in April. It advised a German currency reform which would establish the Reichsmark at 20 to the pound, the bank of issue being free from governmental interference. To prime the pump Germany would receive a foreign loan of £40 million and a more moderate scale of annual instalments of reparations was to be introduced with payments made in German currency. These suggestions were discussed at London in July, and here Stresemann was fortunate in that a Labour administration under Ramsay MacDonald had been formed in Great Britain at the beginning of the year, while in France a radical government under Édouard Herriot had taken over after the fall of Poincaré in May. The left wing in Great Britain and France were inclined to be more conciliatory towards Germany, and the recommendations of the Dawes Committee were accepted without great difficulty. In October 1924 the foreign loan was floated, much of it being raised in the United States, and in November French and Belgian troops were finally withdrawn from the Ruhr.

These clashes with the west, principally over reparations, were not the only factor in Germany's foreign policy at this time. Her geographical position had always enabled her to look east as well as west, and as relations with France had grown more hectic, it was natural that nationalist arguments should be voiced in favour of a deal with Russia. The climax of this had come in April 1922, when an international economic conference at Genoa ran into difficulties over Russia's demand for a cancellation of war debts and over her refusal to grant compensation for the nationalization of private property after the revolution. In the same month Germany and Russia concluded the treaty of Rapallo which re-established diplomatic and commercial relations between the two countries including a mutual renunciation of war debts.

Rapallo at once gave rise to some alarm in the west, where it was seen as an embryo treaty of alliance which could well mean a threat to the frontiers of Poland, and it probably helped to harden the French determination to occupy the Ruhr at the beginning of 1923. Later interpretations have even tended to regard it as a shadowy forerunner to the eventual Ribbentrop-Molotov pact of 1939 (see p. 426). It is true that no German government regarded the frontiers of eastern Europe as final and the easterner school of thought did advocate a positive treaty of alliance with Russia. In September 1922 General von Seeckt, the head of the German army, had presented a masterly statement of their viewpoint, suggesting nothing less than a new partition of Poland. 'The restoration of the frontier between Russia and Germany is a necessary condition before both sides can become strong. The 1914 frontier between Russia and Germany should be the basis of any understanding between the two countries.'

It seems unlikely, however, that Joseph Wirth, who had become German Chancellor in May 1921, was thinking in such far-reaching terms. The purpose of the treaty was largely immediate. It removed the threat of any Russian demand for reparations under Article 116 of the Treaty of Versailles; it opened up the prospect of markets for German goods and it made any attack by Poland less likely. There was a more sinister secret agreement whereby the German army could establish training areas in Russia, but at the time this evasion of the military clauses of Versailles did not represent the forming of a military bloc in the east, and Wirth himself certainly did not intend to abandon the policy of the fulfilment of Versailles with the west. Even so, the growing difficulties with the French naturally delighted the easterner lobby, and the existence of Rapallo was a comforting reassurance for the German government when they embarked on the policy of non-cooperation during the French occupation of the Ruhr in 1923.

The German right wing were less pleased when Stresemann brought that policy to an end, but the Dawes plan, the eventual French evacuation of the Ruhr and the subsequent return of economic prosperity all combined to usher in a new more constructive period of international relations. Stresemann ceased to be Chancellor in December 1923, but remained Foreign Minister in subsequent administrations until his death in 1929 and throughout these years he worked subtly to translate the policy of fulfilment into a diplomatic concert which would relax the tensions in the west, while still leaving Germany's options open in the east.

He was assisted in this by the recent failure of two attempts on the part of the French to strengthen their defence by revising the machinery of the League of Nations. In 1923 they had strongly supported a draft Treaty of Mutual Assistance which was based on the assumption that a state of general security must precede any scheme for world-wide disarmament. The plan was to make military sanction *obligatory* for member States against any country stigmatized as an aggressor by the Council of the League; on the other hand, this duty to intervene was to be restricted to those States situated in the continent where the aggression had taken place. The terms of the treaty naturally suited the French with their new system of alignments to the east of Germany, but for the British the complication of the Commonwealth made such a sub-division of regional responsibilities unacceptable and the proposal lapsed. In 1924, however, a meeting between the two Prime Ministers, Ramsay MacDonald and Herriot, at Geneva led to a reformulation of the scheme. The main purpose of the Geneva Protocol was to strengthen the League's power of intervention in two ways. The existing arrangement precluded any action by the League, if the Council were not unanimous or if a dispute came within the domestic jurisdiction of one of the parties. The Protocol now laid down a system whereby disputes in either of these cases would be bound to be subject to some form of arbitration, although it made no mention of obligatory military sanctions. Once again, the French pressed for acceptance of the scheme, since any dispute over treaty revision was specifically excluded from its terms and hence any enforcement of the settlement of 1919 would not be at the mercy of arbitration. And once again consideration for the Commonwealth caused the British to hold back, since they saw that it would give the Japanese an opportunity to demand the right of immigration into Australia, New Zealand, and Canada, whose governments had prohibited their entry. In March 1925 Austen Chamberlain, Foreign Secretary in the new Baldwin administration in Great Britain, accordingly announced his country's rejection of the Geneva Protocol.

Thus the time was ripe for a return to more traditional forms of diplomacy. In February 1925 Stresemann delivered a memorandum to the Allies and in the course of the year negotiations led in October to an important conference at the Swiss lakeside resort of Locarno where agreement was reached over a set of treaties which were later signed in London. These included mutual guarantees of the Franco-German and Belgo-German frontiers between Great Britain, France, Belgium, Germany and Italy. The permanent demilitarization of the Rhineland was reaffirmed and Great Britain and Italy would assist France if there should be any 'flagrant violation' of this. At the same time Germany signed arbitration treaties with Czechoslovakia and Poland, both of whom were to be reinsured by treaties of mutual defence with France in the case of German aggression. The election of Hindenburg as President of the German Republic after the death of Ebert in February 1925, and the fall of the Herriot government in France in April had at first seemed likely to make agreement more difficult, but despite the resistance of the easterner school of thought in Germany, Stresemann managed to gain the necessary support from Hindenburg and the *Reichstag* for this settlement with the west.

The attractive feature of Locarno was that it gave the impression of opening up a new period of reconciliation. It did, however, retain within its terms most existing alignments, and there was one particular implication that might have aroused a sense of unease. The absolute guarantee of Germany's western frontiers in contrast to the arbitration treaties with Poland and Czechoslovakia suggested that Great Britain, at least, accepted the fact that Germany's eastern frontiers were less firm than those in the west. This distinction between Germany's possible attitudes towards the east and the west was emphasized during negotiations in 1926 over her entry into the League of Nations. It was originally proposed that she should join Great Britain, France, Italy and Japan as a permanent member of the Council, but when Poland, Spain and Brazil were also to be given permanent seats, German protests resulted in Poland becoming only a semi-permanent member, and Spain and Brazil withdrew from the League. This resistance to equality of status for Poland coincided with a renewal, in April, of the Treaty of Rapallo between Germany and Russia, whereby each agreed to remain neutral in the event of the other being attacked, and it was abundantly clear that the Locarno pact had not entirely laid the ghost of the German easterners' policy.

Still, Locarno, coupled with returning prosperity, did usher in a short period of stability which greatly heartened the pacifism of the idealists. For the next four years the new French foreign minister Briand, Austen Chamberlain and Stresemann formed a triumvirate of foreign ministers who were able to give some substance to the spirit of concord with which public opinion associated the pact. It was Stresemann who made the greatest gains from all this, since by soothing the suspicions of the French he was now able to achieve a revision of some of the terms of Versailles affecting disarmament, the payment of reparations and the occupation of the Rhineland.

The most startling aspect of his success concerned the army, which under the skilful direction of von Seeckt was being reorganized throughout the 1920s on a far wider basis than had been stipulated by the Allies. The Treaty of Versailles had ruled that its size should not be greater than 100,000 men, of whom only 4,000 were to be officers, but it had made no mention of the number of N.C.O.s. Von Seeckt took advantage of this to concentrate on the training of leaders, creating some 40,000 N.C.O.s out of 96,000 other ranks, who were to be rehearsed for far higher command than their rank would suggest, and the smallness of the force based on voluntary enlistment enabled him to insist upon the highest standards of physique and education. The General Staff simply continued to exist under another name and set to work almost at once on a new revolutionary technique of war based on mobility, the use of armour, and air support which was to bring about the remarkable German victories in the early years of the second World War. Plans were made for the ultimate equipping of 63 divisions—later reduced to 21, although even this was three times greater than the number allowed by the Treaty of Versailles; much of this was covered by secret business agreements in Austria, Switzerland, Sweden, Spain, the Netherlands, and Italy, but in Germany also the Krupp works made a pact, in January 1922, with the German Ministry of Defence 'jointly to circumvent . . . the provisions of the Treaty of Versailles'. Commercial aviation, gliding clubs, and paramilitary organizations such as labour battalions and the Prussian police force were all used to the same end, and in 1922 the Treaty of Rapallo with the Soviet Union enabled von Seeckt to set up tank and flying schools in Russia. It was an essay in evasion which far surpassed the achievement of Scharnhorst and Gneisenau after the disaster of Jena in 1806. The extraordinary thing is that the Allied military control commission was aware of many of these activities and had reported accordingly, yet so skilful had Stresemann been in gaining the confidence of the western governments that they turned a blind eye to this contravention of the treaty, and in 1927 the Allied commission was withdrawn.

He could hardly expect the same success over reparations, but in 1929 a committee under an American banker, Owen D. Young, did establish a new basis for payment which marked a very considerable reduction on that demanded by the Dawes plan. This was finally established at a conference at the Hague. Here Stresemann gained an additional concession with the complete evacuation of the Rhineland five years ahead of schedule, and by 1930 the occupying forces had been withdrawn.

This new confidence in Germany also affected political alignments, since it led to a gradual weakening of France's interest in her Polish alliance. In Poland Pilsudski, who had seized power in 1926, was mistrustful of France and began to move towards better relations with Germany. Stresemann was quick to seize on this, although their conversations had to avoid the question of the frontier which Stresemann had been careful not to guarantee. Indeed, he had already admitted privately that he hoped to regain Danzig and the Polish Corridor, and since he had also spoken of incorporating Austria within Germany, it might seem that there is a direct continuity between Stresemann's policies and those later adopted by Adolf Hitler. In fact, there was nothing very remarkable about any German foreign minister contemplating such goals after 1918. The difference was that Stresemann's hopes for revision were based on peaceful diplomatic means working through a constitutional democracy rather than on the bombastic aggressiveness of the single party Nazi State. He aimed simply to restore Germany to the position of a great Power who could remain on good terms with the west and with Soviet Russia. To do this, he had to resist the less subtle demands of German nationalists as well as to allay foreign hostility, and the extent to which he had been able to accomplish this by the time of his death in 1929 is the measure of his effectiveness as a European statesman.

Chapter 30

The Great Depression

1. Economic disaster

In 1929 the economy of the entire world outside Russia was stricken by a period of depression more dramatic and widespread in its political consequences than any similar crisis in the nineteenth century. The fundamental causes of this catastrophe remain the subject of some debate, but it seems probable that they lie in the cumulative effects of the over-production of raw commodities such as foodstuffs throughout the 1920s. The irony of the story is that there were still many regions in the world where poverty and hunger were endemic. The farmer with his living to make, however, had to depend upon those markets where he could sell, and since these were ultimately limited in their demand, an excess of agricultural produce soon led to falling prices. It was in order to check this decline that produce was actually kept off the market, with the result that world stocks of food left over at the end of the year rose from 8.9 million tonnes in 1925 to 16.1 million tonnes in 1929. This drop in agricultural prices naturally meant a considerable reduction in the purchasing power of the farming population, but although this was in turn bound to affect the market for industrial goods, the inevitable time lag in the economic process enabled the industrial world to continue to enjoy the boom of the later half of the 1920s and the shock was thus all the greater when it eventually came.

This disparity of tendencies within the economy was most marked in the United States. American agricultural prices had been falling since 1926, yet in the world of industrial investment optimism continued to soar. The average price of stock rose by 25 per cent in 1928 and by a further 35 per cent in 1929, an orgy of speculation in which a great deal of much-needed capital was attracted away from Europe. An example of the corresponding output is provided by the automobile industry, which in the single year 1929 produced nearly five-and-a-half million cars. Then with appalling suddenness the industrialists awoke to the fear that the market might become saturated; production had to be checked and the consequent sense of doubt turned almost at once into a great panic to withdraw investments. On one day, 24 October 1929, thirteen million shares were sold on Wall Street, the financial centre of the U.S.A.; one firm after another crashed as their credit failed, and by the end of the month American investors who had sold too late had lost some 40,000 million dollars. Unemployment mounted, purchasing power collapsed, and so the avalanche rolled on into utter disaster.

It has been seen how throughout the nineteenth century Europe had grown increasingly sensitive to the vicissitudes of American economy (see pp. 90, 225), and in the 1920s, as never before, her fate was utterly dependent upon the prosperity of the United States. The immediate consequence of the Wall Street crash was that the American businessman in his frantic need of capital could lend no more to Europe and even began to call in his existing short-term loans. With this enormous source of credit suddenly cut off, European banks had to meet their obligations through the catastrophic shrinking of American purchasing power, and so Europe, too, became caught up in the vicious circle of depression—pessimism leading to the withdrawal of capital, with the consequent bankruptcies and unemployment which spread pessimism still further.

In Austria the *Kreditanstalt*, a bank whose name was a byword for financial stability, was near collapse by May 1931 and was only saved for the moment by an advance of 150 million schillings from the Bank of England. German economy had hinged almost entirely on foreign loans; in 1927 and 1928, for instance, she had borrowed almost five times as much as was due in reparations payments. By July 1931 the *Reichsbank* had exhausted its reserves of foreign paper money and in three weeks £50 million in gold had been drained from the country. In the same month the *Darmstädterbank* had to close, and in November came the collapse of a great Berlin bank. There were few savings or reserves in Germany with which to meet the crisis, and the figures for trade between 1929 and 1932 tell their own story, exports dropping from £630 million to £280 million, imports from £670 million to £230 million. By the summer of 1931 the Bank of England was losing gold at the rate of £2½ million a day, and in one week at the end of July £21 million were withdrawn. In September Great Britain left the gold standard, which by this time had become purely theoretical throughout most of Europe, and the consequent fall in the value of sterling brought the pound to 30 per cent below par. France did not feel the full shock until 1932 owing to the greater self-sufficiency of her economy, but in the agricultural regions of eastern Europe, which depended upon their export of foodstuffs, the fall in prices meant growing debts for the small peasant farmers.

The social scene was of a modern industrial world that had run calamitously to a halt through a breakdown in the machinery of credit and financial exchange. Small businesses were caught up in the ruin of great ones; thousands of investors lost everything, and in the industrial towns millions of unemployed workers wandered about the streets outside the gates of the silent empty factories. In 1932 there were nearly 6 million workless in Germany, nearly 3 million in Great Britain, and nearly 14 million in the United States. By 1933 France had 1,300,000, while the American figure had risen to 15 million.

Although the disaster was world-wide, international cooperation played only a small part in the attempts to find a solution. There were certain regional agreements, such as the Oslo group formed by the Scandinavian countries or the British Commonwealth discussions at Ottawa in 1932. And an end was brought, not before its time, to the senseless cycle of payments that had been in operation since the end of the war. In July 1932 the Lausanne Convention cancelled all further reparations in return for a single payment by Germany of £150 million in 5 per cent redeemable bonds. The United States had announced in June 1931 a moratorium for one year on all war debts, but when payment was due to be resumed in December 1932, France, indignant at the cancellation of reparations, defaulted, although Great Britain, while making no demand on her own debtors, paid her full instalment in gold to the United States. In 1933 Great Britain could make only a token payment and most other countries defaulted, except Finland, who paid her instalment in full; in 1934 the whole process finally petered out.

Beyond this all attempts at general cooperation were defeated by the continued pursuit of individual national interests. In August 1930, at the conference of Warsaw, the Danubian states had failed in their efforts to persuade the governments of Europe to establish a system of tariffs which would protect their agricultural produce from American competition, and at Stresa in 1932 another scheme for protection among themselves was eventually undermined by German and Italian suspicions over the possible growth of French economic influence in the Balkans. In 1931 French objections prevented the creation of a Customs Union between Germany and Austria, and in June 1933 a World Economic Conference at London came to nothing when the American government, who had left the gold standard in April, refused to agree over a policy of currency stabilization.

In the main, each country tried to work out its own solution for itself. This took the form generally of protecting home production by higher tariffs, at the same time attempting to improve the chances of selling abroad by a devaluation of the currency. This highly competitive approach to the problem was to have a continuing effect upon economic relations; even as late as 1938 tariff walls were still hampering the full development of trade and foreign investment among the great Powers, and there was a general abandonment of the gold standard by most European countries in the early 1930s.

In the United States the new President, Franklin D. Roosevelt, inaugurated his policy of the New Deal. Government controls encouraged certain sections of the economy, while monetary inflation was used to promote higher prices; a vast programme of public works was started to reduce the millions of unemployed, and schemes for a minimum wage and social insurance were introduced to alleviate the worst distress. In Great Britain in 1931 part of the Labour administration formed a coalition with the Conservatives in a National government which cut State expenditure by 10 per cent and embarked upon a policy of Protection with Imperial preference for the Commonwealth countries—the final repudiation of the nineteenth-century gospel of Free Trade. France preferred to rely upon a quota system of imports, and Germany and Italy both turned to the development of national self-sufficiency, whereby they would be less dependent upon foreign production, although this policy was as much due to political and military requirements as to the needs of the economic situation. Fortunately for them all, there comes a point in any slump when the curve of depression ceases to sink so sharply and after 1933 signs of returning confidence were to be seen in the gradual revival of industry and agriculture aided by these government measures.

2. The political consequences

Economic recovery might eventually reduce the vast numbers of unemployed; it could not, however, undo the psychological and political consequences of the great slump. With all the technical resources of the twentieth century as its disposal an unrestricted system of free enterprise had completely broken down, depriving millions throughout the world of their livelihood, and such a catastrophe inevitably gave rise to a fierce questioning of the very principles that had emerged from the turmoil of the nineteenth century. The idea that governments should simply concern themselves with the liberty of the individual through parliamentary institutions, entrusting the general prosperity to *laissez-faire* capitalism now appeared utterly inadequate. Men and women caught up in an economic disaster that they could not explain knew only that they wanted firm efficient leadership, and it was natural that their angry despair should bring about a sudden strengthening of the forces of Communism and Fascism which had been quiescent in the democracies during the second half of the 1920s.

In Great Britain, France, Switzerland, Belgium, the Netherlands, Scandinavia, and Czechoslovakia parliamentary systems survived the ordeal, although there was now a new awareness of the extent to which governments must watch over economic developments, and the antagonism between right and left became considerably sharpened. This last effect was particularly marked in France, where governments changed with even greater rapidity than usual, while in Czechoslovakia the Sudeten Germans, who maintained that they had been victimized by the Czech administration during the slump, began to organize themselves under the leadership of Konrad Henlein, a gymnastics instructor, whose party, the Sudeten German Home Front, gained the support of 62 per cent of the German voters in Czechoslovakia in the elections of 1935.

The existing dictatorships, through their power to suppress opposition and their greater control over State economy were on the whole strengthened in their position. In Italy Mussolini survived the depression without difficulty; in Poland a junta of army colonels continued authoritarian rule after Pilsudski's death in 1935, and in Yugoslavia King Alexander was able to put down any popular stirrings caused by economic distress. In Portugal Salazar, who had been Finance Minister since 1928, took over as Prime Minister in 1932, formed an administration of experts and turned the parliament into nothing more than an advisory Chamber. 'The people', remarked Salazar, 'have less need of being sovereign than of being governed'—a comment which would have been heartily endorsed by the monarchs of the nineteenth century.

Spain provided the only instance of a dictatorship actually undermined by the depression. There Primo de Rivera, who had seized power in 1923 (see p. 217), had already lost the support of the universities and the intellectuals, and when he found that with the onset of the slump he no longer had the confidence of the army, he left Spain for Paris. In 1931 municipal elections revealed such an overwhelmingly republican vote that King Alfonso XIII also quitted the country and a new liberal constitution was devised with a single-chamber Assembly elected by universal suffrage for men and women over the age of twenty-two. The Church was disestablished, the Jesuits expelled, and a system of primary education organized, and in 1932 laws were passed restricting the power of the army and inaugurating land reforms whereby small holdings could be leased to the peasantry.

In contrast to this anti-clerical leftward tendency in Spain, the majority of changes consequent on the depression in Europe were in the direction of a right-wing authoritarianism, either through an outright surrender to Fascism as a defence against resurgent Communism, or through attempts to bolster up a wavering parliamentary régime. In Rumania, where King Carol II returned to the throne in 1930, strong-arm government was established through the Iron Guard. In Bulgaria a military dictatorship was finally set up in 1934; in the same year the executive power was greatly strengthened in Latvia and Estonia, and in Greece General Metaxas became dictator in 1936 with the consent of King George II, who had recently been restored to his throne (see genealogical table. p. 486).

In Austria the emotions of economic distress seemed to place the survival of parliamentary government at the mercy of three antagonistic armed forces—the *Schutzbund* of the Social Democrats, the Austrian Nazis, and the right-wing *Heimwehr*, the private army of Prince von Starhemberg. The gains made by the Austrian Nazis in the municipal elections of May 1932 were emphasized by the spreading of rioting and gang warfare, and in March 1933, after Hitler's advent to power in Germany, the Chancellor, Dr Dollfuss, whose diminutive size earned him the name of *Millimetternich* among his opponents, decided to rule by decree, relying upon the support of Starhemberg's *Heimwehr*. In June the Nazi party was prohibited and, after conversations with Mussolini, Dollfuss announced his intention to set up a corporative State on an authoritarian basis. This was virtually a declaration of war on the Social Democrats, and in February 1934 the left-wing forces were crushed after three days of fighting between the *Heimwehr* and the *Schutzbund*, during which the besieged working-class district of Vienna was bombarded with artillery.

The most disastrous aspect of the great depression was to be seen in Germany, where Adolf Hitler emerged as Chancellor in January 1933—not as the result of a revolutionary *coup*, but by presidential appointment in accordance with the provisions of the Weimar constitution. This superficially 'respectable' rise to power was due to a combination of unfortunate circumstances. In July 1930 Heinrich Brüning, leader of the Catholic Centre party and Chancellor since the previous March, put forward a programme of cuts in expenditure, affecting government salaries, pensions and social insurance benefits. He was unable to gain a majority for this in the *Reichstag* and with unemployment mounting to three million, Brüning felt justified in asking President Hindenburg to invoke Article 48 of the constitution, whereby his measures could be enforced by presidential decree. Hindenburg complied, but since the *Reichstag* strongly objected to this action, Brüning and his successors throughout the depression were henceforth to remain dependent upon the whim of the President.

This first factor has a considerable bearing on the second. The Weimar Republic had now come close to the position of the short-lived Second Republic in France; too few of the men in authority had any deep faith in its survival. The most significant figure behind the scenes at this time, General Kurt von Schleicher, was hoping for a perpetuation of presidential rule, backed by the strength of the army, and by the autumn of 1931 Brüning himself was thinking in terms of a restoration of the Hohenzollern monarchy within a con-

stitutional framework—mainly as a means of robbing the Nazis of
some of their support. Thus, it was not Hitler alone who was envisaging a radical alteration of the system of government; yet the
atmosphere of intrigue in a situation in which the Chancellor
depended purely upon the President's support robbed these conservatives of the chance of finding a firm alternative which would
enable them to stand against the Nazis.

The third overwhelmingly significant factor was the enormous
increase in electoral support for the Nazi party. When in September
1930 Brüning, hoping to gain a more amenable *Reichstag*, rashly
asked for a dissolution, the Nazis won six and a half million votes
in the subsequent election, which raised the number of their seats
from 12 to 107. The simultaneous growth of Communist representation from 54 to 77 seats might suggest the beginning of a polarization, but the Nazi success was not achieved at the expense of the
two major parties. The Social Democrats lost 10 seats, but still
remained the largest party in the *Reichstag* with 143 seats; the Catholic Centre party actually made slight gains. The principal losses
were suffered by the various liberal parties, including the People's
Party (D.V.P.) greatly weakened since Stresemann's death. Naturally, the Nazi victories were assisted by the widespread unemployment, but they do not seem to have been due primarily to working-
class support. Manual workers at this time only account for just
over a quarter of the party and the bulk of the membership was
drawn from the lower middle class of white-collar workers, shopkeepers and junior civil servants, together with small farmers suffering from the decline in agricultural prices—a *Mittelstand* fearful
of losing their position in society. The young, many of them voting
for the first time, were also attracted, unimpressed by the prospects
offered to them by the Weimar Republic.

Still, even if the principal parties remained strong, the growth of
the Communist vote to four and a half million was extremely helpful
for Hitler in his efforts to win over some of the army officers, and
more particularly industrialists, many of whom had already supported other right-wing organizations and who by 1932 were making
considerable contributions to the Nazi party funds. These negotiations were typical of Hitler's technique of aligning himself with the
real centres of power, but they had to be kept secret from radicals
in the Nazi party such as Gregor Strasser who still believed that
Hitler was aiming at a genuine social revolution.

These new funds which enabled Goebbels to organize a prodigious nationwide publicity campaign, the violent tactics of Hitler's
private army, the S.A., the fear of Communist revolution, and the
presence of nearly six million unemployed, all combined to bring
the Nazi party to the peak of its popularity in 1932. Membership
had leapt up to 800,000 and the S.A. numbered about 300,000. In

March Hindenburg, standing for re-election as President against Hitler, just failed to gain the necessary absolute majority and was successful only in a second election in April in which Hitler nevertheless won nearly thirteen-and-a-half million votes. In the same month local elections in Prussia, whose territory comprised two-thirds of the whole of Germany, made the Nazis the strongest party in the Diet.

By this time von Schleicher had decided to get rid of Brüning, who had already alarmed Hindenburg with a proposal that the bankrupt estates of East Prussia should be taken over by the State with compensation for the owners and distributed to the landless peasantry. Still relying on his presidential prerogative, Hindenburg now chose Franz von Papen as Brüning's successor in the hope that he could come to terms with the Nazis—a task which was inescapable after the *Reichstag* elections in July 1932 when they became the most powerful party in the Assembly with 230 seats. A working agreement proved impossible, however, since Hitler was demanding the Chancellorship for himself, and although a second *Reichstag* election in November reduced the Nazi seats to 196, von Papen reckoned that he could not carry on without a declaration of a state of emergency. Von Schleicher refused to support him in this and on von Papen's resignation became Chancellor himself. With the offer of the Vice-Chancellorship to Gregor Strasser he hoped to win the Nazis to his side, but after Hitler had forced Strasser to resign from the party, von Schleicher did not last long. On 4 January 1933 von Papen, determined to get his own back, met Hitler at the house of von Schroeder in Cologne, and when von Schleicher failed to gain the trade unions and the peasantry in an attempt to form a coalition in the face of continued Nazi opposition, he resigned on 28 January.

The Nazis were still open to the highest bidder and von Papen who, as the President's personal favourite, was entrusted with the negotiations, had to make haste to forestall any further manoeuvres by von Schleicher. Hitler, it was agreed, should have the Chancellorship, but only two other members of the party should have seats in the cabinet—Frick as Minister of the Interior and Goering as Minister without Portfolio. With von Papen as Vice-Chancellor and General von Blomberg as Minister of Defence, as well as six other cabinet posts at their disposal, it was the hope of the conservatives behind the scenes that they could effectively smother the independent action of the Nazis, at the same time as gaining their cooperation. In this they sadly misjudged the man with whom they had to deal, and the appointment of Adolf Hitler as Chancellor on 30 January 1933 was to have the most fateful consequences for Germany and for the world.

Chapter 31

Aspects of Totalitarianism

1. Hitler's Third Reich

The Weimar Republic did not long survive Hitler's appointment as Chancellor. It had always been his intention to establish the dictatorship of the Nazi party from a position of power within the State, and the first step was to secure a *Reichstag* that would be amenable to its own destruction. Having carefully failed to come to terms with the Catholic Centre party, he was able to convince Hindenburg that there would have to be one more dissolution, and in the subsequent election Hitler declared openly that he would ask for the suspension of parliamentary government for the next four years. 'The struggle is a light one now,' wrote Goebbels in his diary, 'since we are able to employ all the means of the State. Radio and press are at our disposal.' They had more than that. Goering as Prussian Minister of the Interior formed an auxiliary police force of 25,000 S.A. men and 15,000 S.S. who carried out a campaign of violence against all opposing parties, in which at least fifty people were killed and many hundreds injured. Then, on the night of 27 February, a further opportunity presented itself when the *Reichstag* building was gutted by fire. A young Dutchman, van der Lubbe, was arrested on the spot and the Nazis announced at once that he had been the dupe of Communist conspirators. The Communists returned the charge against the Nazis and for many years the democratic world believed that the fire was the work of the S.A. attempting to create a Communist scare. In fact, it now seems possible that van der Lubbe was really acting on his own account, but whatever the truth may be, the fire provided Hitler with the excuse to issue a decree on 28 February suspending the Weimar constitution's guarantee of individual liberty and thus enabling the Nazis to intensify their activities against their opponents.

The elections in March gave the Nazis 288 seats which with the support of Hugenburg's Nationalist party only ensured them a bare majority, but the arrest of most of the Communist deputies under the decree of 28 February and an unwise agreement by the Catholic Centre party to work in cooperation with the Nazis supplied Hitler with the two-thirds majority necessary for a constitutional amendment. At the first meeting of the *Reichstag* in the Kroll Opera House nothing could stop the passage of the Enabling Bill which would free the government from all forms of constitutional and parliamentary control for a period of four years. 'I do not want your votes,' sneered Hitler at the Social Democrats, the only party that had the courage to oppose him in a hall lined with S.A. men, and when the Bill was carried by 441 votes to 94, the Nazis burst exultantly into the Horst Wessel song.

The way was now open to a process of *Gleichschaltung* (coordination) which finally established the supreme rule of the Nazi party. In the provinces the Nazis were already strongly represented in the *Länder* assemblies, and even before the passing of the Enabling Bill Frick as Minister of the Interior had appointed Reich Police Commissioners who took over the provincial governments in Württemberg, Saxony, Hesse and Bavaria. From April 1933 the local representative assemblies retained little parliamentary control and at the beginning of 1934 were abolished. Already by July 1933 all other political parties had been banned, including the Catholic Centre, who could now only rely on a Concordat which the Nazi Government made with the Vatican promising to leave the Roman Church unmolested. Meanwhile, a firm grip had been established over the civil service with the law of 7 April 1933 which led to the removal of officials who were thought to be politically unreliable or who were of Jewish descent, and on the same day a similar law regulated entry into the legal profession. The collapse of the trade unions was total and immediate. The high level of unemployment had seriously reduced their funds and made the prospect of any successful strike action very unlikely, and for the time being their principal aim was simply to preserve the existence of their organizations in the hope that the Nazi régime would not last long. Constant attacks by the S.A. throughout March and April, however, soon made their weakness apparent to Hitler and convinced him that it would be quite safe to act against them. On 2 May 1933 trade union offices were occupied by government forces and a little later a German Labour Front under Robert Ley took charge of all working-class matters.

The speed and ruthlessness with which Hitler had acted during these weeks were entirely in accord with the statement which he had made of his intentions at Leipzig in September 1930. 'The constitution only maps out the arena of battle, not the goal', he had said. 'We enter the legal agencies and in that way will make our party the determining factor. However, once we possess the constitutional power, we will mould the State into the shape that we hold to be suitable.' This is exactly what had happened. The size of the Nazi party in the *Reichstag* after the elections of 1932 had made it the determining factor and had led to his legal appointment as Chancellor. And even though the Enabling Act had been debated in an atmosphere of violence, it had at least been passed as a constitutional measure. Thus Hitler did not seize power. He merely exploited what he had been given, when the sheer brutality with which the S.A. and the S.S. imposed his will revealed how easily the forces of uninhibited gangsterism could kick aside the restraints with which the conservatives had hoped to curb their newly-appointed Chancellor. By the end of July there were already some 27,000 political prisoners held in concentration camps, and the policy of terror made it unlikely that there could be any protest or resistance.

Yet for all his unscrupulousness in dealing with his opponents Hitler knew well that there were two sections of the community with whose support he could not yet dispense—the industrialists and the army. And here he was to be increasingly embarrassed by the crude menace of the S.A., now numbering between two and three million men, under their commander Ernst Roehm. These brownshirts had believed that the success of the party would be followed by a social revolution in which the jobs and positions of profit at present still in the hands of the old order would be theirs for the asking. Hitler, however, had no intention of pandering to their wishes at the cost of his good relations with his new friends. The S.A. had by now served his purpose, and when their impatience had almost led to an open breach, he resolved to make an end. At some time early in 1934 he struck a bargain with the Minister of Defence, General von Blomberg, whereby the army would support him in gaining the Presidency on Hindenburg's death, while he would ensure that the S.A. ceased to be a danger to the existing social order.

Both sides honoured the pact. On 29 June Hitler arrived at Munich by air to superintend the execution of S.A. leaders, while Himmler and Goering carried out a similar purge in Berlin; for the next thirty-six hours the firing squads of the S.S. shot down the men who had been among Hitler's closest associates during the struggle for power—77 according to Hitler himself, 401 according to the *White Book* published in Paris. Roehm, three S.A. *Obergruppenführer* and Gregor Strasser all perished—as well as a number of political opponents including General von Schleicher, his wife, and two of von Papen's assistants. Von Papen himself probably only escaped death on account of his position as Vice-Chancellor and his close friendship with Hindenburg. The General Staff offered their congratulations on such a speedy solution to the problem, and when Hindenburg finally died on 2 August, did not shirk their part of the bargain. Hitler, it was agreed, should combine the offices of President and Chancellor, and was to be supreme Commander-in-Chief of the armed forces whose officers and men were to take a personal

oath of loyalty to him. Thus the surrender of the Army followed on
that of the *Reichstag* and this new triumph for Hitler was rounded
off by a plebiscite in which almost 90 per cent of the electorate gave
their assent.

During the subsequent years the growth of Nazi control seemed
to make the party increasingly synonymous with the State. In Jan
uary 1935 it was decreed that in future all mayors would be
appointed from above and already almost half of those who held
posts in local administration were party members, as were some
three-quarters of all civil servants by 1937. Naturally, education was
an important weapon for the inculcation of the Nazi ideology and
under the direction of the party this was to concentrate on the fan-
ning of German nationalism and the racial mystique of Aryanism.
During the first five years of the régime nearly 3,000 professors and
instructors were dismissed from their posts; many more, however,
felt compelled to conform and in the autumn of 1933 almost a thousand took a public vow in support of Hitler. 'True physics is the
creation of the German spirit,' wrote the Director of the Institute
of Physics at Dresden, '. . . in fact, all European science is the fruit
of Aryan, or better, German thought.' 'In reality,' said Professor
Lenard of Heidelberg University, 'science, like every other human
product, is racial and conditioned by blood.' Paramilitary youth
organizations proliferated, and as early as May 1933 sections of the
student population were sufficiently enthusiastic to participate in a
great burning of books written by liberals, pacifists, and Jews, cast-
ing into the flames the works of Thomas Mann, Stefan Zweig,
Remarque, Freud, and Einstein as well as those of H. G. Wells, Gide,
Zola, and Proust. For the schools, textbooks were vetted and often
rewritten, although this was to some extent a gradual process and
it was not until 1944 that the Nazis finally imposed a single history
textbook to be used in all schools in Germany—*Der Weg zum Reich*
which naturally brought the story to a triumphant climax with the
rise of the Third Reich, listing in heavy type the names of all those
who had fallen during the Munich *putsch* of 1923.

This unfettered power of the executive might well suggest a monolithic system of totalitarian rule. In fact, Nazi government was not
remotely monolithic. It encouraged an untidy proliferation of separate party agencies whose functions overlapped and conflicted,
while running parallel with existing institutions of State. Hitler
himself had three chancelleries, one of them the Party Chancellery
under Rudolph Hess, and their spheres of responsibility were never
precisely defined. Similarly, the Ministry of Labour found itself
entangled with Ley's German Labour Front, Goebbels as minister
of propaganda was constantly at loggerheads with the press chiefs
whom Hitler appointed, and the professionals at the Foreign Ministry were hampered by the rise of various agencies, each interested

in conducting its own foreign policy. This strange dualism suited Hitler perfectly well, since it strengthened his own position to act as the final arbiter between leading Nazis engaged in domestic squabbles. The ultimate safeguard of his authority, however, lay in the S.S., which under Heinrich Himmler had grown to 20,000 by the end of 1938 and which through its control of police activities and the running of the concentration camps provided the true key to Hitler's régime.

The most startling and horrifying feature of these years was the treatment of the Jews. Here Hitler showed that he had meant literally what he had said. In 1933 they had already been excluded from holding public office and from the professions of journalism, teaching and the civil service, and in 1934 this was extended to the stock exchange and in 1938 to medicine. The Nuremberg laws of 1935 deprived them of German citizenship, forbade Jewish-Aryan marriages, and prohibited any Jew from employing female Aryan servants under the age of thirty-five. This was the doctrine which the later success of Hitler's foreign policy was to carry beyond the frontiers of Germany; the first consequences of his acquisition of Austria in 1938, for instance, included the looting of Jewish possessions and the forcing of Jews out of their homes to scrub the streets and descended to such trivialities as forbidding them to sit on public seats in the parks. While international opinion had still to be considered, Hitler could not yet give full rein to his hatred which, during the Second World War, was to lead to the mass extermination of some six million European Jews. In November 1938, however, there was a glimpse of what was to come, after a Polish Jew had killed a German diplomatic secretary in Paris. Through official instigation many German cities succumbed to a fury of destruction—*Kristallnacht*—during which 7,000 Jewish stores and synagogues were wrecked, a hundred Jews were killed, thousands were beaten up and 35,000 sent to concentration camps and later, if they were lucky, forced to emigrate. It was hardly surprising that by that year a quarter of Germany's 550,000 Jews had fled abroad.

Against this deployment of power there was very little that any opposition could do. The executives of left-wing labour groups could only operate from outside Germany and their position was still further weakened by the continuing mistrust between Communist and non-Communist. Among churchmen there were many instances of individual courage, such as the Protestant pastors Martin Niemöller and Dietrich Bonhoeffer or the Catholic bishop von Galen, whose sermon in August 1941 forced the government to abandon its policy of euthanasia; yet as institutions none of the Churches in Germany took a positive stand against the movement. In the main they felt that the only hope was to maintain their existing organizations and accordingly concentrated their efforts on defending their publications and religious and educational activities against increasing interference.

Only the army might have been a source of serious resistance. Its expansion after 1933 (see p. 405) meant the recruiting of a large number of junior officers who might have been affected by the Nazi philosophy, but Hitler was well aware that at the top there remained considerable dislike and mistrust. The problem for him was that the army was the one institution with which he could not dispense, and consequently the most that he could do was to undermine its independence. Thus, in January 1938 he managed to get rid of both the head of the army, von Fritsch, and the Minister of Defence, von Blomberg, as well as a great many other generals through retirement or transfer, and while von Brauchitsch replaced Fritsch, Hitler declared that he himself would personally exercise immediate command over the armed forces.

Even so, not every problem could be resolved by the consolidation of Hitler's power and the brute force of the S.S. The Nazis had gained their votes by promising an economic recovery and almost at once they did bring about a drastic reduction of the unemployment which had helped to undermine the Weimar Republic. This was partly accomplished by organizing public works with the building of great motorways (*Autobahnen*), a method also being adopted elsewhere in the United States and Sweden. The particular feature of German recovery, however, was that it rested on Hitler's plans to place the country on a military footing. This meant more than a great expansion of the armaments industry; he was determined to establish German economic self-sufficiency, so that she might be immune from any future blockade, and there was consequently great investment in the production of synthetic rubber, oil and dye stuffs. The key figure behind this regeneration of the economy was Hjalmar Schacht who as President of the *Reichsbank* and Minister of Economics was prepared to offer all the credit needed through the issue of so-called *Mefobills*, which were simply bills of exchange at 4 per cent.

The extent to which this enabled Hitler to fulfil his promises to his supporters varied. The idea of dismantling the large industrial and commercial units in favour of small concerns was never seriously attempted, since Hitler was greatly in need of the major elements of German industry. On the other hand, the fall in the level of unemployment was dramatic—from six million in 1932 to one million in 1936 with virtually full employment by 1938, and this together with the provision of recreational facilities and subsidized holiday schemes largely reconciled the workers to the authoritarian discipline of the German Labour Front which had taken the place of their trade unions.

In the long term the effect on the German economy was more debatable. Total production rose by 25 per cent between 1929 and

1938. There were some remarkable achievements in the creation of synthetic materials, but their price was so high that they could not possibly have competed in the open market. That was unimportant from Hitler's point of view. What mattered more was that they had not enabled Germany to attain self-sufficiency. By 1938 she still needed to import half of her oil requirement and two-thirds of her iron ore. Agriculture, too, showed little increase, being hampered by a series of regulations that were actually supposed to enhance the social status of the small farmers, and the cost of continuing food imports had to be offset against the 19 per cent increase in exports between 1934 and 1936.

At the same time the finances of the government were under increasing strain with the immense investment in rearmament and in the search for synthetics, and as early as December 1935 Schacht warned General von Blomberg that if, as Hitler insisted, food imports were to be maintained, this could only be at the expense of rearmament. Yet Hitler was determined to have both. In August 1936 he wrote: 'the German army must be operational in four years. The German economy must be capable of supporting war in four years,' and in September Hermann Goering was put in charge of a Four Year plan which was supposed to achieve this. Thus Nazi economic policy has some bearing on any assessment of Hitler's fundamental intentions, since clearly it was not simply aimed at recovery; it was geared to the probability of war, and the confiscation of Austrian and Czech assets after the acquisition of Austria in 1938 and of Czechoslovakia in March 1939 (see p. 416) suggested that plunder would provide one means whereby such a policy might finance itself.

2. Russia under Stalin

Meanwhile, further east another form of totalitarianism had been established. Long before the Russian revolution Trotsky had predicted that the dictatorship of the Bolshevik party would eventually be succeeded by the emergence of a single dictator and this prophecy was now about to be fulfilled. By 1929 Stalin had finally outmanoeuvered his political rivals within the central organization of the Communist party in Russia. From then on his word was law and throughout the 1930s he was to use this power to accomplish the most extraordinary and brutal transformation of agriculture and industry, at the same time killing off most of his former associates.

Only a few years after the introduction of the New Economic Policy (see p. 372) independent farming had created a wide range of levels of prosperity among the peasantry. The most successful, the *Kulaks*, numbered about two million, the middle peasantry between 15 and 18 million, and the poor, who still used wooden ploughs, between five and eight million. Harvests had been reasonably good, but the peasantry were inclined to hoard their grain in order to get higher prices. In 1928 the consequent food shortage in the cities had led to a policy of forcible requisitioning, and within the party there had been growing criticism of the *Kulaks* and of the whole philosophy of N.E.P.

Stalin himself was becoming convinced that the time was ripe to extend the system of large collective farms. He seems at first to have envisaged a fairly gradual process, but by the end of 1929 he had decided that the *Kulak* was the most likely obstacle to such a development and in January 1930 a resolution of the Central Committee demanded 'the liquidation of the *Kulak* as a class'. Led by local officials and detachments of troops and workers from the cities, the poorer peasants were encouraged to help themselves to their richer neighbours' possessions. The *Kulaks* were not even allowed to join the new collectives, since they would probably have gained a predominant influence in them, and in any case they were needed as an example that it was not wise to become a wealthy peasant. Thus, amid a mounting furore through the Ukraine and across the plains of Russia some two million *Kulak* families were killed, imprisoned or deported to Siberia, or in some cases, as a merciful concession, merely transferred to a small patch of infertile land.

The hope of the authorities had been that by stimulating this rural class war they might make the move to collectivization acceptable to the less prosperous majority. In this they were disappointed. The rest of the peasantry put up a ferocious resistance to the idea of working as wage labourers on the collective farms and slaughtered their livestock by the million rather than see them commandeered. When it became clear by March 1930 that prolonged warfare in the countryside was playing havoc with the spring sowing, Stalin felt compelled to relax the pressure and in a statement entitled 'Dizzy with Success' accused the officials of having gone too far. This did nothing to save the *Kulaks*, but it did slow down the process of collectivization and by 1933 only slightly more than half the holdings had been reorganized in this way. There were, too, some concessions in that the members of a collective were to have a share in the profits of the farm as well as being allowed some land for private cultivation.

Nevertheless, it was hardly an auspicious beginning for agrarian Socialism. The farming of the new vast units demanded the use of tractors and in 1929 there were only 35,000 of these in the whole of Russia. By 1934 the resistance of the peasantry had resulted in the slaughter of 18 million horses, 30 million cattle and 100 million sheep and goats and many years were to elapse before this loss was made up. It was small wonder that in 1933 there should be famine and the government was pushed back once again to a policy of requisitioning. Over the years, however, the supply of tractors steadily increased, as did the number of personnel trained to handle agricultural machinery, and collectivization was almost universal by 1937, although total output from the land had still barely regained the levels reached in the 1920s. Certainly the larger units were likely to prove a more effective economic base for the future than the 24 million tiny holdings that they replaced, but the cost had been appalling and during the second World War Stalin admitted to Winston Churchill that probably some ten million people had perished through coercion and starvation.

While the struggle over collectivization was intensifying, Russia had also embarked upon a new stage of her industrial revolution. Now that N.E.P. had brought about a recovery from the devastation suffered during the civil war, the party had been contemplating for some time the need for a great expansion of industrial production under State control. The first Five Year Plan had been put into operation in October 1928, but the plan never remained static and the target figures for oil, coal, iron ore, pig iron and electric power were always being made more ambitious. 'We are fifty or a hundred years behind the advanced countries,' declared Stalin in February 1931. 'We must make good this lag in ten years. Either we do it or they crush us.'

And so more and more heavy industrial works proliferated in the Urals and the remoter regions of Russia; the great Dnieper dam was built for the generating of electric power and a vast new complex Magnitogorsk was established in Siberia. Naturally, aspiration constantly outstripped practical possibilities and the ugly note of the police state sounds through the accusations of sabotage which were intended to explain this discrepancy. In 1933 Stalin claimed that the first Five Year Plan had achieved 93 per cent of its objectives, and although this was probably an exaggeration, it does seem that the output of production goods had multiplied by some four times, consumer goods rather less than double. The frenetic sense of urgency, with which the first Five Year Plan was pursued, was less marked in the second, but by 1937 production goods had increased by a further two and a half times and consumer goods had doubled.

The great storm of this planned industrialization was bound to involve hardship. The concentration on production goods made life particularly bleak in the cities, whose growth added to the difficulties of poor overcrowded housing. The need to encourage the specialist technician led to considerable differentials in pay, but there was little on which he could spend his money. Workers were drafted to any part of the country where they were needed, and some projects such as the White Sea-Baltic canal, the Moscow-Volga canal and the Baikal-Amur railway were built with forced labour from the camps run by the political police. Nevertheless, there is a visionary element in the story of industrialization under Stalin, distinguishing it from the murderous process of agrarian collectivization; the imagination of young people was fired by the immensity of the task, and thousands volunteered to participate in what they regarded as a great Socialist experiment.

Meanwhile, the history of the party had entered a macabre phase in which idealism played little part. The changes in agriculture and industry were indicative of the power that Stalin wielded and he was now about to consolidate his position with a series of purges, in the course of which most of the original Bolsheviks were wiped out. The reign of terror started in December 1934 when S. Kirov, who had been sent to Leningrad to deal with opposition to Stalin's policy, was shot down by a young Communist, and Stalin responded to this with executions and the deporting of thousands of party members to Siberia from cities all over Russia. Zinoviev and Kamenev were forced to admit that Kirov's assassin might indirectly have been influenced by them and after a secret trial they were given sentences of penal servitude. The filling of the consequent vacancies enabled Stalin to complete his control over the party machine and soon afterwards a series of public and secret trials eliminated any other sources of opposition. In August 1936 Zinoviev and Kamenev, in January 1937 Radek and Piatakov and in March 1938 Bukharin were among the many who were accused of treason and conspiracy. Most of them were shot, although a few were sent to camps where they did not survive long. And down through the ranks of the party tens of thousands, who had owed their position to these leading figures, suffered a similar fate. The full extent of the holocaust was only revealed publicly by Nikita Khrushchev in 1956 after Stalin's death (see p. 477), but Stalin himself stated in 1939 that there had been over 500,000 new appointments since 1934. At the same time a separate purge of the Army began in June 1937, when a number of high-ranking officers were arrested and shot, including the Commander-in-Chief Tukhachevski, a hero of the civil war, and by the end of 1938 most of the high command of the army, the navy and the airforce and about half the entire officer corps had been dispatched—perhaps some 35,000 men.

There are many extraordinary features of this appalling period. Virtually no evidence could be brought against the service officers, although it has been maintained that some of them may have been contemplating a *coup* against Stalin. Many of the party members were tried in secret, or not tried at all. The charges brought against those who were tried publicly were largely without substance and in view of their life-long dedication to the cause of Communism seem nonsensical. Yet one after another these convinced Bolsheviks confessed in the dock to the most implausible crimes of treason and subversion, and the only explanation would seem to be torture or the hope that their lives or those of their relatives might be spared, although a more ingenious solution has been suggested in Arthur Koestler's novel *Darkness at Noon*.

It is natural to ask why Stalin should have embarked upon this tremendous blood-letting. He may have simply wanted scapegoats for the inadequacies of his economic programme, as, for example, when British specialists working in Russia had been accused of sabotage in 1933. Yet that would hardly explain the scale of the purge. It is more likely that, once committed to the vast operation of collectivization and the Five Year Plan, he genuinely feared that any opposition would be bound to attempt to remove him from power and to undo the processes at work. From abroad a periodical produced by Trotsky kept up an unrelenting denunciation, and Stalin knew that this was being smuggled into Russia and must be circulating in government circles, since he was able to read it himself. It is noticeable that at the trials the prosecution was always careful to depict Trotsky as the instigator of the alleged conspiracies. And as the terror continued, so it was likely to stimulate further desperate opposition, which in turn must be rooted out. There was also a danger in that the growth of German power under Hitler now pointed to the eventual prospect of war and this might create greater opportunities for his potential opponents to get rid of him. And so he swept the slate clean in an orgy of executions, torture and imprisonment, depriving the régime of its most experienced administrators and officers and ensuring that all positions of authority were held only by Stalinists. The purge did not continue after 1938, but there was still one last episode when Trotsky was murdered in Mexico in August 1940, and with that it could be said that the revolution had finally devoured almost all its parents and a good many of its children.

Chapter 32

The end of collective security 1933–8

1. Hitler's destruction of the Treaty of Versailles

Hitler had never made any secret of the fundamental aims of his foreign policy. In contrast to Bismarck he believed fervently in *Grossdeutschland* and was consequently not interested in simply regaining the frontiers of 1914; 'they were temporary frontiers', he had written in *Mein Kampf*, 'established in virtue of a political struggle that had not been brought to a finish', and this revival of old German ambitions naturally implied that the memory of the Treaty of Brest Litovsk was to be as insignificant for the future as the hatred of the Versailles settlement. For the moment, however, he had to proceed with caution, and during the first few years of his Chancellorship, before the possession of a strong army made him more careless of the risk of war, Hitler, despite his lack of formal training, displayed a remarkable diplomatic skill, assisted by a gambler's instinct.

First, he was determined to rearm. As has been seen (see p. 397), this was an integral part of his domestic policy and had considerable support from many sections of society, since rearmament meant employment for the workless, a greater army for the General Staff and, above all, a gesture of defiance at the victors of the first World War. Germany, he claimed, was the only country that had really disarmed. She had no aggressive intentions, but he must insist that she could only accept continued restrictions on the size of her forces as part of an agreed international programme. As he well knew, this was a fairly safe stipulation. Great Britain and the United States had already run their military machines down to a mere shadow, and French activity was entirely concerned with defence; yet the official Disarmament Conference had utterly failed to arrive at a general formula, and with this excuse, in October 1933, Hitler finally withdrew Germany from the Conference and from the League of Nations. Thus he could now begin to rearm openly in direct contravention of the terms of the Treaty of Versailles, and he struck his attitude of moral righteousness with such insight that when Winston Churchill stated in the House of Commons in 1934 that the German *Luftwaffe* would equal the strength of the R.A.F. by 1935, the warning went unheeded.

His second step was the announcement of a ten-year non-aggression pact with Poland in January 1934. The Poles' gradual lack of confidence in their alliance with France (see p. 383) was confirmed in March 1933, when the French government had rejected their suggestion for a preventive war against Germany, and they turned now to bolstering their position by friendship with her instead. From a German point of view the pact was certainly not in accordance with the policy outlined by von Seeckt in 1921 (see pp. 379–80), but for Hitler it was simply a temporary measure. In terms of propaganda it was a useful advertisement of his peaceful intentions, while at the same time it struck a blow at the French security system in eastern Europe. More important, it left him free to deal with affairs nearer home, and until the quarrel over Danzig in 1939 the Polish pact remained the linchpin of Hitler's foreign policy.

In 1934, however, he did suffer a couple of setbacks. In Austria the local Nazi party had been making their own plans for taking over the government, and on 25 July they attacked the Chancellery at Vienna, shot down Dr Dollfuss and occupied the radio station. The Austrian authorities, however, succeeded in frustrating the *coup*, and when Mussolini openly supported them by strengthening his forces on the Austro-Italian frontier, Hitler had publicly to disown any German interest in the conspiracy. The murderers of Dollfuss, who had fled to Germany, were surrendered and the German minister at Vienna was replaced by von Papen, who as a conservative and a Roman Catholic might quieten Austrian suspicions of German designs on their country.

Since the evacuation of the Rhineland the French had already shown their mistrust of German ambitions in embarking upon the construction of a vast fortification known as the Maginot Line running between the Belgian and Swiss frontiers, and now Louis Barthou, their Foreign Minister, made a tour of eastern Europe attempting to repair the damage done to the French system by the German-Polish pact. His efforts to create some sort of eastern Locarno agreement were hindered by Poland's suspicion of the Soviet Union, but in September he did succeed in gaining Russia's admission to the League of Nations. In October, however, Barthou died from his wounds when King Alexander of Yugoslavia on a State visit to France was assassinated at his side in Marseilles, and although his successor, Pierre Laval, did not immediately abandon the policy of eastern alliances against possible German expansion, he chose to concentrate on reaching agreement with Italy by a treaty in January 1935 settling some of their colonial differences and guaranteeing the independence of Austria.

For his next achievement Hitler had only to abide by the Treaty

of Versailles, when in January 1935 the fifteen-year separate administration of the Saar expired and a plebiscite gave an overwhelming
vote in favour of reunion with Germany. In March, however, Hitler
took a more hazardous step when he announced the introduction
of conscription which would give Germany an army of thirty-six
divisions with 550,000 men. Even the German General Staff would
probably have preferred a smaller army to manage at the beginning
of a programme of rearmament, but Hitler claimed as justification
the fact that the French had just greatly increased their own military
forces by doubling their length of service. Diplomatic reactions
among the other Powers to this open defiance of the Treaty of
Versailles were almost immediate. In April at Stresa Great Britain,
France, and Italy mutually confirmed the treaties of Locarno; the
League of Nations censured this new step by Germany, and in May
France concluded a pact with Russia for mutual assistance. At the
same time Russia made a similar pact with Czechoslovakia on the
understanding that Russian support would follow on a French
initiative.

Hitler at once set to work to remove all suspicions and in a masterly speech—given before the meaningless *Reichstag*, and really for
foreign consumption—he drew on all the vocabulary of the League
of Nations to protest his utter horror at the thought of war and to
emphasize the harmlessness of German policy. At the same time he
was able to make skilful use of the very fears that he had aroused
to break up the apparent unity of this new front against Germany.
In June an Anglo-German naval agreement was signed, limiting the
tonnage of the German fleet to 35 per cent of the British, although
U-boat construction was to be allowed to reach 100 per cent of British submarine strength. It seemed a peaceful move and it certainly
reassured the British, yet it was utterly disastrous for the maintenance of the Stresa front, since Great Britain had consulted neither
France nor Italy, who regarded the agreement as an open recognition of Germany's right to rearm.

The complete disunity of Germany's opponents was finally
revealed in October 1935 when Mussolini embarked upon the
invasion of Abyssinia (see p. 407). The measures proposed by the
League of Nations appeared utterly ineffectual; the hesitations of
Great Britain and France in their attitude towards this Italian attack
undermined the hopes for any positive action in accordance with
the doctrine of collective security, and with this object lesson before
him Hitler resolved to go forward with the greatest gamble of his
life—the military reoccupation of the Rhineland.

The ruling laid down in the Treaty of Versailles that the Rhineland as well as the territory fifty kilometres to the east of the Rhine
should remain permanently demilitarized had been restated in the
Locarno pact of 1925 and confirmed in 1929 at the time of the final

withdrawal of the Allied occupation forces. Hitler, however, had already shown that he was prepared to ignore the Treaty of Versailles by his open announcement of German rearmament, and he had seen that the Franco-Soviet treaty of May 1935 could be denounced as an aggressive alliance in contravention of the Locarno pact. The final ratification of the Franco-Soviet treaty by the French Chamber gave him the excuse that he needed. On 7 March 1936 German troops marched into the demilitarized zone of the Rhineland at the same time as Hitler informed the western Powers that as a consequence of French diplomatic action he regarded Germany as no longer bound by the Locarno pact, although he was careful to make a specific exception of the arbitration treaties with Poland and Czechoslovakia.

In purely military terms it was a suicidal move, for the French, Poles, and Czechs could between them mobilize 190 divisions in war, and it was hardly surprising that the German General Staff were absolutely appalled at the risk. 'I ran into General von Blomberg,' wrote an American correspondent in his diary on the night of 7 March; 'his face was white, his cheeks twitching.' Yet in the event Hitler's reading of the political scene proved correct. The French General Staff, obsessed by now with a purely defensive strategy behind the Maginot Line, were as cautious and pessimistic as their German counterparts over an offensive operation in the Rhineland. Flandin, the French Foreign Minister, was determined on resistance, but the British government, more concerned over the Abyssinian war at this time, held him back from presenting an ultimatum and insisted that the question should be settled at a diplomatic level. In any case, the most that Great Britain could promise in the way of active aid was two divisions fifteen days after the opening of hostilities. Russia and Poland, conscious of these hesitations in the west, also held back; clearly nothing would happen unless France took the first step alone and this she would not do.

Still, if judgement is to be passed, it can be said that at least a part of the French government had wanted to act. In Great Britain both government and public opinion flatly refused to countenance the thought of military intervention; such a prospect had awoken unhappy memories of the French occupation of the Ruhr in 1923 and there was even a certain sympathy with the German action. 'After all, they're only going into their own back garden,' was a comment that appealed strongly, and among the right wing— already suspicious of the French treaty with Soviet Russia—there was always the lurking thought that a powerful Germany would act as a bulwark against Communist expansion.

There is now little doubt that the reoccupation of the Rhineland could have been successfully resisted, as Hitler had every reason to know. 'The forty-eight hours after the march into the Rhineland,' he said long afterwards, 'were the most nerve-racking in my whole life.' The occupation had been carried out with purely token forces and the French General Staff had wildly overestimated the strength of the German army. It is harder to assess what the political consequences of an Anglo-French intervention might have been. It is, of course, tempting to imagine that it might have led to the overthrow of Hitler, but it is equally possible that German patriotic sentiment might have rallied to him, just as the Weimar Republic had enjoyed its greatest popularity at the time of the passive resistance to the French occupation of the Ruhr. On the other hand, the German generals were beginning to have second thoughts about Hitler by this time and a failure in the Rhineland might have strengthened their hand sufficiently to get rid of him.

As it was, Hitler had enormously bettered his position at home and on the Continent as a whole. He had proved his generals wrong and had demonstrated to the world the weakness of the forces that opposed him. Not merely had he watched the west lose a supreme opportunity to check him; he could ensure that in future such an opportunity would not recur, for Germany was now free to construct the Siegfried Line of fortifications along her western frontier, creating, as Winston Churchill said in the House of Commons, 'a barrier across Germany's front door which will leave her free to sally out eastwards and southwards by the other doors'.With this single outrageous gamble Hitler had turned Germany's back on the past and opened the way to the future, and when in January 1937 he officially withdrew his country's signature from the Treaty of Versailles, he was doing no more than registering what was already a *fait accompli*.

✳ 2. The Abyssinian war 1935–6 ✳

The Anglo-German naval pact and the Franco-Soviet treaty had certainly played a considerable part in weakening the united front that the British and the French might have presented to Hitler when he sent his troops into the Rhineland. The principal factor in the undermining of the policy of collective security, however, was Mussolini's invasion of Abyssinia in October 1935.

Like most European Powers who had entered the race for colonial acquisitions Italy had found that the profits of empire were to be measured more in terms of prestige than of actual economic gain. The organization of her settlements in Libya was costing her 107 million lire in 1921 and as much as 530 million lire by 1930. Somaliland and Eritrea, however, seemed more promising, since their geographical position might enable her to establish economic influence over Abyssinia, with whom she accordingly fostered good relations. It was due to Italian representations that Abyssinia in

1923 was made a member of the League of Nations, and in 1928 a treaty of friendship was signed between the two countries. Unfortunately Mussolini's hopes were disappointed when the Emperor Haile Selassie showed that he wished to encourage other competitors and concluded a commercial treaty with Japan in 1930. Shortly after this disillusionment Mussolini began to consider the possibility of war which would not only establish Italian control throughout Abyssinia, but would also provide his régime with the glory of a cheap victory which would wipe out the memory of the Italian defeat at the hands of the Abyssinians at Adowa in 1896 (see p. 261).

There followed, inevitably, an incident—a skirmish at the oasis of Wal-Wal within Abyssinian territory in December 1934—after which the Italian government demanded an indemnity and the Emperor appealed to the League of Nations. Neither Great Britain nor France was charitably disposed towards the idea of Italian control over Abyssinia—Great Britain, because she did not wish the sources of the Nile, fundamental to Egyptian economy, to fall into their hands; France, because of her own economic interests there. Yet two other factors placed great obstacles in the way of giving wholehearted support to the Emperor. First, the dangerously low level to which the British had run down their military machine and the concentration of the French on the defence of their eastern frontier would make direct resistance to an Italian expeditionary force extremely problematical; second, the foreign policy of Laval at that time was based on gaining the friendship of Italy in order that Mussolini might continue to guarantee Austria's independence against Germany, as he had done at the time of Dollfuss's murder in July 1934, and the Franco-Italian treaty of January 1935 (see p. 404) had given some encouragement to these hopes.

It was this ambivalence of attitude that was to bedevil all subsequent policy throughout the crisis. Mussolini was clearly not going to desist and did his best to delay the appointment of arbitrators, while building up his forces in Eritrea and Italian Somaliland. Yet Hitler's announcement of conscription in Germany in March 1935 made it even more essential for the west that Mussolini should not be driven into his arms, and when Great Britain, France, and Italy met at Stresa in April the Abyssinian question was tactfully left unmentioned—from which Mussolini assumed a general acquiescence. Thus, when in June Anthony Eden proposed the cession of the Abyssinian province of Ogaden to Italy, offering to compensate Abyssinia with the use of a port in British Somaliland, Mussolini rejected the suggestion and in August refused to allow the dispute to be settled by the League of Nations. Finally, on 2 October 1935 Italian forces invaded Abyssinia.

The reaction of the League a fortnight later was to impose a moderate form of economic sanctions, but since the embargo did not include the two vital commodities, coal and oil, this measure was largely ineffectual. In any case, Russia continued to supply Italy, and as neither Germany nor the United States were members of the League, they were not bound by the ruling. Thus, while these half-hearted measures made very little impact on Mussolini's war effort, they did rouse his anger sufficiently against Great Britain and France to cause him to denounce the Franco-Italian treaty and the Stresa agreements.

In fact, the only obstacle to Italian success during the opening months of the campaign was their own military incompetence. The Abyssinian army remained intact and it was becoming doubtful whether the Italians would gain control of the railway line to the capital Addis Ababa before the rainy reason in 1936. Yet, despite the time gained by this long-drawn-out resistance and strong public opinion in Great Britain in favour of full sanctions, the British and French diplomats continued to struggle to find some way of attaining the contradictory ends of forcing the Italians to stop, at the same time as regaining their friendship. Already in September 1935 Sir Samuel Hoare and Pierre Laval had agreed that there should be no military sanctions, mainly because the British naval authorities had expressed strong doubts over their ability to hold the Suez canal against the Italian fleet, and in December the Hoare-Laval pact proposed further concessions that would have given approximately two-thirds of Abyssinia to Italy; the remaining third would be allowed a small outlet to the sea which even *The Times*, although hardly an advocate of resistance to the dictators, described as 'a corridor for camels'.

The Hoare-Laval pact came to nothing. In Great Britain there was an outcry of indignation and Hoare himself had to resign. Nor would Mussolini settle for two-thirds, when he believed that he could gain all without any resistance from the Powers. The Italian army met with greater success in 1936 after the commander, De Bono, had been replaced by Badoglio, and the use of aerial bombardment and poison gas against tribesmen armed with spears soon put the issue beyond doubt. Addis Ababa was occupied by Italian troops at the beginning of May and the Emperor was forced to flee. Thus, at a cost of 1,537 Italians killed in action, Mussolini added the largest of the remaining independent territories of Africa to his empire, and with the ending of sanctions in July the world officially accepted this new state of affairs.

The whole of the Abyssinian episode was an appalling political defeat for Great Britain and France and meant nothing less than the utter bankruptcy of the League of Nations and the ideal of collective security. By antagonizing Italy and yet failing to resist her, the two western Powers had fallen hopelessly between two stools and their evident lack of firmness of purpose had shown Hitler that he might safely risk the reoccupation of the Rhineland at a moment when they were unhappily involved elsewhere. Furthermore, the collapse of the Stresa agreements naturally caused Mussolini to turn to friendship with Hitler. By a treaty signed in October 1936 their two countries were in future to cooperate over foreign policy, and a year later, after Mussolini had paid an official visit to Germany, he joined the Anti-Comintern Pact which Germany and Japan had already formed against Russia. This was mainly to Hitler's advantage, since good relations with Italy suggested that Austria might not be able to rely upon continued Italian support against Germany. For Mussolini, on the other hand, the immediate gain from his Abyssinian adventure was negligible and the eventual outcome disastrous. The Italian administration of Abyssinia proved extremely corrupt and by 1939 Italy's trade with all her African colonies only amounted to 2 per cent of her total trade. Even the prestige of success did him little good, for his flouting of Great Britain and France gave him an ill-founded opinion of his own strength, and his friendship with Hitler was the beginning of a policy that was to culminate in the invasion of his country and an ignominious death for himself.

3. The growing cleavage of opinion: the Spanish Civil War 1936–9

By now the existence of two fundamentally opposed forms of police state in Germany and Russia naturally affected political feelings in the western democracies, creating a growing cleavage of opinion between right and left. Many of the right, although doubtful of many aspects of Fascism, saw Germany and Italy as efficient powerful States which could offer an effective resistance to Communism; on the left, many liberals and mild Socialists, regarding the immediate background of slump, unemployment, and hunger marches as the final condemnation of *laissez-faire* capitalism, leaned increasingly in the direction of Communist Russia, who seemed to be the only non-Fascist country that was prepared to take an unambiguous stand against the racialism and national aggressiveness of the right-wing dictatorships of Germany and Italy.

The practical outcome of these attitudes varied. In Great Britain they played their part in the formation of views throughout the country, but they had only a minor effect on the official policies of the parties. The Conservatives were governed by many other motives than fear of Communism in attempting the appeasement of the Fascist countries (see pp. 414–15), while the Labour party, as was natural for Socialists who accepted the principle of parliamentary constitutionalism, was equally mistrustful of the political implications of revolutionary Communism.

In France and Spain, however, the clash between the two views was translated into direct political action. On the French right wing a number of organizations had been formed of a Fascist type—*Action française*; the oldest of them, which included Charles Maurras, Léon Daudet, and Jacques Bainville, *Croix de feu* led by Colonel de la Roque, and *Solidarité Française*—all authoritarian, appealing to ex-servicemen and strongly anti-Communist and anti-Semitic. The membership of each of the groups was no more than about 100,000, but in 1934 a domestic crisis revealed the lengths to which they might be prepared to go. At the beginning of that year members of the French government were known to have been involved in the fraudulent transactions of a Russian-Jewish business man, Serge Stavisky, and when Stavisky who was due for trial was discovered dead in his villa at Chamonix, apparently through suicide, the right-wing leagues launched a great attack on the government in Paris, declaring that he had been killed in order that embarrassing disclosures might be avoided. On 6 February they fought a pitched battle with the police in the Place de la Concorde in an attempt to break through to the Palais Bourbon where the Assembly had its seat. Constitutional government survived this test, but the left wing, mindful of the lessons offered by Italy and Germany, took warning. In January 1936 Radicals, Socialists, and Communists combined to form a party, the *Rassemblement Populaire Français*, and when the elections of April 1936 gave them a majority, a new government under Léon Blum embarked on a series of left-wing measures, including a forty-hour week, holidays with pay for workers, and the nationalization of munition factories. Employers had to agree to a system of collective negotiation and to wage increases, and the right-wing leagues were outlawed.

In Spain the cleavage between right and left was equally marked in the new freedom of political life that the constitution of 1931 (see p. 388) allowed. Governments had risen and fallen with the speed customary in countries that had just embarked upon an experiment in constitutional rule, but the elections of February 1936 revealed the formation of two composite groups: on the left, Republicans, Socialists, Syndicalists, Anarchists, and Communists combined to create a Popular front; on the right, the Falange Española was supported by the Roman Catholic Church, the army, and the industrialists. In these elections the right gained slightly more votes, but owing to the workings of the electoral system the left actually held a majority in the assembly, the *Cortes*. The outcome was the opening of the civil war in Spain, when a military rising in Spanish Morocco under General Franco in July 1936 was followed by rapid successes on the mainland. By November Franco's forces were established in the south, west, and north of Spain and had set up a new government at Burgos, while the Republicans had withdrawn the seat of the official government to Barcelona and centred their resistance on Catalonia, Valencia, and the two Basque provinces of the north.

Within Spain itself the struggle was only incidentally one between Fascism and Communism. On the right the principal elements were the military and the monarchists, although they naturally included Fascist organizations; nor was the left primarily Communist. Yet to the Powers of Europe it appeared such a struggle. None of them could remain indifferent to it, partly because of Spain's geographical position, partly because both sides in the war were in urgent need of men and supplies. Germany and Italy both favoured Franco-Italy, because she hoped to establish naval bases in the Balearic Isles and to weaken Great Britain's hold on Gibraltar; Germany, because a victory for Franco might create embarrassment for France on her southern frontier—an attitude reminiscent of Bismarck's dabbling in the question of the Spanish succession in 1870. Naturally the consequence of these aims was to swing the western democracies away from supporting Franco, but the presence of Communists among the Republicans inhibited the British government in particular from sending help to the forces that were resisting him. In France, Blum would have liked to intervene on the side of the left, but divisions in his cabinet as well as the attitude of the British compelled him to compromise with a scheme for a general guarantee of non-intervention, and in August 1936 an agreement was signed to this effect by Great Britain, France, Germany, Italy, and Russia.

In fact, none of the dictatorships honoured the agreement. In November Mussolini and Franco reached an understanding over economic support and political collaboration in the western Mediterranean, and before long thousands of rifles and machine-guns were being shipped from Italy to Franco. By January 1937 there were 44,000 Italian troops in Spain and by the following October 60,000. In March 1937 Franco came to a similar agreement with Hitler, whereby he was to have the services of German pilots and technicians together with a great deal of war material. This violation of the principle of non-intervention naturally provided the Soviet government with all the justification that it needed to announce openly in October that Russian help would be sent to the Republican forces. In France the extreme left of the *Rassemblement Populaire* advocated direct intervention on behalf of the Republicans—as eventually did the Labour party in Great Britain—but the governments of the western democracies remained unwilling to make what seemed to be a choice between a Communist and a Fascist cause.

In Spain the war had almost reached a stalemate by the end of 1937 after Franco had been checked at Madrid and Teruel, but in 1938 the superiority pf his forces in numbers and equipment due to the assistance of Germany and Italy enabled him to strike through to the east coast. Barcelona fell in January 1939, Madrid in March, and in April Franco declared that hostilities were officially at an end.

Although the bitterness of the struggle had left Spain far too exhausted to participate in any further warfare, the victory of Franco certainly seemed to represent an overwhelming success for the Fascist dictators. In March 1939 he formed a definite alliance with Germany and Italy, and France was now faced with the possibility of a hostile neighbour beyond the Pyrenees. The prospects for the west of regaining Italian friendship were more remote than ever; the efforts of Neville Chamberlain, who in May 1937 had replaced Baldwin as Prime Minister in Great Britain, met with little success in drawing Italy away from her involvement with Germany, and resulted only in the resignation of Anthony Eden, the Foreign Secretary.

These considerations were naturally important, yet the two most significant aspects of the Spanish Civil War were emotional rather than diplomatic. First, it provided an object lesson in a new form of total war; the ferocity of the fighting, the sufferings of the civilian population, the bombing of cities such as Guernica, the activity of resistance groups behind the lines, all gave a glimpse of the fate that might one day engulf the entire Continent. Second, to many for whom Spain in these years appeared like an arena in which the two extremes of left and right were at last in open conflict, it seemed that there could no longer be any further neutrality in the crisis of ideological loyalty, and with this hardening of opinions over Fascism many of those of more moderate outlook in the western countries, watching the gradual advance of Franco's armies, knew at last in their hearts where their ultimate decision lay.

Chapter 33

Germany's Advance Eastwards 1938–9

By the beginning of 1938 the initiative appeared to be firmly in the hands of the Powers of the Anti-Comintern Pact. The Japanese invasion of Manchuria in 1931, the Italian conquest of Abyssinia, the German reoccupation of the Rhineland, and the supplying of General Franco in the Spanish Civil War, all suggested that the objections of Great Britain and France might be safely defied and the authority of the League of Nations ignored. Certainly the smaller countries of Europe interpreted events in this light. In eastern Europe, except for Czechoslovakia, they began to trim their sails towards Berlin; the Netherlands and the Scandinavian nations announced that they could not in future shape their policy in accordance with the requirements of collective security, while in 1936 Belgium had already officially abandoned her alliances in order to revert to strict neutrality.

British and French reactions to the aggressiveness of the dictators took two forms. By 1936 they had both reluctantly begun to rearm. For Great Britain the importance of air defence seemed to the experts to loom as large as the question of naval superiority had done before 1914 (see pp. 289, 295), but this time there was a striking difference, since the British had already lost their lead and plans had to be made for an expansion of the R.A.F. which would enable it to catch up with the German *Luftwaffe*. At the same time work was begun under the Tizard committee on the operational development of radar—perhaps the greatest single factor in the salvation of the country in 1940. The French, obsessed with the thought of German invasion, concentrated their efforts on the Maginot Line, but these purely defensive measures naturally only added to the apprehensiveness of their eastern allies.

The principal policy of the west remained one of appeasement. This simply allowed the dictators to have almost everything their own way, so that Hitler was able in 1938 to absorb Austria and the Czech Sudetenland, and in 1939 Slovakia and the Memelland, until his attempt to gain Danzig led to the outbreak of the second World War. Appeasement eventually became so discredited that the word itself retained a pejorative flavour long after the end of the war, but at the time it was a policy which had the support of a considerable body of public opinion in the west. The fundamental reason for this lay in the appalling memory of the first World War. 'Never again' was the all-consuming thought of the western democracies—particularly among ex-servicemen whose families were by now reaching military age. And for the British there was in addition a confused sense of guilt over the Treaty of Versailles, strengthened by their irritation with the French in the 1920s. They were consequently not entirely unconvinced by Hitler's arguments over German minorities, and it was not until the partition of the non-German regions of Czechoslovakia in March 1939 that the electorates of Great Britain and France awoke to the belated realization that paying the Danegeld—or, rather, making others pay—meant no limit to what would ultimately be demanded.

Appeasement, however, was based on practical considerations as well as emotional. British mildness in their relations with the Italians over the Abyssinian war was due mainly to a desire to prevent a German–Italian alliance which would add to their problems in the Mediterranean. Over Germany the predominating consideration in 1938 and 1939 was not merely the general military weakness of the west, but also the fact that the Siegfried Line, flanked by a neutral Belgium and Switzerland, shut Great Britain and France out from any effective intervention that might prevent Hitler's expansion eastwards. The only hope seemed to lie in the creation of a league of states in eastern Europe who would stand firm with the west against Germany, but by now the eastern states, increasingly impressed by Hitler's handling of the west, preferred to play his game for him in furthering their individual ends; thus Poland and Hungary each annexed Czech territory in 1938, and Hungary did so again in March 1939.

In the last analysis any firm resistance would depend upon some form of western agreement with Russia—a recreation of the Triple Entente of 1907—but here national and political considerations acted as a powerful brake. The right wing in both Great Britain and France remained highly suspicious of Communist Russia and even saw Nazi Germany as a dam raised against the Bolshevik flood, as Hitler in a speech in 1936 had suggested that they would; 'better Hitler than Blum' was the comment of some French conservatives. In eastern Europe the mistrust of Russia was even stronger; in the crisis of September 1938 the Czechs did not relish the idea of dependence on the Red Army and in any case neither Poland nor Rumania would have allowed it a free passage through their lands to defend Czechoslovakia; in the summer of 1939, when the German demands on Poland were mounting, the Poles were adamant that there could be no alliance with Russia.

Thus, throughout these crises Neville Chamberlain, the British

Prime Minister, was haunted by the thought that even if general
war in resistance to Hitler did ensue, nothing could be done to save
the country over whom it had broken out. In 1938 there was in
addition the realization that public opinion, particularly in the
Commonwealth, was as yet unprepared to accept the appalling consequences of an outbreak of war, and that in any case the west was
still lagging too far behind in rearmament to bring effective pressure
to bear on Germany. On this last point it has sometimes been
argued that the surrender of the Sudetenland at Munich in 1938
was simply an attempt to gain time. Chamberlain was not so
Machiavellian. He was certainly aware of the desperate need to be
able to argue from a position of strength, but he still hoped after
Munich that war might be averted. In this he clearly misjudged
Hitler; on the other hand, when war was finally forced upon him
over the Danzig crisis in 1939, his earlier efforts to preserve peace
did at least ensure him the full support of public opinion, and the
immediate fall of Poland and the military disasters for the west in
1940 would suggest that his appreciation of the difficulties that
had prompted his policy of appeasement had not been entirely
unrealistic.

1. The Austrian *Anschluss*, March 1938

Hitler's own avowal in *Mein Kampf* had made it clear that the first
stage in his revision of the frontiers of 1919 would be the absorption
of Austria within Germany. There is, however, little to indicate that
the actual circumstances of the *Anschluss* (union) of March 1938 were
due to any long-premeditated plan; it seems probable that Hitler
was content to rely upon the activity of the Austrian Nazi party to
bring about such a union with Germany by peaceful invitation, but,
as was his way, he was always ready to seize an opportunity which
the growing tension might present. The Austrian Chancellor, von
Schuschnigg, had hoped to buy time with an agreement with Germany in July 1936, at the same time vainly trying to strengthen
Austria's ties with the '*little entente*' (see p. 376) but when his police
unearthed plans for an Austrian Nazi *coup d' état* in January 1938,
he decided that the moment had arrived for a new negotiation with
Hitler. Von Papen, the German ambassador at Vienna, was recalled
at the beginning of February, but on hearing of von Schuschnigg's
willingness to come to terms, Hitler sent him back to Vienna, where
a meeting was arranged between the two Chancellors at the Berghof,
Hitler's residence in the Obersalzberg. Their conversations on 12
February consisted of no less than a series of demands by Hitler that
Austrian Nazis should be reinstated in their official posts, that
Seyss-Inquart, one of their leading members, should become Minister of the Interior—consequently with control over the police—

and that close economic and military relations should be established between the two countries. Von Schuschnigg, impressed by the presence of German generals at the Berghof, duly gave way. 'I am happy to be able to tell you, gentlemen,' Hitler announced in the *Reichstag* on 20 February, 'that during the past few days a further understanding has been reached with a country that is particularly close to us for many reasons.' Four days later, however, von Schuschnigg made it clear in a speech of his own before the Austrian *Bundestag* that a halt must be called to German demands and on 8 March he announced a plebiscite on the question of union with Germany.

Hitler did not hear of this until 10 March and it seems that he was taken by surprise. The result of the plebiscite, due to be held on Sunday 13 March, would almost certainly deprive him of his argument that the Austrians were longing for reunion with Germany and he was determined to forestall it. Three German army corps and the air force were mobilized at once and Prince Philip of Hesse was dispatched to Mussolini with a letter to dissuade him from rallying to the support of Austria, as he had done at the time of the murder of Dollfuss. On 11 March Goering demanded through Seyss-Inquart that the plebiscite should be called off, but when von Schuschnigg finally agreed, this was followed by an ultimatum that Seyss-Inquart must replace Schuschnigg as Chancellor. Later that night Prince Philip of Hesse telephoned from Rome to say that Mussolini had agreed not to resist German action, and Hitler knew that the way was open.

Shortly before midnight President Miklas finally surrendered, but the orders for an occupation had already been given, and early on 12 March German forces crossed the frontier into Austria, where local Nazi groups were now taking over the local administration. On 13 March union with Germany was proclaimed and on the next day Hitler arrived at Vienna to take possession of the capital in which he had once lived in poverty and degradation. He might indeed feel triumphant. At the price of abandoning the Tyrolese to continued rule under Italy he had taken the first step in realizing the old dream of *Grossdeutschland*, and Austria with a population of seven million, resources of iron, steel, and magnesite, and frontiers that opened a door to the Balkans, was now to be no more than a province of the German Reich.

Plebiscites in Germany and Austria—held under government auspices and naturally overwhelmingly in favour of the *Anschluss*— were mainly for the purpose of conciliating foreign opinion, but in fact reactions abroad to the *coup* were remarkably slight. Poland and Czechoslovakia acquiesced, while France at this time was actually without a government. In Great Britain the public felt vaguely that the Austrians were German anyway, and despite the warning sounded by Winston Churchill in the House of Commons, there was no sense of outrage when the British government contented itself with an official protest.

2. The Sudetenland crisis and the Munich pact, August–September 1938

There could be little doubt where the next blow would fall. The successful accomplishment of the Austrian *Anschluss* awoke a great excitement among the Sudeten Germans in Czechoslovakia, and before the end of March their leader Konrad Henlein was in consultation with Hitler, Ribbentrop, and Hess in Berlin. Immediately after the Austrian crisis Neville Chamberlain had turned down any suggestion of British guarantee for Czechoslovakia, as well as a Russian proposal for a four-Power conference, and when Henlein in a speech at Karlsbad on 24 April outlined eight points demanding autonomy for the Sudetenlanders, it seemed as if there might be very little western resistance to Nazi plans.

Then suddenly in the middle of May Hitler encountered unexpected difficulties. The Czechs, suspicious of German troop-movements near their frontiers, mobilized part of their forces; the British and French governments supported them with the strongest diplomatic warnings, while the Russians reassured the French that they would stand by the agreements of May 1935 in defence of Czechoslovakia. Thereupon Hitler decided to hold back, but this momentary interference with his policy only confirmed him in his hatred of the Czechs as Slav *Untermenschen*; on 30 May he informed the General Staff that 'it is my unalterable decision to smash Czechoslovakia by military action in the near future', and gave orders for the preparation of a military invasion by 1 October.

Throughout the summer, as the tension over the Sudetenland continued to mount, the British and French governments attempted to mediate, asking Hitler to moderate his demands and putting pressure on the Czechs to make concessions to the Sudetenlanders. On 4 September President Beneš granted Henlein's eight points, but by now Hitler was convinced that the west would not fight, and a week later at the Nuremberg Party Rally he launched a savage attack on the Czech President. 'The Germans in Czechoslovakia are neither defenceless, nor are they deserted, and people should take notice of that fact.'

Then, when the crisis was at its height, Neville Chamberlain announced on 13 September his intention of flying to Germany to initiate direct conversations with Hitler. At Berchtesgaden Hitler stated an outright demand that the Sudetenland be ceded to Germany. Back in London Chamberlain and the French decided to agree to a transference of territory where the population was more than 50 per cent German, and the Czechs were forced to accept this. On 22 September Chamberlain returned to Germany by air, this time to Godesberg on the Rhine, only to find that Hitler now wanted more. The Poles and the Hungarians must also receive concessions and the Sudetenland must be placed under immediate German military occupation. These fresh demands seemed to wreck even Chamberlain's hopes of avoiding war. The British cabinet refused to accept them, the French government called up 600,000 reservists, and the Czechs had already mobilized during the Godesberg conversations. These were facts that Hitler did not ignore; his General Staff were already advocating extreme caution, and he had himself noticed the atmosphere of gloom among the crowds in Berlin. At any rate, despite a virulent speech against the Czechs on 26 September, he did not break off negotiations with London, and when the French put forward a proposal involving slight modifications of his Godesberg demands, Mussolini, who dreaded the possibility of being dragged into a European war, was prompted by the British to persuade him to accept this as a basis for discussion. And so on 29 September Hitler, Mussolini, Chamberlain, and Daladier met in conference in the *Führerbau* at Munich and reached an agreement that gave Hitler almost the whole of what he had demanded. The Czechs were not invited and their ambassador was afterwards simply informed by Chamberlain and Daladier that they would have to submit.

Thus, in an ultimately fruitless attempt to preserve European peace Great Britain and France abandoned Czechoslovakia to the German dictator. The Czechs were compelled to give up the horseshoe-shaped western edge of their frontier which contained all their mountain fortifications, and nearly a million Czechs who lived among the German Sudetenlanders found themselves under Nazi rule. Immediately afterwards Poland seized the Teschen district, while Hungary extended her own frontier northwards (see maps, pp. 420–1) each glad to settle grievances that had rankled since the end of the war. In his own way Hitler had harnessed local national animosity to his policy as effectively as the Habsburgs had done in the past.

For France Munich was a flagrant breach of a treaty of alliance. Great Britain had had no treaty with the Czechs; on the other hand, she had taken the initiative in organizing the surrender. It had been open to the British government to create a firm diplomatic front with France and Russia, yet they refused to contemplate cooperation with the Soviet Union; they would not even commit themselves to joining France against Germany, unless she was actually invaded by German forces. Instead, by conscious choice Chamberlain preferred to negotiate with Germany on the assumption of Hitler's good faith, and it was not unnatural that the Russians should suspect the forming of a European alignment that would eventually leave them

Sudetenland

Territory gained by Hungary 1938-40

European countries neutral during second world war

UNITED KINGDOM

NORWAY

SWEDEN

Trondhe

DENMARK

Lübeck

Liverpool

Coventry

Bremen

Hamburg

London

Dunkirk

Arnhem

Berlin

Plymouth

Boulogne

Rotterdam

Cherbourg

Arras

Paris

Reims

SAAR

Tours

Munich

Vienn

Berch
gade

Bordeaux

Vichy

SWITZERLD

UNOCCUPIED FRANCE 1940-42

BO
MOR

Burgos

PORTUGAL

SPAIN

Madrid

Marseilles

Rome

Barcelona

Valencia

Anzio

Naples

Balearic Is

Salerno

Gibraltar

Algiers

Oran

Tunis

Syracuse

Casablanca

Malt

MOROCCO

ALGERIA

Scale 0   600 km

LIBYA

FINLAND

KARELIA
(ceded to
Russia 1940)

Viipuri

anko

ESTONIA

Novgorod

Leningrad

LATVIA

nel LITHUANIA

O E.
PRUSSIA

Brest
Litovsk

rsaw

P O L A N D

Kiev

Moscow

Smolensk

Voronezh

Stalingrad

Dnieper

Kharkov

Don

Rostov

Volga

VAKIA

Budapest TRAN-
SYLVANIA

BARY

grade

RUMANIA

UGO-
LAVIA

BULGARIA

Yalta

ALBANIA

GREECE

ento

T U R K E Y

SYRIA

Cape
Matapan

Crete

Cyprus

IRAQ

PALESTINE

Tobruk

Sidi Barrani

Port
Said

TRANS-
JORDAN

Benghazi

El
Alamein

Cairo

Suez

SAUDI
ARABIA

El Agheila

E G Y P T

Legend:

— Furthest line of German advance Oct. 1942

- - - German advance in 1941

××××× French Maginot line

-·-·- Partition line in Poland 1939

to face a German onslaught in isolation.

Unhappy though it was, however, not every criticism that has been made of Munich is entirely sound. It has been claimed, for example, that Hitler was only bluffing. It is true that the German General Staff were strongly opposed to war and at the Nuremberg trials after the war General Keitel declared that they would not have been strong enough to fight in September 1938. Yet Hitler had continually overruled his General Staff. The secrecy of his partial mobilization on 27 September does not suggest bluff; he had been in a black mood at Munich and his remark to the S.S. afterwards that 'that fellow Chamberlain has spoiled my entry into Prague' implied that he really had been hoping for an excuse 'to smash Czechoslovakia'. Mussolini's attitude may have given him cause to think, but if the west had stood firm in refusing concessions, it is impossible to see how he could have retreated from the public statements that he had already made.

Another criticism that the Germans have constantly stressed since 1945 is that the west's surrender to Hitler at Munich wrecked the chances of a plot that was being hatched among German generals and politicians who were hoping to oust the Nazis. Certainly there was a tentative scheme to get rid of Hitler in September 1938, of which the British government was aware through secret emissaries from Germany, but they could hardly be expected to shape their policy simply on the strength of such information. One must not underestimate the technical difficulties, the personal risk, and the struggle of divided loyalties involved in any attempt to supplant Hitler; yet if Munich did ruin a plan to remove him, it is legitimate to ask why the eventual resistance of the west twelve months later did not favour a similar *coup*. In fact, none materialized until July 1944 and was then a failure—as indeed the doubts and perplexities of the conspirators suggest it would have been in September 1938, even if it had been attempted.

Of course, it is possible that Hitler might have succumbed to a *coup d'état*. Certainly on that assumption Munich can be blamed for the appalling holocaust of the second World War. It seems much more probable, however, that if the west had supported Czechoslovakia, Hitler would have remained in power and that war would have ensued. Beyond that it is difficult to speculate. The French General Staff were highly pessimistic over their chances of penetrating the Siegfried Line; 'une bataille de la Somme modernisée', General Gamelin predicted gloomily. The thirty-six divisions of the Czech army, aided by their Sudetenland fortifications, would have given a good account of themselves, but they would have had to fight without any immediate aid. Despite her protestations to the contrary Russia might have been content to remain neutral while the European Powers exhausted themselves in war, but even if she had been prepared to throw in her lot with the west and if the Czechs had accepted her support, Poland and Rumania would have resisted the passage of the Red Army through their territories. Indeed, the Czechs would have been fortunate if Poland and Hungary had not joined in the attack against them, and on the face of it there is every likelihood that war in September 1938 would have given Hitler possession of the whole of Czechoslovakia in a matter of weeks.

3. The destruction of Czechoslovakia, March 1939, and the change in western policy

'We have sustained a total and unmitigated defeat', declared Winston Churchill in the House of Commons, yet despite the revolt of a small section of the Conservatives at Westminster, there is little doubt that the majority of the public in Great Britain and France were conscious of an overwhelming sense of relief. They preferred to believe that 'it is peace in our time', as Chamberlain announced from the windows of Downing Street on his return from Munich, and for a short while events gave some encouragement to this wishful thinking. In December a Franco-German declaration was issued confirming the agreement at Munich; in January 1939 Chamberlain and his Foreign Secretary, Lord Halifax, paid an official visit to Italy, while in Spain it was clear that the civil war was almost at an end.

It was not long, however, before disillusionment finally dawned. After Munich President Beneš had resigned and left the country, and Czechoslovakia had been converted into a federal state with autonomy for Slovakia and Ruthenia, except over matters of defence and foreign policy. This soon led to domestic disputes until, early in March 1939, President Hacha, Beneš' successor, dismissed the two premiers of Slovakia and Ruthenia, one of whom, Father Tiso of Slovakia, appealed to Hitler in Berlin. Once again Hitler, although taken by surprise at the time, seized the chance when it came. A German demand for Slovak independence brought President Hacha to Berlin, where, through the same techniques as had been employed against von Schuschnigg the year before, he was browbeaten into placing the whole of Czechoslovakia under German protection. Almost at once Bohemia and Moravia, where military occupation had already begun, were annexed to Germany, Slovakia became a German protectorate, and Ruthenia was handed over to the Hungarians. As Hitler announced in delight, Czechoslovakia had ceased to exist, and he followed up this advance a week later by forcing Lithuania to yield the Memelland to East Prussia, and by concluding a trade agreement with Rumania which would ensure oil supplies for Germany.

The west took no direct action, using the excuse that the changes had come about with the consent of the Czech and Lithuanian governments. Yet these events in March 1939 were to be of momentous significance in the history of Europe, for with this further annexation Hitler unwittingly created an extraordinary revolution in official and public opinion in the west. Now, even the most pacific-minded realized at last that the issue of German minorities was merely a screen for a consistent march eastwards which only diplomatic or military pressure could halt. The destruction of Czechoslovakia had finally demonstrated the utter bankruptcy of the policy of appeasement. 'Is this, in fact, a step in the direction of an attempt to dominate the world by force?' demanded Chamberlain in a speech at Birmingham on 17 March. However mild, his question sounded a new note. A week later Great Britain and France agreed that they would resist any German agression in the Netherlands, Belgium, or Switzerland, and at the end of the month Chamberlain stated in the House of Commons that Great Britain would stand with France in supporting Poland with whom Hitler was already beginning to pick a quarrel over Danzig.

This remarkable change of attitude on the part of the west was confirmed almost immediately by Mussolini, when on Good Friday Italian troops began the occupation of Albania. It was a fairly pointless operation, since Albania was economically already in Italy's pocket; indeed, Ahmed Zogu had been able to have himself proclaimed King Zog in 1928 mainly because of Italian support. Mussolini, however, with a Fascist dictator's concern for prestige, was jealous of Hitler's recent successes and was, furthermore, anxious over the growth of German influence in the Balkans. In their new mood the British and the French at once gave guarantees of support to Greece and Rumania and made similar offers to the Netherlands, Switzerland, and Denmark who, however, rejected them. Then, on 26 April, for the first time in her history Great Britain, as a result of French persuasion, introduced universal military conscription. The length of service was only to be six months and made little immediate difference to the state of the British forces, yet as a symbol it marked the extraordinary alteration in general feeling since the previous September.

4. Danzig and the outbreak of war, September 1939

'It would be wrong', wrote the German ambassador in London on 18 March, 'to cherish any illusions that a fundamental change had not taken place in Britain's attitude towards Germany,' but if Hitler saw this, it had little effect on his actions in the summer of 1939. At the beginning of April his General Staff had already received orders to prepare for a campaign against Poland, and in a speech in the

Reichstag at the end of the month he demanded the return of Danzig to Germany, at the same time denouncing the German–Polish non-aggression pact of 1934 and the Anglo-German naval agreement of 1935. On 22 May the so-called Pact of Steel between Germany and Italy was published, each promising to support the other in war and to collaborate over the acquisition of *Lebensraum*. On the next day Hitler outlined his plans before an audience of senior officers. 'We cannot expect a repetition of the Czech affair. There will be war. Our task is to isolate Poland. The success of this isolation will be decisive . . . there must be no simultaneous conflict with the western Powers.' A week later Mussolini secretly informed Hitler that despite the Pact of Steel Italy could do nothing for the next three years. This was of little significance to Hitler, however, since the overriding diplomatic consideration now was not Italy, but Russia.

There is little doubt that the west could have gained a Russian alliance that summer. On 16 April the Russians had actually proposed a three-Power agreement with Great Britain and France, including Poland as well, if possible, but the offer had been rejected because the west, suspicious themselves of Russian designs, knew well the fears that Poland, Rumania, Finland, and the Baltic states entertained of a Communist advance westwards. Critics in the House of Commons urged an immediate alliance. 'You are in it up to the neck already,' declared Winston Churchill, 'and the question is how to make your system effective, and effective in time.' Indeed, the only hope of saving Poland was an Anglo-French-Russian alliance, but the Poles would not hear of it, and after the rejection of their offer of 16 April the Soviet government was confirmed in its conviction that the western Powers were hoping to leave Russia to face Germany alone. On 3 May the pro-western Russian Foreign Minister, Litvinov, was replaced by Molotov and, throughout the summer, negotiations with the west continued at a snail's pace. On 29 June the west did agree to the ominous Russian proposal that if the alliance were formed, it should include a guarantee of Finland and the Baltic States, but subsequent military conversations in August broke down over the Polish refusal to allow Russian bases in Poland.

This failure on the part of the west to come to terms with Russia played into the hands of Germany. It might seem that there could be nothing more incongruous than a pact between a Nazi and a Communist government, yet there were arguments in favour of it on both sides. For Germany it would simply be a reversion to the policy of the nineteenth century which von Seeckt had advocated in 1921, and it would effectively seal the fate of Poland; for Russia it would enable her to gain the spheres of influence which her negotiations with the west did not seem likely to provide. For both it would be a cynical bargain whereby each manoeuvred for a better position in the war that each knew would one day break out between them. Initially, contacts were established through trade talks in May, but by July conversations in Berlin were moving in the direction of a political alliance and on 22 August Ribbentrop arrived by air at Moscow to complete the negotiations. That same night the treaty of alliance between Russia and Germany was finally signed. The first part which was made public was simply a non-aggression pact; the second part was a secret agreement over the division of the spoil. Poland was to be partitioned roughly along the line originally proposed by Lord Curzon as her eastern frontier in 1920 (see p. 351). Lithuania and Vilna were to come within the German sphere of influence, Finland, Estonia, and Latvia within the Russian, while Germany agreed to turn a blind eye to Russian interests in the Rumanian province of Bessarabia.

Hitler was naturally overjoyed at the news of the Molotov–Ribbentrop pact and hailed his Foreign Minister on his return from Moscow as 'a second Bismarck'. Indeed, both Hitler and the statesmen of the west had taken action as soon as they had known that the signing of the pact was imminent. On 22 August Hitler had lectured his generals on the certainty of war with Poland. 'I am only afraid,' he said, 'that some *Schweinehund* will make a proposal for mediation.' On the same day the British cabinet met to issue a *communiqué* that a Soviet–Nazi pact 'would in no way affect their obligation to Poland', and immediately afterwards Chamberlain dispatched a personal letter to Hitler to the same effect. This left Hitler unmoved, but on 25 August the announcement of a definite Anglo-Polish treaty, coupled with a further warning from Mussolini that Italy would be unable to give Germany direct military support, did cause him to hesitate and he ordered a temporary postponement of the attack on Poland.

During these last few days of peace Chamberlain, despite his mistrust of Hitler, was still hoping for some compromise agreement, but for Hitler this seemed no more than an opportunity to detach the west from Poland. He insisted that he had no designs on the British Empire, but over the immediate issue he demanded that a Polish plenipotentiary should be sent to Berlin with powers to accept whatever Germany wanted. This would clearly mean a repetition of the interviews that Hitler had held previously with Schuschnigg and Hacha, and the British government would not countenance it, although they still urged the Poles to continue to negotiate. On 31 August Hitler came to his fateful decision. He issued the final directive to his supreme commander and on 1 September German forces invaded Poland.

To the growing dismay of the British House of Commons the reaction of the west was not immediate. There were reasons for this.

Mussolini had made one last frantic attempt at mediation and the coordination of British and French military measures was not easy to arrange by telephone. The principal difficulty was the demand of the French General Staff for a delay of forty-eight hours in which they could carry out their mobilization without interference from German air attack. By 2 September, however, members of all parties in the House of Commons had grown so impatient that Chamberlain forced the French to overrule their generals and at eleven o'clock on 3 September, after Nevile Henderson had presented an ultimatum at Berlin, a state of war existed between Great Britain and Germany. A French declaration followed later the same day.

Thus, after having for so long failed to face up to the realities of Hitler's aims, the west had at last committed themselves to calling a halt to German expansion. It was an unavoidable step, yet the diplomatic follies of previous years now placed them in a position far worse than in 1914. This time Italy was far more closely linked with Germany; worse still, the Molotov–Ribbentrop pact had freed Germany from the likelihood of a prolonged war on two fronts. As it turned out, this was to have disastrous consequences for Russia as well as for the west. Russia's aim had been to keep Germany embroiled with the west, just as she had suspected the west hoped to see Germany and herself exhausting each other's energies in the east. In the event she overestimated the strength of the west, and the Russo-German alliance enabled Hitler to concentrate all his forces on knocking France out of the war in the summer of 1940, after which he was able to turn them against Russia in 1941.

5. The controversy over Hitler's aims

Even when one makes all due allowance for contemporary prejudice, it is hard to see how Germany can escape the full burden of responsibility for the outbreak of the second World War. This was, of course, largely the work of one man. There was little sense of jubilation among the German public or the professionals; indeed, it might be argued that war broke out in 1914 because the German General Staff had too much power, and in 1939 because they had too little.

For many years after the war the orthodox interpretation of Hitler's aims was that he intended to establish a great German empire throughout eastern Europe stretching as far as the Black Sea, and in very general terms it was reckoned that the evidence for this was to be found in a series of his own statements spanning much of his active life. In 1924 he had declared in *Mein Kampf*: 'We put an end to the perpetual Germanic march towards the south and west of Europe and turn our eyes towards the east. We finally put a stop to the colonial and trade policy of pre-war times and pass over to

The Crisis of Liberal Democracy 1921–45

the territorial policy of the future. But when we speak of new territory in Europe today, we must principally think of Russia and the border states subject to her. Destiny itself seems to wish to point out the way for us here.' Then on 5 November 1937, nearly five years after he had come to power, he gave a long analysis of the options open to Germany before a small group—von Blomberg, von Fritsch, Admiral Raeder, Goering and von Neurath, who was then still Foreign Minister—a statement later recorded by Colonel Hossbach, by whose name the memorandum is consequently usually known. And again later, after the invasion of Russia his *Table Talk* drifted over the great reorganization of Russian territory that he proposed to bring about.

Of all these the Hossbach memorandum is the most interesting, since the speech was delivered just before the beginning of Hitler's annexations and was concerned with tactical moves as well as general goals. The central theme was Germany's need for living space (*lebensraum*). Autarky alone within her existing frontiers could not be expected to supply all her requirements, and an increased participation in the world economy was an unsatisfactory alternative, since it could leave her dangerously dependent on overseas trade routes. Hence the only possible programme was to gain more food-producing regions 'in immediate proximity to the Reich', rather than overseas. He reckoned that Great Britain and France would be the main opponents to such a policy and that Germany would have to act no later than the period 1943–5, since after that she would have lost her advantage in the equipping and arming of her forces. Her immediate objective must be the simultaneous seizure of Czechoslovakia and Austria. An opportunity for this might occur, if France were to be incapacitated by internal strife or involved in a war with another Power, but in any case he did not believe that France would move without British support and he suspected that Great Britain had already written off Czechoslovakia. Thus the Hossbach memorandum would seem to be a remarkable blueprint for the immediate future, highly relevant to the acceleration of Hitler's programme in 1938 and 1939, and it was hardly surprising that in 1946 the prosecution should have made great play of it at the Nuremberg tribunal, when the principal surviving Nazis were charged with having deliberately brought about the war.

In 1961, however, A. J. P. Taylor produced a study of the origins of the second World War which challenged these assumptions. In Taylor's view Hitler, although guilty of appalling crimes against humanity, had in the realm of diplomacy behaved like any other European statesman, seeking to improve his country's position as the opportunity arose. He saw no evidence of a general plan of annexation and certainly no consistency between the Hossbach memorandum and *Mein Kampf* in which, for example, Hitler spoke of Great Britain and Italy as Germany's natural allies. And any scheme to dominate the Continent by military force was hardly feasible, since his forces were considerably less than what he claimed they were. Most striking of all, the Hossbach memorandum was clearly of very dubious validity. The original record was written up from memory by Hossbach several days after the meeting; its contents were never confirmed by those who had attended; and Hitler himself apparently showed little interest in it. Indeed, the original version was never discovered and the one used at Nuremberg was merely a copy of a copy. In any case, none of the contingencies mentioned by Hitler actually came about; hence, Taylor maintained, the Hossbach memorandum can hardly be considered a blueprint and the statement was no more than Hitler dreaming aloud in a way that might distract Goering and von Blomberg from a current dispute over the detail of rearmament. There was nothing very remarkable in this, since Hitler never really made any plans; he was merely a supreme opportunist, who with enormous strength of nerve took advantage of situations created by others; thus, for example, in March 1938 it was von Schuschnigg and in March 1939 Hacha who made the initial moves, from which Hitler was able to gain.

It was understandable that the book should provoke considerable comment on its publication. It contained many brilliant insights into European inter-war diplomacy and it certainly stimulated a fresh look at the evidence. Yet its critics could not accept the idea that in the diplomatic field Hitler had been no different to any other European statesman. It might be that his armaments were less than he said, yet he had had something of a lead, enough for the rapid type of *Blitzkrieg* that he envisaged. And although the Hossbach memorandum had its weakness as a piece of evidence, the meeting that it recorded was nevertheless followed by other events suggesting that its contents did represent a genuine programme. A month afterwards, on 7 December 1937, a military operation order—Plan Green—was amended to make the occupation of Czechoslovakia and Austria a principal objective. And two months later von Fritsch, von Blomberg and von Neurath, all of whom had expressed some disagreement with Hitler's views, were removed from office (see p. 397) and replaced by von Brauchitsch as head of the army and Ribbentrop as Foreign Minister. The main objection of Taylor's critics, however, was that his thesis was based narrowly on the diplomatic documents and they maintained that the true picture could only be seen in the whole context of the Nazi régime—an economy which could ultimately only be sustained by conquest, and a party dogma which idealized the use of force and which spawned similar parties abroad whose activities had forced Schuschnigg and Hacha to respond as they had.

In fact, the two interpretations of Hitler's aims are not entirely incompatible. The value of the Taylor thesis is that it does stress the great flexibility of manoeuvre which Hitler retained throughout each crisis. This meant that the precise detail of Germany's alignments was hardly likely to be as stated in a book written in 1924; it meant also that the taking of Austria and Czechoslovakia did not come about exactly as predicted in the Hossbach memorandum. Yet the fact remains that they *were* taken, and when reiterated statements about the need to gain living space in the east are followed by a series of thrusts in that direction in 1938 and 1939, it would seem a remarkable coincidence if there were no connection between the two. Of course, Hitler may well have hoped to avoid a major war over Poland. 'The men of Munich will not take the risk,' he had said in the middle of August, according to General Halder's diary, and the postponement of the German attack on 25 August suggests that another Munich might have suited him perfectly well. As it was, the ultimatum from the British and French now faced him with what one German biographer has called 'the wrong war'—against the west rather than in the east. In the last analysis, however, Hitler was simply determined to get his own way either by the complete surrender of his opponents or, if need be, by general war when the balance of forces was greatly in his favour.

The causes of the war, however, rest on something more than the whim of one man, for the roots of Hitler's ambition stretch back into the nineteenth century. His annexations during the previous eighteen months had been no more than a ruthless pursuit of the *Grossdeutschland* ideal, inflated with the pan-Germanism of the second half of the nineteenth century. It had been this prospect that had caused the Bohemians in 1848 to pin their hopes to the survival of the Habsburg Empire. 'If the Austrian Empire did not exist,' Palacky had said, 'it would be necessary to create it.' But after 1918 the Austrian Empire had existed no longer and all that had been created in its stead had been a jumble of nation states, too weak to stand alone, too discordant to stand together. In 1848 the springtime of nations had lasted little more than a year; after Versailles the collapse of Germany and Russia had given them a brief life of twenty years, but now they were to become the victims or the satellites of Nazi Germany, and then, after 1945, of Communist Russia. Nearly a century after the year of revolutions Palacky's assessment of the situation in central Europe was still valid.

Chapter 34

The Second World War 1939–45

Even after the outbreak of the second World War the memory of
the first retained its hold upon men's minds. This time there were
no illusions; the war was not going to be over by Christmas and the
thought of the previous carnage imposed a sense of caution alike on
Gamelin and von Brauchitsch, the French and German Commanders-
in-Chief. But whereas in Germany Hitler was able to brush this
aside, the memory of the devastation that the French had suffered
was to contribute greatly to that loss of morale which brought about
their early defeat, and later, even when victory for the Allies seemed
ultimately assured, the western leaders still continued to be haunted
by the fear that the lines would settle down into a static conflict of
attrition.

In fact, the whole character of the second World War was to be
utterly different from the first—more diverse, fast moving, sometimes more desperate, but never as heart-breaking as the 1914–18
deadlock. It was fought out over a vast theatre stretching from the
Pyrenees to the Volga and ended with the complete overrunning of
Germany by the western and Russian armies; it became linked with
another great struggle, when Japan attempted to challenge British
and American power in south-east Asia and the Pacific—truly a
world war. It was, strangely enough in a totalitarian epoch, a war
that allowed the individual a greater range of personal exploits—in
the resistance movements, the paratroop landings, and the new
techniques of combined operations. It never did become static, but
it was fought with an utter savagery on the eastern front and the air
bombardment of cities involved the indiscriminate slaughter of
hundreds of thousands of civilians—although this was small compared with the ruthless extermination of six million Jews by the
Nazis, who could now give free rein to their racial doctrines. A single
chapter cannot do justice to the immensity of this conflict, yet the
general pattern of the war is fundamentally a simple one. Until the
autumn of 1942 the German armies achieved one victory after
another until they held an area greater than that ever before ruled
by Germany, equalling the Napoleonic Empire at its height; after
the autumn of 1942 they knew only defeat as the combined forces

of Great Britain, the United States, and Russia thrust them back to ruin and unconditional surrender.

1. The German victories 1939–42

a) *The defeat of Poland and France, September 1939 to June 1940* ·
During the first eight months of the war Great Britain and France made no move in the west. Had they been ready, their greatest opportunity would have been in September 1939, when the requirements for the German attack on Poland had left only forty-two weak divisions in the Siegfried Line against seventy-two available French divisions. Such a possibility did not last long, for the Polish campaign was over in less than a month—a startling example of the new technique of *blitzkrieg* which the German General Staff under von Seeckt had first envisagd in the 1920s. The Polish army, outnumbered two to one, overwhelmed by German air power and the speed of the armoured Panzer divisions, was cut through and encircled by a three-pronged thrust from East Prussia, Pomerania, and Silesia, and on 20 September the battle of the Vistula completed its destruction.

At the same time the Russians were moving in for their share of the bargain and by 19 September had carried out the occupation of eastern Poland. Stalin was now determined to extend his defences as far west as possible and after a further agreement with Hitler, who could not for the moment object, Russian bases were established in Estonia, Latvia, and Lithuania. At the end of October, still in pursuit of this policy, Russia demanded the Karelian isthmus and the port of Hanko from Finland, and when this was refused, the Russian army crossed the Finnish frontier on 30 November. For three-and-a-half months the Finns under Marshal Mannerheim put up a remarkable resistance to the invader. The spectacle of a tiny country of four million inhabitants fighting alone against the might of Soviet Russia aroused tremendous sympathy in the west, but the British and French governments had inevitably to concentrate on their own war effort; Sweden was determined to remain neutral and Germany remained passive as a matter of policy, since she was still relying on her economic agreements with Russia. Thus, only 11,500 foreign volunteers ever reached Finland, and although the Russian army was successfully repulsed in December, Mannerheim was unable to check a breakthrough on the Karelian isthmus in February 1940. The winter war finally ended on 12 March, when a peace treaty granted Russia the isthmus and the whole province of Viipuri as well as a border territory to the north and a thirty-year lease of the port of Hanko.

Scandinavia was also to be the scene of the next step in the major war, when on 9 April Hitler launched his forces into neutral Denmark and Norway. The Danes made no resistance, while the Norwegians fought back unavailingly. British forces, who were hurriedly landed along the coast a week later, failed to reach Trondheim and although Narvik was recaptured from the Germans, it had eventually to be abandoned. The fundamental cause of Hitler's occupation of Norway was Germany's need of Swedish iron ore. This had been brought down by sea through Norwegian territorial waters, and the objections of the British, who finally began to lay minefields there, seemed to point to possible interference in a region which would threaten Germany's strategic right flank. With the successful conclusion of the military operation Hilter had produced a decisive answer to this problem, but he could hardly have anticipated one immediate consequence. In the House of Commons at Westminster Neville Chamberlain came under fierce attack from all sides over the ineffectiveness of the Norwegian campaign, and on 10 May a coalition government was formed under Winston Churchill who was to continue to lead the nation until the end of the war.

On the same day the storm burst in the west, when the German armies suddenly violated the neutrality of Belgium, the Netherlands, and Luxemburg. Despite the opening of the dykes the Dutch were rapidly overrun, Rotterdam was mercilessly bombed from the air and on 15 May the Dutch army capitulated. At the same time in Belgium the Germans had reached the line of the Maas and a breakthrough near Sedan suddenly revealed the nature of their plan. This was not to be the wide-sweeping right flank movement of 1914; the main thrust had come farther south skirting the Maginot Line and as it broke through the Allied front, threatened to isolate the British and French forces to the north, which had advanced eastwards from their prepared positions to link up with the Belgian army. The question was whether the German Panzers would manage to keep open this gap in the Allied lines and swinging round towards the Channel ports complete the encirclement of the northern forces.

General Weygand now took over as French Commander-in-Chief from General Gamelin and an attempt was made to close the gap, but achieved no more than a slight British advance to the south of Arras. On 23 May Boulogne fell and it seemed as if the whole of the northern armies were doomed. They were, in fact, to be spared as a result of two highly significant decisions. On 24 May the order was given for the German armour to the west of the Allies to halt, although whether this emanated from Hitler or from von Rundstedt has been debated by the generals ever since. And on 25 May Lord Gort, commander of the British Expeditionary Force, doubtful how much longer the Belgians would remain in the war, decided on his own initiative to call off the thrust south and to make for the sea. This was an act of extreme moral courage, and although the French have regarded it as desertion, it was certainly justified by the facts of the political and military situation; indeed, it may be considered one of the great decisions of the war, for if the northern forces had been broken up in the open field, as seemed only too likely, Great Britain would have lost the major part of her army without which it might not have been possible to continue the struggle after the fall of France. It is vital in war to know when to retreat, as the German generals were to learn to their cost in the Russian campaigns of 1943 and 1944.

Gort's decision had been taken only just in time. The German armoured thrust from the west was renewed on 26 May and King Leopold's capitulation on the next day left a great gap on the eastern flank which the Belgians had been holding. The situation was only saved by the defence of Calais to the last round and the extraordinarily skilful withdrawal operation fought by General Brooke enabling the northern forces to fall back on Dunkirk. The R.A.F. managed to hold off the bulk of the German air attack; the sea remained calm, and from the harbour and the bomb-racked beaches of Dunkirk the British navy, aided by every kind of small craft which had put out in response to an Admiralty appeal, succeeded during nine days in bringing back to England 338,000 British and Allied troops.

Meanwhile, the situation in France had deteriorated sharply. On 10 June Mussolini, hoping for a share of the spoils, declared war, but even at this stage the Italians were unable to shake the French resistance in the Alpine regions. Elsewhere, however, the speed of the German penetration, the psychological shock of their massive air power, and the confusion of refugees blocking the roads had all created a sense of inevitable defeat. By 11 June the Germans had reached the Seine, while another thrust southwards was soon to cut off the one-third of the French army still manning the Maginot Line; and on 12 June the government declared Paris an open city and moved to Tours and thence to Bordeaux.

The question now was: how long would France remain in the war? Winston Churchill, who flew to Tours on 13 June, tried every means to persuade the French government to continue the fight, if need be from North Africa. Two British divisions had been sent back to northern France after Dunkirk; there was long discussion over holding a redoubt in Brittany, and at the end he even proposed an indissoluble union between the two countries. It was all in vain. There were strong defeatist elements at work among the French, despairing of any assistance from the United States and mistrustful of Great Britain, who refused to sacrifice her remaining twenty-five fighter squadrons, the last line of her own defence; they were in any case convinced that the British would themselves make peace with Germany. Paul Reynaud, Prime Minister since March, would have been prepared to carry on, but on 16 June he was forced to resign and a new government under Marshal Pétain requested an armistice on the next day. British forces were now left to fend for themselves, but 156,000 were re-embarked, mainly from Cherbourg, and on 18 June General de Gaulle, who as Under-Secretary for National Defence had favoured a continuation of hostilities, was flown from Bordeaux to London, where that same night he broadcast an appeal to the French nation.

Otherwise, the prospect was dark indeed. On 22 June the French Armistice Commission had to sue for peace at Compiègne on the very spot and in the same railway carriage—unearthed by the Germans from a Paris museum—in which Foch had presented his terms in November 1918. All except the south-eastern segment of France was to be under German occupation and all French forces were to be disarmed, while the armistice with Italy signed immediately afterwards stipulated the demilitarizing of zones in the south of France, Tunisia, Algeria, and French Somaliland. Thus, only seven-and-a-half years after he had become German Chancellor Adolf Hitler had finally torn the Treaty of Versailles to shreds and the defeat of Imperial Germany had been avenged by the ex-corporal of the Kaiser's army.

b) The isolation of Great Britain: June 1940–June 1941
By the end of June 1940 the Continent lay under Germany's control from east of the Vistula to the Pyrenees. She had, in addition, drawn in Italy as an active partner and she still retained a somewhat uneasy friendship with Russia; Spain was dallying with thoughts of a German alliance which might give her Gibraltar; there remained the unknown factor of the French fleet. Against this colossus of power Great Britain stood alone, in far worse plight than during the Napoleonic Wars. Her sea routes on which she depended utterly for food and supplies were seriously threatened, and her army, although saved from Dunkirk, lacked all its armament and equipment which had had to be left behind in France. It was a historic moment in every sense, for, had Great Britain surrendered, as Hitler hoped she would, Nazi rule would have been consolidated throughout Europe and with the total force of German arms free to concentrate in the east the eventual attack on Russia might well have resulted in a German victory. It was the British determination to continue the war that made such a concentration impossible. 'Hitler knows', said Winston Churchill in the House of Commons in June, 'that he will have to break us in this island, or lose the war,' and under his magnificent leadership the whole land was consumed with a singleness of purpose remote from the days of appeasement. The manpower and industry of the country were placed on a war footing; local defence volunteers prepared to fight for every village, if invasion should

come, and the government showed that it was prepared to stop at nothing, when French warships in north African ports which refused to place themselves beyond the reach of Germany were attacked and disabled.

The dominating thought in Great Britain that summer was the imminent prospect of invasion. On 2 July Hitler had already given his order for such an operation, but as his service chiefs well knew, the successful crossing of the Channel depended upon command of the air. Throughout July the German air force concentrated on Channel shipping, and then in August the familiar pattern of *blitzkrieg* was repeated as the attack shifted to the airfields of the British fighter squadrons. Here the vital phase of the Battle of Britain was fought out, and by the middle of September the British fighter command under Sir Hugh Dowding had inflicted the first major defeat on Goering's *Luftwaffe*; at the same time incessant bombing raids were being carried out on the invasion barges forming up in French and Belgian ports, and on 17 September the German assault which had been scheduled for a few days later had to be postponed, while in October it was finally called off until the following spring. This change of plan was marked by the shifting of the German air attacks to the large cities. London was bombed almost nightly throughout the winter; Southampton, Plymouth, Bristol, and Liverpool all suffered, and on 14 November the centre of Coventry was utterly destroyed; nearly 22,000 civilians had been killed in these attacks by the end of the year, and a further 19,000 perished in 1941.

Meanwhile, Mussolini was determined to seize his chance in Africa. In August Italian forces invaded British Somaliland and on 13 September Marshal Graziani began an advance along the north African coast into Egypt as far as Sidi Barrani (see map. p. 421). British forces were too small to retaliate immediately, but on 11 November the Fleet Air Arm carried out a great bombing attack on the Italian navy at Taranto. Then on 9 December General Wavell began his own advance on Graziani, and by March 1941 had reached Benghazi and El Agheila, capturing the bulk of the Italian forces. After this, however, hostilities in Greece caused serious reductions in Wavell's forces, which had in any case been far less than the Italians, and the arrival of General Rommel and a German armoured corps forced him to retire to Egypt. Farther south, the British had occupied Eritrea in April and after a short campaign in Abyssinia the Emperor Haile Selassie was once again able to enter his capital, Addis Ababa, on 5 May 1941.

At the same time the war at sea had centred on the maintenance of supplies—an appalling struggle in which the German U-boats sank nearly four million tonnes of British, Allied, and neutral shipping in 1940 and slightly more in 1941. The situation seemed even more desperate when in the spring of 1941 the German battleship, *Bis-*

marck, was at large in the Atlantic and it was not until 27 May that an all-out effort by sea and air succeeded in sinking her. The other major function of the British navy was to impose a blockade, yet with all the Continent at Hitler's disposal this could hardly be effective. Nothing could check the trade of neutrals such as Turkey, Spain, Portugal, and Switzerland with Germany; Russia was still delivering supplies in accordance with the agreements of 1939, and Sweden was even allowing unarmed soldiers as well as supplies to pass through her territory.

The most significant developments of this period, however, lay outside the immediate war areas. In the United States public opinion had become greatly excited at the sight of Great Britain holding the fort against an entire continent dominated by Nazism. By special agreement American destroyers had been handed over for British use in the autumn of 1940, and in January 1941 President Roosevelt introduced a 'Lease-Lend' bill in Congress which was greatly to facilitate the supply of material to Great Britain.

In eastern Europe Russia was continuing to make good use of her opportunities. While Germany had been embroiled in the campaign in France, she had set up Communist governments in Estonia, Latvia, and Lithuania and in June Rumania was forced to surrender Bessarabia and northern Bukovina to her. Eastern European interests remained incorrigibly parochial to the end, for in August Rumania had to give up the south of the Dobruja to Bulgaria, as well as two-thirds of Transylvania to Hungary through German mediation. Then on 28 October Mussolini, still hungry for glory, launched an attack on Greece, but by the end of 1940 had suffered such a repulse at the hands of the Greek forces under General Metaxas that in the early months of the next year he had become dependent, as in North Africa, upon German help. Hitler's troops could reach Greece through Rumania and Bulgaria, but with Yugoslavia partly surrounded the moment seemed to have come for a pact with the Regent Prince Paul, which was duly signed towards the end of March 1941. This was at once followed, however, by an anti-German *coup d'état* in Belgrade with the result that on 6 April the German army invaded Yugoslavia and Greece simultaneously. Breaking through on the Bulgarian frontier they forced the outnumbered Yugoslav forces to capitulate on 17 April, and their mounting attack on Greece eventually overran the Greek defence, despite the support of 58,000 British troops who were sent to their aid from Egypt. The Greek government withdrew to Crete, but here in May a German airborne landing succeeded in capturing the island and the evacuation of British forces was considerably less effective than it had been from Greece. Indeed, the only British success in these months had been a naval encounter off Cape Matapan on 28 March, when four Italian cruisers and three destroyers had been sunk; apart from that, the whole of the British intervention in Greece seemed to be just one more episode in a tale of disaster and retreat.

c) The German invasion of Russia and the entry of the United States into the war

On 22 June 1941 Hitler embarked upon the most fateful venture of his career when he suddenly declared war on Russia. One hundred and fifty German divisions, twenty of which were armoured, began an advance into Soviet territory, striking south towards Kiev and the Ukraine, through White Russia towards Smolensk and Moscow, and through the Baltic states towards Leningrad. This decision of Hitler's was taken against the advice of most of his generals and political associates, who believed that the war should be won in the west before Germany embarked upon the new campaign. Hitler, however, was adamant. He mistrusted the recent gains that Russia had been making in eastern Europe; he hoped for the rapid defeat of Russia, which would finally deprive Great Britain of any chance of an eventual alliance with her, and he reckoned that the territorial gains would more than compensate for the disruption of Russo-German economic agreements.

Except on this last point he was utterly wrong. The lack of Soviet resistance to the growth of German influence in Rumania and Bulgaria hardly suggested any imminent danger, and despite British warnings the Russian army was taken by surprise. On the other hand, once the battle had been joined, the Russian resistance at the front and behind the German lines was so fierce that a rapid victory was soon out of the question; thus, instead of depriving Great Britain of an ally, he actually drove Russia into her arms. On the same day as the German invasion Churchill announced on the radio: 'Any man or State who fights against Nazidom will have our aid', and on 13 July a pact of mutual assistance was signed between the two countries, while in September the United States also agreed to supply Russia. Soon convoys sailing the perilous Arctic route north of Scandinavia began to bring a steady stream of British and American war material to Murmansk and Archangel, and by the end of 1942, 3,276 tanks and 2,665 aircraft had been delivered—at a cost of sixty-four ships sunk by German air and U-boat attack.

By December 1941 the German armies had thrust their way far east of the Crimea; farther north, they had reached the Don and were only fifty kilometres from the suburbs of Moscow, while Leningrad held out under siege. Then winter, still the Russians' greatest ally, came to their aid, and in the early months of 1942 the Germans were pushed back in a series of counter-attacks. Field Marshal von Brauchitsch was dismissed by Hitler, who took over personal command himself, and then when the spring enabled the

Germans to make a new offensive, Field Marshal von Bock swept forward in the south into the Caucasus, although Voronezh on the Don and Stalingrad on the Volga still defied him.

Meanwhile, the British had gained their most significant alliance. Under the guidance of President Roosevelt the United States had been slanting her neutrality increasingly in the interest of Great Britain, and in August 1941 he and Churchill had met in mid-Atlantic to devise the Atlantic Charter which, in answer to the Nazi New Order in Europe, guaranteed the freedom of the nations of the world. It was, however, Japan that finally precipitated the Americans into the war. The Japanese had already taken advantage of the defeat of France to occupy French Indo-China in the summer of 1941, and on 7 December they launched a devastating air attack on American naval forces in Pearl Harbor in Hawaii. For the United States this meant war with Japan and within a few days Germany and Italy had also declared war. For Winston Churchill it meant at last the formation of the Grand Alliance which had been his principal hope since the desperate summer of 1940. That same month he was in Washington; a Combined Chiefs-of-Staff Committee was established to ensure close cooperation in the Anglo-American war effort, and the whole mighty power of American industry was turned over to the defeat of Hitler.

Certainly the ultimate prospect had changed beyond belief; yet the immediate outcome was to be a further series of disasters. On Christmas Day 1941 Hong Kong fell to the Japanese; the Americans lost Wake Island and Guam in the Pacific, and in January 1942 the Dutch East Indies were overrun. On 15 February Singapore itself was forced to surrender; by May American resistance in the Philippine Islands had been crushed, and it was only the American naval victory in the Coral Sea on 4 May that saved Australia from the immediate threat of invasion.

Nor was the news any better elsewhere. In North Africa General Auchinleck, who had assumed command in June 1941, was able to clear the German forces from Cyrenaica by December, but had to withdraw in January 1942 when Rommel was reinforced. In May a new German attack on the British positions met with success, and although Auchinleck was able to check the rout, the British had by July fallen back on El Alamein only 240 kilometres from Cairo. In these last six months three million tonnes of Allied shipping had been sunk; the Japanese had strengthened their hold on south-east Asia and the Pacific, von Bock's great thrust was reaching into the Caucasus, and the British stood at bay on the last line of defence before the Suez canal. Thus the late summer of 1942 marks the blackest moment in the fortunes of the Allied Powers, and Hitler's success was now at its height.

2. Germany in Europe

Between 1940 and 1944 almost the entire Continent lay at Hitler's disposal and in that time he was able to translate into deadly reality the most lunatic racialist dreams that had haunted central Europe in the late nineteenth century. The frontiers of Germany herself were now simply those of *Grossdeutschland* and included Eupen and Malmedy, Luxemburg, Alsace and most of Lorraine, the Polish territories of the Corridor, Posen and Silesia, and, after the invasion of Yugoslavia in 1941, a large part of Slovenia.

In the west the northern and western areas of France as well as Belgium, the Netherlands and Norway were all directly under a German civil administration. There were at first two exceptions to this general pattern. In the south-eastern segment of France Marshal Pétain headed a puppet government at Vichy, and in Denmark, where King Christian X had decided not to go into exile, a Danish government was allowed for a time to remain nominally in charge. In November 1942, however, the Germans extended their occupation to the whole of France, and in August 1943 strikes in Copenhagen caused Hitler to appoint a Reich commissioner for Denmark.

In the east the scene was one of satellites and conquered territory. Hungary, Rumania and Bulgaria were all drawn into an uneasy collaboration with Germany. Yugoslavia was broken up into three states—Croatia, Serbia and Montenegro—and Greece was under military occupation; both countries were theoretically within Italy's sphere, although in reality they were under the supervision of a German military command at Salonica. And after the invasion of Russia had been launched, the eastern territories of Poland were placed under a Nazi governor, Hans Frank.

For Hitler plunder was to be the immediate reward of victory, and when in 1945 the invading armies of the Allies reached Germany after passing through the under-nourished occupied countries, they found the Germans the best fed people on the Continent. In the west the requisitioning was carried out under the screen of occupation agreements, whereby the payment demanded could only be met by the surrender of all forms of plant and industrial and agricultural material. In the east the conquerors simply helped themselves, partly for gain, and partly in order to create an economic wilderness. After the war Frank declared that his orders from Hitler for the governing of his province in Poland were 'to reduce the area as a war zone and a land of booty to complete poverty'. The plunder also included manpower—the deporting of slave labour to Germany; four million by the end of 1941; some seven million by 1944, and a similar number working on German installations in the occupied territories. The more fortunate of these were housed in large camps in the countryside, where they supplied the farms with labour; others were dispatched to factories, where their treatment was so bad that thousands did not survive.

These measures naturally caused appalling hardship for the inhabitants of the occupied territories, and yet it is doubtful whether the Nazi government was making the most effective use of the territory under its control. Certainly Albert Speer, who became Minister of Armaments and Munitions in February 1942, reckoned that it would have been wiser to have allowed the local economies to function normally, so that they might supply stipulated quotas of produce for Germany. These were not his only misgivings. It was one of the peculiar features of the German war effort that for several years Hitler, in contrast to the British, was careful to avoid a total mobilization of resources within Germany. As late as October 1943 some six million Germans were still employed in producing consumer goods and not even the most eloquent appeal by Speer could change this. It was the same over the employment of women. In Speer's view the drafting of women into the factories would have released three million men for military service, but for Hitler this would have been inconsistent with the Nazi image of women's place in the home. He preferred to rely on slave labour. In any case the kind of total civilian mobilization advocated by Speer seemed to suggest a prolonged war and this played no part in Hitler's plans. Instead, he envisaged a series of lightning campaigns, as in Poland and France, and his belief in quick victory is best illustrated by the fact that the forces invading Russia in June 1941 were not supplied with equipment and clothing for a winter campaign.

Plunder, however, was not the only purpose of conquest. In the east it was intended to establish a string of German colonies stretching through the Baltic lands and in the south reaching as far as the Black Sea. Here a part of the local population was to supply the labour for the German master race, while the rest were to be exterminated. In January 1941 Himmler had already told his S.S. that his aim was the death of 30 million Slavs and later that year *Einsatzgruppen* following the German army into Russia proceeded to set up camps, where the slaughter was carried out at first by mass shootings and then later with a cyanide gas, Zyklon B. In these circumstances Russian prisoners of war were hardly likely to receive better treatment and in the course of the war nearly four million died, mostly from starvation.

The racialism which lay behind this appalling inhumanity towards the Slavs was also responsible for the most iniquitous aspect of Hitler's rule. By the middle of 1941 he had decided to embark on what was called the final solution of the Jewish question—a cold, efficient plan devised with bureaucratic thoroughness to kill every Jew in Europe. This meant the establishment of a particular category of extermination camp, as at Auschwitz, Mauthausen and Treblinka, to which Jews, rounded up from every part of Europe, were sent in special trains and where they were gassed and cremated. In all, some six million died and by the end of the war there were only about one million Jews left alive in Europe.

Naturally, the effect of all this horror was to build up a profound sense of antagonism towards German rule. For instance, the stupid brutality of the Germans, when they first entered the Russian border areas in 1941, deprived them of the support of many who would have welcomed release from Communism. Of course, the conquered countries could do little in their own defence, but there was in all of them a growing resistance movement which towards the end of the war in France, Norway, and Yugoslavia had placed whole areas under their effective control, and which in small countries whose topography did not lend itself to such achievements concentrated on the rescue of Jews and assistance to Allied agents and escaping prisoners of war. The risk was appalling, for capture usually meant torture and death; German reprisals often took the form of the shooting of hostages, and in June 1942 the entire village of Lidice in Czechoslovakia was wiped out after the Nazi governor Heydrich had been assassinated. Such methods of retaliation naturally inspired hatred, but they also created mixed feelings over resistance activity, particularly since the most effective elements in the partisan movement were very often Communist; in any case, despite the extraordinary heroism of the resistance, the Continent could only await the outcome of a world conflict in which by the summer of 1942 the hopes for an Allied victory still seemed extremely remote.

3. The defeat of Germany 1942–5

In the autumn of 1942, however, the Allies won two overwhelming victories, at El Alamein and Stalingrad, which together mark the turning point in the course of the war. In August Churchill and General Brooke, Chief of the Imperial General Staff since November 1941, had stopped at Cairo on their way to a conference at Moscow and appointed General Alexander as Commander-in-Chief with General Montgomery in command of the Eighth Army. At the end of the month Montgomery defeated a flanking attack by Rommel at Alam Halfa and continued to prepare for his own assault as reinforcements of American Sherman tanks began to arrive from the long journey round the Cape. On 23 October the battle of El Alamein opened with a tremendous artillery barrage and a frontal assault, reminiscent of the offensives in the first World War, and after twelve days of heavy fighting Rommel was in full retreat, having suffered nearly 30,000 casualties. This great victory was followed almost at once on 8 November by an American landing in Morocco and Algeria under the command of General Eisenhower.

Hitler reacted at once to the resurgence of Allied power in the Mediterranean; Vichy France was occupied, although the French fleet avoided capture by scuttling itself in the harbour of Toulon, and by the middle of November 18,000 German troops had moved into Tunis. None of this could alter the fact that Rommel was now caught between two advancing armies; on 20 March 1943 he was defeated again by Montgomery at Mareth; throughout April there was hard fighting on the German western flank in Tunis, and in May the end came with the capture of a quarter of a million Axis soldiers.

Within a month of El Alamein the Russians sprang their trap on the German forces besieging Stalingrad. On 19 November 1942 thrusts from the north and the south linked up, and although the Germans on Hitler's orders continued a desperate resistance in the appalling winter conditions, Field Marshal von Paulus had eventually to surrender on 31 January 1943. To the north Leningrad was relieved, but in the south the German forces did succeed in escaping from a second trap in the Caucasus, and in March 1943 the Russian offensive was temporarily halted, when Field Marshal von Manstein recaptured Kharkov.

This turn in the fortunes of the Allies naturally necessitated a reconsideration of future western strategy, and at an Anglo-American conference at Casablanca in January 1943 General Brooke was able to gain agreement on its general form. The plan was to concentrate on the Mediterranean with an assault on Italy. This might knock Mussolini out of the war; it would certainly draw more German divisions into Italy and from the point of view of supply it would enable the Allies to dispense with the long route round the Cape. Thus shipping would be freed and the German Command forced to divide their forces, both essential preliminaries to the launching of a cross-Channel invasion on the mainland of the Continent.

At first things moved quickly. In July and August Sicily was overrun, and in Rome a new government formed under Marshal Badoglio after the arrest of Mussolini on 25 July, eventually signed an armistice with the Allies at Syracuse on 3 September. On the same day an Anglo-American landing in the south of Italy in Calabria and at Salerno met with initial success, but the German forces under Field Marshal Kesselring who now held Italy virtually captive began a long stubborn resistance in a countryside ideally suited to defence. Throughout the remainder of 1943 the weary struggle went on, as Alexander edged his way northwards. On 1 October Naples was taken; the rivers Sangro and Garigliano were crossed, but although the Allies attempted to leapfrog up the western coast with a landing at Anzio in January 1944, it was not until May that they were able to link up, and then at last, on 4 June,

Alexander's troops entered Rome, which had been declared an open city.

Meanwhile, in Russia a German summer offensive in 1943 had been successfully resisted and with the autumn the Russian advance was renewed. On 25 September Smolensk was taken, by October they had reached the Dnieper and by February 1944 they were all to the west of Novgorod and were thrusting out in the south. Many factors contributed to these victories. The rapid industrialization of Russia with the five-year plans of the 1930s, aided by the influx of supplies from the west in the Arctic convoys, had enabled the Russians to equip their armies in a way that had been impossible in the first World War. The Germans were faced with mounting demands for troops on their Mediterranean front, and their generals in Russia were hamstrung by the insistence of Hitler, their Commander-in-Chief, that there should never be a strategic withdrawal while there was still time.

Of course, for the Germans all this fighting was on foreign soil. At home, however, their great cities suffered appalling havoc, as the British and American bomber commands brought them under an air bombardment far more concentrated and destructive than anything that they themselves had been able to inflict in the early years of the war. The precise gain from this is difficult to assess. It does not seem that German morale was broken any more than British morale had been broken by the five months of the bombing of London. The major justification was that it might shatter German war production, but these hopes were largely foiled by Hitler's Minister of Armaments, Albert Speer, who by a remarkable organization of dispersal and prefabrication enormously increased output until almost the end of the war. Aircraft production in 1944, for example, was 44,000 in contrast to 12,400 in 1941, and in 1943 Germany was meeting more than half the need for oil with synthetic products. What the bombardment did demonstrate beyond doubt was the total Allied supremacy in the air, at the same time as the Allies were gradually gaining the upper hand on the U-boats attacking their supply lines in the Atlantic.

All these efforts were the essential prelude to the invasion of the Continent from the southern shore of England, and on 6 June 1944—D Day—British, Canadian, and American forces under the command of General Montgomery duly made a landing at various points along the coast of Normandy. Aided by naval and air superiority and by a multiplicity of remarkable devices including a floating harbour, the Allies were able to build up their forces in the bridgehead, and in July, while the British in the eastern sector held the bulk of the German armour, the Americans broke out at the western end, swept south and then north to join up with the British and to catch a considerable portion of Rommel's forces in the

'Falaise pocket'. Hitler's secret weapon—the V1, a pilotless flying bomb—had not been ready in time to have any effect on the invasion armies and with the Germans in full retreat the Allies kept up the pursuit across northern France into Belgium, while in August a landing in the south of France completed the liberation of the French. By September a quarter of a million prisoners had been taken. Fifty-five German divisions were held down on the Italian and Mediterranean fronts, and Russia was continuing to advance into Poland and the Baltic states.

The continuation of hostilities now seemed to threaten Germany with utter disaster, and on 20 July a group of German officers, prompted by the sense of inescapable doom, attempted to assassinate Hitler and to take over the government of the country with the intention of suing for peace in the west. The attempt failed, and in the orgy of executions that followed, Hitler not merely wiped out thousands in Germany who represented a latent opposition to Nazi rule, but also completed his subjugation of the German Officer Corps. It is the paradox of the history of the Third Reich that Hitler's power in Germany had never been so great as it was in the last ten months of the war. Dislike of Nazism and the war policy there may have been; the fact remains that after July 1944 generals and soldiers alike fought on bitterly for Hitler to the end.

At the same time the course of the war had already provoked serious doubts in the minds of Germany's satellites in eastern Europe. In the summer of 1944 their emissaries had been arriving secretly at Cairo to discuss ways of making peace and very soon the advance of the Red Army to their borders had compelled a number of them to change sides. In Rumania on 23 August King Michael suddenly removed the existing government, announced the end of hostilities against Russia and eventually supplied fifteen divisions who fought alongside the Red Army against Germany. In September Bulgaria, who had not officially been at war with Russia, but only with the western allies, was forced to join with the Red Army and lost some 30,000 dead in the continuing thrust westwards. By October Admiral Horthy, the Regent of Hungary, was also keen to make peace, but before he could do this, he was deported to Germany and a Hungarian Fascist party under Szalasi put up a desperate defence until the end of the war during which Budapest was laid waste in a two-month siege.

Meanwhile, in the occupied countries of the east, two different forms of resistance had been at work. In Poland, as the Red Army approached Warsaw, the secret Polish Home Army, non-Communist and in touch with its government in exile in London, launched a major rising in the capital on 1 August 1944. At this point, however, the Russian advance ceased and the Polish Home army, left to fight unaided against the Germans, was finally crushed in October amid the almost total destruction of Warsaw. In Yugoslavia the resistance was also operating on its own, but with greater success, since an army of Communist partisans under their leader Tito swiftly gained control of a large part of the country as the Germans withdrew, and the Red Army was involved in little more than the capture of Belgrade.

Long before this, European statesmen had been well aware that the post-war political scene in Europe was already in the making. Stalin's southern thrust along the Danube into the Balkans may have been prompted by military considerations, yet it did also suggest the re-emergence of the old Eastern Question. Indeed, the main hope of the Germans now was that the realization of this by the west would at last shatter their alliance with Russia. 'They had not counted on our defending ourselves step by step and holding them off in the west like madmen,' said Goering in January, 'while the Russians drive deeper and deeper into Germany.' The Allies, however, had no intention of playing into the Germans' hands in this way, and the only outcome of the prolonged resistance in the west was eventually to place far more of eastern Germany under Russian control. Winston Churchill had long been uneasy about the possible extent of Russian gains, for as early as November 1943 he had proposed at the Teheran Conference that the Allied forces in Italy should push on northwards up into Austria and the Hungarian plainland. Castlereagh and Metternich would have understood his concern, but such a campaign would not have been easy from a military point of view, and Stalin was by now confident of victory on his own front and therefore wanted no western army interfering in eastern Europe. He pressed instead for the Allied landing in the south of France with forces drawn from Italy where the advance was inevitably slowed down.

The only other means of forestalling the Russians lay in breaking into Germany and ending the war in the autumn of 1944, while the Red Army was still some way to the east. Montgomery believed that this could be accomplished with a concentrated Allied thrust through Holland leapfrogging across the Maas and the upper and lower Rhine with airborne landings. General Eisenhower, however, who had now assumed supreme command, favoured an advance on a broad front and when the British attempted the operation on their own in the second half of September, they were checked at Arnhem, the last of the dropping points, which would have taken them over all the water obstacles that separated them from Germany.

After the war statements by German generals lent support to Montgomery's plan for the September thrust, provided that it had been carried out by the whole Allied force. On the other hand, the problem of supply may well have been decisive. The Channel ports were still holding out under siege and with a line of communications stretching back as far as Cherbourg the invasion of Germany in the autumn of 1944 would have been a hazardous undertaking without the use of Antwerp. This had been captured on 4 September, but the estuary of the Scheldt was still held by the Germans and it was not until the end of November after several weeks of hard fighting that the approaches to the port were open to the Allies. Certainly the German General Staff recognized the significance of Antwerp, since it was the principal objective of one last counter-attack launched through the Ardennes by von Rundstedt on 16 December. The attempt was unsuccessful, but it kept the Allies on the defensive until the New Year and it was now clear that the war would continue until the spring.

In February 1945 the Allies met in conference at Yalta in the Crimea. Here it was agreed that the old Curzon line should be the eastern frontier of Poland, who was to be compensated with territory in the west, and that the Poles should have free elections, although there was no provision for these to be supervised by an international force. Churchill was by no means happy about these new frontiers for Poland, nor about the arrangements for the election, but President Roosevelt was anxious to secure Russian support in the Japanese war and, in any case, Stalin was by now in something of the position of Alexander I at the Congress of Vienna. 'His Imperial Majesty', wrote Castlereagh to Lord Liverpool on the Polish problem in October 1814, 'insinuated that the question could only end in one way, as he was in possession.' And in 1950 Edward R. Stettinius, the American Secretary of State at the time of the Yalta meeting, commented: 'What, with the possible exception of the Kuriles, did the Soviet Union receive at Yalta which she might not have taken without any agreement?' Indeed, Stalin was even able to stake a claim to 10,000 million dollars in German reparations, despite the British insistence that no figure should be mentioned.

The war was now moving into its last phase. The German effort in the Ardennes enabled the Russians to advance into eastern Germany early in 1945. In March, when the western Allies crossed the Rhine, the British moved north on to Bremen and Hamburg, crossed the Elbe to capture Lübeck twenty-four hours ahead of the Russians, and sent a small holding force by air to Copenhagen in order to make sure of Denmark. The Americans swept through the centre and the south of Germany, but held back on the Czech border, honouring the agreement that the Russians should take Prague. In April Alexander was victorious in the valley of the Po, and Mussolini, who had been rescued by the S.S. after his arrest and set up as a puppet dictator in north Italy, was captured by the Italian partisans and shot. By 25 April the Russians had surrounded Berlin and five days later Hitler, still in his bunker below the grounds of the Chancellery, committed suicide.

Admiral Doenitz, whom he had appointed as his successor, did not have long in which to enjoy a somewhat embarrassing inheritance. On 2 May nearly a million Germans surrendered to Alexander in Italy; on 4 and 5 May there were local surrenders of the German troops facing the British and American forces in Germany and Austria, and on 7 May General Jodl and Admiral von Friedeburg signed a formal document of unconditional surrender at General Eisenhower's headquarters at Reims before representatives of the United States, Great Britain, Russia, and France. The German nightmare of the ultimate consequence of war on two fronts had finally come to pass; the armies of her enemies had met in the middle of Europe and the Third Reich was no more.

Part 8

Europe after 1945

Chapter 35

The Immediate Problems of Peace

1. Europe in ruin

For the Continent as a whole the death toll of the second World War marks the most terrible slaughter that Europe had known for centuries. The total number of servicemen and civilians killed was well over thirty million, four times as great as the carnage of the first World War, and only Great Britain with 400,000 dead and France with 600,000 had escaped more lightly than before. In Russia eight million servicemen and eleven million civilians had died. Poland and Yugoslavia had lost between 10 and 20 per cent of their population, many of them among the six million wiped out in the German concentration and extermination camps, whose full horror was now revealed. On the German side some three and a half million servicemen and one and a half million civilians were dead or missing.

The material devastation which accompanied these losses was utterly appalling. In May 1945 almost the entire Continent of Europe was in utter ruin. From the Volga across the plains of Russia and Poland and throughout the breadth of Germany town after town had been laid waste in the fighting or by air bombardment, while the progress of the war in the west had left a trail of destruction up the whole of Italy, in Normandy and the south of the Netherlands. Old historic cities—Kiev, Warsaw, Budapest, Berlin, Hamburg, Stuttgart, Dresden, Cologne—had been transformed unbelievably into mountains of rubble and in the south of Russia some six million homes had been destroyed. The girders of smashed bridges poked forlornly from the rivers; three-quarters of those in western Germany were unusable, as were most over the Seine and the Loire, and the canal systems of Belgium and the Netherlands were largely out of action. The state of the railways was still worse. All countries had lost the greater part of their rolling stock and everywhere blocked tunnels, broken viaducts and thousands of kilometres of wrecked track made transport by rail virtually impossible.

Across this scene of havoc there were scattered millions of people who had been uprooted from their homelands. In the west the Allies had to cope with seven million prisoners of war. Some seven million displaced persons, mostly Slavs, who had been brought to Germany for forced labour, now roamed the countryside pillaging, burning and killing in an orgy of revenge, and although two-thirds of them had been sent back within three months, the remainder had no wish to return and some were to linger on for years in great camps of dilapidated wooden huts. At the same time twelve million Germans normally resident in eastern Europe had been moving westwards either to get out of the reach of the advancing Red Army during the last year of the war, or later as a result of expulsion ordered by the new eastern European governments.

Amid this anarchy, in which most recognizable forms of economic life had disintegrated, there was naturally an imminent likelihood of famine. The fact that this was averted was largely due to the work of the United Nations Relief and Rehabilitation Administration (U.N.R.R.A.). This had been created in November 1943 in anticipation of the conditions that would probably confront the Allies after their victory. Financed mainly by the United States and eventually employing 25,000 people U.N.R.R.A. undertook the purchase of some 3,700 million dollars worth of supplies and distributed them wherever they were needed—in China, Poland, Italy, Yugoslavia, Greece, Austria, Czechoslovakia and Russia—and undoubtedly the efficiency and generosity of the scheme, which must have been unprecedented in the history of Europe, helped to save the lives of millions who might otherwise have died of hunger in refugee camps.

Apart from this example of goodwill, however, Europe was an evil place in that summer of 1945, epitomized by the fury with which the liberated countries now turned on their own nationals who had collaborated with the Nazis. Retribution took two forms. Most governments mounted a vast number of public trials, while in the countryside the resistance movements set about their own purges with so-called popular tribunals. The intensity of the operation varied greatly. It was particularly severe in Belgium where 77,000 received sentences from the courts, and in the Netherlands where there were initially 150,000 arrests. In France Marshal Pétain, the head of the Vichy government, was condemned to life imprisonment, and his foreign minister, Pierre Laval, was shot; 120,000 were convicted and out of nearly 5,000 death sentences 2,000 were carried out. In the areas where the French resistance had been strong, however, there were also a great number of summary executions, 4,500 according to the official figure, although this is almost certainly an underestimate and one historian has suggested as many as 40,000. In Austria, on the other hand, only 35 death sentences were passed. In Italy the courts dealt mainly with senior Fascists, but the partisans in the north also killed off several thousand, including Mussolini and his mistress. After the sufferings endured during the war years it was perhaps understandable that there should be such a bitter aftermath, yet the attack on the collaborators was an ugly episode and some of the victims were no worse than their judges and may merely have been the scapegoats for a general uneasiness of conscience.

In Germany the members of Admiral Doenitz's short-lived administration had mostly been placed under arrest. Consequently there was no government at all to take action and the Allies opened their own prosecution of 24 leading Nazis and military commanders at Nuremberg in August 1945. The spectacle of the victors setting up a show trial of the defeated may well appear a somewhat dubious proceeding, and charges such as the attack on Poland in 1939 sounded strange in view of the presence of Russians among the judges. The problem for the Allies was the sheer enormity of the mass murders which had been committed under the Third Reich and it seemed that only some form of judicial examination could assess the evidence for such ghastly events and attempt to define degrees of responsibility. At the end ten of the accused were condemned to death and executed, except for Goering who managed to commit suicide in his cell, and apart from three acquittals, the remainder received prison sentences. This was only the beginning of a long series of other trials concerned with the shooting of prisoners, the brutal treatment of slave labour and the running of the concentration camps, and eventually a newly constituted German government was to continue the work for many years after the end of the war in an effort to redress Germany's own standing in Europe.

2. Aspects of liberation

In September 1945 negotiations began over the new frontiers of Europe, largely conducted by Ernest Bevin, the British Foreign Secretary since the Labour victory of that year, J. F. Byrnes for the United States and Molotov for the Soviet Union. This continued throughout 1946 and most of the peace treaties were signed in 1947, although there was no final settlement over Austria until 1955 and none at all for the whole of Germany.

In the west this meant little more than a return to the position before the war and the only modifications were a slight gain for France on her Italian border near Nice and the granting of Istria to Yugoslavia. Indeed, the major issue was not frontiers, but the nature of the governments that would emerge with the re-establishment of constitutional democracy, and the new factor here was the increased influence of the Communists who had played a prominent part in the various resistance movements after 1941 and might well take advantage of the confused scene during liberation to gain power.

In the smaller countries there seemed little likelihood of this happening. In Denmark a serious break in continuity had been avoided, since the King and the government had remained behind under the German occupation, while in Norway the backbone of the resistance had been patriotic rather than Communist; in both countries the Social Democrats emerged as the strongest political force. The Netherlands and Belgium were for the moment wrapped up in special problems of their own, the Dutch worried over the question of regaining their empire in the East Indies after the defeat of Japan in September 1945, the Belgians harassed by the tension between Walloon and Fleming and by the controversy over King Leopold, who eventually had to abdicate in favour of his son, so that the monarchy could be preserved.

In France, however, there was a far more serious vacuum. In 1940 the assemblies of the Third Republic had surrendered all rights of government to Marshal Pétain, whose subsequent régime had been swept away by the return of the Allies in 1944. Consequently, no legitimate form of government existed and in its place there were two contenders for power—General de Gaulle and the Communists. The Free French movement, which de Gaulle had started in London at the time of the French defeat (see p. 435), had shifted its headquarters to Algiers in 1942, where a consultative assembly had been set up. De Gaulle himself always claimed to speak for France, but this was only his own assertion and on his return with the Allies in 1944 he was confronted by the position that the Communists had established for themselves in the resistance inside France. Indeed, they were by now so powerful within local organizations in the south of France that they could probably have attempted to take over, but while the wartime alliance lasted, Moscow instructed them to work through legal means.

At first, de Gaulle simply included two Communists in the provisional government that he headed, but their main chance seemed likely to come in October 1945, when a constituent assembly was elected. The Communists polled five million votes and the Socialists four and a half million, while a new Catholic party, the Mouvement Républicain Populaire (M.R.P.) gained four and three-quarters of a million. Thus these three groups dominated the assembly which was to devise a constitution for France and all held ministerial posts in a new government, although the Communists were carefully excluded from key positions. Very soon de Gaulle had lost patience with the frustrations of party politics and resigned in January 1946, but the work of creating an acceptable constitution for the Fourth Republic continued throughout a troubled year of referenda until one was finally adopted in October 1946. In the following month a general election produced a legislative assembly with 183 Communists, 166 M.R.P., 103 Socialists and 74 Conservatives. The

Communists now needed an alliance with the Socialists, but the Socialists were wary of this. They preferred to work in conjunction with the M.R.P. and the simmering conflict finally came to a head in May 1947, when the Communist ministers were all dismissed after opposing the government's policy on wages.

In Italy the encouragement of Communism through the partisan movement and the destructiveness of the war, which continued for almost two years after the fall of the Fascist régime, might seem to offer a poor prospect for the restoration of parliamentary democracy. Yet the presence of the Allies was in some ways a stabilizing influence and the only radical development was the end of the monarchy, decided in a referendum in June 1946. At the same time the election of a constituent assembly gave 207 seats to de Gasperi's Christian Democrats with 104 for the Communists and 115 for the Socialists. As a consequence Communists were included for the moment in a governmental coalition, but this only lasted until May 1947, when, as in France, they were dismissed. The Socialists had been divided over joining forces with them and in any case at the general election of January 1948 those who were prepared to do so could only gain a combined representation of 182 seats against de Gasperi's Christian Democrats whose 307 seats gave him an absolute majority. Thus the non-Communist parties of both France and Italy had survived the dangerous period of enforced coalition with the Communists, in marked contrast to their counterparts in eastern Europe.

It was hardly surprising that after the advance of the Red Army had reached the middle of Germany, the eventual readjustment of frontiers in eastern Europe should largely favour Russia. From Finland she gained Petsamo in the north and took back her earlier acquisition of Karelia around the western side of Lake Ladoga. Along the south coast of the Baltic she absorbed Estonia, Latvia, Lithuania and the northern section of East Prussia. From Czechoslovakia she received Ruthenia, and from Rumania Bessarabia and northern Bukovina. Rumania had also to hand over the southern part of the Dobruja to Bulgaria, but received Translyvania from Hungary in compensation for these losses. From Poland, Russia reclaimed those eastern Polish lands which had been her share of the Molotov-Ribbentrop pact of 1939, although this was now justified as being in accordance with the Curzon line orginally proposed in 1920 (see p. 351). Great Britain and the United States had consented to this at Yalta (see p. 447), but there had been less agreement over the precise compensation that Poland should receive. It had been settled that in addition to the southern half of East Prussia she should annex some German territory, but when the war ended, the British had still not accepted the idea that this should extend as far as the line of the Oder and the western Neisse.

As in the west, the real issue was not frontiers, but régimes and the presence of the Red Army was bound to make the western Powers suspicious of the eventual outcome in eastern Europe. The only question had been how far the countries there might retain some element of political independence, and it had been with this in mind that Winston Churchill had suggested to Stalin in Moscow in October 1944 a simple allocation of degrees of influence between them. This took the form of a series of percentages—for Russia 90 per cent in Rumania, 75 per cent in Bulgaria, 50–50 in Hungary and Yugoslavia; and for Great Britain 90 per cent in Greece—all this a forlorn hope to prevent Russia gaining 100 per cent everywhere.

At first, the new governments in these countries consisted of popular front coalitions of Communist and non-Communist parties. These usually established Communists in key ministerial posts and in Hungary led to the introduction of land reforms, as well as in Czechoslovakia where they were little more than a confiscation of the farms of Sudeten Germans who were expelled. In Rumania and Bulgaria, however, the façade of multi-party political life was short-lived. In March 1945 King Michael of Rumania was ordered by the Soviet Deputy Foreign Minister to set up what was effectively a Communist government, and in Bulgaria the agrarian party and the Social democrats had been forced into opposition by the autumn of that year. Over Poland Stalin had already made his own dispositions, when in July 1944 a Polish committee was formed at Lublin as a rival to the Polish government in exile in London. The western Allies, uneasily aware of this, pressed for an agreement that there should be free elections held under international supervision, but as the months went by, the likelihood seemed to become increasingly remote, even after they had made a conciliatory move in accepting the new western frontier for Poland along the Oder-Neisse line.

The only area where these tendencies were reversed was in Greece and this did not rest on percentages, but on the arrival of British forces in October 1944. As elsewhere in occupied Europe, the Greek resistance movement E.A.M. had been predominantly Communist and might well have attempted to take over power as the Germans withdrew; instead, they agreed to cooperate with the government of national unity which the British installed under George Papandreou. Before long, however, serious dissension had broken out and by December British troops were in action against the military wing of E.A.M. Obviously this was an anomalous situation, while the war against Germany was still raging and an armistice was quickly arranged in January 1945. Nevertheless, from now on the survival of non-Communist interests depended on the presence of the British. This certainly gave the right wing the upper hand in government, reflected in an electoral victory in March 1946, but it could not prevent the outbreak of civil war the following autumn, when the Greek Communists took to the mountains and began a long campaign of

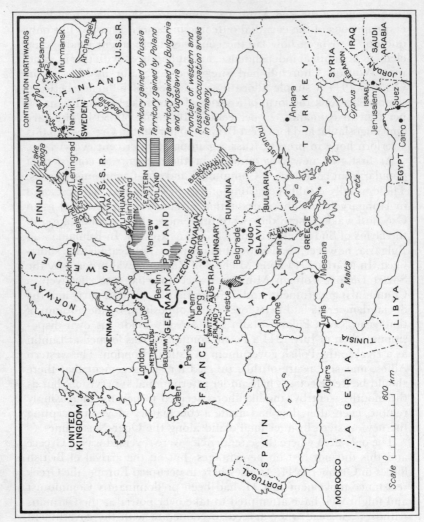

EUROPE AFTER 1945

guerilla warfare supported by the neighbouring governments of Albania, Yugoslavia and Bulgaria.

3. The occupation of Germany

Meanwhile, in Germany central and local government had completely disintegrated. German civilians struggled to survive amid the bomb damage of the cities or in isolated rural communities in a world where all forms of communication had broken down and cigarettes had taken the place of money as a means of exchange. They lay entirely at the mercy of the military commands, whose armies were now proceeding to establish themselves in the zones of occupation already agreed—the Russians in the east, the British in the north-west, the Americans to the south, and the French with two regions in the south-west.

The detail of this did not tally precisely with the position that had been reached by the armies at the end of the fighting, since the Americans in getting as far as the line of the upper Elbe were holding territory between 80 and 240 kilometres further east than what had been originally proposed. Churchill would like to have used withdrawal here as a bargaining counter over the other matters with the Russians, but, as at Yalta, Americans were still keen to ensure Russian support in the continuing war against Japan and accordingly in July withdrew their forces to the line that had been previously settled. At the same time troops from the three western Powers were sent to Berlin to occupy their respective sectors of the city. This was to create further problems, since Berlin lay in the middle of the Russian zone. The western Powers would consequently need special access by road, rail and air in order to maintain contact with their sectors and during the immediate negotiations between the military commanders Marshal Zhukov made considerable difficulties and insisted that the west would be responsible for supplying its own sectors with food and coal.

By the end of the war the Allies had been agreed that there should be a common policy for the whole of Germany, which should ensure that Germany could never again threaten their security. There was, however, already a great divergence of view over how this was to be accomplished. France and Russia, who had felt the full force of German invasion, favoured very positive solutions. The French under de Gaulle wanted total decentralization and the detaching of the Rhineland and Westphalia from Germany. The Russians had already attended to the question of security by pushing the German-Polish frontier as far west as the Oder. Beyond that, they were simply concerned to get compensation for all the damage that they had suffered and demanded reparations up to 10,000 million dollars to be paid in kind with the removal of plant, the use of German labour and the requisitioning of future German production. The British and the Americans had at first toyed with the idea of taking away from Germany all the heavy industry which made it possible for her to wage war, but eventually concluded that this would merely hamper an economic recovery throughout Europe, and preferred to work for the creation of a peaceful German constitutional democracy as the only safeguard for the future. They were also alarmed that Russia's plans would make Germany so destitute that they would be faced themselves with the cost of keeping her alive. The Russians cared less about the fate of the Germans and in any case could reckon that destitution might be a good breeding ground for Communism.

These were some of the problems that Great Britain, the United States and Russia attempted to resolve at the Potsdam Conference in July 1945. Superficially there was a reasonable level of agreement. The west grudgingly had to acknowledge Germany's eastern frontier along the Oder-Neisse line, still hoping that this concession might ensure free elections in Poland. Within Germany it was settled that there should be total disarmament, the banning of the Nazi party and the restoration of democratic political life. It was also accepted that there should be reparations, but this only specified the removal of plant; the requisitioning of future production was not mentioned, even though this had been definitely stated at Yalta, and one clause went so far as to declare that 'payment of reparations should leave enough resources to enable the German people to subsist without external assistance.' The implementing of these decisions was to be in the hands of a Control Commission of the four Powers, but in the absence of any central German administration this had to rely for executive action on the military commands of the four zones of occupation. Thus, in practice it was only too likely that there would be a growing divergence, as each zone went ahead with its own arrangements.

The Russians were the first to embark on the organization of political life. Before the end of the war Walter Ulbricht, a German Communist, had already been flown into the Russian zone to take charge of the Communist party there and by the summer three other parties—Social Democrats, Christian Democrats and Liberal Democrats—had been recognized. Local German governments were established in five provinces (*Länder*), but for the moment the Russians were content that these should consist of broad coalitions, although among local officials the first deputy mayor, the personnel officer and the education officer were all to be Communist. At the same time in July 1945 a land reform was introduced whereby the great estates of the Junkers were broken up to be shared out among existing small farmers including the German refugees from eastern Europe. This scheme had the full support of the Social Democrats, since it was to be based on private ownership rather than any kind of collectivization.

In the western zones German political parties only began to appear in the autumn of 1945. Of these the Social Democrats (S.P.D.) were determined to remain apart from the Communists, and were headed by Dr Kurt Schumacher, a survivor from concentration camps throughout most of the Nazi period. The Christian Democratic Union (C.D.U.) was strongly Catholic, but unlike the old Centre party, included a considerable Protestant element; its policy veered towards a free economy and among its leaders Konrad Adenauer, a Catholic Rhinelander and one-time burgomaster of Cologne, was eventually to emerge as the principal guiding force in the recovery of western Germany. The third, the Free Democratic Party (F.D.P.) also favoured a policy of *laissez faire*, but was anticlerical and middle class in its background. These were the forces on which the later development of the western zones was to depend, but for the moment they could only be active at a provincial level and the immediate future of Germany as a whole still rested on the relations between the victors.

Chapter 36

The Cold War

The American administration had always hoped that their incursion into Europe would be reasonably brief. U.N.R.R.A. was to deal with the immediate problems created by the devastation of war, and once the peace treaties were signed, the United States would be able to withdraw, in the belief that all future disagreements could be settled by the United Nations Organization (U.N.O.)—a refurbished version of the League of Nations—which had already had its inaugural meeting at San Francisco in April 1945.

Before long, however, it was clear that this was not to be. Within a year or two of the end of hostilities the difficult but effective working relationship of the wartime alliance had been undermined by a growing antagonism between Russia and the west, eventually so great that the period became known as the Cold War. In this confrontation the weakness of western Europe made any final withdrawal by the United States impossible, and by 1949 each side had virtually completed the organizing of its own half of the Continent.

Viewed in the perspective of history, it may be that the Cold War needs no explanation. Throughout the nineteenth century the possible expansion of Russia into the Balkans had been a source of international crisis, leading at one point to the Crimean War, and in 1914 to Austria-Hungary's fateful decision to crush Russia's *protégé* Serbia. For the British the threat from Russia had extended beyond the Balkans along her Asiatic borders and on to the Far East, and it was only the emergence of some greater danger on the Continent that could temporarily bring them into alliance. Thus at the beginning of the nineteenth century they had joined forces against Napoleon and, much later, against the German Empire of William II. This partnership, however, had never survived the defeat of their common enemy and in any case the presence of a Communist régime in Russia after 1917 had added a further element of mistrust. Indeed, the thought that Nazi Germany might be a bulwark against her had been one of the arguments in favour of appeasement in the 1930s (see p. 415), and it was only Hitler's invasion of Russia in 1941 that had brought her into a new alliance with the western Powers.

Consequently, once Hitler had been defeated in 1945, it was perhaps inescapable that there should have been suspicion on both sides. Each stood for a political and social system which the other regarded as anathema. For the west the rapid formation of Communist régimes in eastern Europe created a sense of alarm, especially in view of the shakiness of the constitutional governments in western Europe after the war; the west was anxious, too, about the possible growth of Communism in other continents and the Americans were particularly shocked when China became a Communist state in 1949. Equally, the Russians were extremely wary of the intentions of the capitalist world, now armed with the atomic bomb which had brought the Japanese war to an end in September 1945. They suspected that the west was being half-hearted in its treatment of Germany in the hope that she might eventually become part of a bloc against them and in this respect the establishment of Communist states in eastern Europe was not merely the outcome of an ideological crusade; it was aimed at placing a reliable territorial buffer between Russia and the west. In short, the collapse of German power had created a vacuum in central and eastern Europe and across this the old tensions were only too likely to reappear and very quickly to divide the Continent into the two armed camps of the Cold War.

1. The consolidation of Communism in eastern Europe

The process whereby eastern Europe came under Communist control varied a little from country to country, but one historian* has distinguished a general pattern of three stages. The first has already been mentioned—a series of popular front coalitions in which Communist ministers merely gained the key positions that put them in charge of the police, the security forces and the army. The second stage he has described as the bogus coalition, from which peasant and bourgeois parties were excluded and were then harassed by police and censorship, when they attempted to act as an opposition. The third stage was when the Communists moved in for the kill, persuaded the Socialists to fuse with them and then established a single-party government under which all opposition was completely suppressed.

In Yugoslavia and Albania this third stage had already been reached in 1945. In Bulgaria the stage of the bogus coalition came as early as January 1945 and when most other parties had been dealt with, a Soviet type of constitution was approved in December 1947, after which the Socialists agreed to merge with the Communist party. In Rumania the bogus coalition had been set up on Russia's

---

* Hugh Seton Watson, *The East European Revolution*, Methuen 1950.

orders in March 1945, but King Michael's acceptance of this did not save his throne; he was forced to abdicate at the end of 1947 and a totally Communist régime was established early in 1948.

In Poland there were long delays over the holding of elections, and meanwhile a government drawn largely from the Russian-inspired Lublin Committee consolidated the Communist hold, aided by the use of police and the distribution of land to the peasantry, particularly in the western territories gained from Germany. Stanislaw Mikolajczyk, the leader of the peasant party and a principal opponent of the Communists, was also strongly in favour of radical social reforms and believed in good relations with the Soviet Union, but his earlier position as head of the London government in exile made him unacceptable to the Polish Communists. Throughout 1946 his party meetings were disrupted and by the middle of the year he declared that over a thousand of his supporters were under arrest. Despite British and American protests the pressure continued to build up before the parliamentary elections of January 1947, and when these gave a vast majority to the ruling bloc, a new government, nominally under a Socialist, drew up a Soviet type of constitution. A little later Mikolajczyk learnt that his own life was in danger and finally left the country that autumn.

In Hungary the first stage, a four-party coalition, survived rather longer and two members of the small Farmers' Party, its leader Tildy, and Ferenc Nagy, became respectively President and Prime Minister of the Republic. Throughout 1946, however, the Communists worked hard to undermine the Small Farmers' Party with arrests and the closure of newspapers and this eventually led to the enforced resignation of Nagy and a purge of the National Peasant party. The assault on the other parties continued and was rounded off in the middle of 1948 when the Communists absorbed the Social Democrats after those who objected had been expelled.

Brutal and arbitrary as these maneouvres had been, they had concentrated on a gradual erosion of the opposition to the Communists. The striking feature of the change in Czechoslovakia was its suddenness which gave it all the character of a *coup*. Here there appears to have been no second stage at all. After the war Beneš had returned as President of the Republic. Reasonably free elections were held in May 1946, when the Communists gained 38 per cent of the vote, and a coalition government under a Communist premier, Klement Gottwald, continued to represent a variety of parties. The crisis came in February 1948. A majority of the cabinet demanded that the Communist Minister of the Interior should cease packing the police force with his own men, and when Gottwald refused to support them, several non-Communist ministers resigned. On this, Communist detachments of armed factory workers took over various ministries in Prague; in the provinces Communist action committees superseded the all-party people's committees, and on 25 February President Beneš, despairing of assistance from the west and conscious of the need for his country to preserve good relations with Russia, agreed to the forming of a new government dominated by the Communists. Jan Masaryk, the son of the first President of Czechoslovakia, remained Foreign Minister, but was found dead in mysterious circumstances a few days later. Throughout the summer most organizations were purged of non-Communists and the Social Democrats agreed to fuse with the Communist party; in June Beneš finally resigned to be replaced by Gottwald as President and with his death three months later the last vestiges of Czech democracy had vanished.

Throughout the whole of this part of Europe there were only two countries that were able to resist the growth of Russian influence during these years. Firstly, in Finland the process got no further than the first stage, when in March 1945 a popular front coalition of Communists, Social Democrats and agrarians was formed, after parliamentary elections had given the Communists a quarter of the seats. In the elections of July 1948, however, a few months after the events in Czechoslovakia, support for the Communists fell to 19 per cent of the popular vote and their ministers were removed from the government. Secondly, in Yugoslavia there had never been any likelihood of a restoration of the monarchy and Tito had set up a positively Communist régime with a full programme of collectivization. The fact, however, that the Red Army had played only a very small part in the liberation of Yugoslavia gave Tito a greater independence, and Communism became combined with a fierce spirit of nationalism that soon led them to reject any economic subservience to Russia. By 1947 Tito was even contemplating establishing a Balkan federation, and in 1948 the quarrel with Russia finally led to the expulsion of Yugoslavia from the Cominform, a new version of the Third International aimed at assisting the growth of Communism throughout the world.

2. The forming of two Germanies

In Germany the fundamental problem was that if the country was to be treated as a single entity, Russia and the west would eventually have to agree on the nature of the régime to be established there. This was likely to take some time and for the moment they could not even agree on the immediate issues involved in the governing of the occupied territories. Each suspected the other of consolidating a permanent control over its own region and as the mistrust mounted, the two sides began slowly to carry on with their own arrangements in a process that could only lead to the final division of Germany.

The initial quarrel arose over reparations. The Russians had pressed ahead at once with the removal of factory plants from their own zone, but the amount that could be dismantled there was insufficient to cover what they had claimed at Yalta, and during the first year of peace this was made up by deliveries from the western zone. In this respect, at least, Germany was being treated as a single entity and the western Allies had their own reasons for wishing to do so, since their zones were dependent on the food-producing regions of eastern Germany. They soon found, however, that the Russians were not prepared to reciprocate, since most of the current agricultural produce in the Russian zone was being sent back to Russia. As a result, the British and American governments were having to supply one and a half million tons of foodstuffs to maintain a basic minimum for the 47 million Germans in their own zones, and were thus in effect financing a part of the cost of German reparations to Russia. A meeting of the foreign ministers at Paris in April 1946 failed to bring about any change in the Russian attitude and eventually on 26 May General Clay, the American commander, decided that if there was no delivery of food from the east, there should be no further delivery of plant from the United States zone. This naturally created some ill-feeling, but it did not reduce the problems faced by the west. The British economy in particular was simply not equal to maintaining their zone and the consequence was to throw them back on American support, when in July 1946 the American and British zones were merged in order to assist them with the burden.

This hardening of attitudes in the west may also have been hastened by a new development in the eastern zone. Here on 22 April 1946, largely at the behest of the Russians, the fusion of the Social Democrats and the Communists in a Socialist Unity Party (S.E.D.) had been announced. This was rejected by most of the German Social Democrats in the western zones, but in October 1946 the Russians went ahead with new elections in the five provinces under their control. In these the S.E.D. gained almost 50 per cent of the vote and in the consequent reshuffle within the provincial administrations gained most of the positions of local president and minister of the interior.

The growing tension has also to be seen in the world context. Communist intentions in eastern Europe now seemed to be beyond doubt. At the first meeting of the Security Council of the United Nations at London in January 1946 the western Powers had objected to Russian claims to the trusteeship of Libya and the Dodecanese islands and to the continuing presence of Russian troops in northern Iran; at the same time the Russians in their turn complained about British troops in Greece and Indonesia, and French and British troops in Syria and the Lebanon. One of these areas was soon to cause the west to draw still closer together, since in March 1947, after the British had declared that they could no longer afford to finance aid against Communist pressure in Greece and Turkey (see p. 455), President Truman announced that the United States would take over this task with a grant of 400 million dollars.

It was not only the British who were confronted with economic difficulties. By the late spring of 1947, after a particularly severe winter, it was clear that most of western Europe was floundering in a morass of economic stagnation. To remedy this General Marshall, the American Secretary of State, in a famous speech at Harvard in June 1947 proposed a massive programme of financial assistance whereby the United States would pump 17,000 million dollars into the European economy to facilitate a revival of production and purchasing power. The offer was made to the entire Continent, but it was perhaps natural that the Russians should regard the move as a capitalist plot to establish a free economy in eastern Europe. Accordingly, they rejected it and forced the countries under their control to do the same. This included the eastern zone of Germany and since the western zones were to be recipients of Marshall Aid, the division of Germany was still further accentuated. In the west an Organization for European Economic Cooperation (O.E.E.C.) was set up to administer the scheme, and when the French had at last agreed to merge their zone with the British and Americans, it was decided that the west Germans should now proceed with devising a new constitution. The Russian reaction was immediate. In February 1948 the Communists took over in Prague (see p. 462), and in March their delegation under Marshal Sokolovsky withdrew from the Control Commission in Berlin.

This worsening of relations brought another issue to a head. It had long been clear that no economic recovery could take place in Germany until there had been a currency reform, but it had never been possible to reach agreement with the Russians over the creation of a central bank of issue that this would entail. Indeed, the whole debate seemed to epitomize the utter incompatibility of two such opposed philosophies. With the withdrawal of the Russians from the control commission, however, the west decided to take the opportunity to proceed with a currency reform in their regions of Germany and in June 1948 a new German mark was established to be issued by the *Bank Deutscher Länder*, later known as the *Bundesbank*.

The Russians declared at once that the new notes would not be valid in their zone, nor in their sector of Belin, and stigmatized the currency reform and the merging of the three western zones as a deliberate breach of earlier agreements. They were determined to force the west to retract. To do so, they reckoned to exploit the precarious position of the western sectors of Berlin, and on 24 June

1948, they closed all land routes through East Germany on which these sectors depended for the supply of food and coal from the western zones. They then waited for the west to come to terms.

The tightening of Communist control over eastern Europe, however, convinced the west that they must not surrender. An immense ferrying operation by air was organized and during the next ten months some 200,000 flights ensured the delivery of one and half million tons of supplies to Berlin. Both sides were circumspect. The west had no intention of trying to break through by land; the Russians were careful not to interfere with the air corridors on which the airlift depended. Nevertheless, the risk of open hostilities was always present and there was general relief, particularly among the hungry Berliners, when on 12 May 1949 Stalin decided to give up and reopened the land routes. The danger had passed, but the division of Germany was now complete. Within a few weeks of the end of the Berlin blockade a federal two-chamber constitution for west Germany came into force; in the east the Russians had already devised a constitution for a German Democratic Republic but waited for the west to make their move before having it adopted by a People's Congress at Berlin on 30 May.

3. The establishing of the armed blocs

The underlying factor in the attitude of the west was a growing sense of their own weakness in the face of Russian power. The apparently monolithic system of control that was being established through single-party Communist governments in eastern Europe stood in marked contrast to the untidy and changeable processes of democratic rule in the west, and this difference was matched by a considerable military imbalance, since the west had only a few effective divisions immediately available against some 175 divisions of the Red Army. It seemed essential to achieve a greater unity and in March 1948, a month after the Communist *coup* in Prague, Great Britain, France, Belgium, the Netherlands and Luxemburg signed the treaty of Brussels whereby a consultative council of their foreign ministers was to coordinate a system of military defence. A year later in April 1949, when the Berlin blockade had already lasted ten months, a much larger combination was set up, the North Atlantic Treaty Organization (N.A.T.O.), headed by the United States and including Canada, Italy, Iceland, Norway, Denmark and Portugal as well as the Powers of the Brussels treaty. It was a fair measure of the apprehensiveness of Great Britain and the United States that this was the first time in their history that either of them had accepted a direct military commitment on the Continent in peacetime.

Shortly after the establishment of N.A.T.O. the area of tension shifted to the other side of the world. In September 1949 a Communist state was declared in China by Mao Tse-Tung who had finally driven the nationalist leader Chiang Kai-Shek from the mainland to the island of Formosa (Taiwan). Then in June 1950 the Communist government of North Korea launched an invasion of South Korea. The resistance of South Korea depended largely on American forces hastily dispatched from Japan and acting nominally on behalf of the United Nations and for the first year the frontline oscillated to and fro in a contest that eventually threatened to involve China.

Fortunately the war, which continued until July 1953, did not spread, but the fact that the Communist and non-Communist worlds were in open conflict was bound to raise the question which diplomats in western Europe had until now been careful to avoid. In September 1950 Dean Acheson, the American Secretary of State, finally voiced it. In New York at a N.A.T.O. meeting he declared that the western Europeans could only expect American support if they were prepared to include western Germany within the machinery of defence. The proposal gave rise to a good many emotions. For western European countries the memory of the German occupation was still recent. Russia would naturally accuse the west of rearming their common foe against her, and among Germans themselves, living amid the ruin of defeat, there was little desire to become mercenaries of the west.

The new move, however, did provide Konrad Adenauer, the Chancellor of the West German Federal Republic, with an opportunity to bargain for a restoration of national parity with the western allies, although this seemed likely to put the eventual reunification of Germany still further out of reach. In fact, the rehabilitation of West Germany had already been envisaged in other spheres. In May 1949 the dream of a united Europe had been expressed in the creation of a Council of Europe to coordinate social and cultural matters and West Germany had been among the signatories. Then, in May 1950, Robert Schuman, the French Foreign Minister, had suggested a Customs Union of a coal and steel community which was eventually set up in 1952 and consisted of France, West Germany and the smaller countries, Belgium, the Netherlands and Luxemburg, usually known as Benelux. And now in May 1952 the preliminaries to meeting the American demand for German rearmament brought about the ending of the state of occupation and the recognition of full West German sovereignty.

Naturally, the Russians had watched this development with some alarm and three months earlier had tried to halt it by suggesting that Germany should be reunited as a neutral state in the middle of Europe, entirely free of any armed forces. The two sides were eventually to reach such an agreement over Austria in 1955, but in

1952 over Germany the stakes were too high. The west believed that the Russian proposal was simply a delaying tactic; and in any case there was always the danger that a reunited, but unarmed Germany might be drawn into the Communist bloc. And so the treaty with West Germany went ahead, whereupon the East Germans virtually closed their frontier with the west.

The actual rearmament of West Germany, however, proved to be rather more problematical. The original idea had been that she would be included in a European Defence Community with a completely integrated military force. The British, however, would not join this, since they objected to a loss of their own independence of action and in the absence of the British the French feared that they would be unable to cope with a possible revival of German militarism. Later the British put forward an alternative scheme for a Western European Union, merely an alliance between sovereign states, to which they would be prepared to contribute four divisions and some air power, and on this the French gave way. From October 1954 West Germany was to be a part of the western defence against the east and was to supply a force of 500,000 men to N.A.T.O.

Meanwhile, in June 1953, Russia had been faced with a rising in East Germany where a low standard of living had persisted owing to the fact that the Russians had been continuing to take a quarter of the gross national product in reparations. The rising was quelled with Russian tanks, but the west took advantage of the unrest to put forward their own proposals for reunification. Their conditions were that there should be free elections under supervision and that a reunified Germany should have the right to make alliances as she wished. This was hardly the moment for the Russians to contemplate such a solution and the offer simply became one more gambit in the international diplomatic exchange. Then, once the Western European Union was established, the Russians took the next step and in February 1955 created the Warsaw Pact, a military alliance of Russia, East Germany, Albania, Bulgaria, Czechoslovakia, Hungary, Poland and Rumania. Thus, only ten years after the end of the war, the two armed camps had been formed and Europe was divided by an iron curtain running down the middle of Germany.

Chapter 37

Europe in the 1950s

1. Economic recovery

Thus far, the story of post-war Europe would seem to be one of depressing extremes. It opens with a Continent apparently in a state of total ruin, and within a few years moves quickly into a period of Cold War between two hostile blocs. During the next two decades, however, this pattern was to be accompanied by a much more exhilarating extreme—an economic recovery which brought Europe to a position of affluence startlingly in advance of anything known before.

The principal reason for this suggests that although men do not often learn from history, they can do so occasionally. After the First World War the restoration of normal economic life had been hampered by the vicious circle of war debts and financial reparations (see pp. 377–9); now after the second there was in the west a conscious avoidance of such narrow local interests, or at least a realization that those interests would be best served by making the economic system work for all. The most striking and generous example of this was Marshall Aid (see p. 465), which by providing the necessary initial capital had, only three years after its inception, stimulated an increase of 25 per cent of total output in Europe. This, however, was only part of a much broader set of assumptions strongly advocated by the British economist J. M. Keynes. It was argued that market forces on their own could not always automatically ensure prosperity; consequently some form of intervention by governments affecting interest rates, money supply or the control of credit was necessary to turn things in the right direction, and some international organization would be needed for the implementing of these decisions. The general acceptance of these views was reflected in the creation of the International Monetary Fund, the World Bank, as well as the General Agreement on Tariffs and Trade (G.A.T.T.). Within this framework of cooperation there also developed specific regional schemes—in 1952 the coal and steel community, and in 1957 the treaty of Rome which established a common market between France, Germany, Italy and Benelux, and by 1965 had brought the tariffs between them down to one-fifth of the original level.

All these efforts were rewarded with remarkable speed, for the 1950s and 1960s saw a period of boom which would have seemed utterly impossible to an observer in Europe in the summer of 1945. In the 1950s Italy's output grew by 64 per cent, and that of France, the Netherlands, Switzerland and Spain by nearly 50 per cent. The output of chemicals rose by three times. Oil imports had reached 457 million tonnes by 1967, compared with 17 million tonnes in 1929, and there was a great increase in oil-refining capacity. All forms of transport had multiplied. By 1957 the carriage of passengers and freight by rail was almost 60 per cent higher than in 1938, merchant fleets had doubled and the 5 million cars on the road in 1948 had become 44 million by 1965. Altogether, by 1960 western Europe alone was responsible for a quarter of the world's industrial output and for 40 per cent of world trade, and by 1964 industrial output for the entire Continent was two and a half times what it had been in 1938.

Within this scene the most remarkable feature was the economic recovery of the West German Federal Republic under Konrad Adenauer and his Minister of Economics, Ludwig Erhard, who succeeded him as Chancellor in 1963. In these years industrial production in West Germany increased six times, the gross national product three times, eight million dwelling places were constructed, and unemployment which had stood at 9 per cent in 1949 was less than one per cent in 1961. For those who had lived amid the ruin of Germany in 1945 this might well seem an economic miracle, but the miracle does have a rational explanation. The starting point had been the currency reform introduced by the western Allies, the receipt of 1400 million dollars in Marshall Aid and the rapid political rehabilitation of West Germany as a consequence of the Cold War. Most other factors, however, were internal. Factory machinery buried beneath the rubble in the cities was often found to be less damaged than had been supposed and in any case, when it was irreparable, could be replaced with more modern equipment. Naturally, the work of reconstruction demanded an immense labour force and in this respect the additional ten million German refugees from the east, at first thought to be a burden, became an asset. On the other hand, the loss of the eastern territories did not prove to be a serious inconvenience, since the real industrial potential of Germany had always lain in the west. More than anything, there was an enormous incentive to rebuild; trade unions, whose structure had been simplified according to British suggestions, were prepared to accept low wages; businessmen were encouraged by tax reliefs to reinvest their profits and in the 1950s 22 per cent of the gross national product was ploughed back in this way. It is probable, too, that in the circumstances which faced Germany the free economy that Adenauer pursued offered the most appropriate means for meeting her needs as rapidly as possible.

The population was rising everywhere—in western Europe from 264 million in 1940 to 320 million in 1970, and in Russia from 170 million to 234 million. In the west the percentage of people employed on the land was declining, although mechanization and fertilizers had increased agricultural output by 35 per cent, despite the relative smallness of most farms on the Continent. Generally the setting was becoming far more urban, as cities expanded and villages grew into towns, all linked by vast networks of motorways. There was another break with the past in that all governments of whatever political complexion had adopted the idea of the welfare state and the individual enjoyed a far more extensive system of social security for health, education, family allowances and old age pensions.

Meanwhile, in eastern Europe recovery had been slower. The Russians had continued to draw reparations from East Germany until 1954 and the satellite countries were compelled to buy from Russia at high prices and to sell their own produce to her at low ones. Russia herself achieved a considerable expansion, principally in heavy industry and by 1957 her gross national product was 36 per cent of that of the U.S.A., and by 1962 50 per cent. All this was at the price of a scarcity of consumer goods and an apparatus of control that relied upon secret police and labour camps, but after Stalin's death in 1953, his successors Malenkov and then Nikita Khrushchev did make some attempt to liberalize the régime.

At the same time the eastern European countries had embarked upon a greater industrialization, although their economies remained predominantly agricultural. The Russian boast was that the Communist system of planned production would eventually outdo the free economy of the west, but to the inhabitants of East Germany, where per capita consumption had only reached the 1938 level by 1958, it did not seem so. Every week thousands of them made their escape through Berlin to the prosperity of the west, and in the first part of 1961 alone 140,000 crossed over. Then, in the August of that year, the East German government decided that they could not allow this loss of personnel to go on, and began the building of the Berlin wall which finally closed the last remaining chink in the iron curtain—a personal tragedy for the Germans and a tacit admission of defeat on the part of the Russians.

2. The shedding of empire

There was another remarkable phenomenon in the history of Europe during these years. At the same time as Russia was consolidating her hold on eastern Europe, the countries of the west, which sixty years before had competed with each other over the acquisition of empire (see p. 227–33), now began to shed many of their colonial possessions and radically to revise their relationship with those that they retained.

This tranference of power came about largely because of the weakened state of most European countries at the end of the war, and the ease of the operation varied according to the extent to which each was prepared to accept the new situation. One of them had no option. Italy was simply deprived of her African colonies by the treaty of peace, and Libya, Eritrea, Italian Somaliland and Abyssinia all became sovereign states. In Great Britain, however, the Labour government took the initiative over India, and a partition between Hindu and Moslem regions led to the forming of India and Pakistan in August 1947; Burma and Ceylon also gained their independence early in 1948, although, except for Burma, all of them chose to remain within the British Commonwealth. In 1946 Transjordan was recognized as an independent kingdom, but elsewhere in the Middle East the changes were less tidy. In Palestine the British, already war-weary, finally tired of trying to keep the peace between Arab and Jew and in 1948 surrendered their mandate to the United Nations. In Egypt a military *coup* in 1952 removed King Farouk from the scene and in 1954 agreement was eventually reached with the new nationalist leader Colonel Nasser that British forces would depart from the Suez canal zone (see p. 473).

Other countries were not so prepared to accept the inevitable. The Dutch East Indies had been under Japanese occupation during the war, but after the surrender of Japan in September 1945 the local inhabitants had had no wish to return to their former colonial masters. Negotiations over this broke down in 1946 and for the next three years the Dutch fought to regain possession until in 1949 they were forced to recognize the independent republic of Indonesia. Similarly, the French proved more reluctant to let go. They had accepted the independence of Syria and the Lebanon, but in Indo-China they waged a long war against the Communist forces of the Viet Minh, headed by Ho Chi Minh. Eventually, however, in 1954 they had to agree to the loss of North Vietnam in a partition devised by the great Powers at Geneva. In North Africa, too, they were confronted by independence movements which by 1955 had brought them to terms in Tunisia and Morocco, while in Algeria, which the authorities treated as a part of metropolitan France, a civil war dragged on for several years until its later stages brought about the collapse of the Fourth Republic in 1958 (see p. 479).

Of course, these changes had not completely ended European colonialism. Belgium and Portugal continued to exercise a firmly paternalistic rule over their empires in Africa. Great Britain still held vast territories overseas—in Africa, Kenya, Uganda, Tanganyika, Sierra Leone, the Gold Coast and Nigeria as well as a projected federation for Nyasaland and North and South Rhodesia; in Asia, Malaya, Singapore, Hong Kong and North Borneo; and in the Caribbean, the West Indian islands which they hoped to weld into another federation. France, too, retained French West Africa and French Equatorial Africa which covered some four and a quarter million square miles with a population of 21 million, apparently unaffected by movements of independence. Even so, Great Britain and France were aware that the relationship now was a much more delicate one and required a more progressive attitude than before the war. Economically this was to mean a considerable investment by the mother countries in agricultural and industrial development. Politically their methods diverged. The French attempted to create a more compact unit, extending French citizenship and giving their colonies representation in the assemblies of the Fourth Republic in Paris. The British concentrated on developing legislative bodies within each colony as a step towards their eventually achieving Dominion status. For both of them the hope was that a profitable partnership would replace the old colonial tutelage and thus frustrate any Communist attempt to take advantage of dissent; in this way the echoes of the Cold War now ran out to the ends of the earth.

3. Suez and Hungary 1956

There was one area in which those echoes were particularly insistent and that was along the Russian border in the Middle East between Turkey and India. Uncertainty here had been heightened by various indications of a weakening of the hold that Great Britain had previously exercised. In 1951 the Iranian premier Musaddiq had nationalized the Anglo-Iranian oil company and although this scheme was frustrated through his being deprived of any oil tankers, it still took the British two years to get rid of Musaddiq and the subsequent reorganization left Iran with most of the benefits of nationalization. In Egypt, too, there was a radical change in July 1952, when the British puppet monarch Farouk was overthrown in a military *coup*. Within two years Colonel Nasser had emerged as the new ruler determined on national regeneration and resentful of the presence of 80,000 British troops occupying the area of the Suez canal. In 1953, however, the Russians succeeded in exploding a nuclear device, and since this seemed to make all such isolated strategic points hopelessly vulnerable, the British government decided in 1954 to give Nasser what he wanted by withdrawing their forces to Cyprus.

These changed fortunes of Great Britain appeared to suggest a power vacuum in the Middle East which a number of contenders were eager to fill. Under Stalin Russia had not played much part here, but his eventual successors Khrushchev and Bulganin had now seen the possibility of acquiring a few client States through the judicious offer of economic aid. The United States, who in September 1954 had taken a leading part in forming the South East Asia Treaty Organization as a bulwark of mutual defence against Communism, was anxious to create a similar league in the Middle East and by the autumn of 1955 a treaty between Turkey and Iraq had been joined by Great Britain, Iran and Pakistan, the whole being known as the Baghdad Pact.

Among the States of the Middle East themselves there were, too, some hopes of finding an independent role for the Arab world. Unfortunately for these aspirations there was really only one issue which could create a temporary unity among the Arabs—a hatred of the State of Israel. Since 1950 Great Britain, France and the United States had attempted to hold this in check with a Tripartite Declaration. This balanced the supply of arms to each side and guaranteed the armistice lines with which the fighting had ended after the British surrender of the mandate in 1948, but the sense of antagonism persisted. A treaty of 1888 had established the Suez canal as an international waterway, yet Egypt refused to allow Israeli shipping through and was bringing the alternative route up the Gulf of Akaba under fire from Sharm-el-Sheik at the southern extremity of Sinai. Apart from this, however, there were too many internal antagonisms to make it possible to construct an effective Arab League. Saudi Arabia disliked the two states of Iraq and Jordan which had been carved out of territory which she regarded as her own after the first World War; of these two Iraq, enjoying improved oil revenue since 1951, followed her own pro-western policy under King Faisal and his minister Nuri-al-Said. And the modern revolutionary pronouncements of the new Egyptian régime struck a note that was hardly acceptable to the conservative Arab monarchies.

To Nasser the creation of the Baghdad Pact was a characteristic piece of interference by the great Powers and his immediate response was to take advantage of Russia's new interest in the Middle East. In 1955 he made a trade treaty with her and purchased considerable armaments including tanks and planes from Czechoslovakia. Playing Russia off against the west, however, was a risky policy, since he was still hoping to gain a substantial loan from the World Bank with American and British backing for the construction of the Aswan dam on the upper Nile, which would revolutionize the Egyptian economy. In May 1956 he finally overreached himself when he recognized Communist China. In July the British and the Americans decided as a consequence to cancel the loan and this brought the crisis to a head. Nasser, who had had no similar promise from

Russia, now turned to his only remaining asset and announced the nationalization of the Suez canal company.

Reactions to this step varied. The United States, principally concerned with mounting a guard on Russia's Asiatic border, wanted to maintain peace in the Middle East, particularly since an American presidential election was due to take place in November. Hence the American Secretary of State, John Foster Dulles, stressed the need for negotiation through a hastily formed canal-users' association, which argued vainly throughout August and September for the internationalizing of the canal. The British and the French as the two principal shareholders were more belligerent; they were both determined to regain the canal, if possible by bringing about the fall of Nasser, and the French had an added incentive in that they believed that Nasser was subsidizing resistance to their rule in Algeria.

By September they seemed likely to acquire a third partner. Israel, harassed by guerrilla attack from Gaza and anxious over Egypt's recent acquisition of planes and tanks, was keen to launch an attack into Sinai to wipe out the guerrilla bases and to destroy the guns of Sharm-el-Sheik, and the crisis seemed to offer her two allies who would supply her with the necessary air cover over the open spaces of the Sinai desert. For the British and the French the advantage of an Israeli attack would be that they could then pose as mediators, sending an expeditionary force on to the canal in order to separate the combatants. The French under their premier Guy Mollet were perfectly happy to work in conjunction with Israel. The British position was less certain. The Prime Minister, Sir Anthony Eden, knew that it would be fatal for Great Britain's relations with Arab States, such as Iraq and Jordan, if she was seen to be acting in alliance with Israel, and as a consequence the British were always careful to deny such an arrangement. It was equally clear that such a scheme would never be countenanced by the Americans, from whom it would have to be kept secret.

The opening stages went as planned. On 29 October Israel, assured of air and naval cover by the French, advanced into Sinai. On 30 October Great Britain and France declared that the canal was endangered and issued an ultimatum to Egypt and Israel to take up positions respectively sixteen kilometres distant from either side of the canal—a remarkable demand, which required Egypt to surrender the whole of Sinai and which Nasser not unnaturally rejected. In the Security Council of the United Nations the British and French delegates vetoed a resolution calling for an end to force in the region. On 31 October an Allied military and naval expeditionary force set sail for Egypt and the R.A.F. destroyed Nasser's recently acquired air force with bombing attacks on Egyptian airfields.

The need now was for speed, but this was made impossible by two factors. First, the harbours of Cyprus had been inadequate for the loading of such a task force and the main part of it had had to sail from Malta 1440 kilometres away. Second, Eden's scruples over no apparent collusion with Israel had meant that this could not set out until Israel had opened her attack, thus providing Great Britain and France with their pretext that they were taking action in order to separate the combatants. And so for six days the Americans and the Opposition in Great Britain denounced the whole scheme, Bulganin uttered threats about the rocketing of British and French cities and the diplomats warded off efforts to bring about a ceasefire, while an armada of seven aircraft carriers, 150 warships and 80,000 troops slowly lumbered across the eastern Mediterranean. By the time they were in position to carry out landings, after a parachute drop and the bombardment of Port Said at dawn on 6 November, it had become almost impossible to ignore any longer the international demand for a ceasefire. By now the Americans, furious at what they regarded as a colonial adventure, were refusing to allow any withdrawal from the International Monetary Fund by Great Britain, whose gold reserves had fallen by £100 million in a week. In addition, the Israelis, who had never been keen on their proposed role as an aggressor threatening the canal, had not pushed very far across Sinai, but instead had concentrated on a thrust south towards Sharm-el-Sheik. Once the guns there had been captured by the evening of 5 November, they were prepared to obey the call for a ceasefire and this meant that the western allies were deprived of their excuse, since there were now virtually no combatants to separate. Thus on 6 November the British government, to the fury of the French, also agreed to a ceasefire, when their troops were no further than forty kilometres south of Port Said, and a few weeks later the Anglo-French force was replaced by a United Nations peace-keeping contingent.

The British government always maintained that they had achieved a part of their objective, since they had saved the canal. In fact, it does not seem that the canal had been greatly in danger, or if it was, only because of the Anglo-French plan with Israel. Meanwhile, Egypt still retained control of it, although it was now unusable after Nasser had carried out a blocking operation with sunken ships. And Nasser himself had survived, whereas Eden, whose health had finally given way, retired in January 1957 to be succeeded as British premier by Harold Macmillan.

The Suez crisis was not only a fiasco for Great Britain and France. It brought a temporary halt to an improvement in east-west relations. Since Stalin's death his successors had been attempting to modify the harsher aspects of his rule at home and abroad. In 1954 a conference at Geneva ended the fighting in Indo-China with the partition of Vietnam. In 1955 a Soviet delegation including the party secretary Khrushchev visited Yugoslavia in an effort to win her back to the fold and it was soon clear that a notion of 'different roads to Socialism' was likely to ease Soviet pressure on other eastern European countries. The most startling moment of change came in February 1956 when Khrushchev made a speech at the twentieth congress of the Communist Party, denouncing much of Stalin's rule and rehabilitating many of those who had died in the course of it.

In the autumn of 1956 all these promising features appeared suddenly blighted. It was hardly surprising that the Suez crisis should be depicted in the Communist world as a typical piece of western colonialism. Khrushchev's reactions, however, had to be limited to violent utterances, because at precisely the same time the new mood of relaxation had produced an unexpected response in Poland and Hungary.

The issue here was not so much over the existence of a Communist régime, as over the extent to which it should be under Russian domination. In Poland the Stalinist secretary of the Polish Communist party had recently died and after several riots in June 1956 at Posen about the level of factory workers' pay it seemed that Wladislav Gomulka might take the lead in establishing greater freedom from Moscow. Gomulka had fought in the Polish resistance during the war, but had been ousted from the party and later imprisoned during the Stalin period. Now at liberty again and readmitted to the party in August, he seemed likely to be a strong candidate when a new presidium was to be elected by the central committee in October. Not even the appearance of Russian leaders including Khrushchev and Molotov in Warsaw could shake the mood of independence and eventually the Russians accepted the new situation which was soon to bring about the election of Gomulka as party secretary.

This mildness was partly explained by the far greater disturbances that had been taking place in Hungary. Here on 23 October mass demonstrations in Budapest sparked off by university students and factory workers were followed on the next morning by the appearance of Russian troops and tanks, but they could hardly cope with the extent of the rising, which within a short time had thrown open the borders of Hungary to the west. It had also set up a coalition government under a liberal Communist Imre Nagy, who now began to demand the withdrawal of Soviet troops and a new status of neutrality for Hungary in Europe. This was far more ambitious than anything claimed by Gomulka in Poland and was certainly far too much for the Russians. They retaliated by taking up a new Hungarian Communist leader, Janos Kadar, who had the right credentials, since he had been arrested and imprisoned during the Stalin period, but who was now prepared to suppress the rising with the help of Russian tanks.

At first it might seem that the Poles had gained more from these events by showing greater restraint than the Hungarians, but in the long run it was Kadar who introduced a far less strict form of Communism in Hungary, whereas in Poland Gomulka gradually restored many of the controls associated with the earlier period. On the Continent as a whole the Hungarian rising had if anything consolidated the partition of Europe. The west could hardly take advantage of it, since they were so divided over the Suez crisis, yet even without that it seemed that there could have been no question of the west moving into a Russian sphere of influence to go to the assistance of Hungary. The possession of nuclear bombs by both sides now ensured that the iron curtain had become a permanent frontier.

4. General de Gaulle and the fall of the French Fourth Republic 1958

The French Fourth Republic has never enjoyed a very flattering press. Perhaps nineteen successive governments in ten years do suggest an almost exaggerated response to the requirements of democracy. At any rate, it meant that the struggle to recover from wartime occupation and to resolve the problem of overseas possessions had to be carried on in an atmosphere of political instability and horse-trading. In these circumstances it was France who suffered a more lasting damage than Great Britain from the Suez affair and two years later a final crisis over Algeria brought the Fourth Republic to an end and replaced it with a Fifth, whose constitution was tailored to the demands of General de Gaulle.

Nevertheless, it would be wrong to ignore the very positive success of the Fourth Republic. A national economic plan provided guidelines and incentives for private enterprise; as early as 1954 industrial production was 50 per cent higher than before 1939 and the gross national product continued to increase by 5 per cent a year. An extensive system of social security was inaugurated and large family allowances eventually sent France's population up from 41 million in 1938 to 50 million in 1967. All this was in step with the general recovery of western Europe already noted (see pp. 469–71) and ironically the Fifth Republic was eventually to benefit very much from the work of its predecessor.

The record was all the more remarkable in that it was being achieved at a time when the successive governments were dogged with the problems of an empire beset with independence movements. The tragedy was that the governments themselves would have been prepared to find a compromise solution to much of this, but were constantly foiled by their own colonists, members of the colonial administration and the army, who saw negotiated settlements as one more step along the path of retreat which had continued since 1940. Thus, for seven years a war was waged in Indo-China until after the military disaster at Dien Bien Phu the premier Mendès France forced through the settlement that was confirmed at the Geneva Conference in 1954. At the same time a policy of repression had to be abandoned in Tunisia, just when an Algerian nationalist movement, the F.L.N., began its own struggle for independence.

It was here that the Fourth Republic met its downfall. Algeria, administered as a part of metropolitan France and occupied by a million Frenchmen, many of whose families had lived there for several generations, was to prove infinitely more difficult to jettison. The French settlers and their colonial governors were determined that France should fight to preserve them from the F.L.N. and for more than two years French governments did their best to crush the movement, ultimately deploying as many as 350,000 troops in Algeria. In 1958, however, one premier, Felix Gaillard, decided to return to negotiation. With this the French in Algeria took the matter into their own hands and on 13 May an insurrection in Algiers made it clear to the government in Paris that they could no longer rely on their forces there.

From this time on, when it seemed that the Fourth Republic might collapse into some type of neo-Fascist régime, there was increasing mention of de Gaulle as an alternative leader who might satisfy the Algerian French. After his resignation as premier in 1946 the General had formed his own Gaulliste group, R.P.F., but being unable to make headway, had retired from politics in 1955. Now he began issuing his own independent statements, announcing that he would be prepared to accept power, if it was offered to him, but only on condition that the existing system of government was radically changed. This certainly seemed a possibility if the pressures became too great; so naturally it became the concern of Gaullists to see that they did so. On 24 May, Corsica joined the insurrection and rumour spoke of an intended *coup* on the mainland with paratroops landing near Paris. On 28 May the premier, Pierre Pflimlin, after a conversation with de Gaulle resigned, and de Gaulle became Prime Minister on 1 June.

Within a few months a new constitution had been drawn up, whereby the President elected by universal suffrage would have far greater power, particularly over defence and foreign policy. In September 1958 this was accepted overwhelmingly by a plebiscite, in November a new assembly was elected and in December de Gaulle completed his triumph with his own election as President. De Gaulle's rule was to last more than ten years and in many ways

justified the hope of his supporters, giving firm rule which strengthened rather than weakened constitutional processes. There was,
however, one disappointment. The French in Algeria had certainly
expected strong support from him; yet de Gaulle continued to
negotiate with the FLN. Once again the generals resisted, but now
de Gaulle was too well established in metropolitan France to succumb to colonial pressure and in 1962 Algeria became an independent state. More than 130 years before, Charles X had been
unable to save his throne by embarking on the conquest of empire
in Algeria; now the abandonment of that empire had finally demonstrated the strength of the new ruler of the French Fifth Republic.

Appendices

1. ROYAL GENEALOGICAL TABLES

N.B. The family trees have been very much simplified. The dates beneath the Sovereigns refer to their reigns.

FRANCE: THE HOUSES OF BOURBON AND BOURBON–ORLEANS

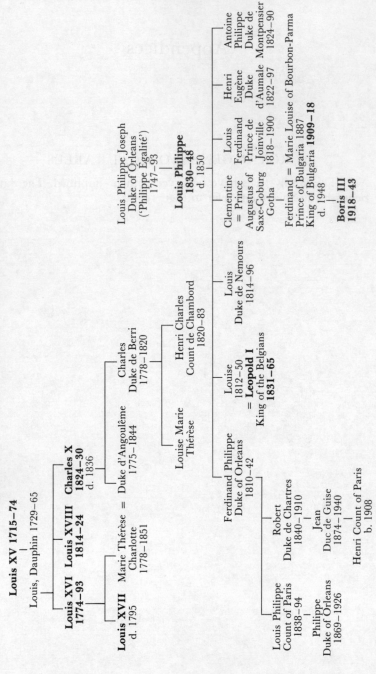

FEANCE: THE HOUSE OF BONAPARTE

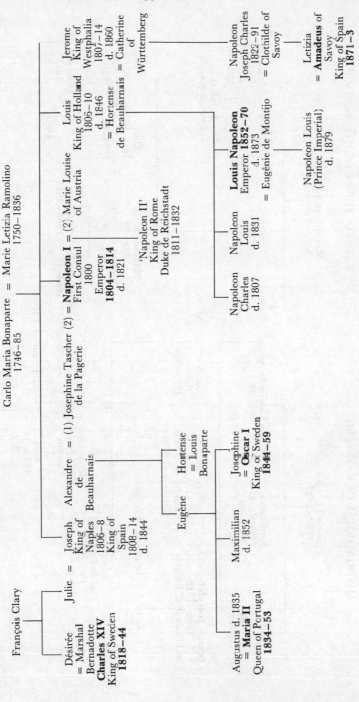

BAVARIA: HOUSE OF WITTELSBACH

AUSTRIA: HOUSE OF HABSBURG

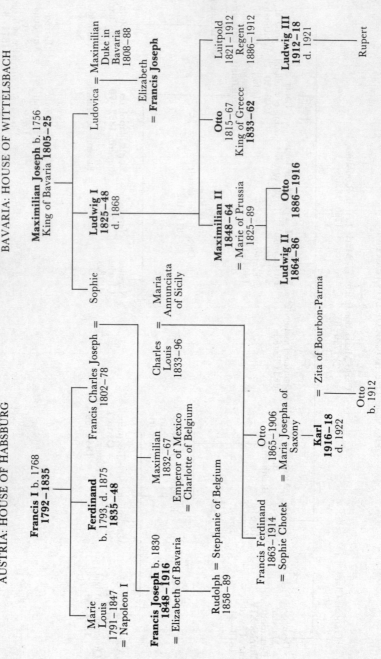

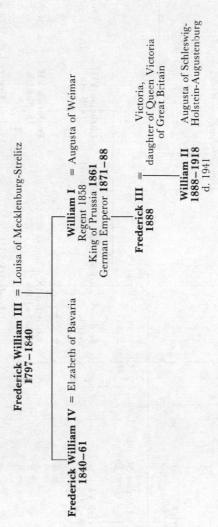

PRUSSIA: THE HOUSE OF HOHENZOLLERN

Frederick William III = Louisa of Mecklenburg-Strelitz
1797–1840

Frederick William IV = Elizabeth of Bavaria
1840–61

William I = Augusta of Weimar
Regent 1858
King of Prussia 1861
German Emperor 1871–88

Frederick III = Victoria,
1888   daughter of Queen Victoria
             of Great Britain

William II = Augusta of Schleswig-
1888–1918   Holstein-Augustenburg
d. 1941

DENMARK: THE HOUSE OF OLDENBURG

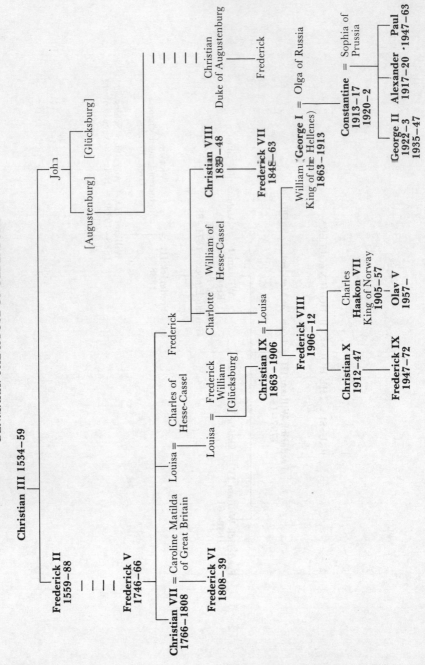

ITALY: THE HOUSE OF SAVOY

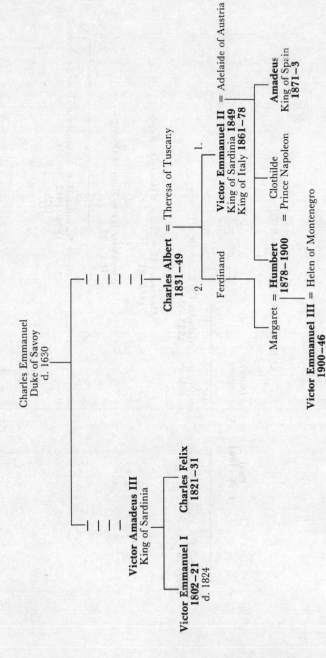

488 *Appendices*

RUSSIA: THE HOUSE OF ROMANOV

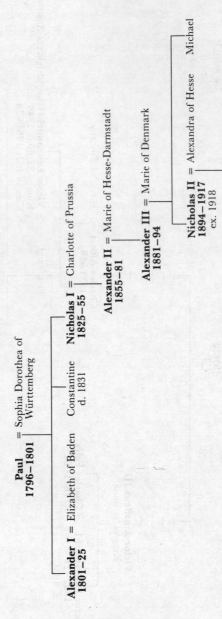

2 POPES

Elected	*Title*	*Family Name*
1800	Pius VII	Chiaramonti
1823	Leo XII	Della Genga
1829	Pius VIII	Castiglion
1831	Gregory XVI	Cappellari
1846	Pius IX	Mastai-Ferretti
1878	Leo XIII	Pecci
1903	Pius X	Sarto
1914	Benedict XV	Della Chiesa
1922	Pius XI	Ratti
1939	Pius XII	Pacelli
1958	John XXIII	Roncalli

3 PRESIDENTS OF THE FRENCH THIRD REPUBLIC
1871–1940

Adolphe Thiers	1871–3
Marshal MacMahon	1873–9
Jules Grévy	1879–87
Sadi Carnot	1887–94
Jean-Paul Casimir Périer	1894–5
Félix Faure	1895–9
Emile Loubet	1899–1906
Armand Fallières	1906–13
Raymond Poincaré	1913–20
Paul Deschanel	1920
Alexandre Millerand	1920–4
Gaston Doumergue	1924–31
Paul Doumer	1931–2
Albert Lebrun	1932–40

4. FRENCH ELECTORAL SYSTEMS 1814–1945

See also: P. Campbell, *French Electoral Systems and Elections 1789–1957*. (1958)

	No. of seats	Deputies' Qualifications Tax	Age	Years of tenure	Electors' Qualifications Tax	Age	Type of constituency	Size of electorate
1814	258	1,000 fr.	40	5 (annual election of $\frac{1}{5}$)	300 fr.	30	Single-member (scrutin d'ar-rondissement)	88,000– 110,000 (1814–30)
1815	402 (395)[1]		25					
1816	258		40					
1817						25	Multi-member (scrutin de liste)	
1820	430						Single-member (172 additional deputies elected by chief tax-payers)	
1824				7 (no $\frac{1}{5}$)				
1830–1	459	500	30	5	200[2]	25	Single-member	166,000– 241,000 (1830–48)
1848	900[3]	—	21	—	Manhood[4] suffrage 21		Multi-member	8 million
1849	750[5]		25	3				10 million[6]
1850					3-year residential			7 million
1852	261[7]			6			Single-member	
1857	267							
1863	283							
1869	292							
1871	768 (738)[8]	—	25	4			Multi-member	10 million
1875	533[9]						Single-member	
1881	541[10]							
1885	569						Multi-member	
1889	560						Single-member	
1919– 20	610[11]						Multi-member	
1927	593[12]						Single-member	12 million
1944					Female suffrage			25 million
1945	586							

[1] Reduction after territorial losses by the second Treaty of Paris.
[2] As well as members of the Institut de France and a small number of retired army officers paying 100 francs in tax.
[3] Including 4 for Algeria and 12 for colonies.
[4] Including soldiers and sailors.
[5] Including 4 for Algeria and 7 for colonies.
[6] Increase of 2 million since 1848 owing to the completion of the registers.
[7] 1 seat per 35,000 electors during the Second Empire.
[8] Reduction after the loss of Alsace and Lorraine. 15 for Algeria and colonies.
[9] Including 7 for Algeria and colonies.
[10] Representation of Algeria and colonies raised to 16.
[11] After regaining Alsace and Lorraine.
[12] Representation of Algeria and colonies raised to 19.

5. GERMAN CHANCELLORS AND PRESIDENTS
1871–1960

1. The German Reich.

   Chancellors:
   Prince Otto von Bismarck 1871–90
   Count Leo von Caprivi 1890–4
   Prince Chlodwig zu Hohenlohe-Schillingsfürst 1894–1900
   Prince Bernhard von Bülow 1900–9
   Theobald von Bethmann Hollweg 1909–17
   Dr Georg Michaelis, July–October 1917
   Count Georg von Hertling, October 1917–September 1918
   Prince Max of Baden, October–November 1918
   Friedrich Ebert, November 1918–February 1919

2. President of the National Assembly:
   Friedrich Ebert, February–August 1919

3. The Weimar Republic.

   Presidents:
   Friedrich Ebert 1919–25
   Field Marshal Paul von Hindenburg 1925–34

   Chancellors:
   P. Scheidemann (SPD) February 1919
   G. Bauer (SPD) June 1919
   H. Müller (SPD) March 1920
   K. Fehrenbach (Centre) June 1920
   J. Wirth (Centre) May 1921
   W. Cuno (non-party) November 1922
   G. Stresemann (People's) August 1923
   W. Marx (Centre) November 1923
   H. Luther (non-party) January 1925
   W. Marx (Centre) May 1926
   H. Müller (SPD) June 1928
   H. Brüning (Centre) March 1930
   F. von Papen (non-party) May 1932
   K. von Schleicher (non-party) December 1932
   A. Hitler (Nat. Soc.) January 1933

4. The Third Reich.

   Chancellor:
   A. Hitler, who assumed the Presidency as well in August 1934

5. Post-war

West Germany	East Germany
President:	*President:*
T. Heuss 1949–59	W. Pieck 1949–60
H. Lübke 1959–69	
	Minister President:
Chancellor:	O. Grotewohl 1949–64
K. Adenauer (CDU) 1949–63	

6. SEATS HELD BY THE PRINCIPAL PARTIES IN THE GERMAN REICHSTAG ELECTIONS 1919–33

Source: K. S. Pinson, *Modern Germany: its History and Civilization.* (1954)

	Jan. 1919	June 1920	May 1924	Dec. 1924	May 1928	Sept. 1930	July 1932	Nov. 1932	Mar. 1933	Nov. 1933
Majority Socialists	165	102	100	131	153	143	133	121	120	—
Independent Socialists	22	84								
Communists	—	4	62	45	54	77	89	100	81	—
Centre party	91	64	65	69	62	68	75	70	74	—
Bavarian People's party	—	21	16	19	16	19	22	20	18	—
Democrats	75	39	28	32	25	20	4	2	5	—
Wirtschaftspartei	4	4	10	17	23	23	2	1	—	—
Nationalists	44	71	95	103	73	41	37	52	52	—
Landbund	—	—	10	8	3	3	2	2	1	—
People's Party	19	65	45	51	45	30	7	11	2	—
National Socialists	—	—	32	14	12	107	230	196	288	661

7. POPULATIONS

Figures given in millions.

	Great Britain	France	Italy	Habsburg Empire	Germany	Russia
1815	18	29	18		26	43
1830	24	32	21		30	50
1840	26	33	22·4		31	55
1850	27·6	35·8	24·3	30·7	35·9	57
1860	29	37·4	25	31·7	38	63
1870	31	37	26	35·8	41	77
1880	35	37	28	38	45	89
1890	38	38	30	41	49	95
1900	41	39	32	45	56	103
1910	45	39	35	50	65	111
1920	42	40	38		58	
						147(1926)
1930	44	42	42		65	170(1939)
			42(1936)		86(1939)[1]	
1940		40				
					64(1945)[2]	
1950	50	41·7	46·3			180
1966	54·9	49·4	51·9		59·6 (west)	227

[1] This includes the acquisition of Austria, the Sudetenland, Bohemia, Moravia, and Memel.
[2] After the Treaty of Potsdam in 1945.

8. THE MIXED POPULATIONS IN THE NEW EASTERN EUROPEAN STATES AFTER 1919

Source: H. Seton–Watson, *Eastern Europe between the Wars 1918–1941.* (1945)
Figures given in thousands.

Date of census	Poland 1921	Czecho-slovakia 1921	Hungary 1920	Rumania 1930	Yugo-slavia 1921	Bulgaria 1934	Austria 1923
Poles	18,814	76		35			
Ruthenians	3,898	462	1	500			
Jews	2,110	181	161[1]	778	68[2]	28	
Germans	1,059	3,124	551	714	506		6,273
Russians	1,116			174		12	
Lithuanians	69						
Czechs	31	} 8,761			} 176[3]		94
Slovaks			142	27			5
Magyars		745	7,147	1,464	468		25
Rumanians		14	24	11,545	231	16	
Croats			37		}8,912		} 47
Serbs			17	53			
Slovenes			6		1,020		43
Bulgarians				351		5,275	
Turks				222		618	
Albanians					440		
Italians					13		
Armenians						23	
Gypsies				133		81	

[1] According to the census of 1941.
[2] According to the census of 1931.
[3] This figure also includes Ruthenians.

9. EMIGRATION FROM EUROPE TO THE UNITED STATES 1831–1930

Source: S. E. Morison and H. S. Commager, *The Growth of the American Republic.* (1942)

Countries refer to the last place of permanent residence.

Figures given in thousands.

	1831–40	1841–50	1851–60	1861–70	1871–80	1881–90	1891–1900	1901–10	1911–20	1921–30
Austria-Hungary				8	73	354	593	2,145	896	
France	45·5	77	76	36	72	50·5	31	73	62	49·5
Germany	152·5	434·5	951·5	787·5	718	1,453	505	341·5	144	412
Great Britain[1]	283	1,048	1,338	1,042·5	985	1,463	660	865	487·5	551
Italy	2	2	9	12	56	307	652	2,046	1,109·5	455
Russia	0·5	0·5	1·5	4·5	52	265	602	1,597	922	78·5
Total European	495·5	1,597·5	2,452·5	2,046·5	2,262	4,731·5	3,559	8,136	4,376·5	2,478

[1] Including Ireland.

10. COAL, IRON, AND STEEL PRODUCTION OF THE GREAT POWERS 1850–1960

Sources: A. J. F. Taylor, *The Struggle for Mastery in Europe 1848–1918.* (1954)
Encyclopaedia Britannica. (1959 edn.)
United Nations Statistical Office: *The Growth of World Industry 1953–1965.* New York 1967
Figures given in millions of metric tonnes.[1]

	1850	1860	1870	1880	1890	1900	1910	1914	1920[2]	1929[2]	1935	1944	1953[3]	1960[3]
COAL														
Germany	6	12	34	59	89	149	222	277	275	348	319	404	226	239
Austria-Hungary	1·2	2·3	8·5	15	26	39	47	47						
France	5	8·3	13·3	19·4	26·1	33·4	38·4	40	37	57	52	29	54	58
Great Britain	57	81	112	149	184	228	268	292	265	250	249	216	227	197
Russia		0·15	0·75	3·2	6	16·2	24·9	36·2	12	34	121	130	300	513
PIG-IRON														
Germany			1·3	2·5	4·1	7·5	9·5	14·7	6·9	13·2	12·6	14·2	13	25
France	0·5	0·9	1·2	1·7	2	2·7	4	4·6	3·4	10·2	5·7	2·8	8	14
Great Britain	2·2	3·9	6	7·8	8	9	10	11	8	7·6	6·4	6·7	11	15
Russia			0·4	0·4	0·9	2·9	3	3·6	0·11	3·9	12·4	7·6	27	46
STEEL														
Germany				0·7	2·3	6·7	13·8	14	8·4	16	16·1	16·2	18	34
France				0·4	0·7	1·6	3·4	3·5	3	9·5	6·2	3	9	17
Great Britain				1·3	3·6	5	5·9	6·5	9	9·6	9·8	12·1	17	24
Russia					0·4	1·5	3·5	4·1	0·1	4·9	12·3	11·8	38	65

[1] 1 metric tonne = 1,000 kg. = 19 cwt. 12 oz. 5 dwt.
[2] The figures for coal in 1920 are based on an average for the years 1920–4, and in 1929 on an average for the years 1925–9.
[3] The figures for Germany refer to West Germany.

GLOSSARY OF PLACE-NAMES

Place-names loom large in Continental emotions. An inhabitant of Lausanne once expressed indignation to the author at the English habit of calling Lac Léman the Lake of Geneva; after the Anglo-French crisis of 1898 (see p. 232) the name of Fashoda was changed to Kodok, so that further mention of the place might not awaken unpleasant memories, and at the beginning of the first World War the German-sounding St Petersburg was changed by the Russians to Petrograd. Since 1945 an ideological element has been added to the confusion in eastern Europe with the naming of cities after leading Communists. For example, Königsberg in East Prussia is now Kaliningrad, and the cartographer has to keep pace with the shifts in the official Russsian interpretations of recent history. For the student of nineteenth-century Europe, however, the principal significance of place-names is that they reflect the rivalries of linguistic nationalism. A dispassionate viewpoint would demand an anglicized form, but too often a satisfactory one does not exist, and the following glossary simply gives the alternative forms of the place-names that occur in the text.

Danzig (German)	Gdansk (Polish)	
Dorpat (German)	Tartu (Estonian)	Yuryev (Russian)
Fiume (Italian)	Rijeka (Yugoslav)	
Gorizia (Italian)	Görz (German)	Goriska (Yugoslav)
Hanko (Finnish)	Hangö (Swedish)	
Helsinki (Finnish)	Helsingfors (Swedish)	
Kaunas (Lithuanian)	Kovno (Russian)	

Königgrätz: The battle of 1866 is sometimes called Sadowa, particularly by French historians. This is not an alternative place-name, but simply another town not far from Königgrätz.

Laibach (German)	Ljubljana (Yugoslav)	
Lemberg (German)	Lwow (Polish)	Lvov (Russian)
Memel (German)	Klaypeda (Lithuanian)	
Olmütz (German)	Olomouc (Czech)	
Porvoo (Finnish)	Borgå (Swedish)	
Posen (German)	Poznan (Polish)	
Pressburg (German)	Pozsony (Hungarian)	Bratislava (Czech)
Ragusa (Italian)	Dubrovnik (Yugoslav)	
Reval (German)	Talinn (Estonian)	

Schleswig–Holstein: This involves a particular difficulty, since a hyphenated form implies the German nationalist view of the indivisibility of the duchies, while the separation of the two supports the Danish claim. I have retained the hyphen, since this seems to be customary in English, but have used the Danish Slesvig rather than the German Schleswig (although one historian has suggested Sleswick as an earlier English form).

Teschen (German)	Těšin (Czech)	Cieszyn (Polish)
Vilna (German)	Vilnyus (Lithuanian)	Wilno (Polish)
Viipuri (Finnish)	Viborg (Swedish)	Vyborg (Russian)
Zagreb (Croat)	Agram (German)	

GLOSSARY OF TECHNICAL TERMS

Anschluss: Union, usually referring to that of Germany and Austria, accomplished in 1938. See p. 416

Ausgleich: The Compromise of 1867, creating Austria–Hungary. See p. 200.

Barshchina: Compulsory labour performed by privately-owned Russian serfs.

Blitzkrieg: Lightning war, a German technique of attack in the second World War, based on close cooperation of infantry, armour, and air power.

Bundesrat: Federal Council representing the states in the German Reich of 1871 (see pp. 200, 254), and the cantons in the Swiss constitution of 1848.

Bundesstaat: Any federal organization in which the central government has definite power over the member states: e.g. Switzerland after 1848, and the German Reich of 1871. This is in contrast to a *Staatenbund,* a confederation in which the member states enjoy far greater independence: e.g. the German and Swiss Confederations of 1815.

Bundestag: (1) Diet of the German Confederation of 1815. See p. 31. (2) Federal Parliament of Austria after 1918.

Consulta: An advisory council.

Cortes: Spanish Parliament.

Diet: A general term to describe a representative assembly of: (1) the states of a confederation, or (2) a single country, usually meeting in the form of three or four Estates of the realm (*Stände* in German). See p. 32.

Duma: Russian national Parliament established after the revolution of 1905. See p. 269.

Landtag (plur. -e): A provincial Diet.

Métayage: A system of farming whereby the owner of the land and the farmer shared the profits.

Mir: The community of the peasant village in Russia.

Obruk: Payment made in cash or in kind by Russian serfs for the right to farm.

Reichsrat: (1) Austrian constitutional assembly whose powers were gradually increased in the second half of the nineteenth century. (2) Upper House representing the provincial governments in the constitution of the Weimar Republic. See p. 361.

Reichstag: Lower representative House in the constitutions of the North German Confederation of 1867, the German Reich of 1871, and the Weimar Republic.

Reichswehr: The German army.

Riksdag: Swedish Diet. The four Estates were transformed into a bi-cameral Parliament in 1866, but the institution retained the same name.

Risorgimento: Resurgence, the Italian word applied to the movement of Italian nationalism.

Staatenbund: See Bundesstaat.

Staatsrat: Council of State.

Storting: Norwegian Parliament.

Zemstvo (plur. -va,: District or provincial assembly established by Tsar Alexander II in Russia in 1864. See p. 205.

Zollverein: Customs Union. See p. 61.

Further Reading

1. Bibliographies

A. Bullock and A. J. P. Taylor, *Select Lists of Books on European History 1815–1914* (2nd edn), Oxford U.P. 1957.

W. N. Medlicott, *Modern European History 1789–1945*, (Historical Association Pamphlet.)

2. General Works

D. Thomson, *Europe since Napoleon,* 2nd edn. Longman 1962.

E. Barker, G. N. Clark, and P. Vaucher, (eds), *The European Inheritance.* Vol. III, Oxford U.P. 1954.

E. L. Woodward, *War and Peace in Europe 1815–70.*

G. A. Kertesz (ed.), *Documents of the Political History of the European Continent, 1815–1939,* Oxford U.P. 1968.

The following series each contain several volumes on the period:

The New Cambridge Modern History, Cambridge U.P.

The Rise of Modern Europe, Harper; Hamish Hamilton.

Peuples et Civilisations, Presses Universitaires de France.

A General History of Europe, Longman.

The Fontana History of Europe, Fontana/Collins.

3. Diplomatic

a) Official documents

A. Oakes and R. B. Mowat (eds), *Great European Treaties of the 19th Century* (2nd edn), Oxford U.P. 1921.

H. W. V. Temperley and L. M. Penson, *Foundations of British Foreign Policy, from Pitt to Salisbury*, Cambridge U.P. 1938.

R. H. Lord, *Origins of the War of 1870*, Harvard U.P. 1924.

G. Bonnin, *Bismarck and the Hohenzollern Candidate for the Spanish Throne*, Chatto 1958.

A. F. Pribram, *The Secret Treaties of Austria–Hungary 1879–1914*, Harvard U.P.; Oxford U.P. 1920.

A. B. Keith, *Speeches and Documents on International Affairs 1918–37* (2 vols), Oxford U.P. 1938 (World's Classics).

b) Secondary sources

P. Renouvin, *Histoire des Relations Internationales: Le XIXe siècle*, (2 vols), 1954–5; *le XXe siècle* (2 vols), Hachette 1958.

A. J. P. Taylor, *The Struggle for Mastery in Europe 1848–1918*, Oxford U.P. 1954 (Oxford History of Modern Europe).

C. K. Webster, *The Congress of Vienna, 1814–1815*, Bell 1934.

W. E. Mosse, *The European Powers and the German Question 1848–71*, Cambridge U.P. 1958.

A. F. Pribram, *England and the International Policy of the Great Powers 1871–1914*, Oxford U.P. 1931 (Ford Lectures).

W. L. Langer, *The Diplomacy of Imperialism 1890–1902* (2 vols), New York 1935.

L. Albertini, *The Origins of the War of 1914*, trans. I. M. Massey (3 vols), Oxford U.P. 1952–7.

G. M. Gathorne–Hardy, *A Short History of International Affairs 1920–39* (4th edn), Oxford U.P. for R.I.I.A. 1950.

A. J. P. Taylor, *The Origins of the Second World War*, Hamish Hamilton 1961.

E. M. Robertson (ed), *The Origins of the Second World War: Historical Interpretations*, Macmillan 1971.

J. W. Hiden, *Germany and Europe 1919–1939*, Longman 1977.

K. Middlemas, *The Diplomacy of Illusion. The British Government and Germany 1937–1939*, Weidenfeld & Nicolson 1972.

K. Robbins, *Munich 1938*, Cassell 1968.

4. Economic

C. M. Cippola (ed.), *The Fontana Economic History of Europe. Vol. 4. The Emergence of Industrial Societies; Vol. 5. The Twentieth Century; Vol. 6. Contemporary Economies*, Harvester Press, Barnes & Noble.

J. H. Clapham, *The Economic Development of France and Germany 1815–1914* (4th edn), Cambridge U.P. 1936.

W. O. Henderson, *The Industrial Revolution on the Continent 1800–1914*, F. Cass 1961.

L. H. Jenks, *The Migration of British Capital*, Cape 1938.

W. Ashworth, *A Short History of the International Economy, 1850–1950*, Longman 1952.

W. A. Lewis, *Economic Survey 1919–39*, Allen & Unwin 1949.

5. Religious and Ideological

a) Original writings

J. J. Rousseau, *Du contrat social* (1762), (various translations).

J. G. Fichte, *Reden an die deutsche Nation* (1808), trans. R. F. Jones and G. H. Turnbull, The Open Court Publishing Co. 1922.

L. Blanc, *L'organisation du travail* (1839), English edn Sir J.A.R. Marriott 1913.

G. Mazzini, *The Duties of Man* (1844–58), Everyman's Library.

Napoleon III, *Des idées napoléoniennes* (1838), trans. as *The Mind of Napoleon*, Pennsylvania U.P. 1955.

K Marx, *Das Kapital* (1867–94), (various translations).

K. Marx and F. Engels, *The Communist Manifesto* (1848), (various translations).

b) Secondary sources

A. R. Vidler. *The Church in an Age of Revolution*, Penguin 1961 (Pelican History of the Church).

E. E. Y. Halles, *The Catholic Church in the Modern World*, Eyre & Spottiswoode and Burns Oates 1958.

R.I.I.A., *Nationalism*, Oxford U.P. 1939.

P. Henry, *Le problème des nationalités* (2nd edn), Armand Colin 1949.

J. Ancel, *Slaves et Germains* (2nd edn), Armand Colin 1947.

G. de Ruggiero, *European Liberalism*, trans. R. G. Collingwood, Oxford U.P. 1927.

J. Plamenatz, *German Marxism and Russian Communism,* Longman 1954.

R. N. Carew Hunt, *The Theory and Practice of Communism*, (5th edn), Bles 1956.

G. D. H. Cole, *History of Socialist Thought*, Macmillan.

D. McLellan, *Karl Marx: his life and thought*, Macmillan 1973.

J. Joll, *The Second International 1889–1914*, Weidenfeld & Nicolson 1955; *The Anarchists*, Eyre & Spottiswoode 1964.

F. L. Carsten, *The Rise of Fascism*, Batsford 1967.

D. Smith, *Left and Right in Twentieth Century Europe*, Longman 1970.

6. History of France

a) Memoirs

F. R. de Chateaubriand, *Mémoires d' outre-tombe* (1849–50), ed. A. H. Thompson, Cambridge U.P. 1920.

A. de Musset, *Confession d'un enfant du siècle* (1836).

G. Sand, *Histoire de ma vie* (1854–5), adaptation de Noelle Roubaud, Librairie Stock 1960.

Nassau Senior, *Conversations with Thiers and Guizot* (2 vols), Hurst 1878.

V. Hugo, *Choses vues* (1887–1900), Collection Nelson.

A. de Tocqueville, *Souvenirs* (*1893*): trans. as *Recollections*, ed. J. P. Mayer, Harvill 1948.

E. Renan, *Souvenirs d'enfance et de jeunesse* (1892), Paris, Calmann Lévy; trans. C. B. Pitman, Routledge 1929.

R. Baldick, ed. *Pages from the Goncourt Journal*, Oxford U.P. 1962.

b) Novels

H. de Balzac, *Le Colonel Chabert* (1832); *Le Père Goriot* (1834); *César Birotteau* (1838), (all in various translations).

G. Flaubert, *L'éducation sentimentale* (1869), trans. Goldsmith, Dent (Everyman's Library).

E. Zola, *Germinal* (1885); *La terre* (1877), (various translations).

A. France, *Ile des pingouins* (1908).

M. Proust, *A la recherche du temps perdu* (1913–27), trans. C. K. Scott Moncrieff as *Remembrance of Things Past*, Chatto 1922–31.

G. Duhamel, *Le notaire du Havre*, Mercure de France 1933.

c) Secondary sources

J. P. T. Bury, *France 1814–1940* (3rd edn) (including an appendix with the successive French constitutions), Methuen 1954.

D. W. Brogan, *The Development of Modern France 1870–1939*, Hamish Hamilton 1939.

E. L. Woodward, *French Revolutions*, Oxford U.P. 1934.

J. Plamenatz, *The Revolutionary Movement in France 1815–71*, Longman 1952.

P. Campbell, *French Electoral Systems and Elections 1789–1957*, Faber 1958.

A. R. Vidler, *Prophecy and Papacy: A Study of Lamennais, The Church and the Revolution*, S.C.M. 1954.

Duff Cooper, *Talleyrand*, Cape 1932.

D. O. Evans, *Social Romanticism in France 1830–48*, Oxford U.P. 1952.

T. E. B. Howarth, *Citizen King. The Life of Louis Philippe*. Eyre & Spottiswoode 1961.

F. A. Simpson, *The Rise of Louis Napoleon* (3rd edn), Longman 1950; *Louis Napoleon and the Recovery of France, 1848–56* (3rd edn), Longman 1951.

T. Zeldin, *The Political System of Napoleon III*, Macmillan 1958.

M. Howard, *The Franco-Prussian War*, Hart-Davis 1961.

A. Horne, *The Fall of Paris*, Macmillan 1965.

J. Hampden Jackson, *Clemenceau and the Third Republic*, E.U.P. 1946 (Teach Yourself History).

R. Aron, *The Vichy Régime 1940–44*, Putnam 1958.

P. M. Williams, *Crisis and Compromise: Politics in the Fourth Republic*, Longman 1964.

P. M. Williams and M. Harrison, *De Gaulle's Republic*, Longman 1960.

7. History of Austria

a) Original writings

Lord Sudley (ed.), *The Lieven–Palmerston Correspondence 1828–56*, Murray 1943.

S. Zweig, *The World of Yesterday*, Cassell 1943.

b) Secondary sources

A. J. P. Taylor, *The Habsburg Monarchy 1809–1918*, Hamish Hamilton 1948.

G. de Bertier de Sauvigny, *Metternich and his Times*, trans. P Ryde, Darlon 1962.

A. J. May, *The Habsburg Monarchy 1866–1914*, Harvard U.P.; Oxford 1951.

C. A. Macartney, *The Habsburg Empire 1790–1918*, Weidenfeld & Nicolson 1969.

E. Crankshaw, *The Fall of the House of Habsburg*, Longman 1963.

L. Valiani, *The End of Austria–Hungary*, Secker & Warburg 1973.

F. R. Bridges, *From Sadowa to Sarajevo*, Routledge & Kegan Paul 1972.

C. A. Gulick, *Austria from Habsburg to Hitler* (2 vols), Univ. of California 1948.

8. History of Germany

a) Original writings

O. Von Bismarck, *Reflections and Reminiscences. Gedanken und Erinnerungen*, ed. A. M. Gibson, Cambridge U.P. 1940 (in German).

G. Ritter, ed. *The Schlieffen Plan*, trans. A. and E. Wilson, O. Wolff 1958.

Prince Max of Baden, *Memoirs*, trans. W. M. Calder and C. W. H. Sutton, Constable 1928.

A. Hitler, *Mein Kampf* (1925–27) (various translations), full edn trans. J. Murphy, Hurst & Blackett 1939.

J. Noakes & G. Pridham, *Documents on Nazism 1919–1945*, Cape 1974.

b) Novels

T. Mann, *Buddenbrooks*, trans. H. L. Porter, Secker 1937, Penguin 1957.

T. Fontane, *Effi Briest*, Eng. trans. Penguin 1967.

c) Secondary sources

G. Mann, *History of Germany since 1789*, trans. M. Jackson, Chatto & Windus 1968.

G. A. Craig, *Germany 1866–1945*, Oxford U.P. 1978; *The Politics of the Prussian Army 1640–1945*, Oxford U.P. 1955.

T. S. Hamerow, *Restoration, Revolution, Reaction: Economics and Politics in Germany 1815–71*, Princeton U.P. 1958.

W. O. Henderson, *The Zollverein*, Cambridge U.P. 1939.

H. Friedjung, *The Struggle for Supremacy in Germany*, trans. A.J.P. Taylor and M.L. McElwee, Macmillan 1935.

V. Valentin, *1848: Chapters of Germany History*, trans. E. T. Scheffauer, Allen & Unwin 1940.

J. Droz, *Les Révolutions allemandes de 1848*, Presses Universitaires de France 1949.

F. Eyck, *The Frankfurt Parliament 1848–49*, Macmillan 1968.

A. J. P. Taylor, *Bismarck: The Man and the Statesman*, Hamish Hamilton 1955.

E. Eyck, *Bismarck and the German Empire*, Allen & Unwin 1950.

O. Pflanze, *Bismarck and the Development of Germany 1815–71*, Princeton U.P. 1963.

W. M. Simon, *Germany in the Age of Bismarck*, Allen & Unwin 1968.

E. L. Woodward, *Great Britain and the German Navy*, Oxford U.P. 1935.

F. Fischer, *German Aims in the First World War*, Chatto & Windus 1967.

A. Rosenberg, *The Birth of the German Republic*, trans. I. F. D. Morrow, Oxford U.P. 1931.

R. Coper, *Failure of a Revolution: Germany in 1918–1919*, Cambridge U.P. 1955.

J. Hiden, *The Weimar Republic*, Longman 1974.

J. W. Wheeler–Bennett, *The Nemesis of Power: The German Army in Politics 1918–1945*, Macmillan 1953.

A. Bullock, *Hitler*, Oldhams 1952.

J. C. Fest, *Hitler*, Penguin 1977.

K. D. Bracher, *The German Dictatorship*, Weidenfeld & Nicolson 1971.

W. Carr, *Arms, Autarky and Aggression*, Arnold 1972.

M. Cooper, *The German Army 1933–1945*, Macdonald & Jane's 1978.

M. Balfour, *West Germany*, E. Benn 1968.

W. F. Hanrieder, *West German Foreign Policy 1949–1963*, Stanford U.P. 1967.

T. Prittie, *Adenauer: A Study in Fortitude*, Tom Stacey Ltd 1972.

P. Nettl, *The Eastern Zone and Soviet Policy in Germany 1945–50*, Oxford U.P. 1951.

K. Stolper, K. Hauser, K. Borchardt, *The German Economy: 1870 to the Present*, Weidenfeld & Nicolson 1967.

9. History of Italy

a) Original writings

G. S. Abba, *The Diary of one of Garibaldi's Thousand*, trans. E. R. Vincent, Oxford U.P. 1962.

G. Di Lampedusa, *The Leopard*, English trans. Harvill, Collins 1962.

O. Russell, *The Roman Question: Extracts from Despatches from Rome 1858–1870*, ed. N. Blakiston, Chapman 1962.

b) Secondary sources

A. J. Whyte, *The Evolution of Modern Italy, 1715–1920*, Blackwell 1944; *The Political Life and Letters of Cavour 1848–61*, Oxford U.P. 1930.

E. E. Y. Hales, *Mazzini and the Secret Societies*, Eyre & Spottiswoode 1956; *Pio Nono* (2nd edn), Eyre & Spottiswoode 1956.

D. Mack Smith, *Cavour and Garibaldi in 1860*, Cambridge U.P. 1954; *Garibaldi*, Hutchinson 1947; *Italy 1860–1960*, Univ. of Michigan Press 1959; *Mussolini's Roman Empire*, Longman 1976.

C. Seton Watson, *Italy from Liberalism to Fascism 1870–1925*, Methuen 1967.

10. History of Russia

a) Original writings

G. Vernadsky (ed.), *A Source Book for Russian History*, Vols 2 and 3, Yale U.P. 1972.

D. Mackenzie Wallace, *Russia on the Eve of War and Revolution*, A. A. Knopf/Random House, New York 1961.

V. I. Lenin, *What is to be done?* eds S. V. & P. Utechin, Oxford U.P. 1963.

N. Sukhanov, *The Russian Revolution 1917*, ed. J. Carmichael, Oxford U.P. 1955.

J. Reed, *Ten Days That Shook the World*, Penguin 1966.

b) Novels and plays

L. N. Tolstoy, *The Cossacks*, trans. V. Traill, Hamish Hamilton, new edn 1949; *Resurrection*, trans. L. and A. Maude, Oxford U.P. 1916 (World's Classics).

I. Turgenev, *A Sportsman's Sketches*, trans. Dent 1932; *On the Eve; Smoke; Literary Reminiscences* (including several short stories); *Virgin Soil; Fathers and Sons; A Month in the Country* (all in various translations).

N. Gogol, *Dead Souls* (1842), trans. G. Reavez, Oxford U.P. (World's Classics); trans. C. J. Hogarth, Dent (Everyman's Library); *The Inspector General*, trans. D. J. Campbell, Heinemann.

F. Dostoevsky, *The House of the Dead*, trans. C. Garnett, Heinemann 1915; *Crime and Punishment* (various translations).

A Chekhov, *The Cherry Orchard; Uncle Vanya; The Three Sisters* (various translations).

B. Pasternak, *Doctor Zhivago*, Collins 1958.

c) Secondary sources

J. W. Westwood, *Russian History 1812–1971*, Oxford U.P. 1973.

H. Seton–Watson, *The Russian Empire 1801–1917*, Oxford U.P. 1967.

T. Szamuely, *The Russian Tradition*, Secker & Warburg 1974.

W. E. Mosse, *Alexander II and the Modernization of Russia*, E. U. P. 1959 (Teach Yourself History).

T. Emmons, *The Russian Landed Gentry and the Peasant Emancipation of 1861*, Cambridge U.P. 1968.

A. B. Ulam, *Lenin and the Bolsheviks*, Fontana/Collins 1969.

E. H. Carr, *The Bolshevik Revolution 1917–23*, Macmillan; *The Russian Revolution from Lenin to Stalin*, Macmillan 1979.

A. Nove, *An Economic History of the U.S.S.R*, Allen Lane, The Penguin Press 1969.

L. Schapiro, *The Communist Party of the Soviet Union*, Methuen 1970.

I. Deutscher, *Stalin*, Oxford U.P. 1949.

11. History of Eastern Europe

C. A. Macartney and A. W. Palmer, *Independent Eastern Europe*, Macmillan 1962.

H. Seton–Watson, *Eastern Europe between the Wars 1918–41*, Cambridge U.P. 1945.

C. A. Macartney, *Hungary and her Successors 1919–37*, Oxford U.P. 1937; *Hungary: A Short History*, Edinburgh U.P. 1962.

W. F. Reddaway (ed.), *Cambridge History of Poland 1697–1935*, Cambridge U.P. 1941.

R. Hiscocks, *Poland, Bridge for the Abyss*, Oxford U.P. 1963.

H. W. V. Temperley, *History of Serbia*, Bell 1917.

J. Remak, *Sarajevo*, Weidenfeld & Nicolson 1959.

R. West, *Black Lamb and Grey Falcon*, Macmillan 1942.

R. W. Seton–Watson, *History of the Roumanians*, Cambridge U.P. 1936.

E. S. Forster, *Short History of Modern Greece 1821–1956* (3rd edn), Methuen 1957.

A. J. Toynbee and R. Kirkwood, *Turkey*, Benn 1926 (Nations of the Modern World).

A. J. Toynbee, *A Study of History* (10 vols), Oxford U.P. 1935–54; Vol. VIII, pp. 216–72 (on Turkey).

12. History of Scandinavia

B. J. Hovde, *The Scandinavian Countries 1720–1865* (2 vols), Cornell U.P. 1950.
J. Danstrup, *History of Denmark*, Bailey 1949.
K. Larsen, *History of Norway*, Princeton U.P.; Oxford 1948.
I. Anderson, *History of Sweden*, trans. C. Hannay, Weidenfeld & Nicolson 1956.
J. Hampden Jackson, *Finland* (2nd edn), Allen & Unwin.

13. History of the Low Countries

H. Pirenne, *Historie de Belgique*, Vols. VI and VII, 1926, 1932.
G. J. Renier, *The Dutch Nation*, Allen & Unwin 1944.
E. H. Kossmann, *The Low Countries 1780–1940*, Oxford U.P. 1978.

14. History of Switzerland

C. Hughes (ed.), *The Federal Constitution of Switzerland*, Oxford U.P. 1954.
J. Burckhardt, *The Letters of Jacob Burckhardt*, ed. A. Dru, Routledge 1955.
E. Bonjour, H. S. Offler, and G. R. Potter, *A Short History of Switzerland*, Oxford U.P. 1952.

15. History of Spain and Portugal

H. V. Livermore, *History of Spain*, Allen & Unwin 1958.
G Brenan, *The Spanish Labyrinth*, Cambridge U.P. 1943.
E. Allison Peers, *The Spanish Tragedy 1930–36*, Methuen 1936.
H. Thomas, *The Spanish Civil War*, Eyre & Spottiswoode 1961.
G. L. Steer, *The Tree of Gernika*, Hodder & Stoughton 1938.
G. Orwell, *Homage to Catalonia*, Secker 1938.
H. V. Livermore, *History of Portugual*, Cambridge U.P. 1947.

16. The Revolutions of 1848

F. Fejto (ed.), *The Opening of an Era: 1848*, Wingate 1948.
F. Ponteil, *1848* (2nd edn), Armand Colin 1947.
A. Whitridge, *Men in Crisis: The Revolutions of 1848*, Scribner's 1950.
L. B. Namier, *1848: The Revolution of the Intellectuals*, Oxford U.P. 1944.
P. N. Stearns, *The Revolutions of 1848*, Weidenfeld & Nicolson 1974.

17. The First World War

C. R. M. F. Cruttwell, *History of the Great War 1914–18* (2nd edn), Oxford U.P. 1936.

C. Falls, *The First World War*, Longman 1960.

W. S. Churchill, *The World Crisis 1911–1918* (4 vols), Butterworth 1923–9.

F. P. Chambers, *The War behind the War, 1914–1918: The History of the Political and Civilian Fronts*, Faber 1939.

A. Moorehead, *Gallipoli*, Hamish Hamilton 1956.

J. W. Wheeler–Bennett, *Hindenburg. The Wooden Titan*, Macmillan 1936.

C. Barnett, *The Sword Bearers*, Eyre & Spottiswoode 1963.

18. The peace settlement of 1919

J. W. Wheeler–Bennett, *The Forgotten Peace: Brest Litovsk, March 1918*, Macmillan 1936.

Harold Nicolson, *Peacemaking 1919* (rev. edn), Constable 1945.

F. L. Carsten, *Revolution in Central Europe 1918–19*, Temple Smith 1972.

J. M. Keynes, *The Economic Consequences of the Peace*, Macmillan 1919.

E. Mantoux, *The Carthaginian Peace, or the Economic Consequences of Mr Keynes*, Oxford U.P. 1946.

19. The Second World War

J. F. C. Fuller, *The Second World War 1939–1945* (3rd edn), Eyre & Spottiswoode 1954.

C. Falls, *The Second World War, A Short History* (3rd edn), Methuen 1950.

B. H. Liddell Hart, *History of the Second World War*, Cassell 1970.

W. S. Churchill, *The Second World War* (6 vols), Cassell 1948–52.

C. Wilmot, *The Struggle for Europe*, Collins 1952.

C. de Gaulle, *War Memoirs*, 1954–9.

E. Maclean, *Eastern Approaches*, Cape 1949.

Lord Alanbrooke, *The Turn of the Tide*, ed. A. Bryant, Collins 1957; *Triumph in the West*, ed. A. Bryant, Collins 1959.

A. Clark, *Barbarossa: The Russo–German Conflict 1941–1945*, Penguin 1966.

A. and V. M. Toynbee (ed.), *Hitler's Europe*, Oxford U.P. for R.I.I.A. 1954.

H. R. Trevor Roper, *The Last Days of Hitler* (3rd edn), Macmillan 1956.

20. Europe After 1945

W. Knapp, *A History of War and Peace 1939–1965*, Oxford, U.P. 1967.

R. Mayne, *The Recovery of Europe*, Weidenfeld & Nicolson 1970.

W. Laqueur, *Europe since Hitler*, Penguin 1972.

H. Seton–Watson, *The Eastern European Revolutions*, Methuen 1950.

D. F. Fleming, *The Cold War and its Origins 1917–1960*, Allen & Unwin 1961.

R. Douglas, *From War to Cold War 1942–48*, Macmillan 1981.

M. Balfour, *The Adversaries: America, Russia and the Open World 1941– 62*, Routledge & Kegan Paul 1981.

21. Miscellaneous

a) Maps
J. Ramsay Muir, *Historical Atlas, Medieval and Modern* (8th edn), G. Philip, 1959.

J. F. Horrabin, *An Atlas of Current Affairs* (covers much of the inter-war years).

I. Richards, J. B. Goodson, and J. A. Morris, *A Sketch-map History of the Great Wars and after, 1914–60* (rev. edn), Harrap 1961.

b) Photographs
H. and A. Gernsheim, *Historic Events 1839–1939*, Longman 1960.

c) Collections of Essays
L. B. Namier, *Vanished Supremacies*, Hamish Hamilton 1958.

A. J. P. Taylor, *From Napoleon to Stalin*, Hamish Hamilton 1950.

A. O. Sarkissian (ed.), *Studies in Diplomatic History and Historiography in honour of G. P. Gooch*, Longman 1961.

R. Pares and A. J. P. Taylor (eds), *Essays presented to Sir Lewis Namier*, Macmillan 1956.

The *Problems in European Civilization* series (D. C. Heath; Harrap) includes the following:

1848 – A Turning Point?; The Outbreak of the First World War—Who was Responsible?; The Russian Revolution and Bolshevik Victory—Why and How?; The Versailles Settlement—Was it foredoomed to Failure?; The Nazi Revolution—Germany's Guilt or Germany's Fate?

Index of Principal Countries

General Index

Treaties and Congresses are listed together alphabetically. Dates after rulers refer to their reigns.